Almanac of the Unelected
Staff of the U.S. Congress

23rd Edition
2011

CONTRIBUTORS

John Filar Atwood
Katherine Boyle
Jessica Brady
Elizabeth Brotherton
Dena Bunis
Matt Canham
Michael Coleman
Michelle Davis
Lisa Friedman
Malia Rulon Herman
Nathan Hurst
Evan Lehmann
Mike Lillis
Kenneth Maguire
Lauren Markoe Kolko
John McArdle
Lauren Morello
John Mulligan
Aryeh Natter
John Seidenberg
Adam Snider
Mike Soraghan
Nicole Thompson
Patricia Turner
Emily Walker
Jessica Wehrman
Dana Wilkie
Jordy Yager

Almanac of the Unelected
Staff of the U.S. Congress

23rd Edition
2011

Edited by
Suzanne Struglinski and Lisa Friedman

Lanham, MD

Published in the United States
of America by Bernan Press,
a wholly owned subsidiary of
The Rowman & Littlefield
Publishing Group, Inc.
4501 Forbes Boulevard, Suite 200
Lanham, Maryland 20706

Bernan Press
800-865-3457
info@bernan.com
www.bernan.com

Copyright © 2011 by Bernan Press

All rights reserved. No part of this publication may be reproduced, stored in a retrieval system, or transmitted in any form or by any means, electronic, mechanical, photocopying, recording, or otherwise, without the prior permission of the publisher.

ISBN: 978-1-59888-416-6 (cloth)
978-1-59888-418-0 (paper)
E-ISBN: 978-1-59888-417-3
ISSN: 1047-0999

∞ The paper used in this publication meets the minimum requirements of American National Standard for Information Sciences—Permanence of Paper for Printed Library Materials, ANSI/NISO Z39.48-1992.

Manufactured in the United States of America.

TABLE OF CONTENTS

Preface ... vii
How to Get a Job on Capitol Hill ... ix
The Congressional Calendar Made Easy ... xi
How a Bill REALLY Becomes a Law ... xiii
Life After Congress ... xv

United States House of Representatives ... 1

    Leadership ... 3
    Committee on Agriculture ... 43
    Committee on Appropriations ... 63
    Committee on Armed Services ... 91
    Committee on the Budget ... 111
    Committee on Education and the Workforce ... 127
    Committee on Energy and Commerce ... 145
    Committee on Financial Services ... 169
    Committee on Foreign Affairs ... 185
    Committee on Homeland Security ... 197
    Committee on House Administration ... 209
    Committee on the Judiciary ... 217
    Committee on Natural Resources ... 233
    Committee on Oversight and Government Reform ... 243
    Committee on Rules ... 253
    Committee on Science, Space and Technology ... 263
    Committee on Small Business ... 283
    Committee on Standards of Official Conduct ... 297
    Committee on Transportation and Infrastructure ... 303
    Committee on Veterans' Affairs ... 329
    Committee on Ways and Means ... 343
    Permanent Select Committee on Intelligence ... 363
    Select Committee for Energy Independence and Global Warming ... 367

United States Senate — 371

- Leadership — 373
- Committee on Agriculture, Nutrition and Forestry — 403
- Committee on Appropriations — 413
- Committee on Armed Services — 439
- Committee on Banking, Housing, and Urban Affairs — 451
- Committee on the Budget — 461
- Committee on Commerce, Science and Transportation — 475
- Committee on Energy and Natural Resources — 483
- Committee on Environment and Public Works — 517
- Committee on Finance — 543
- Committee on Foreign Relations — 563
- Committee on Health, Education, Labor and Pensions — 573
- Committee on Homeland Security and Governmental Affairs — 591
- Committee on the Judiciary — 603
- Committee on Rules and Administration — 613
- Committee on Small Business and Entrepreneurship — 617
- Committee on Veterans' Affairs — 631

Select, Special, and Other Committees — 641

- Committee on Indian Affairs — 643
- Special Committee on Aging — 651
- Select Committee on Ethics — 657
- Select Committee on Intelligence — 663

Joint Committees — 669

- Joint Committee on the Library — 671
- Joint Committee on Printing — 675
- Joint Committee on Taxation — 679
- Joint Economic Committee — 685

Name Index — 690

Preface

The 112th Congress—not yet half over—already has earned a reputation as one of the most politically tumultuous sessions in recent history.

After four years in the minority, Republicans blew back into power in the 2010 midterm elections. With the Tea Party wind in their sails, the GOP took back the majority in the House of Representatives and claimed a bigger margin in the Senate, prompting President Obama to admit responsibility for what he called the Democrats' "shellacking." The new political dynamic was instantly palpable on Capitol Hill as the parties engaged in a months-long budget showdown, barely averting a government shutdown as they agreed at the eleventh hour to complete a long-overdue spending package from the previous year.

The new Republican majority also set in motion fundamental organizational changes to committees and sweeping legislative initiatives. Most were aimed at rolling back the Obama administration's agenda, particularly the health care overhaul. But with the May killing of Osama bin Laden in Pakistan, Obama's fortunes appear to have changed drastically. Campaign watchers already have their eyes trained on the 2012 elections, and many wonder whether the bump Obama saw in the polls will have a transformative impact on the political landscape.

Throughout it all, hundreds of Capitol Hill staffers kept the country's legislative wheels turning. Traditionally seen but not heard, Hill aides are the unnamed men and women scurrying through the House and Senate office buildings with their thumbs surgically connected to their Blackberries. They write thousands of pieces of legislation each year, juggling knowledge on everything from the arcane federal appropriations process to military base closures to ethanol subsidies. They write speeches, respond to constituent requests, and often are charged with thoroughly researching a brand new issue—the alternative minimum tax or the political situation in Bahrain—to be turned into a single television-worthy sound bite for their bosses within hours. Their role on congressional committees is particularly key, doing everything from writing the questions House and Senate members ask on the dais to forging compromises with the other side of the aisle on bills.

"The Almanac of the Unelected" was designed to help readers make sense of the rapid-fire changes on Capitol Hill and to inform the public about the hundreds of men and women who make the legislative process tick. In addition to contact information and other pertinent information for all the leading House and Senate committee and leadership aides, the Almanac is constantly updating itself to give readers the most up-to-date information about Congress' ever-shifting legislative agenda. Through one-on-one interviews with staffers and in-depth profiles, the Almanac works to ensure that its readers have the most up-to-date information about what issues aides are handling and what bills are expected to pass through their desks in the coming year.

Both of us want to thank the staff members who patiently took time to explain their roles and guide readers through the way work gets done on Capitol Hill. And to the Almanac team who tirelessly tracked down aides, made dozens of phone calls to procure a single five-minute interview and helped put together another fantastic edition of "The Almanac of the Unelected": you have our most sincere gratitude.

—Suzanne Struglinski and Lisa Friedman

How to Get a Job on Capitol Hill

Every year, thousands of people who want to help improve their country—or just earn a steady paycheck with good benefits—inundate Capitol Hill with resumes.

Only a small percentage will ever land a job in one of the 535 House and Senate offices or dozens of congressional committees. So, what's the secret? Relevant experience, a good plan of attack and, of course, knowing the right people can all be a big help, said Brad Traverse, president and CEO of The Traverse Group, a leading Capitol Hill job search firm.

"Networking is terribly important," Traverse said. "Decide what member of Congress (or committee) you'd like to work for and find some connection there. Maybe you've got a third cousin whose best friend went to college with the member. Get them to put in a good word for you."

If you don't have connections within the offices or committees, don't despair. Get your name on one of myriad Capitol Hill internet job lists. It's an excellent way to keep abreast of where the openings are. While Hill job hopefuls might see an occasional position advertised on the back pages of the Hill, Roll Call or Politico, three Capitol Hill-based newspapers, there are many, many more included on a slew of vacancy lists operated by current or former Hill staffers.

Traverse, who runs one of the most expansive and popular lists, charges $5 for inclusion on his list. Others are free. Perhaps the fastest way to find your way onto a few of these lists is to simply do an internet search for "capitol hill job lists." Clotureclub.com operates a good one with frequent postings. Another frequently updated Hill jobs site is at www.google.com/group/capitol-hill-job-list-by-mr-baker.

Of course, there are more formal places to find Hill job listings. The official Senate job site, which only includes a fraction of available jobs, is online at www.senate.gov/employment/po/positions.htm. For U.S. House of Representative jobs, applicants can upload a resume at www.house.gov/cao-hr/. But those who decide to go that route and wait by the phone can usually expect a very, very long wait.

For recent college graduates—or even those still in college—an internship in a House or Senate office is frequently the best way to get your foot in the door. Traverse advised young people taking on an internship to do more than is asked of them once on the job.

"What you do in that internship is probably just as—or more than—important than getting it," he said. "Work your tail off. Offer to do more than what's given to you—make an impression. You talk to a lot of people who are staffers now and they started as an intern."

He also advised having fun, but not too much.

"The danger of an internship is that it's a heck of a lot of fun," he said. "If you've never been to a big city before and you've never been to the nation's capitol—the allure of Georgetown and Dupont circle is pretty strong. Be responsible."

The Congressional Calendar Made Easy

The congressional work schedule looks pretty appealing on paper.

Members of Congress work in their Washington, D.C. offices roughly four days per week, and most years they leave Washington for the majority of January and August. They also take a two-week break for Easter, usually in March or April and typically another two weeks for Thanksgiving. Congress even adjourns for a week in honor of President's Day in February.

But the congressional calendar can be deceiving.

The fact is most members of Congress and their staffs—especially in the U.S. House—work as much or more than the average American, especially when you count all of the time they spend traveling and meeting with constituents in their districts. At the outset of the 112th Congress, House Majority Leader Eric Cantor, R-Va., unveiled a new House calendar that eschewed the longstanding Tuesday-Thursday House work week, which allowed members to fly home to their districts on Friday and return on Monday.

Instead, the new House calendar pretty much banishes the three-day workweek. The schedule requires members to stay in session for two weeks, followed by roughly one week off.

"In total, it contains 123 days and 32 weeks of session," Cantor wrote in a letter to his House colleagues in late December. "While the number of days in session is consistent with first sessions in years past, the number of weeks in session represents an 11 percent drop, resulting in less travel for members and potential (tax money) savings."

The Senate calendar is not as rigidly formed, but the chamber usually convenes on Monday afternoon and works occasional Fridays.

In fact, Fridays are usually pretty low-key on Capitol Hill (unless there are rare votes scheduled), and many members fly home to far-flung districts on that day, instead of putting in a full work day. On Monday morning, the members are often flying back to Washington. Senators, who only run for office every six years as opposed to two, tend to spend less time in their districts than House members.

Many members of Congress have dubbed their weeks-long recesses, such as at Thanksgiving, July 4th or Easter, as "district work periods." That means they're hosting events such as town hall meetings, or meeting with constituents and engaging in other activities that keep them in minds of voters. Lobbyists hoping to score a meeting with a key congressional staffer might consider that the August or January recesses present a good opportunity to get some face-time. The pace around Capitol Hill offices often slows considerably during these periods.

The congressional calendar is not set in stone. For example, in 2009, members had hoped to adjourn in early December but Senate disagreement over the massive health care reform bill kept members of that chamber in session until Christmas Eve.

Capitol Hill has its own "seasons" too. The president kicks off the winter with the January State of the Union Address, followed quickly by the traditional introduction of the federal budget in February. Budget debate and appropriations committee hearings dominate the spring, while other committees hear from a variety of witness—from top Pentagon Officials to A-list celebrities—on other bills under consideration by the House and Senate.

There is usually a big push to get legislation done before the Memorial Day recess and if not done then, to try to cram as much as possible between Memorial Day and July 4.

August is a ghost town around Washington and the lawmakers head home for a month-long district work period and Capitol Hill slows down. This doesn't last long though as the fall is full of getting those appropriations bill done before the end of the fiscal year, and in election years, getting things done in time for those up for re-election to go back home to campaign.

November and December are wrap-up months, with lawmakers—and staff—eager to get home for the holidays but also wanting to make sure they can keep the government funded if a budget bill did not get past before the end of the fiscal year and any other legislation they want to see move does so before the session adjourns.

Then in January it starts all over again.

How a Bill REALLY Becomes a Law

Millions of Americans are familiar with how a bill becomes a law thanks to the now-legendary *Schoolhouse Rock* cartoons that aired on Saturday morning television from 1973 until about 1999.

The brilliantly simple skit and song, with its bluesy refrain "I'm just bill and I'm sitting here on Capitol Hill," taught millions of Americans the basics of how laws get made. But anyone who has actually spent time on Capitol Hill knows the reality is much more complicated than the cartoon.

"The biggest misconception is how much more difficult it is to actually get a bill though the House and Senate," said Rich Galen, a former press secretary for ex-House Speaker Newt Gingrich. "People just don't understand how hard it is."

Galen said Schoolhouse Rock gets the fundamentals right, but aside from bickering congressmen many other hurdles await any piece of legislation.

"The one part of it that is true is that a bill is introduced by someone who thinks it's a good idea," Galen said.

After introduction, the bill is referred to a committee that has jurisdiction over its subject matter. For example, a tax bill would be referred to the Senate Finance Committee, or the House Ways and Means Committee. Sometimes a bill might be referred to more than one committee. Then, the committee chairman might assign the bill to a subcommittee for initial debate. The subcommittee may or may not amend it.

If the subcommittee decides to "report" the bill back the full committee, then the full committee will debate its merits—sometimes for days—and often make additional changes. This process is referred to as a "mark-up" because members are marking-up or changing the text of the bill.

Once the mark-up is finished, the committee votes to kill it, or pass it and send it to the floor of the full House or Senate.

"That's where things really get tricky," Galen said. "Many pitfalls await."

In the House, the bill has one more stop before the floor—the Rules Committee. This panel decides how long and under what rules the full House will debate. In the Senate, there is no Rules Committee—the majority leader decides when, or if, the bill gets a floor vote.

If a bill passes the full Senate, it goes to House where the process starts all over again. If it passes the Senate, it goes to the House. If a bill ultimately passes both the House and Senate, chances are it won't have identical language because of the amendment process in each chamber. However, the House and Senate versions of a bill must be identical before the president can sign it into law.

Enter the conference committee, where negotiators appointed by the House Speaker and Senate Majority Leaders hash out differences.

"This is when they go into some room and trade stuff, especially in appropriations (spending) bills," Galen explained.

When the conference committee is finished, the bill goes back to each chamber for a final vote. Once approved, the legislation heads to the White House. If the president signs the bill, or simply waits 10 days without signing it while Congress is in session, it becomes a law.

Life After Congress

These days, it seems almost every new candidate for Congress runs as a Washington "outsider."

These candidates usually denounce incumbents, or "insiders," as lacking fresh ideas and beholden to special interests. But the fact is, some members of Congress have been elected in recent years despite (or perhaps because of) their previous status as the ultimate insiders: Capitol Hill staffers.

At least 70 former Hill staffers are now members of Congress, including Rep. Paul Ryan, a Wisconsin Republican who wrote speeches as a member of late New York Rep. Jack Kemp's staff, Sen. Barbara Boxer, a California Democrat who succeeded her boss in the U.S. House, and Sen. Lamar Alexander, a Tennessee Republican who worked for former Senate Majority Leader Howard Baker, also of Tennessee.

Ari Fleischer, a former communications director for ex-Sen. Pete Domenici, R-N.M., went on to become a spokesman for the House Ways and Means Committee in the late 1990s. He then went served as the first press secretary for President George W. Bush.

Fleischer, a New York native, has since returned to his home state where he runs a sports media consulting business representing professional athletes. He said working as a Capitol Hill staffer has upsides and downsides for aspiring members of Congress.

"There's no question it gives you a heads up on how Congress works," Fleischer said. "On the other hand, in this era where outsiders and people who want to change things have a high value, it can be a handicap.

During the mid-1990s, Paul Hernsson, director of the Center for American Politics and Citizenship at the University of Maryland at College Park, conducted a study of staffers who became members of Congress. He found that former Hill staffers had a significantly higher election rate than those who had never worked for a House or Senate member or committee.

"What an aide has in terms of advantages is knowledge of the issues, knowledge of politics in general and a lot of contacts that can be useful in running a congressional campaign," Hernsson said. "They get in and they hit the ground running because they know how Congress works. They also know virtually everybody because congressional aides do a lot of the work."

However, the fact that staffers are expected stay behind the scenes and not eclipse their bosses in the public arena can be a disadvantage. Most members of Congress win election after having served in some form of high-profile position in their community. Maybe they've been a county commissioner or school board member, or worked in a high-profile corporate job or some other visible post.

"What (staffers) don't have that most elected officials have is public recognition, and that's a tremendous advantage," Hernsson said.

Rep. Joe Bonner, R-Ala., worked for Rep. Sonny Callahan, also an Alabama Republican, from 1985 to 2002. He began as press secretary and then became Callahan's chief of staff in 1990. Bonner said having Capitol Hill experience has been invaluable to him in his job as congressman.

"Working on the Hill for so long enabled me to develop the kind of relationships back in the district—once I became a candidate—that proved especially helpful in a campaign with eleven other candidates," he recalled.

He also said he came to office with immense respect for his staff.

"You more fully appreciate the critically important role of the staff…and you make sure you have that team in place on day one," he said.

Princella Smith, a former staffer for Republican ex-Louisiana Rep. Joseph Cao, ran for a U.S. House seat in her home state of Arkansas in 2010. Smith, who was just 26 at the time, won the endorsement of Arkansas' largest newspaper, but was unable to win the Republican primary. Now employed in the Arkansas Secretary of State's Office, Smith said she plans to make another run for Congress, possibly in 2012. She also sees very few political downsides to having served on the staff of a congressman.

"When you campaign you are interviewing for a job and you need to understand where you're saying and doing," she said. "The immediate help was that I knew the culture. Also, when you work on the Hill you learn who the power players in your party are. It made me feel like I was ready to do this."

United States House of Representatives

Leadership
http://www.house.gov

MAJORITY MEMBERS

John Boehner, OH-8th, Speaker of the House
Eric Cantor, VA-7th, Majority Leader
Kevin McCarthy, CA-22nd, Majority Whip
Pete Sessions, TX-32nd, Chairman, National Republican Congressional Committee
Jeb Hensarling, TX-5th, Chairman, Republican Conference
Tom Price, GA-6th, Chairman, Republican Policy Committee

MINORITY MEMBERS

Nancy Pelosi, CA-8th, Minority Leader
Steny Hoyer, MD-5th, Minority Whip
James E. Clyburn, SC-6th
John Larson, CT-1st, Chairman, Democratic Caucus
Xavier Becerra, CT-31st, Vice Chairman, Democratic Caucus
Rosa DeLauro, CT-3rd, Co-Chairman, Democratic Steering Committee
George Miller, CA-7th, Co-Chairman, Democratic Steering Committee

HOUSE LEADERSHIP

The elections of 2010 were not kind to the majority Democrats of the 111th Congress. Amid a fragile economy and sky-high unemployment, Rep. Nancy Pelosi, D-Calif., and the Democrats were trounced at the polls in November, losing 63 seats and delivering House control back to the Republicans after just four years in power.

The election "shellacking," in the headline-grabbing description of President Barack Obama, has set the tone for the 112th Congress. The shake-up at once threw the brakes on the Democrat's ambitious legislative agenda, forced a heated discussion about appropriate levels of federal spending, and launched a national debate about how much government is good for the country.

The power switch creates considerable complications for Obama, who had enjoyed commanding Democratic majorities in both chambers through the first two years of his White House tenure. Over that span, House Democrats were able to pass some of the most consequential legislation in decades, including Wall Street reform, an economic stimulus package, and an overhaul of the nation's healthcare system—all very partisan bills that the new GOP majority is fighting to scale back or overturn altogether.

The year began civilly enough. In passing the Speaker's gavel to Rep. John Boehner in January, Pelosi hailed the Ohio Republican as "a man of conviction, a public servant of resolve, and a legislative leader of skill."

Boehner responded modestly.

"Thank you," he said. "It's still just me."

Since then, the two parties haven't agreed on much. Democrats blamed the bad economy for their election drubbing, while Republicans cited the healthcare law and soaring federal deficits. The Democrats think more government spending is necessary to create jobs, while Republicans say steep cuts are required to unshackle the hiring powers of private enterprise.

It's the latter disagreement that's sure to consume the most oxygen this year.

"Our spending has caught up with us, and our debt soon will eclipse the entire size of our national economy," Boehner said as he took the gavel. "Hard work and tough decisions will be required of the 112th Congress. No longer can we fall short."

Assisting Boehner this Congress are Majority Leader Eric Cantor, R-Va., and Majority Whip Kevin McCarthy, R-Calif.—two of the so-called "young guns" of the GOP. With that label, they're hoping to create a youthful image in contrast to the top Democratic leaders, all a generation older.

Democrats, meanwhile, kept their top leadership team intact, with Pelosi now the minority leader, Rep. Steny Hoyer, D-Md., stepping into the minority whip role, and Rep. James Clyburn, D-S.C., assuming the No. 3 spot.

The decision to keep the roster unchanged wasn't without controversy.

Fearing Pelosi is too controversial a figure to lead the party back to the majority next year, Blue Dog Rep. Heath Shuler, D-N.C., challenged her leadership position. Pelosi won by an overwhelming margin, however—an indication that most Democrats intend to continue fighting this year for the liberal-leaning reforms that defined the last four.

Boehner and the Republicans have their own internal issues to deal with. More than 80 GOP freshmen arrived on Capitol Hill this year—an enormous figure that left party leaders scurrying to get them up to speed on the arcane rules and routines of the lower chamber.

Additionally, many freshmen were backed by the staunchly conservative Tea Party movement, and are sure to pressure Boehner against too much compromise with Democratic leaders in the White House and Senate.

HOUSE LEADERSHIP

Differing leadership styles between Boehner and Pelosi will also help define the 112th Congress. Whereas Pelosi had a hand in everything—particularly the legislation that reached the floor, which tended to come directly from her office—Boehner is much more willing to let the committees and rank-and-file members dictate the discussion.

Indeed, on the first major spending bill of the year, Boehner opened the floor to almost unlimited amendments. The move—unheard of in recent House history—attracted more than 500 proposals and kept lawmakers voting practically around the clock for three days straight.

"I think that the House working its will is what the Founders have envisioned," Boehner said at the time.

HOUSE LEADERSHIP

John Ashbrook

Staff Director
S-229 U.S. Capitol
Phone: (202) 228-6397
John_ashbrook@mcconnell.senate.gov

Personal: Born 05/02/1981 in Cincinatti, Ohio.

Education: B.S., Business, Miami University (Ohio), 2004.

Professional: 2004–2005, field representative, Rep. Rob Portman, R-OH. 2005–2006, deputy chief of staff, Rep. Jean Schmidt, R-OH. 2006, senior communications coordinator, House Republican Conference. 2007–2010, communications advisor/press secretary, Senate Republican Communications Center, 2010, staff director, Senate Republican Communications Center.

Expertise: Communications.

As Senate Minority Leader Mitch McConnell, R-Ky., tested the new strength of Republican gains from the 2010 elections, he reorganized his staff for the 112th Congress, promoting then-Deputy Spokesman John Ashbrook to the post of communications director.

That was not the end of the bonuses the Ohio native found in the fortified Republican conference.

"Not only did we pick up a number of seats, it's an all-star lineup of new members," Ashbrook said.

The freshmen class of GOP senators "brought an incredible level of talent to the table: Folks with business backgrounds, folks with backgrounds in local government, folks with grass-roots backgrounds, longtime public servants with experience in the executive branch, in the House, in state government," Ashbrook said.

The new members will mesh well, he said, with McConnell's continuing emphasis on "spreading the Republican message in traditional and non-traditional ways."

The GOP communications center's staff breaks down into such specialties as print, radio and TV, and new media.

"Our mission is to amplify and advocate for arguments that our members are making, and to feature members who are participating in the debate," Ashbrook said

"The top issue is jobs," Ashbrook said. "Spending by the federal government will also be a key issue. One of the reasons many voters sent conservatives into the government was that they want Congress to address spending. They want congress to limit this government over-reach."

In addition, Ashbrook said, the Democratic health care overhaul that President Barack Obama signed into law in 2010 "will continue to be a huge issue."

In a sense, Ashbrook's step up to become McConnell's minority communications director brings him back to his roots. Ashbrook came to Capitol Hill right out of college as a staffer to Ron Portman, the congressman who represented the suburban Cincinnati area where he grew up. Now a senator, Portman is part of that "wide variety," as Ashbrook called it, that is represented in the new class of Republican senators.

"An understanding of how the House typically operates" will be an asset, Ashbrook said, as McConnell and the new House Speaker, John Boehner, R-Ohio, continue their longstanding partnership—with a major infusion of clout. "Their relationship translates into [a] good working relationship at the level of the floor and policy staffs," Ashbrook said.

HOUSE LEADERSHIP

Katie Beirne

Staff director, Democratic Policy and Communications Center

S-318 U.S. Capitol

Phone: (202) 224-2939

Katie_Beirne@dpcc.senate.gov

Personal: Born 12/26/1975 in Cleveland, Ohio.

Education: B.A., Government and International Studies, University of Notre Dame, 1998. M.A., Comparative Ethnic Conflict Regulation, Queens University Belfast, 1999. M.Sc., Comparative Politics, London School of Economics, 2000.

Professional: 2000-2002, Investment Banking associate, Lehman Brothers, New York. 2003-2005, Competition Policy Associates, vice president. 2005-2006, policy director, Democratic Senatorial Campaign Committee. 2007, Joint Economic Committee, deputy staff director. 2008-2011, Sen. Charles E. Schumer, legislative director.

Expertise: Policy development.

As staff director of the newly formed Democratic Policy and Communications Center, Katie Beirne's business is to help assemble the Senate Democratic legislative agenda, from its very inception, in terms that connect directly with the public.

The newly-revamped DPCC, chaired by New York Senator Chuck Schumer, merged the Senate's communications center with the Democratic Policy Center. The goal of the reorganization was to allow for greater coordination between communications, policy, and research "so that you'd have the right hand coordinating with the left hand" from the outset, said Beirne, a longtime legislative aid for Schumer.

Under Beirne's direction, the DPCC is focused on arming the caucus with a crisper message and policy ideas that resonate with the middle-class voters that Democrats need to target. In February, the DPCC organized a three-day caucus strategy session that culminated in the launching of the Senate Democrats "Winning the Future" jobs agenda. Within weeks, the Senate passed three of the bills from this agenda.

Early in the 112th Congress, DPCC began to show members and their aides "how to prove to real people the gains they receive from the policies we're delivering," said Beirne. To guide her, Beirne repeats Schumer's key take-away from the 2010 elections, "people will choose a government that works for them over no government at all, but they would rather have no government than a government that works for somebody else," Beirne said.

The DPCC training grounds include daily brainstorming sessions for the staff of more than 20, the senators' weekly caucus luncheons, and weekly meetings of senior aides. There, the DPCC provides members and aides localized data to help demonstrate the benefits of each policy and generate positive local press coverage.

Beirne sees her personal background as an asset to the DPCC's new mission. She's the second of eight children of middle-class parents in the Cleveland suburbs who worked hard to put all of their children through college. She worked for several years in finance and economic consulting before she got into politics.

The business experience, Beirne said, has attuned her to a fact that Democrats need to do more to appeal to engage the private sector: "Middle-class voters trust businesses that hire them in their local communities, often more than they trust the government. We need to leverage that."

HOUSE LEADERSHIP

Stacey Farnen Bernards

Deputy Chief of Staff
House Minority Whip Steny Hoyer
H-148, The Capitol
Phone: (202) 225-3130
stacey.bernards@mail.house.gov

Personal: Born 08/11/1974 in Albany, N.Y.

Education: B.A., foreign affairs; French, University of Virginia, 1996.

Professional: 1998, field coordinator, Wisconsin Democratic Coordinated Campaign. 1998–2000, deputy press secretary and legislative correspondent, Rep. Dave Obey, D-Wisc. 2000–2001, associate and senior producer, Home Front Communications. 2001–2002, press secretary, Rep. Steny Hoyer, D-Md. 2002–2006, press secretary, House Minority Whip Steny Hoyer, D-Md. 2007–2009, communications director, House Majority Leader Steny Hoyer, D-Md. 2009–present, deputy chief of staff, House Majority Leader Steny Hoyer, D-Md.

Expertise: Communications.

The 111th Congress was the first for Stacey Farnen Bernards in a new role as deputy chief of staff under Rep. Steny Hoyer, D-Md. It was an eventful time to step into the role.

With a broad majority, House Democrats were able to pass a number of sweeping reforms—from climate change legislation, to Wall Street reform, to a health care overhaul. And Hoyer, then the majority leader, was at the front lines of all the action.

"We worked on almost every major piece of legislation that moved through the House," Bernards said.

Through it all, Bernards—who worked in Hoyer's press shop for eight years prior—advised on strategy and helped coordinate the various aspects of Hoyer's operation. Working closely with Chief of Staff Terry Lierman, her focus included items as diverse as policy, the floor schedule, member services, outreach, and, of course, communications.

Those responsibilities have carried over into the 112th Congress—with a big exception: although Hoyer, as minority whip, remains the second-ranking Democrat, he no longer controls the chamber's floor calendar.

The change has not discouraged Bernards, however, who's constantly searching ways to gain traction for the various proposals on Hoyer's legislative wish-list.

"We are working on other ways to build support for his priorities and have them brought to the floor," Bernards said, without volunteering details.

Part of Bernards' task is to identify those priorities and drive the staff to stay focused on them. This year, the first half of that equation won't be difficult. As Hoyer reminds reporters frequently, his primary focus this year is the so-called "Make It in America" agenda, a series of proposals designed to tackle the lingering jobs crisis by discouraging outsourcing.

Getting it passed from the minority will be a test of the Democrats' talents.

HOUSE LEADERSHIP

Neil L. Bradley

Deputy Chief of Staff

Republican Leader Eric Cantor, R-Va.

H-329, The Capitol

Phone: (202) 225-4000

Personal: Born 10/29/1975 in Sapulpa, Okla.

Education: B.A., Georgetown University, 1998.

Professional: 1995–99, various positions, Rep. Tom Coburn, R-Okla. 1999–2004, executive dir., Republican Study Cmte. 2004–2008, policy dir., House Republican Whip Roy Blunt, R-Mo. 2009–2010, policy dir., House Republican Whip Eric Cantor, R-Va. 2011–present, deputy chief of staff, House Republican Leader Eric Cantor, R-Va.

Expertise: Budget, tax and spending matters, legislative process.

Neil Bradley will serve in the 112th Congress as deputy chief of staff for new House Republican Leader Eric Cantor, R-Va.

The promotion comes after Bradley served for five and a half years as policy director for the Republican Whip, under both Cantor and former Rep. Roy Blunt, R-Mo. In that role, he became known as one of the most powerful back room players on the Hill.

Part of Bradley's job is to help Cantor highlight weaknesses in the Democrats' proposals and offer alternatives that are appealing to the Democrats most likely to cross the aisle. He also helps identify areas in which Republicans and Democrats can work together on advancing legislation.

But Bradley is most known for pioneering the use of a once-overlooked procedural vote known as motion to recommit, or "MTR" as policy wonks call it. The MTR is requested before a final vote on a bill as a way to kill the bill or amend it so that opponents are forced to vote against their own bill.

"We use it almost every occasion we can, either to try to stop the bill from moving forward, to highlight the kind of policies we would be pursuing if we were in charge, or frankly to highlight some really absurd, bad choices that are being made by the majority," Bradley told *Doublethink* in 2009, the official magazine of America's Future Foundation, a young conservatives organization.

Prior to going to the Whip's office, Bradley was executive director of the Republican Study Committee. At age 24, he was the youngest person to hold the position.

Bradley started his Capitol Hill career as an intern in the office of then-Rep. Tom Coburn, R-Okla., whom he worked for while attending Georgetown University. He joined Coburn's staff after graduating in 1998.

Bradley is married to Kiki Bradley, a welfare expert for The Heritage Foundation. They have a newborn son.

HOUSE LEADERSHIP

Guy Cecil

Executive director, Democratic Senatorial Campaign Committee

120 Maryland Avenue NE

Phone: (202) 224-2447

Personal: Born in Miami, Fla.

Education: B.A., political science, University of Florida, 1996.

Professional: 2000, field director, Missouri Democratic Coordinated Campaign. 2001, national field director, Children's Defense Fund. 2002, director, Arkansas Democratic Coordinated Campaign. 2003–2004, principal, grassroots campaign practice, Dewey Square Group. 2005–2006, political director, Democratic Senatorial Campaign Committee. 2007–2008, national political and field director, Hillary Clinton for President. 2009–2010, chief of staff, Sen. Michael Bennet. 2010, executive director, Democratic Senatorial Campaign Committee.

Expertise: Political organization, field operations.

As executive director of the Democratic Senatorial Campaign Committee for the incoming chairwoman, Sen. Patty Murray of Washington, Guy Cecil brought a rare variety and wealth of experience to what loomed as a challenging 2012 election cycle for her fellow Senate Democrats.

The numbers alone were daunting. Democrats were to defend 23 seats, against only 10 for the Republicans, so their majority in the 2010 elections was in peril. Democrats had made such gains in the 2006 and 2008 elections that the new President, Barack Obama, got much of what he wanted from a "filibuster-proof," 60-vote Democratic majority in the Senate until early in 2010. But Massachusetts Republican Scott Brown's win in a special election for the seat long-held by the late Sen. Edward M. Kennedy previewed the strong GOP gains to come.

As the 112th Congress convened, the Democrats claimed majority control with 53 seats (counting those of independent Senators Joseph I. Lieberman of Connecticut and Bernard Sanders of Vermont). The roster of retiring Democrats included some, such as Senators Kent Conrad of North Dakota and Jim Webb of Virginia, from Republican-leaning states.

But Cecil had a track record that Senate Democrats considered auspicious. He took the job at the DSCC after a key victory in a swing state, during a bad year for the party. Cecil "was instrumental" to the reelection of Sen. Michael Bennet, the Colorado Democrat said. "My colleagues in the Senate will soon find out how fortunate they are to have him on their side."

Majority Leader Harry Reid made note of another asset: having served as political director of the DSCC six years earlier, Cecil "has the added benefit of having worked with this particular class of senators. I worked with Guy when we won the majority in 2006 and I look forward to working with him to keep it."

Before entering politics, Cecil served as a high school teacher, a minister, and an organizer for such causes as educating the disadvantaged.

In 2000, Cecil served as a staffer on Vice President Al Gore's New Hampshire primary campaign, the director of his Vermont primary campaign, and general election field director for the party's coordinated effort in the perennial swing state of Missouri.

Cecil has since held key posts at public, private, and non-government organizations, including national political and field director for presidential candidate Hillary Clinton in the 2008 primary campaigns.

HOUSE LEADERSHIP

Daniel P. Coughlin

Chaplain, U.S. House of Representatives
HB-25, The Capitol
Phone: (202) 225-2509
Fax: (202) 225-0204

Personal: Born 11/08/1934, in Ill.

Education: S.T.L., sacred theology, St. Mary of the Lake University, 1960. D.D., pastoral studies, Loyola University, 1968. Honorary doctorate, theology, Lewis University, 2004.

Professional: 1960–65, associate pastor, St. Raymond Parish (Mount Prospect, Ill.). 1965–68, associate pastor, Holy Name Cathedral (Chicago, Ill.). 1969–84, director, Office for Divine Worship, Archdiocese of Chicago. 1984–85, sabbatical, scholar-in-residence, North American College (Rome, Italy). 1985–90, pastor, St. Francis Xavier Parish (La Grange, Ill.). 1990–95, director, Cardinal Stritch Retreat House (Mundelein, Ill.). 1995–2000, vicar for priests, Archdiocese of Chicago. 2000–present, chaplain, U.S. House of Representatives.

Expertise: Public speaking.

As the House chaplain, Daniel P. Coughlin is the chamber's spiritual rock. But the 76-year old Roman Catholic priest says he couldn't do it without the support and inspiration from the thousands of staff who work in the House.

"They are such inspiring young people," Coughlin said. "They come here out of a sense of desire to help people and a hope that they can better the world. There's a certain openness and generosity amongst them that is so wonderful to be around."

Coughlin played an instrumental role in the wake of the shooting that left Rep. Gabrielle Giffords, D-Ariz., wounded and killed her director of community outreach, Gabe Zimmerman. In the weeks following, Coughlin was the House's spiritual lighthouse, providing countless hours of moral support for staffers who had seemingly unanswerable questions.

Counseling the grieving during moments of great tragedy is just one of Coughlin's roles as the chamber's chaplain.

Coughlin opens every formal session of the House with a prayer and he actively promotes the guest chaplain program in which members of Congress invite clergy from their congressional districts to offer the daily prayer. The program highlights the richness of America's spiritual heritage, Coughlin said.

Coughlin was appointed in March 2000, the first Roman Catholic priest to serve as House chaplain. Since then he has been sworn in for five subsequent Congresses and has become part of the Chamber's fabric, providing spiritual guidance and ministry to members and staff.

In the 112th Congress, Coughlin has made it a priority to familiarize himself with the largest freshman class in 60 years. After more than a decade as the House's chaplain, though, Coughlin has said that he is not planning on staying in the position beyond the 112th Congress.

HOUSE LEADERSHIP

Brad Dayspring

Communications Director
House Republican Leader Eric Cantor, R-Va.
H-329, The Capitol
Phone: (202) 225-4000
Twitter: @BDayspring
brad.dayspring@mail.house.gov

Personal: Born 03/10/1977 in Paterson, N.J.

Education: B.A., political science, Villanova University, 1999.

Professional: 1999–2000, deputy press secretary, House Budget Cmte. Chairman John Kasich, R-Ohio. 2000, West Virginia director of communications, Bush/Cheney 2000. 2001–2003, deputy director of press advance, White House. 2004–2005, director of media relations, National Restaurant Association. 2005–2006, communications director, Rep. Chris Smith, R-N.J. 2006–2009, communications director, Rep. Jeb Hensarling, R-Texas. 2009–2010, Press Secretary, House Republican Whip Eric Cantor, R-Va. 2010–present, communications director, House Republican Leader Eric Cantor, R-Va.

Expertise: Media relations, new media, political strategy.

Brad Dayspring started the 112th Congress moving up in rank, just as his boss Rep. Eric Cantor, R-Va., did. Dayspring served as press secretary for then-Whip Cantor. After Republicans won the House, Cantor became Republican Leader and Dayspring was named Cantor's communications director.

A release about the appointment said: "In his new role, Brad will develop and implement a long-term communications strategy as well as manage all day-to-day communications and press operations."

Dayspring talks to reporters daily and posts tweets to Twitter constantly, pushing out Republican talking points. "Brad is laser-focused and extremely competitive, which is what you want in a media relations guy," Texas Rep. Jeb Hensarling, told Politico in 2008.

Dayspring is no stranger to Republican message-making. Before Cantor, he worked for three years as press secretary for Hensarling, who was chairman of the conservative Republican Study Committee.

Dayspring's first job on Capitol Hill was in the press shop of former Budget Chairman John Kasich, R-Ohio. He then served as West Virginia press secretary for the George W. Bush presidential campaign. After the election, Dayspring became deputy director of press advance at the White House. That experience gave him a better understanding of, and appreciation for, journalists, he said.

After two years at the White House, he joined the Bush reelection campaign. A year later, he joined the National Restaurant Association, returning to the Hill in 2005 as communications director for Rep. Chris Smith, R-N.J. In 2006, Hensarling offered him the RSC job; he moved to Cantor's office after Cantor became Whip.

A native of Pompton Lakes, N.J., Dayspring was captain of Villanova University's hockey team before he graduated in 1999. He is a lifelong fan of the New York Yankees, New York Rangers, and New York Jets.

HOUSE LEADERSHIP

Nadeam Elshami

Communications Director/Senior Advisor

House Speaker Nancy Pelosi

H-204, The Capitol

Phone: (202) 226-7616

nadeam.elshami@mail.house.gov

Personal: Born 04/29/1970 in Nashville, Tenn.

Education: B.A., international business, University of Evansville, 1991.

Professional: 1992–94, staff assistant, Senate Mail Room. 1994–99, staff assistant, deputy press secretary, Sen. Barbara Boxer, D-Calif. 1998, deputy communications director, Boxer for Senate. 1999–2005, press secretary, deputy chief of staff, Rep. Jan Schakowsky, D-Ill. 2004, communications director, Up for Victory. 2005, national press secretary, Senate Minority Whip Richard Durbin, D-Ill. 2006–2007, deputy communications director, senior communications advisor, Senate Minority Whip Dick Durbin, D-Ill. 2007–present, deputy communications director, House Speaker Nancy Pelosi. 2011–present, communications director, House Minority Leader Nancy Pelosi, D-Calif.

Expertise: Communications, media relations, media strategy.

From mailroom grunt to messaging guru, Nadeam Elshami has come a long way in his 19 years on Capitol Hill.

The Nashville native, who began his political career delivering mail in the Senate, was tapped this year to lead the communications team for House Minority Leader Nancy Pelosi, D-Calif. The spot opened up when long-time Pelosi aide Brendan Daly left for a public relations firm.

The move puts Elshami in charge of shaping the public image of Pelosi, one of the most effective—but controversial—figures on the Hill. He also manages messaging for the entire caucus, which includes reaching out to reporters; coordinating strategy with the White House and Senate; and working with rank-and-file members to polish talking points ahead of district visits.

The goal is "ensuring that everyone stays on message and that we're operating in clear contrast to the Republicans," Elshami said.

The task is hardly new to Elshami, who was Pelosi's deputy communications director between 2007 and 2010. During the time frame, House Democrats moved some major legislation, including a climate change bill, health care reform, and a stimulus package.

"The country had major problems," Elshami said. "We were trying to sell to the voters why the Democrats' policies were an appropriate response."

Many voters, however, weren't buying. Instead, they put Republicans back in control of the House.

For Elshami, the minority status alters the game a bit. Democrats don't control the floor, but they can attack whatever the Republicans bring there. This year, the fight will focus on spending cuts.

"Wherever there's an opportunity to contrast who we are with the Republicans, we'll do it," Elshami said. "You're still attempting to legislate, but you're also pointing out where the differences are."

Elshami and his wife Stacy live in Alexandria, Va., with their three children.

HOUSE LEADERSHIP

Brian Fallon

Chief Spokesman, Democratic Policy and Communications Center

S-318 U.S. Capitol

Phone: (202) 224-2939

brian_fallon@dpcc.senate.org

Personal: Born in Lowell, Mass.

Education: B.A., Harvard University, 2003.

Professional: 2003–2004, spokesman, Democratic National Convention. 2007–2009, National press secretary, Sen. Charles E. Schumer. 2009–2010, communications director, Sen. Charles E. Schumer. 2011, chief spokesman, Democratic Policy and Communications Center.

Expertise: Communications.

In the wake of his party's losses in the 2010 elections, Sen. Chuck Schumer, D-NY, tapped spokesman Brian Fallon to assist in the task of conducting the diverse chorus of Senate Democrats from a single policy hymnal.

Under Chairman Schumer, the Democratic Policy and Communications Center merged the party's message shop—modeled after the Clinton administration's rapid-response "war room"—with the old Democratic Policy Committee, which traced its roots to Lyndon B. Johnson's leadership of Senate Democrats in the 1950s.

The goal, in the words of DPCC chief spokesman Fallon, was to fashion the party's "Three Ps"—policy, politics and press—under one roof. "Members wanted to see us be more strategic, and they wanted to see us go on offense more" in the 112th Congress, said Fallon. The new House GOP majority's free-swinging attacks on federal spending offered a foil for the DPCC.

A relatively small legislative chore—reauthorization of the Federal Aviation Administration—was an early test of the DPCC. In answer to Arizona Republican Sen. John McCain's push for program cuts, the DPCC's researchers "excavated" nuggets of concrete effect: less aid to specific rural airports around the country, said Fallon. DPCC communications staff of about 15 organized news events for Democratic senators to critique the cuts in their localities. The DPCC thus honed an obscure federal program—but one cherished by the many thousands of travelers who depend on it—to sharpen the Democratic message of budget-cutting prudence in a highly specific way. The FAA bill passed with a bipartisan majority.

Fallon said the DPCC would deploy Senate Democrats to voice party policy on a broad array of issues in 2011 and 2012. A likely focal point: the tension between the need to create jobs and buoy the fragile economic recovery and the need to address the federal deficit.

A full bill of tough policy fights awaited, from reauthorization of the "No Child Left Behind" education program and the federal highway-building system, to the GOP attacks on Obama's health care overhaul, to the federal spending and taxation issues implicit in almost every debate.

Reared in the fading Merrimack Valley mill town of Methuen, Mass., Fallon jumped into politics soon after he graduated from Harvard, serving on the staff of the Democratic National Convention that nominated Sen. John F. Kerry for president in 2004.

HOUSE LEADERSHIP

Kristie Greco

Communications Director

Assistant Democratic Leader James Clyburn, D-S.C.

H-132, The Capitol

Phone: (202) 226-3210

kristie.greco@mail.house.gov

Personal: Born 02/21/1975 in Voorhees, N.J.

Education: B.A., English, Villanova University, 1997.

Professional: 1995, intern, The White House. 1996, intern, Rep. Tim Holden, D-Pa. 1997, associate, Goodyear Government Relations. 1998–2000, legislative correspondent, Rep. Tim Holden, D-Pa. 2000–2006, press secretary, Rep. Peter DeFazio, D-Ore. 2006, communications director, House Democratic Caucus Chairman James Clyburn, D-S.C. 2007–2011, communications director, House Majority Whip James Clyburn, D-S.C. 2011–Present, communications director, Assistant Democratic Leader James Clyburn, D-S.C.

Expertise: Communications.

Kristie Greco is in charge of handling the media for the highest-ranking African American congressman, Rep. James Clyburn, D-S.C.

Greco has taken on a new role in the 112th Congress as Clyburn shifted from being the Democratic Whip to becoming the Assistant Democratic Leader, the third-highest ranking Democrat.

Clyburn's leadership position was created in an effort to prevent a division within the Democratic leadership as they shifted from the majority to the minority in the 112th Congress. Democrats lost the position of Speaker when they lost control of the House, which left former Democratic Majority Leader Steny Hoyer, D-Md., and Clyburn jockeying for the House Minority Whip position.

After a briefly contentious battle, Clyburn ceded power to Hoyer and became the Assistant Democratic Leader, which ensured his seat at leadership meetings and kept intact the leadership team that brought the Democrats success in the previous two Congresses.

In the new role, Greco helps craft the Democratic message while they retain the minority, a job that is tactfully different than when Democrats were in the majority.

"In the minority, you spend the day trying to break through and convince the public what you're doing is relevant," Greco said.

Greco grew up in nearby Springfield, Virginia, and says her interest in politics was piqued by growing up in the shadow of the Capitol.

"When we were studying Congress, we went to see Congress in session," Greco recalled. "It made it very exciting and immediate."

In 2000, Greco began working as Rep. Peter DeFazio's, D-Ore., press secretary and hasn't looked back since.

"After working in an office, I realized [communications] was the best job in the office," Greco said. "It's fast-paced, you never know what you're going to get, and I was more interested in dealing with all the issues."

HOUSE LEADERSHIP

Karen Lehman Haas

Staff Clerk, U.S. House of Representatives
Speaker of the House John Boehner, R-Ohio
H-154, The Capitol

Personal: Born 04/13/1962 in Baltimore, Md.

Education: B.S., University of Maryland, 1984.

Professional: 1984–94, executive legislative assistant, Minority Leader Robert H. Michel, R-Ill. 1995–98, dir. of government relations, ABC, Inc. 1998–99, senior legislative analyst, The Walt Disney Company. 1999–2005, director of GOP Steering Committee, Speaker of the House J. Dennis Hastert, R-Ill. 2005–2006, clerk of the House, U.S. House of Representatives. 2007–2008, executive director, Republican Conference Chairman Adam Putnam, R-Fla. 2009–2011, staff director, House Minority Committee on Small Business. 2011–Present, clerk of the House, U.S. House of Representatives.

Expertise: Rules, House procedures, administration.

Karen Haas is the 34th individual to serve as the Clerk of the House of Representatives and was sworn in by House Speaker John A. Boehner, R-Ohio in January 2011.

As Clerk, the 49-year old Haas oversees operations on the House floor, including the recording of votes, the creation and certification of all legislative documents and sending and receiving official messages from the Senate and the White House.

The House elects a new clerk every two years when it reconvenes for a new Congress. The majority and minority caucuses nominate candidates for the House officer positions after the election of the Speaker. The full House adopts a resolution to elect the officers, who will begin serving the Membership after they have taken the oath of office, according to the Clerk's office.

But this isn't Haas' first time being the chamber's Clerk. In 2005, she also served in the post after being appointed by former House Speaker J. Dennis Hastert, R-Ill.

A native of Catonsville, Md, Haas graduated from the University of Maryland with a bachelor's degree in political science and a minor in economics. She resides in Maryland with her husband and two children.

For more than a decade Haas has been a fixture in the House. Most recently Haas served as the Republican staff director for the House Small Business Committee in the 111th Congress. And in the 110th Congress she served as executive director of the House Republican Conference.

"Lawmakers on both sides of the aisle have long known and respected Karen—as much for her in depth knowledge of legislative procedure as for her tireless dedication to the work of the people's House," Boehner said. "For as long as I can remember, Karen always seemed to be on the floor of the House when I arrived and was still there working after most Members and staff had left the chamber."

Among Haas' many duties, she oversees the House's art collection and the House Page Program, which has been under close scrutiny since 2007, when four pages were expelled from the program, two for allegedly shoplifting and two others for allegedly engaging in public sex acts.

At the request of the House leadership, House inspector general James Cornell investigated the page program, finding that additional supervision was needed at the page dorm, located just off the congressional campus.

HOUSE LEADERSHIP

Drew Hammill

deputy communications director

House Minority Leader Nancy Pelosi, D-Calif.

H-204, The Capitol

Phone: (202) 225-0100

drew.hammill@mail.house.gov

Personal: Born 07/09/1978 in Marion, Ill.

Education: B.A., political science and communications, University of Illinois at Champaign-Urbana, 2001. M.Phil., comparative politics, London School of Economics, 2003.

Professional: 2002, national development associate, New Democrat Network. 2003, press assistant, Rep. Rahm Emanuel, D-Ill. 2004–2006, press secretary, Rep. Kendrick Meek, D-Fla. 2006, deputy press secretary, House Minority Leader Nancy Pelosi, D-Calif. 2007–2010, press secretary, House Speaker Nancy Pelosi, D-Calif. 2011–present, deputy communications director, House Minority Leader Nancy Pelosi, D-Calif.

Expertise: Communications, messaging strategy, energy, the environment..

Drew Hammill is no stranger to the Democrats' Capitol Hill message machine. The Illinois native cut his teeth in the press shops of former-Reps. Rahm Emanuel, D-Ill. (2003), and Kendrick Meek, D-Fla. (2004-2006), before landing with Rep. Nancy Pelosi, D-Calif., in 2006.

The quick ascension didn't come without a good deal of elbow grease. Hammill recalls waiting tables at a Capitol Hill bistro when Meek called with an urgent request for a press release.

"I kept up with my tables while taking any free moment to type up the release and email back and forth with the congressman," he said. "Got the whole release out within the hour and still made good tips that night."

The hard work has paid off. In 2011, Hammill was promoted as Pelosi's deputy communications director, where he works with Communications Director Nadeam Elshami to develop a messaging strategy to counter the Republicans' legislative offensive. Hammill focuses on the day-to-day operations, corresponding directly with reporters and ensuring a rapid response to criticism and current events.

As communications become ever-more sophisticated and technology-based, Hammill said he's constantly searching for "unique ways" to use the press to reach those demographic groups vital to the Democrats' election chances in 2012. Performing that task from the minority, he said, "has its pros and cons."

"It's very hard work translating a legislative text into the benefits it provides," Hammill said, "but being in the minority has a certain scrappiness that I love."

As Pelosi's press secretary in the last Congress, Hammill focused much of his attention on the Democrats' climate change bill, a controversial measure that passed the House but was never taken up in the Senate. His proudest work, however, was promoting a repeal of the long-standing Pentagon policy barring gays from serving openly in the military. After years of contentious debate, Congress yanked that ban last year.

Hammill said he has no regrets about the Democrats' reform strategy last Congress, even if it was rejected by a good number of voters. He blamed the Democrats' election drubbing on the struggling economy, not their legislative agenda.

"There's nothing you can do to counter that level of unemployment," Hammill said. "We made historic achievements for the American people, and history will remember Speaker Nancy Pelosi got the job done."

Hammill is married to Jason Mida. The couple live on Capitol Hill.

HOUSE LEADERSHIP

Jerry Hartz

Director of Floor Operations
House Minority Leader Nancy Pelosi, D-Calif.
H-204, The Capitol
Phone: (202) 225-0100

Personal: Born 03/30/1958 in Pleasantville, Iowa.

Education: B.A., history, Central University of Iowa, 1980.

Professional: 1981–86, legislative dir., Committee for a SANE Nuclear Policy. 1987–91, associate staff, House Rules Cmte. 1991–2001, executive floor asst., Democratic Whip David Bonior, D-Mich. 2001–2002, executive floor asst., Democratic Whip Nancy Pelosi, D-Calif. 2003–2006, executive floor asst., Democratic Leader Nancy Pelosi, D-Calif. 2007–present, director of floor operations, House Speaker Nancy Pelosi, D-Calif.

Expertise: Floor procedure, House rules, appropriations, labor, health.

Few people spend more hours on the House floor than Jerry Hartz. The director of floor operations for Minority Leader Nancy Pelosi, D-Calif., Hartz is ever-present in the chamber, helping manage members and promote bills.

In the last Congress, when Pelosi was Speaker and the Democrats controlled the schedule, that meant crafting strategy, advising members on the chamber's arcane procedures and coordinating bills with the Senate and the White House.

"When the Speaker and the leadership decided to move legislation, the leadership floor team worked collectively to make sure it got done," Hartz said. "The last Congress was historic in its accomplishments."

This year, instead of rallying the troops around Democratic proposals, Hartz now helps coordinate opposition to GOP bills.

"Being in the minority is always hard. But the goal is to be an alternative voice that holds the majority's feet to the fire," he said. "An organized and unified House minority is a potent force. It speaks for at least half the country and it's what makes democracy work."

Hartz has been part of Pelosi's floor team since 2001, when his old boss, former Democratic Whip David Bonior, D-Mich., stepped down to run for governor. The job grants Hartz some influence over every major proposal the House considers—a situation that suits him just fine.

"One of the great things about working on the House floor is that you lend a hand on all major legislation," Hartz said. "It's why I love this job."

After more than 20 years on the Hill, Hartz said he's never seen the country more divided—a testimony to the "wrenching economic and political times as America redefines itself for this century."

"The days of long-tenured majorities are over," he said. "But political engagement is much better than apathy, so we all have to let democracy work...and take nothing for granted."

HOUSE LEADERSHIP

George Kundanis

Deputy Chief of Staff

House Minority Leader Nancy Pelosi, D-Calif.

H-204, The Capitol

Phone: (202) 225-0100

Personal: Born 02/13/1950 in Chicago, Ill.

Education: B.A., Northwestern University, 1971. M.A., University of Wisconsin, 1972. Ph.D., University of Wisconsin, 1982.

Professional: 1976–77, fellow, American Political Science Association. 1977, legislative asst., Rep. Thomas Foley, D-Wash. 1977–80, asst. to the chairman, House Democratic Caucus. 1981–86, floor asst., House Majority Whip Thomas Foley, D-Wash. 1986–89, executive floor asst., Majority Leader Thomas Foley, D-Wash. 1989–94, executive dir., House Democratic Steering and Policy Cmte. 1995–2002, special asst., House Minority Leader Richard Gephardt, D-Mo. 2002–2006, special asst., House Minority Leader Nancy Pelosi, D-Calif. 2007–present, deputy chief of staff, House Speaker Nancy Pelosi, D-Calif..

Expertise: Democratic politics.

As deputy chief of staff for House Speaker Nancy Pelosi, D-Calif., in the 111th Congress, George Kundanis helped the Democrats pass some of the most significant bills the country has seen in decades. From Wall Street reform, to a climate change bill, to an overhaul of the nation's health care system, Kundanis had a direct hand in every major proposal that came to the floor.

"It was a historic Congress with a historic record of achievement," Kundanis said.

Ask Kundanis about his personal role in the success of those bills, and he's quick to downplay it. He is, he said, "just part of a staff team."

Ask anyone else, however, and they'll likely tell a different story. Indeed, Kundanis is one of the most respected staffers on the Hill, having built a reputation as the leadership's go-to man for policy advice and political strategy. The Chicago native is a master of floor procedure, a key messaging strategist, and an able tactician in crafting policies that can pass a closely divided House.

Kundanis—who this year remains deputy chief of staff for Minority Leader Pelosi—will need all of those skills if the minority Democrats hope to win any legislative victories in the 112th Congress. Working closely with Pelosi Chief of Staff John Lawrence, Kundanis's responsibilities include floor strategy and communicating with rank-and-file members.

"Our primary focus in the minority is to work with the majority when we can, and expound clear alternatives when we cannot," Kundanis said. "We do not control the floor or the agenda. We have to react not create."

For more than 30 years, Kundanis has worked in leadership as a top aide for Pelosi, former Minority Leader Dick Gephardt, D-Mo., and former House Speaker Tom Foley, D-Wash. He's been there so long that members and aides affectionately joke that he, like the furniture, comes with the office.

HOUSE LEADERSHIP

John A. Lawrence

Chief of Staff
House Minority Leader Nancy Pelosi, D-Calif.
H-204, The Capitol
Phone: (202) 225-0100
John.Lawrence1@mail.house.gov

Personal: Born 07/05/1949 in Paterson, N.J.

Education: A.B., Oberlin College, 1970. Ph.D., history, University of California at Berkeley, 1979.

Professional: 1971–74, research and teaching asst., University of California, Berkeley. 1975–93, administrative asst. and legislative dir., Rep. George Miller, D-Calif. 1979–83, staff dir., Subc. on Labor Standards. 1983–89, associate staff, House Cmte. on the Budget. 1993–94, staff dir., House Cmte. on Resources. 1995–2005, staff, Democratic Policy Cmte. 1997–2000, Democratic staff dir., House Cmte. on Resources. 2001–2005, Democratic staff dir., House Cmte. on Education and the Workforce. 2005–2006, chief of staff, House Minority Leader Nancy Pelosi, D-Calif.. 2007–present, chief of staff, House Speaker Nancy Pelosi, D-Calif..

Expertise: Democratic politics, education, environment and energy, labor.

As chief of staff to Minority Leader Nancy Pelosi, D-Calif., John Lawrence is the most influential staffer for the most powerful Democrat in the House.

Lawrence supervises all areas of operation within Pelosi's office, including policy initiatives, floor strategy, public messaging and communications within the caucus. He plots strategy with Senate leaders, and also acts as chief liaison between Pelosi and the White House.

In the 111th Congress, Lawrence oversaw enactment of some of the most sweeping new laws in decades, including a health care overhaul and Wall Street reform. Now, in 2011, without the power to bring legislation to the floor, he and the Democrats have necessarily altered their routine.

"We're in a more reactive role," Lawrence said. "We're focusing a good deal on message and communications to let people know what our alternatives are. It's much harder when you don't control the floor, and so you've got to put much greater emphasis into communications."

The Democrats' message this year is three-pronged, with the emphasis on job creation, deficit reduction and strengthening the middle class. They've proposed immediate hikes on education and infrastructure funding, and warned that Republican efforts to slash federal spending will cost jobs amid a fragile economic recovery.

"We're still not seeing any jobs legislation on the floor," Lawrence said. "That's our greatest frustration."

The focus on jobs plays into one of Lawrence's key strengths. Prior to joining Pelosi's team in 2005, he spent decades in the office of Rep. George Miller, D-Calif., a long-time member of the House labor committee who's now its senior Democrat.

Born in New Jersey, Lawrence lives in Washington with his wife, Deborah Phillips, a professor of psychology and public policy at Georgetown University. They have two children.

HOUSE LEADERSHIP

Terry Lierman

Chief of Staff

House Minority Whip Steny Hoyer, D-Md.

H-148, The Capitol

Phone: (202) 225-3130

terry.lierman@mail.house.gov

Education: B.A., political science, Winona State University, 1969. M.A., University of Wisconsin, 1971.

Professional: 1971–72, management intern, National Institutes of Health. 1972–73, administrative officer for Drug Research and Development, National Cancer Institute, National Institutes of Health. 1973–75, staff member, Office of the Director, National Cancer Institute, National Institutes of Health. 1975–77, professional staff member, Senate Subc. on Labor, Health and Human Services Appropriations. 1976–79, staff director, Senate Subc. on Labor, Health and Human Services and Education Appropriations. 1979–81, staff director/chief clerk, Senate Cmte. on Appropriations. 1981–84, Director of Washington Office, Carley Capital Group. 1984–2001, founder and president, Capitol Associates, Inc. 1990–2002, vice chair, Employee Health Programs. 1994–2001, partner, TheraCom. 1999–2000, candidate for U.S. House of Representatives, 8th District of Maryland. 2001–2004, managing partner, Health Ventures. 2003–2004, National Finance Co-Chair and State Organizer, Howard Dean for President Campaign. 2004–2007, state chair, Maryland Democratic Party. 2007–present, chief of staff, House Majority Leader Steny Hoyer, D-Md.

Expertise: Health care, policy, management.

Terry Lierman is one of the most influential staffers on Capitol Hill—and among the busiest. As chief of staff to Minority Whip Steny Hoyer, D-Md., Lierman oversees not only Hoyer's leadership office, but his personal and campaign offices as well.

That puts the Wisconsin native in charge of balancing policy goals, political strategy, and management for the second-ranking Democrat in the House. He's also Hoyer's point man for outside groups that want to weigh in on bills before Congress.

In the 112th Congress, Lierman said little has changed in his daily routine despite the Democrats' new minority role.

Still, one difference is glaring: Hoyer this year has lost the authority to set the legislative calendar—a power he had as majority leader in the last two Congresses. The change means that, if House Democrats hope to move any of their policy priorities this year, they'll be relying more than ever on the affable Hoyer to forge ties and cut deals with those who can help.

It's a dynamic Lierman recognizes well.

"In the minority, Mr. Hoyer's role as a bridge builder to all parts of our Caucus, the Senate, the White House, and House Republicans is more important than ever," Lierman said. "Our staff is continuing to highlight that."

On the policy side, last Congress Liermen helped the Democrats pass some of the most far-reaching, if controversial, laws Congress has managed in decades, including Wall Street reform and a health care overhaul. He coordinates frequently with John Lawrence, chief of staff to House Minority Leader Nancy Pelosi, D-Calif.

This year, Lierman will focus largely on promoting the central plank of the Democrats' economic recovery platform: the so-called "Make It in America" agenda. The program includes a series of tax, trade, and regulatory reforms designed to discourage outsourcing and create jobs.

HOUSE LEADERSHIP

Wilson Livingood

Sergeant at Arms

H-124, The Capitol

Phone: (202) 225-2456

Personal: Born 10/01/1936 in Philadelphia, Pa.

Education: B.S., police administration, Michigan State University, 1961.

Professional: Positions included (33 years): special agent, U.S. Secret Service, Dallas Field Office. asst. to the special agent in charge, U.S. Secret Service, Presidential Protective Division. asst. special agent in charge, U.S. Secret Service, Office of Protective Forces. special agent in charge, U.S. Secret Service, Office of Protective Forces. inspector, U.S. Secret Service, Office of Inspection. special agent in charge, U.S. Secret Service, Houston Field Office. deputy asst. dir., U.S. Secret Service, Office of Training. 1989–95, executive asst. to the director, U.S. House of Representatives. 1995–present, sergeant at arms, U.S. House of Representatives.

Expertise: Security.

Wilson Livingood, who for 16 years has held the House's top security post, honed his craft during more than three decades in the Secret Service. He began his work on former Vice President Lyndon Johnson's detail and by the time he retired was the last agent on the force who had been on active duty the day President John F. Kennedy was assassinated.

Livingood started as House sergeant-at-arms under Republican House Speaker Newt Gingrich, R-Ga. who was looking for a non-political person with a law-enforcement background. Democratic House Speaker Nancy Pelosi, D-Calif., asked him to stay on in 2007. This year, Speaker John Boehner, R-Ohio, did the same.

Livingood has seen a lot during his long career in law enforcement but said he was still shocked by the sudden and vicious shooting rampage this year in Arizona that left six people dead and Rep. Gabrielle Giffords, D-Ariz, critically injured.

"It is an emotional thing for me because I care for everyone up here," said Livingood. "They are my family and it's my responsibility to protect them and I know that."

Nevertheless, Livingood said the challenge facing security officials on Capitol Hill has not changed. "It's keeping a really good secure environment and having as much openness as possible," he said. "It's that balance."

Livingood's responsibilities also include: parking security, chamber security, IDs, enforcing the rules regulations of floor of House, and coordinating the visits of dignitaries on the House side of the Capitol.

As he goes about that work, Livingood said one of his strongest attributes is his ability to interact with members and staff, who he believes play a vital role in the security of Capitol Hill.

"I've been very fortunate in always having an outstanding relationship with members and staff," he said.

HOUSE LEADERSHIP

Mike Lynch

Chief of Staff
Sen. Charles E. Schumer, D-NY
322 Hart Senate Office Bldg.
Phone: (202) (202)224-4654
Mike_Lynch@schumer.senate.gov

Personal: Born 06/02/1967 in Neubrucke, Germany.

Education: B.S., political science and social science, James Madison University, 1989.

Professional: 1990–93, staff assistant, legislative assistant, senior legislative assistant, Rep. Les Aspin, D-Colo. 1993, Legislative specialist, Defense Secretary Les Aspin. 1994, Field director, Herb Kohl for U.S. Senate. 1995, Director of strategic plans, Sen. Herb Kohl, D-Wisc. 1996, Coordinated campaign director, Democratic Party of Wisconsin. 1997, Midwest political director, Democratic National Committee. 1998, Field director, Schumer for U.S. Senate. 1999–2002, State director, Sen. Charles E. Schumer, D-N.Y. 2002–2005, Staff director, Sen. Charles E. Schumer, D-NY. 2005–2007, Country director, Serbia, National Democratic Institute. 2007, Chief of staff, Sen. Charles E. Schumer, D-NY.

Expertise: Political strategy, congressional management.

As chief of staff to Sen. Chuck Schumer, D-N.Y., Mike Lynch saw the scope of his responsibilities broaden substantially in the 112th Congress when his boss became the chairman of the newly-organized Democratic Policy and Communications Center.

Lynch remained anchored in the veteran Democrat's office, but he also had a foot in the camp of the retooled leadership organization, because a number of key Schumer aides continued to answer to him when they took staff positions there.

"There's not a lot of separation," said Lynch, among the policy arenas under his purview: issues related to Schumer's home state of New York, to the Senate Democratic caucus, and to the Senate Rules Committee, which the Brooklyn native also chairs. "The chief of staff's job is to make sure they all get the attention they need," Lynch said.

Schumer brings to the newly-created DPCC "a talent for strategy" that has long marked his career, according to Lynch. In the 112th Congress, "the challenge is finding the balance between offense and defense to advance your agenda and make sure people know what you stand for," Lynch said.

As the 2011 session got underway, it appeared likely that the legislative agenda would influence the senator's strategic policy and communications agenda as DPCC chairman. Some measures—a new highway bill and a new farm bill, for example—were slated for reauthorization. Others, including tax reform, loomed as potential fields of action after President Obama mentioned them in his first State of the Union address of the new Congress. Taxes "are not necessarily left or right issue," so they offer a chance of bipartisan action, Lynch said.

"Clearly the economy" loomed over all legislative issues, Lynch said. He foresaw another balancing act on that front. Because the Democrats lost several Senate seats in the 2010 elections, "we don't have the numbers" for as broad and ambitious an agenda as President Obama launched in the 111th congress, Lynch said.

So Democrats planned to adopt "a more aggressive style" in critiquing Republican budget priorities and in "putting out our view and our vision of things we want to accomplish," he said. At the same time, however, Lynch envisioned "more collective efforts" by Senate Democrats to work toward "a consensus budget bill."

HOUSE LEADERSHIP

John Murray

Deputy Chief of Staff
Republican Leader Eric Cantor, R-Va.
H-329, The Capitol
Phone: (202) 225-4000

Personal: Born 1972 in Seattle, Wash.

Education: B.A., Franklin and Marshall College, 1994. Masters, health policy and management, Johns Hopkins Bloomberg School of Public Health, 2000.

Professional: 1995–96, deputy political director, Dole for President, Washington, DC. 1996, special assistant to convention manager, Republican National Committee Convention. 1996–2000, director, Strategic Planning and Public Affairs, America's Health Insurance Plans, Washington, DC. 2000–2001, manager, Public Affairs Practice, Burson-Marsteller, Washington, DC. 2000, communications operations, Republican National Committee Convention. 2001–2002, director, Government Relations Director, Government Relations, Freddie Mac, McLean, VA. 2002–2003, deputy vice president, Strategic Communications and Public Affairs, Pharmaceutical Research and Manufacturers of America, Washington, DC. 2003–2007, chief operating officer, Pharmaceutical Care Management Association, Washington, DC. 2007–2008, founder & partner, AB+M Partners, LLC, Washington, DC. 2009–present, deputy chief of staff, House Republican Leader Eric Cantor, R-Va.

Expertise: Communications, strategy.

John Murray will serve in the 112th Congress as deputy chief of staff for House Republican Leader Eric Cantor, R-Va., after doing his part to help Republicans win back the majority.

A news release about his appointment as deputy chief of staff said, "In this capacity John will oversee national strategic planning and initiatives, communications and press operations."

Murray first joined Cantor's office as communications director, after Cantor was elected Minority Whip in November 2008. Cantor had been looking to bolster his press shop after two bruising elections and the loss of the White House.

Murray was hired out of the private sector to run Cantor's ramped up communication office. Murray had the credentials. He was founder and partner of AB+M Partners, a strategic communication and public affairs consulting firm.

"Our job is to articulate in no uncertain terms what the Republican agenda is and what our policy positions are for America, and to do that as aggressively and actively as we can every single day of the week," Murray said at the time.

Effective messaging requires communicating with the various leadership aides on a regular basis. "Coordinating and communicating constantly is something we take very seriously," Murray said.

Murray came to the Hill after spending 14 years in various public relations/management positions in the pharmaceutical and health care industry. He also played senior roles at the 1996 and 2000 Republican National Conventions as well as with Sen. Bob Dole's presidential campaign in 1996.

He is a graduate of Franklin and Marshall College in Pennsylvania and Johns Hopkins' School of Advanced International Studies. He lives and his wife Joanna, a native of Melbourne, Australia, and their daughter Isabella in Alexandria, Va.

HOUSE LEADERSHIP

Kyle Nevins

Deputy Chief of Staff

Republican Leader Eric Cantor, R-Va.

H-329, The Capitol

Phone: (202) 225-4000

kyle.nevins@mail.house.gov

Personal: Born 11/23/1979 in Manhattan, N.Y.

Education: B.A., history, Duke University, 2002.

Professional: 2002–2003, associate, Dawson, McCarthy, Nelson Media. 2003, personal aide, House Majority Whip Roy Blunt, R-Mo. 2004–2006, floor assistant, House Majority Whip Roy Blunt, R-Mo. 2006–2007, chief floor assistant, House Majority Whip Roy Blunt, R-Mo. 2007–2009, floor director, House Minority Whip Roy Blunt, R-Mo. 2009–2010, floor director, House Minority Whip Eric Cantor, R-Va. 2010–present, deputy chief of staff, House Majority Leader Eric Cantor, R-Va.

Expertise: floor operations, vote counting.

After spending nearly a decade in the GOP whip office counting votes, Kyle Nevins starts the 112th Congress in a new position and new office. He's deputy chief of staff to House Majority Leader Eric Cantor, R-Va.

A news release announcing the position said, "Kyle has eight combined years of experience in Republican Whip Offices, serving in floor, coalitions, and Steering Committee capacities for Congressman Cantor as well as former Republican Whip and newly-elected senator, Roy Blunt."

To his new role, Nevins brings his extensive experience of vote counting. That will come in handy when Cantor needs to quickly find out where the GOP caucus stands on certain issues and which members he can depend on.

Nevins has good relationships with GOP members. In the whip office, he relied on face-to-face, member-to-member communication on the House floor.

"He doesn't play checkers; he plays chess," Rep. Patrick McHenry, R-N.C., told Politico for a profile on Nevins. "He's a very intelligent operator."

As floor director for the minority, Nevins worked to make sure that no Republicans supported a Democratic bill. He succeeded on President Barack Obama's $787 billion economic stimulus bill. The bill still passed, but with zero Republican support.

Nevins had been interested in the whipping operation since he interned in the office of then-Majority Whip Tom DeLay, R-Texas, after his freshman year in college. He later worked for Blunt, R-Mo.

Counting votes, he said, is more than simply asking members for a thumbs-up or down. It's figuring out ways to get a large cast of individuals to support the party agenda.

"You're judging personalities, relating to their districts and applying it to votes," Nevins said.

Nevins is a native of North Carolina and a graduate of Duke University. He and his wife, Kristan, live in Washington, D.C.

HOUSE LEADERSHIP

Jay Pierson

Floor Assistant
House Speaker John Boehner, R-Ohio
H-232, The Capitol
Phone: (202) 225-0600

Personal: Born 06/25/1947 in Santa Barbara, Calif.

Education: B.A., English literature, Westmont College, 1969. M.A., English literature, California State University, Long Beach, 1972. Ph.D., English literature, University of Maryland, 1978.

Professional: 1978–79, journal clerk, House Minority Leader John Rhodes, R-Ariz. 1979–86, asst. manager, Republican cloakroom under John Rhodes, R-Ariz., and Bob Michel, R-Ill. 1986–94, floor asst., House Minority Leader Bob Michel, R-Ill. 1995–98, floor asst., House Speaker Newt Gingrich, R-Ga. 1999–2006, floor asst., House Speaker J. Dennis Hastert, R-Ill. 2007–present, floor assistant and parliamentarian, House Republican Leader John Boehner, R-Ohio.

Expertise: Floor procedures.

Jay Pierson is the floor assistant to House Speaker John Boehner, R-Ohio, for the 112th Congress. Last Congress, he worked in the same position for Boehner, who was minority leader.

As the speaker's floor assistant, Pierson's the in-house expert, instructor and coach for Republican members on the traditions, history, rules and procedures of the House. As Republicans look to use their floor time to move their agenda, Pierson's knowledge will be crucial.

Pierson started in the journal clerk's office in 1978 under then-Minority Leader John Rhodes, R-Ariz. He served in the minority in his current position for many years prior to the 1994 Republican take over of the House, then enjoyed life in the majority for 12 years before returning to the minority. Now that Republicans are back in the majority, Pierson knows how to play both ways.

Every day Pierson writes up a description of each vote and posts a daily and weekly tip sheet (his educated guess on the floor calendar) so that members can plan their own schedules.

Pierson holds a doctorate in English literature. As he was graduating, Pierson's wife—who worked for Rhodes—tipped him off to an opening on the House floor under the minority leader.

Originally intending to teach English, one of the things Pierson said he likes most about his job is telling the congressional pages, the high school students who intern on the Hill, about the history and traditions of the Capitol and those who work there.

Pierson learned the intricacies of House rules and procedures firsthand by keeping the official minutes of the House for the journal clerk's office. In 1979, he began a seven-year stint in the House Republican cloakroom. From 1986 to 1994, he worked as a floor assistant to House Minority Leader Bob Michel, R-Ill., a job he also held under former House Speakers Newt Gingrich, R-Ga. and Dennis Hastert, R-Ill.

HOUSE LEADERSHIP

Reva Price

policy advisor

House Minority Leader Nancy Pelosi, D-Calif.

419-B, The Capitol

Phone: (202) 225-0100

Fax: (202) 226-0938

reva.price@mail.house.gov

Personal: Born in Kisco, N.Y.

Education: B.A. history; Jewish studies, State University of New York - Binghamton, 1982.

Professional: 1984–87, administrator, Religious Action Center of Reform Judaism. 1987–97, associate director, B'nai B'rith International Center for Public Policy. 1997–2005, Washington director, Jewish Council for Public Affairs. 2005–2010, advisor to the Speaker, House Speaker Nancy Pelosi, D-Calif. 2011–present, policy advisor, House Minority Leader Nancy Pelosi, D-Calif.

Expertise: Outreach.

Outside groups play an enormous role in shaping legislation and influencing its success on Capitol Hill. In the office of Minority Leader Nancy Pelosi, D-Calif., it's Reva Price who manages relations with these organizations.

For the 112th Congress Price will continue to reach out to interest groups and forge alliances in hopes of building support for the Democrats' agenda. The affiliations are designed to be symbiotic: Interest groups have policy priorities just like lawmakers do. A large part of Price's task is to locate areas where the priorities intersect—spots where working together could prove mutually beneficial.

She is no stranger to the sport. Prior to joining Pelosi's office in 2005, when Pelosi was Speaker of the House, Price was Washington director of the Jewish Council for Public Affairs, a coalition of groups advocating for the Jewish community. The position offered plenty of practice in the art of juggling communications, outreach, politics and special interest advocacy—skills central to her task today.

According to the New York-based Jewish Daily Forward, Pelosi's office had sought to make the Jewish portfolio a higher-profile position, and applicants were told they were seeking a "Reva Price type." As it turned out, Price sought the job herself.

After the move, the Forward hailed Price as "the policy matchmaker between the Jewish community and Democratic lawmakers."

"Price has the chance to bring the Jewish community's hot topics to the ear of true power," the Forward wrote.

But her outreach role extends far beyond Jews, to include other faith-based groups, business interests, and countless other coalitions and individuals who are working on Pelosi's pet issues.

"Outreach is communication," Price once said. "We want to know what their agenda is, and tell them what our agenda is. We try to find where we can work together."

HOUSE LEADERSHIP

Wendell E. Primus

Senior Policy Advisor

House Minority Leader Nancy Pelosi, D-Calif.

H-204, The Capitol

Phone: (202) 225-0100

wendell.primus@mail.house.gov

Personal: Born 1946 in Eldora, Iowa.

Education: B.A., economics, Iowa State University, 1968. Ph.D., economics, Iowa State University, 1975.

Professional: 1975–76, part-time consultant, House Agriculture Cmte. 1977–86, staff economist, House Ways and Means Cmte. 1987–93, chief economist, House Cmte. on Ways and Means. 1991–93, staff dir., Subc. on Human Resources, House Cmte. on Ways and Means. 1993–96, deputy asst. secretary for Human Services Policy, Dept. of Health and Human Services. 1997–2003, dir. of income security, Center for Budget and Policy Priorities. 2003–2004, Democratic staff dir., Joint Cmte. on Economics. 2005–2006, senior policy advisor, House Minority Leader Nancy Pelosi, D-Calif. 2007–present, senior policy advisor, House Speaker Nancy Pelosi, D-Calif.

Expertise: Federal budget, Medicare, Medicaid and health issues, welfare, income and poverty issues.

From one fierce policy battle to the next, Wendell Primus always seems to be at the heart of the mix. As senior policy advisor to Rep. Nancy Pelosi, D-Calif., Primus was at the front lines of the toughest debates of the 111th Congress, including those over the stimulus and health care bills.

This year promises to be little different. As the parties spar over how to rein in soaring deficits, Primus—a distinguished economist with years of experience on budget issues—will be in the thick of things again.

"We have two major economic problems," said the soft-spoken Primus. "Our jobs deficit...and then the budget deficit."

Those problems aren't in dispute; the solutions are. The Republicans want to slash federal spending immediately, while the Democrats would delay the biggest cuts until the economy is more stable.

Despite the House power switch, Primus was quick to note that the Democrats are hardly helpless in fighting the legislative wishes of the majority Republicans.

"We still have a Democratic president and we still have a Democratic Senate," he said. "Yes, we are in the minority—and believe me, we understand that—but it's not like the Democrats are without power."

Primus has plenty to draw on as the budget debate evolves. In the early 1990s, he served as chief economist for the Ways and Means Committee. He was staff director of the Joint Economic Committee in the mid-2000s. In between, he served in Bill Clinton's health department, where he focused largely on child welfare.

A fierce defender of liberal policies, Primus is not afraid to confront other Democrats in the heat of debate. Indeed, he famously clashed with former White House Chief of Staff Rahm Emanuel during the health care battle. And in 1996 he resigned from his Department of Health and Human Services post to protest Clinton's overhaul of the nation's welfare system.

HOUSE LEADERSHIP

Donald A. Ritchie

Historian, Senate Historical Office
201 Hart Senate Office Bldg.
Phone: (202) 224-6900
don_ritchie@sec.senate.com

Personal: Born 12/23/1945 in New York, N.Y.

Education: B.A., City College of New York, 1967. M.A., University of Maryland, 1969. Ph.D., University of Maryland, 1975.

Professional: 1976–2009, associate historian, Senate Historical Office. 1990–2000, Adjunct professor, Cornell in Washington program. 2009, Historian, Senate Historical Office.

Expertise: History, United States and U.S. Senate.

Donald A. Ritchie has been watching the world's greatest deliberative body for long enough to have some perspective on the partisan strife that ushered in the 112th Congress: It's been worse.

A Queens native, Ritchie is a graduate of the City College of New York, a former Marine and a veteran of decades in the Senate Historical Office.

"Right from the start people recognized that they were dealing with highly emotional issues" that tended to invite harsh conflict, said Ritchie, who succeeded retiring Senate Historian Richard Baker in 2009. That is why Vice President Thomas Jefferson exhorted members in the Senate's first set of rules to address one another with elaborate courtesy. The admonition persists in such antique locutions as "the distinguished senator from Such-and-Such a state," said Ritchie.

Such ostensibly arcane knowledge is at the heart of the Senate historian's job—"explaining the Senate to the non-specialist—to people who don't really understand how Congress works," as he put it.

Ritchie said he strives "to get to the nub of what distinguishes the Senate from the House." He offered one of the unvarnished illustrations that have made him popular with generations of researchers and reporters: The old sections of the Capitol have no room numbers bearing the prefix "C," because "Congress," per se, is an ephemeral thing. A room is either "S" for Senate or "H" for House, the "very separate" bodies that do the people's business, said Ritchie. The two do meet, but only rarely, as in the annual joint session for the president's State of the Union Address.

Ritchie is the author of several books, including well-regarded studies of the role of the press in the Capitol. He has been deeply involved in recent years in creating historical exhibits and services for the new Capitol Visitors Center. Ritchie expressed the public's indebtedness to the staff of the Historical Office, including associate historian Betty Koed and photo historian Heather Moore.

While Ritchie has seen harder lines of partisan division in the Senate in recent years, he is quick to point out another facet of the picture.

"For all the divisiveness, the Senate still does the majority of its work by unanimous consent," Ritchie said. "The rules and procedures and ethos of the Senate require it" because its protection of minority rights extends to the individual senator—who has the power to delay any floor action simply by objecting.

HOUSE LEADERSHIP

Brian Romick

Whip Director and Senior Advisor
House Minority Whip Steny Hoyer, D-Md.
H-148, The Capitol
Phone: (202) 225-3130
brian.romick@mail.house.gov

Personal: Born 11/10/1976 in Cleveland, Ohio.

Education: B.A., government and politics, University of Maryland, 1998.

Professional: 1996, campaign volunteer, Hoyer for Congress. 1998, field director, Hoyer for Congress. 1998–2002, special assistant, House Administration Cmte. 1998, staff assistant, Rep. Steny Hoyer, D-Md. 2002–2006, floor assistant, House Minority Whip Steny Hoyer, D-Md. 2007–2010, member services director, House Majority Leader Steny Hoyer, D-Md. 2011–present, whip director, House Minority Whip Steny Hoyer, D-Md.

Brian Romick is no stranger to counting votes. As member services director for Rep. Steny Hoyer, D-Md., in the last two Congresses, the Cleveland native was in charge of outreach to rank-and-file members—managing their relations with leadership and taking their temperature on legislation. Counting votes was a big part of his job.

Now in 2011, as whip director, it got even bigger.

With Republicans controlling the House in the 112th Congress, Hoyer has stepped into the role of minority whip. With that switch, Romick said, "counting votes is much more important."

The central battle lines are being drawn over where to cut federal spending – and by how much. Although the Republicans have a comfortable majority, many conservatives threaten to oppose their own party's spending bills if the cuts aren't deep enough. In that environment, the vote-counting prowess of Democrats could prove crucial if they're to have any chance of blocking GOP bills.

Romick said Democrats will constantly be searching for ways to play spoiler.

"It's not our responsibility to pass things," he said. "So there's more flexibility."

Making Romick's job a bit easier, the Democratic Caucus is more liberal this year. That's because a number of conservative-leaning Blue Dogs were defeated in November. The change means fewer Democrats will cross the aisle, and leaders will have an easier time uniting behind a single message.

"We want to call the Republicans out when they're doing extreme things," Romick said.

Romick has spent his entire political career with Hoyer. He first joined the Maryland Democrat's district campaign staff while he was still a student at the University of Maryland in the late 1990s. Later, as Hoyer's floor assistant in 2006, he helped fend off a leadership challenge from the late-Rep. John Murtha, D-Pa., who was also vying for the majority leader spot.

HOUSE LEADERSHIP

David Michael Schnittger

Deputy Chief of Staff for Communications Operations

House Speaker John Boehner, R-Ohio

H-232, The Capitol

Phone: (202) 225-0600

Twitter: @OhSchnitt

dave.schnittger@mail.house.gov

Personal: Born 1/22/1971 in Cincinnati, Ohio.

Education: B.A., political science and economics, University of Dayton, 1993.

Professional: 1993, executive dir., Montgomery County, Ohio, Republican Party. 1994–96, field rep., Rep. John A. Boehner, R-Ohio. 1996–2000, press secretary, Rep. John A. Boehner, R-Ohio. 2000, regional communications coordinator, Republican National Committee Victory 2000. 2001–2005, communications dir., House Cmte. on Education and the Workforce. 2005–2006, chief of staff, Rep. John Boehner, R-Ohio. 2006–present, deputy chief of staff, House Majority/Minority Leader/Speaker John Boehner, R-Ohio.

Expertise: Communications strategy, member services, coalitions.

As a college freshman, David Schnittger started as volunteer for his home-district congressman in 1990. After graduating, he rose through the ranks to his current position: Deputy Chief of Staff for Communications Operations. That hometown congressman also rose through the ranks: House Speaker John Boehner, R-Ohio.

Schnittger spent many years as Boehner's main conduit with the press, working as Boehner's press secretary from 1996 to 2000. He served as communications director for the House Education and the Workforce Committee when Boehner was chairman from 2001 to 2005.

Through his years working with the media, Schnittger learned first-hand how to interact with reporters. Although he no longer deals directly with the press, Schnittger maneuvers behind the scenes to help craft the overarching "message" for the Republican conference and speaker. He also leads the communication team's efforts to push out Republican talking points on social media platforms, such as Twitter.

"My part of the operation is responsible for the Speaker's overall message – conceiving it, developing it, and disseminating it, in coordination with other House Republican leaders," Schnittger said. "Press relations, digital media, speechwriting, booking of TV and radio appearances, advance work, photography and video production, preparation of the Speaker's remarks to internal House Republican meetings, outreach to grass-roots organizations—all of these activities fall under me. I spend most of my time coordinating all these moving parts both within our operation and with other House Republican offices."

Schnittger, who attended Boehner's high school, Archbishop Moeller High School in West Chester, Ohio, now lives in South Riding, Va., with his wife, Stephanie, and four children: Ella (8), Kayla (6), Julia (5), and Andrew (1).

HOUSE LEADERSHIP

Kevin Smith

Communications Director
House Speaker John Boehner, R-Ohio
H-232, The Capitol
Phone: (202) 225-0600
Twitter: @KG_Smith
Kevin.Smith@mail.house.gov

Personal: Born 12/30/1971 in Springfield, Ore.

Education: B.S., political science and business administration, Oregon State University, 1995.

Professional: 1995–96, legislative assistant, Rep. Randy Tate, R-Wash. 1997–99, legislative analyst, Rep. John Boehner, R-Ohio, House Republican Conference. 2000–2001, senior editor, Voter.com. 2001–2005, senior communications advisor, House Cmte. on Education and the Workforce. 2005–2006, communications director, House Cmte. on Education and the Workforce. 2006–present, communications director, House Majority/Minority Leader/Speaker John Boehner, R-Ohio.

Expertise: Communications strategy.

As communications director for House Speaker John Boehner, R-Ohio, Kevin Smith has spent the last five years honing his media strategy to help achieve GOP goals.

"We have intensified our outreach efforts to White House correspondents and reporters, as well as other reporters covering administration beats to ensure Republican news is reported in a timely manner and GOP reaction is included in every story." Smith said.

He added, "We have placed an increased emphasis on using new technologies to communicate and deliver our message, efforts which are already paying off."

Indeed, Smith and his communications staff are among the most active Hill offices on Twitter. They frequently tweet out Boehner talking points and news, working around the clock to push GOP strategy and refute criticism or misinformation.

During negotiations in early 2011 over the continuing resolution, Smith's Twitter feed featured a nonstop flow of comments over media links and efforts to win the message war, such as this March 30 post:

"On MSNBC, liberal WaPo columnist Eugene Robinson admits Republicans are winning the messaging war over spending cuts," Smith wrote.

Smith started working for Boehner when the Ohio Republican was chairman of the House Education and the Workforce Committee. As Boehner became majority leader in 2006, then minority leader, and finally house speaker in 2011, Smith has been there at his side.

While in the minority, Smith was responsible for working to mold the public debate so that Republicans were seen as putting forth ideas and not simply shooting down Democratic measures. Now that Republicans are in the majority again, he's focused on passing the GOP agenda in the House.

"Kevin works hard, is solid and is real smart," Boehner said.

Smith is an Oregon State University graduate. He and his wife, Kara, live in Washington, D.C., with their new baby.

HOUSE LEADERSHIP

Mike Sommers

Deputy Chief of Staff for Leadership Operations

House Speaker John Boehner, R-Ohio

H-232, The Capitol

Phone: (202) 225-0600

Twitter: @ironmikesommers

Personal: Born 01/30/1975 in Westchester, Pa.

Education: B.A., political science, Miami University (Ohio), 1997.

Professional: 2000–2002, legislative director, Rep. John Boehner, R-Ohio. 2002–2005, chief of staff, Rep. John Boehner, R-Ohio. 2005–2006, special assistant to the president, White House National Economic Cmte. 2006–2010, policy director, House Majority/Minority Leader John Boehner, R-Ohio. 2011–present, deputy chief of staff for leadership operations, House Speaker John Boehner, R-Ohio.

Expertise: Agriculture and trade policy, floor procedure.

Mike Sommers is House Speaker John Boehner's, R-Ohio, deputy chief of staff for Leadership Operations. It's a new title, which comes after Sommers spent four years as Boehner's policy director. For Sommers, the mission is similar: use floor speeches and other strategies to get the Republican message across – and thwart the Democrat's efforts. That shouldn't be hard, now that Republicans control the House.

When Republicans were in the minority from 2007 through 2010, Sommers helped develop strategies to oppose legislation advanced by the Democrats, such as the "motion to recommit," a once arcane tactic that Republicans used effectively to kill bills. But Sommers has also served in the majority. He was first appointed as Boehner's policy director in February 2006, after Boehner became majority leader.

Sommers prepares the agenda for the Republican leaders' weekly meeting and is responsible for the leadership effort on Republican amendments on bills that come to the floor. Boehner's policy staff also coordinates Republican committee efforts at hearings and markups.

Sommers is among a handful of close-knit staffers in Boehner's office who have been with him since graduating college. Sommers started in Boehner's office as an intern in 1997, moved up to legislative director, and became chief of staff of Boehner's personal office in 2002. As Boehner's chief of staff, Sommers was named one of Capitol Hill's most influential staff members, making the "35 Under 35" list in *The Hill* 2006 and the *Roll Call* "Fabulous Fifty" list.

Sommers, an expert on agriculture and trade policy, left the Hill in 2005 to serve as special assistant to the president for national economic policy at the White House during the Bush administration.

Sommers, who lives in Alexandria, Va., is married to Jill Maycumber, a former commissioner on the Commodity Futures Trading Commission.

HOUSE LEADERSHIP

Jo-Marie St. Martin

General Counsel/Director of Legislative Operations
House Speaker John Boehner, R-Ohio
H-232, The Capitol
Phone: (202) 225-0600
Jo-Marie.St-Martin@mail.house.gov

Personal: Born 02/10/1960 in Kingsport, Tenn.

Education: B.S., Phi Beta Kappa, final honors and highest distinction, Mary Washington College, 1982. J.D., University of Tennessee, 1985.

Professional: 1985–86, attorney/advisor, The Honorable E. Earl Thomas, U.S. Dept. of Labor. 1986–92, minority education counsel, House Cmte. on Education and Labor. 1992–95, Wilson, Worley & Gamble (Tenn.). 1995–98, parliamentary counsel, House Cmte. on Education and Labor. 1998–2006, general counsel, House Cmte. on Education and the Workforce. 2006–present, general counsel/director of legislative operations, House Speaker John Boehner, R-Ohio.

Expertise: Parliamentary procedure.

As general counsel and director of legislative operations for Speaker John Boehner, R-Ohio, Jo-Marie St. Martin is the highest ranking female staffer in the House. She has been in Boehner's inner circle for the past 11 years and is a senior aide with whom the new speaker consults on most major decisions.

"Jo-Marie is an invaluable counselor who helps ensure the House truly functions—as it should—as the Peoples' House," Boehner told *Roll Call* newspaper.

It's St. Martin's job to advise Boehner about parliamentary procedure and legal issues. She also advises members on how to effectively get that week's message across. St. Martin told Roll Call that she sees her role as a "caretaker"—making sure Boehner's vision for the House is carried out.

"What I provide for him is that expertise and guidance about what it is that is regular order under the House rules and what it is we should be doing and how we should be doing it," she told Roll Call.

St. Martin played a big role in overseeing the continuing resolution debate in the House in early 2011. That bill was debated in an unusual open rule process that allowed hours of debate on hundreds of amendments. The bill's passage was seen as an important success for House Republicans.

While in the minority, St. Martin helped Republicans launch a protest in August 2008 in which GOP lawmakers spoke during recess to a darkened chamber about expanding oil drilling to lower gas prices. After weeks of protest, House Democrats allowed a vote on parts of the GOP plan; it was seen as a procedural win for Republicans.

"We were very creative in how we went about it, in using the House rules in the best way possible to get the message out," she said.

St. Martin has known Boehner for the past 21 years and worked for him for 11 of those years, even since he was chairman of the House Education and the Workforce Committee.

HOUSE LEADERSHIP

Michael Steel

Press Secretary
House Speaker John Boehner, R-Ohio
H-204, The Capitol
Phone: (202) 225-0600
michael.steel@mail.house.gov

Personal: Born 02/05/1977 in Durham, N.C.

Education: B.A., journalism, University of North Carolina at Chapel Hill, 1999. M.S., journalism, Columbia University, 2003.

Professional: 2000–2002, editorial assistant, correspondent, National Journal News Service. 2003–2005, press secretary, Rep. John Shadegg, R-Ariz. 2005–2006, comm. dir., Republican Policy Committee. 2006, press secretary, Rep. Jim McCrery, R-La. 2007, Republican communications dir., House Cmte. on Ways and Means. 2008–2011, press secretary, House Minority Leader John Boehner, R-Ohio. 2011–Present, press secretary, House Speaker John Boehner, R-Ohio.

Expertise: Communications.

As John A. Boehner, R-Ohio, ascended to become the House Speaker in the 112th Congress, Michael Steel became the chamber's most powerful press secretary.

The transfer of power that ceded the majority to Republicans brought Steel a dramatically heightened workload and a much more visible role as the spokesman responsible for crafting Boehner's comments on a wide variety of daily issues.

Steel is no stranger to members of the Fourth Estate and prides himself at being very prompt in returning the dozens, sometimes hundreds, of requests for comment he receives each day.

The 34-year old North Carolina native began his career as a print reporter on Capitol Hill writing for the *National Journal News Service* and earned a masters degree in journalism from Columbia University before taking on a government job.

Steel joined Boehner's team in 2008 and has the difficult task this Congress of delivering the Republican's message in a way that sets it apart from the Democratic platform, but remains legislatively effective. With Republicans in the minority in the Senate, the House GOP's chances at passing major legislation are significantly diminished unless they strike conciliatory tones with Democrats.

Formerly the communications director for the powerful House Ways and Means Committee's Republican members, Steel embraces the long hours and spends a lot of time coordinating with his House and Senate leadership counterparts to review the message of the day and how they intend to craft it.

Steel works in tandem with Boehner's longtime communications director Kevin Smith. Steel is typically responsible for dealing with the day-to-day stories and can frequently be seen talking with reporters in the House Speaker's Lobby during the chamber's votes, while Smith handles the longer-term strategy aspect of crafting a message.

HOUSE LEADERSHIP

Jonathan Stivers

Senior Advisor
House Minority Leader Nancy Pelosi, D-Calif.
H-204, The Capitol
Phone: (202) 225-0100
jonathan.stivers@mail.house.gov

Personal: Born 12/10/1973 in Birmingham, Mich.

Education: B.S., international relations, Michigan State University, 1992. Masters of International Policy & Practice (MIPP), Asian Relations, George Washington University, 2008.

Professional: 1996, campaign assistant, David Bonior for Congress. 1997–99, floor staff assistant, House Minority Whip David Bonior, D-Mich. 2000–2001, legislative director, Senior, Press Secretary, Rep. Nancy Pelosi, D-Calif. 2002, policy advisor, House Minority Whip Nancy Pelosi, D-Calif. 2003–2006, advisor, House Minority Leader Nancy Pelosi, D-Calif. 2007–Present, senior advisor, House Speaker Nancy Pelosi, D-Calif.

Expertise: Foreign policy, democratic politics.

The Democrats' economic platform in the 112th Congress revolves around the "Make It in America" program, a series of reforms designed to promote exports and create jobs. Central to that agenda are proposals to curb unfair trade practices abroad; central to those efforts is Jonathan Stivers.

As point man on international trade for Rep. Nancy Pelosi, D-Calif., Stivers focuses on export financing and monetary policy, with a particularly close eye on China. In the 111th Congress, he helped the House pass a bill to discourage Chinese currency manipulation. It died in the Senate, but the Democrats are vowing to try again this year.

"There will be opportunities to make the case for our ideas," Stivers said hopefully.

Stivers also focuses on foreign aid and human rights concerns, which puts him at the front lines of issues as diverse as sanctions on Burma and earthquake assistance to Haiti. It also means he'll have a hand in the response to the March earthquake, tsunami, and nuclear disaster in Japan. Pelosi described the event as a tragedy "beyond biblical proportions."

Stivers also plays a political role in the House. He serves as a liaison between Pelosi and other Democrats on the chamber floor, and manages member requests, committee assignments, and the Steering and Policy Committee.

A Michigan native, Stivers worked for Rep. David Bonior, D-Mich., before joining Pelosi's office in 1999 as senior legislative assistant. Later, as legislative director, Stivers helped organize a campaign against permanent normal trade relations (PNTR) with China. He's also worked with Pelosi on efforts to increase global AIDS funding and debt relief for poor countries.

With Republicans vowing sharp spending cuts this year, Stivers said he's particularly concerned with cuts to overseas programs "to levels that undermine our national security."

HOUSE LEADERSHIP

Steve Stombres

Chief of Staff

Republican Leader Eric Cantor, R-Va.

H-329, The Capitol

Phone: (202) 225-4000

Personal: Born 06/23/1970 in Washington, D.C.

Education: B.A., Virginia Polytechnic Institute, 1993.

Professional: 1987–present, intelligence officer, U.S. Army Reserve. 1993–94, staff asst., House Cmte. on Science. 1994–95, legislative corresp., Rep. Bob Walker, R-Pa. 1995–97, legislative asst., Rep. Bob Walker, R-Pa. 1997, legislative asst., Rep. Elton Gallegly, R-Calif. 1997–98, legislative asst., Rep. Herbert Bateman, R-Va. 1998–2001, legislative dir., Rep. Herbert Bateman, R-Va. 2001–present, chief of staff, House Republican Leader Eric Cantor, R-Va.

Expertise: Military affairs, legislative policy.

Steven Stombres is not only chief of staff for House Republican Leader Eric Cantor, he's the Virginia Republican's right hand man who has been at Cantor's side since he was sworn into office in 2001.

Stombres started in Cantor's office as legislative director, quickly moving up to chief of staff. When Cantor served as chief deputy whip from 2003-2008, Stombres moved into Cantor's new leadership office. When Cantor rose to GOP Whip, Stombres was right there as his leadership office's chief of staff. When Republicans won back the House in 2010, Cantor became majority leader and Stombres became the top staffer for the No. 2 Republican in the House.

As such, Stombres has regularly been named on lists of Capitol Hill's most powerful staffers.

Prior to joining Cantor's staff, Stombres worked as the legislative director for National Security Affairs for Rep. Herbert H. Bateman, R-Va.

But when Stombres is not handling the latest issues in the halls of the Capitol, he is handling issues affecting the residents of Fairfax, Va. Stombres is serving his second term as a member of Fairfax's City Council having won re-election to another two year term ending on June 30, 2012. He also serves on the Northern Virginia Transportation Commission representing the City of Fairfax.

Stombres enlisted in the United States Army Reserves in 1987 and is a 1995 Graduate of Officer Candidate School. In 2003, Mr. Stombres was mobilized in support of Operation Iraqi Freedom and served the Joint Chiefs of Staff as an Iraq Analyst for the Iraq Intelligence Task Force.

Stombres graduated in 1993 with a bachelor of arts in history from Virginia Tech. As a member of the U.S. Army Reserves, he attended Officer Candidate School and served as a military intelligence officer in various assignments during his 20-year career in the Army Reserves. He and his wife Kristen have three children.

HOUSE LEADERSHIP

John V. Sullivan

Parliamentarian

H-209, The Capitol

Phone: (202) 225-7373

John.Sullivan@mail.house.gov

Personal: Born 1952 in Chicago, Ill.

Education: B.S., U.S. Air Force Academy, 1974. J.D., University of Indiana School of Law, 1977.

Professional: 1974–84, active duty, U.S. Air Force. 1984–87, counsel, House Armed Services Cmte. 1987–94, assistant parliamentarian, U.S. House of Representatives. 1994–2004, deputy parliamentarian, U.S. House of Representatives. 2004–present, parliamentarian, U.S. House of Representatives.

Expertise: Parliamentary procedure, military affairs.

As House parliamentarian, John Sullivan treads a delicate line. In a political body filled with partisan rhetoric, Sullivan and his staff are strictly non-partisan and responsible for establishing and updating the House's procedural precedent.

As in past session, for the 112th Congress, every morning Sullivan and his staff go through the congressional record of the previous day and mark incidents that lend some bearing to congressional precedent. When the House isn't in session, Sullivan and his staff write analysis of these changes in precedent, maintaining a chronological scrapbook of events so future parties can research the various rules.

This practice also provides members and their staff with a standard for what to expect during floor proceedings.

"The idea is that fidelity to precedent promotes the consistency and predictability that fosters legitimacy in the parliamentary practices of the House," said Sullivan. "So our job is to put the House in a position to stand by its procedural decisions by being rigorous about what constitutes precedent and by recording the precedents."

Sullivan and his staff of lawyers and clerks also tally votes and maintain order on the House floor.

Members and their staff often ask Sullivan's office to review drafts of bills and amendments in confidence before they are introduced to gauge whether they conform to the House rules. Once introduced, the parliamentarian recommends which committee has jurisdiction over the subject matter.

The complexity of Sullivan's job requires up to four years of apprenticeship and parliamentarians tend to stay in the job for long stretches. The previous parliamentarian, Charles Johnson, served for 10 years before Sullivan. William Holmes Brown served as parliamentarian for 20 years before Johnson was appointed to the post, and Lewis Deschler held the job for 46 years before Brown.

HOUSE LEADERSHIP

Jon Summers

Communications director, Democratic Policy and Communications Center

S-318 U.S. Capitol

Phone: (202) 224-3929

jon_summers@dpcc.senate.gov

Personal: Born 09/28/1070 in Houston, Texas.

Education: B.A., University of Central Florida, 1996.

Professional: 1996–99, Reporter, KPNX Television. 1999–2003, Reporter, KLAS Television. 2003–2005, Nevada State Democratic Party, communications director. 2005–2006, Democratic Governors Association, communications director. 2006–2010, communications director, Senate Majority Leader Harry Reid. 2011, Democratic Policy and Communications Center, communications director.

Expertise: Communications.

After Majority Leader Harry Reid, D-Nev., closed with a convincing victory in a 2010 election cycle that also brought costly losses in his caucus, the senator tapped his chief campaign spokesman, Jon Summers, to take over as communications director of a retooled Senate Democratic leadership organization.

Summers, who traveled the state and worked closely with Reid during his come-from-behind campaign against Tea Party Republican Sharron Angle, quickly set about publicizing an agenda for the 112th Congress, rarely passing up an opportunity to use the word "jobs."

With Illinois Sen. Dick Durbin continuing as his Democratic whip, Reid created a new umbrella organization under the chairmanship of New York Sen. Chuck Schumer: the Democratic Policy and Communications Center. Summers is communications director of the DPCC.

On the topic of the staff reorganization—which essentially merges the old Democratic policy and communications shops—Summers said, "We wanted to do a better job of coordinating policy and press, to make sure that the policy folks are communicating with the press folks—not only on crafting a policy agenda but also on getting it out," Summers said. "We wanted to do a better job defining what it is we stand for."

A signal moment in that effort came early, with the unveiling of the Senate Democratic "Jobs Agenda," in February, 2011. "It focuses on making the American economy more competitive, embracing the pillars of President Obama's State of the Union Address," said Summers, referring to the president's pledge to "out-innovate, out-educate and out-build the rest of the world."

"We are focused like a laser on the future of our country, and on jobs. We are not interested in joining battles for the past," Summers said, referring to the Republican push, early in 2011, for a vote to repeal the health care overhaul that Reid shepherded through the Senate for President Obama in 2010. The Democrats handily defeated that effort.

On the first major showdown of the new Congress—an extension of a temporary spending measure that had continued financing the government after the close of the lame duck session of Congress in 2010—"We tried hard to set a tone of bipartisanship," Summers said.

HOUSE LEADERSHIP

Matt Wasniewski

House Historian

B-56 Cannon House Office Bldg.

Phone: (202) 226-5525

Personal: Born 02/1969 in Alexandria, Va.

Education: B.S., James Madison University. M.A., James Madison University. Ph.D., University of Maryland.

Professional: 2002–2010, publications specialist, Office of History and Preservation. 2010–Present, historian, U.S. House of Representatives.

Expertise: U.S. history.

Dr. Matt Wasniewski is the House's fourth Historian and, at 42-years old, its youngest.

Former House Speaker Nancy Pelosi, D-Calif., with input from incoming Speaker John Boehner, R-Ohio, and an advisory committee, appointed Wasniewski at the end of the 111th Congress.

"Dr. Wasniewski brings enormous experience and energy to the job of House Historian," Pelosi said. "His knowledge of congressional history, and his familiarity with cutting edge research and archival techniques make him the perfect candidate for this position."

Boehner said that "Wasniewski's interest in the history of the federal government, and his long-time association with the House, make him an excellent choice who will continue to find innovative ways to not only help the public be better engaged with their House, but to help Members better perform their duties through an understanding of the history of the institution."

Wasniewski replaced Dr. Robert Remini, who had served as the historian for five years. Remini wrote the definitive book on the House of Representatives, entitled "The House: The History of the House of Representatives."

Wasniewski's passion for history dates back to his childhood.

"My dad, in his spare time, had a metal detector, so we would go metal detecting on a private farm field and find these Civil War bullets, and that really got my interest going," said Wasniewski, who grew up in the northern Virginia area.

After a brief foray as a journalist in his undergraduate years at James Madison University, Wasniewski began pursuing history with full fervor, eventually earning his Ph.D. from the University of Maryland. Soon after receiving his doctorate he began an eight-year stint working for the Clerk of the House's Office of History and Preservation, which he now wants to integrate with the Office of the Historian.

One of Wasniewski's duties is recording the oral histories of lawmakers, which in 2011 he is hoping to expand. He talks to incoming House members of the 112th Congress and their staff about the importance of keeping records of their papers and ongoing events.

Every summer the Historian's office takes two groups of high school teachers under its wing for a week to teach and show them what the U.S. House of Representatives does and how it operates. Wasniewski's office gained a new responsibility in 2008 educating tour guides of the Capitol Visitor Center, which opened in December, about the Capitol's history.

HOUSE LEADERSHIP

Yelberton Watkins

Chief of Staff

Assistant House Minority Leader James Clyburn, D-S.C.

2135 Rayburn House Office Bldg.

Phone: (202) 225-3315

yelberton.watkins@mail.house.gov

Personal: Born 05/19/1964 in Columbia, S.C.

Education: B.S., biology, Duke University, 1986. J.D., Georgetown University School of Law, 1991.

Professional: 1986–87, staff assistant, Sen. Terry Sanford, D-N.C. 1991–92, staff attorney, Washington, D.C., City Council. 1993–94, staff assistant, Rep. James Clyburn, D-S.C. 1994–2006, chief of staff, House Democratic Caucus Chairman James Clyburn, D-S.C. 2007–2010, chief of staff, House Majority Whip James Clyburn, D-S.C. 2011–present, chief of staff, Assistant House Minority Leader James Clyburn, D-S.C.

Expertise: Communications strategy, legislative policy.

Yelberton Watkins enters his 18th year as chief of staff for Rep. James Clyburn, D-S.C. But his role in the 112th Congress is slightly different from the one he played during the past few years.

Clyburn had served from 2007 to 2010 as House Majority Whip, which meant Watkins was in charge of making sure the Democratic leadership has the votes to pass its agenda.

But when Democrats lost the majority in 2010, former House Speaker Nancy Pelosi, D-Calif., became minority leader, setting up a potential showdown between Clyburn and former House Majority Leader Steny Hoyer, D-Md., over who would serve as minority whip. To keep both Hoyer and Clyburn within Democratic leadership, Pelosi created the Assistant House Minority Leader position for Clyburn. The position makes Clyburn the No. 3 Democrat in the House.

That shouldn't change Watkins' clout on Capitol Hill. He has been named for several years by *Roll Call* newspaper as one of the top 50 staffers on the Hill. Plus, he is so close to his boss that he has been described as Clyburn's alter-ego.

Watkins, who is known as "Yebbie," has worked for Clyburn since the day Clyburn was sworn in. He grew up in Clyburn's district and was friends with the congressman's daughter, Mignon.

Originally planning to study medicine, Watkins became interested in politics when visiting friends working on Capitol Hill. So he "pounded the pavement" and landed a job with then-Sen. Terry Sanford, D-N.C. Watkins then left the Hill to earn his law degree at Georgetown University.

He clerked for two D.C. law firms and worked as an associate for a Columbia, S.C., firm before landing a job as staff attorney with the Washington, D.C., City Council. He joined Clyburn's office when the congressman was elected the following year.

"My career has been one of opportunities rather than grand design," he said.

Committee on Agriculture

1301 Longworth House Office Bldg.
Washington, DC 20515
Phone: (202) 225-2171
Fax: (202) 225-8510
http://agriculture.house.gov
agriculture@mail.house.gov

Ratio: 26/20

MAJORITY MEMBERS

Frank D. Lucas, OK-6th, Chairman

Bob Goodlatte, VA-6th
Timothy V. Johnson, IL-15th
Steve King, IA-5th
Randy Neugebauer, TX-19th
K. Michael Conaway, TX-11th
Jeff Fortenberry, NE-1st
Jean Schmidt, OH-2nd
Glenn W. Thompson, PA-5th
Thomas J. Rooney, FL-16th
Marlin Stutzman, IN-3rd
Bob Gibbs, OH-18th
Austin Scott, GA-8th
Stephen Lee Fincher, TN-8th
Scott R. Tipton, CO-3rd
Steve Southerland, FL-2nd
Rick Crawford, AR-1st
Martha Roby, AL-2nd
Tim Huelskamp, KS-1st
Scott DesJarlais, TN-4th
Renee L. Ellmers, NC-2nd
Christopher P. Gibson, NY-20th
Randy Hultgren, IL-14th
Vicky Hartzler, MO-4th
Robert T. Schilling, IL-17th
Reid J. Ribble, WI-8th

MINORITY MEMBERS

Collin C. Peterson, MN-7th, Ranking Member

Tim Holden, PA-17th, Vice Chairman
Mike McIntyre, NC-7th
Leonard L. Boswell, IA-3rd
Joe Baca, CA-42nd
Dennis A. Cardoza, CA-18th
David Scott, GA-13th
Henry Cuellar, TX-28th
Jim Costa, CA-20th
Timothy J. Walz, MN-1st
Kurt Schrader, OR-5th
Larry Kissell, NC-8th
Bill Owens, NY-12th
Chellie Pingree, ME-1st
Joe Courtney, CT-2nd
Peter Welch, VT-At Large
Marcia L. Fudge, OH-11th
Gregorio Kilili Sablan, MP-At Large
Terri A. Sewell, AL-7th
James McGovern, MA-3rd

HOUSE AGRICULTURE

JURISDICTION

(1) Adulteration of seeds, insect pests, and protection of birds and animals in forest reserves.
(2) Agriculture generally.
(3) Agricultural and industrial chemistry.
(4) Agricultural colleges and experiment stations.
(5) Agricultural economics and research.
(6) Agricultural education extension services.
(7) Agricultural production and marketing and stabilization of prices of agricultural products and commodities (not including distribution outside of the United States).
(8) Animal industry and diseases of animals.
(9) Commodity exchanges.
(10) Crop insurance and soil conservation.
(11) Dairy industry.
(12) Entomology and plant quarantine.
(13) Extension of farm credit and farm security.
(14) Inspection of livestock, poultry, meat products, and seafood and seafood products.
(15) Forestry in general and forest reserves other than those created from the public domain.
(16) Human nutrition and home economics.
(17) Plant industry, soils, and agricultural engineering.
(18) Rural electrification.
(19) Rural development.
(20) Water conservation related to activities of the Department of Agriculture.

HOUSE AGRICULTURE

The U.S. House of Representatives Committee on Agriculture is focusing on myriad projects and issues in 2011. But in order to see them through, they'll have to survive the deep budget cuts being made by Republican lawmakers in the 112th Congress.

In a letter outlining the committee's goals for the year, Chairman Frank Lucas, R-Okla., said he sees the cuts his party heralds as a positive challenge.

"I view our current budget situation as an opportunity to make our agriculture policy even more efficient while allowing farmers and ranchers continued access to the risk management tools vital to producing the safest, most abundant, and most affordable food and fiber supply in the world. While streamlining our programs, we must be careful not to jeopardize the stability of the agricultural industry, which will play a key role in feeding an estimated 9 billion people by the year 2050," Lucas wrote in the panel's "views and estimates" letter outlining the committee's budget recommendations for the year.

Meanwhile, his counterpart Rep. Collin Peterson, D-Minn., has expressed deep concerns.

"The Agriculture Committee is prepared to make our fair contribution toward deficit reduction. We have already reduced commodity program spending over the course of several farm bills and crop insurance through the SRA process that was done in May. I don't believe, however, that our Committee should bear a disproportionate share of the cuts. Everything should be on the table," Peterson said.

When not fighting to keep their programs funded, the Agriculture Committee expects to be doing a lot of oversight on reauthorizing programs from the 2008 Farm Bill, which is set to expire in 2012. They will also be planning for the next Farm Bill. The Committee put together a massive Farm Bill in 2008. The legislative process for that bill was a long one, involving negotiations between the House and Senate, a veto from then President George W. Bush, and a final override.

In 2010, the House Agriculture Committee played an instrumental role in derivatives reform and the Dodd-Frank Wall Street Reform and Consumer Protection Act. The legislation, passed in July 2010, addresses what officials said were concerns about excessive speculation in commodity markets and brings greater oversight over financial derivatives instruments—such as credit default swaps. Now with the 112th Congress, the committee will be spending a lot of time working on oversight regarding the implementation of the Dodd-Frank Act.

Both Lucas and Peterson have also expressed an interest in looking into the regulatory burden placed on American agriculture by the Environmental Protection Agency (EPA) and other agencies.

"The 2008 Farm Bill provided assistance for producers for their voluntary efforts to improve management practices and water quality," Lucas said at a discussion of the EPA's proposed regulations for the Chesapeake Bay Watershed. "The EPA is clearly reaching beyond its authority under current law and failing to comprehend the economic impact of these regulations at the local level."

HOUSE AGRICULTURE

Andrew W. Baker

Democratic Chief Counsel

1305 Longworth House Office Bldg.

Phone: (202) 225-3069

Fax: (202) 225-8510

Personal: Born 03/16/1961 in Shreveport, La.

Education: B.A., University of Virginia, 1983. J.D., University of Georgia, 1986.

Professional: 1986–88, attorney-advisor, Office of Administrative Law Judges, Dept. of Labor. 1988–90, trial attorney, Office of the General Counsel, Dept. of Agriculture. 1990–97, Democratic professional staff member/associate counsel, House Cmte. on Agriculture. 1998–2005, deputy Democratic counsel, House Cmte. on Agriculture. 2005–present, Democratic counsel, House Cmte. on Agriculture.

Expertise: Trade, international development, legal issues.

Andrew Baker is Democratic chief counsel for the House Committee on Agriculture, specializing in trade, international development, and of course, legal issues.

A Shreveport, La., native, Baker is a graduate of the University of Virginia. After earning his bachelor's, he went on to attend law school at the University of Georgia. He earned his J.D. in 1986.

After finishing law school, Baker came to the Department of Labor's Office of Administrative Law Judges, where he worked as an attorney-advisor for two years. He then moved to the Office of the General Counsel at the Department of Agriculture as a trial attorney for two years, until 1990.

Since then, Baker has been with the Democratic staff of the House Committee on Agriculture. He started off as an associate counsel and has now worked his way to the top as chief counsel for the minority Democratic Party. When he joined the committee in 1990, he had to jump in to key issues with both feet right away. As a Democratic counsel, he has worked on the 1990, 1996, 2002 and 2008 Farm Bills.

In the 112th Congress, the committee will be handling oversight for the 2012 Farm Bill, as the 2008 Farm Bill comes to its expiration date. The committee will also attempt to keep agriculture programs from receiving an unfair amount of cuts in the 112th Congress's attempt to slash billions from the federal budget. Another key goal, under Democratic Ranking Member Collin Peterson, D-Minn., is to examine the regulatory burden that the EPA and other agencies put on American agriculture.

HOUSE AGRICULTURE

Patricia Barr

Deputy Counsel

1301 Longworth House Office Bldg.

Phone: (202) 225-2171

patricia.barr@mail.house.gov

Personal: Born 02/18/1981 in Washington, DC, D.C.

Education: J.D., The George Washington Law School, 2007. B.A., political science, College of the Holy Cross, 2003.

Professional: 2003–2004, staff assistant, Sen. Pete Domenici, R-N.M. 2007–present, deputy counsel, House Committee on Agriculture.

Expertise: Conservation, forestry, livestock, fruits and vegetables, food safety.

Patricia Barr, deputy counsel for the House Committee on Agriculture, focuses on a variety of issues, including food safety, a hot-button issue after President Obama kicked off the 112th Congress signing a $1.4 billion food safety bill into law.

The law—which focuses on preventing food-borne outbreaks rather than just reacting to them—is expected to bring the most sweeping changes to the nation's food system in decades. It gives the Food and Drug Administration the authority to issue mandatory recalls if businesses do not voluntarily recall harmful foods and improves disease surveillance so outbreaks can be discovered earlier.

The law requires close collaboration between the Agriculture Department, the Centers for Disease Control and Prevention, and the FDA.

The Obama administration is asking for $183 million in 2012 to begin carrying out the new law, but House Republicans have objected to doling out money for food-safety measures, often arguing that the United States has the safest food production system in the world, so it's unnecessary to hire the thousands of new food inspectors mandated by the law.

Barr also works on forestry issues.

The 2008 Farm Bill included funds to help private forest owners implement conservation initiatives and rebuild habitat, and reauthorized a program to address the use of forest biomass in energy production.

"Today, our nation's forests cover about one-third of the country, provide 51 percent of the nation's demand for water, provide wood and paper products, provide habitat for threatened and endangered species and other wildlife, and offer beautiful settings for billions of recreation visits," Jay Jensen, deputy undersecretary for Natural Resources and the Environment at the U.S. Department of Agriculture, told the committee.

Current issues facing forests are invasive species including bugs and weeds. The demand for forest products, such as lumber to build new homes, also declined during the economic recession.

HOUSE AGRICULTURE

Mike Dunlap

Staff Director, Subcommittee on Rural Development, Research, Biotechnology, and Foreign Agriculture

Subcommittee on Specialty Crops, Rural Development and Foreign Agriculture

1301 Longworth House Office Bldg.

Phone: (202) 226-1188

mike.dunlap@mail.house.gov

Personal: Born 07/03/1978 in Loudon County, Va.

Education: B.S., Dairy and Animal Science, Virginia Tech University, 2003. M.A., International Commerce and Policy, 2008.

Professional: 2003–2005, staff assistant, House Committee on Agriculture. 2005–2009, legislative assistant, House Committee on Agriculture. 2009–present, staff director, Subcommittee on Rural Development, Research, Biotechnology, and Foreign Agriculture.

Expertise: Rural development, biotech, foreign agriculture.

Mike Dunlap, the staff director for Subcommittee on Rural Development, Research, Biotechnology, and Foreign Agriculture, deals with biotechnology, focusing on ensuring biotech approvals are done in a "science-based manner."

Dunlap held a public meeting in early 2011 on Roundup Ready Alfalfa, a biogenetically engineered alfalfa that can resist the weed killer, Roundup.

Soon after the meeting, the Agriculture Secretary Tom Vilsack announced the USDA would deregulate Roundup Ready Alfalfa, which was a victory for the House Agriculture Committee.

"Genetically engineered alfalfa has been subjected to an extensive multi-year review and the conclusion has always been the same: it's safe," said House Committee on Agriculture Chairman Frank Lucas, R-Okla.. "A product that has been repeatedly found to be safe should be deregulated."

Dunlap's subcommittee will continue to focus on the hot-button issue of biotechnology farming products during the 112th Congress. While biotech products hold potential, some are concerned about health and environmental risks of certain products, such as genetically-modified foods.

"Biotech is so critical to American agriculture not only because it provides us with new tools to be more efficient, but it allows us to use less pesticides," Dunlap said. "And it allows us to provide a lot more on a lot less land."

Dunlap also handles foreign agriculture and trade issues for the full committee, as well as food aid programs.

"Emergency food aid is a huge help all over the world," he said. "There is also a huge emphasis on helping agricultural communities be sustainable and not rely on food aid."

In August 2010, Dunlap and several staffers took a trip to observe committee-approved farming programs in Kenya and Uganda, which was a moving experience for Dunlap.

"It's very different seeing firsthand how the projects are being implemented, how they're being run, and seeing how these projects are effecting peoples' lives."

Dunlap also works on school lunch programs, feed programs, teaching farmers better techniques, and reviewing United Nation's world food programs.

Dunlap grew up not far from Washington, DC, in western Loudon County where he worked on farms, and then at a farming cooperative. He earned a dual Bachelor's Degree in animal science and dairy science from Virginia Tech. He went on to earn a Master's Degree in international commerce and policy from George Mason University in 2008.

HOUSE AGRICULTURE

Liz Friedlander

Minority Communications Director

1305 Longworth House Office Bldg.

Phone: (202) (202) 225-1564

liz.friedlander@mail.house.gov

Personal: Born in Hazen, N.Dak.

Education: B.S., mass communications, emphasis in public relations and advertising, Minnesota State University Moorhead, 2004.

Professional: 2003, intern, Sen. Kent Conrad, D-ND, . 2004–2005, paid intern/temp. employee, Rep. Earl Pomeroy, D-ND, . 2005–2006, communications coordinator, National Farmers Union. 2006–2009, communications director, National Farmers Union. 2009–2010, press secretary, Senate Cmte. on Agriculture, Nutrition and Forestry. 2010, deputy communications director, House Cmte. on Agriculture. 2010–present, communications director, House Cmte. on Agriculture.

Expertise: Communications.

Liz Friedlander is the communications director for the minority Democratic Party at the House of Representatives Committee on Agriculture. She joined the panel in 2010, at the end of the 111th Congress.

A native of Hazen, N.D., Friedlander earned a degree in mass communications, emphasizing in public relations and advertising, in 2004 from Minnesota State University Moorhead.

Both during college and after graduating, Friedlander spent time on Capitol Hill, working for representatives and senators from her home state. She started as an intern for Democratic Sen. Kent Conrad, now North Dakota's senior senator and chairman of the Senate Budget Committee. After graduating, Friedlander went on to work for Rep. Earl Pomeroy, who was defeated in the 2010 election by Republican Rick Berg.

Friedlander left the Hill in 2006 to serve as the communications coordinator for the National Farmers Union in their government relations office. There she assisted the director of communications in implementing programs to positively position the organization with agricultural, legislative and consumer audiences. She eventually went on to become the group's director of communications, helping to get the group's message out on a range of issues including the 2008 Farm Bill, climate change and biofuels.

She returned three years later to take a position as press secretary for the Senate Agriculture, Nutrition and Forestry Committee, before moving in 2010 to the House of Representatives Committee on Agriculture.

In her current role, Friedlander handles all communications for the Democratic minority. She also handles press releases for the committee's Ranking Member, Rep. Collin C. Peterson (D-MN), on committee issues, and media inquiries.

Issues Friedlander has recently dealt with as the Agriculture Committee's minority communications director include Environmental Protection Agency (EPA) regulation, budget cuts to programs under the Agriculture Committee's jurisdiction, and implementation of the Dodd-Frank Wall Street Reform and Consumer Protection Act.

HOUSE AGRICULTURE

John J. Goldberg

Senior Professional Staff Member

1002 Longworth House Office Bldg.

Phone: (202) 225-2171

john.goldberg@mail.house.gov

Personal: Born 04/29/1966 in Philadelphia, Pa.

Education: B.S., Rutgers University, Cook College, 1988. M.S., University of Vermont, 1991. Ph.D., University of Vermont, 1993.

Professional: 1993–94, postdoctoral research associate, Pennsylvania State University. 1994–95, congressional sciences fellow, Federation of American Societies of Food Animal Science. 1995–2006, professional staff member, House Cmte. on Agriculture. 2007–present, senior professional staff, House Cmte. on Agriculture.

Expertise: Animal and plant health, food safety, dairy issues.

John J. Goldberg, senior professional staff member for the House Agriculture Committee, focuses on animal and plant health, animal welfare, livestock, agriculture security, pesticide policy, and organic architecture, an architectural practice that promotes harmony between buildings and nature.

Goldberg also works on issues affecting the dairy industry, which was hit particularly hard by the economic recession.

The number of dairy farms has shrunk by 44 percent since 2000, according to the Center for Dairy Excellence. There are now about 55,000 dairy farms in the United States, and the bulk of the nation's milk supply comes from 15,800 farms, according to the group.

Goldberg also works on pesticide policy for the committee, which in the 112th Congress means he will be dealing with the aftermath of court ruling requiring pesticide users, including farmers, ranchers, and state and local governments to obtain a permit under the Clean Water Act or face a fine up to $37,500 per day. Another law already mandates obtaining pesticide permits. Several members of the House Agriculture Committee, including Chairman Frank Lucas, R-Okla., co-sponsored a bi-partisan bill in the 112th Congress that would eliminate the requirement to obtain a second permit, which opponents say is duplicative and overly burdensome for pesticide users.

"The last thing producers need is more regulation and this bill will relieve producers from meeting a costly regulatory burden that would have little to no environmental benefit," said House Agriculture Committee ranking member Collin Peterson, D-Minn, also a co-sponsor of the bill.

After doing postdoctoral research at Pennsylvania State University, Goldberg, a Philadelphia native, first came to the committee on a fellowship with the American Association for the Advancement of Science in 1994.

HOUSE AGRICULTURE

Tamara Hinton

Majority Communications Director

1305 Longworth House Office Bldg.

Phone: (202) 225-0029

Tamara.Hinton@mail.house.gov

Personal: Born in Stanton, Va.

Education: B.A., economics and history, University of Mary Washington, 1999.

Professional: 1999–2001, teacher, Peace Corps, Uzbekistan. 2001–2004, loan officer, Hinton Mortgage Company (Waynesboro, VA). 2004–2008, general assignment reporter, NBC29 (Charlottesville, VA). 2008–present, Republican communications director, House Cmte. on Agriculture.

Expertise: Communications.

Tamara Hinton, communications director for the House Agriculture Committee Republican staff, is no stranger to foreign lands. Possessing a passion for travel and adventure, Hinton has said "throw a dart on a map and send me there!"

In 2010, Hinton and another congressional staffer ran a marathon in the world's oldest desert in Namibia, exceeding their fundraising goal of $10,000 for a children's organization in Nepal, and braving extreme temperatures for the 26-mile run.

But Namibia and Nepal aside, Hinton is still impressed with the sights right at her doorstep, and is consistently in awe when she reports to work in the U.S. Capitol.

"Every time I walk into the rotunda, I always think it's stunning," she said. "You're reminded of your part in history and that the work you're doing has an impact on history."

That sense of history is her favorite part of her job, which in the 112th Congress will include work on the Farm Bill, said Hinton, who majored in history and economics at the University of Mary Washington.

Hinton had wide-ranging experience as a journalist before taking on the government job. She was a general assignment reporter with NBC29 News, an NBC affiliate based in Charlotte, Va.

Since becoming communication director for the Agriculture Committee in 2008, she said she still works hard to tell stories, as she did in her days as a journalist.

"One of the challenges we face is telling the story of how farmers and ranchers produce our food," Hinton said. "We have the safest, most abundant, most affordable food supply, and sometimes that fact is taken for granted because you can go to the grocery store and the shelves are always full. Having traveled in a few developing countries, that's not the case for many places in the world."

HOUSE AGRICULTURE

Craig Jagger

Chief Economist
1305 Longworth House Office Bldg.
Phone: (202) 225-1130
craig.jagger@mail.house.gov

Personal: Born 08/16/1952 in Salina, Kans.

Education: B.A., Kansas State University, 1974. M.S., Kansas State University, 1982. Ph.D., Cornell University, 1986.

Professional: 1985–87, agricultural economist, Economic Research Service, Department of Agriculture. 1987–89, agricultural economist, General Accounting Office. 1989–95, agricultural economist, Farm Service Agency, Department of Agriculture. 1995–2001, principal analyst, Congressional Budget Office. 2001–present, chief economist, House Cmte. on Agriculture.

Expertise: Budget and cost analysis, economic and policy analysis, commodity programs.

Craig Jagger, economist for the House Agriculture Committee Democrats, is ready to tackle his fifth farm bill. But this time, his role will be different. Having worked for two Republican and one Democratic Chairmen during the last 10 years, it's Jagger's first time in the minority. He hopes to use his expertise on the agriculture budget and the budget process to help Ranking Member Collin Peterson, D-Minn. The Committee's tradition of bipartisanship should help, he said.

"We have 37 programs or provisions from the 2008 farm bill that will need funding after 2012 to continue," Jagger said. "Reducing costs of other ag programs is the only certain source of funding. Tighter budget rules have closed traditional funding sources and we've used up other options."

"As my boss, Mr. Peterson, has said, the country's serious budget problems have to be addressed and everyone needs to contribute. The Agriculture committee has already contributed $6 billion in crop insurance reductions through Office of Management and Budget (OMB) administrative actions last summer and $7.5 billion in Changes in Mandatory Proposals (CHIMPs) during the last 8 years."

Jagger grew up on the wheat farm in Kansas that his great-grandparents homesteaded 145 years ago. He started his education in a two-room country school. He earned a B.A. in technical theater at Kansas State University and did two national tours with a theater company before returning to his farming roots. He then earned an M.S. in agricultural economics at Kansas State and a Ph.D. at Cornell University.

His wife, Joy W. Harwood, heads an economist group at the USDA's Farm Service Agency where Jagger worked during the early 1990s. The couple raises two daughters they adopted from China. His eldest, 10, "outranks me" in Tae Kwon Do, he said, laughing.

In his spare time, Jagger plays the drums and teaches Sunday school.

HOUSE AGRICULTURE

Kevin Kramp

Republican Chief Counsel

1301 Longworth House Office Bldg.

Phone: (202) 225-0025

kevin.kramp@mail.house.gov

Personal: Born 02/09/1969 in Chicago, Ill.

Education: B.A., Cornell College (Mt. Vernon, Iowa), 1991. J.D., Catholic University of America, 2002.

Professional: 1991–93, staff asst., Rep. Jim Nussle, R-Iowa. 1993–94, systems manager, Rep. Bob Goodlatte, R-Va. 1994–96, agriculture legislative asst., Rep. Bob Goodlatte, R-Va. 1997–2000, staff dir., Subc. on Dept. Operations, Oversight, Nutrition and Forestry, House Cmte. on Agriculture. 2003–2006, chief counsel, House Cmte. on Agriculture. 2007–present, Republican chief counsel, House Cmte. on Agriculture.

Expertise: Operations, nutrition, energy.

Kevin Kramp, Republican chief counsel for the House Agriculture Committee, focuses on federal commodity programs as well as energy and nutrition issues.

In the farming community, growers can use derivatives, or agricultural swaps, to protect themselves from swings in the prices of crops, or farming machinery.

The Dodd-Frank Wall Street Reform and Consumer Protection Act (named for Democratic Sen. Chris Dodd of Connecticut and Rep. Barney Frank of Massachusetts), signed into law in July 2010, was intended to bring oversight to the swaps market, but there is bi-partisan concern within the House Agriculture Committee that the financial reform law will have an unintended effect on growers.

Republicans have criticized the U.S. Commodity Futures Trading Commission (CFTC) for moving too fast with writing new rules authorized by Dodd-Frank.

Meanwhile, some U.S. agriculture-based businesses have argued they should be exempt from some of the CFTC rules because they use derivatives only to hedge risks from price wings in the agriculture market and that they are not at risk of destabilizing the financial system.

As GOP chief counsel, Kramp has seen it all: criticism and complements of committee leadership and different views of an administration, depending what party is in charge. He has been on the committee since 1997, giving him experience in both the minority and now the majority.

Kramp was raised outside Chicago, and has a B.A. from Cornell College in Iowa and a law degree from Catholic University in Washington. He is an avid Cubs fan.

When he isn't rooting for his favorite professional team he roots elsewhere—he coaches baseball for his sons.

HOUSE AGRICULTURE

Rob Larew

Chief of Staff

1305 Longworth House Office Bldg.

Phone: (202) 225-0317

rob.larew@mail.house.gov

Personal: Born 1966 in Greenville, W.Va.

Education: B.S., dairy science, Virginia Tech, 1989. Graduate study, Pennsylvania State University, 1992.

Professional: 1994–96, legislative assistant/press secretary, Rep. Collin Peterson, D-Minn. 1996, legislative assistant, Sen. Paul Wellstone, D-Minn. 1997–2004, legislative director, Rep. Collin Peterson, D-Minn. 2004–2005, congressional and pub. affairs director, USDA Food Safety and Inspection Service. 2005–2006, Democratic staff director, House Cmte. on Agriculture. 2007–present, chief of staff, House Cmte. on Agriculture.

Expertise: Legislative affairs.

Rob Larew started working for Rep. Collin Peterson, D-Minn., over a decade and a half ago as a legislative assistant and press secretary. Now, he is in his fourth year as chief of staff under Peterson on the House Committee on Agriculture.

Larew is involved in many facets of the committee's work, from derivatives legislation to implementation of the $286 billion, five-year Farm Bill that became law in 2008 after intense negotiations following two presidential vetoes. Larew says it's the most significant project he's worked on at the Agriculture Committee.

"It's what I live for, you know, working here and to work on a project like that," Larew said. "It's a lot of hard work, a lot of effort, but nobody put in more effort than Chairman Peterson. And so we were all glad to do our part."

Now in the 112th Congress, Larew expects to be doing a lot of oversight on reauthorizing programs from the 2008 Farm Bill, as it is set to expire in 2012, and planning for the next Farm Bill. He says Rep. Peterson is also interested in looking into the regulatory burden placed on American agriculture by the EPA and other agencies, as well as cutting the budget without letting agriculture "bear an undue cost of that."

Larew grew up on a dairy farm near Greenville, W.Va., and has spent almost his entire career working on agricultural issues. He has first-hand international agriculture experience from his time as a Peace Corps livestock specialist in Tanzania.

He got his start on Capitol Hill in the early 1990s, but left in 2003 to work as a congressional liaison at the Department of Agriculture's Safety and Inspection Service. There he was briefly at the center of the "mad cow" disease storm.

HOUSE AGRICULTURE

Pam Miller

Senior Professional Staff

Subcommittee on Horticulture and Organic Agriculture

1301 Longworth House Office Bldg.

Phone: (202) 226-1097

Pam.Miller@mail.house.gov

Personal: Born 05/09/1976 in Emporia, Kans.

Education: B.S., Texas Tech University, 1998.

Professional: 1998–99, legislative corresp., Rep. Larry Combest, R-Texas. 1999–2003, legislative asst., House Cmte. on Agriculture. 2003–2007, staff director, Sbcmt. on Livestock and Horticulture Subcommittee, House Cmte. on Agriculture. 2007–present, senior professional staff, House Cmte. on Agriculture.

Expertise: Fruits and vegetables, honey and bees.

Not many people can say they are experts in the policy of "honey and bees" but Pam Miller will continue to focus much of her time in the 112th Congress on those two interconnected and often overlooked areas in her role as senior professional staff member.

Colony collapse disorder is a major problem and a mysterious trend that causes worker bees to disappear from their hives, ultimately leading to the collapse of the colony. The problem has caused at least one-third of all U.S. honey bees to vanish, according to a number of sources, mostly affecting mobile hives that beekeepers transport to pollinate crops. Bees are vital because they pollinate many crops that Americans rely on, including watermelons, apples, cucumbers, and squash, Miller said. They also pollinate clover, a crucial feed source in the cattle industry.

Research on the cause of colony collapse disorder is needed, Miller said, and the 2012 Farm Bill could be the vehicle to try and funnel money to research on why the honey bees are disappearing.

Miller also works to protect U.S. honey producers, who face competition from imported honey. Miller said much of the honey shipped in from other countries may not be pure honey. Miller was successful at getting a provision in to the 2008 Farm Bill that requires any honey stamped with the USDA mark to also display the country of origin.

A Texas native, Miller was born in rural Kansas but moved south during elementary school. Like many farm committee staffers, she's a farm kid herself: her family raised sheep, hogs, and goats, and Miller and her siblings were active in 4-H. She thought she'd become an agriculture reporter after college, but said was drawn to government instead.

"I've found I have really enjoyed it and what we do here makes a big impact on ranchers and growers," she said.

HOUSE AGRICULTURE

Clark Ogilvie

Senior Professional Staff
Subcommittee on General Farm Commodities and Risk Management
1305 Longworth House Office Bldg.
Phone: (202) (202) 225-0720
clark.ogilvie@mail.house.gov

Personal: Born 02/14/1969 in Memphis, Tenn.

Education: B.A., Rhodes College, 1991. J.D., George Washington University, 2004.

Professional: 1992–95, legislative asst., Rep. Jim Sasser, D-Tenn. 1995–98, dep. dir. of correspondence, Vice President Al Gore. 1998–2000, legislative analyst, Hogan & Hartson law firm. 2000–2005, legislative asst., Rep. Bob Etheridge, D-N.C. 2005–2006, professional staff, House Cmte. on Agriculture. 2007–2010, subc. staff dir., Subc. on General Farm Commodities and Risk Management, House Cmte. on Agriculture. 2010–present, senior professional staff, House Cmte. on Agriculture.

Expertise: Crop insurance, commodity exchanges.

Clark Ogilvie is in his sixth year with the House Committee on Agriculture. Starting on the panel in 2005 as professional staff, he is now senior professional staff for the minority Democratic Party.

Ogilvie has been active with working on the Commodity Exchange Act and with the Commodity Futures Trading Commission (CFTC). He also deals with crop insurance issues.

Ogilvie worked with the House Agriculture Committee when they were playing an instrumental role in derivatives reform and the Dodd-Frank Wall Street Reform and Consumer Protection Act. "That was the biggest thing we did in the previous congress," Ogilvie said.

The legislation addresses what officials said were concerns about excessive speculation in commodity markets and brings greater oversight over financial derivatives instruments—such as credit default swaps.

Now with the 112th Congress, Ogilvie will be spending a lot of time working on oversight regarding the implementation of the Dodd-Frank Act. In the fall, he will be gearing up to work on the next farm bill.

This won't be Ogilvie's first time working on a farm bill. During the 110th session of Congress, he participated in conference committee negotiations regarding the 2008 Farm Bill, "particularly with regard to farm safety net programs and crop insurance."

When Ogilvie was working as a legislative assistant for Rep. Bob Etheridge, D-N.C. in the early '00s, he worked on issues involving the House Agriculture Committee for the Congressman. It was a natural extension for him to then come to work for the Agriculture Committee, he said.

Clark Ogilvie grew up in Memphis, where he could see barges full of cotton plying the Mississippi, taking it from surrounding farms down river to international ports.

Coming to Washington right after graduation from Rhodes College allowed Ogilvie's early interest in farm policy to blossom.

"Memphis is a cotton town," he said. "I was very aware of cotton and the role it plays in American agriculture."

Now Ogilvie is the subcommittee staff director for the subcommittee on general commodities and risk management. The panel oversees crop subsidies for cotton, and the other traditional row crops: corn, rice, soy, and wheat, and as such, serves as a lightning rod for criticism from farmers who worry about the future and structure of federal government subsidies and from free trade advocates and budget hawks who argue that crop payments distort free trade and waste money.

To gear up for the farm bill debate, Ogilvie attended five field hearings on the issue in 2006.

Legislation authorizing the Commodities Futures Exchange Commission, which regulates speculative trading in farm products, expired in 2005. The House passed a reauthorization by voice vote during the 109th Congress, but the full Senate did not take up a corresponding bill. A debate on how to regulate market volatility in energy markets, and whether that volatility is necessarily the result of market manipulation, is like to continue as the committee takes another shot at the reauthorization. But it probably won't get to it until 2008, because there are more pressing matters. "We're going to come back to that again during this Congress," Ogilvie said, "but the farm bill has the top priority."

The federal crop insurance program does not need reauthorization this year, but debate on it will likely spill into Ogilvie's subcommittee. Under President Bush, the U.S. Department of Agriculture has long tried to boost participation in the program as a way to reduce farmers' reliance on disaster payments when their crop or livestock yield declines as a result of a natural disaster. "They're trying to drag crop insurance into the farm bill," Ogilvie said.

Ogilvie earned his law degree at George Washington University, taking classes at night, while he worked on agriculture issues for Rep. Bob Etheridge, D-N.C. during the day.

HOUSE AGRICULTURE

Nicole Scott

Staff Director

1305 Longworth House Office Bldg

Phone: (202) 225-0029

nicole.scott@mail.house.gov

Personal: Born in Waurika, Okla.

Education: J.D., University of Oklahoma College of Law, 1994. B.A., University of Oklahoma, 1991.

Professional: 1999–2001, legislative assistant, Former Rep. J.C. Watts, R-Okla. 2001–2003, legislative director, House Committee on Agriculture. 2003–2009, deputy chief of staff, House Committee on Agriculture. 2009–present, staff director, House Committee on Agriculture.

Margaret "Nicole" Scott, staff director for the House Agriculture Committee, started working for Frank Lucas, R-Okla., in 2001. By 2009, she had worked her way up from legislative director to deputy chief of staff.

When Lucas became the ranking Republican on the committee in 2009, he hired Scott as minority staff director, and when Lucas took over the chairmanship of the committee in 2010, Scott's position became majority staff director, a position she still holds in the 112th Congress.

"Nicole has been a valuable member of my staff for the last 10 years, and I know that her knowledge and experience will serve the committee well," Lucas said in a press release announcing Scott's new role as minority staff director in 2009.

Scott has seen a number of foreign countries during her time working for Lucas. She's traveled with Lucas and other staff to Turkey, Israel, Tunisia, Germany, and England for various purposes including to tour ocean ports, chemical plants, nuclear facilities, and farms and to learn about those countries political and economic structures.

In accepting the position on the Agriculture Committee, Scott said she was "honored" and looked forward to her new role on the committee, serving the people of Oklahoma, which is her home state. She was born in Waurika, Oklahoma, and graduated from the University of Oklahoma University in 1991. She earned her law degree from University of Oklahoma's law school in 1994.

The major piece of legislation that the House Agriculture Committee works on—the Farm Bill—isn't up for reauthorization until 2012. Until then, the committee will focus most of its time on holding oversight hearings and investigation whether programs authorized in the 2008 Farm Bill are living up to their promise. In addition, the committee will talk with its constituency and hear what concerns the nation's farmers, ranchers, and growers would like addressed in the next Farm Bill.

As another committee staffer said, it's nearly impossible to have a conversation on the committee without bringing up the Farm Bill.

HOUSE AGRICULTURE

Anne Simmons

Senior Policy Advisor

Subcommittee on Conservation, Credit, Energy and Research

1305 Longworth House Office Bldg.

Phone: (202) 225-1494

Anne.Simmons@mail.house.gov

Personal: Born in Spencer, Iowa.

Education: B.S., Cornell College, 1986.

Professional: 1987–88, staff assistant, House Cmte. on Armed Services. 1988–93, legislative assistant, Rep. Tim Johnson, D-S.Dak. 1993–94, staff director, Subc. on General Farm Commodities, House Cmte. on Agriculture. 1994–95, staff dir., Subc. on Conservation, Credit, Rural Development, and Research, House Cmte. on Agriculture. 1995–96, consultant, Subc. on Resource Conservation, Research, and Forestry, House Cmte. on Agriculture. 1997–2004, professional staff member, House Cmte. on Agriculture. 2005–2006, senior professional staff member, Subc. on Conservation, Credit, Rural Development, and Research, House Cmte. on Agriculture. 2007–2010, senior professional staff, Subc. on Conservation, Credit, Energy, and Research, House Cmte. on Agriculture. 2010–present, senior policy advisor, House Cmte. on Agriculture.

Expertise: Commodity, conservation, farm credit programs.

Anne Simmons is Democratic Senior Policy Advisor with the House Committee on Agriculture. She works for the minority Democratic Party under ranking member Rep. Collin Peterson D-Minn.

In the 112th Congress, Simmons expects to be working on continued oversight of the 2008 farm bill, as well as the new 2012 farm bill. She notes past farm bills as some of her most important projects.

Simmons also helped work to transfer budgetary responsibilities for the census of agriculture from the Census Bureau to the United States Department of Agriculture (USDA) in 1997. The census of agriculture has collected data on agriculture in the U.S. separate from the decennial census since 1840 and is now conducted in years ending in "2" and "7."

Simmons has been responsible for Agriculture Committee issues related to program crops, conservation, energy, credit and research for Peterson. She was responsible for the same issues for the former Rep. Charlie Stenholm, D-Tex., when he was the committee's ranking member, and former Chairman Eligio "Kika" De la Garza, also of Texas.

Simmons has been with the Agriculture Committee since 1993 and served as staff director of several subcommittees under then-Rep. Tim Johnson, D-S.D. Johnson is now in the U.S. Senate.

Prior to joining the Agriculture Committee, Simmons was a member of Johnson's congressional staff. She grew up on a farm that raised corn, soybean, and livestock near Spencer, Iowa, and graduated from Cornell College. Now, she says she has the "best of both worlds," getting to work on agriculture policy even though she didn't stay on the farm.

HOUSE AGRICULTURE

Pelham Straughn

Senior Professional Staff Member

1002 Longworth House Office Bldg.

Phone: (202) 225-4916

Personal: Born 03/21/1975 in Birmingham, Ala.

Education: B.A., Hampden-Sydney College, 1997.

Professional: 1997–1998, legislative corresp., Rep. Terry Everett, R-Ala. 1998–2001, legislative asst., Rep. Terry Everett, R-Ala. 2001–2006, staff dir., Subc. on Specialty Crops and Foreign Agriculture Programs, House Cmte. on Agriculture. 2007–present, sr. professional staff, House Cmte. on Agriculture.

Expertise: Conservation, tobacco, and peanuts.

Until the House Agriculture Committee begins the heavy lifting on the 2012 Farm Bill, senior professional staff member Pelham Straughn is working oversight hearings on issues such as conservation and the Environmental Protection Agency's proposed regulations for the Chesapeake Bay Watershed.

Straughn worked on the conservation sections of the 2008 Farm Bill and also handles issues surrounding specialty crops, including tobacco, which has been majorly impacted by the 2009 passage of a bill that gave the Food and Drug Administration (FDA) regulatory control over tobacco products.

The FDA now has the power to regulate the manufacturing, distribution, advertising, promotion and sale of cigarettes as well as smokeless tobacco. The law puts the FDA in the position of being "on the farm micromanaging farmers," said House Agriculture Committee Chairman Frank Lucas, R-Okla., who was the ranking Republican on the committee when the landmark anti-smoking bill was signed into law by President Obama.

"Producers will bear the brunt of this legislation," Lucas said prior to passage of the bill. "FDA will tell producers what type of seeds they can plant, the methods in which they cultivate those seeds, the records they must keep and on and on and on."

The 2008 Farm Bill provided assistance for producers for their voluntary efforts to improve management practices and water quality, and states and localities have had success in improving runoff and water quality, argued Lucas.

Straughn also works on peanuts, a crop that contributes more than four billion dollars to the U.S. economy each year. Americans eat more than 600 million pounds of peanuts and about 700 million pounds of peanut butter each year, according to the National Peanut Board, a research and promotion group funded by the peanut industry.

HOUSE AGRICULTURE

Pete Thomson

Senior Professional Staff Member

1301 Longworth House Office Bldg.

Phone: (202) 225-0029

Personal: Born 09/01/1957 in Norfolk, Va.

Education: B.A., Virginia Tech, 1980. M.P.A., Virginia Tech, 1982.

Professional: 1983–1990, legislative asst. and legislative dir., Rep. Bob Smith, (R-Ore). 1990–1993, minority staff member, Subc. on Conservation, Credit, and Rural Development, House Cmte. on Agriculture. 1994–1995, minority consultant, Subc. on Dept. Operations and Nutrition, House Cmte. on Agriculture. 1995–1997, staff dir., Subc. on Livestock, Dairy and Poultry, House Cmte. on Agriculture. 1997–1999, legislative dir., House Cmte. on Agriculture. 1999–present, senior professional staff member, House Cmte. on Agriculture.

Expertise: Food safety, livestock issues, animal health, agricultural business.

Pete Thomson is a senior professional staff member involved in food safety and livestock issues for the House Agriculture Committee.

Animal feed availability issues will loom large in the 112th Congress as the increasing use of grains in everything from ethanol production to food, has driven up costs.

"There is more demand that supply," Thomson said.

That presents an issue for ranchers, because "The vast majority of the cost to raise a pig or a cow is feed," he said.

Thomson also will focus on the Grain Inspection, Packers and Stockyards Administration, which facilitates the marketing of agricultural products.

Thomson said money for agricultural projects and proposals might be scarce in the 112th Congress.

"This is a Congress where a lot of people were elected to cut spending," he said. "There's a feeling that that's a lot of what we'll see this year."

Thomson said he's spent about equal time being in the minority as in the majority, but being in the majority now has its perks, such as setting the weekly agenda, which allows him to have a little more certainly about what his day will entail.

There is not a dramatic shift in the fundamental policy agenda when Democrats are in charge versus when Republicans are in charge, Thomson said.

"This is a constituent-oriented committee, while there are occasionally partisan divides, mostly alignments occur along commodity, regional or other dimensions," he said.

Unlike many of his colleagues, Thomson did not grow up on a farm. His father was in the Navy and moved the family all over the country. After graduate school, he interned for Rep. Bob Smith, R-Ore., and convinced the lawmaker to overlook his lack of farm experience and to take him on as a legislative assistant.

"I'm certainly jealous of the farm kids, but what we're doing here is public policy, not farming," he said.

HOUSE AGRICULTURE

Michelle Weber

Staff director, Subcommittee on Livestock, Dairy, and Poultry

1301 Longworth House Office Bldg.

Phone: (202) 225-4453

michelle.weber@mail.house.gov

Personal: Born 04/28/1983 in Hastings, Nebr.

Education: J.D., University of Nebraska, 2008. B.S., Animal Science, University of Nebraska, 2005.

Professional: 2008–2009, Nebraska Attorney General's Office. 2009–2011, legislative aide, Sen. Mike Johans, R-Neb. 2011–present, staff director, Subcmte. on Livestock, Dairy, and Poultry.

Expertise: Livestock, dairy, poultry, animal welfare.

Michele Weber is staff director of the Subcommittee on Livestock, Dairy, and Poultry, which focuses on inspection, marketing, and promotion of meat and dairy, as well as seafood. The subcommittee also has jurisdiction over animal welfare and grazing.

For the 2012 Farm Bill, Weber's subcommittee will focus on the animal ID system, country of origin labeling, and a controversial proposal dealing with the Grain Inspection, Packers & Stockyards Administration (GIPSA). The 2008 Farm Bill directed GIPSA to create a set of rules to address competitive marketing among livestock and poultry producers, but Republicans on the Agriculture Committee worry the provision will hurt farmers.

"GIPSA's proposed rule governing livestock and poultry marketing practices will have costly, unintended consequences for our nation's livestock producers, leading to higher consumer prices, lower producer income and reduced competitiveness," said Subcommittee Chairman Thomas Rooney, R-Fla.

Weber knows a thing or two about cattle and farming, because like many other Agriculture Committee staffers, Weber grew up on a farm. Her family still raises corn, soybeans, wheat, and cattle on a farm near Blue Hill, Nebraska.

Rural America has seen a major decrease in farms of all kind, but the loss has been particularly pronounced in the cattle industry, which as has declined significantly in the past 30 years. In 1980, there were more than 1.6 million cattle farms, and now there are roughly 950,000 cattle farms in the United States.

Weber studied animal science at the University of Nebraska, a background that makes her well-suited to dealing with animal welfare issues tackled by the committee.

The 2008 Farm Bill contained a number of animal welfare provisions, including creating a framework for animal disease traceability "a critical component of quick and successful disease response," Edward Avalos, under secretary for Marketing and Regulatory Programs at the U.S. Department of Agriculture, told the subcommittee.

"The new approach will also incorporate strengthening protections against the entry and spread of disease, more strictly enforcing existing disease control regulations, and finding ways to provide more resources to the States to combat diseases when they emerge," Avalos said.

Committee on Appropriations

H-307, The Capitol
Washington, DC 20515
Phone: (202) 225-2771
Twitter: @AppropsDems (Democrats)
http://appropriations.house.gov

Ratio: 29/26

MAJORITY MEMBERS

Harold Rogers, KY-5th, Chairman

C.W. Bill Young, FL-10th
Jerry Lewis, CA-41st
Frank R. Wolf, VA-10th
Jack Kingston, GA-1st
Rodney P. Frelinghuysen, NJ-11th
Tom Latham, IA-4th
Robert Aderholt, AL-4th
Jo Ann Emerson, MO-8th
Kay Granger, TX-12th
Michael K. Simpson, ID-2nd
John Abney Culberson, TX-7th
Ander Crenshaw, FL-4th
Dennis R. Rehberg, MT-At Large
John Carter, TX-31st
Rodney Alexander, LA-5th
Ken Calvert, CA-44th
Jo Bonner, AL-1st
Steven C. LaTourette, OH-14th
Tom Cole, OK-4th
Jeff Flake, AR-6th
Charles Dent, PA-15th
Mario Diaz-Balart, FL-25th
Steve Austria, OH-7th
Cynthia Lummis, WY-At Large
Tom Graves, GA-9th
Kevin Yoder, KS-3rd
Steve Womack, AR-3rd
Alan Nunnelee, MS-1st

MINORITY MEMBERS

Norman D. Dicks, WA-6th, Ranking Member

Marcy Kaptur, OH-9th
Peter J. Visclosky, IN-1st
Nita M. Lowey, NY-18th
José E. Serrano, NY-16th
Rosa L. DeLauro, CT-3rd
James P. Moran, VA-8th
John W. Olver, MA-1st
Ed Pastor, AZ-4th
David E. Price, NC-4th
Maurice D. Hinchey, NY-22nd
Lucille Roybal-Allard, CA-34th
Sam Farr, CA-17th
Jesse L. Jackson Jr., IL-2nd
Chaka Fattah, PA-2nd
Steven R. Rothman, NJ-9th
Sanford D. Bishop, GA-2nd
Barbara Lee, CA-9th
Adam Schiff, CA-29th
Mike Honda, CA-15th
Betty McCollum, MN-4th
Steve Israel, NY-2nd
Tim Ryan, OH-17th
C.A. Dutch Ruppersberger, MD-2nd
Ben Chandler, KY-6th
Debbie Wasserman Schultz, FL-20th

HOUSE APPROPRIATIONS

JURISDICTION

(1) Appropriation of the revenue for the support of the government.
(2) Rescissions of appropriations contained in appropriations Acts.
(3) Transfers of unexpended balances.
(4) Bills and joint resolutions reported by other committees that provide new entitlement authority as defined in section 3(9) of the Congressional Budget Act of 1974 and referred to the committee under clause 4(a)(2).

The committee shall include separate headings for "Rescissions" and "Transfers of Unexpended Balances" in any bill or resolution as reported from the committee under its jurisdiction specified in subparagraph (2) or (3), with all proposed rescissions and proposed transfers listed therein; and shall include a separate section with respect to such rescissions or transfers in the accompanying committee report. In addition to its jurisdiction under the preceding provisions of this paragraph, the committee shall have the fiscal oversight function provided for in clause 2(b)(3) and the budget hearing function provided for in clause 4(a).

HOUSE APPROPRIATIONS

The 112th Congress is sure to be a unique one in the history of the Appropriations Committee as it becomes ground zero in the spending wars between Republicans and Democrats. That battle could consume the balance of the year and beyond. Gone is the focus on congressionally-directed funds, with members on both sides of the aisle agreeing to a two-year moratorium on earmarks.

Panel members, and particularly senior members, have long held some of the most powerful positions in Washington. But a number of recent scandals associated with the spending process, as well as a focus on the skyrocketing debt has blunted the allure of the committee. The past panel chairman, Democrat Rep. David Obey, D-Wisc., resigned rather than face what many experts predicted would be a nearly-impossible re-election campaign.

With the sharpening focus on reducing the nation's debt and deficit, the committee will have to contend with dramatic differences between Republicans who control the House and Democrats the Senate, resulting in what many think will be a tug-of-war between short-term funding measures to avert a government shutdown to the 13 annual spending bills that fund the government for the next fiscal year.

"The Appropriations Committee will have a huge job ahead to drastically cut government spending, stop our exploding deficit, root out waste and unnecessary funding, and get our nation onto a responsible budget path," Chairman Hal Rogers, R-Ky., said after he was tapped to lead the panel for the 112th Congress.

Unlike the last Congress, when the spending panel crafted an $814 billion stimulus bill, under the guidance of the Democratic majority, Chairman Rogers was faced right away with the Herculean task of slashing $61 billion from non-defense, discretionary spending, a GOP campaign promise. Democrats decried the cuts as "draconian," and not one voted for the measure.

"The result, after more than four days of debate over hundreds of amendments, is a bill that is regrettably even worse than when it was introduced, and it is now encumbered with an array of ideologically-driven provisions that will surely render it dead on arrival in the other body and virtually impossible for the President to sign it into law," Ranking Democrat Norm Dicks, D-Wash., said.

The process of crafting the annual spending bills has been crippled in the past decade by the growing partisan environment in Washington and now more so with a divided Congress. So difficult, in fact, that not since 1996 has Congress passed the spending measures before the beginning of the fiscal year on October 1, and for many years, an all-encompassing omnibus appropriations bill was needed to complete business before the end of the year.

Rogers attempted to set the tone by slashing his own panel's budget four percent more than every other office at the start of the 112th Congress.

Because the size and complexity of appropriations bills often goes beyond the normal expertise of most lawmakers, appropriators tend to give significant deference to their committee's staff, many of whom have remained in the 112th Congress.

Members will have to find the balance they need for federal spending against the strong push to reign in the deficit and debt, all under the ever-watchful eye of the Tea Party, which largely supports Republicans and has become a force in U.S. politics. One strong force for the possibility of compromise in this committee is the fact that Chairman Rogers and Rep. Dicks are said to be close. They're going to need it to navigate the treacherous spending waters ahead.

HOUSE APPROPRIATIONS

Dena Baron

Chief Clerk

2358A Rayburn House Office Bldg.

Phone: (202) 225-2141

dena.baron@mail.house.gov

Personal: Born in Minneapolis, Minn.

Education: B.A., University of Minnesota. M.P.A., The George Washington University.

Professional: 1999–2010, staff assistant, Subc. on Transportation, Housing and Urban Development, House Cmte. on Appropriations. 2010–present, chief clerk, Subc. on Transportation, Housing and Urban Development, House Cmte. on Appropriations.

House Transportation, Housing and Urban Development Appropriations Subcommittee Chairman Tom Latham, R-Iowa, said in early January that he planned "to get to work immediately looking for ways to scale back the federal budget and give American families and businesses the economic certainty they're demanding." And that's exactly what he did, with the help of Clerk Dena Baron.

Baron, a 12-year veteran of the spending panel, and the staff slashed 23 percent from last year's spending levels and achieved a $16.3 billion, or 24 percent, reduction from the White House's fiscal year 2011 request. Cuts made to the transportation and housing section of the House Republican leadership's $61 billion government funding bill, called a continuing resolution, totaled $52.4 billion.

The chairman made clear that spending cuts and budget reform would be Baron and her staff's prime focus during the 112th Congress, as Republicans look to drastically reduce the nation's deficit and debt, putting the spending panel on a collision course with the president, who has stated that innovation is a top priority this year with projects like high-speed rail.

"Over the last several years, programs within THUD experienced tremendous growth—an approximate 38 percent increase since 2008—primarily in grant programs and new Obama Administration initiatives such as high-speed rail and the National Infrastructure Investments Program," Latham noted, adding, "the continuing resolution slashes spending but maintains the funds necessary to meet priorities such as renewing every housing voucher and contract and keeping up with the country's transportation infrastructure needs."

Baron will also work Latham's plans to pursue unallocated stimulus funding, something Republicans promised to target during the recent midterm campaign.

In 2010, much to her surprise, Baron, a Minnesota native, got some on-the-record time at a hearing on her subcommittee's spending bill. Rep. Jerry Lewis, R-Calif., announced to panel members, "Dena Baron wants us to get through quickly. She's just about ready to give delivery to her second child. For those who are curious, about all of that, Dena is planning to deliver us a baby girl. And Dena, it's a delight."

HOUSE APPROPRIATIONS

Taunja Berquam

Chief Clerk

2362B Longworth House Office Bldg.

Phone: (202) 225-3421

taunja.berquam@mail.house.gov

Personal: Born in Portland, Ore.

Professional: In 2005, Taunja Berquam arrived at the House Appropriations Subcommittee on Energy and Water Development from the U.S. Army Corps of Engineers. She was detailed to the panel for a time and is now its chief clerk during the 112th Congress.

Her résumé includes a tour of duty in Iraq and as the Corps' program manager in her home town of Portland, Oregon.

In a 2004 Army Corps of Engineers' publication titled, "Essayons Forward," Berquam is described as "flexible and able to adapt to change," and she added, "Once you manage a program, the business processes are enough alike that you can manage something entirely different."

"Here (in Iraq) the work is very different; we're master planning 14 bases and identifying future camp needs," Berquam went on. "In the beginning these bases will be used by US troops and then will be turned over to the Iraqi Armed Forces.... The workload is going to be massive."

Experience with a massive workload and her program management skills are sure to help this Energy and Water panel's chief clerk manage a staff responsible for defending agencies under their jurisdiction against majority Republicans who are sparing no nook or cranny of the federal budget as they drive to reduce the nation's skyrocketing debt and deficit. The panel has jurisdiction over the Department of Energy is a ripe GOP target, a cabinet post that some Republicans have suggested does not need to exist.

One popular entity under the subcommittee's jurisdiction Berquam is extremely familiar with, the Army Corps of Engineers, is likely to be spared the budgetary knife. The Corps remains a highly-popular federal agency with members who often like to tout its projects underway in their districts.

Berquam, according to "Essayons Forward," said she went to Iraq for a variety of reasons. "I wanted to see firsthand what the circumstances were. I think the adventure of being here was a definite reason. I knew I would grow professionally, and I guess it was based a little on being patriotic. Did I get what I came for? Yes, absolutely, my experience here met my expectations." From Mosul to Baghdad, Berquam served as the Military Program Manager responsible for "a $350 million program that included 30 military bases throughout Iraq."

Her commander at the time, Command Sgt. Maj. Mike Balch, is also quoted as saying, "Someone will have to fill some large shoes when she's gone."

HOUSE APPROPRIATIONS

Rob Blair

Chief Clerk

2362B Rayburn House Office Bldg.

Phone: (202) 225-3421

rob.blair@mail.house.gov

Personal: Born in Alexis, Ill.

Education: B.A., regional planning, Cornell University, 1994. M.A., regional planning, Tufts University, 2000. M.A., Tufts University, Fletcher School of Law and Diplomacy, 2001.

Professional: 2001–2003, staff, oil and energy industry, U.S. Dept. of State. 2003–present, chief clerk, Subc. on Energy and Water, House Cmte. on Appropriations.

The Energy and Water Subcommittee will deal with a number of explosive topics in 2011, from energy policy and rising fuel prices to funding for the nation's effort to keep nuclear weapons out of the hands of terrorists—an effort that was hit early this year by the budgetary ax as House leaders sought to dramatically reduce the nation's deficit in a stopgap government funding bill.

Rob Blair, top Republican staffer on the panel with previous oil and gas industry experience at the State Department, is uniquely positioned to deal with that challenge, as well as the subcommittee's responsibility to purchase and maintain bomb-grade nuclear weapons.

Republican aides predict that the major flashpoints in this first session of the 112th Congress will be on nuclear weapons modernization and the 12 percent increase the Obama Administration is seeking for the Department of Energy in the fiscal year 2012 budget request.

This subcommittee also funds the U.S. Army Corps of Engineers, which is responsible for navigation, flood control, environmental protection and disaster response, a highly-popular entity for members and their home states. The panel also must allocate federal tax dollars for Energy Department scientific research and the 16 national laboratories. "These laboratories house 30,000 scientists and conduct cutting edge research," according to Subcommittee Chairman Rodney P. Frelinghuysen, R-N.J.

But nuclear nonproliferation is expected to dominate the subcommittee's focus, as Blair works with Frelinghuysen, to balance competing agendas, from GOP desires to slash spending, and the Administration's drive to fund the Energy Department's non-proliferation programs.

And though subcommittee aides say that the chairman is likely to focus on rising gas prices, there is little the committee can do to affect any change in that arena.

Blair, an Illinois native, served in the Peace Corps in Africa and is a member of Pi Kappa Alpha, a secret social fraternity, one of the top 10 largest and oldest fraternities in the United States.

HOUSE APPROPRIATIONS

Anne Marie Chotvacs

Chief Clerk

HB-26, The Capitol

Phone: (202) 225-2041

Fax: (202) RepKayGranger

annemarie.chotvacs@mail.house.gov

Personal: Born in Barnwell, S.C.

Education: B.S., Presbyterian College. M.P.A., University of Georgia.

Professional: 1999–2001, staff, National Oceanic and Atmospheric Administration. 2001–2004, staff, Department of Commerce. 2004–present, chief clerk, Subc. on State and Foreign Operations, House Cmte. on Appropriations.

As the top Republican aide on the Appropriations Subcommittee on State and Foreign Operations, Anne Marie Chotvacs, will have a full plate in the 112th Congress with growing unrest in the Middle East, the continued wars in Iraq and Afghanistan, and ongoing operations with strategic U.S. ally, Pakistan.

On top of that, Chairwoman Kay Granger, R-Tex., has made clear that she will focus toward slicing excess from the budgets of agencies under the committee's jurisdiction.

"Our debt is the greatest threat to our national security," Granger said at a recent hearing, echoing a statement made recently by Joint Chiefs of Staff Chairman Admiral Mike Mullen. And a statement released from her office early this year said, "All programs under the subcommittee's jurisdiction will be under heavy scrutiny, and projects that are not achieving intended results will be subject to cancellation."

With Secretary of State Hillary Clinton lobbying hard for not only flexibility in her current budget to deal with the mounting crises abroad but also for new money for overseas operations, Chotvacs, with seven years of experience on this panel, will have to work long hours to deal with competing priorities. Budgets under the subcommittee's purview have increased by 33 percent since 2008, according to the chairwoman, and Republicans have said that will not continue.

And now, with the crisis in Japan resulting from a trio of catastrophes, from a massive earthquake followed by a tsunami and resulting nuclear reactor crisis, this subcommittee will be deeply involved in trying to find money to help this close ally.

Chotvacs' boss also will continue strict oversight on civilian funds used in Afghanistan, after reports indicated corruption and misuse of U.S. taxpayer dollars.

Chotvacs has also been tasked with reviewing and reconsidering plans to increase the staff at the State Department and the U.S. Agency for International Development, as well as a boost in lending by international banks.

This South Carolina native stays connected to her home state through her alma mater, Presbyterian College, supporting the school's "833 Fund," a society formed to help fund college scholarships and campus groups that promote educational growth.

HOUSE APPROPRIATIONS

Liz Dawson

Chief Clerk

Subcommittee on Military Construction, Veterans' Affairs, and Related Agencies

H-147, The Capitol

Phone: (202) 226-7252

liz.dawson@mail.house.gov

Personal: Born 10/12/1958 in Ft. Rucker, Ala.

Education: B.S., George Mason Univ., 1980.

Professional: 1983–1986, aide, Rep. Mickey Edwards, R-Okla. 1986–1991, aide, Rep. Bill Lowrey, R-Calif. 1991–1995, Republican staff, Subc. on Military Construction, House Cmte. on Appropriations. 1995–2001, clerk, Subc. on Military Construction, House Cmte. on Appropriations. 2001–2005, staff assistant, Subc. on the Legislative Branch, House Cmte. on Appropriations. 2005–2010, Republican professional staff member, Subc. on Military Construction, Veterans' Affairs, and Related Agencies, House Cmte. on Appropriations. 2010–present, chief clerk, Subc. on the Legislative Branch, House Cmte. on Appropriations.

Expertise: Appropriations, housing.

Liz Dawson, a 25-year veteran of Congress, got a new boss on the Appropriations Subcommittee on the Legislative Branch, Rep. Ander Crenshaw, R-Fla., and the two made news right out of the gate in the 112th Congress. Newly in the majority, Republican leaders emphasized that nearly every corner of the federal budget was ripe for spending cuts, and Chairman Crenshaw put forward a $194 million spending reduction that will affect a wide variety of congressional operations.

"I've asked offices and programs to share the pain of tough spending cuts," said Crenshaw, and with that, Congress abruptly approved cuts to its own budget.

"Our nation is at a cross-road with clear choices in the months and years ahead: fiscal responsibility or continued reckless, big-government spending." Crenshaw added, "Congress must enact reforms to return confidence and transparency to the appropriations process...at the Legislative Branch Subcommittee...we'll take the same steps that American taxpayers have taken to do more with less by cutting committee, leadership, and member office budgets."

Dawson, the subcommittee's chief clerk, was on the subcommittee when lawmakers approved a massive addition to the Capitol complex, the new visitor's center that opened in late 2008. And one issue that Dawson dealt with in that Congress could be undone by Republicans in this session. Then-Speaker Nancy Pelosi, D-Calif, worked to "green" the Capitol, but Republicans have said the effort was too costly and have already begun to roll back the energy efficiency efforts.

Dawson, an Alabama native, received her undergraduate degree from George Mason University in 1980.

HOUSE APPROPRIATIONS

Martin Delgado

Chief Clerk

Subcommittee on Agriculture, Rural Development, Food and Drug Administration, and Related Agencies

Subcommittee on Military Construction, Veterans' Affairs, and Related Agencies

2362A Rayburn House Office Bldg.

Phone: (202) 225-2638

martin.delgado@mail.house.gov

Personal: Born 07/15/1962 in Santa Rosa, N.Mex.

Education: B.A., New Mexico Highlands University, 1988.

Professional: 1991–1992, staff, Office of Management and Budget (OMB). 1992–1996, staff, U.S. Dept. of Agriculture. 1997–1998, professional staff asst., Subc. on Interior, House Cmte. on Appropriations. 1998–2003, staff asst., Subc. on Agriculture, Rural Development, Food and Drug Administration, and Related Agencies, House Cmte. on Appropriations. 2004–2008, clerk, Subc. on Agriculture, Rural Development, Food and Drug Administration, and Related Agencies, House Cmte. on Appropriations. 2008–2010, chief clerk, Subc. on Military Construction, Veterans Affairs, and Related Agencies, House Cmte. on Appropriations. 2010–present, chief clerk, Subc. on Agriculture, Rural Development, Food and Drug Administration, and Related Agencies, House Cmte. on Appropriations.

Expertise: Appropriations, Agriculture.

After several years on the Military Construction and Veterans' Affairs panel, Martin Delgado returns to the Subcommittee on Agriculture, Food and Drug Administration under its new chairman, Republican Rep. Jack Kingston of Georgia. In addition to the U.S. Department of Agriculture and the Food and Drug Administration, Delgado's new assignment involves oversight of the budgets for the Farm Credit Administration, the Farm Credit System Financial Assistance Corporation, and the Commodity Futures Trading Commission.

Much of the discussion this year is expected to focus on how lawmakers are going to make cuts without stifling the future of the industries under its purview. That could get dicey, as highly-popular federal farm subsidies come under the budgetary magnifying glass. According to a subcommittee GOP aide, this will include "taking a hard look at the presidential terminations list." This was a list submitted by the Administration in its fiscal 2012 budget which proposed more than 200 program terminations, much of them duplicative, in an effort to save $33 billion.

The chairman announced that he plans to use his panel's "power of the purse over a centerpiece of the controversial financial market reform enacted last year—the Commodity Futures Trading Commission." A regulatory body designed to battle fraud and manipulation in the commodities market, with a focus on agricultural futures, today oversees futures in the massive energy and financial futures industries.

Kingston, upon being named to the job, said, "In all that we do, the focus of this subcommittee will be to ensure that we are good stewards of taxpayer dollars."

Delgado, a New Mexico native, joined the Appropriations Committee in 1997, first working for the Agriculture Subcommittee.

HOUSE APPROPRIATIONS

Martha Foley

Chief Clerk

Subcommittee on Agriculture, Rural Development, Food and Drug Administration, and Related Agencies

2362-A Rayburn House Office Bldg.

Phone: (202) 225-2638

martha.foley@mail.house.gov

Professional: 1994–2001, associate director, legislative affairs, Office of Management and Budget (OMB). 2001–2005, Democratic staff asst., Subc. on Agriculture, Rural Development, Food and Drug Administration, and Related Agencies/Subc. on Transportation, Treasury, and Independent Agencies, House Cmte. on Appropriations. 2005–2007, Democratic staff asst., Subc. on Agriculture, Rural Development, Food and Drug Administration, and Related Agencies/Subc. on Transportation, Treasury, and Housing and Urban Development, the Judiciary, District of Columbia, House Cmte. on Appropriations. 2007–present, clerk, Subc. on Agriculture, Rural Development, Food and Drug Administration, and Related Agencies, House Cmte. on Appropriations.

Expertise: Appropriations.

With nearly 20 years of experience dealing with the contentious budget process in Washington, Martha Foley will be well-positioned to deal with the Republican majority determined to slash federal government spending significantly in this session of Congress.

As the top staffer for Democrats on the Appropriations Subcommittee on Agriculture, Foley, together with new Ranking Member Rep. Sam Farr, D-Calif., will work with Republicans on funding the U.S. Department of Agriculture, as well as the Food and Drug Administration.

Foley and the subcommittee determine federal spending on food safety, agricultural research, some conservation programs, and the special nutrition program for women, infants and children known as WIC. And though the subcommittee does not have direct jurisdiction over mandatory programs, like farm subsidies and food stamps, it occasionally cuts into the mandatory programs to pay for other priorities. Aides expect Democrats and Republicans alike to try to trim back farm subsidies in an effort to bring down the nation's deficit.

Foley is breathing a sigh of relief in 2011, as Congress will not have to deal with the farm bill, a product that typically consumes nearly an entire year of work by multiple committees, including Foley's. Congress succeeded in passing the last farm bill over the veto of then-President Bush in 2008, and Foley had a front-row seat in that battle.

She is a former high-level executive in the Administration of former President Bill Clinton, with positions of senior advisor to White House Chief of Staff Leon Panetta and deputy assistant to the president and associate director for legislative affairs in the Office of Management and Budget.

HOUSE APPROPRIATIONS

Kate Hallahan

Clerk

Subcommittee on Transportation, Treasury, and Housing and Urban Development, The Judiciary, District of Columbia

2358 Rayburn House Office Bldg.

Phone: (202) 225-2141

Kate.Hallahan@mail.house.gov

Personal: Born 1962 in Clarksville, Ind.

Education: B.A., political science, Univ. of Washington, Seattle, 1985. B.A., speech communication, Univ. of Washington, Seattle, 1985.

Professional: 1989–1993, sr. legislative asst. Secretary for Public Affairs, Rep. Al Swift, D-Wash. 1994–1995, professional staff member, Subc. on Transportation and Hazardous Materials, House Cmte. on Energy. 1995–1996, sr. congressional relations officer, U.S. Dept. of Transportation. 1996–1997, special asst. to the secretary, U.S. Dept. of Transportation. 1997–2000, sr. policy advisor to deputy secretary, U.S. Dept. of Transportation. 2000–2001, deputy asst. administrator, Office of Govt. and Industry Affairs, Federal Aviation Administration. 2001–2006, professional staff member, Subc. on Transportation, Treasury, the Judiciary, Housing and Urban Development, Senate Cmte. on Appropriations. 2006–2007, professional staff member, Subc. on Transportation, Treasury, and Housing and Urban Development, the Judiciary, the District of Columbia, House Cmte. on Appropriations. 2007–present, clerk, Subc. on Transportation, Housing and Urban Development, and Related Agencies, House Cmte. on Appropriations.

Expertise: Transportation appropriations issues.

Kate Hallahan has had her hand in transportation policy since 1989, and now in 2011, as top Democratic clerk on the committee, she will have a lot on her plate as Republicans look to trim massive savings out of the federal budget during the 112th Congress.

At the start of the legislative session, newly-empowered Republican leaders announced massive cuts in the transportation sector as part of their $61 billion government funding bill, and Hallahan's boss, Rep. John Olver, D-Mass., was livid, foreshadowing a major fight to come.

"While the Republican 'slash-and-burn' approach certainly reduces the numbers on paper, the reality is extremely costly," Olver said, "Under the Republican's proposal, 10,000 new vouchers in funding for homeless veterans are eliminated....This will severely hinder communities' ability to offer basic services and implement local economic development projects, resulting in 45,000 lost jobs."

Hallahan and other Democratic subcommittee aides said the panel, this year, will also have to contend with Republicans attempts to strip all funding for high speed rail, a presidential priority.

"The Republican budget ensures we will remain behind countries like Japan and China in infrastructure investments, placing us at a serious disadvantage for winning the future," Olver said.

Hallahan is no stranger to a tough budget fight, as she led her staff through the epic fights over the creation of the Democrats' $814 billion economic stimulus bill and its many "shovel-ready" transportation projects.

This subcommittee has jurisdiction of the Department of Transportation, including the Federal Aviation, Federal Highway Administration, Federal Transit Administration, Federal Railroad Administration and Amtrak. It is also responsible for the annual budgets of the Department of Housing and Urban Development.

HOUSE APPROPRIATIONS

Jennifer Hing

Communications Director

1016 Longworth House Office Bldg.

Phone: (202) 226-7007

JHing@mail.house.gov

Personal: Born in Tigard, Ore.

Education: B.S., Oregon State University, 2002.

Professional: 2000–2002, House congressional staff, Oregon State Legislature. 2004–2005, press secretary, Rep. Jack Kingston, R-Ga.. 2005–2007, communications dir., Rep. Joe Knollenberg, R-Mich. 2007–2008, press secretary, Office of Transportation Secretary Mary E. Peters. 2008–present, communications dir., Republican staff, House Appropriations Cmte.

Expertise: Communications.

House Republicans ushered in the 112th Congress with a new chairman atop the Appropriations Committee. Rep. Hal Rogers, R-Ky., carries with him a new mission to drastically reduce non-discretionary spending back to FY2008 funding levels and to preclude all earmarks, once the signature of power for this panel.

The voice of this mammoth goal is Jennifer Hing, who will remain on the committee under its new leadership.

Hing joined the committee in 2008 when her boss, former Rep. Joe Knollenberg, R-Mich., joined the panel. Hing had worked for the congressman as his communications director before serving as press secretary for former Transportation Secretary Mary Peters in 2007.

Hing had a front-row seat to the major fights in 2010 over the $814 billion stimulus bill and the unsuccessful GOP efforts to rescind the funding. She can expect to be in the thick of GOP efforts in 2011 to defund the health care reform legislation passed in early 2010. Many GOP lawmakers have described defunding the health care bill as a chance make a serious dent in the legislation, more so than any effort to fully repeal it.

Earmark reform could prove the most difficult task for the panel, as Rogers is known for his ability to bring home money for this Bluegrass state. Still he, along with all House Republicans, voted to ban earmarks.

Hing said Republicans plan to pass all 13 appropriations bills this year, rather than the all- encompassing omnibus bill that has become the norm.

In addition to her work inside Congress, Hing took time during the 2008 election cycle to serve as spokeswoman on the campaign of Rep. Virgil Goode, R-Va., but he ultimately lost his bid to Rep. Tom Perriello, D-Va.

An Oregon native, Hing is married to Hill veteran John Scofield who formerly served as a spokesman for the Appropriations Committee. The two live on Capitol Hill.

HOUSE APPROPRIATIONS

Laura Hogshead

Chief Clerk

2358A Rayburn House Office Bldg.

Phone: (202) 225-3481

laura.hogshead@mail.house.gov

Personal: Born in Matthews, N.C.

Education: B.A., journalism and political science, University of North Carolina, Chapel Hill, 2000. Masters, public administration, University of North Carolina, Chapel Hill, 2002.

Professional: 2002–2005, policy analyst, presidential fellowship, US Department of Housing and Urban Development. 2005–2006, assistant dir., UNC Center on Poverty, Work and Opportunity. 2007–present, chief clerk, Subc. on Financial Services, House Cmte. on Appropriations.

As top Democratic staffer for the Subcommittee on Financial Services, Laura Hogshead will fight Republican efforts to dismantle the recently passed financial regulatory reform bill, as well as the stated goal of the chairwoman, Rep. Jo Ann Emerson, R-Mo., to gut the IRS enforcement component of the president's health care reform legislation.

Hogshead worked her way to Washington from a small town in North Carolina. She volunteered for Habitat for Humanity, interned in New York City at the social service agency Project Renewal, and in her junior year in college, Hogshead said in an online résumé that she hoped "to eventually work in the non-profit world as an administrator."

A top student at the University of North Carolina at Chapel Hill, Hogshead became a presidential management fellow at the U.S. Department of Housing and Urban Development. She took on social policy issues as a fellow to the House Appropriations Committee, as well, and a career in Congress was born.

The panel has wide ranging jurisdiction from the Treasury Department, to the District of Columbia, the Judiciary and Executive branches, the Federal Communications Commission, the Federal Deposit Insurance Corporation, and the Securities and Exchange Commission, several of them ripe targets for Republican efforts to dramatically reduce both the size of the deficit and the scope of government.

Hogshead has proudly touted the Democrats 2009 federal stimulus bill, which she helped to craft, but she recently told the Council of Large Public Housing Authorities that she was disappointment in the Administration's FY2011 budget request for the public housing capital fund—$500 million less than the FY2010 budget. The organization quoted her as saying, "Don't be shy about making the case for the public housing backlog."

Hogshead, with a degree in journalism and political science, perhaps naturally gravitated back to her alma mater just three years after graduation to be deputy director of the University of North Carolina at Chapel Hill Center on Poverty, Work and Opportunity. The center is the brainchild of former senator and vice presidential candidate John Edwards.

A tennis, soccer, and gymnastics buff, in her online college résumé, Hogshead noted that she was no sports buff. Photography, travel, and yard work were also tops on her list of favorite pastimes.

HOUSE APPROPRIATIONS

William Inglee

Chief Clerk/Staff Director

Phone: (202) 225-2771

william.inglee@mail.house.gov

Personal: Born in Malone, N.Y.

Education: Georgetown University. Carleton University, Ottawa, Canada.

Professional: 1978–1985, staff, Rep. Tom Coleman, R-Mo. 1985–1990, staff, House Cmte. on Foreign Affairs. 1990–1993, dep. asst. secy., Department of Defense. 1993–1995, staff, House Wednesday Group. 1995–1998, staff, House Cmte. on Appropriations, Foreign Ops Subcmte. 1998–2000, natl. security policy advisor, House Speaker Dennis Hastert, R-Ill. 2000–2010, vice president for global security Policy, Lockheed Martin Corp. 2010–present, chief clerk/staff director, House Cmte. on Appropriations.

Expertise: Defense policy, National security, Foreign affairs.

Bill Inglee, a veteran congressional policy advisor, returned to Capitol Hill in January as chief clerk and staff director of the Appropriations Committee after a decade working for Lockheed Martin Corp., for a time lobbying the spending panel he now leads.

Inglee is known to many in Washington after his nearly 20-year career in Congress, all of it spent in the House of Representatives. A defense and national security expert, Inglee returns at a time when many lawmakers are focused on drastic reductions in spending, rather than on the traditional push for more. Some senior Republicans have even said the Pentagon's budget should not escape the knife—scrutiny that will require a combination of Inglee's well-honed skills in the defense industry and Hill knowledge.

Inglee might also call on his experience in the House Wednesday Group, a forum of moderate Republicans that helped bridge the gap with the more conservative elements in the party, to navigate the GOP goal of cutting the federal budget by $100 billion.

Chairman Hal Rogers, R-Ky., made "a very smart choice," said John Feehery, who worked alongside Inglee in the Speaker's office in the late 1990s.

"He (Inglee) understands inside and out both the Appropriations and Authorization process, but his real expertise is in defense policy," Feehery said, adding, "He is simply one of the most knowledgeable, thoughtful, and wise people I know."

Inglee served House Speaker Dennis Hastert, R-Ill., for two years as a national security policy advisor where he played a key role in forming the Mexico City policy language that blocks U.S. funds from international organizations that provide abortions. President Obama reversed it in early 2009.

As an assistant secretary at the Pentagon in the early 1990's, Inglee focused on international security policy, conventional forces, and arms control policy. At Lockheed, according to the company, he focused on defense industry relations with the executive and legislative branches as well as defense think tanks.

Inglee is an avid rugby fan, according to Hill sources. He has served on a number of prestigious boards and was awarded the Secretary of Defense Medal for Outstanding Public Service and the Order of Merit Officer's Cross, First Class for his contributions to German-American relations, the highest honor awarded by the German government.

He holds degrees from Georgetown University and Carleton University in Ottawa, Canada.

HOUSE APPROPRIATIONS

Paul Juola

Clerk

H-149 The Capitol

Phone: (202) 225-2847

paul.juola@mail.house.gov

Personal: Born in Duluth, Minn.

Education: B.S., University of Minnesota. M.A., Speech, University of North Texas.

Professional: 1990–93, civilian analyst, Department of Defense. 1995–2009, Staff Assistant, Subc. on Defense, House Cmte. on Appropriations. 2009–present, Clerk, Subc. on Defense, House Cmte. on Appropriations.

The House Appropriations Subcommittee on Defense could be in for an interesting ride in the 112th Congress, as lawmakers, both Democrat and Republican, cast about for areas in the massive federal budget in which to enact deep spending cuts to reduce the skyrocketing national debt. Once thought to be sacrosanct, the more than $700 billion defense budget is now being dragged into the spotlight, and its chief Democratic clerk, Paul Juola, will have a front row seat for what promises to be a stormy struggle.

Long a protégé of a defense industry champion, the late Rep. John "Jack" Murtha, D-Pa., Juola, dubbed "Mr. Army" by a Washington magazine, got a new boss in 2010 on the highly-coveted defense panel, Ranking Appropriations Committee Member Norman Dicks of Washington. Dicks is known as a friend to the defense industry, as well, so it's not likely Juola will experience a major change in his work focus. And with major defense contractor Boeing's heavy presence in Dicks' home state, it's not likely massive cuts will go down easily.

The spending panel, in this session, will also have to contend with the Administration's goal of bringing home a substantial number of combat troops from Afghanistan, a move increasingly supported by the American electorate in early 2011 polls. Republicans, and some moderate Democrats, have, in the past, fought such withdrawals not based on ground conditions.

Juola, in the last Congress, worked on a top Obama goal of procurement reform enacting changes the acquisition cycle based on cost containment and work schedule slippage.

Juola, under Murtha, was responsible for purchases of ground-combat equipment and helicopters for the Army and Marines and learned to balance the clashing demands of the world's busiest armed service. Juola worked as a civilian analyst for the Pentagon comptroller before his service on the Hill.

HOUSE APPROPRIATIONS

David LesStrang

Chief Clerk

B-308 Rayburn House Office Bldg.

Phone: (202) 225-3081

david.lesstrang@mail.house.gov

Personal: Born 02/22/1963 in Ann Arbor, Mich.

Education: B.A., English, Hillsdale College (Mich.), 1985.

Professional: 1985–2002, press secretary/legislative dir., Rep. Jerry Lewis, R-Calif. 2002–2005, government affairs manager, EMC Corporation. 2005–present, chief clerk, Subc. on the Interior, House Cmte. on Appropriations.

Expertise: Member services, communications, appropriations.

One of the prime responsibilities of the Interior Subcommittee, under the chairmanship of Rep. Mike Simpson, R-Idaho, is squeezing the federal budgets of agencies it oversees as Republican leaders seek to bring down the nation's rising debt and deficit. Chief Clerk Dave LesStrang has remained on board for the Herculean task.

In the 112th Congress, the first legislation authored by the new Republican majority slashed discretionary spending by $61 billion. Simpson played a major role in that undertaking. The chairman reduced his subcommittee's budget by over $4.5 billion, 14 percent below the President's fiscal year 2011 budget request. Cuts to the Environmental Protection Agency, which the subcommittee oversees, comprised 69 percent of the government funding bill. The GOP legislation also terminated 27 programs within the subcommittee's jurisdiction.

"I realize that many of these cuts will not be popular, but the simple truth is that you can't spend money you don't have," Simpson said.

Republicans are on an all-out mission to strip funding from the EPA, and LesStrang will have a front-row seat as the committee clashes with the Obama Administration over its stated goal of reducing the nation's greenhouse gases, possibly through executive action.

"The EPA is the scariest agency in the federal government, an agency run amok," Simpson said. "Its bloated budget has allowed it to drastically expand its regulatory authority in a way that is hurting our economy."

LesStrang is no stranger to tough spending battles. He worked with Simpson as Republicans in the previous Congress unsuccessfully fought the Democrats' $814 billion economic stimulus bill, with Simpson saying at the time, "Our country needs repair, it needs help. People are losing their jobs and their homes—we need to act. However, we need to act in a thoughtful manner."

HOUSE APPROPRIATIONS

John Martens

Chief Clerk

B-300 Rayburn House Office Bldg.

Phone: (202) 225-7245

john.martens@mail.house.gov

Personal: Born in Reistertown, Md.

Education: B.A., Randolph-Macon College. MPA, Troy State University.

Professional: 1991–94, budget analyst, Naval Sea Systems Command, U.S. Navy. 1994–2002, staff, Administrative Office of the U.S. Courts. 2002–present, chief clerk, Subc. on Financial Services, House Appropriations Cmte.

Rep. Jo Ann Emerson, R-Mo., is poised to play a significant role in the 112th Congress in her new job as chairwoman of the Appropriations Subcommittee on Financial Services. The congresswoman has made clear that she intends to scrutinize the budgets of agencies under her jurisdiction with an eye toward what can be sliced away, and she has kept John Martens in place as the top Republican staffer to help her do the job.

"You have to take every single line item separately, looking at the missions and goals for particular programs and asking, do we even need these things anymore?" Emerson told her hometown paper, the St. Louis Dispatch.

In a position that oversees controversial federal government agencies, including the Internal Revenue Service and the Security and Exchange Commission, Martens is expected to be at ground zero for Republican efforts to defund the financial regulatory reform bill passed by the last Congress, as well as efforts to loosen the tightening regulatory grip of the SEC.

"The financial reform bill, that's definitely going to be the big fight," predicted one senior Democratic aide whose boss sits on the subcommittee. "Others may include social riders for Washington, D.C.," the aide said, referring to a top GOP priority to block all federal funding for abortion and needle exchange programs in the district, which is controlled by the federal government.

Martens is also likely to find himself in the middle of an unexpected fight, as well, as Republicans look to block the implementation of the 2010 health care reform bill by every means possible. Emerson has already said she intends to scrutinize closely recent IRS rules, including some of those related to the health-care law.

Emerson's committee has wide jurisdiction from the regulatory agencies to the Federal Election Commission and beyond, making it a ripe location for those hoping to dramatically reduce the nation's discretionary spending.

Martens brings a discipline to the job from several years as a budget analyst for the U.S. Navy in its Sea Systems Command. The Reistertown, Maryland, native worked in the court system for a short time before heading to Capitol Hill where he has served nine years on the Financial Services Subcommittee.

HOUSE APPROPRIATIONS

Tom McLemore

Clerk

1016 Longworth House Office Bldg.

Phone: (202) 225-2847

Personal: Born in Baltimore, Md.

Education: Mathematics, Washington College. MPA, George Mason University.

Professional: 1996–2003, budget analyst, Air Force. 2003–2009, staff assistant, Subc. on Defense, House Cmte. on Appropriations. 2009–present, clerk, Subc. on Defense, House Cmte. on Appropriations.

Expertise: Armed Forces, Homeland Security.

Rep. C.W. Bill Young, R-Fla., remains at the helm of the powerful Defense Subcommittee in the 112th Congress, having secured a special waiver from term limits on leadership posts from Speaker John Boehner, R-Ohio. Tom McLemore, Young's aide, has remained in place atop the staff hierarchy, as well.

Young, the 79-year-old lawmaker, first elected in 1970, oversaw the defense subcommittee from 1995 to 1998 and 2005 and 2006. McLemore joined in 2003 after a 12-year career as a budget analyst in the U.S. Air Force.

Many watchers of the Appropriations Committee think Young will have a particularly difficult time with the two-year moratorium on earmarks, as the lawmaker has been prolific in and an ardent defender of the practice, particularly in the defense industry. He recently noted that congressionally-targeted spending to a defense contractor gave birth to the now-famous unmanned Predator drones being used in Afghanistan and Pakistan.

With McLemore's decade of experience in the armed forces, he brings first-hand knowledge of the funding needs for the Defense Department. This will be key as many lawmakers, both Democrat and Republican, turn to the once-sacrosanct defense budget looking to dramatically shrink the nation's more than $14 trillion debt.

"The major issue is affordability," McLemore told the Almanac, "Can we afford to buy everything that needs to be bought?"

The highly-popular defense spending bill is one of the few that actually still make it through Congress solo, though 2011 is sure to see a battle over how to fund the ongoing wars in Iraq and Afghanistan and whether to accept the Obama Administration's plans to draw down combat troops in the later.

HOUSE APPROPRIATIONS

Darek Newby

Chief Clerk

H-309, The Capitol

Phone: (202) 225-3351

darek.newby@mail.house.gov

Personal: Born in N.C.

Education: B.A., Davidson College, 1988.

Professional: 2000–2010, legislative dir., Rep. David Price, R-NC. 2010–present, chief clerk, Subc. on Commerce, Justice, Science, and Related Agencies, House Appropriations Cmte.

After working for Rep. David Price, D-NC, for nearly 12 years, Darek Newby took a new job last February working for the House Appropriations Committee, focusing on the Departments of Justice and Commerce.

Newby's newest boss, Rep. Chaka Fattah, D-Pa., touted his new assignment as top Democrat on the prestigious Commerce, Justice Science Subcommittee (CJS), saying that along with funding for the National Science Foundation, of particular importance to health care industry-heavy Pennsylvania, "We're talking about funding for the FBI, ATF, the DEA and the United States Attorney's office. It wields considerable influence."

National Aeronautics and Space Administration (NASA), the Commission on Civil Rights, the Equal Employment Opportunity Commission (EEOC), and the International Trade Commission, also fall under the jurisdiction of the panel.

"We're going into lean times, but that means active participation in smart choices and job-building, not just going along on what to cut. We must be sensible in our spending and precise in our priorities," Fattah said of his new assignment.

Newby honed his skills in the justice and homeland security arena working for Price who lead the House Homeland Security Committee for years.

The subcommittee, whose staff Newby will lead as chief clerk, will manage a budget of roughly $70 billion in 2011. It is all but certain, as Republicans look for cuts, though much of the CJS panel will be off limits, particularly the FBI and Department of Justice, more broadly, Newby and his colleagues will have to work overtime to defend against cuts in other areas, particularly Alcohol, Tobacco, and Firearms, according to a panel source.

As for policy related to the Justice Department, Newby recently told *The Crime Report* in 2010, that it will be difficult to get members behind some of the latest gains made in evidence-based anti-crime measures.

Newby said that in today's budget climate, "it is difficult for new anticrime programs to gain a budget foothold and replace current programs that have political support even if they aren't backed by research results," according to the publication.

Newby is a native of North Carolina.

HOUSE APPROPRIATIONS

Ben Nicholson

Chief Clerk

B-307 Rayburn House Office Bldg.

Phone: (202) 225-5834

ben.nicholson@mail.house.gov

Personal: Born in Baltimore, Md.

Education: B.S., U.S. Coast Guard Academy. M.S., resource policy and behavior, University of Michigan. M.S., naval architecture and marine engineering, University of Michigan.

Professional: 1996–2005, officer, U.S. Coast Guard. 2001–2004, congressional fellow, Subc. on Homeland Security, House Cmte. on Appropriations. 2005–present, chief clerk, Subc. on Homeland Security, House Cmte. on Appropriations.

Helping to secure the nation's homeland has been the primary career focus of Ben Nicholson, top Republican staffer on the House Appropriations Subcommittee on Homeland Security.

With nearly a decade of experience as an officer in the U.S. Coast Guard, Nicholson spent three years as a congressional fellow detailed to the Homeland Security Subcommittee at one of the more extraordinary periods in Congressional history. Just eight months after he joined the panel, terrorists struck the United States on September 11, 2001. His subcommittee assignment, a first for the panel, would give him a front row seat as Congress worked to respond to the attack, from war to surveillance policy changes.

Nicholson, according to a staffer who worked on the committee in 2004, was a "top notch guy, performing every duty we asked of him with pinpoint accuracy, always turning in work ahead of schedule."

In taking the gavel for the first time, incoming Chairman Robert Aderholt of Alabama said, "Coming up on the 10-year anniversary of 9/11, the matters facing our nation's intelligence community and law enforcement agencies are significant."

The subcommittee is responsible for about $50 billion in federal spending on the Department of Homeland Security, which includes Customs and Border Protection, the Federal Emergency Management Agency, Citizenship and Immigration Services, Immigration and Customs Enforcement, the Transportation Security Administration, the U.S. Coast Guard, and the Secret Service.

In the Coast Guard, Nicholson performed engineering and policy work at its headquarters and operations in the Caribbean as both a Deck Watch and Engineering Division Officer aboard the Cutters *Decisive* and *Resolute*. Ben has earned two Master's degrees from the University of Michigan and as Bachelor's degree from the U.S. Coast Guard Academy.

This former officer is a member of The Council for Emerging National Security Affairs (CENSA), which, according to its mission statement, is "a non-partisan, not-for-profit organization established in 1999 with the following purpose: To shape U.S. national security policy by advancing the innovative perspectives and long-range planning concepts of a select group of non-partisan professionals."

HOUSE APPROPRIATIONS

Ryan Nickel

Press Secretary

1016 Longworth House Office Bldg.

Phone: (202) 225-3481

ryan.nickel@mail.house.gov

Personal: Born in Baltimore, Md.

Education: B.A., political science, Calvin College, 2006.

Professional: 2007–2009, info tech staff, Catalyst LLC. 2009–present, press secretary, House Cmte. on Appropriations.

After interning in the office of Senator Carl Levin, D-Mich., Ryan Nickel settled on a career dealing with Capitol Hill reporters. "It just stuck with me. Haven't looked back since," Ryan told the Almanac.

As the lead communications contact for the incoming ranking member, Rep. Norm Dicks of D-Wash., Nickel will have his work cut out for him getting out his party's message. The year is likely to keep the committee in the spotlight with lawmakers grappling over how to reduce the nation's skyrocketing debt, while also trying to keep the sluggish economy from deteriorating.

Early in the 112th Congress, Democrats, led by Dicks, unsuccessfully fought the Republican leadership's attempt to slash discretionary spending by more than $61 billion. Dicks helped to field hundreds of proposed Democratic amendments in one of the first wide-ranging, open floor debates in years, though his GOP counterparts, with a sizeable majority, were able to defeat each provision. Through it all, Nickel addressed scores of questions from reporters, who describe the press aide as "helpful" and "quick to respond."

Of particular note, the major fight of the year in the Appropriations Committee is expected to be not on its 13 annual spending bills, but rather on GOP efforts to defund the health care reform legislation passed in early 2010. Republicans are expected to target the billions of dollars needed to run the programs authorized by the controversial legislation.

Nickel is no stranger to dealing with fierce opposition to a bill. He was on the Appropriations Committee when Democrats pushed through the controversial $814 billion stimulus bill that passed in 2009 without a single Republican vote.

Before making the move to Capitol Hill, Nickel worked in the information and technology services industry as an executive assistant for Catalyst, LLC, a company with a national, subscription-only database of voting-age Americans that Democrats can access to target and communicate more efficiently and effectively in political campaigns.

In his spare time, Nickel says he is an avid reader of history and contemporary fiction. And to shake off the stress of the high-octane job, Nickel plays in Washington, D.C. and Maryland soccer leagues on the Caballeros soccer team. He also describes himself as "a very big Liverpool FC fan."

Nickel was raised in the Republic of Ireland from age two to 17.

HOUSE APPROPRIATIONS

Tim Peterson

Chief Clerk
H-143, The Capitol
Phone: (202) 225-3047
tim.peterson@mail.house.gov

Personal: Born 02/02/1955 in Lincoln, Nebr.

Education: B.A., history, international affairs, economics, University of Nebraska, 1979. M.B.A., finance, American University, Kogod School of Business, 1982.

Professional: 1980–1988, budget analyst, Dept. of the Navy, Office of the Comptroller. 1989–1995, staff assistant, Subc. on Defense, House Cmte. on Appropriations. 1995–2003, staff assistant, Subc. on Veterans' Affairs, Housing and Urban Development and Independent Agencies, House Cmte. on Appropriations. 2003–2010, clerk, Subc. on Veterans' Affairs, Housing and Urban Development and Independent Agencies, House Cmte. on Appropriations. 2010–present, chief clerk, Subc. on Military Construction and Veterans' Affairs, House Cmte. on Appropriations.

Expertise: Appropriations.

Since 1989, Tim Peterson has had some connection to funding the nation's military, be it on the Defense or Veterans' Affairs, Housing and Urban Development spending subcommittees, and that track record continues in the 112th Congress as Peterson takes the helm of the Military Construction and Veterans' Affairs subcommittee under a new chairman, Rep. John Culberson of Texas.

"As our men and women in uniform continue fighting two wars overseas, it is vital that they have the most up-to-date training facilities and that the veterans who have served receive expedited care at top notch hospitals," Culberson said when tapped to lead the panel.

But the chairman made clear, the GOP focus on deep spending cuts would not elude his new post. "With the third largest subcommittee budget on the Appropriations Committee, it is equally important to eliminate any inefficient programs and cut initiatives that are not producing results. Our military and our veterans deserve the very best we can provide," Culberson said.

Peterson and his staff found $462 million in cuts to construction projects and the Veterans Administration budget in the GOP's $61 billion spending reduction plan.

Aides to the subcommittee said that Peterson and Culberson are poised for a fight with labor unions as they look for federal savings. The chairman is looking to roll back a key union priority, the Davis–Bacon Act of 1931. This measure now requires "prevailing" union wages be paid on all federal construction projects, including military projects.

In his previous job atop the Veterans' Affairs panel, Peterson spent much of his time on NASA's space programs.

Before coming to Congress, Peterson was a budget analyst for the U.S. Navy.

HOUSE APPROPRIATIONS

David Pomerantz

Staff Director

1016 Longworth House Office Bldg.

Phone: (202) 225-3481

David.Pomerantz@mail.house.gov

Personal: Born 02/22/1952 in Los Angeles, Calif.

Education: B.A., Dickinson College, 1973. M.A., Vanderbilt University, 1975. Ph.D., philosophy, Vanderbilt University, 1980.

Professional: 1979–1982, asst. professor, State University of New York at Stony Brook. 1982–1983, fellowship, Rep. Richard Gephardt, D-Mo., American Assoc. for the Advancement of Science/American Philosophical Assoc. 1983–1992, professional staff member, House Cmte. on Rules. 1993–2001, Democratic deputy staff director, House Cmte. on Rules. 2001–2005, Democratic professional staff member, Subc. on Commerce, Justice, State, and the Judiciary, House Cmte. on Appropriations. 2005–2007, Democratic professional staff member, Subc. on Science, the Departments of State, Justice, and Commerce, and Related Agencies, House Cmte. on Appropriations. 2007–2010, deputy staff director, House Cmte. on Appropriations. 2010–present, staff director, House Cmte. on Appropriations.

Expertise: Budget process, appropriations.

With more than two decades of experience in Congress, David Pomerantz takes the helm of the House Appropriations Committee's Democratic staff at a turbulent time when the focus is more on reductions than spending.

Pomerantz's career path to the House was somewhat unorthodox but could prove useful in the increasingly partisan environment. He started out as a political philosophy professor at State University of New York, before joining the college's program which sent two such professors to work on the Hill. "I took advantage of that in the early 80s, and caught Potomac fever," Pomerantz once told an interviewer.

Before joining the spending panel, Pomerantz gained a significant understanding of the arcane House floor procedures as he helped lead the staff of the Rules Committee. As well, his boss placed a high priority on knowing all members, regardless of party affiliation.

That rather unique skill set is sure to come in handy now as the battle over deficit reduction likely remains at the boiling point throughout the session. And as the Democratic staff director for incoming Ranking Member Norm Dicks of Washington, Pomerantz will be at the tip of the legislative spear for the minority, trying to hold back the desire of Republicans to implement steep spending cuts only in the discretionary side of the budget.

The committee must also pass its 13 annual spending bills to fund the departments and agencies of government, a process for which Pomerantz will be responsible. One notably absent chore, however, will be dealing with members' earmarks after Congress enacted a two-year moratorium on the time-honored practice.

"Dave is part of the building. He knows where all the bodies are buried and how they were buried. Not only that, he's a nice guy to boot. We're lucky to have him," said one long-time Democratic leadership aide.

HOUSE APPROPRIATIONS

David J. Reich

Chief Counsel

Subcommittee on Labor, Health and Human Services, Education, and Related Agencies

H-218 Capitol

Phone: (202) 225-2771

Twitter: @rosadelauro

david.reich@mail.house.gov

Personal: Born 01/27/1954 in New York, N.Y.

Education: B.A., economics, University of California at Santa Cruz, 1975. M.A., economics, American University, 1978. J.D., Georgetown University Law Center, 1991.

Professional: 1976–1979, analyst, Dept. of Labor. 1979–1981, acting dir. and economist, Center to Protect Workers Rights. 1981–1987, legislative analyst, House Democratic Study Group. 1987–91, research dir., House Democratic Study Group. 1991–1993, associate, Shea & Gardner. 1993–1996, chief counsel, House Cmte. on the Budget. 1996–2006, Democratic staff asst., Subc. on Labor, Health and Human Services, Education, and Related Agencies, House Cmte. on Appropriations. 2007–2008, Democratic staff asst., House Cmte. on Appropriations. 2009–2010, Chief Counsel, Subcommittee on Financial Services and General Government Appropriations. 2010–present, chief counsel, Subc. on Labor, Health and Human Services, House Cmte. on Appropriations.

Expertise: Budget, appropriations.

A 27-year veteran of Capitol Hill, with most of that time spent on various Appropriations subcommittees, David Reich is no stranger to the process. This knowledge will be put to good use as Reich faces one of the toughest spending battles in the 112th Congress as the top Democratic staffer on the subcommittee where Republicans have vowed to starve the Obama Administration's new health care reform law of funding.

Reich's House Appropriations Labor, Health and Human Services, and Education Subcommittee is responsible for the lion's share of the federal dollars needed for the legislation, and the panel's chairman, Rep. Denny Rehberg, R-Mont., has vowed to stop it.

"I'm going to fulfill my promise to the people of Montana that to the best of my ability, I will defund Obamacare if we're not able to repeal it," Rehberg said.

The spending panel is responsible for funding not only the Labor, Health and Human Services, and Education Departments, but also for mandatory programs, like Medicaid, Medicare, and Social Security.

Reich's new boss, Rep. Rosa DeLauro, D-Conn., who is close to the Democratic leadership and has been a member of the panel for 16 years, has vowed to fight back against Republican efforts.

"The work of this subcommittee has always reflected our nation's priorities and the highest moral obligation of our government - providing health care services, educating our children, advancing scientific research to find the cures of tomorrow, and strengthening job training programs, which are especially critical in this tough economy," DeLauro said.

Fiscal hawk Republicans have vowed to take a budgetary ax to man of these same areas as they look for massive savings in all areas of federal spending. Many Tea Party Republicans have even vowed to shutter the Education Department, so Reich's job is sure to be a tough one this session.

HOUSE APPROPRIATIONS

Michael Ringler

Clerk

Subcommittee on Commerce, Justice, Science, and Related Agencies

H-307, The Capitol

Phone: (202) 225-2771

Mike.Ringler@mail.house.gov

Personal: Born 1963 in Rector, Pa.

Education: B.S., foreign service, Georgetown University, 1985. M.P.I.A, University of Pittsburgh, 1987.

Professional: 1987–1989, presidential management intern, U.S. Information Agency. 1989–1996, program and budget officer, U.S. Information Agency. 1996–1997, budget officer, Broadcasting Board of Governors. 1997–2001, staff asst., Subc. on the Depts. of Commerce, Justice, State, the Judiciary, and Related Agencies, House Cmte. on Appropriations. 2002–2004, clerk, Subc. on the Depts. of Commerce, Justice, State, the Judiciary, and Related Agencies, House Cmte. on Appropriations. 2005–2006, clerk, Subc. on Science, the Depts. of State, Justice, and Commerce, and Related Agencies, House Cmte. on Appropriations. 2007–present, chief clerk, Subc. on Commerce, Justice, Science, and Related Agencies, House Cmte. on Appropriations.

Expertise: Appropriations, commerce, justice, and science programs, international affairs.

Mike Ringler continues work under Rep. Frank Wolf, R-W.Va., who returns as chairman of the Commerce, Justice, Science Subcommittee after a two-year stint as the top Republican on the State-Foreign Operations panel.

"As chairman of the CJS subcommittee, Wolf will...focus on job creation by boosting American exports, bringing jobs back to the U.S. and rebuilding the manufacturing sector," a Wolf spokesman said, "In science and technology, he will work to prioritize science, technology, engineering and math education and invigorate NASA's manned space exploration program. He also will work with the FBI to focus on U.S. counterterrorism strategy and fighting crime."

Ringler's Commerce-Justice-Science Subcommittee is responsible for funding the Commerce and Justice Departments, the National Aeronautics and Space Administration, the National Science Foundation, and other related agencies.

Wolf has made no secret that he is ready for a fight over spending cuts, though he did, after the President's State of the Union address, tell reporters that he is sympathetic to Obama's calls for increased funding the area of innovation. Wolf said, "You've got to invest in basic research," adding that lawmakers cannot balance the federal budget by "hacking away" at the budgets of agencies like the National Science Foundation and NASA.

Ringler has amassed an extensive resume on a variety of issues during his time on the spending panel.

In 2009, Ringler not only was the lead GOP staffer for Commerce, Justice, and Science, but he also dealt with funding for the United Nations, peacekeeping, international law enforcement, and public diplomacy issues, a task aided by his masters degree in foreign service from Georgetown University.

HOUSE APPROPRIATIONS

Stephen Sepp

Budget analyst
Phone: (202) 226-7270
Fax: (202) 226-7174
stephen.sepp@mail.house.gov

Personal: Born in Forth Worth, Texas.

Education: B.S., political science, University of North Texas.

Professional: 1999–2002, legislative assistant, Sen. Phil Gramm, R-Tex. 2002–2006, legislative assistant, Sen. John Cornyn, R-Tex. 2006–2007, legislative director, Rep. Jeb Hensarling, R-Tex. 2007–2010, budget analyst, House Budget Cmte., Republican staff. 2010–present, budget analyst, House Appropriations Committee.

Expertise: Budget review.

Those who know Stephen Sepp describe him as the quintessential numbers cruncher, someone who intrinsically understands the archaic language of the budget and all the inner workings of the appropriations process.

"It's a foreign language, and he is fluent," said Don Stewart, senior spokesman for Senate Minority Leader Mitch McConnell, R-Ky. Stewart and Sepp worked together for Sen. John Cornyn, R-Tex, back in the early 2000's, and Senate Budget Committee Chairman Phil Gramm, R-Tex, before that. "He has an ability to cut through it and tell you what it actually means," Stewart added.

In 2007, Sepp left the Senate to work for fiscal hawk Rep. Jeb Hensarling, R-Tex., who led, for a time, the conservative Republican Study Committee. As the legislative director, Sepp helped Hensarling and other Budget Committee members craft a $2.7 trillion budget that members said, at the time, held the line on discretionary spending.

As a House Budget Committee analyst for three years, Sepp aided in the creation of "A Roadmap for America's Future" by Rep. Paul Ryan, R-Wisc., a fiscal blueprint still touted by Ryan in his new position as the panel's chairman.

Rep. Jerry Lewis, top Republican on the Appropriations Committee in 2010, tapped Sepp to work for the spending panel as a budget analyst. That put Sepp in the middle of the raucous battles over President Obama's $814 billion stimulus bill.

This year, incoming Committee Chairman Hal Rogers, R-Ky., retained Sepp to help with the herculean task of slashing billions from the federal budget. The committee hit the ground running in the 112th Congress, eventually crafting a continuing resolution with $61 billion in cuts. With Senate Democrats balking at that level of cuts, Congress has already had to grapple with two emergency stopgap spending measures, each containing spending cuts, and there are some who fear this could be the way lawmakers must fund the budget for much of the year.

With a college major in political science and a concentration in quantitative statistics, Sepp has found the perfect niche working for members focused on the federal budget.

Colleagues describe the budget guru as impeccably dressed and always professional. "He's the kind of guy who would wear a suit and tie in a pool…He was always there to work," one former colleague said.

Sepp is married with two children.

HOUSE APPROPRIATIONS

Will Smith

Deputy Staff Director

Phone: (202) 225-2771

will.smith@mail.house.gov

Personal: Born in Beattyville, Ky.

Education: B.A., Emory University.

Professional: 1994–96, staff, Sen. Mitch McConnell, R-Ky. 1997–98, staff, Sen. Appropriations Cmte., Foreign Operations Subc. 1998–2010, chief of staff, Rep. Hal Rogers, R-Ky.

Will Smith joins the staff of the House Appropriations Committee after 12 years in the personal office of the panel's incoming chairman, Rep. Hal Rogers, R-Ky. Smith served as the Roger's chief of staff, a position colleagues say will help him guide the spending panel through its many difficult battles this session.

"He's a pretty easy-going guy, a southern gentleman with a good sense of humor," one former colleague described the Beattyville, Kentucky native, adding, "And in this environment, he's going to need it."

Starting off his career in 1994, Smith joined the staff of a fellow Kentuckian, GOP Sen. Mitch McConnell, as one of his so-called "Men of the Wheel," a nickname McConnell staffers have given to the now-famous fraternity of chauffeurs. The senator has an uncanny record with his drivers, many of whom have gone on to prestigious jobs as chiefs of staff or in top posts in the Bluegrass state's political climes.

"It opened a lot of doors for me, and I learned a lot," Smith once told an interviewer.

During his four years with McConnell, Smith went on to become a member of the professional staff of the Senate Foreign Operations Appropriations Subcommittee, and a career on the prestigious spending panel was born.

As deputy staff director, Smith has the challenging task of shepherding stop-gap funding resolutions that keep the federal government as well as finding steep cuts in the panel's 13 annual appropriations bills that will satisfy the conservative wing of a Republican party hungry for a major reduction in the nation's more than $14 trillion debt.

Smith and the committee will work to honor a two-year moratorium on earmarks approved in both houses of Congress early in the 112th session. This ban, coupled with a backlash against spending among the American electorate, saw a drop-off in interest in the panel, so much so that a number of freshmen landed once-highly-coveted positions on the committee.

Chairman Rogers said he expects the committee's job in 2011 to be a challenging one.

"The Appropriations Committee will have a huge job ahead to drastically cut government spending, stop our exploding deficit, root out waste and unnecessary funding, and get our nation onto a responsible budget path," Rep. Rogers said in a press release. "These staffers are highly qualified and dedicated individuals, and the Committee, the Congress, and the American people will be well served by having them aboard."

HOUSE APPROPRIATIONS

Lesley Turner

Deputy Staff Director

1016 Longworth House Office Bldg.

Phone: (202) 225-3481

lesley.turner@mail.house.gov

Professional: 2000–2004, interior specialist, Rep. Norman Dicks, D-Wash. 2004–2005, staff assistant, House Committee on Appropriations. 2005–2006, legislative director, Rep. Patty Murray, D-Wash.. 2006–present, deputy staff director, House Committee on Appropriations.

Democrats on the House Appropriations Committee, where Lesley Turner has served since 2004, will have their work cut out for them in 2011, as Republicans have made clear they plan to squeeze the federal budget of every drop of spending they can possibly find in order to bring down the nation's skyrocketing debt and deficit.

Democrats have said they support spending cuts, but clashes in the 112th Congress came early and loudly when Republicans sought to ax $61 billion from the discretionary budget in a government funding bill, H.R.1.

"When the House approved H.R.1 earlier this month, despite the overwhelming opposition of the Democratic Caucus, it was clear to me that gaining agreement on a compromise version of a full-year Continuing Resolution would be very difficult, at least before the expiration of the current Continuing Resolution.," Ranking Member Norm Dicks of Washington said. "We opposed H.R.1 because we believe it would have the effect of slamming on the fiscal brakes too abruptly, resulting in higher unemployment and threatening our nation's economic recovery. There is no dispute that cutting federal spending too deeply and too quickly, before the economy has fully recovered, risks slowing growth and losing jobs. "

Turner will be part of the government funding debate likely to dominate the remainder of the year, unless Congressional Democrats and Republicans can agree on a long-term funding bill. The Appropriations Committee, responsible for crafting the legislation, could remain on the precipice of a government shutdown if not.

Committee Chairman, Rep. Hal Rogers of Kentucky, has said he is determined to pass the 13 annual spending bills that fund the various departments and agencies of government. Dicks and Rogers are known to have a good relationship, and that could help Turner as she and her staff try to find common ground with their GOP counterparts.

Colleagues describe Turner as "hard-nosed" and "determined." One former aide who worked with her when she was legislative director for Sen. Patty Murray, D-Wash., said, "She's incredibly tough and strong-willed and knows the process and knows how to get things done."

Turner could be aided in her fight by her close connections to the Obama White House. She is known to enjoy a close relationship with top congressional liaison, Rob Nabors, a former long-time Appropriations Committee staffer.

Committee on Armed Services

2120 Rayburn House Office Bldg.
Washington, DC 20515
Phone: (202) 225-4151
Fax: (202) 225-9077
http://armedservices.house.gov

Ratio: 35/27

MAJORITY MEMBERS

Howard (Buck) McKeon, CA-25th, Chairman

Roscoe G. Bartlett, MD-6th
Mac Thornberry, TX-13th
Walter B. Jones, NC-3rd
W. Todd Akin, MO-2nd
J. Randy Forbes, VA-4th
Jeff Miller, FL-1st
Joe Wilson, SC-2nd
Frank A. LoBiondo, NJ-2nd
Michael R. Turner, OH-3rd
John Kline, MN-2nd
Mike Rogers, AL-3rd
Trent Franks, AZ-2nd
Bill Shuster, PA-9th
Michael K. Conaway, TX-11th
Doug Lamborn, CO-5th
Rob Whittman, VA-1st
Duncan D. Hunter, CA-52nd
John Fleming, LA-4th
Mike Coffman, CO-6th
Tom Rooney, FL-16th
Todd Russell Platts, PA-14th
Scott Rigell, VA-2nd
Chris Gibson, NY-20th
Vicky Hartzler, MO-4th
Joe Heck, NV-3rd
Bobby Schilling, IL-17th
Jon Runyan, NJ-3rd
Austin Scott, KY-8th
Tim Griffin, AR-2nd
Steve Palazzo, MI-4th
Allen West, FL-22nd
Martha Roby, AL-2nd
Mo Brooks, AL-5th
Todd Young, IN-9th

MINORITY MEMBERS

Adam Smith, WA-9th, Chairman

Silvestre Reyes, TX-16th
Loretta Sanchez, CA-47th
Mike McIntyre, NC-7th
Robert A. Brady, PA-1st
Robert Andrews, NJ-1st
Susan A. Davis, CA-53rd
James Langevin, RI-2nd
Rick Larsen, WA-2nd
Jim Cooper, TN-5th
Madeleine Z. Bordallo, GU-At Large
Joe Courtney, CT-2nd
David Loebsack, IA-2nd
Gabrielle Giffords, AZ-8th
Nicki Tsongas, MA-5th
Chellie Pingree, ME-1st
Larry Kissell, NC-6th
Martin Heinrich, NM-1st
William L. Owens, NY-23rd
John Garamendi, CA-10th
Mark Kritz, PA-12th
Tim Ryan, OH-17th
C.A. Dutch Ruppersberger, MD-2nd
Hank Johnson, GA-4th
Kathy Castor, HI-11th
Betty Sutton, OH-13th
Coleen Hanabusa, HI-1st

HOUSE ARMED SERVICES

JURISDICTION

(1) Ammunition depots; forts; arsenals; Army, Navy, and Air Force reservations and establishments.
(2) Common defense, generally.
(3) Conservation, development, and use of naval petroleum and oil shale reserves.
(4) The Department of Defense generally, including the Departments of the Army, Navy, and Air Force generally.
(5) Interoceanic canals generally, including measures relating to the maintenance, operation, and administration of interoceanic canals.
(6) Merchant Marine Academy and State Merchant Marine Academies.
(7) Military applications of nuclear energy.
(8) Tactical intelligence and intelligence-related activities of the Department of Defense.
(9) Armed Services aspects of merchant marine, including financial assistance for the construction and operation of vessels, the maintenance of the U.S. shipbuilding and ship repair industrial base, cabotage, cargo preference, and merchant marine officers and seamen as these matters relate to the armed services.
(10) Pay, promotion, retirement, and other benefits and privileges of members of the armed services.
(11) Scientific research and development in support of the armed services.
(12) Selective service.
(13) Size and composition of the Army, Navy, Marine Corps, and Air Force.
(14) Soldiers' and sailors' homes.
(15) Strategic and critical materials necessary for the common defense.

HOUSE ARMED SERVICES

The House Armed Services Committee will face a rather unique dynamic in the 112th Congress. The Republican Party is in power and members are eager to keep campaign promises to reduce federal spending, jumpstart the economy and rein in the national debt. But if there is one area they are least excited to cut, it's the military.

The committee is led by Chairman Howard "Buck" McKeon, R-Calif., who has said that a military budget in decline portends an America in decline. He has no intention of seeing that happen on his watch, not while the fight continues in places like Iraq and Afghanistan.

"America's sons and daughters have been fighting on the frontlines for nearly a decade; and our brave troops and their families pay a heavy burden on behalf of a grateful nation. The Armed Services Committee will focus our oversight on equipping, training and empowering our warfighters to do their jobs effectively and return home to their families," McKeon said shortly after becoming chairman.

"We will utilize the bipartisan tradition of the Committee and the talents of our members to also go to work for the American taxpayer by rigorously scrutinizing the Pentagon's budget to ensure every defense dollar is spent wisely."

McKeon may be willing to scrutinize the budget, but he isn't going to be supportive of any massive budget cuts. He responded with anger when Defense Secretary Robert Gates proposed $78 billion in reductions over the next five years. McKeon argued the cuts would hurt the Marines ability to make amphibious landings, because of the cancellation of the expeditionary fighting vehicle, and he worried the cuts would mean less soldiers.

"This is a dramatic shift for a nation at war and a dangerous signal from the Commander in Chief," McKeon said after the announcement of the proposed cuts. "I remain committed to applying more fiscal responsibility and accountability to the Department of Defense, but I will not stand idly by and watch the White House gut defense when Americans are deployed in harm's way."

Beyond budget cuts, the committee is likely to spend time on the areas of cyber security, the unrest in the Middle East, detainee policy, and emerging threats.

HOUSE ARMED SERVICES

Paul Arcangeli

Minority Staff Director

Subcommittee on Readiness

2340 Rayburn House Office Bldg.

Phone: (202) 225-4158

Fax: (202) 225-3623

paul.arcangeli@mail.house.gov

Personal: Born 1965 in Huntsville, Ala.

Education: B.S., biology, North Georgia College, 1987. M.S., information technology management, United States Naval Postgraduate School, 1997.

Professional: 1987–99, United States Army. 2001–2004, dir. of humanitarian demining training, Dept. of Defense. 2004–2008, professional staff member, Subc. on Readiness, House Armed Services Cmte. 2009–2010, deputy staff director, House Armed Services Cmte. 2010–2011, staff director, House Armed Services Cmte. 2011–present, minority staff director, House Armed Services Cmte.

Expertise: Military readiness.

After a drag-out political fight that focused more on the military's "don't ask, don't tell" policy than on needed defense projects, the Senate and House came to an agreement. Just a week away from New Year's, Congress approved the Ike Skelton National Defense Authorization Act, named in honor of the chairman of the House Armed Services Committee, who lost his bid for reelection in the 2010 midterms.

Paul Arcangeli is a long time friend of Skelton's who served as his staff director in the waning months of the congressman's political career. Arcangeli remains with the committee as the Democratic staff director for the committee's ranking member, Rep. Adam Smith, D-Wash.

Arcangeli joined the committee in 2004 after leaving the Department of Defense as the director of the Humanitarian Demining Training Center in Fort Leonard Wood, Miss. An Alabama native, he spent 13 years in the U.S. Army serving in explosive ordnance disposal, information technology, and maintenance and logistics.

He was the deputy staff director when he received a promotion in May 2010 because then staff director Erin Conaton became an undersecretary of the Air Force. In announcing the switch, Skelton expressed his feelings for Arcangeli and the professional trust he places in him.

"I have come to know Paul well over the course of many years, since his time as an officer in the U.S. Army. Paul has consistently demonstrated his ability to lead, and his dedication to our men and women in uniform is unparalleled," Skelton said. "He is a trusted friend and advisor and an expert on national security issues."

Arcangeli will likely advise Smith as the committee reviews potential savings identified by Defense Secretary Robert Gates, who has announced a plan to cut $78 billion from the budget. Smith's initial reaction is that the plan "appears to be a good first step in the right direction."

HOUSE ARMED SERVICES

Kari Bingen

Staff Director

Subcommittee on Strategic Forces

2120 Rayburn House Office Bldg.

Phone: (202) 225-4151

Fax: (202) 225-0858

kari.bingen@mail.house.gov

Personal: Born in Falls Church, Va.

Education: B.S., aeronautics and astronautics, Massachusetts Institute of Technology, 1999.

Professional: 1999–2005, space systems analyst, SRA International. 2005–2006, space systems analyst, The Aerospace Corporation. 2006–2010, professional staff member, Subc. on Strategic Forces, House Cmte. on Armed Services. 2011–present, staff director, Subc. on Strategic Forces, House Cmte. on Armed Services.

Expertise: Missile defense, nuclear weapons, space and intelligence.

When it comes to the missile programs meant to protect Americans at home and its friends abroad, the point person in the House is Kari Bingen. She is the staff director of the Subcommittee on Strategic Forces and the main advisor to subcommittee Chairman Michael Turner, R-Ohio.

The Senate ratified the new START treaty in late 2010 and Turner is concerned that the administration is already considering future efforts to reduce the nation's nuclear arsenal. In the subcommittee's first hearing of the 112th Congress, Turner said: "We should slow down, let the treaty ink dry, and assess where we are. Our security requirements should guide the feasibility and desirability of further reductions, not the other way around."

Like most of Congress, the committee will search for areas of cost savings, but Turner warned that could only go so far in the Defense Department.

"I am committed to working with the department to identify efficiencies and better ways of doing business," he said. "With that said, we are a nation fighting two wars. And, it is our subcommittee's responsibility to ensure our strategic forces are kept viable in both the good years and the bad."

The subcommittee also oversees the proposed missile defense system in Europe, though there are differences surrounding how much of the cost should be shouldered by the United States. At a 2010 conference hosted by the Atlantic Council, Bingen said Republicans in Congress questioned why the United States was paying so much when the shield would primarily defend Europeans.

Bingen came to the hill from The Aerospace Corporation where she was a senior space policy analyst at the company's Center for Space Policy and Strategy. She served as an expert on space protection and vulnerabilities. In 2005, while working at Aerospace, Bingen was awarded the James E. Haywood Award for Excellence from the Federation of Galaxy Explorers for her volunteer efforts to get children involved in science.

At the time she said: "I have been fortunate to have a few great people in my life who have influenced me and encouraged me to pursue my interests in space. I see this as my way of returning the favor."

She previously worked at SRA International and as a 2002 National Reconnaissance Office Technology Fellow

HOUSE ARMED SERVICES

John D. Chapla

Professional Staff Member
Subcommittee on Military Personnel
Subcommittee on Tactical Air and Land Forces
2340 Rayburn House Office Bldg.
Phone: (202) 225-6521
Fax: (202) 226-0789
john.chapla@mail.house.gov

Personal: Born 06/06/1947 in Cleveland, Ohio.

Education: B.A., Virginia Military Institute, 1968. M.A., University of North Carolina, 1978.

Professional: 1968–1990, retired as lt. colonel, U.S. Army. 1990–1994, professional staff member, House Armed Services Cmte. 1995–present, professional staff member, Subc. on Military Personnel, House Armed Services Cmte.

Expertise: Personnel readiness.

Leading the staff of the Military Personnel Subcommittee is nothing new for John Chapla. He did it for a dozen years before the Democrats took power in 2006. Now that Republicans are back on top in the 112th Congress, so is he.

"It is familiar territory," he said. "I've got a good team here in terms of a veteran staff."

He said the subcommittee has always acted on a largely bipartisan basis whether he was serving in the majority or minority and he doesn't see that changing now, even with the tough issues that they face.

General concerns about federal spending are sure to impact the Defense Department budget. Chapla predicts that the House will keep the core pay and benefits intact, but bonuses and recruiting dollars may face some reductions.

"The bottom line is we are looking at the budget for potential efficiencies," he said. "The other big issue we will deal with is the Department of Defense's proposal for health care cost control."

That plan seeks to save $8 billion over five years and includes such ideas as a TRICARE fee increase for military retirees under the age of 65, a reduction in contract support personnel and a push for members of the military to use mail order pharmacies as opposes to traditional retail stores. Chapla said all of these ideas will impact military families and he expects some to become politically controversial.

The Military Officers Association of America gave Chapla the 2007 Col. Paul W. Arcari meritorious service award for his support of military personnel. Chapla retired as a U.S. Army lieutenant colonel in 1990 after service for 22 years and immediately began working for the committee. Chapla, who is a Civil War history buff, is also the author of three books in the Virginia Regimental Histories series, focusing on the 42nd, 48th and 50th infantry units.

HOUSE ARMED SERVICES

Jaime Cheshire

Senior Advisor

2120 Rayburn House Office Bldg.

Phone: (202) 225-4151

jaime.cheshire@mail.house.gov

Personal: Born in Farmington, Conn.

Education: B.A., political science, University of Connecticut, 1999.

Professional: 2000–2006, legislative assistant, Office of Rep. Nancy L. Johnson, R-Conn.. 2006–2007, legislative director, Office of Rep. Nancy L. Johnson, R-Conn.. 2007–2009, legislative director, Office of Rep. Buck McKeon, R-Calif. 2009–present, senior advisor, House Cmte. on Armed Services.

Expertise: Member services.

Jaime Cheshire is the go to staffer for House members and veterans groups who want to get in contact with House Armed Services Chairman Howard "Buck" McKeon, R-Calif.

Cheshire holds the title as senior advisor and her responsibilities are in the areas of member services, communications and coalition outreach. She joined the committee in the fall of 2009, moving from McKeon's personal staff.

"Jaime brings a wealth of Capitol Hill experience to the Armed Services Committee," McKeon said at the time. "Her knowledge of the legislative process and experience in guiding complex policy into law will aid our members on the committee; and ultimately, Jaime's work will directly benefit the men and women of our military and their families."

A native of Farmington, Conn., Cheshire got her start on Capitol Hill with the staff of Rep. Nancy Johnson, R-Conn. in 2000 and later served as legislative director before moving to McKeon's office in 2007.

On the committee, she has focused on helping McKeon develop legislative and communication strategies and works to build coalitions on Capitol Hill and with industry partners, trade associations, and defense-related policy organizations to push GOP priorities.

In the 112th Congress, the top priority is protecting the national defense budget from harmful budget cuts, while also looking for ways to be more efficient. The committee Republicans will also work to block any potential detainee shifts from Guantanamo Bay to the United States, and make sure the service members in Afghanistan and Iraq are equipped and supported adequately.

"Members and staff work on the Armed Services Committee because they care deeply about national security and want to provide the best available resources and support to the men and women of the military. I look forward to building on that tradition," Cheshire said.

HOUSE ARMED SERVICES

Michael R. Higgins

Professional Staff Member
Subcommittee on Military Personnel
2339 Rayburn House Office Bldg.
Phone: (202) 225-7560
Fax: (202) 226-0789
michael.higgins@mail.house.gov

Personal: Born 05/23/1947.N.J..

Education: B.A., Davis and Elkins College, 1969. M.S., Troy State University, 1978.

Professional: 1970–1990, personnel officer (retired as lt. col.), Military Personnel Center/Office of the Secretary, Legislation Liaison Division, U.S. Air Force. 1990–1993, professional staff member, House Cmte. on Armed Services. 1993–1994, professional staff member, Subc. on Readiness, House Cmte. on Armed Services. 1995–present, professional staff member, Subc. on Military Personnel, House Cmte. on Armed Services.

Expertise: Military personnel.

Few things are less partisan than the pay of the nation's military personnel, so Michael Higgins works for the party in the majority whether it is the Democrats in the last Congress or now the Republicans in the 112th Congress. What has changed is Higgins' title. He is no longer the staff lead on the Subcommittee on Military Personnel.

"I fall back to my role as a resident technician," he said.

Higgins focuses almost exclusively on the pay and benefits provided to the military and is an advocate for reducing the gap between military wages and those in the private sector.

In the 111th Congress, the committee wanted a 0.5 percent military pay raise in the areas of hostile fire and family separation. In a tough budget year, both financially and politically, that proposal didn't get as much traction in the Senate as it did in the House.

"They did get a pay raise, but not the enhanced pay raise envisioned by the House," Higgins said.

He expects the sluggish economy and the Republican drive to lower federal spending to impact areas of military compensation in 2012, but he doubts he will see cuts to military recruiting or retention efforts. It could, however, spur Congress and the Pentagon to look for areas of redundancy.

"An era of austerity is going to be in place over military personnel," Higgins said. "As we look forward, the national economic downturn is the premier issue and it reaches out and touches all other issues to some degree."

Higgins has worked for members of Congress from both parties since joining the committee staff in 1990. He is a retired lieutenant colonel with the U.S. Air Force and he worked in the legislation liaison division before joining House Armed Services. In 2005, he received the military Offices Association of America's highest award given to people "who strongly support military men and women and their families."

HOUSE ARMED SERVICES

Alexander Kugajevsky

Professional Staff Member
Subcommittee on Emerging Threats and Capabilities
2120 Rayburn House Office Bldg.
Phone: (202) 225-4151
Fax: (202) 225-0858
Alexander.Kugajevsky@mail.house.gov

Personal: Born in Washington, D.C.

Education: B.A., economics and B.A., psychology, Dartmouth College, 1993. MBA, Wharton School, University of Pennsylvania, 2011.

Professional: 1993–2005, officer, U.S. Army. 2006–2010, professional staff member, House Armed Services Cmte. 2011–present, staff director, Subc. on Emerging Threats and Capabilities.

Expertise: Counterterrorism, special operations.

Among his responsibilities as staff director of the newly renamed Emerging Threats and Capabilities Subcommittee, Alex Kugajevsky oversees special operations forces and he does so with plenty of personal experience. Kugajevsky spent 12 years in the Army and his assignments included two stints with special forces groups, work as a CIA liaison, and a deployment with the Defense Attache Office in Lima, Peru.

The subcommittee, led by Rep. Mac Thornberry, R-Texas, has a full plate that goes far beyond the oversight of special operations. Kugajevsky will also work on counter-terrorism, defense-related management programs, cyber operations, and "ensuring the [Department of Defense] is making the necessary investments in science and technology programs," Kugajevsky said.

Thornberry, who also serves as the vice chairman of the full committee, described the role of his subcommittee this way: "We are to look out into the future and help see that the United States is prepared to deal with those national security challenges that are still emerging—those that we are still learning about, such as terrorism and cyber warfare."

He is particularly interested in cyber security, a charge handed down from House Speaker John Boehner, R-Ohio, himself.

"Cyber is a new domain of vandalism, crime, espionage, and yes, warfare, but we are not very well equipped to deal with any of those challenges," Thornberry said in a recent hearing. "As we look for solutions, we want to be smart, careful and true to our values, but we need to act to improve our security."

Beyond the issues in the subcommittee, Kugajevsky is also the full committee expert on technology investment and small business innovations, having just received his master of business administration from the University of Pennsylvania's Wharton school. He concentrated his studies on other areas such as private equity and venture capital.

Kugajevsky is a native of Washington, D.C., who earned degrees in economics and psychology from Dartmouth College before he was commissioned in 1993 through the Army ROTC program. He joined the House Armed Services Committee promptly after leaving the service in 2006, having worked as the Republican lead staffer on what was previously called the Terrorism Unconventional Threats and Capabilities Subcommittee.

HOUSE ARMED SERVICES

Mark R. Lewis

Professional Staff Member

Subcommittee on Emerging Threats and Capabilities

2340 Rayburn House Office Bldg.

Phone: (202) 226-4295

Fax: (202) 225-9077

mark.lewis@mail.house.gov

Personal: Born 04/08/1965 in Durham, N.C.

Education: B.S., Georgetown University, 1991. M.A., Georgetown University School of Foreign Service, 2003.

Professional: 1984–1990, infantryman, United States Army. 1991–1999, infantry officer, United States Army. 1999–2000, defense policy analyst, BAI, Inc. 2000–2004, research staff member, Institute for Defense Analysis. 2004–2009, professional staff member, House Cmte. on Armed Services. 2009–2010, senior policy advisor, House Cmte. on Armed Services. 2011–present, professional staff member, Subc. on Emerging Threats and Capabilities.

Expertise: National defense policy, defense transformation, joint professional military education.

Many in U.S. defense circles have kept a close eye on the deepening unrest in Africa and the Middle East and the toppling of more than one autocratic ruler. Mark R. Lewis is one of them. As the top Democratic staffer on the Emerging Threats and Capabilities Subcommittee, he's focused on the role played by U.S. special operations forces in any hot spot throughout the globe.

"The first priority is to pay attention to our special operations forces engaged throughout the global, with Afghanistan being primary, but elsewhere as well," he said.

It's a new role for Lewis, who served as the senior policy advisor to former chairman Ike Skelton, D-Mo., in the 111th Congress. Now that Republicans have regained control, he has shifted over to a subcommittee where he can lean on his practical experience. Lewis served 11 years on active duty with the Army, including a stint with a Ranger special operations unit. He's now will help Ranking Member James Langevin, D-R.I., make sure such units are properly trained and equipped.

Lewis said the subcommittee also will address cyber security issues, focusing first on preparing the military while also exploring the potential military role in protecting the broader cyber community.

In 2010, Lewis focused on the training and equipping of foreign partners including Iraq and Afghanistan, but also countries in Africa and the Pacific. He also worked on the quadrennial defense review, which outlines the nation's approach to national security.

Before joining the committee, Lewis worked as a research staff member at the Institute for Defense Analysis focusing on strategy, forces and military resources. He is a Russian speaker with a master's degree in national security studies and has published scholarly articles about the status of the military in several journals, including Joint Force Quarterly and Armed Forces & Society.

HOUSE ARMED SERVICES

Tom MacKenzie

Staff Director

Subcommittee on Seapower

2120 Rayburn House Office Bldg.

Phone: (202) 225-4151

Fax: (202) 225-0858

Tom.MacKenzie@mail.house.gov

Personal: Born 08/03/1948 in Baltimore, Md.

Education: B.S., United States Naval Academy, 1970. M.S., University of Southern California, 1987.

Professional: 1970–1999, member, U.S. Navy. 1999–2003, professional staff member, Subc. on Airland Forces, Senate Cmte. on Armed Services. 2003–2005, professional staff member, Subc. on Seapower, Senate Cmte. on Armed Services. 2005–2010, vice president of naval programs, Northrop Grumman. 2011–present, staff director, Subc. on Seapower and Projection Forces, House Cmte. on Armed Services.

Expertise: Naval programs.

The new staff director for the Subcommittee on Seapower and Projection Forces has had successful careers in the military, Congress, and most recently in the private sector. Tom MacKenzie spent the past five years at Northrop Grumman, most recently serving as a vice president of naval programs, acting as a conduit between the massive shipbuilder and its biggest customer—the U.S. Navy.

But with changes in the military and more competition from other firms, Northrop Grumman decided to sell off its ship building unit, a move approved by its board in March 2011. Seeing the writing on the wall, MacKenzie made a jump back to Capitol Hill.

"Basically, it was a reorientation, their biggest customer is no longer going to be their biggest customer," he said.

MacKenzie spent 29 years in the U.S. Navy and is a long-acknowledged expert in fixed-wing tactical aviation. He ended his flying career as a commander of a squadron of F-14 Tomcats. He first came to Capitol Hill in 1999, taking a spot on the Senate Armed Service Committee's panel on airland forces. Four years later, he switched to Seapower. He now has a spot on the House version of the same subcommittee.

"It is exciting. It is a different type of organization. The processes are a little different, but the end result is the same—the National Defense Authorization Act," he said.

The subcommittee, led by Chairman Todd Akin, R-Mo., will continue to oversee the military's shipbuilding accounts and essential research and development programs. Even while the Department of Defense is striving to cut costs, the Navy has a requirement to have at least 313 ships. Right now, it is in the 280s. The fiscal year 2012 budget includes 10 more ships; a move MacKenzie called "the first steps" toward reaching the goal.

Akin expressed some concerns in a hearing early in the 112th Congress saying that the Navy's planned development "will require near-perfect execution in cost control, schedule adherence and risk mitigation efforts to obtain the force structure necessary to deter hostile threats, show force when needed and as a last resort, employ lethal operations."

HOUSE ARMED SERVICES

Catherine McElroy

Counsel
2120 Rayburn House Office Bldg.
Phone: (202) 225-4151
Fax: (202) 225-0858
catherine.mcelroy@mail.house.gov

Personal: Born in Charlestown, Md.

Education: B.A., foreign affairs, University of Virginia, 2002. J.D., American University, 2005.

Professional: 2006–2010, assistant general counsel, Central Intelligence Agency. 2010–2011, Republican Counsel, House Permanent Select Committee on Intelligence. 2011–present, counsel, House Armed Services Cmte.

Expertise: National intelligence.

The House Armed Services Committee has a new staffer with a specialized portfolio that includes the nation's intelligence community and detainee policy. Catherine McElroy is an attorney who will primarily assist the committee's general counsel in the 112th Congress, having transferred from the House Permanent Select Committee on Intelligence.

She has been tasked with three goals. The first is to make sure the Department of Defense has the legal authority to meet the evolving international threats to the United States. The second is to safeguard the nation's detention system, which hold terrorists and seeks to provide warfighters with needed intelligence about potential terrorist plots. The third is to make sure the troops in places like Iraq and Afghanistan have the time-sensitive intelligence necessary to successfully complete their missions.

"There's nothing more important to me than supporting our men and women in uniform during a time of war," McElroy said. "I'm the daughter of a retired career submarine officer and grew up on a lot of different military bases so I also understand the hardships faced by our troops and their families."

McElroy took a job with the Central Intelligence Agency after getting her law degree from American University. At the CIA, she focused largely on the protection of national security information in counterterrorism prosecutions.

She joined the Intelligence Committee staff on Intelligence in 2010 as the Republican counsel on the Subcommittee on Oversight and Investigations. She also oversaw the budget and national security activities of the Federal Bureau of Investigations.

Now on the Armed Services Committee, McElroy works for a chairman who has made it very clear that he supports the continued use of the military detention facility at Guantanamo Bay.

Chairman Buck McKeon, R-Calif., led an effort to block the transfer of detainees held in Guantanamo to the United States, which President Barack Obama proposed as part of his plan to shutter the facility.

"Our nation has invested millions of dollars in building state-of-the-art humane and safe facilities to detain and prosecute the terrorist detainees at Guantanamo," he told reporters in January 2011. "It would be fiscally and morally irresponsible to shutter the facility and invest in new facilities in the United States."

HOUSE ARMED SERVICES

Michele A. Pearce

Staff Director

Subcommittee on Oversight and Investigations

2120 Rayburn House Office Bldg.

Phone: (202) 225-4151

Fax: (202) 225-0858

michele.pearce@mail.house.gov

Personal: Born in Oakdale, Ala.

Education: B.A., Mount Holyoke College, 1992. J.D., University of Connecticut School of Law, 1996.

Professional: 1996–1999, assistant staff judge advocate, Office of the Staff Judge Advocate, Mountain Home Air Force Base. 2000–2002, area defense counsel, Cannon Air Force Base. 2002–2004, chief, military justice and operations law, Office of the Staff Judge Advocate, Nellis Air Force Base. 2004–2005, assistant executive, Judge Advocate General, Pentagon. 2005–2006, associate deputy general counsel, Personnel and Health Policy, Office of the General Counsel, Pentagon. 2006–2009, aide, Secretary of the Air Force. 2009–2010, advisor, Chief Judge Andrew S. Effron, U.S. Court of Appeals for the Armed Forces. 2010–present, staff director, Subc. on Oversight and Investigations, House Cmte. on Armed Services.

Expertise: Military law.

A lawyer steeped in just about every aspect of the complex military legal system now serves as the staff director of the subcommittee designated with investigating the nation's armed services, keeping an eye out for waste, fraud, and abuse.

That lawyer is Michele Pearce, who has held this post since mid 2010, after transferring from the appellate court that services the military. She is teaming with the new chairman of the Subcommittee on Oversight and Investigations, Rep. Rob Whitman, R-Va., as they prepare for the unexpected in the year to come.

Whitman has served on the Oversight as well as the sea power subcommittees in years past. Shortly after accepting the post from committee Chairman Buck McKeon, R-Calif., Whitman said, "As our nation's budget remains tight, it is critical that we continue to focus on defense policies and budgets by the strategic needs of this nation."

While the other subcommittees perform oversight of the areas within their jurisdiction, it's this subcommittee's responsibility to coordinate a broader oversight role with the goal of identifying the best practices and areas of potential savings. What that is in particular is often hard to gauge ahead of time. The subcommittee is often reactive in nature.

In the 111th Congress, the subcommittee focused on an extensive study of sexual assaults in the armed forces, issues of child custody, and the contempt authority for military judges.

Pearce joined the committee with extensive experience in military law, particularly when it comes to the Air Force. After obtaining her legal degree, she worked at Mountain Home Air Force Base in Idaho, Cannon Air Force Base in New Mexico, and Nellis Air Force Base in Nevada alternating between prosecuting crimes and serving as counsel to the defendant.

She then moved to Washington, D.C., in 2004, working for the Judge Advocate General, the Pentagon's general counsel, and the secretary of the Air Force. Immediately before joining the committee, Pearce served as an advisor to Chief Judge Andrew S. Effron of the U.S. Court of Appeals for the Armed Service. Her job was to conduct legal research and analysis.

HOUSE ARMED SERVICES

Douglas C. Roach

Staff Director

Subcommittee on Tactical Air and Land Forces

2120 Rayburn House Office Bldg.

Phone: (202) 225-4151

Fax: (202) 225-0858

doug.roach@mail.house.gov

Personal: Born in Mich.

Education: B.A., business, University of Michigan, 1964. M.A., government, national security, Georgetown University, 1982. National War College, 1982.

Professional: 1965–91, officer, U.S. Air Force. 1991–97, professional staff member, House Cmte. on Armed Services. 2001–present, professional staff member, House Cmte. on Armed Services.

The Subcommittee on Tactical Air and Land Forces, with its staff director Douglas Roach, has undergone a thorough review of military efforts to equip the nation's warfighters, particularly in the ongoing missions in Afghanistan and Iraq, during the first few months of the 112th Congress.

Roach and the subcommittee worked on hearings—some classified, some public—that reviewed the military's slow response to improvised explosive devices and its rapid development of the Mine Resistant Ambush Protected Vehicle. Subcommittee Chairman Roscoe Bartlett, R-Md., said the top priority of the subcommittee is making sure the military has implemented the process necessary to equip services members in an ever-changing environment.

"There is no doubt that the equipment, body armor, and processes that our soldiers and marines have and use today is saving lives and has greatly improved during this past decade," Bartlett said. "I've often wondered though if we would have taken just five percent of what was spent on the now terminated Future Combat Systems program and applied it to lessoning the weight of what our soldiers carry, where would we be today?"

Roach is one of the committee's most experienced staffers and he has plenty of first hand experience with the military. He served 26 years in the Air Force and retired as a colonel in 1991. He flew 516 combat missions in F-15s and F-4s and for a time was a demonstration pilot with the Thunderbirds. For two years in the late 1980s, Roach served as the commander of U.S. Central Air Forces in Dhahran and Riyadh, Saudi Arabia.

Roach also served two stints as a legislative affairs officer interacting with Congress. He made the jump to Capitol Hill after his military service ends and has been the staff director of various subcommittees on House Armed Services including Research and Development and Air and Land Forces.

Roach was also the first ever recipient of the Civil Air Patrol's Spaatz award, named for the first chief of staff of the U.S. Air Force. It is the highest cadet honor and only 1,500 cadets have received it since Roach was honored in 1964.

HOUSE ARMED SERVICES

David Sienicki

Professional Staff Member
Subcommittee on Readiness
2120 Rayburn House Office Bldg.
Phone: (202) 225-4151
Fax: (202) 225-0858
David.Sienicki@mail.house.gov

Personal: Born 1965 in Jacksonville, Md.

Education: bachelors of mechanical engineering, Georgia Institute of Technology, 1987. Master of engineering, University of Florida, 2000.

Professional: 1987–2007, officer, Civil Engineer Corps., U.S. Navy. 2007–present, professional staff member, Subc. on Readiness.

Expertise: Military installations.

Whether the Republicans are in power or the Democrats, military construction work continues and David Sienicki's keeps on top of it all for the House Armed Services Committee, who describes the job as "bipartisan and very local."

The biggest piece of Sienicki's portfolio within the Readiness Subcommittee remains the implementation of the 2005 Base Closure and Realignment Commission decisions, more commonly referred to as BRAC 2005. The non-partisan plan to close bases and move military units was more ambitious and expansive than any in the nation's history and even six years out the work continues. The statutory goal is to relocate 123,000 personnel impacting more than 800 defense locations by Sept. 15, 2011. A Government Accountability Office report said it was unlikely that all of the projects would be completed on time, while many others are likely to be finished in the days just before the deadline.

Sienicki will work on the military's ever evolving global military posture, particularly in light of the ongoing financial struggles within the country and the nation's large national debt. Admiral Michael Mullen, chairman of the Joint Chiefs of Staff, appeared before the committee in early 2012 to address the military's posture.

"For too much of the past decade we have not been forced to be disciplined with our choices. This must change, and it already has," he said. "We have identified a number of efficiencies in our budget and have reduced spending, while also retaining the combat readiness, force structure, essential modernization, and personnel programs we need."

Mullen said more needs to be done. Some in Congress agree. Sienicki said he expects part of his job to entail a hunt for "contracting efficiencies."

Sienicki was commissioned as an ensign in the U.S. Navy in 1987 and served as the gunnery on the USS Blakely. He transferred to the Civil Engineer Corps where he worked in Philadelphia, Mississippi and Italy. In 2001, he received a legislative fellowship in the office of Rep. Gene Taylor, D-Miss.

Afterward, Sienicki went to the Pentagon and served as a planner for BRAC 2005 and as a Navy staffer focused on installations and facilities. He made the leap to the House Armed Services Committee in 2007.

HOUSE ARMED SERVICES

Jenness Simler

Policy Advisor
2120 Rayburn House Office Bldg.
Phone: (202) 225-4158
Fax: (202) 225-0858
Jenness.Simler@mail.house.gov

Personal: Born 07/03/1973 in Okinawa, Japan.

Education: B.S., Millsaps College, Jackson, Miss., 1995. M.B.A., University of Maryland, 2005.

Professional: 1996–2000, program manager, The Navy's Center of Excellence for Composites Manufacturing Technology. 2001–2004, program officer, Manufacturing Technology Program, Office of Naval Research. 2004–2005, deputy, Combating Counterterrorism Technology Task Force, Office of the Secretary of Defense, Acquisition, Technology & Logistics. 2005–2010, professional staff member, House Cmte. on Armed Services. 2011–present, policy advisor, House Cmte. on Armed Services.

Expertise: Procurement.

Despite looming budget cuts, unrest in the Middle East or the threat of sophisticated cyber security, the fundamental job of the House Armed Services Committee never changes. As Jenness Simler, the committee's new policy advisor puts it: "The first order of business is always to determine what the needs of the war fighter will be."

Born in Okinawa, Japan, but raised in Jackson, Miss., Simler has been immersed in the world of the Armed Forces for years. Most recently she served as the Republican staff lead on the Seapower and Expeditionary Forces Subcommittee, which has been renamed the Seapower and Projection Forces Subcommittee. With the shift in power, new Chairman Buck McKeon, R-Calif., broadened Simler's responsibility.

Her primarily job will be to help the committee conduct oversight on the ongoing operations in Afghanistan and Iraq, making sure the military has the tools necessary to complete its mission and return the troops home safely. After that, she expects to work on the dominate issue in the House—federal spending.

"I anticipate that much of my time will be devoted to assisting the committee in balancing the need to reduce federal spending with the need to provide adequately for the nation's defense in the current threat environment," Simler said.

She will also make sure the policy staff is focused on emerging threats, such as what the military has dubbed Anti-Access/Area Denial challenges or AA/AD, where a potential adversary attempts to block American access to areas of interest, whether it is closing access to a vital waterway or a needed air strip.

Simler loves kayaking and cooking and recently became a mother. She previously worked for the Navy's Center for Excellence for Composites Manufacturing and in the Office of Naval Research. She spent a year at the Defense Department as a deputy on the Combating Counterterrorism Technology Task Force, before she joined Armed Services in 2005.

In an interview with *Roll Call*, Simler professed her love for her job and her view that its public service. "The staff here is so much fun," she said. "We work long, tough days, and we view this as our way of giving back."

HOUSE ARMED SERVICES

Bob Simmons

Chief of Staff

2120 Rayburn House Office Bldg.

Phone: (202) 225-9648

Fax: (202) 225-0858

bob.simmons@mail.house.gov

Personal: Born 09/03/1955 in Murfreesboro, Tenn.

Education: B.S., electrical engineering, San Diego State University, 1978.

Professional: 1978–2002, chief executive officer, Senior Aerospace. 2003–2005, professional staff member, House Cmte. on Armed Services. 2005–2010, Republican staff director, House Cmte. on Armed Services. 2011–present, chief of staff, House Cmte. on Armed Services.

Expertise: Army procurement, defense industrial base, oversight and investigations.

The top Republican on the House Armed Services Committee has changed twice in recent years, but the top Republican staffer remains the same. Bob Simmons has held that role since 2005 and with the shift in power from Democrats to the GOP, he is now the committee's chief of staff, working with the new Chairman Buck McKeon of California.

Like McKeon, Simmons is cognizant of the tough financial conditions in the nation but concerned about potential budget cuts resulting in the loss of needed weapon systems and the potential impacts on combat readiness.

The committee will also oversee the elimination of the military's "don't ask, don't tell" policy involving the service of gay men and women. It was a move that McKeon disagreed with because he worried such a cultural shift in the middle of war actions could negatively impact a force that is already stretched thin. Another issue Simmons will oversee is the planned end to military operations in Iraq by 2012 and the debate over whether that time frame is reasonable.

Roll Call described Simmons' leadership style as friendly, saying he tries to establish a laid-back environment that's also as family friendly as possible for a committee that must stay long hours while putting together the massive defense authorization bill.

"I'm not a legacy Hill person. And to get results here, I manage employees' needs, and that includes ensuring the staff has time to spend with their family," he told *Roll Call*.

An electrical engineer by training, Simmons spent 26 years in the aerospace industry making jet engine components before joining the Armed Services Committee staff in 2003. He accepted the job at the insistence of former Rep. Duncan Hunter, R-Calif. Simmons described his committee work as public services in a previous interview. "I came here because I didn't serve in the military," he said. "This is my military service."

HOUSE ARMED SERVICES

Debra S. Wada

Professional Staff Member
Subcommittee on Military Personnel
2340 Rayburn House Office Bldg.
Phone: (202) 226-5662
Fax: (202) 225-3623
debra.wada@mail.house.gov

Personal: Born 10/31/1962 in Honolulu, Hawaii.

Education: B.A., political science and economics, Drake University, 1984.

Professional: 1987–1999, legislative asst. for defense and veterans' affairs, Sen. Daniel Akaka, D-Hawaii. 2000–2010, professional staff member, House Armed Services Cmte. 2010, deputy staff director, House Armed Services Cmte. 2011–present, professional staff member, House Armed Services Cmte.

Expertise: National security, personnel.

Congress has repealed the military's "don't ask, don't tell" policy that allowed gay service members to stay enlisted as long as they kept their sexuality quiet, but this policy does not just evaporate with President Barack Obama's signature. The Defense Department will slowly implement the change and committee Democratic staff member, Debra Wada, will follow this closely.

Wada also will work on the military's health care program, known as TRICARE, and on the recruitment and compensation of those servicing in each branch.

In the 111th Congress, former Armed Services Chairman Ike Skelton, D-Mo., promoted Wada to deputy staff director saying that "Debra has a deep understanding of what makes this committee tick and an impressive knowledge of our nation's military," but with the Republican takeover of the House in the 112th Congress, Wada returned to the Military Personnel subcommittee as a professional staff member.

This is familiar territory for Wada, who spent nine years on the subcommittee, earning repeated honors for her work. In 2004, the Enlisted Association of the U.S. National Guard gave Wada the Militia Award, which then-ranking member Skelton referenced on the House floor saying: "Millions of Americans in uniform owe the improvement of their pay and benefits to Debra and her foresight and dedication."

The Military Officers Association of America honored Wada and her colleague Michael Higgins in 2005 with the Col. Paul W. Arcari Meritorious Achievement Award for their work on pay equity, health care, and the survivor benefit plan. The Military Coalition, a consortium of veterans groups, gave Wada the Freedom Award in 2007.

Before joining the committee, Wada, a Hawaii native, spent a dozen years working as a legislative assistant to Sen. Daniel Akaka, D-Hawaii. She specialized in Medal of Honor winners, VA loans, and small business affairs.

HOUSE ARMED SERVICES

Lynn Williams

Staff Director

Subcommittee on Readiness

2120 Rayburn House Office Bldg.

Phone: (202) 225-4151

lynn.williams@mail.house.gov

Personal: Born in Marfa, Texas.

Education: B.S., computer science, Embry-Riddle Aeronautical University, 1993. Master of Aeronautical Studies, Embry-Riddle Aeronautical University, 2007.

Professional: 1993–2005, officer, U.S. Air Force. 2005–2010, professional staff member, Subc. on Readiness, House Cmte. on Armed Services. 2011–present, staff director, Subc. on Readiness, House Cmte. on Armed Services.

Expertise: Military operations and maintenance.

Rep. J. Randy Forbes, R-Va., is worried that the military is headed toward a disaster, with equipment becoming antiquated and replacements are nowhere in sight. Averting that crisis is a top priority for the new chairman of the Subcommittee on Readiness and that means that Lynn Williams, the subcommittee's staff director, is all over the issue.

Williams is a Hill staffer with plenty of practical experience in her field. She is an Air Force lieutenant colonel, with 18 years of total military services. Most of that was active duty as an officer and pilot of the F-15C. Williams left active duty in January 2005, when she accepted a post on the House Armed Services Committee. Since then she has worked as a professional staff member on the readiness panel, though she also handled the aviation procurement and modernization programs for the Seapower and Tactical Air and Land subcommittees.

She has degrees in computer science and aeronautical studies, which she relies on as she oversees the subcommittee's diverse jurisdiction. The Readiness Subcommittee manages the operation and maintenance funding of the military, while also overseeing energy and environmental policy, services contracting, military construction and depot policies.

But for Forbes, the top issue is the state of the military's technology. Shortly after becoming the subcommittee's chairman in 2011, Forbes held two hearings entitled "Are we ready?" which took the unusual step of having a roundtable conversation with leading members of the armed services.

"It was reinforced today that the equipment used by our nation's Armed Forces is quickly approaching a 'geriatric state' and our force levels are disproportionate to the needs that our men and women in uniform are called to serve," Forbes said at the start of the hearings. "When it comes to our military, Congress must be able to answer one simple question: 'are we ready?' We need to avert the impending 'train wreck' that defense experts have said is coming."

Forbes has also expressed concern about the Defense Department's plan to reduce its budget, saying he thinks it will reduce the capabilities of what he considers the world's best military. He also has repeatedly expressed his concerns about the military buildup in China.

HOUSE ARMED SERVICES

Roger Zakheim

Deputy Staff Director and General Counsel

Subcommittee on Oversight and Investigations

2120 Rayburn House Office Bldg.

Phone: (202) 226-4444

Fax: (202) 225-9077

roger.zakheim@mail.house.gov

Personal: Born in Silver Spring, Md.

Education: B.A., Columbia University, 2000. M.Phil., international relations, Cambridge University, 2003. J.D., NYU School of Law, 2005.

Professional: 2005–2007, counsel, House Cmte. on Armed Services. 2007–2008, Republican counsel, House Cmte. on Armed Services. 2008–2009, deputy assistant secretary of defense for coalition affairs, Department of Defense. 2009–2010, Republican counsel, House Cmte. on Armed Services. 2011–present, deputy staff director and general counsel, House Cmte. on Armed Services.

Expertise: Homeland defense, terrorism.

Roger Zakheim is partial to one of House Armed Services Committee Chairman Howard "Buck" McKeon, R-Calif., oft-quoted lines: "A defense budget in decline portends an America in decline."

As the committee's deputy chief of staff and general counsel, Zakheim's role is to McKeon, at least keep America on an even keel.

That means Zakheim will help search for savings but guard against cuts in the overall defense budget. It also means making sure that the nation's fighting force has the tools necessary as it winds down operations in Iraq and keeps the pressure on in Afghanistan. But Zakheim said the committee is aware of the House's overall goal to attack waste.

Given the fiscal environment, we need to be very aggressive going after efficiencies and being better stewards of the taxpayers' dollar," he said

In the last Congress, Zakheim served as the Republican counsel where he delved into an array of policy issues involving everything from the ongoing conflicts to security issues in Europe. With the change in power, Zakheim has given over most of his policy responsibilities to take a larger role in overseeing the entire committee operation.

He anticipates the budget debate will dominate the agenda, but also said the committee will continue its focus on detainee issues and Guantanamo Bay as well as some regional concerns involving the military capabilities of Iran and China.

Zakheim has published articles in the New York University's Journal of International Law and Politics, where he once served as a senior editor, and in the Forward, on such varied topics as the Israeli peace process, homeland security issue, and the United Nations. A former House intern, Zakheim joined the committee in August 2005. He served a brief stint as the deputy assistant secretary of defense for coalition affairs in 2009.

Committee on the Budget

207 Cannon House Office Bldg.
Washington, DC 20515
Phone: (202) 226-7200
Fax: (202) 225-9905
http://budget.house.gov
budget.democrats@mail.house.gov

Ratio: 21/17

MAJORITY MEMBERS

Paul Ryan, WI-1st, Chairman

Scott Garrett, NJ-5th
Mike Simpson, ID-2nd
John Campbell, CA-48th
Todd Akin, MO-2nd
Tom Cole, OK-4th
Tom Price, GA-6th
Tom McClintock, CA-4th
Jason Chaffetz, UT-3rd
Marlin Stutzman, IN-3rd
James Lankford, OK-5th
Diane Black, TN-6th
Reid Ribble, WI-8th
Bill Flores, TX-17th
Mick Mulvaney, SC-5th
Todd Young, IN-9th
Tim Huelskamp, KS-1st
Justin Amash, MI-3rd
Todd Rokita, IN-4th
Frank Guinta, NH-1st
Rob Woodall, GA-7th

MINORITY MEMBERS

Chris Van Hollen, MD-8th, Ranking Member

Allyson Y. Schwartz, PA-13th, Vice Chairman
Marcy Kaptur, OH-9th
Lloyd Doggett, TX-25th
Earl Blumenauer, OR-3rd
Ken Calvert, CA-4th
Betty McCollum, MN-4th
John Yarmuth, KY-3rd
Bill Pascrell, NJ-8th
Mike Honda, CA-15th
Tim Ryan, OH-17th
Debbie Wasserman Schultz, FL-20th
Gwen Moore, WI-4th
Kathy Castor, FL-11th
Heath Schuler, NC-11th
Paul Tonko, NY-21st
Karen Bass, CA-33rd

HOUSE BUDGET

JURISDICTION

(1) Concurrent resolutions on the budget (as defined in section 3(4) of the Congressional Budget Act of 1974), other matters required to be referred to the committee under titles III and IV of that Act, and other measures setting forth appropriate levels of budget totals for the United States government.
(2) Budget process generally.
(3) Establishment, extension, and enforcement of special controls over the federal budget, including the budgetary treatment of off-budget federal agencies and measures providing exemption from reduction under any order issued under part C of the Balanced Budget and Emergency Deficit Control Act of 1985.

HOUSE BUDGET

When the Republicans took control of the House following the 2010 midterm elections, they promised to reign in federal spending and reform entitlement programs. The heart of this effort lies in the House Budget Committee, chaired by the youthful and fiscally-minded Rep. Paul Ryan, R-Wis.

Ever since he first came to Congress in 1999, Ryan has pushed for a major revamp of government spending. In 2008, he released his Roadmap for America's Future, a comprehensive legislative action plan aimed at eliminating the deficit and national debt, creating jobs and altering the funding of programs such as Social Security. Ryan is expected to push the ideas from his roadmap during his tenure as committee chairman.

Ryan also is expected to put up a fight when it comes to the budget itself. When President Barack Obama released his budget proposal in early February 2011, Ryan immediately criticized it, arguing it didn't do enough to cut government spending. "The President's budget spends too much, taxes too much, and borrows too much—stifling job growth today and leaving our children with a diminished future. In this critical test of leadership, the President has failed to tackle the urgent fiscal and economic threats before us," Ryan said in a statement.

Defending Obama's budget on the committee is the panel's new ranking member, Rep. Chris Van Hollen, D-Md., successor of Rep. John Spratt, D-S.C., who lost a re-election bid. Much like Ryan, Van Hollen is considered a rising star in his party, and has pushed for a reduction in federal spending. But Van Hollen has urged restraint when it comes to spending cuts, arguing that slashing money for valuable federally-funded programs will be harmful in the long-term and prevent Americans from receiving valuable services.

The pair is almost certain to tussle over entitlement reform. Ryan has said Republicans will propose fundamental changes to the way Medicare and Medicaid programs are funded, although he had yet to offer specifics by March 2011. He also expressed disappointment Obama didn't include reforms for the programs in his fiscal 2012 budget proposal. But Van Hollen stepped up to defend Obama, saying reforms, while important, could wait until another budget.

HOUSE BUDGET

Timothy Flynn

Chief Economist

207 Cannon House Office Bldg.

Phone: (202) 226-7270

Fax: (202) 226-7174

tim.flynn@mail.house.gov

Personal: Born 10/16/1974 in Chicago, Ill.

Education: B.A., magna cum laude, English literaure, Loyola University of Chicago, 1996. M.S., international relations, Johns Hopkins University, School of Advanced International Studies, 2000.

Professional: 2000, Summer intern, Federal Reserve Bank of Chicago economic research dept. 2000–2006, Senior economist, Treasury Department, office of economic policy. 2007–present, Chief economist, House Cmte. on the Budget, minority staff.

Expertise: Economics.

As the House Budget Committee looks for ways to institute policy that will stabilize the economy during the 112th Congress, they can look to the expertise of staffer Tim Flynn. The chief economist for the Republican team, Flynn advises Chairman Paul Ryan, R-Wisc., on the condition of the economy and the direction of the financial markets.

Flynn first joined the panel on loan from the Treasury Department. But he never left, and has ended up advising Ryan during debates on the economic stimulus and the Troubled Asset Relief Program, among other issues. Flynn also worked on Ryan's Roadmap for America's Future, comprehensive legislation to cut spending and entitlements and balance the budget.

"It was a little more fast paced over here; a lot of things going on," Flynn has said of leaving the Treasury Department for the committee. "I enjoyed the political favor of things, putting the wonky esoteric numbers and theories into use in real life."

This Congress, Flynn is likely to help Ryan find ways to cut government spending in order to strengthen the economy in the long-term. Ryan and his team have argued that sacrifices must be made in the short term in order to ensure financial success in the upcoming decades.

Flynn also has advised other policy makers and economic experts. In 2010, he took part in a panel discussion at an economic policy conference moderated by Stan Collender, the managing director of Qorvis Communications. Flynn reasserted that there is a need to reduce debt in order to keep the economy moving in the long run.

Flynn is an avid traveler who has spent significant time in Italy. He studied there in college and, after graduate school, he likes to get back there as often as he can.

HOUSE BUDGET

Jim Herz

Budget Analyst

207 Cannon House Office Bldg.

Phone: (202) 226-7270

jim.herz@mail.house.gov

Education: B.S., electrical engineering, University of Colorado, 1999. B.A., liberal arts, University of Colorado, 1999. M.B.A., Rice University, 2006.

Professional: 1999–2002, engineer, Seatgate Technology LLC. 2002–2004, engineer, Quadros Systems Inc. 2006–2008, analyst, Office of Management and Budget. 2008–present, analyst, House Cmte. on the Budget.

Expertise: Net interest, allowances, undistributed offsetting receipts.

As a budget analyst for the House Budget Committee's Republican staff, Jim Herz oversees how the overall budget affects the state of the federal government. As such, Herz said he is able to analyze "just about everything that happens in government."

"The budget's interesting, because it impacts everything," he explained. "I get to look at the entire big picture."

Herz, a former engineer, left the private sector in 2004 and earned an M.B.A., enabling him to switch to working on public policy issues. After a stint with the Office of Management and Budget, he joined the committee in 2008, where he spent several years looking at how federal energy programs affect the overall budget.

Herz has new duties in the 112th Congress, charged with studying not just the energy parts of the budget but "the overall numbers." Herz said he likes his new position, because he can dip his toes in a variety of issues. "It's quite exciting," he said.

In the 111th Congress, Herz and his fellow staffers combed the federal budget looking for items that Republican members could perhaps amend.

But now with the Republicans in the majority for the 112th session, Chairman Paul Ryan, R-Wis., will be setting the committee's agenda. So far, Ryan has pushed for major entitlement reform and a huge reduction in federal spending, and has been highly critical of President Barack Obama's fiscal year 2012 budget, meaning Herz's job could see him combing through the budget looking for funding to cut entirely. Hearings early on included studying how health care reform could affect the nation fiscally and the overall state of the U.S. economy.

Herz has said he left the private sector for government work because he wanted to dive into the world of public policy." "I just felt like it was time to make more of a bigger difference in the world around me," he said.

HOUSE BUDGET

Charlotte Ivancic

Counsel and Budget Analyst

207 Cannon House Office Bldg.

Phone: (202) 226-7270

Fax: (202) @civancic

charlotte.ivancic@mail.house.gov

Personal: Born 09/09/1977 in Phoenix, Ariz.

Education: BA, English literature, philosophy, Wheaton College (Norton, Ma.), 1999. JD, health law, Boston University School of Law, 2003.

Professional: 1999–2003, program administration, Children's Hospital Boston/Harvard Medical School. 2003–2004, associate, Reed Smith, LLP, Washington, D.C. 2005, legislative counsel, Sen. Jim DeMint. 2006, health policy counsel, Senate Majority Leader Bill Frist. 2007–present, counsel and budget analyst, House Budget Cmte, Republican staff.

Expertise: Health care, Medicare.

Charlotte Ivancic does not have what one might consider the typical background for a senior Capitol Hill staffer. Unlike many of her colleagues, who spend years working in several Hill offices before landing a senior position, Ivancic worked at a health care law practice prior to becoming a congressional aide.

These days, Ivancic works as counsel and budget analyst for the House Budget Committee, charged with studying how health care legislation and Medicare affects the federal budget. It's a big priority for her boss, Chairman Paul Ryan, R-Wis., who told the Associated Press in March 2011 that his party will lead efforts to drastically reform Medicare and Medicaid as the 112th Congress continues.

Ivancic will surely advise Ryan on those issues, as she's specifically tasked at looking how to get entitlement spending under control.

In past Congresses, Ivancic worked on a number of health care topics, including Ryan's "Roadmap for America's Future," a blueprint of the Republican's vision for health care reform entitlements, and on the re-authorizations of the State Children's Health Care Insurance Program, better known as SCHIP.

Although Ivancic left private practice for government service, her heart remains with her old days as a Washington lawyer—sort of. Ivancic met her husband, Nicholas, during the time the pair worked together at the same law firm. When the legal lovebirds were married in California wine country in 2004, their ceremony was featured in the wedding magazine The Knot. The two welcomed a son in 2009.

HOUSE BUDGET

Thomas Kahn

Democratic Staff Director/Chief Counsel

B-71 Cannon House Office Bldg.

Phone: (202) 226-7200

Fax: (202) 226-7174

tom.kahn@mail.house.gov

Personal: Born 10/20/1955 in Boston, Mass.

Education: B.A. magna cum laude, Tufts University, 1977. Postgraduate work, Russian language and Soviet studies, University of Leningrad, 1978. J.D. magna cum laude, Georgetown University Law Center, 1984.

Professional: 1978-1982, legislative asst., Rep. Barbara Mikulski, D-Md. 1984-1985, corporate attorney, Sullivan and Cromwell (N.Y.). 1986, research asst., Rep. Jim Florio, D-N.J. 1987-1992, legislative counsel, Rep. John Spratt, D-S.C. 1993-1995, chief counsel, Subc. on Commerce, Consumer and Monetary Affairs, House Cmte. on Government Operations. 1995-1996, professional staff member, House Democratic Policy Cmte. 1997-present, Democratic staff dir. and chief counsel, House Cmte. on the Budget.

Expertise: Budget issues.

When Rep. Chris Van Hollen, D-Md., took over as ranking member of the House Budget Committee from retiring Rep. John Spratt, D-S.C., one of the first things the incoming committee leader did was make sure Thomas Kahn stayed on as the Democrats' top staffer.

"He has the perfect combination of policy smarts and deep understanding of the Congressional budget process," Van Hollen said in a statement. "His insight will be invaluable as we work to tackle the important issues facing our economy and put our country on a fiscally sustainable path."

Kahn is a longtime Hill aide, having served Congress for more than 25 years and the budget committee for more than 14 years. In the 112th Congress, he is expected to further Van Hollen's efforts on the committee, which is to reduce government spending while also preventing Republicans from slashing certain government programs in haste.

For example, Van Hollen introduced the "Reduce Unnecessary Spending Act" in March 2011, a measure that would allow the president propose eliminating specific pieces of spending from legislation and send those items back to Congress for expedited votes. But Van Hollen also criticized the Republican's February 2011 proposal of a continuing resolution to fund the federal government, calling the plan "reckless."

After well over a decade of service, Kahn has significant experience tackling budget committee matters, including the annual budget resolution. Off Capitol Hill, Kahn sits on the Council on Foreign Relations and served as a national vice president of the American Jewish Committee, of which he remains a member of the Board of Governors.

Kahn and his wife Susana Schwartz have two young sons, Benjamin and Daniel.

HOUSE BUDGET

Patrick L. Knudsen

Policy Director

207 Cannon House Office Bldg.

Phone: (202) 226-7270

Fax: (202) 226-7174

pat.knudsen@mail.house.gov

Personal: Born 02/05/1951 in Milwaukee, Wis.

Education: B.A., English, University of Wisconsin-Milwaukee, 1974.

Professional: 1974–1976, advertising salesperson, Post Newspapers (West Allis, Wis.). 1979–1982, reporter/editor, Community Newspapers (Oak Creek, Wis.). 1982–83, reporter, *Milwaukee Journal*. 1983–1987, business reporter, *Times-Union* (Rochester, N.Y.). 1987–1988, reporter, Washington, D.C. 1988–1989, research dir., House Wednesday Group. 1989–1990, legislative dir., Rep. Fred Upton, R-Mich. 1991–1994, editor/analyst, House Cmte. on the Budget. 1995–2003, dir. of budget policy, House Cmte. on the Budget. 2004–present, policy dir., House Cmte. on the Budget.

Expertise: Budget policy.

As policy director for the House Budget Committee majority staff, Patrick Knudsen oversees Republican policy documents on budget-related matters. He also helps craft the budget resolution the panel's majority staff releases each year.

Although it can be a challenge to explain complicated budget topics, Knudsen has the skills. Before he came to Capitol Hill, he worked for 14 years as a journalist, giving him the writing and editing tools needed to explain often hard-to-understand matters in a clear and concise way.

There will be plenty for Knudsen to help explain in the 112th Congress, as Budget Committee Chairman Paul Ryan, R-Wis., is aiming to drastically alter longstanding government policy in a number of areas. Ryan's main policy goals early on appeared to be reforming entitlement programs such as Medicare and Social Security, paying down the national debt and drastically cutting government spending.

During the 111th Congress, Knudsen worked extensively to promote Ryan's ambitious fiscal plans, a challenging task given Republicans were then in the minority. Knudsen worked with other staffers on the panel to help draft Ryan's "Roadmap for America's Future," a comprehensive legislative plan to reshape government spending and the nation's fiscal future. He also assisted Ryan in his efforts to promote the work and institute some of the recommendations of National Commission on Fiscal Responsibility and Reform, among other policy-related tasks.

Writing and editing is not Knudsen's only skill set, as he also is a folk singer and guitar player who has been known to perform at open mic nights.

HOUSE BUDGET

Gail Millar

General Counsel

B-71 Cannon House Office Bldg.

Phone: (202) 226-7200

Fax: (202) 225-9905

Gail.Millar@mail.house.gov

Personal: Born 08/09/1955 in New York, N.Y.

Education: B.A., political science and economics, State University of New York at Buffalo, 1977. J.D., State University of New York at Buffalo, 1980.

Professional: 1981–1984, chief counsel, Senate Cmte. on the Budget. 1984–1988, asst. parliamentarian, U.S. Senate. 1989–2000, general counsel, Congressional Budget Office. 2000–2002, clerk, Subc. on Commerce, State, Justice, the Judiciary and Related Agencies, House Cmte. on Appropriations. 2002–2005, associate dir. for budget policy and management, Office of Technical Assistance, U.S. Dept. of Treasury. 2005–2007, general counsel, Senate Cmte. on the Budget/Sen. Judd Gregg, R-N.H. 2007–present, general counsel, House Cmte. on the Budget.

Expertise: Budget process, procedure.

There was much talk of the need for bipartisanship at the start of the 112th Congress. For a lesson in getting along across party lines, perhaps lawmakers and Hill staffers alike should turn to House Budget Committee general counsel Gail Millar.

These days, Millar serves Democrats by assisting Committee Ranking Member Chris Van Hollen, D-Md., on the technical aspects related to the budget resolution, amendments and a variety of legislative topics.

Millar also had worked for Van Hollen's predecessor, Rep. John Spratt, D-S.C., as a budget staffer. But before that, Millar served in the Department of Treasury under President George W. Bush and for Sen. Judd Gregg, R-N.H., on the Senate Budget Committee.

In the 111th Congress, Millar helped out on the budget resolution and also worked on issues related to the Pay-Go rule, adjusting it so it could align more closely with the Senate's version, putting some of her experience from the other chamber to use.

Millar's duties often see her answering technical questions from Members of Congress, including those who are not her boss. During debate on the budget resolution in 2009, for example, then-ranking member Paul Ryan, R-Wis., asked Millar on the House floor about committees who had been directed to produce $1 billion in deficit reduction by 2014.

In the 112th Congress, Millar is likely to assist Van Hollen in his efforts to reduce government spending while also protecting certain programs from getting hit with devastating cuts. He introduced the technically-minded "Reduce Unnecessary Spending Act" in March 2011, for example. This measure would allow the president to propose specific spending cuts in legislation that reach his desk for signature, sending his request back to Congress for an expedited vote.

HOUSE BUDGET

Andrew S. Morton

Deputy Staff Director

207 Cannon House Office Bldg.

Phone: (202) 226-7270

Personal: Born 05/08/1955 in Seattle, Wash.

Education: B.S., Iowa State University, 1977. Ph.D., Iowa State University, 1982.

Professional: 1979–1982, research assoc., Center for Agricultural and Rural Development. 1983–1992, economist, Congressional Budget Office. 1992–1995, Democratic staff economist, Senate Cmte. on Agriculture, Nutrition and Forestry. 1995–2003, Democratic economist, Senate Cmte. on Agriculture, Nutrition and Forestry. 2003–2007, chief economist, Senate Cmte. on Agriculture, Nutrition and Forestry. 2007–2008, budget analyst, House Cmte. on the Budget. 2011–present, deputy staff director, House Cmte. on the Budget.

Expertise: Futures trading, commodity programs.

After a few years away from Capitol Hill, longtime staffer Andy Morton returned to the congressional hallways in the 112th Congress, this time to serve as the No. 2 staffer on the House Committee on the Budget.

Morton, the deputy chief of staff, said the best part about returning to Capitol Hill after a brief stint working in the executive branch is the ability to work alongside new Budget Committee Chairman Paul Ryan, R-Wisc. "I am working along with the rest of our staff to develop, communicate and help pass the through the House the [fiscal] 2012 budget resolution," Morton wrote in an e-mail to the Almanac.

Morton is likely to stay busy this session, as Ryan has an ambitious plan that not only affects the budget committee's work, but the future of federal spending. The young chairman is seeking a dramatic overall of federal spending, which he has laid out in his comprehensive legislation, Roadmap for America's Future. The plan seeks to reduce the deficit by reshape entitlement programs such as Social Security, among other initiatives.

Although Morton's last stint on Capitol Hill was as an analyst for the House budget panel, he spent many years working for the Senate Agriculture, Nutrition and Forestry Committee. There, he helped with efforts to reauthorize the Commodity Futures Trading Commission, took part in discussions surrounding the farm bill and helped out on developments in the Doha round of World Trade Organization negotiations.

Morton spent the first decade of his career as a staffer for the nonpartisan Congressional Budget Office, experience that is likely to come in handy as he helps Ryan develop and pass this year's budget resolution.

HOUSE BUDGET

Kimberly Overbeek

Director of Budget Review

B-71 Cannon House Office Bldg.

Phone: (202) 226-7200

Fax: (202) 225-9905

Kimberly.Overbeek@mail.house.gov

Personal: Born 08/26/1971 in Seoul, Korea, Republic of.

Education: B.A., Yale University, 1993.

Professional: 1994–1995, program instructor, Close Up Foundation. 1995–1998, legislative asst., Rep. David Minge, D-Minn. 1998–2000, legislative dir., Rep. David Minge, D-Minn. 2000–present, dir. of budget review, House Cmte. on the Budget.

Expertise: Budget policy.

As director of budget review for the House Budget Committee's minority staff, Kimberly Overbeek is charged with looking at the big picture when it comes to the budget resolution. The longtime Hill aide must look at what all the numbers in the resolution actually mean for the nation, and then explain it in a way that makes sense to Members and her fellow staffers.

In the 112th Congress, Overbeek will likely help ranking member Chris Van Hollen, D-Md, in his plans to reduce the federal deficit and cut government spending while also ensuring that certain programs are not destroyed by anti-spending measures. Van Hollen has praised President Barack Obama's budget proposal, saying it makes "smart choices" about where spending cuts should take place. Overbeek also is certain to help Van Hollen during the budget resolution process, as the minority often puts forth amendments to the language drafted by the majority.

In past Congresses, Overbeek has assisted on other measures designed to keep government spending down. She helped on Pay-Go, for example, ensuring that congressional committees had a plan for paying for any spending measures they approve. Overbeek also helped on legislative efforts that were designed to get the economy back on its feet in the wake of the financial crisis.

Although Overbeek is an expert in the federal budget, it wasn't always so. She majored in sociology while in college, and just sort of fell into budget work when she was hired by the committee after her onetime boss, Rep. David Minge, D-Minn., lost his re-election bid. Overbeek moved to the committee in 2000.

HOUSE BUDGET

Courtney Reinhard

Counsel/Budget Analyst

207 Cannon House Office Bldg.

Phone: (202) 226-7270

Fax: (202) 226-7174

courtney.reinhard@mail.house.gov

Personal: Born in Sacramento, Calif.

Education: B.A., history and political science, University of California, Davis, 1997. J.D., George Mason School of Law, 2006.

Professional: 1997–1998, staff assistant/legislative correspondent, Rep. Brian Bilbray, R-Calif. 1998–1999, legislative assistant, Rep. Gary Miller, R0Calif. 2004–2005, senior legislative assistant, Rep. John Shimkus, R-Ill. 2005–2006, legislative assistant, Sen. Sam Brownback, R-Kan. 2006–2009, legislative assistant, Sen. Jim DeMint, R-S.C. 2009–present, counsel, budget analyst, House Cmte. on the Budget, Republican staff.

Expertise: Telecommunications, education, job training, commerce.

As a budget analyst on the House Budget Committee's majority staff, Courtney Reinhard advises Republican committee members on the fiscal impact of a wide-variety of pieces of legislation. She also works with her fellow staffers to help craft the panel's annual budget resolution.

Reinhard is tasked with monitoring a long list of issues that affect the federal budget, including commerce, telecommunications, transportation, education, and job training programs, as well as monitoring the fiscal impact of spectrum auctions. Although Reinhard is charged with becoming an expert of an eclectic mix of subjects, she has some experience, as she analyzed their monetary implications for the Republicans' alternative budget proposal in the 111th Congress.

But her work in the 112th Congress will be a tad different. Now that Republicans are in the majority, they will get to do more than put forth alternative ideas. "I am proud to be working for House Budget Committee Chairman Paul Ryan at this pivotal point, where the FY2012 Budget Resolution will start our nation on a path to solvency," she wrote in an e-mail.

Reinhard also oversaw the crafting of Title VII of Ryan's "Roadmap for America's Future," a comprehensive legislative proposal for the future of government spending. Title VII aims to bring greater accountability and improved results to federal job training programs.

A California native, Reinhard first wanted to work on Capitol Hill after participating in the Presidential Classroom program when she was 15. Her first official job was as a legislative correspondent and staff assistant for Rep. Brian Bilbray, R-Calif., where she was charged with answering constituent mail, updating the website and managing the internship program.

HOUSE BUDGET

Paul Restuccia

Chief Counsel
207 Cannon House Office Bldg.
Phone: (202) 226-7270
Fax: (202) 226-7174
Paul.Restuccia@mail.house.gov

Personal: Born 07/29/1964 in Ann Arbor, Mich.

Education: B.A., Kenyon College, 1986. J.D., Loyola University of Chicago School of Law, 1990.

Professional: 1991, law clerk, Edelman and Edelman, Chicago, Ill. 1992–1995, legislative asst., Rep. John R. Kasich, R-Ohio. 1995–1996, budget analyst, House Cmte. on the Budget. 1996–2001, asst. counsel and budget analyst, House Cmte. on the Budget. 2001–2005, deputy chief counsel, House Cmte. on the Budget. 2005–present, chief counsel for the minority, House Cmte. on the Budget.

Expertise: Budget enforcement, banking, housing and community development.

Paul Restuccia is one of the House Budget Committee's longest serving staffers, having been with the panel since the early 1990s. These days, he serves as chief counsel for the majority, charged in part with helping Chairman Paul Ryan, R-Wis., craft the language of a variety of pieces of legislation that hit the House floor.

Restuccia no doubt will help on the budget resolution expected to put forth by the majority. He also likely will help with any legislation introduced by Ryan, who is expected to push measures designed to reduce government spending, reform entitlement programs such as Medicare and Social Security and begin to pay down the national debt.

In the 111th Congress, Restuccia helped on the Republicans' budget substitute and assisted on amendments that the Republicans brought to the floor when the budget was considered. He also has helped Ryan on his Roadmap for America's Future, a comprehensive legislative plan designed to drastically reshape government spending and the nation's fiscal policy.

Restuccia's work with the committee has not gone unnoticed. When Ryan took to the House floor to speak about the budget resolution during the 111th Congress, for example, he personally thanked Restuccia and a handful of other budget staffers for their hard work.

Restuccia said in 2009 that he has remained with the budget committee for so many years because he likes being a part of the institution of Congress. "I like how legislation is developed. I guess that's why I've never lost interest," he said.

HOUSE BUDGET

Austin Smythe

Republican Staff Director
207 Cannon House Office Bldg.
Phone: (202) 226-7270
Fax: (202) 226-7174
austin.smythe@mail.house.gov

Personal: Born 06/29/1956 in Charleston, S.C.

Education: B.A., University of Texas. M.A., University of Texas.

Professional: 1980–1983, assistant project manager, Hart Associates. 1983–1988, analyst, Senate Budget Cmte. 1988–1999, assistant staff director, Senate Budget Cmte. 1999–2007, executive associate director, Office of Management and Budget. 2007–present, Republican staff director, House Cmte. on the Budget.

Expertise: Budget process, Congressional and Executive.

The federal budget process can be complicated to explain, even to the most informed policy wonks. But if there is one man who is an expert on its intricacies, it is Austin Smythe, staff director for the House Budget Committee's majority staff.

Smythe has been a part of the budget process in both chambers and on both sides of Pennsylvania Avenue, having worked for the Senate Budget Committee and Office of Management and Budget. Now he's working as the top staffer on the panel for Chairman Paul Ryan, R-Wis., who is pushing to drastically reshape the nation's fiscal future through major entitlement reform and cuts in government spending.

Smythe assists Ryan in developing big picture plans for the panel and budget policy in general. Smythe has helped Ryan put together a number of pieces of legislation, including Ryan's Roadmap for America's Future— a comprehensive measure that would drastically alter the nation' fiscal policy and entitlement programs.

Ryan's top budget aide is well-respected among budget experts and government observers alike. Then-OMB Director Josh Bolton told GovernmentExecutive.com in 2005 that Smythe is "among the nation's leading experts on the budget process." Politico named Smythe to their "Who's who" list of congressional staffers in 2010, noting he has become something of "an alter ego" to Ryan in the budget committee's office.

Politico's assessment likely wasn't too far off. For example, in 2010 Ryan appeared at the non-profit Brookings Institution to explain his ideas to reshape federal entitlement programs such as Medicare and Social Security. After his speech, Ryan couldn't stay for a panel discussion on the subject because he had business on Capitol Hill, so Smythe remained to speak for him.

HOUSE BUDGET

Conor Sweeney

Communications Director

207 Cannon House Office Bldg.

Phone: (202) 226-7270

FB: facebook.com/conorbsweeney

conor.sweeney@mail.house.gov

Education: B.A., economics, Marquette University, 2007.

Professional: 2007, office administrator, Rep. Paul Ryan, R-Wis. 2007, staff asst., Rep. Paul Ryan, R-Wis. 2007–2008, legislative corre., Rep. Paul Ryan, R-Wis. 2008–2010, press secretary, Rep. Paul Ryan, R-Wis.. 2010–present, communications director, House Budget Cmte.

Expertise: Communications.

Conor Sweeney has been loyal to his boss, House Budget Committee Chairman Paul Ryan, R-Wis., ever since he first came to Capitol Hill as a lowly office administrator in 2007. But the Wisconsin native quickly moved up the ranks on Ryan's team, becoming the congressman's press secretary in 2008 and communications director for House Budget Committee Republicans in 2010.

In this role, Sweeney is charged with delivering Ryan's message of major fiscal reform and the need to revamp entitlement spending programs such as Medicare and Social Security. Sweeney regularly speaks to members of the media on behalf of Ryan, both promoting his boss's much talked about message as well as defending it when needed.

The 112th Congress should prove to be a busy time for Sweeney. By March 2011, Ryan already had held six hearings on various budget-related matters, and planned at least two more by April. The panel also released several press releases a week, and Ryan wrote several op-eds on fiscal matters for newspapers and other publications, an effort Sweeney certainly played a role in. Plus, Ryan's status as a popular figure on Capitol Hill meant that the congressman regularly appeared on cable television programs.

Between 2008 and 2010, Sweeney pulled double duty for Ryan, working with the media and handling communications matters for both the budget committee staff and in Ryan's personal office. Sweeney helped out on a variety of Ryan initiatives, including the role-out and promotion of the Roadmap for America's Future, a comprehensive legislative plan to drastically reshape America's fiscal policies and government spending. E-mail exchanges about the plan between Sweeney and journalists appeared on-line, with *Forbes'* magazine's website featuring a note between Sweeney and writer Brian Wingfield.

Sweeney attended Marquette University in Milwaukee on a Raynor Scholarship. In an article posted to the university's website, Sweeney discussed how the scholarship enabled him to visit locales such as South Africa and China and volunteer during trips to Jamaica, Kenya, and Kentucky. He is married to Ruth Burke Sweeney and lives in Washington, D.C.

HOUSE BUDGET

Greg Waring

Budget analyst
B-71 Cannon House Office Bldg.
Phone: (202) 226-7200
Fax: (202) 225-9905
greg.waring@mail.house.gov

Personal: Born 01/27/1977 in Washington, D.C.

Education: B.A., economics, University of Maryland, Baltimore County, 1999. M.P.A., domestic policy, Princeton University, Woodrow Wilson School of Public and International Affairs, 2002.

Professional: 2000–2001, budget/management analyst, Prince George's County, Md., Office of Management and Budget. 2002–2007, budget analyst, Congressional Budget Office. 2008–present, budget analyst, House Cmte. on the Budget.

Expertise: Budget analysis.

Compared to most of his coworkers, Greg Waring is relatively new to the House Budget Committee's Democratic staff, having joined as a budget analyst in 2008. But he's quickly become a policy pro on a number of important issues, including immigration, transportation, commerce, and housing credits.

The 112th Congress marks Waring's first time in the minority. As a majority staffer, Waring was charged with helping to defend Democratic spending on his areas of expertise. Now, he'll need to study ways that Democrats such as committee ranking member Chris Van Hollen, D-Md., can go after the Republicans' budget proposal by introducing amendments on these issues.

Waring also has served as a resource to those off Capitol Hill on his issues of expertise, including when spoke about transportation at a March 2011 conference sponsored by the American Association of State Highway and Transportation Officials.

Prior to joining the budget committee, Waring worked as a budget analyst for the Congressional Budget Office, an agency his current employer has jurisdiction over. Waring said in 2009 that he wanted to leave the nonpartisan agency in order to help craft an agenda with a congressional office.

"I was familiar with the budget so I could see things from the other side," Waring said.

Waring is a proud alumnus of Princeton University's Woodrow Wilson School of Public and International Affairs. He even appears in a video on the school's website, noting how "the WWS experience gave him the analytical, writing, and quantitative skills that serve him well in his current position as budget analyst."

Committee on Education and the Workforce

2181 Rayburn House Office Bldg.
Washington, DC 20515
Phone: (202) 225-3725
Fax: (202) 225-9571
http://edworkforce.house.gov

Ratio: 22/17

MAJORITY MEMBERS

John Kline, MN-2nd, Chairman

Thomas E. Petri, WI-6th
Howard P. (Buck) McKeon, CA-25th
Judy Biggert, IL-13th
Todd Russell Platts, PA-19th
Joe Wilson, SC-2nd
Virginia Foxx, NC-5th
Duncan D. Hunter, CA-52nd
David P. Roe, TN-1st
Glenn G.T. Thompson, PA-5th
Tim Walberg, MI-7th
Scott DesJarlais, TN-4th
Richard Hanna, NY-24th
Todd Rokita, IN-4th
Larry Buschon, IN-8th
Trey Gowdy, SC-4th
Lou Barletta, PA-11th
Kristi Noem, SD-1st
Martha Roby, AL-2nd
Joe Heck, NV-3rd
Dennis Ross, FL-12th
Mike Kelly, PA-3rd

MINORITY MEMBERS

George Miller, CA-7th, Ranking Member

Dale E. Kildee, MI-5th
Donald M. Payne, NJ-10th
Robert E. Andrews, NJ-1st
Robert C. (Bobby) Scott, VA-3rd
Lynn C. Woolsey, CA-6th
Rubén Hinojosa, TX-15th
Carolyn McCarthy, NY-4th
John F. Tierney, MA-6th
Dennis J. Kucinich, OH-10th
David Wu, OR-1st
Rush D. Holt, NJ-12th
Susan A. Davis, CA-53rd
Raúl M. Grijalva, AZ-7th
Timothy H. Bishop, NY-1st
Dave Loebsack, IA-2nd
Mazie Hirono, HI-2nd

HOUSE EDUCATION AND LABOR

JURISDICTION

(1) Child labor.
(2) Gallaudet University and Howard University and Hospital.
(3) Convict labor and the entry of goods made by convicts into interstate commerce.
(4) Food programs for children in schools.
(5) Labor standards and statistics.
(6) Education or labor generally.
(7) Mediation and arbitration of labor disputes.
(8) Regulation or prevention of importation of foreign laborers under contract.
(9) Workers' compensation.
(10) Vocational rehabilitation.
(11) Wages and hours of labor.
(12) Welfare of minors.
(13) Work incentive programs.

HOUSE EDUCATION AND LABOR

Education is front and center for the House Education and the Workforce Committee during the first session of the 112th Congress. Committee chairman, Rep. John Kline, R-Minn. and ranking member Rep. George Miller, D-Calif., both have said they are committed to reworking the overdue Elementary and Secondary Education Act, also known as the No Child Left Behind Act (NCLB).

Miller is one of the original "gang of four" architects of the law, but he and fellow Democrats, as well as Republicans, said the federal K–12 education statute needs to be revamped. NCLB aims to close the achievement gap between minority and white students, as well as between higher-income and disadvantaged students on a K–12 level. But the law also emphasizes standardized testing and puts penalties in place for schools that fail to meet annual achievement goals.

"Anyone who has talked to a superintendent or teacher understands that federal law can stand in the way of innovative solutions and meaningful reform," Kline said during a hearing in March.

Miller said the educational landscape has changed since the law was adopted and that its focus must shift to a performance-based system that uses common data, across the state, to evaluate how schools are doing.

Pell Grants are also up for discussion this year, with Kline saying the growth of the program that helps low-income students with the costs of higher education is unsustainable, and Miller pushing for its increase. For the 2011–12 school year, the Pell Grant scholarship is a maximum of $5,550 per student.

The committee is also examining the for-profit education sector, with Kline expressing concerns over gainful employment regulations in this area.

On the workforce side, the Workforce Investment Act is up for reauthorization. The Act oversees federal employment, training, and adult education programs for adults, dislocated workers and youth, seeks to promote employment, job retention, increased earnings and occupational skills.

The committee will also look at healthcare items related to the Employee Retirement Income Security Act, which sets minimum standards for most voluntarily established pension and health plans in private industry to provide protection for individuals in these plans.

Mine safety, a perennial concern of Miller's, also continues to be on the agenda, following a series of deadly mining disasters in the last few years, including the 2010 deaths of 29 miners at Massey Energy's Upper Big Branch mine in West Virginia. Before the explosion that killed the miners occurred, Massey Energy's Big Branch mine was cited for numerous safety violations.

HOUSE EDUCATION AND LABOR

James Bergeron

Director for Education and Human Services Policy

2181 Rayburn House Office Bldg.

Phone: (202) 225-4527

Fax: (202) 226-1010

james.bergeron@mail.house.gov

Personal: Born 08/11/1973 in Houma, La.

Education: B.A., University of Louisiana at Lafayette, 1995.

Professional: 1990–2001, legislative director, Rep. Tom Tancredo, R-Colo. 1995–99, legislative assistant, Rep. Bob Livingston, R-La. 2001–2004, legislative director, Rep. Howard P. "Buck" McKeon, R-Calif. 2004–2006, vice president, MARC Associates. 2006–2011, deputy director for education and human services policy, House Cmte. on Education and Labor. 2011–present, director for education and human services policy, House Cmte. on Education and the Workforce.

Expertise: K-12 education, higher education.

James Bergeron took on a new role in the 112th Congress as director for education and human services policy. It's a post that covers familiar ground for Bergeron but also puts him in some new territories.

Bergeron now oversees the Republicans' education team and helps set legislative and policy priorities for the committee in education. He's carrying out the committee's agenda in the realm of K-12 education, which Bergeron had focused on for the committee in his previous role, but also will tackle a new topic by handling higher education issues.

Bergeron also will be involved with action as The Elementary and Secondary Education Act, also known as the No Child Left Behind Act, takes center stage on the education agenda this session. The law, which aims to close the achievement gap between student groups, has come under fire for the penalties it imposes when schools and students don't meet annual educational benchmarks, called Adequate Yearly Progress (AYP).

Bergeron said accountability and assessment issues, teacher quality, charter schools, and school choice will all be up for discussion. "I definitely think there's going to be a lot more state and local flexibility around whatever happens when schools don't make AYP," he said.

Bergeron has also turned his attention to higher education issues, which this session will focus more on oversight and regulations. The committee is looking at how to define "gainful employment" when it comes to for-profit higher education institutions. Committee Chairman John Kline, R-Minn. said the "gainful employment" criterion prevents students from having more educational choice.

Also in the higher education arena, the committee is examining the growth of Pell Grants for low-income students seeking higher education. Bergeron said the growth of program is unsustainable.

HOUSE EDUCATION AND LABOR

Jody Calemine

Minority Staff Director

2101 Rayburn House Office Bldg.

Phone: (202) 225-3725

jody.calemine@mail.house.gov

Personal: Born 1974 in Morgantown, W.Va.

Education: B.A., American Government, Philosophy, University of Virginia, 1995. J.D., University of Virginia, 1999.

Professional: 1999–2003, headquarters counsel, Communications Workers of America. 2002–2003, associate counsel, Zwerdling, Paul, Liebig, Kahn & Wolly. 2003–2006, labor counsel, House Subcmte. on Employer-Employee Relations. 2007–2011, deputy labor policy director, House Cmte. on Education and Labor. 2009–2011, general counsel, House Cmte. on Education and Labor. 2011–present, staff director, House Cmte. on Education and the Workforce.

Expertise: Labor law and policy.

Since joining the Committee on Education and the Workforce in 2003, Jody Calemine has had the chance to get a wide range of experiences in a number of positions. This session he's taken on a new role as Democratic staff director.

His new responsibilities include directing staff and operations on behalf of the committee's ranking Democrat, Rep. George Miller, D-Calif.

Miller has put job creation and job quality at the forefront of his agenda during the first session of the 112th Congress. In January, Miller called on committee members to focus on solutions to help grow and strengthen America's middle class.

"All across the nation, communities are confronting a lack of highly skilled workers, even as unemployment is high," he said. "We must support these local efforts to create jobs, stay competitive, and act decisively nationally to build and maintain a highly skilled workforce."

Calemine is also continuing a focus on mine and occupational safety and health reform, following a series of deadly mining disasters in the last few years, including the 2010 deaths of 29 miners at Massey Energy's Upper Big Branch mine in West Virginia. Before the explosion that killed the miners occurred, Massey Energy's Big Branch mine was cited 515 times and ordered to shut down operations on 52 occasions. In March, Miller urged action on the Robert C. Byrd Mine Safety Protection Act, which would give the Mine Safety and Health Administration new tools to keep miners safe and hold mine operators accountable for putting workers in danger. The bill was blocked by Republicans in the 111th Congress.

The overdue reauthorization of the Elementary and Secondary Education Act, often referred to as the No Child Left Behind Act under President George W. Bush's administration, is also on the table. Miller is one of the original architects of the law, which calls for schools and student to reach annual benchmarks in reading and math or face penalties. But the law has been controversial and Democrats have pledged to take a new look at its requirements.

Calemine said he is also working on reauthorization of the Workforce Investment Act, as well as issues surrounding the protection of workers' rights.

HOUSE EDUCATION AND LABOR

Jamie Fasteau

Deputy Director of Education Policy

2101 Rayburn House Office Bldg.

Phone: (202) 225-3725

jamie.fasteau@mail.house.gov

Education: B.A., Claremont-McKenna College.

Professional: 2000–2003, lobbyist, National Association of University Women. 2003, lobbyist, National PTA. 2007–2010, vice president for federal advocacy, Alliance for Excellent Education. 2010–present, senior education policy advisor, House Cmte. on Education and the Workforce. 2011–present, deputy director of educational policy, House Cmte. on Education and the Workforce.

Expertise: Education issues.

Jamie Fasteau is building on a long career in education policy in her new position as deputy director of education policy. Before coming to the Committee on Education and Workforce, she spent several years as vice president for federal advocacy for the Alliance for Excellent Education, which works to improve national and federal education policy with the goal of boosting secondary school academics.

The organization focuses in particular on at-risk students who are most likely to leave school without a diploma or to graduate unprepared for higher education or a career. In her capacity at the Alliance, Fasteau led the organization's federal policy efforts on secondary school reform and also served as the director of policy, managing the Alliance's legislative agenda

Fasteau has her hands full this year as the committee turns its focus to the overdue reauthorization of the Elementary and Secondary Education Act, known as the No Child Left Behind Act. The law has come under fire from both Republicans and Democrats who say its reliance on standardized testing and penalties are counterproductive. Fasteau's boss, ranking member Rep. George Miller, D-Calif., was one of the original architects of the law, but at a hearing in March he said the measure needs to be revamped.

Asked late last year about prospects for reauthorization, Fasteau told an Education Week panel, "There won't be conflict over the content of a new bill, but over the details instead." She also noted that Miller has rejected proposals for a quick-fix or "patch" approach to reauthorization.

Fasteau's experience with the No Child Left Behind Act is extensive. Before joining the Alliance, she worked as a legislative assistant on education issues for Sen. Patty Murray, D-Wash., and before that served as the senior lobbyist at the National PTA where she worked on implementation of No Child Left Behind as well as school vouchers, education funding, and other issues.

HOUSE EDUCATION AND LABOR

Ruth J. Friedman

Director of Education Policy

230 Ford House Office Bldg.

Phone: (202) 226-2068

ruth.friedman@mail.house.gov

Personal: Born 12/25/1970 in Hong Kong.

Education: B.A., Pomona College, 1992. M.A., Arizona State University, 1996. Ph.D., Arizona State University, 1999. M.A., University of Chicago, 2000.

Professional: 1999–2000, postdoctoral fellow, Northwestern University. 2000–2001, American Psychological Association fellow, House Cmte. on Education and the Workforce. 2001–2007, committee staffer, House Cmte. on Education and Labor. 2007–2011, senior education policy advisor, House Cmte. on Education and Labor. 2011–present, director of education policy, House Cmte. on Education and the Workforce.

Expertise: Early childhood education, child welfare, juvenile justice.

Ruth Friedman has taken on a new role with the House Committee on Education and the Workforce in the first session of the 112th Congress. After focusing on education issues for several years, she is now the committee's director of education policy.

One of the first items on Friedman's agenda this session is the overdue reauthorization of the Elementary and Secondary Education Act, commonly known during the last administration as the No Child Left Behind Act. Since its adoption in 2001, the law has come under fire from both Republicans and Democrats. In early March at a hearing on the role of the federal government in education, Miller called for an outcomes-based approach to federal education policy and pointed to a need for an upgraded and aligned data system.

"We've evolved to a system where we have to hold a school responsible for what they can accomplish and not punish them for what they can't," Miller said. "The time has come to start thinking about how you transition to an information- and performance-based system."

Friedman is also working on several other pieces of legislation, including the Juvenile Justice and Delinquency Prevention Act, which provides the major source of federal funding to improve states' juvenile justice systems.

In addition Friedman is working on the Early Learning Challenge Fund which calls for states to develop new methods and raise the bar in early learning settings for children to ensure that more children enter kindergarten ready to learn.

HOUSE EDUCATION AND LABOR

Edwin J. Gilroy

Director of Workforce Policy

230 Ford House Office Bldg.

Phone: (202) 225-7101

Fax: (202) 225-9571

ed.gilroy@mail.house.gov

Personal: Born 04/17/1958 in Palos Verdes Estates, Calif.

Education: B.S., public administration, University of Southern California, 1981.

Professional: 1993–1997, professional staff member, House Cmte. on Education and the Workforce. 1997–2000, dir. of legislative affairs, American Trucking Associations. 2000–2001, vice president of legislative affairs, American Trucking Associations. 2001–present, dir. of workforce policy, House Cmte. on Education and the Workforce.

Expertise: Labor and employment policy, employee benefits.

With a faltering economy and high unemployment on the horizon, Director of Workforce Policy Ed Gilroy has a long list of items to focus on while working for Education and Workforce Committee Chairman John Kline, R-Minn.

In January, Gilroy worked on a hearing Kline held on the state of the American workforce, where the chairman expressed strong concerns on Obama administration's proposals and policies that he said have a chilling effect on job creation. He urged lawmakers to rethink policies that may undermine efforts by entrepreneurs and small business owners to invest in new opportunities and hire new workers.

During the hearing, committee members examined challenges facing the economy and the private-sector job market and heard testimony from witnesses regarding the challenges facing states, manufacturers and small business owners.

In February, Gilroy also worked on a hearing regarding policies and priorities at the U.S. Department of Labor, following up on allegations that policy actions taken by the National Labor Relations Board were skewed to toward special interests and impeded job creation.

Gilroy will also be watching so-called "card check" legislation, which took up much of his time during the 111th Congress. The Employee Free Choice Act would allow a union to be certified as the official union to bargain with an employer if union officials collect signatures of a majority of workers. But the legislation failed to become law during the 111th Congress.

The bill would have removed the present right of the employer to demand an additional, separate ballot where over half of employees have already given their signature supporting the union. Republicans have said the card check method is unreliable and would have opened workers to intimidation, coercion and the threat of retribution.

HOUSE EDUCATION AND LABOR

Amy Jones

Education Policy Counsel and Senior Advisor

2257 Rayburn House Office Bldg.

Phone: (202) 202-225-6558

amy.jones@mail.house.gov

Personal: Born 11/11/1976 in Milwaukee, Wis.

Education: B.A., political science and justice, American University, 1999. J.D., Washington College of Law at American University, 2003.

Professional: 1999–2000, legislative assistant, Dean Blakey Attorneys at Law. 2003–2005, attorney, Dean Blakey Attorneys at Law. 2005–present, education policy counsel and senior advisor, House Cmte. on Education and Labor.

Expertise: Higher education.

Amy Jones always had a fascination with policy and a yearning to work on Capitol Hill. She turned this interest into a career when she came to the House Committee on Education and the Workforce and became education policy counsel and a senior advisor to Republicans on the committee.

Growing up with a mother who was a teacher, Jones had a passing interest in education—but after graduating from college and earning her law degree she worked at a law firm specializing in education policy.

Before coming to the committee, Jones specialized in the higher education sector, working on issues related to the Pell grant program, representing the Consumer Bankers Association's Education Funding Committee and advising them on lending practices and representing their interests to the U.S. Department of Education.

That experience translates to Jones' current position where she is looking at higher education policies and regulations. During the first session of the 112th Congress Jones is monitoring gainful employment regulations for the for-profit education sector. The regulations include requirements that try to determine how many students become gainfully employed when they graduate from these programs, Jones said.

In February, Committee Chairman John Kline, R-Minn., Jones's boss, called for a new approach to gainful employment regulation for the for-profit education sector.

"Students should be empowered to make an informed decision about their education and we must ensure they have the information they need without targeting an entire sector of colleges and harming our economy," he said.

Kline is concerned that this type of regulation doesn't reflect the quality of the institution, Jones said. In addition, this sector is currently flourishing and the regulations proposed by the U.S. Department of Education could stifle that vitality.

The Department of Education is also in the process of implementing a full-scale direct loan program, known as the William D. Ford Direct Loan Program, which Jones is monitoring. The lender in this case is the Department of Education rather than a private bank.

During the 111th Congress, Jones worked on issues that included student aid, proposals that affected proprietary colleges, and teacher training policy.

Jones said she enjoys the fast pace of work on the Hill. "You never get through your to-do list and there's always something going on," she said, "but I thrive in this type of environment."

HOUSE EDUCATION AND LABOR

Barrett Karr

Republican Staff Director

2181 Rayburn House Office Bldg.

Phone: (202) 225-4527

barrett.karr@mail.house.gov

Personal: Born 09/23/1972 in Fort Worth, Texas.

Education: B.A., international relations, Texas Christian University, 1994. M.A., legislative affairs, George Washington University, 1998.

Professional: 1997–2005, chief of staff, U.S. Rep. Kay Granger, R-Tex.. 2000–2010, deputy assistant to the president, White House Legislative Affairs. 2005–2009, assistant to the president, White House Legislative Affairs. 2009–present, staff director, House Cmte. on Education and the Workforce.

Expertise: K-12 education, appropriations, higher education, workforce training, healthcare.

Barrett Karr landed at the House Committee on Education and the Workforce after spending years in the White House working under the Bush administration.

As Republican staff director for the committee, Karr manages about 50 people with expertise in all jurisdictions, makes policy recommendations to Chairman John Kline, R-Minn., monitors administrative hearings on related committee issues, and sets the committee schedule for hearings and markups.

In 2010, Karr described her management philosophy to *The Hill* newspaper as "Hire good people and let them do their jobs."

During the first session of the 112th Congress, Karr is working on reauthorization of the Elementary and Secondary Education Act. The law requires schools, districts, and states to collect a large amount of data on students and their progress, with mandates that they report the same data on multiple occasions in multiple areas. In March, the full committee held a hearing to analyze how compliance with data collection mandates creates unnecessary hurdles for K-12 schools, colleges, and universities.

Aside from education, Karr is focusing on healthcare items related to the Employee Retirement Income Security Act, which sets minimum standards for most voluntarily established pension and health plans in private industry to provide protection for individuals in these plans. Karr is also working on workforce training reform.

After leaving the White House, Karr got the inside track on the staff director job at the committee in 2009 when she was on maternity leave and heard that Kline, who she had gotten to know through her work with the White House, would be the next chairman. She told *The Hill* newspaper that she took her then four-month old daughter with her to drop off a good-luck note to him. When Kline's chief of staff called Karr a few days later to ask for recommendations for a staff director, she put her own name forward.

An avid swimmer, Karr also enjoys mountain biking and can ride a unicycle.

HOUSE EDUCATION AND LABOR

Richard D. Miller

Senior Labor Policy Advisor

2101 Rayburn House Office Bldg.

Phone: (202) 202-225-3725

richard.miller@mail.house.gov

Personal: Born in Boston, Mass.

Education: B.A., University of Massachusetts at Amherst.

Professional: 1984–2000, policy analyst, Oil, Chemical & Atomic Workers Union. 2001–2007, senior policy analyst, Government Accountability Project. 2007–2009, investigator, House Energy and Commerce Cmte. 2009–present, senior labor policy advisor, House Cmte. on Education and Labor.

Expertise: Worker health and safety, labor policy.

Richard Miller has a long history advocating on behalf of workers and looking at worker safety issues. As senior labor policy advisor for the Committee on Education and the Workforce, Miller is continuing that mission.

During the first session of the 112th Congress, Miller is focusing much of his time on mine safety issues. At a hearing in March, Miller's boss, Rep. George Miller, D-Calif., heard from the Mine Safety and Health Administration to examine its recent regulatory and enforcement actions.

Rep. Miller has made mine safety a high priority since a series of deadly mine accidents have taken place in the last few years. In 2010, 29 miners were killed in an explosion at Massey Energy's Upper Big Branch mine in West Virginia, even after the company was repeatedly cited for safety violations and ordered to shut down operations. Rep. Miller has said that shortcomings in mine safety law allowed some mine operators to find loopholes in mine safety regulations and the mine inspections system.

In March, Rep. Miller urged Congress to take action. During the last session mine safety legislation proposed by Rep. Miller and Rep. Lynn Woolsey, D-Calif. was blocked by Republicans. In January, Rep. Miller praised a proposal from the Mine Safety and Health Administration to revamp sanctions surrounding a "pattern of violation" for mining companies, in order to hold chronic mine safety violators accountable. He said the proposal was similar to provisions in the legislation he and Woolsey had proposed in the Robert C. Byrd Miner Safety and Health Act.

Senior Labor Policy Advisor Miller is also working closely with his boss on budget issues. Early in the year, Rep. Miller blasted Republicans for proposing cuts to the pre-K education program Head Start, aimed at preparing low-income students for kindergarten, as well as to job training and workplace safety programs. He urged the GOP to instead consider cuts aimed at big industry and financial institutions instead of targeting programs aimed at poor and minority citizens.

"It is simply irresponsible to leave working Americans without the critical services they need," Rep. Miller said.

During the first session of the 112th Congress, Richard Miller is also working on occupational safety issues and labor policy.

HOUSE EDUCATION AND LABOR

Megan O'Reilly

General Counsel

2101 Rayburn House Office Bldg.

Phone: (202) 225-3725

megan.oreilly@mail.house.gov

Personal: Born in Exeter, N.H.

Education: B.A., American University. J.D., DePaul University College of Law.

Professional: legislative assistant, Rep. Anna G. Eshoo, D-Calif. 2007–2011, labor policy advisor, House Cmte. on Education and Labor. 2011–present, general counsel, House Cmte. on Education and the Workforce., law clerk, Illinois Department of Children and Family Services.

Expertise: Labor policy.

Serving in a new position on the House Education and the Workforce Committee this year, Megan O'Reilly is expanding the issues on her plate.

Formerly labor counsel for the committee, O'Reilly was named general counsel in January. In that position, O'Reilly is advising ranking member Rep. George Miller, D-Calif., on parliamentary procedures, committee jurisdiction, and legislative planning and drafting. That means she's looking closely at a wide range of priorities for Democrats.

O'Reilly will be helping Miller as he focuses his energy in a number of areas: everything from reauthorization of the Elementary and Secondary Education Act, to mine safety and job creation.

In naming her to the new position, Miller noted in a press release that O'Reilly helped lead the panel in drafting and passing health care reform in 2010, and has extensive experience in both the public and private sector, having worked on the Hill in various capacities, as a law clerk at the Illinois Department of Children and Family Services and at the law firms McCarthy Duffy and Baker and McKenzie

At a hearing on the state of the American workforce in January, Miller called on the committee to work on solutions to help grow and strengthen the middle class. He said the federal government must support local efforts to create jobs, stay competitive, and increase the number of people in the skilled workforce.

Miller has also been outspoken in his continued support for strengthening mine safety regulations. Though Congress failed to pass the Robert C. Byrd Miner Safety and Health Act, which Miller authored in the 111th Congress, the committee's senior Democrat continues to push the issue forward. Early in the first session of the 112th Congress, the federal Mine Safety and Health Administration issued a proposal to revamp the so-called "pattern of violations" sanctions, which created loopholes for mining companies that repeatedly violated safety regulations. That proposal was similar to one contained in the Miner Act.

As one of the original architects of the federal No Child Left Behind Act, Miller also called for its reauthorization early in the session.

HOUSE EDUCATION AND LABOR

Julie Peller

Deputy Staff Director

2101 Rayburn House Office Bldg.

Phone: (202) 225-3725

julie.peller@mail.house.gov

Personal: Born in Glastonbury, Conn.

Education: B.A., political science, George Washington University, 2002. M.P.P., Georgetown University, 2004.

Professional: 2004–2006, budget analyst, U.S. Department of Education. 2006–2008, education policy advisor, House Cmte. on Education and Labor. 2008–2011, senior education policy advisor, House Cmte. on Education and Labor. 2011–present, deputy staff director, House Cmte. on Education and the Workforce.

Expertise: Higher education.

Specializing in higher education, Julie Peller continues to have her eye on some of the hot button issues in that arena, including making college more affordable and accessible to more students.

As senior education policy advisor to Rep. George Miller, D-Calif., Peller spent much of her time early in the first session of the 112th Congress looking at Pell Grants. Those federal grants for higher education are targeted at students from low-income families, and Miller has campaigned for years to increase funding for the program.

Unlike a loan, Pell Grants do not have to be repaid and are considered a foundation of federal financial aid, to which aid from other federal and nonfederal sources might be added. Students can receive up to two consecutive Pell Grant awards during a single award year to accelerate their program toward their degree.

Early in the year, the U.S. Department of Education announced that Pell Grant scholarships for the 2011-12 school year would be a maximum of $5,550 per students. In addition the department also announced that need-based student loan interest rates would drop to 3.4 percent. That fulfilled a 2006 Democratic promise to cut interest rates on need-based student loans in half, Miller said in February.

"With the maximum Pell Grant at a continued all-time high, we must continue our effort to make college affordable, to invest in students and keep college costs transparent," Miller said.

Peller was the lead staffer on the Student Aid and Fiscal Responsibility Act, which was included in the health care reconciliation bill that passed on March 21, 2010 by a vote of 220-211 and signed into law on March 30, 2010.

Prior to joining the Committee in 2006, Peller worked at the Department of Education as a Presidential Management Fellow in the Budget Service, where she served as a program and policy analyst for a portfolio of elementary and secondary education programs.

HOUSE EDUCATION AND LABOR

Amanda Schaumburg

Oversight Counsel

2257 Rayburn House Office Bldg.

Phone: (202) 225-6558

mandy.schaumburg@mail.house.gov

Personal: Born 01/08/1973 in Arlington, Texas.

Education: B.A., University of Wisconsin, 1995. J.D., Hamline University, 1999.

Professional: 1999–2001, deputy legal counsel, Gov. Tommy G. Thompson, R-Wis. 2001–2002, deputy legal counsel, Gov. Scott McCallum, R-Wis. 2003–2005, legal counsel, Office of Rep. Mark Green, R-Wis. 2003, chief legal counsel, Gov. Scott McCallum, R-Wis. 2005–2006, education policy counsel, House Cmte. on Education and the Workforce. 2006–2008, deputy assistant secretary, Office of Planning, Evaluation and Policy Development, U.S. Department of Education. 2008–2011, education policy counsel, House Cmte. on Education and Labor. 2011–present, oversight counsel, House Cmte. on Education and Labor.

Expertise: School Choice, charter schools, faith-based initiative, student privacy.

Mandy Schaumburg has a new title and new job duties after taking on the post of oversight counsel for Republicans on the House Education and Labor Committee.

As oversight counsel, Schaumburg looks at how programs are working and how policies are being implemented by several different agencies. The wide variety of issues she's working on during the first session of the 112th Congress includes job creation and American competitiveness as well as school and workplace concerns.

Early in 2011, Committee Chairman John Kline, R-Minn., was fighting hard against new regulations targeted at the for-profit education sector. These regulations try to determine how many students become gainfully employed when they graduate from these programs, but Kline has said the formula used is arbitrary and is stifling the growth of such programs.

Schaumburg and the committee also will focus on labor issues, with a number of hearings early in the session that included looking at the impact of the Occupational Safety and Health Administration's regulations on job creation.

During the 111th Congressional Session, Schaumburg worked towards reauthorization of the No Child Left Behind Act, also known as the Elementary and Secondary Education Act, which is yet to be reauthorized, as well as the successful reauthorizations of the Child Nutrition Act and the Child Abuse Prevention and Treatment Act.

This is Schaumburg's second stint with the committee and she also served as deputy assistant secretary in the Office of Planning, Evaluation and Policy at the Department of Education where one of her major issues was charter schools.

HOUSE EDUCATION AND LABOR

Michele Varnhagen

Chief Policy Advisor/Labor Policy Director

2101 Rayburn House Office Bldg.

Phone: (202) 225-3725

Michele.Varnhagen@mail.house.gov

Personal: Born 1960 in New York, N.Y.

Education: B.A., economics, New York University, 1982. J.D., Catholic University Law School, 1985.

Professional: 1984–1988, professional staff, Subc. on Labor Management. 1989–1994, professional staff, Subc. on Labor, Senate Cmte. on Health, Education, Labor, and Pensions. 1995–1998, USAID, former Soviet Union. 1999–2011, Democratic labor coordinator/counsel, House Cmte. on Education and Labor. 2011–present, chief policy advisor/labor policy director, House Cmte. on Education and the Workforce.

Expertise: Workforce development, pensions, health.

Michele Varnhagen spent most of her time in the 111th Congress working on healthcare legislation. In the 112th Congress Varnhagen has a new title—chief policy advisor/labor policy director—and she continues her work on healthcare.

During the last session, Congress passed a package of health insurance reforms as part of the Affordable Care Act on March 21, 2010. The healthcare package was aimed at protecting Americans from poor insurance industry practices, offering the uninsured and small businesses the opportunity to obtain affordable health care plans, and covering 32 million uninsured Americans.

But in 2011 the healthcare reforms came under attack from Republicans. In early February, Republicans attempted to repeal the law, but their efforts were blocked by Democrats. However, the GOP continued attempts to repeal aspects of the law or impede aspects of its implementation.

As part of her healthcare work, on behalf of Ranking Rep. George Miller, D-Calif., Varnhagen focused on a hearing in March before the Subcommittee on Health, Employment, Labor and Pensions examining the pressures of rising costs on employer-provided health care. In February, the full committee held a hearing on the impact of the health care law on the economy, employers and the workforce.

At February hearing, Miller acknowledged that the law did not contain all the provisions that he would have wanted and that it contained many provisions that the GOP did not like But he said, "The new law has unquestionably begun to deliver positive results, for small businesses, large employers, individuals, children and families, and the elderly."

Miller said the law is protecting workers and their families from discrimination by insurers based on preexisting conditions, that it's easing costs for prescription drugs and lowering other health care expenses.

HOUSE EDUCATION AND LABOR

Daniel Weiss

Chief of Staff/Special Advisor to the Ranking Member

2205 Rayburn House Office Bldg.

Phone: (202) 225-2095

daniel.weiss@mail.house.gov

Personal: Born 1962 in New York, N.Y.

Education: B.A., University of California at Santa Cruz, 1985.

Professional: 1985–1988, reporter, *States News Service*. 1987, freelancer, Santiago, Chile. 1988–1993, press secretary, Rep. George Miller, D-Calif. 1993–2006, senior advisor/chief of staff/special assistant, Rep. George Miller, D-Calif./House Cmte. on Education and the Workforce. 2007–present, chief of staff/special Assistant to the chairman, George Miller, D-Calif./House Cmte. on Education and the Workforce.

Expertise: Strategy, communications, healthcare, Elementary and Secondary Education Act.

After three years helping to set the agenda of the Committee on Education and the Workforce and driving the issues, both Daniel Weiss and his boss, U.S. Rep George Miller, D-Calif. are adjusting to a new reality.

Miller, now the ranking member of the committee, served as its chairman from 2007 to 2010. But the Republican takeover of Congress changed the dynamics.

Weiss acknowledged that "the specific legislative agenda of the committee, of course, will be determined" by the current chairman, Rep. John Kline, D-Minn. and the GOP.

But the savvy Weiss is not to be underestimated in getting Miller's priorities to the table. In January 2009, the Capitol Hill newspaper Roll Call listed Weiss, who serves as both chief of staff and special advisor to Miller, as on the top 50 movers and shakers behind the scenes

During the 112th Congress, Weiss said Miller's main focus is "creating jobs and growing the economy." Miller helped kick that effort off with a hearing before the House Democratic Steering and Policy Committee, of which Miller is a member, on the subject.

Though Miller acknowledged economic progress, it was not enough, he said. "That's why job creation must become priority number one for the new Congress as it already is for the American people," he said.

During the 111th Congress, Weiss saw success with a number of the pieces of legislation championed by Miller. Congress enacted the Lilly Ledbetter Fair Pay Act of 2009, the first bill signed into law by President Barack Obama, which amends the statute of limitations in the Civil Rights Act of 1964 when it comes to equal pay discrimination lawsuits. The 111th Congress also enacted the Affordable Care Act, part of the overall health care reform efforts of 2010, and the American Recovery and Reinvestment Act, designed to create new jobs spur economic activity and long-term growth.

HOUSE EDUCATION AND LABOR

Michael C. Zola

Chief Investigative Counsel

H2-230 Ford Office Bldg.

Phone: (202) 226-2068

michael.zola@mail.house.gov

Personal: Born 09/25/1965 in Trenton, N.J.

Education: B.A., Rider College (now Rider University), 1987. M.A., public and international affairs, University of Pittsburgh's Graduate School of Public and International Affairs, 1988. J.D., cum laude, Catholic University of America's Columbus School of Law, 2002.

Professional: 1989–2002, analyst, Government Accountability Office. 2002–2005, attorney, Office of General Counsel, Government Accountability Office. 2006–present, chief investigative counsel, House Cmte. on Education and Labor.

Expertise: Oversight, special investigations.

Though the legislative agenda in the House is being driven by a Republican majority in the 112th Congress, Chief Investigative Counsel Michael Zola said there are some issues that he, on behalf of Democrats on House Education and Workforce Committee, was sure to tackle this session.

Zola said he continues his work from previous sessions investigating instances of "sexual abuse associated with certain child care facilities and child abuse at K–12 public and private schools."

As part of that, Zola is working toward building bi-partisan support will for legislation similar to H.R. 6547, the Protecting Students from Sexual and Violent Predators Act, which passed the House last session The bill called for public schools to conduct comprehensive background checks for any employee using state criminal and child abuse registries and the FBI's fingerprint database. It would also prohibit schools from hiring or retaining anyone who had been convicted of certain violent crimes.

A 2010 report released by the Government Accountability Office found that individuals with histories of sexual misconduct were hired or retained, and in at least one instance broke existing state laws that prohibit offenders from being near children or on school grounds.

"It's hard not to support such legislation in light of what our investigative work with GAO has uncovered," Zola said.

Zola had significant success with the legislation he worked on during the 111th Congress. The House passed the Stop Child Abuse in Residential Programs for Teens Act of 2009, which seeks to protect teens attending treatment programs; the Keeping All Students Safe Act, which creates minimum standards for safe and limited use of seclusion and restraint techniques in some public and private schools; and the Protecting Students from Violent Predators Act.

Committee on Energy and Commerce

2125 Rayburn House Office Bldg.

Washington, DC 20515

Phone: (202) 225-2927

Twitter: @HouseCommerce

http://energycommerce.house.gov

Ratio: 31/23

MAJORITY MEMBERS

Fred Upton, MI-6th, Chairman

Joe Barton, TX-6th
Cliff Stearns, FL-6th
Ed Whitfield, KY-1st
John Shimkus, IL-20th
Joseph R. Pitts, PA-16th
Mary Bono Mack, CA-45th
Greg Walden, OR-2nd
Lee Terry, NE-2nd
Mike Rogers, MI-8th
Sue Wilkins Myrick, NC-9th
John Sullivan, OK-1st
Tim Murphy, PA-18th
Michael Burgess, TX-26th
Marsha Blackburn, TN-7th
Brian P Bilbray, CA-50th
Charles F Bass, NH-2nd
Phil Gingrey, GA-11th
Steve Scalise, LA-1st
Bob Latta, OH-5th
Cathy McMorris Rodgers, WA-5th
Gregg Harper, MS-3rd
Leonard Lance, NJ-7th
Bill Cassidy, LA-6th
Brett Guthrie, KY-2nd
Pete Olson, TX-22nd
David McKinley, WV-1st
Cory Gardner, CO-4th
Mike Pompeo, KS-4th
Adam Kinzinger, IL-11th
Morgan Griffith, VA-9th

MINORITY MEMBERS

Henry A. Waxman, CA-30th, Ranking Member

John D. Dingell, MI-15th
Edward J. Markey, MA-7th
Edolphus Towns, NY-10th
Frank Pallone Jr., NJ-6th
Bobby L. Rush, IL-1st
Anna G. Eshoo, CA-14th
Eliot L. Engel, NY-17th
Gene Green, TX-29th
Diana DeGette, CO-1st
Lois Capps, CA-23rd
Mike F. Doyle, PA-18th
Jan Schakowsky, IL-9th
Charles A. Gonzalez, TX-20th
Jay Inslee, WA-1st
Tammy Baldwin, WI-2nd
Mike Ross, AR-4th
Anthony D. Weiner, NY-9th
Jim Matheson, UT-2nd
G.K. Butterfield, NC-1st
John Barrow, GA-12th
Doris Matsui, CA-5th
Donna Christensen, VI-At Large

HOUSE ENERGY AND COMMERCE

JURISDICTION

(1) Biomedical research and development.
(2) Consumer affairs and consumer protection.
(3) Health and health facilities (except health care supported by payroll deductions).
(4) Interstate energy compacts.
(5) Interstate and foreign commerce generally.
(6) Exploration, production, storage, supply, marketing, pricing, and regulation of energy resources, including all fossil fuels, solar energy, and other unconventional or renewable energy resources.
(7) Conservation of energy resources.
(8) Energy information generally.
(9) The generation and marketing of power (except by federally chartered or federal regional power marketing authorities); reliability and interstate transmission of, and ratemaking for, all power; and siting of generation facilities (except the installation of interconnections between government waterpower projects).
(10) General management of the Department of Energy and management and all functions of the Federal Energy Regulatory Commission.
(11) National energy policy generally.
(12) Public health and quarantine.
(13) Regulation of the domestic nuclear energy industry, including regulation of research and development reactors and nuclear regulatory research.
(14) Regulation of interstate and foreign communications.
(15) Travel and tourism.
(16) The committee shall have the same jurisdiction with respect to regulation of nuclear facilities and use of nuclear energy as it has with respect to regulation of nonnuclear facilities and use of nonnuclear energy.

HOUSE ENERGY AND COMMERCE

Following a contentious campaign to lead the powerful House Energy and Commerce Committee, Rep. Fred Upton, R-Mich., beat back a challenge from, among others, Rep. Joe Barton, R-Texas, who had once headed the panel, to gain the chairmanship in 2011. Barton was given a largely ceremonial position as chairman emeritus with a seat on each of the six subcommittees.

One of Upton's first acts was to restructure the subcommittees by splitting the former Energy and Environment Subcommittee into two panels: the Energy and Economy, Oversight and Investigations, and the Energy and Power subcommittees.

The Environment and Economy Subcommittee, headed by Rep. John Shimkus, R-Ill., has jurisdiction over drinking water, nuclear waste, toxic substances, the Clean Water Act, Superfund, and chemical issues. The Energy and Power Subcommittee, chaired by Rep. Ed Whitfield, R-Ky., oversees energy regulation, the Clean Air Act, electricity transmission issues, and carbon limits.

In seeking the chairmanship, Upton faced some conservative criticism, including from tea party allies, over his past approach to environmental issues and support for an energy savings bill.

But with the full committee's authority over energy, health care, telecommunications, consumer safety, and trade, the new Republican majority in the House has gone about efforts to scale back environmental regulations and limit the power of the Environment Protection Agency, specifically in the area of reducing greenhouse gas emissions from power plants and other large industrial facilities.

"It is the goal of the House Committee on Energy and Commerce to remove the roadblocks to reliable energy," Upton wrote in *The Hill* newspaper. "More freedom for north American energy supplies means more freedom for consumers and businesses to use the affordable energy they need."

The change on the committee is "like night and day," said Jeremy Symons, senior vice president of the National Wildlife Federation, a nonpartisan organization that lobbied the committee to stem greenhouse gas emissions. "In the past, the committee majority viewed the Clean Air Act as an effective way to protect the public," Symons said. "Now the committee treats the Clean Air Act and the EPA as if they are the enemy."

Upton faces a formidable opponent on the committee with the former chairman and current ranking member, Rep. Henry Waxman, D-Calif., who is fighting to defend EPA's carbon programs and slow other GOP efforts, including on health care.

The full House voted 245-to-189 in January 2011 to repeal the Patient Protection and Affordable Care Act which President Barack Obama signed into law in March 2010. Republicans acknowledge the measure has little chance of passing the Senate. Still, they are pushing ahead on steps to cut off funding to enact some of the law's provisions, such as enforcement of the requirement that most Americans carry health insurance, expansion of the Medicaid program for the poor, and subsidies to offset the cost of buying insurance for lower-income workers.

HOUSE ENERGY AND COMMERCE

Kristin Lawes Amerling

Democratic Chief Counsel

2322A Rayburn House Office Bldg.

Phone: (202) 225-3641

kristin.amerling@mail.house.gov

Personal: Born in North Adams, Mass.

Education: B.A., Harvard College, 1987. J.D., Boalt Hall School of Law, University of California, Berkeley, 1995.

Professional: 1987–1988, production assoc., Interlock Media Assoc., Cambridge, Ma. 1988–1990, legislative asst., Rep. Ted Weiss, D-N.Y. 1990–1992, press secretary, Sen. George Mitchell, D-Maine. 1995–1997, associate, Steptoe & Johnson LLP. 1997–2007, minority counsel, House Cmte. on Government Reform. 2007–2008, chief counsel, House Cmte. on Oversight and Government Reform. 2009–present, chief counsel, House Cmte. on Energy and Commerce.

Expertise: Government affairs.

Kristin Amerling, Democratic chief counsel on the House Energy and Commerce Committee, is in the panel's minority for the first time since joining the committee staff in 2009 with her boss, ranking member Henry Waxman, D-Calif. Now much of her work in support of Waxman involves facing off against the contrary objectives of the Republican majority.

While no longer having the authority to direct a climate change bill through Energy and Commerce, Waxman can still expound on his views about legislation and investigations. "I think that we're always looking to find out the facts, and while we can't call a hearing and we can't issue subpoenas, we still have the ability to ask the right questions and we will continue to do that," Waxman told Environment & Energy Daily.

Amerling now assists her boss in making the case on such issues as why the U.S. EPA should not have its authority taken away—as the GOP favors—to regulate greenhouse gas emissions under the Clean Air Act. One of the Waxman staff's moves this year was to distribute a 2008 letter from then-EPA Administrator Stephen Johnson to President George W. Bush supporting a finding that greenhouse gases were detrimental to humans.

In her prior capacity as counsel for the House Oversight and Government Reform Committee, Amerling participated in the resurgence of congressional oversight activities under Waxman on everything from Iraq war contracts and false reporting on friendly fire deaths in combat to the outing of CIA operative Valerie Plame and steroid use in baseball.

The Maine native earned her B.A. from Harvard College and a juris doctorate from Boalt Hall School of Law at the University of California at Berkeley. During her Hill career, Amerling has been a senior Stennis congressional staff fellow and a presidential scholar.

HOUSE ENERGY AND COMMERCE

Gary J. Andres

Staff Director

2125 Rayburn House Office Bldg.

Phone: (202) 225-2927

gary.andres@mail.house.gov

Personal: Born in Medinah, Ill.

Education: B.A., Wheaton College, 1977. M.A., University of Illinois, 1980. Ph.D, public policy, University of Illinois, 1983.

Professional: 1982–1984, legislative assistant, Rep. Tom Corcoran, R-Texas. 1984–1985, vice president, Prudential Securities. 1985, executive director, federal relations, Southwestern Bell Corp. 1989–1993, deputy assistant, legislative affairs, Executive Office of the President, George H.W. Bush administration. 1993–2011, vice chairman, public policy and research, Dutko Worldwide, Inc. 2011–present, staff director, House Cmte. on Energy and Commerce.

Expertise: Health care issues, financial services, public policy, lobbying.

House Energy and Commerce Committee Staff Director Gary Andres has held previous congressional positions, but also comes from an extensive lobbying background and prior work for two Republican presidents.

Andres is no stranger to Capitol Hill, having provided public opinion research and analysis widely used there and elsewhere from his time as vice chairman at the Washington lobbying firm of Dutko Worldwide.

Much of his attention was on health care and financial services while at Dutko, in representing health care organizations and Fortune 500 corporations. Andres also made his views known in writing regularly for *The Weekly Standard Online*, *National Review*, *Real Clear Politics*, *Roll Call*, and *Politico*, in addition to publishing a book in 2008 titled **Lobbying Reconsidered**.

Andres was singled out as one of Washington's top lobbyists by *The Hill* newspaper in 2007. He was a deputy assistant for legislative affairs during the George H.W. Bush administration and later advised the transition team for incoming President George W. Bush on Senate confirmations. For the first half of 2001, he also worked on the White House Legislative Affairs staff as confirmation coordinator.

In his current role, Andres is at the center of Republican efforts on the committee to dismantle President Barack Obama's health care law and contest new climate change measures. In a 2009 column for *Politico* on climate change options, Andres said the administration could "dramatically scale back the bill passed by the House and craft a "climate change lite" or "enhanced energy" package, focusing more on energy exploration, nuclear power expansion, and alternative energy incentives than the more controversial cap-and-trade regulations."

Prior to joining Dutko Worldwide, Andres was Vice President for Washington Research at Prudential Securities and Executive Director of Federal Relations at Southwestern Bell Corp. He has been a research fellow at the American University Center for Congressional and Presidential Studies in Washington and was a floor coordinator at the 2004 Republican National Convention.

Andres worked for two Republican members of the Energy and Commerce Committee (Tom Corcoran of Illinois and Carlos Moorhead of California) following graduate school. Additionally, he has served as an advisor to Resurgent Republic, a 501(c)(4) organization involved in the debate over the proper role of government.

HOUSE ENERGY AND COMMERCE

Michelle Ash

Chief Counsel

2322A Rayburn House Office Bldg.

Phone: (202) 225-3641

michelle.ash@mail.house.gov

Personal: Born in Pittsburgh, Pa.

Education: B.A., economics, University of Michigan, 1988. J.D., University of Pittsburgh, 1992.

Professional: 1993–1997, legislative advisor, Rep. Ben Cardin, D-Md. 1997–2006, minority counsel, House Cmte. on Government Reform. 2006–2008, chief legislative counsel, House Cmte. on Oversight and Government Reform. 2009–2011, chief counsel, Subcmte. on Commerce, Trade, and Consumer Protection, House Cmte. on Energy and Commerce. 2011–present, chief Democratic counsel, Subcmte. on Commerce, Manufacturing, and Trade, House Cmte. on Energy and Commerce.

Expertise: Legislative procedure.

Democratic Chief Counsel Michelle Ash of the House Commerce, Trade and Consumer Protection Subcommittee, while now in the minority, is focusing her efforts on consumer protection topics she worked on as a majority staffer for Rep. Henry Waxman, D-Calif., the full committee's ranking member in the 112th Congress.

One of those areas remains reauthorizing of the Toxic Substances Control Act (TSCA), first enacted in 1976 to give the Environmental Protection Agency authority to regulate hazardous chemical use. The lack of timeliness in some of the TSCA provisions is considered one reason why toxic chemicals are present in children's toys and baby bottles. Industry and environmental can't agree on requirements for industry to provide exposure and toxicity data.

Another significant undertaking for Ash has been National Highway Traffic Safety Administration reform legislation. Waxman was the principal drafter of the NHTSA measure and offered a proposal allowing the NHTSA administrator to order a stop to all manufacturing, sales, and advertising of a vehicle determined to pose "an imminent hazard to public safety."

Although that provision came in response to the Toyota Motor Corp.'s safety recalls in the wake of a series of vehicle sudden accelerator incidents, the automobile industry opposes granting that power.

A related development regarding monitoring of deceptive and fraudulent conduct is the Consumer Product Safety Commission's launch of a product safety database for publicly available information. Questions were raised as to information accuracy in reports indicating harm about products and who could file reports.

A major sticking point was protection of confidential business information and possible disclosure of trade secrets or product misidentification. Ash worked on their resolution prior to launch of the database in March 2011.

HOUSE ENERGY AND COMMERCE

Phil Barnett

Democratic Staff Director

2322A Rayburn House Office Bldg.

Phone: (202) 225-3641

phil.barnett@mail.house.gov

Education: B.A., Princeton University, 1979. J.D., Harvard Law School, 1983.

Professional: 1983–1984, law clerk, U.S. Court of Appeals, 9th Circuit. 1984–1988, staff attorney, Sierra Club Legal Defense Fund, Alaska. 1988–1989, counsel, Subc. on Transportation and Hazardous Materials, House Cmte. on Transportation and Infrastructure. 1989–1994, counsel, Subc. on Health and Environment, House Cmte. on Energy and Commerce. 1995–1996, counsel, Rep. Henry A. Waxman, D-Calif. 1996, director of policy research, U.S. Food and Drug Administration. 1997–2003, chief Democratic counsel, House Cmte. on Government Reform. 2004–2008, Democratic staff dir., House Cmte. on Government Reform. 2009–present, Democratic staff director, House Cmte. on Energy and Commerce.

Expertise: Government affairs.

Phil Barnett, the Democratic staff director on the House Energy and Commerce Committee, has worked for Rep. Henry Waxman, D-Calif., the ranking member, since 1989. After being a lawyer for the Sierra Club in Alaska, he came to Washington and joined the House Transportation and Infrastructure Subcommittee.

A decade of his service to Waxman was on the House Government Oversight Committee, where he also worked with Waxman Chief of Staff Phil Schiliro. When Schiliro left to accept a position as congressional liaison and later special advisor for President Barack Obama, Barnett became Energy and Commerce staff director after Waxman secured the committee's chairmanship in 2009.

His influence and standing with Waxman brings Barnett into contact with every legislative measure the congressman pursues. After his boss became ranking member this year, Barnett worked on release of documents criticizing the Republicans' contention that Environmental Protection Agency regulation of carbon dioxide is unneeded and economically harmful.

A frequent move of the Democratic committee staff under Barnett is to release details of Republican positions on issues before hearings, giving Waxman an opportunity to criticize the proposals and enable a forum for his arguments. The staff also will introduce past GOP support for measures such as a clean energy standard to try to bridge some of the differences of opinion.

With last year's health care enactment, Barnett is helping Waxman counter House Republican efforts to change mandatory spending in the Patient Protection and Affordable Care Act to discretionary levels, and to lift state Medicaid eligibility.

In 2010, Barnett was proposed as a possible candidate to head the Government Accountability Office given his extensive oversight experience. But Republicans vetoed the idea saying that he would be too partisan a choice.

HOUSE ENERGY AND COMMERCE

James D. Barnette

General Counsel

2125 Rayburn House Office Bldg.

Phone: (202) 225-2927

jim.barnette@mail.house.gov

Personal: Born in New Haven, Conn.

Education: B.A., Political Science, Yale College, 1985. J.D., Georgetown Univ., 1990.

Professional: 1985–1987, legislative assistant, Sen. Arlen Specter, R-Pa. 1990–95, associate, Weil, Gotshal & Manges LLP. 1995–1998, majority counsel, House Cmte. on Energy and Commerce. 1998–2005, general counsel, House Cmte. on Energy and Commerce. 2003–2005, deputy staff director, House Cmte. on Energy and Commerce. 2005–2006, private practice, Collier Shannon Scott, PLLC. 2006, private practice, Scott Group, PLLC. 2007–2010, partner, government affairs and public policy, Steptoe & Johnson LLP. 2011, general counsel, House Cmte. on Energy and Commerce.

Expertise: Environmental law, telecommunications, health care, energy.

Jim Barnette, who served as House Energy and Commerce Committee general counsel in the last Republican-led House, assumed that same position with the committee at the start of the 112th Congress. During part of his time away, he was with the Washington lobbying firm of Steptoe & Johnson as a partner representing some of the industries he had helped to regulate.

Barnette, who previously served as general counsel and, for part of that time, deputy staff director, stepped down from the panel in March 2005 to join the Washington law firm of Collier, Shannon & Scott. He had worked under the chairmanships of Reps. Tom Bliley, R-Va., Billy Tauzin, R-La., and Joe Barton, R-Texas.

In that capacity, Barnette functioned as legal advisor on legislation pertaining to Medicare, health care, consumer protection, accounting improprieties in the energy sector, bioterrorism, medical malpractice, telecommunications, and e-commerce. He worked on passage of the Medicare Modernization Act and the Gramm-Leach-Bliley financial services law.

In late 2010, Barnette accepted an offer from incoming Chairman Fred Upton, R-Mich., to come back. "Chairman Upton called me in December to tell me he was thinking about revoking my leave of absence from the Committee. Although I was very happy at a premier international law firm, Steptoe & Johnson, I was thrilled by the challenge resulting from the Republican takeover of the House."

As the committee's lawyer, he is involved in everything from legislative drafting to ethics to parliamentary procedure. "Because I've been around a while, I'll serve as something of the institutional memory for Committee Republicans in developing policy."

One of those areas this year was Upton's own bill to bar the Environment Protection Agency from regulating greenhouse gas emissions under the Clean Air Act, in response to Republicans' concern the Obama administration would try and obtain through administrative action and regulation what it didn't achieve through the legislative process.

Barnette earned his law degree from Georgetown University in 1990 and his Bachelor of Arts degree from Yale College in 1985. After graduation from Yale, he was a legislative assistant for two years when Sen. Arlen Specter of Pennsylvania was a Republican

HOUSE ENERGY AND COMMERCE

Michael M. Beckerman

Deputy Staff Director

2125 Rayburn House Office Bldg.

Phone: (202) 225-2927

michael.beckerman@mail.house.gov

Education: B.A., George Washington Univ., 2001.

Professional: 2002, campaign field director, Rep. Fred Upton, R-Mich. 2003, legislative correspondent/special projects director, Rep. Fred Upton, R-Mich. 2003–2004, legislative director, Rep. Jack Quinn, R-N.Y. 2005–2007, legislative director, Rep. K. Michael Conaway, R-Texas. 2007–2011, policy director, Rep. Fred Upton, R-Mich. 2011–present, deputy staff director, House Cmte. on Energy and Commerce.

Expertise: Environmental issues, Technology, Telecommunications, Business Affairs, Energy, International Affairs.

Michael Beckerman, formerly policy director on the office staff of Rep. Fred Upton, R-Mich., became deputy staff director for the House Energy and Commerce Committee in 2011 when Upton assumed the chairmanship under Republican House control for the 112th Congress.

Beckerman first worked for the lawmaker when Upton was the chairman of the Energy and Commerce Telecommunications and Internet Subcommittee, as well as a senior member of the Energy and Air Quality Subcommittee. Beckerman handled legislative correspondent responsibilities then.

He came to the job having been the field director for Upton's 2002 primary campaign in Michigan. Later he joined the office of former Rep. Jack Quinn, R-N.Y., as legislative director for the Northeast-Midwest Congressional Coalition, a congressional member organization. Prior to rejoining Upton's staff, he was Rep. K. Michael Conway's, R-Texas, legislative director.

Now Beckerman is helping the panel's Republican members implement their legislative policy agenda, with considerable emphasis on preventing the Environmental Protection Agency from imposing greenhouse gas regulations in 2011. A constituent of Upton, who once met with Beckerman at the congressman's office in Washington, described the staffer afterward to a Michigan newspaper as thinking it's possible to find a balance between climate legislation and the economic crisis but as also saying that environmental action comes at the expense of the economy.

The majority on the committee is working toward the permanent blocking of EPA regulations of greenhouse gases under the Clean Air Act. Upton favors tapping into domestic oil-and-gas resources, arguing that restrictions harm jobs and increase the price of gasoline.

Beckerman also is helping Republicans as they pinpoint spending reductions for other agencies.

Before getting into politics, Michael was a water ski instructor for at-risk youth and a volunteer lifeguard. Once, on a sailing trip in Belize, he saved a young girl from drowning.

HOUSE ENERGY AND COMMERCE

Michael D. Bloomquist

Deputy General Counsel

2125 Rayburn House Office Bldg.

Phone: (202) 225-2927

Personal: Born in Royal Oak, Mich.

Education: B.A., history, Hamilton College (N.Y.), 1991. J.D., Washington University (St. Louis), 1995. LL.M., environmental law, George Washington University, 1997.

Professional: 1997–1999, attorney, Office of the Solicitor, Dept. of the Interior. 1999–2003, associate, environmental law, Patton Boggs, LLP. 2003, associate general counsel, House Cmte. on Science and Technology. 2003–2005, chief counsel, House Cmte. on Science and Technology. 2005–2007, deputy general counsel, House Cmte. on Energy and Commerce. 2007–2008, of counsel, Patton Boggs, LLP. 2008–2011, of counsel, Wiley Rein, LLP. 2011–present, deputy general counsel, House Cmte. on Energy and Commerce.

Expertise: House and committee procedures, legislative drafting, natural resources, pollution control law.

Deputy General Counsel Michael Bloomquist returned to that position on the Energy and Commerce Committee in the 112th Congress after a four-year absence.

"The great thing about my job is I get to work on all the biggest issues," the Republican staffer said.

He works for Chairman Fred Upton, R-Mich., and assists on legislative operations and jurisdictional questions. Part of his responsibilities are helping the subcommittees prepare for legislative markups, anticipating amendments, issuing follow-ups, and preparing for floor debate.

Bloomquist likes to say he works on bills from their birth to conclusion on the House floor. His first tour on the Hill had been his only one until returning in early 2011.

He left energy and commerce in 2007 to return to Patton Boggs where he had worked previously before moving to Wiley Rein. Bloomquist had been with the Science and Technology Committee and the Interior Department before becoming a lobbyist.

While in private practice he concentrated on energy, environmental, and climate matters. Most of his congressional interaction while away from the Hill was on the Senate side in handling issues for his clients.

Since coming back to the committee, Bloomquist has worked on health care, climate change, and network neutrality. When he was with the panel before, he also was involved in net neutrality during consideration of a broadband bill.

While telecommunications and internet issues are a big part of Wiley Rein's business, Bloomquist during his time at the firm didn't work on net neutrality specifically as his practice then was climate and energy.

House Republicans have opposed the idea of the federal government being able to regulate the internet or telecommunications. Other related subjects on which Bloomquist is working include looking at reallocation of broadcast spectrum, auctioning, and cyber security.

HOUSE ENERGY AND COMMERCE

Maryam Sabbaghian Brown

Chief Counsel, Subcmte. on Energy and Power

2125 Rayburn House Office Bldg.

Phone: (202) 225-2927

maryam.brown@mail.house.gov

Education: B.S., Louisiana State Univ., 1997. J.D., Louisiana State Univ., 2000.

Professional: 2000–2004, associate, Pillsbury Winthrop Shaw Pittman. 2004–2006, staff director, House Cmte. on Energy and Commerce. 2006–2008, policy counsel, House Subcmte. on Energy and Mineral Resources, House Cmte. on Natural Resources. 2008–2010, manager for policy and strategic planning, ConocoPhillips. 2010, policy counsel, Senate Republican Policy Committee. 2011–present, chief counsel, Subcmte. on Energy and Power, House Cmte. on Energy and Commerce.

Expertise: Energy and power issues.

Maryam Sabbaghian Brown returned to the House Energy and Commerce Committee in 2011 as Republican chief counsel for the newly created Energy and Power Subcommittee. It was formed out of the Energy and Environment Subcommittee with the establishment of a new Environment and Economy Subcommittee.

In between prior House and Senate tenures, Brown was manager for public policy at ConocoPhillips. She also worked on energy and environmental issues with the Senate Republican Policy Committee and was with the House Energy and Mineral Resources Subcommittee.

Her current jurisdiction includes national energy policy, energy regulation, and regulation of nuclear power plants. Of paramount concern are the possible actions of the Environmental Protection Agency related to energy costs and U.S. competitiveness.

As reported in *National Journal* in 2011, Brown challenged the contention of Energy and Commerce Ranking Member Henry Waxman, D-Calif., that curtailing the EPA's ability to regulate greenhouse gases under the Clean Air Act could also jeopardize fuel economy standards. She "retorted that the National Highway Traffic Safety Administration's fuel-efficiency regulations would not be impacted."

In the wake of cap-and-trade legislation failing to pass in the 111th Congress, the industry fears the EPA may attempt a similar agenda through a series of regulations, Brown told a Bipartisan Policy Center program. House Republicans don't believe the Clean Air Act is an appropriate tool for regulation of greenhouse gases, she stressed.

Utilities do not know what federal environmental regulations they could face on carbon dioxide and other emissions, Brown stated at the policy forum. That may hinge in part on how aggressively the new Republican majority seeks to curtail the EPA's rule-making, she noted.

Republican members this year ask whether energy industry regulations address health benefits or worsen economic and competitiveness problems. Consequently, Republican and some Democratic members wonder whether additional environmental regulations are necessary if the United States is facing real economic competition from China. It has far more coal consumption and is building nuclear plants when the United States is not, Brown has said in public comments. It also consumes a large amount of hydroelectricity.

In addition, Energy and Commerce is looking at the Federal Energy Regulatory Commission rule-making regarding transmission lines.

HOUSE ENERGY AND COMMERCE

Howard Cohen

Chief Health Counsel

2125 Rayburn House Office Bldg.

Phone: (202) 225-2927

howard.cohen@mail.house.gov

Education: B.A., Illinois University. Ph.D, psychology, University of Massachusetts. J.D., George Washington University.

Professional: 1988–1999, health counsel, House Cmte. on Energy and Commerce. 1999–2001, lobbyist, Greenberg Traurig LLP. 2001, lobbyist, Verner, Liipfert et al. 2001–2010, president, HC Associates. 2011–present, chief health counsel, House Cmte. on Energy and Commerce.

Expertise: Health policy, health insurance.

House Energy and Commerce Committee Chief Health Counsel Howard Cohen returned to his former position in 2011 after more than a decade away as a health care lobbyist. He had headed the Washington lobbying firm of HC Associates and represented members of the pharmaceutical and private insurance industries as well as their trade groups, hospitals, and other health care providers.

Cohen was the committee's chief counsel from 1988–1999 when Republicans were last in charge of the House. Then many of his duties revolved around federal regulation of health insurance and also pharmaceuticals under the Food, Drug, and Cosmetic Act, as well as Medicare and Medicaid.

He again is working on health care policy, this time in re-opening the discussion of health care reform with the ongoing GOP effort to repeal the Obama health care law enacted in 2010. Republicans also have criticized the administration's granting of waivers to states for the annual dollar limit requirements affecting low-cost health, without which states could not afford to participate under the law's coverage rules.

"Cohen has long been considered a go-to person on health care policy on K Street and has represented a number of clients that will have interests before the committee in 2011," Kaiser Health News stated. "[In 2010] he was registered to lobby for America's Health Insurance Plans, Amgen, Federation of American Hospitals, Genzyme, Group Health Cooperative, Health Net and PhRMA [Pharmaceutical Research and Manufacturers of America], according to the Senate Office of Public Records."

Cohen has come in for criticism at times over his lobbying activities. Public Citizen's Congress Watch for June 2003, focusing on drug company representatives, said he "parlayed a decade" of Hill work "into more than $1 million in lobbying income from dug companies [in 2002]."

Aside from his time as president of HC Associates, Cohen was a health policy consultant with the law firm of Greenberg Traurig. He received his bachelor's degree from Illinois University, a doctorate from the University of Massachusetts in Psychology, and a law degree from George Washington University.

HOUSE ENERGY AND COMMERCE

Gregory J. Dotson

Chief Environmental and Energy Counsel

2322A Rayburn House Office Bldg.

Phone: (202) 225-3641

greg.dotson@mail.house.gov

Personal: Born in Charleston, S.C.

Education: B.A., Virginia Tech, 1992. J.D., Univ. of Oregon, 1995.

Professional: 2000–2007, Democratic counsel, House Cmte. on Oversight and Government Reform. 2007–2009, chief environmental counsel, House Cmte. on Oversight and Government Reform. 2009–2011, Democratic chief counsel, Subcmte. on Energy and Environment, House Cmte. on Energy and Commerce. 2011–present, Democratic chief counsel for environment, House Cmte. on Energy and Commerce.

Expertise: Environmental and energy issues.

Greg Dotson's role as Democratic environmental and energy counsel on the House Energy and Commerce Committee has shifted back to the full committee with his boss, Rep. Henry Waxman, D-Calif., now the ranking member. Waxman, while chairman, had named him chief counsel to the then-Subcommittee on Energy and Environment in the 111th Congress.

But with Republicans winning House control in the November 2010 elections, and Waxman again becoming ranking member, current Chairman Fred Upton, R-Mich., choose to split energy and environment into two subcommittees: Environment and Economy and Energy and Power.

As a recognized energy staffer Dotson, who first joined Waxman's staff in 1996, has worked actively on climate change legislation, energy policy as well as the energy provisions in the American Recovery and Reinvestment Act of 2009, and public health and food and water safety. In 2010, he assisted Rep. Edward Markey, D-Mass., in his investigation of the causes of the BP oil spill in the Gulf of Mexico.

Dotson moved with Waxman in 2009 to the energy and commerce committee from the House Oversight and Government Reform Committee which the congressman had previously chaired.

This year Dotson is facing Republican resistance to cap-and-trade legislation as well as U.S. EPA regulations to lower greenhouse gases, along with the GOP's de-emphasis on clean energy standards. The impetus instead is on more oil and gas extraction and removing restrictions on oil drilling.

One potential area for compromise with House Republicans may be the curtailing of regulation of coal-fired power plants and additional industrial facilities. But any such measure would likely include blocking the EPA's authority to regulate emissions, something that Waxman, and Dotson acting on his behalf, will oppose.

HOUSE ENERGY AND COMMERCE

Neil Fried

Republican Chief Counsel, Subcommittee on Communications and Technology

2125 Rayburn House Office Bldg.

Phone: (202) 225-2927

neil.fried@mail.house.gov

Personal: Born in New York, N.Y.

Education: B.S., Northwestern University, 1991. J.D., Washington University of St. Louis, 1994.

Professional: 1996–2000, attorney, Common Carrier Bureau, Federal Communications Commission. 2000–2002, associate, Verner, Liipfert, Bernard, McPherson & Hand. 2002–2003, associate, Paul, Hastings, Janofsky & Walker. 2003, telecommunications counsel, House Cmte. on Energy and Commerce. 2003–2007, counsel, House Cmte. on Energy and Commerce. 2007–2011, senior telecommunications counsel, House Cmte. on Energy and Commerce. 2011–present, chief counsel, Subcmte. on Communications and Technology, House Cmte. on Energy and Commerce.

Expertise: Telecommunications.

Neil Fried, a House Energy and Commerce Committee staff member since August 2003, continues in his position as the Republican chief counsel for the Subcommittee on Communications and Technology. He advises Rep. Fred Upton, R-Mich., chairman of the full committee, and Rep. Greg Walden, R-Ore., the subcommittee chairman, on media, telecommunications, spectrum, and internet-related matters.

A vocal critic of net neutrality rules who has compared the Federal Communications Commission's order to the Ministry of Truth in George Orwell's "1984," Fried thinks a resolution nullifying the order could pass in the current Congress. At the same time, Fried views the 2010 election outcome as reflecting the public's support for less government intervention, including in the communications industry.

As telecommunications counsel, he is keeping a wary eye on online privacy protection and internet entrepreneurs. "I don't see the issue [of privacy] going away," Fried told a State of the Net conference panel in early 2011.

Two energy and commerce members, Reps. Edward Markey, D-Mass., and Joe Barton, R-Texas, asked Facebook founder Mark Zuckerberg about the privacy implications of a Facebook data request feature that would enable Web sites and application developers to obtain user's home addresses, phone numbers, and other such information.

Both lawmakers were concerned over the misuse of unique identifiers, known as UIDs, which are paired with Facebook profiles.

Fried worked on the legislation for the 2009 conversion to digital television and spent three years in private practice specializing in telecommunications. Aside from working as an attorney for four years with the FCC's Common Carrier Bureau implementing the Telecommunications Act of 1996, he was a law fellow for the Reporters Committee for Freedom of the Press.

HOUSE ENERGY AND COMMERCE

Karen L. Lightfoot

Senior Policy Advisor and Communications Director

2322A Rayburn House Office Bldg.

Phone: (202) 225-3641

karen.lightfoot@mail.house.gov

Personal: Born in Bethesda, Md.

Education: B.A., Yale University, 1990. M.P.P., Princeton University, 1992.

Professional: 1977–1985, staff, House Majority Whip Thomas S. Foley, D-Wash. 1992–1997, lobbyist, Center on Budget and Policy Priorities. 1997–2002, professional staff member, Democratic senior policy advisor, House Cmte. on Government Reform. 2002–2007, Democratic senior policy advisor/communications dir., House Cmte. on Government Reform. 2007–2008, senior policy advisor and communications director, House Cmte. on Oversight and Government Reform. 2009–present, senior policy advisor and communications director, House Cmte. on Energy and Commerce.

Expertise: Oversight, health care, consumer issues.

Karen Lightfoot continues as senior advisor and communications director for the House Energy and Commerce Committee with the accompanying differences of Democrats now being in the minority. Her boss, Rep. Henry Waxman, D-Calif., moved from chairman to ranking member as House Republicans regained the majority in the 2010 elections.

The Republicans are undertaking intensified challenges to last year's passage of the health care law and to the existence of global climate change. Republican members are trying to strip the Environmental Protection Agency of the authority to regulate greenhouse gas emissions.

In her job, Lightfoot reiterates Waxman's frequent opposition to Republicans on health care and energy and their attempts to reverse prior legislative action under Democrats. In 2010, Lightfoot had to acknowledge an existing gap in the new health care law's protection of children, with insurance companies still able to refuse new coverage to them because of preexisting medical problems.

If a child was accepted by a health plan or was already covered, the insurer could not bar payment for a specific illness, Lightfoot pointed out.

Waxman has rebuked Republicans on the committee and elsewhere in the House for voting to repeal the health law and for being "the party of science deniers" regarding climate factors. When he headed the energy committee in 2009, he helped manage passage of a House climate bill that did not advance to the Senate but has subsequently said he would necessarily call for the same carbon caps in any new legislation.

Lightfoot is assisting the committee Democrats this year in arguing for a clean energy standard and in questioning whether some extensive GOP document requests of agencies are largely attempts to thwart the departments from carrying out their designated functions.

HOUSE ENERGY AND COMMERCE

Ryan Long

Chief Counsel, Subcommittee on Health

2125 Rayburn House Office Bldg.

Phone: (202) 225-2927

ryan.long@mail.house.gov

Education: B.A., Univ. of North Carolina, 1997. J.D., Catholic University, 2005.

Professional: 1999, legislative correspondent, Rep. Charlie Norwood, R-Ga. 1999–2003, legislative assistant, Rep. Joe Barton, R-Texas. 2003–2004, legislative director, Rep. Joe Barton, R-Texas. 2004–2006, professional staff member, Subcmte. on Oversight and Investigations, House Cmte. on Energy and Commerce. 2007–2011, chief health counsel, House Cmte. on Energy and Commerce. 2011–present, chief health counsel, Subcmte. on Health, House Cmte. on Energy and Commerce.

Expertise: Health policy issues.

Ryan Long joined the House Energy and Commerce Committee staff in April 2004, working on health issues mostly in the areas of the Food and Drug Administration and Medicare. He became chief health counsel in 2006 and will continue that role in the 112th Congress for the Subcommittee on Health devoting his efforts to health policy.

The health care law implementation is the primary focus for the subcommittee this year. With that too comes work on Medicare physician payment, trying to have more flexibility for states in their Medicaid programs as they face budget shortfalls, and monitoring the FDA.

But the emphasis is on the Patient Protection of Affordable Care Act that President Barack Obama signed into law in March 2010 because of its wide ranging effects on the entire health care system and the federal budget.

A major part of Long's focus is the Republican effort to repeal the health care law with the House voting to do that in early 2011. "It's such a wide ranging law with so many different components that we'll be examining all of those different components as well as what we view as better solutions than the health care law," he said.

While wholesale repeal remains part of the GOP agenda, so many elements have so many ramifications for different sectors of the health care industry that the subcommittee also is looking at individual sections of the law. One such area is the requirements on states to maintain their Medicaid eligibility in return for federal funds.

The absence of a public plan option does not remove existing problems of the health care law as it was passed in 2010, Long said. "The public plan was probably one avenue that supporters saw to get to their end result," he said.

Still some of the remaining parts of the law have what Republican members view as damaging effects on the private health care sector regardless of the public plan's exclusion.

Issues related to the FDA will be significant, he added, leading up to creating the foundation for reauthorizing both the prescription drug user fee and the medical device user fee.

Prior to going to Energy and Commerce, Long was legislative assistant and later legislative director for Rep. Joe Barton, R-Texas. He dealt then with energy issues, agriculture, defense, and most subjects outside of telecom. He began his Hill career in the office of the late Rep. Charlie Norwood, R-Ga.

HOUSE ENERGY AND COMMERCE

Alexa Marrero

Communications Director

2125 Rayburn House Office Bldg.

Phone: (202) 225-2927

alexa.marrero@mail.house.gov

Personal: Born in Baraboo, Wis.

Education: B.A., Creighton University, 2002.

Professional: 2002–2006, deputy communications director, House Cmte. on Education and Labor. 2006–2007, vice president, communications and industry relations, Education Finance Council. 2007–2011, communications director, House Cmte. on Education and Labor. 2011–present, communications director, House Cmte. on Energy and Commerce.

Expertise: Communications, education, health care, energy, labor.

Republican Communicators Director Alexa Marrero assumed a similar role on the Energy and Commerce Committee in 2011 from the position she had held before on the House Education and Labor Committee (the title of which was changed to Education and the Workforce just prior to her leaving). She came on board with Rep. Fred Upton, R-Mich., assuming the chairmanship.

"Communicators tend to be jacks of all trades," she said.

One dominant issue before energy and commerce on which Marrero worked previously for the education committee is health care. The objective for most Republicans in the current Congress is to repeal and replace the health care law passed in 2010.

The GOP is seeking what it considers more affordable health reforms. The committee's focus is on looking at the law piece by piece and at the consequences of its existing provisions of which the general public may not have been aware, Marrero said.

As the spokeswoman she divides her time among all the issues before the panel this year. Marrero works with the all subcommittees as well because of the amount of work done at that level, she noted. "[In] holding a hearing at the subcommittee level you have fewer members, which means you have more time to ask additional rounds of questions to really get information from the witnesses."

Another subject on which Marrero represented the views of GOP committee members was their support for halting the Federal Communications Commission's network neutrality regulations. The FCC passed the measure in December 2010 to bar broadband providers from blocking access to internet content and services that may compete with them.

The full House ultimately voted to repeal the net neutrality rules in maintaining that they would be a disincentive for phone and cable companies to upgrade their networks in not being able to offer expanded premium services.

HOUSE ENERGY AND COMMERCE

David McCarthy

Chief Energy Counsel

2125 Rayburn House Office Bldg.

Phone: (202) 225-2927

david.mccarthy@mail.house.gov

Education: B.A., University of Notre Dame, 1974. J.D., George Mason University School of Law, 1980.

Professional: 1980–1988, assoc. staff member, House Cmte. on Appropriations, Subcommittee on Energy and Water Development. 1988–1989, attorney, Baker & Daniels. 1989–1993, counsel, House Cmte. on Standards and Official Conduct. 1994–1995, private practice. 1996–2001, assistant general counsel, Indianapolis Power & Light (Washington, D.C.). 2002–2003, counsel, House Select Cmte. on Homeland Security. 2004–2005, chief of congressional and legislative affairs, U.S. Bureau of Reclamation. 2005–2006, deputy commissioner, U.S. Bureau of Reclamation. 2006–2008, chief energy counsel, House Cmte. on Energy and Commerce. 2008–2011, vice president, Algenol Biofuels. 2011–present, chief energy counsel, House Cmte. on Energy and Commerce.

Expertise: Energy, appropriations.

David McCarthy, the Republican chief counsel to the Subcommittee on Environment and the Economy, returned to Capitol Hill in 2011 having left and resumed the congressional staff positions previously.

"I'm the bad penny that keeps coming back," he said.

McCarthy held the same position with the Energy and Commerce Committee between 2006 and 2008 when he departed to become vice president for government affairs and business strategy at Algenol Biofuels, a private start-up alternative fuels firm specializing in developing ethanol from algae.

His congressional tenure extends back to January 1980 with the House Appropriations Subcommittee on Energy and Water Development. He remained until going into private law practice before again returning to the Hill as counsel on the House Committee on Standards and Official Conduct.

Returning to the private sector, he worked primarily as an assistant general counsel for Indianapolis Power and Light doing legal work, some lobbying, and corporate strategic planning.

In his current position on the subcommittee, he is working on the regulation of nuclear waste, toxic substances, and solid waste disposal including Superfund; soil and water contamination; mining, oil, gas, and coal combustion wastes; drinking water; and industrial plant security.

A related subject before the committee this year is consideration of extending the Chemical Facility Anti-Terrorism Standards Program (CFATS) for seven years, authorizing the Homeland Security Department to continue its security efforts at U.S. chemical plants.

McCarthy is reluctant to prioritize any one of the issues but noted the dominance of the nuclear waste question following the crisis with Japan's tsunami-ravaged Fukushima Nuclear Power Plant in March 2011.

HOUSE ENERGY AND COMMERCE

Karen Nelson

Deputy Democratic Staff Director, Subcommittee on Health

2322A Rayburn House Office Bldg.

Phone: (202) 225-3641

karen.nelson@mail.house.gov

Personal: Born in Elgin, Ill.

Education: B.A., Cornell University.

Professional: 2000–present, special assistant, Rep. Harry Waxman, D-Calif. 2007–2009, health policy director, House Cmte. on Oversight and Government Reform. 2009–present, deputy committee staff director, Subcmte. on Health, House Cmte. on Energy and Commerce.

Expertise: Health care policy.

Karen Nelson, the long-serving senior health policy advisor to Rep. Henry Waxman, R-Calif., has had little time this year to rest on her legislative laurels with passage of the new health care law in 2010. While a signal achievement for Nelson and her boss, the ranking member of the House Energy and Commerce Committee, Republicans who now control the House are at work on attempting to repeal the law.

Knowing the Senate is unlikely to follow suit, House Republicans are seeking to cut off funding for certain of the law's provisions, such as the requirement that most Americans carry health insurance.

A dominant issue for Nelson this year is the Obama administration's one-year waivers granted to limited benefit plans. House Republicans criticized the Department of Housing and Human Services for allowing the waivers to four states: Florida, Tennessee, New Jersey, and Ohio—and to more than 900 health plans.

President Barack Obama said he would support giving states authority to apply for waivers from provisions of the health care law beginning in 2014, instead of in 2017 as the law now requires, if states could create plans with coverage as comprehensive and affordable as that offered under other means.

Republicans on the Energy and Commerce Subcommittee on Oversight and Investigations said the waivers demonstrate the health law has serious problems, while Democrats on the panel accused them of trying to block implementation of the law. Waxman disputed that the waivers were made for political allies.

Another ongoing issue for Nelson is responding to GOP support for Medicaid block grants to control program costs by giving states an established dollar amount for Medicaid, instead of a percentage of costs.

HOUSE ENERGY AND COMMERCE

John S. O'Shea

Senior Health Policy Advisor

Rep. Fred Upton, R-Mich.

2322 Rayburn House Office Bldg.

Phone: (202) 225-2927

John.OShea@mail.house.gov

Education: M.A., History and Sociology of Science, University of Pennsylvania, 2002. M.A., Public Administration, John F. Kennedy School of Government, Harvard University, 2006.

Professional: 2006–2007, graduate fellow in Health Policy, Heritage Foundation. 2009–2010, assistant professor of Surgery, Montefiore Medical Center, Albert Einstein Medical College. 2011–present, senior health policy Advisor, House Committee on Energy and Commerce.

Expertise: Health Policy, Medicare, Medicaid, Physician Payment.

A former practicing general surgeon and Health Policy Fellow at the Heritage Foundation in Washington, John O'Shea joined the House Energy and Commerce Committee in 2011 as a senior Republican health policy advisor.

O'Shea said his professional experience—which includes 17 years in private practice in New Jersey—and not specifically the passage of the Obama health care law in 2010, drew him to the committee. O'Shea's view is that too much government involvement exists already in the doctor-patient relationship with the potential for more. In his past writings, O'Shea has favored doctors being able to contract with patients and determine their own prices.

"I think a lot of the provisions in the new health reform law sort of drive a wedge between the patient and their doctor and interfere with the traditional patient-doctor relationship," O'Shea said.

He is bringing his work both as a medical practitioner and a health policy specialist to the Energy and Commerce Committee in considering ways to reform health care. "Once you get finished with the policy issues and the economic and political impact of policies, then the bottom line is that reforming the health care system is about taking care of patients," he said.

The principal policy issues for him are the Medicare physician payment system, Medicaid quality and access, and ways to reform the emergency medical delivery system to relieve the burden on hospital emergency rooms.

O'Shea also hopes to achieve some results in medical malpractice reform in terms of reducing adverse consequences for medical professionals by providing relief from malpractice lawsuits in the delivery of hospital emergency care to uninsured patients.

He is concerned about the growing numbers of patients who come for care and are unable to pay for it, with the resulting impact on taxpayers and those with private health insurance. During his Heritage fellowship, he wrote that private insurance should move away from having the government determine health benefits to a defined contribution structure instead.

Medicare could begin to control expenses if it provided more for the specific needs of seniors, in his opinion. O'Shea doesn't believe that universal health care can be achieved by increasing the government's role or in mandating universal coverage.

While he has given up his own direct participation in medicine, O'Shea said he thinks it has become more common for medical professionals to be working in Congress now as lawmakers and staff.

HOUSE ENERGY AND COMMERCE

Roger C. Sherman

Democratic Chief Counsel, Subcommittee on Communications and Technology

2322A Rayburn House Office Bldg.

Phone: (202) 225-3641

roger.sherman@mail.house.gov

Personal: Born in New York, N.Y.

Education: B.A., Amherst College, 1988. J.D., Harvard, 1995.

Professional: 1988–1989, staff assistant, Senate Subc. on Labor. 1989–1990, legislative aide, Sen. Alan Cranston, D-Calif. 1990–1992, legislative assistant, Rep. Henry Waxman, D-Calif. 1995, legal intern, White House Office of Legal Counsel. 1995–1997, associate, Wiley, Rein & Fielding. 1997–2007, senior attorney/director, Sprint Nextel Corp. 2007–2009, deputy chief counsel, House Cmte. on Oversight and Government Reform. 2009–present, chief counsel, Subcmte. for Communications and Technology, House Cmte. on Energy and Commerce.

Expertise: Telecommunications.

Roger Sherman, the Democratic chief counsel for the House Energy and Commerce Subcommittee on Communications and Technology since January 2009, is concentrating in 2011 on the Federal Communications Commission's network neutrality rules. The issue divides Republicans and Democrats in Congress and on the FCC, with House GOP members seeking to dismantle the rules deeming them governmental interference with network management.

Sherman thinks President Barack Obama would veto any congressional effort to overturn the rules with net neutrality being part of the technology platform he campaigned on, but Sherman expects a court challenge and seems less sure about that outcome.

With a 2010 release of the first National Broadband Plan and the first set of rules to maintain open internet access, the FCC is trying to make major changes under intensified congressional scrutiny. The broadband proposal calls for freeing up more airwaves for wireless connectivity by way of incentive auctions.

Sherman also works on the reform of the $8 billion a year Universal Service Fund, a topic which divides rural and urban interests in the deployment of broadband in rural America. The fund now subsidizes basic phone service in low-income areas and sparsely populated regions.

Before his present position, Sherman worked on financial and corporate accountability issues for Rep. Henry Waxman, D-Calif., on the House Oversight and Government Reform Committee, and then went with Waxman to the Energy and Commerce Committee.

Sherman also was as a legislative assistant to Waxman, a legislative aide to Sen. Alan Cranston, D-Calif., and a staff assistant on the Senate Labor Subcommittee. In between his jobs on Capitol Hill, he was a director of regulatory affairs and senior attorney for a wireless telecommunications company and spent two years in private practice at a Washington law firm.

HOUSE ENERGY AND COMMERCE

Alan M. Slobodin

Republican Chief Counsel
Subcommittee on Oversight and Investigations
2322A Rayburn House Office Bldg.
Phone: (202) 225-5631
Alan.Slobodin@mail.house.gov

Personal: Born in Holmdel, N.J.

Education: B.B.A., Temple University, 1979. J.D., George Washington University, 1984.

Professional: 1984–1985, attorney, Ross, Dixon and Masback. 1985–1986, assistant general counsel, Washington Legal Foundation. 1986–1989, minority counsel, Subc. on Civil and Constitutional Rights, House Cmte. on the Judiciary. 1989–1995, president/general counsel, legal studies division, Washington Legal Foundation. 1995–2006, oversight counsel, House Cmte. on Energy and Commerce. 2007–present, Chief Republican counsel, Subc. on Oversight and Investigations, House Cmte. on Energy and Commerce.

Expertise: Oversight, investigation, EPA.

Alan Slobodin, chief investigative counsel for the House Subcommittee on Oversight and Investigations, says his role resembles a chief operating officer with the panel's investigative team. He works with the subcommittee's chief counsel, Todd Harrison, who functions in effect as the chief executive officer, Slobodin said.

Republicans moving to the majority brought additional responsibility and work as well as more staff.

"The oversight is not strictly the oversight investigations subcommittee although we certainly will be very, very involved in a lot of the major oversight business of the committee, and all of the other subcommittees as well," he said.

Their oversight involves follow up work after a law is passed to see how it's being implemented and administered or if some issues exist that should be addressed through more legislation or administrative fixes.

From time to time some investigations will identify an issue that isn't really addressed adequately under current law, Slobodin noted. One past example of that was the emergence of date rape drugs.

In 2010, the oversight subcommittee dealt with the Deepwater Horizon BP oil spill in the Gulf of Mexico. It continues to monitor the aftermath with issues related to the Obama administration's original response.

The overall subcommittee priorities in 2011 are the new health care reform law, regulatory actions of the Environmental Protection Agency and issues related to energy development, and oversight of the stimulus funds.

While with the House Judiciary Subcommittee on Civil and Constitutional Rights in the 1980s, Slobodin participated in investigative activity on judicial impeachments which then had not occurred in some 50 years. In a short period of time, three such major impeachment investigations went through the Judiciary Committee of which he was involved in two.

HOUSE ENERGY AND COMMERCE

Alexandra Teitz

Senior Democratic Counsel, Environment and Energy

2322A Rayburn House Office Bldg.

Phone: (202) 225-3641

alexandra.teitz@mail.house.gov

Personal: Born in Oakland, Calif.

Education: B.A., Oberlin College, 1988. M.E.S., Yale School of Forestry and Environmental Studies, 1991. J.D., University of California, Berkeley, 1994.

Professional: 1994–2001, attorney, Environmental Protection Agency, Office of General Counsel. 2001–2006, environmental counsel, House Cmte. on Oversight and Government Reform. 2007–2008, senior environmental counsel, House Cmte. on Oversight and Government Reform. 2009–present, senior counsel, environment and energy, House Cmte. on Energy and Commerce.

Expertise: Environmental regulation.

Alexandra Teitz, senior counsel for environment and energy with the Democratic staff of the House Energy and Commerce Committee, works on issues affecting the power industry regarding carbon dioxide and other greenhouse gas emissions. Still she views regulation as simply one factor in the equation.

"But the arguments on the Hill are being framed as saying that environmental regulation threatens blackouts," she told a Bipartisan Policy Center workshop in 2011. Even if the Environmental Protection Agency did nothing on climate change, questions about related future actions would remain, in her view.

Teitz's boss, Rep. Henry Waxman, D-Calif., ranking committee member and former chairman, realizes this continuing uncertainty is a burden for utilities and wants to move forward on new generation capacity.

The Waxman-Markey clean energy and climate legislation the House passed in the 111th Congress would have encouraged coal use and enabled yearly funding for carbon capture and storage, while helping to avoid the impact of drastic changes for the industry, Teitz said. That's why former Democratic Rep. Rick Boucher, a committee member who represented a coal mining district in Southwest Virginia for 28 years before losing his 2010 re-election, supported the measure, she added.

Power providers have to consider certain issues as they retire or clean up plants, Teitz said. Local, state, and regional entities must assist them in taking needed steps.

The current Congress is unlikely to resolve the issue of a future price on carbon. The House Republican focus is on attempts to repeal or delay EPA's existing authority on greenhouse gases and blocking EPA from implementing greenhouse gas regulations under the Clean Air Act. Doing that would not solve the power sector's problems with inaction in the face of climate change, Teitz said.

Committee on Financial Services

2129 Rayburn House Office Bldg.
Washington, DC 20515
Phone: (202) 225-2502
http://financialservices.house.gov

Ratio: 33/32

MAJORITY MEMBERS

Spencer Bachus, AL-6th, Chairman

Jeb Hensarling, TX-5th, Vice Chairman
Peter King, NY-3rd
Edward R. Royce, CA-40th
Frank D. Lucas, OK-6th
Ron Paul, TX-14th
Donald A. Manzullo, IL-16th
Walter B. Jones, NC-3rd
Judy Biggert, IL-13th
Gary G. Miller, CA-42nd
Shelley Moore Capito, WV-2nd
Scott Garrett, NJ-5th
Randy Neugebauer, TX-19th
Patrick T. McHenry, NC-10th
John Campbell, CA-48th
Michele Bachmann, MN-6th
Thaddeus McCotter, MI-11th
Kevin McCarthy, CA-22nd
Stevan Pearce, NM-2nd
Bill Posey, FL-15th
Michael G. Fitzpatrick, PA-8th
Lynn Westmoreland, GA-3rd
Blaine Luetkemeyer, MO-9th
Bill Huizenga, MI-2nd
Sean P. Duffy, WI-7th
Nan A.S. Hayworth, NY-19th
Jim Renacci, OH-16th
Robert Hurt, VA-5th
Robert J. Dold, IL-10th
David Schweikert, AZ-5th
Michael G. Grimm, NY-13th
Francisco R. Canesco, TX-23rd
Steve Stivers, OH-15th

MINORITY MEMBERS

Barney Frank, MA-4th, Ranking Member

Maxine Waters, CA-35th
Carolyn B. Maloney, NY-14th
Luis V. Gutierrez, IL-4th
Nydia M. Velázquez, NY-12th
Melvin L. Watt, NC-12th
Gary L. Ackerman, NY-5th
Brad Sherman, CA-27th
Gregory W. Meeks, NY-6th
Michael E. Capuano, MA-8th
Rubén Hinojosa, TX-15th
William Lacy Clay, MO-1st
Carolyn McCarthy, NY-4th
Joe Baca, CA-43rd
Stephen F. Lynch, MA-9th
Brad Miller, NC-13th
David Scott, GA-13th
Al Green, TX-9th
Emanuel Cleaver, MO-5th
Gwen Moore, WI-4th
Keith Ellison, MN-5th
Ed Perlmutter, CO-5th
Gary Peters, MI-9th
Andre Carson, IN-7th
Joe Donnelly, IN-2nd
Jim Himes, CT-4th
Ed Perlmutter, CO-7th
Joe Donnelly, IN-2nd
John Carney, DE-At Large
Andre Carson, IN-7th
Jim Himes, CT-4th
Gary Peters, MI-9th

Almanac of the Unelected, 2011

HOUSE FINANCIAL SERVICES

JURISDICTION

(1) Banks and banking, including deposit insurance and federal monetary policy.
(2) Economic stabilization, defense production, renegotiation, and control of the price of commodities, rents, and services.
(3) Financial aid to commerce and industry (other than transportation).
(4) Insurance generally.
(5) International finance.
(6) International financial and monetary organizations.
(7) Money and credit, including currency and the issuance of notes and redemption thereof; gold and silver, including the coinage thereof; valuation and revaluation of the dollar.
(8) Public and private housing.
(9) Securities and exchanges.
(10) Urban development.

HOUSE FINANCIAL SERVICES

Republicans swept into the House majority pledging to undo in the 112th Congress some of the major legislative initiatives that were enacted during the previous session. While health care reform was at the top of that list, the major financial regulatory overhaul known as Dodd-Frank was another top priority for Republicans to pare down. Under the control of Rep. Spencer Bachus, R-Ala., the powerful Financial Services Committee will be at the center of that debate during the 112th Congress.

"Individual initiative and free markets have long been the recipe for our dynamic economy. Unfortunately, the new regulatory structure created by Dodd-Frank will redefine the way our economy operates in the future, constricting jobs and punishing Main Street businesses that did nothing to cause the crisis," Bachus said at a January hearing about government policies and job creation.

Bachus warned: "We all know that inadequate underwriting and loose credit standards contributed to the financial crisis, but the pendulum has swung too far towards regulatory micromanagement."

With Democrats still holding the majority in the Senate, a complete repeal of Dodd-Frank is unlikely. But House Republicans have set out to pare down the sweeping bill piece by piece, from postponing a provision on debit card "swipe fees" to changing the structure of the Consumer Financial Protection Bureau (CFPB) from an agency run by one individual to a bipartisan board.

"We can achieve consumer protection without a credit czar," Bachus said in March after introducing legislation to reform the CFPB.

Bachus has pledged to conduct scrupulous oversight of the Obama administration and his committee has also set out to identify duplicative regulations, a priority that all legislative committees have been charged to do under the new GOP majority. In March, the Financial Services panel voted to end four different foreclosure programs; and heard testimony from Federal Reserve Chairman Ben Bernanke regarding monetary policy.

Bachus has long fought criticism of not being forceful enough as the top Republican on the Financial Services panel. In 2008, the panel was at the center of the debate in crafting the Emergency Economic Stabilization Act, which created the Troubled Assets Relief Program. Rep. Barney Frank, D-Mass., who was chairman during that time, remains the top Democrat on the committee and remains as outspoken as he was when his party was in the majority. Shortly after the committee voted to end the foreclosure programs, Frank introduced legislation that would charge financial institutions to cover the costs for those same housing initiatives. He has been a fixture on the House floor as Members have considered legislation both pertaining to his committee and out of its purview, and he will remain an outspoken supporter of the 2010 Dodd-Frank bill, particularly since it's other author, Sen. Chris Dodd, D-Conn., is now retired.

Other top priorities to be considered by the committee in the 112th Congress are a full reauthorization of the National Flood Insurance Program and a review of government-sponsored enterprises such as Fannie Mae and Freddie Mac, which Republicans complained were not addressed in the Dodd-Frank measure. Indeed, Bachus blasted the Obama Administration in February for not producing a plan to reform the institutions in the wake of the housing crisis and pledged to take the issue up in his panel.

"While there is no legitimate reason for failing to have a plan, the Democrats always offer an excuse for not meeting deadlines, even those they impose themselves," Bachus said in a statement. "It is clear the administration cannot make any tough choice required to protect taxpayers."

HOUSE FINANCIAL SERVICES

Michael Borden

Senior Counsel

2129 Rayburn House Office Bldg.

Phone: (202) 225-7502

Michael.Borden@mail.house.gov

Personal: Born 1977 in Tarzana, Calif.

Education: B.A., with distinction, Yale University, 1999. J.D., University of Chicago, 2003.

Professional: 2004–2007, legislative assistant, Rep. Jim Leach, R-Iowa. 2007–present, senior counsel, House Cmte. on Financial Services. 2007, counsel, House Cmte. on Financial Services.

Expertise: Financial institutions, consumer credit issues, government sponsored enterprises.

As the financial industry watches for Rep. Spencer Bacchus, R-Ala. to peel away provisions in the sweeping Dodd-Frank regulatory reform bill in 2011, Michael Borden will head the team that makes strategic decisions on how Republicans can pick away at the law.

Borden, a senior counsel for the majority staff, said Republicans would go after the Dodd-Frank law that was enacted in 2010, and specifically target the so-called "Volcker Rule" that bars banks from engaging in proprietary trading.

"Even [Treasury] Secretary Geithner said this had no bearing on the financial crisis," Borden told the American Bar Association on Nov. 5, according to The Deal magazine.

Bacchus has already led an active committee in early 2011, presiding over hearings on Dodd-Frank, Fannie Mae and Freddie Mac and reform of government-sponsored enterprises. All three topics will be common threads for Republicans during the 112th Congress as the GOP seeks to highlight what they charge are legislative failings aimed to bolster the economy. Borden has said that reform of Freddie and Fannie will also be a primary focus this year. The federal government bailed out both companies, private entities backed by the government, during the 2008 financial crisis.

In a January 31 statement, Bacchus said that House Republicans want to reform "the housing finance system in a way that does not rely on government guarantees, that does not make private investors and creditors wealthy while saddling taxpayers with losses, and that does not set the stage for the next financial crisis."

Borden joined the committee as counsel in 2007 after his former boss, Rep. Jim Leach, R-Iowa, was defeated in the 2006 election. He was promoted to senior counsel after the departure of Dina Ellis. The California native graduated with distinction from Yale and has his J.D. from the University of Chicago.

HOUSE FINANCIAL SERVICES

Jim Clinger

Republican Chief Counsel

2129 Rayburn House Office Bldg.

Phone: (202) 225-7502

Jim.Clinger@mail.house.gov

Personal: Born 04/04/1961 in Warren, Pa.

Education: B.A. (high distinction), University of Virginia, 1983. J.D., University of Virginia, 1987.

Professional: 1987–1995, associate, Sutherland, Asbill & Brennan. 1995–2001, senior counsel/asst. staff dir., Subc. on Oversight and Investigation, House Cmte. on Banking and Financial Services. 2001–2005, senior banking counsel, House Cmte. on Financial Services. 2005–2006, deputy assistant attorney general for legislative affairs, U.S. Dept. of Justice. 2006–2007, acting associate attorney general, Office of Legislative Affairs, Justice Dept. 2007–present, Republican chief counsel, House Cmte. on Financial Services.

Expertise: Financial institutions and banking.

Republican Chief Counsel Jim Clinger will help carry out the House Republicans instructions to committee chairman to review laws enacted by the Obama administration and search for extraneous and harmful provisions.

Clinger, who specializes in financial institutions and banking, was a senior staffer to Rep. Spencer Bachus, R-Ala., during the debates over the federal bailout program and Dodd-Frank bill. Now with the Republicans in the majority for the 112th Congress, Bachus will use his committee gavel to criticize the Obama administration for over-regulating the financial industry and ultimately hurting job growth.

"The burden of these regulations will almost certainly limit access to credit for small businesses and consumers," Bachus said in February during floor debate over a resolution tasking committee's to scrub Obama's regulatory structure. "And they will divert private sector resources that should be going to expanding businesses and creating jobs."

Clinger first worked for the committee from 1995 until 2005, when Republicans where in the majority. When he returned in 2007, Republicans were in the minority but after the November 2010 election change over, Clinger will stay busy looking into the Obama administration's regulations and helping craft Republican alternatives.

In between his committee stints, Clinger worked at the Justice Department where he took part in the investigations into the allegedly improper messages between former Rep. Mark Foley, R-Fla., and congressional pages. Prior to working for the Justice Department, Clinger had served as senior banking counsel to former chairman Mike Oxley, R-Ohio.

Clinger is a graduate from the University of Virginia, both for his undergraduate degree and his law degree. His father was Rep. William Clinger, R-Pa., who served as chairman of the House Government Reform and Oversight Committee.

HOUSE FINANCIAL SERVICES

Jeff Emerson

Deputy chief of staff

2129 Rayburn House Office Bldg.

Phone: (202) 202-225-7502

jeff.emerson@mail.house.gov

Education: B.A., journalism and political science, University of Alabama, 1991.

Professional: 1992–1995, leg. asst., press secretary, Rep. George (Buddy) Darden, R-Ga. 1995–1997, acct. exec., Odell, Roper & Simms, Inc. 1997–2003, chief of staff, press secretary, Rep. Spencer Bachus, R-Ala. 2003, deputy director, Alabama Association of Realtors. 2003–2011, communications director, Gov. Bob Riley, R-Ala.. 2011–present, deputy chief of staff, House Cmte. on Financial Services.

Expertise: Communications.

Jeff Emerson is a new addition to the House Financial Services Committee for the 112th Congress, but the University of Alabama graduate comes to the panel with deep southern roots and previous experience working with Committee Chairman Spencer Bachus, R-Ala.

Before joining the committee in 2011, Emerson worked for eight years in Montgomery, Ala., for Gov. Bob Riley, a Republican, and former House member, who served two terms. Emerson was Riley's communications director, and brings those skills to Bachus's office, where he now serves as the deputy chief of staff for communications. As one of two deputy chiefs on the panel, Emerson's media savvy and Alabama ties will no doubt help Bachus steer a busy committee during the 112th Congress.

Emerson has carried out similar duties for Bachus before, when he served as the Congressman's chief of staff and press secretary from 1997 to 2003. During that time, Emerson worked to increase Bachus's national profile and maintain his ties back in the state, where the Congressman has been a fixture since his days as a state legislator.

Now with the chairman's gavel, Bachus has outlined an ambitious agenda that includes reviewing the Dodd-Frank bill, reviewing housing and mortgage programs and reforming government sponsored enterprises. In pursuing those goals, the Bachus will depend on a savvy press operation, which includes Emerson, to win public support and serve as a foil to the Democratic-controlled White House.

"Obviously the Democrats control the Senate and the White House but that shouldn't keep Republicans from doing what the American people sent them here to do, which is to end these failed government programs and cut spending," Emerson told the Birmingham News in March.

Indeed, Bachus's committee already got to work early in the legislative session reviewing provisions in Dodd-Frank legislation, conducting oversight of the Housing and Urban Development Department and looking into policy initiatives to boost job growth.

HOUSE FINANCIAL SERVICES

Marisol Garibay

Communications Director

2132 Rayburn House Office Bldg.

Phone: (202) 225-7502

Fax: (202) 226-4301

Marisol.Garibay@mail.house.gov

Education: B.A., political science and sociology, University of Minnesota.

Professional: 2004–2005, staff assistant, Sen. Peter Fitzgerald, R-Ill. 2005–2007, communications specialist, House Cmte. on Financial Services. 2007–2008, special assistant for banking and finance in the Office of Legislative Affairs, Treasury Department. 2008–present, communications director, House Cmte. on Financial Services.

Expertise: Communications.

Marisol Garibay has been the communications director for the House Financial Services Committee for three years, and 2011 marks the first time she will serve as the spokeswoman for a committee chairman.

With the Republicans taking over the majority of the House, Garibay focuses on driving the message of Chairman Spencer Bachus, R-Ala., and responding to countless media inquiries on the potential repeal of Dodd-Frank and overhaul of mortgage companies Fannie Mae and Freddie Mac.

The panel voted in March to dismantle the pair of housing programs in a broader attempt by Republicans to terminate the Home Affordable Modification Plan, a foreclosure-prevention program that has drawn the ire of GOP members and particularly Bacchus.

"These programs, while well-intentioned, are actually doing more harm than good for many struggling homeowners," Bachus said after the committee voted to zero out the programs.

Within days of that committee vote, the full House voted largely along party lines to end two other Obama administration housing programs, indicating the high profile status that financial services matters will have during the 112th Congress. Garibay will play a major role in shaping the messaging debate for her boss.

But Garibay is used to it. She handled the media during the 2009 drafting of the Dodd-Frank financial regulatory reform bill, and before that in 2008 during the financial crisis. Garibay also has previous experience in explaining financial matters. She was a special assistant for banking and finance in the Office of Legislative Affairs at the Treasury Department.

Before her Treasury Department job, Garibay was an assistant communications director on the House Financial Services Committee. She also worked as a staff assistant to former Sen. Peter G. Fitzgerald, R-Ill., and was an intern for former Sen. Norm Coleman, R-Minn.

HOUSE FINANCIAL SERVICES

Clinton C. Jones

Senior Counsel
Subcommittee on Insurance, Housing and Community Opportunity
2129 Rayburn House Office Bldg.
Phone: (202) 225-6634
Fax: (202) 225-6635
Clinton.Jones@mail.house.gov

Personal: Born 07/20/1962 in Kaiserslautern, West Germany.

Education: B.A., University of North Carolina at Chapel Hill, 1984. J.D./M.R.P., University of North Carolina at Chapel Hill, 1988.

Professional: 1988–1993, attorney/advisor, Office of the General Counsel, Insured Housing and Finance, U.S. Department of Housing and Urban Development. 1990–present, adjunct professor, Howard University. 1993–1996, counsel, House Cmte. on Banking and Financial Services. 1996–2001, senior counsel, House Cmte. on Banking and Financial Services. 2001–2006, senior counsel, House Cmte. on Financial Services. 2007–2008, vice president for industry relations & legislative Policy Counsel, Fannie Mae. 2008–2011, general counsel/parliamentarian, House Cmte. on Financial Services (Minority Staff). 2011–present, general counsel, House Cmte. on Financial Services.

Expertise: Mortgage finance, urban policy, insurance, community and economic development.

Clinton Jones came back to Capitol Hill after a two-year stint at Fannie Mae, and has been a longtime fixture on the House Financial Services Committee.

As the lead staffer for the Insurance, Housing & Community Opportunity Subcommittee, Jones will be responsible for managing a panel that will make housing finance a top issue this year. The National Flood Insurance Program (NFIP) is up for reauthorization this year, and Rep. Judy Biggert, R-Ill., who chairs the subcommittee, said in March, "There is no question that the program is in dire need of reform."

"We must work toward a long-term plan for flood insurance that eliminates taxpayer risk," Biggert told a subcommittee hearing. "In the near-term, important reforms to the NFIP must improve its financial stability, reduce the burden on taxpayers, and examine ways to increase private market participation."

Before Republicans took the majority in 2010, Jones was the parliamentarian for the minority staff under Rep. Spencer Bachus, R-Ala. In that role, Jones "kept the trains running" during committee meetings and mark ups.

"I was all about process, about moving the bills through committee, the hearing structures, all that came under my purview," Jones said.

Now, Jones will focus on policymaking for a high profile committee that has already been active in the first few months of the 112th Congress. The Financial Services Committee voted to roll back four foreclosure programs and will continue to look for duplicative programs and regulations, which is a top focus for all committees this year. Indeed, the first hearing of the Insurance and Housing subcommittee in 2011 was titled "Are There Government Barriers to the Housing Market Recovery?"

Jones was an experienced housing advisor to former committee chairman Rep. Michael Oxley, R-Ohio, and worked on problems facing the Rural Housing Service, Section 8 housing choice vouchers, and will resume the effort to reform the Federal Housing Administration (FHA). Some of those areas, particularly FHA, are expected to be a focus of the committee this year.

HOUSE FINANCIAL SERVICES

Larry Lavender

Republican Chief of Staff

2129 Rayburn House Office Bldg.

Phone: (202) 225-7502

Fax: (202) 226-4301

Larry.Lavender@mail.house.gov

Personal: Born 2/24/1944 in Birmingham, Ala.

Education: B.S., administration, University of Alabama at Birmingham, 1970. M.B.A., University of Alabama at Birmingham, 1972.

Professional: 2001–2007, chief of staff, Rep. Spencer Bachus, R-Ala. 2007–present, Republican chief of staff, House Cmte. on Financial Services.

Expertise: Financial institutions, capital markets.

Larry Lavender has been the chief of staff for his hometown Congressman, Rep. Spencer Bachus, R-Ala., since 2001. As the Republican take over of the House in the 112th Congress sent Bachus to lead the House Financial Services, Lavender will now lead the committee's staff and play a major role in shaping the committee's focus during the next two years.

From reviewing provisions in the sweeping Dodd-Frank financial reform bill, looking into financial regulations carried out by the Obama administration, or hearing from Federal Reserve chairman Ben Bernanke on monetary policy, Lavender will make decisions on what areas the committee focuses on and when. As the chief of staff he has a managerial role, but as a staffer with experience in financial issues he will help carry out the chairman's legislative priorities for the year.

Rep. Ed Royce, R-Calif., challenged Bachus for the committee gavel, although the Alabamian ultimately won out. Some Republicans have privately grumbled that Bachus was not vocal enough while he served as ranking member. After the GOP won control of the House in November, Bachus assured colleagues he would be a force as the committee's chair. It will be Lavender's job to help follow through on that.

Lavender, who was born just outside of Birmingham, graduated from the University of Alabama. He moved from Bachus' personal office to the House Financial Services Committee office in 2007 as the chief of staff when Bachus became ranking member on the financial services panel. He has a background in finance. He was chief of staff to the mayor of Birmingham, helping run the city and its finances.

Before he came to Washington, Lavender was in the private sector as a business owner. He said that gives him a unique perspective when it comes to dealing with financial institutions and businesses.

HOUSE FINANCIAL SERVICES

Frank Medina

Republican Senior Counsel

2129 Rayburn House Office Bldg.

Phone: (202) 225-7502

Fax: (202) 226-4301

Frank.Medina@mail.house.gov

Professional: 2007–present, senior counsel, House Committee on Financial Services.

Expertise: Banking/financial institutions.

With special expertise in banking and financial institutions, Republican Counsel Frank Medina stands to be a marquis player on the staff of the Financial Services Committee in 2011 as the panel conducts oversight of the sweeping Dodd-Frank bill enacted in 2010.

Republicans widely opposed the bill and continued to blast its provisions after it was enacted. Medina will work with Chairman Spencer Bachus, R-Ala., to conduct strong oversight of the Obama administration law.

"As in many other areas of Dodd-Frank, Congress has broadly delegated authority to Federal regulatory agencies to write the rules, so it is incumbent upon this Committee to exercise rigorous oversight of that process," Bachus said at a Feb. 15 hearing examining the law's regulations of the derivatives market.

Medina will also work with Bachus to look into the Consumer Financial Protection Bureau, led by Elizabeth Warren. Republicans blasted Obama's move to appoint the former Harvard University professor to the high profile post and were angrier that Warren did not have to win Senate approval before taking on the top job in the administration. Bachus said the move "undermined" the Constitution and he is sure to focus on Warren's tenure atop the CFPB.

Meanwhile, Medina served on the panel during the 2008 bailout debate and assisted Republican members and staff on investigations. The Financial Services also kicked off a busy March schedule with separate hearings featuring Treasury Secretary Timothy Geithner and Federal Reserve President Ben Bernanke, and in each case the Obama administration's monetary policies were a central focus.

HOUSE FINANCIAL SERVICES

Scott R. Olson

Democratic Professional Staff Member

2129 Rayburn House Office Bldg.

Phone: (202) 225-4247

Fax: (202) 225-6952

scott.olson@mail.house.gov

Education: B.A., Stanford University, 1977. M.B.A., University of California, Los Angeles, 1980.

Professional: 1981–1985, investment banker, Birr, Wilson & Co. 1986, mortgage banker, Birr, Wilson & Co. 1987–1988, investment banker, Johnston, Lemon & Co. 1989–1991, mortgage banker, Johnston, Lemon & Co. 1992–1996, legislative dir., Rep. Bill Orton, D-Utah. 1997–1998, Democratic professional staff member, Subc. on Housing and Community Opportunity. 1999–2001, Democratic professional staff member, House Cmte. on Banking and Financial Services. 2001–present, Democratic professional staff member, House Cmte. on Financial Services.

Expertise: Housing.

As an expert in housing issues, Professional Staff Member Scott Olson worked on high profile issues when Rep. Barney Frank, D-Mass., led the Financial Services Committee. Frank made housing a centerpiece of his Congressional career, and in 2008 he sought to address the subprime mortgage lending industry during the sweeping financial crisis.

But now with the Democrats in the minority in the 112th Congress, Republicans have sought to undo some of Frank's—and Olson's work. Already in 2011, the House approved a bill to terminate four different foreclosure programs that Republicans charged have not helped bolster the housing industry.

"In an era of record-breaking deficits, it's time to pull the plug on these programs that are actually doing more harm than good for struggling homeowners," Rep. Spencer Bachus, R-Ala., the committee's chairman, said in a February statement. "These programs may have been well-intentioned but they're not working and, in reality, are making things worse."

With that, Republicans have already unraveled some of Olson's work from the last several years and they are working step by step undo many parts of other laws. The Emergency Economic Stabilization Act of 2008, which created the Troubled Assets Relief Program (TARP), allowed the government to bail out troubled institutions, like banks, which were hit hard by the housing crisis. While Frank played a central role in drafting the legislation, he and other lawmakers did not like how the $700 billion in funds were distributed. The sweeping Dodd-Frank bill, signed into law in 2010, also sought to provide increased consumer protections to stave off predatory lending and provide additional oversight of the financial industry.

Olson has been a part of the committee since 2001. Before becoming a Congressional staffer in 1992, he worked in the mortgage and investment banking industry.

HOUSE FINANCIAL SERVICES

Joe Pinder

Senior Professional Staff Member

2129 Rayburn House Office Bldg.

Phone: (202) 225-7502

joe.pinder@mail.house.gov

Personal: Born 01/06/1951 in Grinnell, Iowa.

Education: B.S., Boston University, 1972.

Professional: 1972–1974, education editor, *Grinnel (Iowa) Herald-Register*. 1979–1988, reporter, *Worcester (Mass.) Telegram*. 1988–1993, press secretary, Rep. Jim Leach, R-Iowa. 1990–1992, adjunct professor in journalism, American University. 1993–1994, Republican press secretary, House Cmte. on Banking. 1995–1996, Republican deputy communications director, House Cmte. on Banking. 1996–present, sr. professional staff, House Cmte. on Financial Services.

Expertise: Coins, medals, domestic and international policy.

Joe Pinder brings an interesting background and diverse experience to a committee that will have its hands full during the 112th Congress.

The onetime journalist, college professor, and press secretary boasts an expertise in coins and medals and is an overall valued senior staffer on the House Financial Services Committee.

Pinder joined the committee as a press secretary just before the 1994 Republican Revolution, so beyond his other areas of expertise he can provide additional guidance as Republicans once again adjust to managing a much larger caucus in the majority following the sweeping 2010 midterm elections.

During the 112th Congress, Pinder will be the top staffer on the Domestic Monetary Policy and Technology Committee. The subcommittee, chaired by Rep. Ron Paul, R-Texas, is expected to be an active one in 2011. Already, the panel has held hearings exploring the relationship between monetary policy and job creation and the cause for rising prices in the United States.

Pinder played a central role in 2007 when President Bush signed into law S. 2271, the Sudan Accountability and Divestment Act of 2007. In House debate on the bill, then committee Ranking Member Rep. Spencer Bachus, R-Ala., said the legislation "has the potential to give hundreds of thousands of peaceful and unarmed men, women, and children in Darfur an increased chance of surviving the genocide."

As a senior professional staff member on the House Financial Services Committee, Pinder was among the aides whom Bachus thanked for their work on the issue on the floor of the House. He also was praised by the committee's chairman, Rep. Barney Frank, D-Mass., at a February hearing related to a signing statement Bush attached to the bill.

HOUSE FINANCIAL SERVICES

Jeanne M. Roslanowick

Democratic Staff Director/General Counsel

2129 Rayburn House Office Bldg.

Phone: (202) 225-7141

Fax: (202) 225-6952

jeanne.roslanowick@mail.house.gov

Personal: Born 08/31/1948 in Erie, Pa.

Education: B.A. (magna cum laude), political science and English, Marquette University, 1970. M.P.A., University of Massachusetts, Amherst, 1972. J.D., Yale Law School, 1979.

Professional: 1972–1976, staff member, Dept. of Public Welfare (Boston, Mass.). 1980–1983, associate, Patton, Boggs, and Blow (Washington, D.C.). 1983–1987, counsel, Subc. on Economic Stabilization, House Cmte. on Banking and Financial Services. 1987–1993, senior counsel, House Cmte. on Small Business. 1993–1994, staff dir., House Cmte. on Small Business. 1995–1997, Democratic staff dir., House Cmte. on Small Business. 1998–2001, Democratic staff dir./general counsel, House Cmte. on Banking and Financial Services. 2001–present, Democratic staff dir./general counsel, House Cmte. on Financial Services.

Expertise: International finance and development, financial services, consumer protection, housing.

Jeanne Roslanowick joined the House Committee on Financial Services in 2002 while Democrats were in the minority. She enjoyed a four-year stint in the majority, but in the 112th Congress will be back in familiar territory as the Democratic staff director on the powerful panel.

During the time that Rep. Barney Frank, D-Mass., wielded the committee gavel, Roslanowick was a key player in the 2008 legislative debate over the $700 billion bank bailout, known as the Troubled Asset Relief Program. Responding to critics of the Bush administration's performance in distributing the first $350 billion, Roslanowick and the staff worked hard as Frank sought to push a new set of regulations to be followed by President Barack Obama shortly after he took office. Among Frank's suggestions was requiring the government to devote at least $50 billion toward preventing foreclosures. Frank has made housing a marquis issue during his Congressional career, and likewise, Roslanowick specializes in housing issues.

Now in the minority, the outspoken Frank is in the position of having to defend many of the Democratic priorities he helped to craft during the last two Congresses. As Frank's staff director, Roslanowick will assist the Massachusetts Democrat in those pursuits.

Roslanowick also specializes in consumer protection, a central issue in the debate over financial regulatory reform in the 111th Congress. The Dodd-Frank bill, which became law in 2010, created a Consumer Financial Protection Bureau and required advisors of private equity funds to register with the Securities and Exchange Commission. Democrats described the legislation as the most sweeping in reforming the financial sector in a generation, while Republicans maintained it would stifle the business sector and was a governmental overreach.

HOUSE FINANCIAL SERVICES

David A. Smith

Chief Economist

2129 Rayburn House Office Bldg.

Phone: (202) 225-4247

David.Smith@mail.house.gov

Education: bachelor's degree, Tufts University. master's degree, education, Harvard University, 1972.

Professional: 1980s, Democratic staffer, Sen. Edward Kennedy, D-Mass. 2003, legislative aide, Rep. Sam Farr, D-Calif. 2007–present, chief economist, House Cmte. on Financial Services.

Expertise: Domestic economics, International economics.

Chief Economist David A. Smith has extensive experience helping craft some of the most high profile financial legislation in recent years, but the longtime staffer had not served in the minority on the Financial Services Committee, until now.

While Smith is a trusted confidante of Rep. Barney Frank, D-Mass., the committee's ranking member, his reach will be limited while Republicans run the powerful panel in the 112th Congress. Still, Frank is no shrinking violet on the dais and Smith's expertise will not be wasted.

As Frank's chief economist since 2007, Smith boasts steep knowledge on the domestic and international fronts. In 2008, this committee took the lead on the Emergency Economic Stabilization Act of 2008, which paved the way for $700 billion to help shore up America's troubled economy. Smith was equally involved during the 2009 crafting of the economic stimulus package that passed shortly after President Barack Obama was sworn into office.

Before joining the committee, Smith worked for Sen. Edward Kennedy, D-Mass. Smith also worked for the AFL-CIO as the director of the public policy department, where he dealt with a wide range of domestic and international issues with a special emphasis on economics, including the World Trade Organization. He was also a fellow at Demos, a New York City think tank that concentrates on election reform and economic security, with a special emphasis on the development of a broad, stable future middle class. While working at Demos, Smith co-edited a book, **Inequality Matters**, which focused on a realistic policy path to a more just and humane economy.

Smith was on the faculty of the College of Public and Community Service at the University of Massachusetts for most of the 1970s and has taught at the New School. He has written and lectured widely on issues of development, labor, and tax and income policy.

HOUSE FINANCIAL SERVICES

Warren Tryon

Deputy chief of staff

2129 Rayburn House Office Bldg.

Phone: (202) 225-7502

warren.tryon@mail.house.gov

Education: University of Vermont, 1991.

Professional: 1993–1995, Sen. Slade Gorton, R-Wash. 1995–1997, Rep. Linda Smith, R-Wash. 1997–2000, Rep. Rick Hill, R-Mont.. 2000–2006, Leg. aide, Rep. Spencer Bachus, R-Ala. 2006–2010, Republican dep. staff dir., House Cmte. on Financial Services. 2011–present, deputy chief of staff, House Cmte. on Financial Services.

Warren Tryon began working his way up the ladder in Alabama Rep. Spencer Bachus's office since 2000, when he started as a financial services legislative aide in the Republican's personal office. Little more than a decade later, Tryon is now the deputy chief of staff for the new committee chairman.

With the Republican's taking over the House for the 112th Congress, Tyron is part of the chairman's senior management team and will play a role in planning hearings and setting the committee's agenda. This is a busy job for the University of Vermont graduate; already the committee has looked in to the Dodd-Frank bill and Bachus has made government sponsored enterprises and the government's role in the mortgage industry top focuses for the 112th Congress. Bachus has also promised to make Congressional oversight central to his chairmanship, and ending what the Republicans see as failed and ineffective housing foreclosure programs. Already in 2011, the Financial Services Committee marked up four separate pieces of legislation on that issue.

"In an era of record-breaking deficits, it's time to pull the plug on these programs that are actually doing more harm than good for struggling homeowners," Bachus said in a statement in February. "These programs may have been well-intentioned but they're not working and, in reality, are making things worse."

Tryon also will be kept busy with unemployment issues as Bachus plans to use his panel to look at growing the job sector, which has been suffering since the 2008 financial crisis.

"The Financial Services Committee and House Republicans are committed to sweeping away unnecessary, repetitive or intrusive government-imposed obstacles to recovery and hiring," Bachus said in February. "We will look to remove the confusing impediments the Dodd-Frank Act places in the way of a freely operating and safe financial services industry."

Tryon became deputy staff director for Financial Services Republicans in 2006; he previously worked for Sen. Slade Gorton, R-Wash.

Committee on Foreign Affairs

2170 Rayburn House Office Bldg.
Washington, DC 20515
Phone: (202) 225-5021
Fax: (202) 225-2035
http://foreignaffairs.house.gov

Ratio: 25/20

MAJORITY MEMBERS

Ileana Ros-Lehtinen, FL-18th, Chairman

Christopher H. Smith, NJ-4th
Dan Burton, IN-5th
Elton Gallegly, CA-24th
Dana Rohrabacher, CA-46th
Donald A. Manzullo, IL-16th
Steve Chabot, OH-1st
Edward R. Royce, CA-40th
Ron Paul, TX-14th
Mike Pence, IN-6th
Joe Wilson, SC-2nd
Connie Mack, FL-14th
Jeff Fortenberry, NE-1st
Michael T. McCaul, TX-10th
Ted Poe, TX-2nd
Gus Bilirakis, FL-9th
Jean Schmidt, OH-2nd
Bill Johnson, OH-6th
David Rivera, FL-25th
Mike Kelly, PA-3rd
Tim Griffin, AR-2nd
Tom Marino, PA-12th
Jeff Duncan, SC-3rd
Ann Marie Buerkle, NY-25th
Renee Ellmers, NC-2nd

MINORITY MEMBERS

Howard L. Berman, CA-28th, Ranking Member

Gary L. Ackerman, NY-5th
Eni F.H. Faleomavaega, AS
Donald M. Payne, NJ-10th
Brad Sherman, CA-27th
Eliot L. Engel, NY-17th
Gregory W. Meeks, NY-6th
Russ Carnahan, MO-3rd
Albio Sires, NJ-13th
Gerald E. Connolly, VA-11th
Theodore Deutch, FL-19th
Dennis Cardoza, CA
Ben Chandler, KY-6th
Brian Higgins, NY-27th
Allyson Y. Schwartz, PA-13th
Christopher S. Murphy, CT-5th
Frederica Wilson, FL-17th
Karen Bass, CA-33rd
William Keating, MA-10th
David Cicilline, RI-1st

HOUSE FOREIGN AFFAIRS

JURISDICTION

(1) Relations of the United States with foreign nations generally.
(2) Acquisition of land and buildings for embassies and legations in foreign countries.
(3) Establishment of boundary lines between the United States and foreign nations.
(4) Export controls, including nonproliferation of nuclear technology and nuclear hardware.
(5) Foreign loans.
(6) International commodity agreements (other than those involving sugar), including all agreements for cooperation in the export of nuclear technology and nuclear hardware.
(7) International conferences and congresses.
(8) International education.
(9) Intervention abroad and declarations of war.
(10) Diplomatic service.
(11) Measures to foster commercial intercourse with foreign nations and to safeguard American business interests abroad.
(12) International economic policy.
(13) Neutrality.
(14) Protection of American citizens abroad and expatriation.
(15) The American National Red Cross.
(16) Trading with the enemy.
(17) United Nations organizations.

In addition to its legislative jurisdiction under the preceding provisions of this introduction (and its general oversight function under clause 2(b)(1)), the committee shall have the special oversight functions provided for in clause 3(d) with respect to customs administration, intelligence activities relating to foreign policy, international financial and monetary organizations, and international fishing agreements.

HOUSE FOREIGN AFFAIRS

Ileana Ros-Lehtinen's, R-Fla., rise to head of the powerful House Foreign Affairs Committee coincided with swift talks of reforming the United Nations, deep cuts to the State Department and Foreign Aid budgets, and strengthened support for Israeli nationalists.

Shortly after the 2010 midterm elections put Ros-Lehtinen in charge, the Republican Study Committee produced a plan that cut federal spending by $2.5 trillion over a decade. A staggering amount of that money would come—with the new chairwoman's blessing—from those areas over which Foreign Affairs has jurisdiction: $1.39 billion from the U.S. Agency for International Development; $250 million from economic assistance to Egypt; $17 million from the International Fund for Ireland; and $55 million from the U.S. Trade Development Agency, a cut that would all but eliminate it.

One of Ros-Lehtinen's clear targets is the United Nations, which many Republicans believe has become ineffective and unaccountable to those—including the United States—that keep it financially afloat. The United States' dues make up 22 percent of the U.N. budget.

Early in 2011, she arranged a committee hearing on a bill designed to make U.N. dues voluntary in hopes of pressuring the U.N. into making changes.

"U.S. policy on the United Nations should be based on three fundamental questions: Are we advancing American interests? Are we upholding American values? Are we being responsible stewards of American taxpayer dollars?" reads a statement from Ros-Lehtinen, who also wants investigations into possible U.N. corruption and mismanagement. "Unfortunately, right now, the answer to all three questions is 'No.'"

One of Congress' first votes on the matter didn't go well for the new chairwoman: In February 2011, the House rejected her "United Nations Tax Equalization Refund Act," which would have ordered the U.N. to pay $179 million of U.S. overpayments to a special U.N. fund. The committee's former chairman, Rep. Howard Berman, (D-Calif.), argued that the legislation would not save money and would only threaten "critical security upgrades at the United Nations headquarters."

As for U.S. policy on Israel, the chairwoman has long been a spokesperson for Israeli nationalists—one who has called for cutting off funding for the Palestinian Authority and the expulsion of all PLO representatives from the United States—until Palestinians agree to recognize Israel as a Jewish state.

Early in 2011, she introduced the Holocaust Insurance Accountability Act of 2011, which would allow Holocaust survivors or their representatives to sue European life insurers for Holocaust-era claims. After World War II, many insurance companies rejected claims from Holocaust survivors or their heirs for lack of proper documentation, including death certificates.

Whether the chairwoman will follow Berman's lead on rewriting foreign aid policy remains to be seen: During the two years before he relinquished his chairmanship, Berman was negotiating an agreement under which the Foreign Affairs Committee would ease up on specific foreign policy directions and congressional earmarks, provided the White House gave the committee more details about its international development plans. Some credit Berman's efforts with convincing the White House to launch two major policy reviews—the Quadrennial Diplomacy and Development Review being run by the State Department and a National Security Council review of foreign aid.

HOUSE FOREIGN AFFAIRS

Doug Anderson

General Counsel
2170 Rayburn House Office Bldg
Phone: (202) 226-5021
Fax: (202) 226-7629
doug.anderson@mail.house.gov

Personal: Born 11/12/1967 in La Mesa, Calif.

Education: A.B., University of Chicago, 1989. J.D., The University of Chicago Law School, 1992.

Professional: 1992–1995, attorney, Meyer Hendricks Victor Osborn & Maledon. 1996–2001, counsel, House Subc. on International Operations and Human Rights. 2001–2006, senior counsel, House Cmte. on International Relations. 2007–2010, GOP chief counsel, House Cmte. on Foreign Affairs. 2011–present, general counsel, House Cmte. on Foreign Affairs.

Expertise: Asia, the Pacific, State Department, Executive Branch, Human Rights.

For Doug Anderson, State Department authorization and United Nations reform are among the big-ticket items he will help the House Committee on Foreign Affairs address during the 112th Congress.

With the GOP takeover of the House in the 2010 midterm elections, Anderson became the lead attorney on the committee, having served as Republican chief counsel since 2007.

He will be responsible for legal, legislative, and procedural matters that come before the committee, which is now being run by his boss, Ileana Ros-Lehtinen, R-Fla.

Anderson will take a lead role on the legal end of State Department authorization, which provides funding for the department so it can carry out its diplomacy and development programs. Such reauthorization acts tend to do more than just continue an agency's existence. For instance, the State Department's 2009 reauthorization bill that came out of the House Foreign Affairs Committee also provided money to promote foreign assistance programs that fight poverty and disease, create economic opportunity, and highlight American values in poor countries.

That was when the committee was run by Democrats, however. Under new GOP leadership, the reauthorization agenda is likely to be different. Regardless, it won't be new terrain for Anderson, who has, in the past, drafted, planned, and negotiated State Department budget authorization bills.

As for United Nations reform, Anderson will no doubt be in the thick of debates over how to ensure that the United States does not continue to find itself on the losing side of U.N. debates and votes. Some congressional Republicans have called for withholding federal spending on the United Nations to try to pressure the body to pay closer attention to U.S. interests, particularly by linking specific demands with financial withholding.

HOUSE FOREIGN AFFAIRS

Doug Campbell

Deputy Staff Director

Phone: (202) 225-5021

doug.campbell@mail.house.gov

Personal: Born 01/04/1967 in Glendora, Calif.

Education: B.A., political science, University of California, Berkeley, 1989. M.A., international relations, Yale University, 1992.

Professional: 1992–1993, campaign/transition staff, Clinton/Gore Presidential Campaign. 1993–1997, legislative assistant, Rep. Howard L. Berman (D-Calif.). 1993, international trade analyst, U.S. Department of Commerce. 1997–2008, legislative director, Rep. Howard L. Berman (D-Calif.). 2008, deputy staff director, House Committee on Foreign Affairs. 2008, senior policy advisor, House Committee on Foreign Affairs.

Doug Campbell has been with the House Foreign Affairs Committee a tender two years, but in that time, he has been immersed in legislation involving Pakistan, Afghanistan, and Iran, as well as issues covering terrorism, proliferation of weapons of mass destruction, export controls, national missile defense, and public diplomacy, which will likely continue during the 112th Congress.

During the 111th Congress, the deputy staff director for the committee worked on negotiating the Anti-Counterfeiting Trade Agreement (ACTA), which was designed to help protect intellectual property in the global economy.

Piracy and counterfeiting are believed to cost U.S. citizens and businesses billions of dollars each year. ACTA was written to improve international standards for protecting intellectual property rights.

To help increase "transparency" after some complained about secrecy surrounding ACTA, negotiators created an ACTA Web page on the USTR Web site with a summary of issues being negotiated and agendas for each ACTA meeting.

Despite his relative "newcomer" status, Campbell worked in the legislative office of former committee chairman Howard Berman, D-Calif., more than a decade before moving to the committee in 2009. Berman in 2011 relinquished the chairmanship to Ileana Ros-Lehtinen of Florida following Republican gains in the 2010 midterm elections.

A Yale graduate, Campbell came to the committee with strong international credentials, having studied abroad as an exchange student at Scotland's University of St. Andrews, earned a master of international relations from Yale in 1992 and worked as a fellow at the United Nations in New York in the summer of 1991, where he wrote reports on human rights and the principle of "humanitarian intervention."

HOUSE FOREIGN AFFAIRS

Joan O. Condon

Senior Professional Staff Member
Subcommittee on Africa, Global Health and Human Rights
B-360 Rayburn House Office Bldg.
Phone: (202) 225-5068
Fax: (202) 226-7296
joan.condon@mail.house.gov

Personal: Born 04/17/1974 in Westmont, N.J.

Education: B.A., Western Maryland College, 1996. M.A., government and politics, Johns Hopkins University.

Professional: 1996–1999, committee staff, Maryland House of Delegates. 1999–2000, staff associate, House Cmte. on International Relations. 2000–2001, travel coordinator and research associate, House Cmte. on International Relations. 2001–2010, Republican professional staff member covering Africa, House Cmte. on Foreign Relations. 2011–present, senior professional staff member, House Cmte. on Foreign Affairs.

Expertise: African affairs.

Joan Condon has been working for the House Foreign Affairs Committee since June of 1999, and specializing in the committee's work in Africa since 2001. With expertise in North and Sub-Saharan Africa, U.N. Peacekeeping and global HIV/AIDS, she has traveled to 25 of the 53 countries she covers and visited seven United Nations peacekeeping operations.

In her job as a senior professional staff member for the committee, she is responsible for advising Republican members on matters relating to 53 countries or territories in Africa, United Nations peacekeeping and global HIV/AIDS. She also manages the oversight of the $50 billion PEPFAR program.

The challenges that lie ahead during the 112th Congress, she said, include South Sudan's transition into its own nation; the spread of the Lord's Resistance Army's terrorizing to the Democratic Republic of Congo and Central African Republic; and the illicit trade in minerals that has fueled a brutal war in the eastern Congo.

"A major challenge this year will be working to address legitimate humanitarian, development and security needs in Africa in extraordinarily tight fiscal environment," said Condon, whose transition into the majority in 2011 should make her feel better about having had "little opportunity to set the agenda" when Republicans were in the minority.

"Difficult decisions on funding will have to be made, and a number of programs will face steep cuts, including in Africa," she said. "Despite this daunting challenge, I am looking forward to rigors of returning to the majority. Fortunately, complacency was never an option during our four years in the minority and so our staff is well-equipped to hit the ground running."

Condon is married with two daughters, ages three and four.

HOUSE FOREIGN AFFAIRS

David Fite

Professional Staff Member
2170 Rayburn House Office Bldg.
Phone: (202) 225-6735
Fax: (202) 225-5674
David.Fite@mail.house.gov

Personal: Born 06/17/1961 in Tallahassee, Fla.

Education: B.A., anthropology/sociology, Amherst College, 1983. M.A., international relations, Georgetown University, 1987.

Professional: 1990–1992, presidential management fellow, Bureau of Intelligence and Research, U.S. State Department. 1992–1999, specialist, Arms Control and Disarmament Agency. 1999–present, Democratic professional staff member, House Cmte. on International Relations.

Expertise: International security and nonproliferation.

David Fite's work as a professional staff member for the House Foreign Affairs Committee has been crammed with nuclear intrigue and international traffic in arms regulations.

After Japan's historic earthquake in March 2011 and resulting nuclear reactor fires, Fite and his colleagues will monitor criticism about the International Atomic Energy Agency (IAEA's) response to Japan's nuclear crisis and its record on monitoring nuclear safety.

The scrutiny has focused on the IAEA secretary general, Yukiya Amano, and his team for long delays in issuing updates on the disaster at Fukushima.

Meanwhile, Fite has collaborated with IAEA staff on safeguards verification in Iran and Syria and the screening of IAEA Technical Cooperation projects for proliferation risk. Fite was in the midst of the November 2010 revelation that Iranian officials withheld from international atomic energy inspectors the original design documents for a secret nuclear reactor suspected of being part of Tehran's plan to build an atomic bomb.

A U.S. embassy cable revealed that inspectors were "not impressed" by the Iranians' continued refusal to elaborate on their denials of evidence pointing to the nuclear program's military intent.

As the lead international security expert on the committee, he also has worked on the State Department authorization act as well as the legislation that gives the president the authority to remove satellites and related components from the U.S. Munitions List.

The legislation passed the House in 2010, but sat for several months in the Senate, raising fears the upper chamber might not consider it. But speaking on an International Traffic in Arms Regulations panel at the Satellite 2010 conference, Fite said things were going "somewhat on schedule" compared to authorization bills in previous Congresses.

HOUSE FOREIGN AFFAIRS

Mark Gage

Deputy Staff Director
B-360 Rayburn House Office Bldg.
Phone: (202) 225-5021
mark.gage@mail.house.gov

Personal: Born in Hudson Falls, N.Y.

Education: B.A., Russian & Eastern European studies, State University of New York at Albany, 1979. certificate in Russian language & culture, Pushkin Institute, 1981.

Professional: 1982–1986, district representative, Rep. Jerry Soloman, R-N.Y. 1986–1991, legislative director, Rep. Jerry Soloman, R-N.Y. 1991–1993, professional staff member, House Rules Cmte. 1993–2001, professional staff member, House Cmte. on International Relations. 2002–2007, senior advisor, Bureau of European & Eurasian Affairs, U.S. State Department. 2007–2008, Republican senior policy advisor/director of European Affairs, House Cmte. on Foreign Affairs. 2008–2009, Republican senior policy advisor/director of European Affairs, House Cmte. on Foreign Affairs. 2009–2010, Minority Deputy Staff Director, House Cmte. on Foreign Affairs. 2011–present , deputy staff director, House Cmte. on Foreign Affairs.

Expertise: U.S. Policy and Foreign Aid, International Relations, U.S.-European Affairs, U.S.-Russian Affairs.

Longtime House Foreign Affairs Committee staffer Mark Gage has moved steadily through the ranks, recently trading his title of "minority deputy staff director" for "deputy staff director"—reflecting his party's move into the majority.

In this new capacity, the New York native helps the staff director manage policy activities and operations. He is the leader aide on foreign aid issues for the committee, including overseeing majority staffers who cover foreign assistance policy, budgeting and programs.

During the 112th Congress, Gage expects to work on foreign aid in a time of declining funding and to examine the core purpose and cohesion of the NATO Alliance.

"Now that key allies are selling advanced weapons to Russia, the Obama administration is pursuing a 'reset' policy with Russia, (and) several allies have exhibited reluctance to engage in support of global security operations outside of Europe, and European defense budgets are being cut," he said.

Finally, he anticipates the committee will examine the "growing influence of the European Union on its member states' approach to foreign policy—and how that will impact traditional United States relations with the major states of Europe."

In the 111th Congress, Gage says his time was primarily focused on Russia's invasion and subsequent occupation of parts of Georgia; proposals for the general reform of the United States' foreign assistance policies and programs; and attempts to identify innovative approaches to foreign aid programs that might achieve results at lower cost to the United States.

In addition to his deputy staff director duties, Gage has long been the committee's director of European Affairs, which requires that he directly oversee those majority staffers who are responsible for issues having to do with Europe and Eurasia.

HOUSE FOREIGN AFFAIRS

Brad Goehner

Communications Director

2170 Rayburn House Office Bldg.

Phone: (202) 202-225-5021

Brad.Goehner@mail.house.gov

Personal: Born 06/13/1983 in Bel Air, Md.

Education: B.A., international studies, with University Honors, American University, 2005.

Professional: 2006–2008 , communications coordinator, Lawyers for Civil Justice, Washington, D.C. 2008–2009, assistant communications director, House Cmte. on Foreign Affairs. 2009–present, communications director, House Cmte. on Foreign Affairs.

Expertise: communications.

As communications director for the House Foreign Affairs Committee, Brad Goehner's primary job is managing the day-to-day activities of the panel's press shop under newly installed Chairwoman Ros-Lehtinen, R-Fla. He works closely with the committee's chief of staff and its policy experts to ensure the chairwoman's positions, priorities, and messages on issues are well articulated and advanced.

The chairwoman, Goehner says, "is very active in press outreach, so a typical day for me might begin by pushing out a statement calling for the enforcement of sanctions on the Iranian regime while simultaneously prepping several more releases on anything from a crisis involving North Korea to the State Department's budget."

In the 112th Congress, Goehner says the chairwoman expects to tackle security threats to the United States and its allies by rogue regimes and extremist groups. She also wants to keep pressure on regimes such as China, Cuba, Iran, North Korea, Syria, and Venezuela while strengthening the nation's alliance with Israel and supporting passage of free trade agreements with Colombia, Panama, and South Korea.

Ros-Lehtinen, long a proponent of increasing sanctions on the Iranian regime, was a driving force behind the sanctions legislation that Obama signed into law July 2010. But because she believes the sanctions in the bill are not being fully enforced, she intends to make their enforcement a key focus in 2011.

Finally, she'll pursue United Nations reform and try to rein in foreign affairs-related spending, which she believes has skyrocketed under the Obama administration.

"One of the best things about my job is the wide variety of topics and issues that I get to work on," says the Baltimore native, who said his only other dream job would be as general manager of the Baltimore Orioles. "I enjoy being involved with all of the hot-button issues, as well as the challenge of keeping up-to-speed on everything within our committee's jurisdiction. Ros-Lehtinen's style is to be very straightforward and direct, and she's very quotable. I try to make sure that everything we put out does her justice by being as clear, concise, and to-the-point as possible."

HOUSE FOREIGN AFFAIRS

Don MacDonald

Professional staff member

Subcommittee on Terrorism, Nonproliferation, and Trade

253 Ford House Office Bldg.

Phone: (202) 225-5911

Fax: (202) 225-5879

don.macdonald@mail.house.gov

Personal: Born 1973 in Boston, Mass.

Education: B.A., Boston Univ., 1995. J.D., American Univ. Law School, 2002.

Professional: 1996, finance director, Brad Sherman for Congress. 1997–2003, legislative assistant, Rep. Brad Sherman, D-Calif. 2003–2007, professional staff member, Subc. on International Terrorism and Nonproliferation, House Cmte. on International Relations. 2007–2010, staff director, House Cmte. on Foreign Affairs. 2011–present , professional staff member, House Cmte. on Foreign Affairs.

Expertise: economic sanctions, nuclear nonproliferation.

Having what he calls "diminished duties" after an election-related turnover on the House Foreign Affairs Committee is nothing new to Don MacDonald, a professional staff member for the panel's Subcommittee on Terrorism, Nonproliferation, and Trade.

On the Hill since 1999 and with the committee the past eight years, MacDonald views the Republican takeover of the House after 2010 with equanimity.

"I'm now just a humble minority professional staff member," said MacDonald, who was until the midterm elections a staff director. "I'm still up to the same tricks, and working on the same issues."

For now, the New England native—he was born in Boston and got his undergraduate degree at Boston University and his law degree at American University Law School—has helped to staff a hearing detailing some of China's unfair trade practices.

"That was certainly something where Sherman had himself shined a light in the past," said MacDonald, who lives in Arlington, Va., with his wife and who likes to fish and golf. "We anticipate that the same focus on critical problems in the three areas of the subcommittee will continue."

MacDonald has long worked for Brad Sherman, the California Democrat who chaired the subcommittee until the GOP takeover put another Californian—Republican Ed Royce—in charge.

"I know Royce's people going back to when we first started working together," MacDonald said. "Nothing has really changed other than that the parties have switched control again."

The committee's priorities will change, naturally, and so might those on the subcommittee that MacDonald serves.

HOUSE FOREIGN AFFAIRS

Yleem Sarmiento de Poblete

Republican Staff Director

B-360 Rayburn House Office Bldg.

Phone: (202) 226-8467

Fax: (202) 226-7269

Yleem.PobleteIR@mail.house.gov

Education: B.A., St. Thomas University, 1987. M.A., University of Miami (Florida), 1990. Ph.D., Catholic Univ. of America, 2006.

Professional: 1993–1994, foreign policy research consultant, Hudson Institute. 1994–1997, contractor, IMF. 1995–1996, advisor on Western Hemisphere issues, Subc. on Africa, House Cmte. on International Affairs. 1997–2001, deputy staff dir./prof. staff member, Subc. on International Economic Policy and Trade, House Cmte. on International Relations. 2001–2002, staff dir., Subc. on International Operations and Human Rights, House Cmte. on International Relations. 2003–2007, staff dir., Subc. on the Middle East and Central Asia, House Cmte. on International Relations. 2007–2010, Republican staff dir., House Cmte. on Foreign Affairs. 2011–present , staff director, House Cmte. on Foreign Affairs.

Expertise: Foreign policy.

In a letter sent in early 2011 to congressional Republican chiefs of staff, Yleem Sarmiento de Poblete tried to quell what she called "misinformation" circulating through Capitol halls about U.S. aid to Israel.

"Congresswoman Ros-Lehtinen wanted to advise your members that…there will be no cuts to security assistance to the Jewish State of Israel," wrote Poblete, the staff director for the House Committee on Foreign Affairs, whose chairwoman—Florida Rep. Ileana Ros-Lehtinen—has Jewish roots. "Speaker Boehner, Majority Leader Cantor, Majority Whip McCarthy, and Appropriations Chairman Hal Rogers have ALL confirmed that Israel will maintain its Qualitative Military Edge. To reiterate, while there will be cuts to the foreign aid and State Department budgets, there will be no cuts to aid to Israel."

Fluent in Spanish, conversant in French and boasting the title of "Dr." in front of her name, Poblete is a clear asset to the committee, where she served as Republican staff director until the 2010 midterm elections boosted her into the staff director's post.

Five years ago, she earned her Ph.D. from the Catholic University of America in world politics and international relations, with expertise on the Middle East. She holds a master's degree in international relations and communications from the University of Miami, and a bachelor's in international relations from St. Thomas University.

Poblete is married to Jason I. Poblete, an international expert and attorney who is himself a former Hill staffer, having worked with former Ways and Means Chairman Bill Thomas (R-Calif.). The two live in Arlington, Va.

HOUSE FOREIGN AFFAIRS

Thomas P. Sheehy

Staff Director, TNT Subcommittee
Subcommittee on Terrorism, Nonproliferation, and Trade
2185 Rayburn House Office Bldg.
Phone: (202) 225-4111
Fax: (202) 226-7269
thomas.sheehy@mail.house.gov

Personal: Born 07/20/1963 in Boston, Mass.

Education: B.A., Trinity College, 1986. M.A., government and foreign affairs, University of Virginia, 1989.

Professional: 1991–1994, policy analyst for African affairs, Heritage Foundation. 1994–1996, Jay Kingham Fellow in International Regulatory Affairs, Heritage Foundation. 1996, legislative dir., Rep. Ed Royce, R-Calif. 1997–2004, staff dir., Subc. on Africa, House Cmte. on International Relations. 2005–2007, staff dir., Subc. on International Terrorism and Nonproliferation, House Cmte. on International Relations. 2007–2010 , professional staff member, Subc. on Terrorism, Nonproliferation, and Trade. 2010–2011 , staff dir., Subc. on International Terrorism and Nonproliferation, House Cmte. on International Relations.

Expertise: U.S. foreign and trade policy, economic development, Africa, terrorism, nonproliferation.

As the lead GOP staffer for the House Committee on Foreign Affairs' Subcommittee on Terrorism, Nonproliferation, and Trade, Thomas Sheehy this year expects to work on a large platter of issues, ranging from new free trade agreements to monitoring Korea's proliferation efforts.

Sheehy recently became staff director for the subcommittee, which oversees the United States' efforts to manage and coordinate international programs to combat terrorism. It also plays a role in bringing international terrorists to justice.

Sheehy's boss is the subcommittee's ranking member, Rep. Ed Royce, D-Calif., who was a conferee on the successful Iran sanctions bill and played an important role in seeing that international arms trafficker Viktor Bout was extradited from Thailand to the United States.

Sheehy chooses and manages staffers who must help members maintain oversight of several issues: international economic and trade policies; commerce with foreign countries; international investment policy; and international financial and monetary institutions such as the Export-Import Bank.

In addition, he and his staff help members oversee the Overseas Private Investment Corporation and the Trade and Development Agency.

This year, Sheehy and his staff expect to work on advancing the South Korea, Panama and Colombia free trade agreements. They will also monitor Chinese policies that harm U.S. investors.

There will also be a great deal of work overseeing the Obama administration's handling of Sudan's status on the state sponsor of terrorism list; U.S. policy toward Pakistan; North Korean proliferation efforts; the State Department's counterterrorism program; and nuclear proliferation policy.

Committee on Homeland Security

176 Ford House Office Bldg.
Washington, DC 20515
Phone: (202) 226-2616
Fax: (202) 226-4499
http://homeland.house.gov
homeland@mail.house.gov

Ratio: 19/13

MAJORITY MEMBERS

Peter King, NY-3rd, Chairman

Lamar S. Smith, TX-21st
Daniel E. Lungren, CA-3rd
Mike Rogers, AL-3rd
Michael T. McCaul, TX-10th
Gus M. Bilirakis, FL-9th
Paul Broun, GA-10th
Candice Miller, MI-10th
Tim Walberg, MI-7th
Chip Cravaack, MN-8th
Joe Walsh, IL-8th
Patrick Meehan, PA-7th
Ben Quayle, AR-3rd
Scott Rigell, VA-2nd
Billy Long, MO-7th
Jeff Duncan, SC-3rd
Tom Marino, PA-10th
Blake Farenthold, TX-27th
Mo Brooks, AL-5th

MINORITY MEMBERS

Bennie G. Thompson, MS-2nd, Ranking Member

Loretta Sanchez, CA-47th
Sheila Jackson Lee, TX-18th
Henry Cuellar, TX-28th
Yvette D. Clarke, NY-11th
Laura Richardson, AZ-37th
Donna M. Christensen, VI-At Large
Danny K. Davis, IL-7th
Brian Higgins, NY-27th
Jackie Speier, CA-12th
Cedric L. Richmond, LA-2nd
Hansen Clarke, MI-13th
William R. Keating, MA-10th

HOUSE HOMELAND SECURITY

JURISDICTION

(1) Overall homeland security policy.
(2) Authority over the Department of Homeland Security's internal administration.
(3) Border and port security, except for immigration policy and non-border enforcement.
(4) Customs (except customs revenue).
(5) Integration, analysis, and dissemination of homeland security information.
(6) Domestic preparedness for and collective response to terrorism.
(7) Homeland security research and development.
(8) Transportation security.

HOUSE HOMELAND SECURITY

Homeland Security Committee Chairman Rep. Peter King, R-N.Y., wasted no time getting the committee's activities in the national spotlight at the onset of the 112 Congress.

King's hearing on Muslim radicalization created a firestorm. Democrats said such a session would stigmatize Muslims in America and around the world. But King held his ground and said the topic was vital to explore.

The chairman had foreshadowed his views in a statement the day after the November, 2010 election when it became clear that he would regain the gavel of the committee he has chaired under previous GOP rule.

"The terror threat has evolved and in many ways is more challenging now than at any time since 9/11," King said then. "We are seeing an increasing number of attacks and plots resulting from radicalization of individuals already residing in the country. The terror threat to our homeland has not waned; our diligence in fighting the terrorists must not wane."

Besides combating domestic radicalization, King's priorities for the new Congress include identifying what must be done to achieve operational control of the border; overseeing the Obama administration's plans for Guantanamo detainees; improving cargo security on passenger planes and on cargo-only planes; strengthening the nation's cyber security; improving communications for first responders; ensuring homeland security grants are effective and risk-based; strengthening the country's defenses against terrorist use of weapons of mass destruction, and conducting rigorous oversight of the Department of Homeland Security to ensure it is operating efficiently and cost-effectively.

A perennial issue for the committee is how to get an authorization bill passed.

Committee members on both sides of the aisle have set this as a goal in repeated Congresses. The Department of Homeland Security hasn't had an authorization bill since the agency's creation in 2003. King has said he plans to introduce such a measure by May. Although the committee has marked up authorization bills in previous Congresses, they either were never passed by the full House or were not taken up by the Senate.

Another complication for the committee has been the many committees that share its jurisdiction. King has tried to get that simplified in the past, but based on the rules adopted in the 112th Congress there won't be any changes in the foreseeable future.

HOUSE HOMELAND SECURITY

Lanier Avant

Democratic Staff Director

117 Ford House Office Bldg.

Phone: (202) 226-2616

lavant@mail.house.gov

Personal: Born 02/20/1978 in Sardis, Miss.

Education: JD, Howard University, 2007. B.B.A., Jackson State University, 2000.

Professional: 2000–2001, communications dir., Rep. Bennie Thompson, D-Miss. 2001–2003, leg. dir., Rep. Bennie Thompson, D-Miss. 2003–present, chief of staff, Rep. Bennie Thompson, D-Miss. 2007–2008, dep. staff dir., House Cmte. on Homeland Security. 2008–2010, staff director, House Cmte. on Homeland Security. 2011–present, Democratic staff director, House Cmts. on Homeland Security.

Expertise: Legislative procedure, political affairs.

For Lanier Avant, having to put "Democratic" before his staff director title for the homeland security committee is a bit liberating.

"The big difference will simply be that we're not in charge of setting the agenda," said Avant. But that also means he won't have the responsibility of scheduling and other administrative duties that he had when his boss, Rep. Bennie Thompson, D-Miss., was the chairman and not the ranking member.

In the last Congress, Avant pointed to some legislative and oversight accomplishments, including passage of a TSA authorization and chemical security measures in the House, although those bills were bottled up in the Senate.

On the oversight front, Avant said it was the committee's work that led to the elimination of the color-coded threat alert system, cancellation of the SBI Net contract on the southern border, and for needed reform in the program that gave contract preferences for the Alaska Native Corporation.

Going forward, the Democratic members, he said, are determined to get the Department of Homeland Security to abide by the portion of the 9/11 bill that calls for a 100 percent cargo screening requirement on ships entering U.S. waters.

"Our ports are still far too vulnerable," Avant said. And he believes the Republican majority will join the Democrats in that effort.

Democrats also want to take a closer look at the number of contractors that DHS uses for work that could be done more efficiently and at less cost by federal employees.

"In this day of saving money to cut costs that has to be on the table," Avant said, particularly as it applies to the protection of federal buildings. Democrats believe far too many of those facilities are protected by contract workers.

Avant, who managed to fit in law school while working for Thompson, has now passed the bar and taken up golf. He still has his bass guitar to keep him company.

HOUSE HOMELAND SECURITY

Mandy L. Bowers

Senior Policy Director
Subcommittee on Border and Maritime Security
H2-176 Ford House Office Bldg.
Phone: (202) 226-8417
Fax: (202) 226-3399
mandy.bowers@mail.house.gov

Personal: Born 01/06/1978 in Sheridan, Mich.

Education: B.A., Calvin College (Mich.), 2000.

Professional: 2000–2003, legislative asst., Rep. Dave Camp, R-Mich. 2003–2008, senior professional staff member, House Homeland Security Cmte. 2009–2010, republican senior policy advisor, House Homeland Security Cmte.

Expertise: Border security, port security, immigration.

As a senior policy director for the homeland security committee, Mandy Bowers has a broad portfolio that includes working with the panel staff to develop hearings, legislation, and committee events, all designed to help the chairman carry out his agenda for the 112th Congress.

This is an expansion of Bower's previous role as a senior professional staff member. In that capacity, she worked primarily on border security issues, including on the Department of Homeland Security's (DHS) efforts to address border violence in Mexico and the U.S. and on interior enforcement programs to identify and remove illegal and criminal immigrants from the U.S. In the last Congress, she also worked on the Coast Guard Authorization Act of 2010, which became law.

Going forward, Bowers says that at the direction of committee Chairman Peter King, R-N.Y., "the panel is refocusing on security and counterterrorism—the very reasons the committee was established."

Its sweeping agenda includes ensuring that DHS has sufficient authority and resources to carry out its missions, that the panel reviews the threat of home grown radicalization, and a concentration on cyber security.

Bowers won't totally put aside her experience with border issues. She expects to work to see if DHS needs more tools or authority to help it gain operational control of the border. She'll also be focusing on legislation to designate spectrum for first responders. And always in the mix is the hope that Congress will do a DHS authorization bill "since the department has not been authorized since the Homeland Security Act in 2002," Bowers said.

An avid outdoors enthusiast, Bowers likes to travel—especially to great dive locations and natural habitats with lots of wildlife. She is a promoter of animal adoption and works actively with animal rescue groups that focus on rescuing dogs from rural shelters.

HOUSE HOMELAND SECURITY

Cherri L. Branson

Chief Oversight Counsel, Democratic Staff

117 Ford House Office Bldg.

Phone: (202) 226-2616

cherri.branson@mail.house.gov

Personal: Born 09/30/1959 in Shepherdstown, W.Va.

Education: B.A., political science, Vassar College, 1981. J.D., Indiana University School of Law- Bloomington, 1985. L.L.M., litigation, Emory University, 1988.

Professional: 1989–1993, legislative counsel, Rep. Edolphus Towns, D-N.Y. 1993–1995, associate counsel, Subc. on Human Resources and Intergovernmental Relations, House Cmte. on Government Operations. 1995–2000, professional staff/counsel, House Cmte. on Government Reform. 2000–2001, legislative officer, Department of Labor. 2001–2002, legislative director, Rep. Eddie Bernice Johnson, D-Texas. 2003–2005, counsel, Rep. Edolphus Towns, D-N.Y. 2005–2006, senior investigative counsel, House Cmte. on Homeland Security. 2007–2010, chief oversight counsel, House Cmte. on Homeland Security. 2011–present, chief oversight counsel, Democratic staff, House Cmts. on Homeland Security.

Expertise: Legal counsel.

As the chief oversight counsel for the Democrats on the Homeland Security Committee, Cherri Branson finds matters to investigate in a variety of ways.

Several years ago she read an Inspector General's report that said the Federal Protective Service wasn't paying contractors on time, which blossomed into an investigation. The investigation led to legislation to start a pilot program, which examined whether it's both cost-effective and safe to continue to use private contractors to guard the highest-risk federal buildings around the country.

The bill didn't move during the 111th Congress, but Branson said ranking member Rep. Bennie Thompson, D-Miss., has reintroduced the measure. She believes it might have a decent chance to go this year.

"I really do believe that many members will have a different understanding of the need for safety in federal buildings, especially after the shooting of Miss (Rep. Gabrielle) Giffords," Branson said. "Even though that shooting didn't occur in a federal place, it made people think that people can be targets just because they work for the federal government."

Branson's panel looked at homeland security's color-coded terror alert system simply because "we never heard anybody say anything good about it." DHS has since modified the program.

In the 112th Congress, Branson doesn't expect Democrats to let up on oversight because they are in the minority.

"I still have pens and paper and all those things...a computer," she joked, "when we were in the minority before we were able to collaborate on a few investigations with the majority. But we also conducted our own reviews."

Branson said that since Thompson is from Mississippi, oversight of the Federal Emergency Management Agency remains a priority.

Branson's interest in government extends beyond Capitol Hill. She is a commissioner for the Montgomery County Redistricting Commission.

HOUSE HOMELAND SECURITY

Rosaline Cohen

Chief Counsel

176 Ford House Office Bldg.

Phone: (202) 226-2616

Fax: (202) 226-4499

rosaline.cohen@mail.house.gov

Personal: Born 04/10/1972 in Tel Aviv, Israel.

Education: B.A., George Washington University, 1994. J.D., University of Houston, 1999.

Professional: 2000–2002, leg. counsel, Rep. Ken Bentsen, D-Texas. 2002–2005, leg. director, Rep. Louise Slaughter, D-N.Y. 2005–2006, counsel and dir. of budget analysis, House Cmte. on Homeland Security. 2007–present, chief counsel, House Cmte. on Homeland Security. 2007, deputy chief counsel, House Cmte. on Homeland Security.

Expertise: Management, aviation.

As Chief Counsel for Legislation, Rosaline Cohen not only has to be up to speed on everything from cyber security to the Coast Guard, but she works for a committee that shares jurisdiction with virtually every other panel on the Hill.

Despite that, she says, in the 111th Congress, the committee got more legislation—or pieces of bills—signed into law than ever in its short history.

Measures such as HR 553, the Reducing Over-Classification Act, authored by Rep. Jane Harman, D-Calif.; HR 730, the Nuclear Forensics and Attribution Act, by Rep. Adam Schiff, D-Calif., and HR 3619, the Coast Guard Authorization Act, written by Rep. James Oberstar, chairman of the Transportation and Infrastructure committee, were signed into law.

The Coast Guard measure is an example, Cohen explains, of one of the many areas where the homeland security panel shares jurisdiction.

Cohen said despite new committee Chairman Peter King's, R-NY, talk of fixing the jurisdiction jumble, the 112th Congress started without any changes. Cohen remembers that back when the panel shepherded the 9/11 bill, she had to negotiate with eight or nine different staffs.

Going forward, Cohen expects ranking member, Rep. Bennie Thompson, D-Miss., to continue to work on cyber security. Within the first legislative month, the panel held hearings on such matters as airport security measures and implementing chemical security regulations.

"Most bills that come out of this committee are bipartisan," Cohen said. Because of that, she and the legislative staff sometimes get a chance to look at the drafts from the Republican staff and "put our members' own little spin on it. Our members have their own legislative goals."

Cohen said her work involves "everything from issue spotting to drafting legislation to give feedback to Democrat committee members to building consensus for Democratic bills."

HOUSE HOMELAND SECURITY

Dena Graziano

Communications Director, Democratic staff

176 Ford House Office Bldg.

Phone: (202) 226-2616

Fax: (202) 226-4499

dena.graziano@mail.house.gov

Personal: Born 11/08/1974 in Trenton, N.J.

Education: B.A., political science, University of Maryland at College Park, 1996.

Professional: 1997–2000, staff assistant and executive assistant, Sen. Edward M. Kennedy, D-Mass. 2000–2006, Democratic communications director, House Cmte. on the Judiciary. 2006–present, Democratic communications director, House Cmte. on Homeland Security.

Expertise: Communications.

As communications director for the Democrats on the homeland security committee, Dena Graziano doesn't believe her job will change much even though her members are no longer in control.

"Unlike some other committees, we try not to make homeland security a partisan issue," she says.

But that doesn't mean Graziano won't be talking to the press about areas where her boss, ranking member Bennie Thompson, D-Miss., doesn't agree with Chairman Peter King, R-N.Y.

Early in 2011 Thompson and King tussled over the chairman's decision to hold hearings on Muslim radicalization. Thompson wanted the panel to also look into groups like white supremacists and neo-Nazis. That didn't fly with King.

Graziano believes the two will be able to put aside differences on such emotional issues when it comes to working on an authorization bill for the Department of Homeland Security, something that has eluded them in previous congresses because the Senate has not passed one.

In the 111th Congress, Graziano fielded attacks from Republicans who didn't like the way Thompson approached the authorization bill—with piecemeal measures, hoping that strategy might be more successful than trying to pass one larger bill. "We had to explain to the media that we were indeed authorizing the department and were fulfilling our duties," she said.

Graziano also oversees Democratic communication for the subcommittees. In 2011 she'll pay particular attention to the freshman members in an effort to make sure they are all on the same page message wise.

In 2011, she's created a Twitter account for the Democratic members. "We're trying to branch out in that area."

When Graziano is not on Capitol Hill she's either tending to her two young children or working with her two partners in her event planning company, founded by her and two former Hill staffers.

HOUSE HOMELAND SECURITY

R. Nicholas Palarino

Staff Director of the Subcommittee on Investigations

H2-176 Ford House Office Bldg.

Phone: (202) 226-8417

Nick.Palarino@mail.house.gov

Personal: Born in Pittsburgh, Pa.

Education: Ph.D. in world politics, The Catholic University of America, 2002. M.A. in international affairs, The Catholic University of America, 1997. M.M.A.S. in international relations, Command and General Staff College, 1980. B.A. in political science/history, Western Kentucky University, 1976.

Professional: 1966–1988, field artilleryman, helicopter pilot and arms control negotiator, U.S. Army. 1988–2000, director of policy analysis, Pacific-Sierra Research Corp. 2000–2008, staff director, senior policy analyst and senior investigator, House Cmte. on Oversight and Government Reform. 2009, country director, International Republican Institute in Pakistan. 2009–2010, senior policy analyst, Office of Rep. Brian Baird, R-Wash. 2010–2011, senior investigator, Senate Cmte. on Homeland Security and Governmental Affairs. 2011–present, staff director of the subcommittee on investigations, House Cmte. on Homeland Security.

Expertise: Middle East issues, national security with a focus on the military.

Nick Palarino joined the House Homeland Security Committee early in the 112th Congress after finishing out the last Congress with the Senate Homeland Security and Governmental Affairs Committee. He specializes in Middle East issues and has made more than 20 trips to Iraq and several to Gaza and Afghanistan.

Palarino is a Vietnam veteran who served in the military from 1966 to 1988 as a field artilleryman, a helicopter pilot, and an arms control negotiator. He said that one of his more memorable duties in Vietnam was serving as commander of a helicopter platoon in the 101st Airborne Division.

The Pittsburgh native is doing oversight and investigations work in 2011 with an eye toward curbing government spending. That includes examining programs at the Department of Homeland Security to ensure that they are operating efficiently.

Addressing the terrorist threat against the United States is another priority for Palarino in the 112th Congress. In this area, he said the committee's responsibility is broader than just homeland security because the threat extends beyond the nation's borders.

The threat emanates from safe havens overseas, Palarino said. Accordingly, the committee is looking at havens in Yemen, the federally administered tribal lands in Pakistan, and in Somalia to find ways to curtail the threat before it reaches the United States.

At the end of the last session, Palarino participated in an examination of the inter-agency collaboration in the areas of counter-terrorism, counter-insurgency post-conflict, and radicalization. No one agency can confront the issues alone, he said.

Palarino and other Senate Homeland Security Committee staff began to address the issue of how government agencies can collaborate on the issues. The committee's goal was to work toward developing legislation that will help enhance inter-agency cooperation.

Palarino teaches at Georgetown University's School of Continuing Studies. He has written numerous classified publications and more than a dozen reports on national security issues. He holds a master's in international affairs and a Ph.D. in world politics.

HOUSE HOMELAND SECURITY

Mike Russell

Staff Director, Chief Counsel
Subcommittee on Oversight, Investigations, and Management
H2-176 Ford House Office Bldg.
Phone: (202) 226-8417
Fax: (202) 226-3399
mike.russell@mail.house.gov

Personal: Born in Northampton, Mass.

Education: B.A., Gettysburg College, 1980. M.A., Vanderbilt University, 1984. J.D., Vanderbilt University, 1984.

Professional: 1984–1985, staff atty., Office of the General Counsel, Dept. of Agriculture. 1985–1987, Counsel, Senate Judiciary subcommittee on juvenile justice. 1987, minority general counsel, Senate Judiciary subcommittee on the Constitution. 1987–1990, legislative director, Sen. Arlen Specter, R-Pa. 1990–93, dep. director, National Inst. of Justice, Dept. of Justice. 1993–1994, acting director, National Institute of Justice, Dept. of Justice. 1994–1996, senior public safety advisor, Corp. for National Service. 1996–2001, dep. chief of staff, Sen. Ben Nighthorse Campbell, R-Colo. 2001–2003, deputy asst. sec. for enforcement policy and budget, Treasury Dept. 2003–2005, staff director, Subc. on Financial Management, the Budget, and International Security, Senate Cmte. on Governmental Affairs. 2005–2006, staff director, Subc. on Management, Integration and Oversight, House Cmte. on Homeland Security. 2007–2008, Republican chief counsel, Cmte. on Homeland Security. 2009–2010, Republican chief counsel, House Cmte. on Homeland Security. 2011–present, staff director, chief counsel, House Cmte. on Homeland Security.

Expertise: Homeland security, international affairs, appropriations and budget.

Mike Russell's duties with the House Homeland Security Committee have changed for two reasons: the Republicans reclaimed the majority and he added staff director to his previous title as chief counsel.

In his new job, Russell has to juggle implementing the agenda of Chairman Peter King, R-N.Y., overseeing the committee staff, and being there when homeland security measures come to the House floor.

Russell said he will work to implement "the chairman's reorganization of the committee to support its work to combat the terrorist threat." His changes include streamlining the subcommittees to sharpen their focus on majority homeland security priorities. King plans to establish a subcommittee specifically focused on counter terrorism and intelligence and create a new office of counter terrorism at the full committee level.

During the 111th Congress, as chief counsel for the Republican staff, Russell worked to push King's agenda that included a comprehensive homeland security authorization bill and House passage of legislation to implement the Securing the Cities initiative, support for House passage of authorization bills for the Coast Guard, the Transportation Security Administration, and DHS Science and Technology. Only the Coast Guard authorization bill made it to the president's desk.

Russell has a long history of working on terrorism issues, including service in the Justice and Treasury departments and as a staffer for former Sen. Ben Nighthorse Campbell, R-Colo., where he worked on the first ever review of federal work in the area of international crime and terrorism.

When Russell is not working to help keep the nation safe from terrorism, he can be found hiking, on weekend getaways, or when the weather isn't good, at gallery openings and other cultural events. He also guest lectures at a local university and volunteers at his alma mater, Gettysburg College.

HOUSE HOMELAND SECURITY

KerryAnn Watkins

Senior Policy Director

H2-176 Ford House Office Bldg

Phone: (202) 226-8417

Fax: (202) 226-3399

kerryann.watkins@mail.house.gov

Personal: Born in Manhassat, N.Y.

Education: B.A., University of Maryland Baltimore County, 1999.

Professional: 2000–2005, legislative aide, Rep. Peter T. King, R-N.Y. 2005–2010, legislative director, Rep. Peter T. King, R-N.Y. 2010–present, senior policy director, House Cmte. on Homeland Security.

Expertise: Homeland security policy.

KerryAnn Watkins may be new to the House Homeland Security Committee but the senior policy director has worked for Chairman Peter King, R-N.Y., for 11 years.

Moving over to the committee staff from King's personal office means she can focus on one topic rather than the myriad of issues she dealt with as King's legislative director.

"This is a welcome opportunity as I look forward to being able to spend more time examining the varying aspects of the issues and gaining a better understanding of the complexities of homeland security policy," Watkins said. "As legislative director I oversaw Mr. King's work on these issues but was unable to [do] the proverbial 'deep dive.'"

"With Mr. King's ambitious agenda this Congress, I really look forward to moving his legislation through Congress and, quite frankly, trying to keep up with him!" Watkins added.

Watkins' key role will be to work with the committee staff to coordinate the chairman's agenda. She'll all work closely with the subcommittee chairs.

Watkins said King wants to return the focus of the committee to what it was named for. His legislative priorities, she said, include: combating domestic radicalization; identifying what is needed for operational control of the border; overseeing the administration's plans for Guantanamo detainees; improving cargo security on passenger planes and on cargo-only planes; strengthening cyber security; improving communications for first responders; ensuring homeland security grants are effective and risk-based; strengthening U.S. defenses against terrorist use of weapons of mass destruction; and doing rigorous oversight of the Department of Homeland Security to ensure it is running efficiently and cost-effectively.

King got a start on his agenda in March when he held a controversial hearing on Muslim radicalization.

During the last Congress, Watkins actually was King's point person on health care, a portfolio she had from the first day she started in his office. Her interest in health care came in handy when she worked on the passage of H.R. 847, the 9/11 Health Bill.

"This was an issue close to my heart and the passage of that was many years in the making," Watkins said.

When Watkins is not at work on the Hill, she enjoys painting and finds time to work on at least one painting a month. She spends lots of time outdoors with her two large dogs. And the native New Yorker frequents museums, street fairs, and farmer's markets.

HOUSE HOMELAND SECURITY

Shane Wolfe

Communications Director

H2-176 Ford House Office Bldg.

Phone: (202) 226-8417

Fax: (202) 226-3399

shane.wolfe@mail.house.gov

Personal: Born 04/20/1973 in Dover, Ohio.

Education: B.S., broadcast journalism, Kent State University, 1997. J.D., University of Akron, 2003.

Professional: 1998–99, general assignment report, anchor, WHIZ-TV, Zanesville, Ohio. 1999–2000, general assignment reporter, WICU-TV, Erie, Pa. 2003–2004, press officer, Department of Defense, Coalition Provisional Authority, Baghdad. 2004–2006, deputy press secretary, Department of the Interior. 2006–2009, press secretary, Department of the Interior. 2009–2010, Republican communications director, House Cmte. on Homeland Security. 2011–present, communications director, House Cmte. on Homeland Security.

Expertise: Media Affairs.

As communications director, Shane Wolfe manages the media coverage of the Homeland Security Committee's hearings and markups and helps members of the press get access to Chairman Peter King, R-N.Y., one of the historically more press-savvy members in Congress.

Since Republicans moved from the minority to the majority, Wolfe says the number of incoming press calls has definitely gone up.

"Whenever there is a terror attack or arrest or a major homeland security-related decision, reporters from around the country seek out the Chairman for his insight," Wolfe said.

Early in the 112th Congress, King called for an investigation into the rise of Muslim radicalization that kept Wolfe busy. King's outspoken nature also sparked press interest during the 111th Congress, particularly after the Obama Justice Department announced in November 2009 that it intended to put Khalid Sheikh Mohammed on trial in a civilian court in lower Manhattan.

King vehemently opposed such a move and said so on television, radio, and in newspaper interviews. The failed Times Square bombing attempt in 2010 and the Christmas 2009 attack on Northwest Airlines Flight 253 also had Wolfe scheduling interviews.

Besides the hearings on radicalization, Wolfe expects an increased number of committee markups this Congress, including one to deal with a Department of Homeland Security authorization bill. The hot topics of border and cyber security will also likely draw a crowd at the press table.

Wolfe is used to being in heated situations. After law school, Wolfe found himself in Saddam Hussein's palace in Iraq as a spokesman for the Bush administration.

An avid Buckeye, the Ohio native tries to get back to Columbus for as many Ohio State football games as possible. When he is indoors, he's a movie buff, slowly working his way through some of the best movie lists.

Committee on House Administration

1309 Longworth House Office Building
Washington, DC 20515
Phone: (202) 225-8281
Twitter: @HouseAdminGOP, @HouseAdm_Dems
http://cha.house.gov

Ratio: 6/3

MAJORITY MEMBERS

Dan Lungren, CA-3rd, Chairman

Gregg Harper, MS-3rd
Phil Gingrey, GA-11th
Aaron Schock, IL-18th
Todd Rokita, IN-4th
Richard Nugent, FL-5th

MINORITY MEMBERS

Robert A. Brady, PA-1st, Ranking Member

Zoe Lofgren, CA-16th
Charles Gonzalez, TX-20th

HOUSE ADMINISTRATION

JURISDICTION

(1) Appropriations from accounts for committee salaries and expenses (except for the Committee on Appropriations); House information resources; and allowance and expenses of members, delegates, the resident commissioner, officers, and administrative offices of the House.
(2) Auditing and settling of all accounts described in subparagraph (1).
(3) Employment of persons by the House, including staff for members, delegates, the resident commissioner, and committees; and reporters of debates, subject to rule VI.
(4) Except as provided in paragraph (q)(11), the Library of Congress, including management thereof; the House Library; statuary and pictures; acceptance or purchase of works of art for the Capitol; the Botanic Garden; and purchase of books and manuscripts.
(5) The Smithsonian Institution and the incorporation of similar institutions (except as provided in paragraph (q)(11)).
(6) Expenditure of accounts described in subparagraph (1).
(7) Franking Commission.
(8) Printing and correction of the *Congressional Record*.
(9) Accounts of the House generally.
(10) Assignment of office space for members, delegates, the resident commissioner, and committees.
(11) Disposition of useless executive papers.
(12) Election of the president, vice president, members, senators, delegates, or the resident commissioner; corrupt practices; contested elections; credentials and qualifications; and federal elections generally.
(13) Services to the House, including the House restaurant, parking facilities, and administration of the House office buildings and of the House wing of the Capitol.
(14) Travel of members, delegates, and the resident commissioner.
(15) Raising, reporting, and use of campaign contributions for candidates for office of representative, of delegate, and of resident commissioner.
(16) Compensation, retirement, and other benefits of the members, delegates, the resident commissioner, officers, and employees of Congress.
(17) Oversight of House Fine Arts Board

HOUSE ADMINISTRATION

Although it is not well known off Capitol Hill, the House Administration Committee wields a significant amount of power on the Capitol campus. As the panel charged with overseeing logistical operations for the House of Representatives, the committee has jurisdiction over everything from staff salaries to distribution of Member office space.

The panel is responsible for oversight of the agencies of Congress including the Capitol Police Department, the Library of Congress, the Architect of the Capitol, the Botanical Gardens, the Smithsonian Institution, and several others. Another major job of the House Administration Committee is to oversee all federal elections and consider all legislation that would impact federal campaigns and elections.

When he took over the committee gavel at the beginning of the 112th Congress, Rep. Dan Lungren (R-Calif.) made it clear in his first statement as chairman that the watch words of this Congress's panel would be fiscal responsibility.

"On November second, the American people spoke loud and clear, and it is our responsibility as members of House Administration to reduce spending and create more cost effective and efficient operations within the House," Lungren said.

That effort began in earnest when the committee made cuts in office salaries and helped move through the House a resolution aimed at reducing printing costs by requiring the Public Printer to make bills and resolutions available to Congressional offices in electronic format only unless hard copies are specifically requested.

But committee members on both sides of the aisle have agreed this year that there is such a thing as cutting too deep.

After an amendment was proposed to the fiscal 2011 funding resolution that called for an across the board 11 percent cut for the legislative branch, both Republicans and Democrats on the panel raised objections noting that such a move could reduce the ability of Members to provide services to constituents and endanger the safety of staff, Members, and visitors.

Meanwhile some cuts have been more controversial than others.

Early in the 112th Congress, Lungren ended the House of Representatives composting program, which had been a key part of the controversial Greening the Capitol initiative.

Started as a pet project of former Speaker Nancy Pelosi (D-Calif.), the Greening the Capitol initiative had been billed as energy efficiency program that would save taxpayer dollars while allowing Congress to lead by example. But Republicans had long viewed the initiative as more of a public relations stunt than a real effort to cut spending.

"After a thorough review of the House's composting operations, I have concluded that it is neither cost-effective nor energy-efficient to continue the program," Lungren said in a statement about the composting program. A few weeks later, Republicans cut all spending for the Greening the Capitol initiative from their continuing resolution spending proposal.

HOUSE ADMINISTRATION

Kyle Anderson

Press Director

1307 Longworth House Office Bldg.

Phone: (202) 225-2061

kyle.anderson@mail.house.gov

Personal: Born 12/28/1967 in Philadelphia, Pa.

Education: B.A., political science, Swarthmore College, 1989.

Professional: 1989–1993, various positions, Prudential Insurance Company of America. 1993–1999, station manager, WHAT radio. 1999–2003, vice president, B&C Associates. 2003–2007, consulting and outreach, ACG Associates. 2007–2010, majority press director, Cmte. on House Administration. 2011–present, minority press director, Cmte. on House Administration.

Expertise: Press relations.

After serving as the spokesman for the Democratic majority on the House Administration Committee for three years, Kyle Anderson stayed on in the 112th Congress to be the voice of the new Democratic minority.

Despite the power shift in the House, Anderson said the goals of the panel remain the same.

Anderson said the committee's job is to provide careful oversight of House operations with a strong emphasis on ensuring the safety and security of visitors, members, and staff. The importance of that responsibility was made especially clear in early 2011 after the shooting of Rep. Gabrielle Giffords, D-Ariz, at a campaign event in her district.

In the wake of that tragedy, the House Administration committee became a focal point for both a barrage of new security proposals and the debate over the balance between security and public access to Members of Congress.

Anderson said that another of the Committee's most important areas of jurisdiction is oversight of federal elections.

"We will continue to advocate for legislation that expands access to the ballot," Anderson said. "This includes voter registration and absentee ballot opportunities for American military personnel and civilians working and living overseas."

Meanwhile, as both parties try to position themselves as watchful stewards of taxpayer dollars, Anderson said that Democrats on the panel are committed to running Congressional agencies and House operations with an eye toward fiscal responsibility.

Anderson, who overcame his fear of public speaking by hosting a show on his father's talk radio station, came to Capitol Hill in 2007 after several different jobs in the private sector. He has held a variety of management positions in the broadcasting industry, worked on grassroots and community outreach on large municipal projects, and spent seven years as a strategic diversity consultant.

HOUSE ADMINISTRATION

Jamie Fleet

Minority Staff Director

1316 Longworth House Office Bldg.

Phone: (202) 225-2061

jamie.fleet@mail.house.gov

Personal: Born 1980 in Gettysburg, Pa.

Education: B.A., Gettysburg College, 2002.

Professional: 2003, special assistant, Pennsylvania Gov. Ed Rendell. 2005, senior administrator, City of Philadelphia, Office of the Controller. 2006, campaign aide, Jonathan Saidel for Mayor of Philadelphia. 2007, campaign aide, Bob Brady for Mayor of Philadelphia. 2009–present, staff director, Cmte. on House Administration.

Expertise: Government administration.

As the Democratic staff director for the House Administration panel, Jamie Fleet serves as panel Ranking Member Robert Brady's, D-Pa., point person in overseeing the operational processes of the House of Representatives. In that capacity, Fleet works closely with the Chief Administrative Officer of the House and Congress's various agencies like the Government Printing Office and Library of Congress.

Congressional security matters, which also fall under the purview of the committee, have also been a major focus of Fleet's efforts this year. The shooting of Rep.Gabrielle Giffords (D-Ariz.) at a campaign event in Tucson, Ariz., earlier this year raised new questions about how best to protect Members and their staff both on and off Capitol Hill. The incident resulted in a slew of new security proposals coming before the Committee. Immediately the incident Brady said he wanted to introduce legislation that made it a crime to make threats against a Member of Congress.

One other area of jurisdiction where Fleet has been particularly active since Brady tapped him to serve on the panel in 2009 has been the oversight of federal elections. Campaigns have been a part of Fleet's life since age 18, when he ran a successful write-in campaign for a spot on the borough council in his hometown of Gettysburg, Pa. After college, Fleet cut his teeth on several state and local campaigns in the Philadelphia area.

During the 111th Congress, Fleet oversaw the committee's review of voter registration guidelines, military and overseas voting issues, and the expansion of technology in voting machines and in campaign outreach tools.

Last year, Fleet played major role in helping to move the DISCLOSE Act through the House. That bill, which sought to provide tough new disclosure requirements on groups that participate in elections, served as the Democratic response to the Supreme Court's ruling in the controversial Citizens United v. Federal Election Commission case. The bill narrowly failed in the Senate.

Fleet and his wife Kate met while working on Brady's 2007 Philadelphia mayoral campaign.

HOUSE ADMINISTRATION

Philip Kiko

Chief of Staff/General Counsel

1309 Longworth House Office Bldg.

Phone: (202) 225-8281

philip.kiko@mail.house.gov

Personal: Born 07/16/1951 in Massillon, Ohio.

Education: B.A., Mount Union College (Alliance, Ohio), 1973. J.D., International School of Law, George Mason University, 1977.

Professional: 1995–1997, associate administrator, Office of the House Chief Administrative Officer. 1997–1999, deputy chief of staff, House Cmte. on Science. 1999–2000, chief of staff/counsel, Rep. F. James Sensenbrenner Jr., R-Wis. 2001–2007, chief of staff/general counsel, House Cmte. on the Judiciary. 2007–2011, senior member, Regulatory and Public Policy Team, Foley and Lardner, LLC. 2011–present, staff director/general counsel, House Administration Cmte.

Expertise: Legal, legislative, and oversight issues.

After a four year stint to work on regulatory and public policy issues for an international law firm, Philip Kiko returned to Capitol Hill in late 2010 to serve as staff director and general counsel for the House Administration Committee.

Kiko serves as Chairman Dan Lungren's, R-Calif., point person in overseeing the operational processes of the House of Representatives. In that capacity, Kiko works closely with the Chief Administrative Officer of the House, the House Sergeant at Arms and Congress's various agencies, including the Capitol Police Department, to ensure that the trains run on time on Capitol Hill. Kiko has plenty of experience in that regard, including two years working under the House's first CAO in the mid-1990's overseeing procurement and purchasing.

Kiko said his two main priorities for the 112th Congress include providing the best possible service to Members of Congress and—in the wake of the tragic shooting of Rep. Gabrielle Giffords, D-Ariz., in early 2011—reviewing security effectiveness and opportunities for improvement "anywhere from the district offices to the House campus."

Compared to other committees, House Administration is one of the less political panels on Capitol Hill and security is one area where both parties usually set their differences aside. But some programs under the panel's jurisdiction, such as former Speaker Nancy Pelosi's, D-Calif., "Greening the Capitol" initiative, do occasionally become the subject of contentious political debate.

Kiko is no stranger to tough political battles.

During his last job on Capitol Hill, Kiko served as chief of staff on the House Judiciary Committee, where he helped craft the USA Patriot Act and pushed for its first two extensions. He has also worked on the bill to ban partial birth abortion and fought legislative battles over immigration reform and class action reform.

HOUSE ADMINISTRATION

Andi Snow

Deputy Staff Director

1309 Longworth House Office Bldg.

Phone: (202) 225-8281

andi.snow@mail.house.gov

Personal: Born in Los Angeles, Calif.

Education: B.S., California State University, Sacramento.

Professional: 1991–1995, deputy press secretary, California Dept. of Justice. 1995–1998, special assistant, Office of California Attorney General. 1999–2009, various positions, Bristol-Myers Squibb Pharmaceuticals. 2009–2010, director of oversight, Cmte. on House Administration. 2011–present, deputy staff director, Cmte. on House Administration.

Expertise: Agency oversight and management.

When Republicans reclaimed control of the House this year they promised to trim $100 billion from the federal budget.

House Administration Committee Deputy Staff Director Andi Snow believes she can do her part in that effort by looking for ways to reduce spending and overlap within legislative branch agencies.

The House administration panel is charged with oversight of Congressional offices and the agencies that keep Congress running. It's an effort that cost about $4.7 billion in 2010. But House Republicans have said this year that they want to trim as much of $200 million from that total.

Snow will play a key role finding those reductions. She joined the committee in 2009 to serve as director of oversight for Republicans. She had previously spent a decade in the private sector at the pharmaceutical company Bristol-Myers Squibb.

Under GOP plans this year, about half of the savings they are hoping to find would come from cuts to three of Congress's largest agencies, the Architect of the Capitol, the Government Accountability Office, and the Library of Congress. Other savings would come from the elimination of smaller legislative branch initiatives like the John C. Stennis Center for Public Service Training and Development.

One high profile reduction that was championed by Republicans on the House Administration panel this year was the elimination of the "Greening the Capitol" initiative. Republicans have long argued that that energy efficiency program for Congress that was started under former Speaker Nancy Pelosi, D-Calif., was more a public relations tool than a true effort to save money.

But one legislative branch agency that isn't likely to fall under the Republican cost cutting scalpel any time soon is the Capitol Police department. Earlier this year, as the GOP rolled out a list of reductions, the agency was targeted for a slight funding increase. Republicans said the increase represents a commitment to security on Capitol Hill, especially in the wake of the shooting of Rep. Gabrielle Giffords, D-Ariz., in Tucson in January.

HOUSE ADMINISTRATION

Salley Wood

Majority Communications Director

1309 Longworth House Office Bldg.

Phone: (202) 225-8281

salley.wood@mail.house.gov

Personal: Born in Washington, D.C.

Education: B.A., political science and communications, University of Dayton.

Professional: 2000–2006, public affairs manager, National Association of Broadcasters. 2006–2010, minority press secretary, House Cmte. on Administration. 2011–present, majority communications director, House Cmte. on Administration.

Expertise: Press relations.

Salley Wood has been handling Republican press operations for the House Administration Committee since mid-2006. As spokeswoman for the panel's Chairman, Rep. Dan Lungren, R-Calif., Wood serves as the voice for the majority's outlook on committee matters.

In the current financial environment, that means that Wood spends a lot of time talking about fiscal restraint when it comes to running House offices and Capitol Hill agencies.

One of Republicans' key campaign promises during the 2010 elections was to rein in out-of-control spending in Washington. And as they looked to implement that agenda, House Administration Committee Republicans were eager to show that cost savings began at home.

During the first week of the 112th Congress, Congress passed a resolution, which was championed by the panel's Republican members, that cut House office budgets by 5 percent. That cut is expected to save taxpayers more than $35 million in 2011.

In the wake of the shooting in Arizona that left Rep. Gabrielle Giffords, D-Ariz, seriously injured, Wood has also become a point-person for informing the public about the Capitol security issues that fall under the committee's purview.

In that capacity, Wood is occasionally forced to explain the delicate balance between providing proper security and allowing the public access to elected leaders.

For instance, two weeks after the shooting, a Republican Congressman submitted a resolution calling for enclosing the visitors' galleries of the House of Representatives with a clear bomb-proof material.

It fell to Collins to explain why the Lungren and the committee did not support such a drastic step.

Collins is a former public affairs manager at the National Association for Broadcasters. She was brought to House Administration in 2006 by then-Chairman Vern Ehlers, R-Mich.

Committee on the Judiciary

2138 Rayburn House Office Bldg.
Washington, DC 20515
Phone: (202) 225-3951
FB: http://www.facebook.com/pages/US-House-Judiciary-Committee/54559691607
Twitter: @HouseJudDems
http://judiciary.house.gov

Ratio: 23/16

MAJORITY MEMBERS

Lamar Smith, TX-21st, Chairman

F. James Sensenbrenner, WI-5th
Howard Coble, NC-6th
Elton Gallegly, CA-24th
Bob Goodlatte, VA-6th
Dan Lungren, CA-3rd
Steve Chabot, OH-1st
Darrell E. Issa, CA-49th
Mike Pence, IN-6th
J. Randy Forbes, VA-4th
Steve King, IA-5th
Trent Franks, AZ-2nd
Louie Gohmert, TX-1st
Jim Jordan, OH-4th
Ted Poe, TX-2nd
Jason Chaffetz, UT-3rd
Tom Reed, NY-29th
Tim Griffin, AR-2nd
Tom Marino, PA-10th
Trey Gowdy, SC-4th
Mike Ross, AR-4th
Sandy Adams, FL-24th
Ben Quayle, AZ-3rd

MINORITY MEMBERS

John Conyers, MI-14th, Ranking Member

Howard Berman, CA-28th
Jerrold Nadler, NY-8th
Robert Scott, VA-3rd
Melvin Watt, NC-12th
Zoe Lofgren, CA-16th
Sheila Jackson Lee, TX-18th
Maxine Waters, CA-35th
Steve Cohen, TN-9th
Hank Johnson, GA-4th
Pedro Pierluisi, PR-1st
Mike Quigley, IL-5th
Judy Chu, CA-32nd
Ted Deutch, FL-19th
Linda Sanchez, CA-39th
Debbie Wasserman Schultz, FL-20th

HOUSE JUDICIARY

JURISDICTION

(1) The judiciary and judicial proceedings, civil and criminal.
(2) Administrative practice and procedure.
(3) Apportionment of representatives.
(4) Bankruptcy, mutiny, espionage, and counterfeiting.
(5) Civil liberties.
(6) Constitutional amendments.
(7) Criminal law enforcement.
(8) Federal courts and judges, and local courts in the territories and possessions.
(9) Immigration policy and non-border enforcement.
(10) Interstate compacts generally.
(11) Claims against the United States.
(12) Members of Congress; attendance of members, delegates, and the resident commissioner; and their acceptance of incompatible offices.
(13) National penitentiaries.
(14) Patents, the Patent and Trademark Office, copyrights, and trademarks.
(15) Presidential succession.
(16) Protection of trade and commerce against unlawful restraints and monopolies.
(17) Revision and codification of the statutes of the United States.
(18) State and territorial boundary lines.
(19) Subversive activities affecting the internal security of the United States.

HOUSE JUDICIARY

The new chairman of Judiciary Committee, Texas Republican Lamar Smith, has a message for the Obama administration: He's watching.

Republicans won control of the House in the 2010 midterms, and Smith wasted no time pledging strict oversight of the White House policies on immigration and border security, healthcare and terrorism, among other issues.

"Right now, we've had one party control all aspects of our government," Smith told San Antonio-area radio station WOAI just before he took the Judiciary gavel. "The result of that is that the American people have only gotten one side of a lot of issues."

That includes immigration, a long-time interest for Smith, who was first elected to the House representing a district that once included several hundred miles of the U.S.-Mexico border in Texas.

The congressman recently disputed Homeland Security Secretary Janet Napolitano's assertion that the federal government's border security enforcement is successful.

"Administration officials are either unaware of the massive holes in security along the southern border or are misleading the American people," Smith wrote in a letter published by Politico.

The Republican has also tried to tie the country's illegal immigration problem to America's current economic woes, arguing that taking a harder line on border security would preserve jobs for American citizens and legal residents.

Smith's priorities also include fighting the spread of child pornography on the Internet, curtailing frivolous lawsuits, and pressing the Obama administration for greater transparency in its decision-making.

He's introduced legislation with Rep. Geoff Davis, R-Ky., that would require Congress to approve any federal regulations that would have an economic impact of $100 million or more, or cause "major increases" in cost or price for consumers. And Smith plans a series of hearings that will examine how the administration implements the sweeping new healthcare law enacted in 2010, as well as the efficacy of using medical malpractice reform to hold down healthcare costs.

Still, Smith says his brand of vigorous oversight doesn't necessarily equal antagonism—"unless the administration chooses not to cooperate," he told the San Antonio Express-News.

HOUSE JUDICIARY

Perry H. Apelbaum

Democratic Chief of Staff and Chief Counsel

B-351 Rayburn House Office Bldg.

Phone: (202) 225-6906

Fax: (202) 225-7682

Personal: Born 10/26/1958 in Akron, Ohio.

Education: B.A., highest distinction, University of Michigan, 1981. J.D., cum laude, Harvard Law School, 1984.

Professional: 1984–91, associate, Covington & Burling. 1992–94, asst. counsel, Subc. on Economic and Commercial Law, House Cmte. on the Judiciary. 1994–2001, Democratic counsel, House Cmte. on the Judiciary. 2001–2003, Democratic chief of staff and chief counsel, House Cmte. on the Judiciary. 2004–present, Democratic chief of staff and chief counsel, House Cmte. on the Judiciary.

Expertise: Antitrust, bankruptcy, tort reform, constitutional law, legal issues.

Perry Apelbaum, the Democratic chief of staff and chief counsel, has spent almost two decades on the Judiciary Committee staff.

Those years of experience have taught Apelbaum—and his longtime boss, Committee Chairman John Conyers, D-Ga.—how to operate when his party is in the minority, which will come in handy during the 112th Congress.

During the 111th Congress, Apelbaum worked with the Democrats as they passed legislation that extended the USA Patriot Act, created new federal penalties for hate crimes and mortgage fraud, reduced sentencing disparities for possession of crack and powder cocaine, and amended the Title VII of the Civil Rights Act and the Age Discrimination in Employment Act to codify anti-discrimination protections. The Committee also completed an investigation into the Bush administration's firing of U.S. attorneys.

This time around, Apelbaum and the panel's Democrats will be playing defense as Republicans push an ambitious agenda that includes immigration policy reform, increased attention to abortion and other social issues, and giving Congress more say over rulemaking at federal agencies.

Republicans have indicated a willingness to work together on some issues, and Committee Chairman Lamar Smith, R-Texas, organized a daylong bipartisan retreat for committee members at the start of the 112th.

"I'm hoping to find some common ground," Smith told the Houston Chronicle; Conyers said the retreat marked "a good kickoff to the new Congress."

Apelbaum earned his undergraduate degree from the University of Michigan and his law degree from Harvard University. He began his professional career as an associate at Covington & Burling before joining the Judiciary Committee staff in 1992 as assistant counsel for the Subcommittee on Economic and Commercial Law.

HOUSE JUDICIARY

George M. Fishman

Republican Chief Counsel

Subcommittee on Immigration Policy and Enforcement

B 353 Rayburn House Office Bldg.

Phone: (202) 225-3926

Fax: (202) 225-7680

george.fishman@mail.house.gov

Personal: Born 12/13/1962 in New York, N.Y.

Education: B.A., University of Illinois, 1985. J.D., University of Michigan, 1988.

Professional: 1988–1989, attorney/advisor, Dept. of the Interior. 1989–1995, legislative counsel, Rep. Henry Hyde, R-Ill. 1993–1995, legislative counsel, House Republican Policy Cmte. 1995–1998, counsel, Subc. on Immigration, Border Security, and Claims, House Cmte. on the Judiciary. 1998–present, chief counsel, Subc. on Immigration, Citizenship, Border Security, and International Law, House Cmte. on the Judiciary.

Expertise: Immigration.

After four years in the minority, Judiciary Committee Republicans are eager to use their newfound power to push for stricter enforcement of immigration law.

As chief Republican counsel for the Immigration Policy and Enforcement Subcommittee, George Fishman will help panel Chairman Elton Gallegly, R-Calif., craft legislation to reach that goal.

For Gallegly, the solution is simple.

"First, we must enforce our laws and secure the border," he said during a February hearing. "Second, we must remove the magnets that encourage illegal immigration. And finally, we must remove the benefits that make it easy for illegals to stay in this country."

Like Committee Chairman Lamar Smith, R-Texas, Gallegly has emphasized tougher immigration enforcement as a means to combat unemployment of American citizens and legal permanent residents, and Fishman's job will be to help lawmakers implement those measures.

He has introduced a measure that would require federal contractors to participate in the government's voluntary E-Verify program. The program, run by the Department of Homeland Security with assistance from the Social Security Administration, offers Internet-based checks of an employee's eligibility to work in the United States.

Fishman, who has worked for the Subcommittee's Republican staff since 1995, began his career as an attorney at the Interior Department before joining the staff of former Rep. Henry Hyde, R-Ill., and working as a legislative counsel for the House Republican Policy Committee in the mid-1990s.

HOUSE JUDICIARY

Daniel M. Flores

Chief Republican Counsel
Subcommittee on Courts, Commercial and Administrative Law
517 Cannon House Office Bldg.
Phone: (202) 226-3951
Fax: (202) 225-7680
daniel.flores@mail.house.gov

Education: J.D., Yale Law School, 1987.

Professional: 1995–2003, trial attorney, senior attorney, Environmental Defense Section, Department of Justice. 2003–2007, acting associate deputy general counsel, acting assistant general counsel, Environmental Protection Agency. 2007–present, chief Republican counsel, Subc. on Courts, Commercial and Administrative Law.

Expertise: Environmental regulation, administrative law.

As Republican counsel for the Courts, Commercial and Administrative Law Subcommittee, Daniel M. Flores will help shepherd legislation that seeks to reform regulatory and tax policy.

First up: The Regulations from the Executive in Need of Scrutiny (REINS) Act, introduced by Rep. Geoff Davis, R-Ky., and Committee Chairman Lamar Smith, R-Texas.

The legislation and its companion Senate bill would require Congress to approve any federal regulation that would have an economic impact of at least $100 billion. Policies that increase costs to consumers or harm American employment, investment, productivity, innovation, or economic competitiveness would also be subject to legislative approval.

"For too long, unelected federal officials have imposed huge costs on the economy and American people through burdensome regulations," Smith said. "Because the officials authorizing the regulations are not elected, they cannot be held accountable by American voters. The REINS Act reins in the costly overreach of federal agencies that stifles job creation and hinders economic growth."

Flores and his colleagues on the panel also have begun examining other aspects of the Administrative Procedures Act, the 65-year-old law that governs how federal agencies propose and establish regulations. It also has also taken up legislation sponsored by Smith that would require a complete analysis of the potential effect of federal regulation on small businesses.

Under Chairman Howard Coble, R-N.C., the subcommittee's docket has also expanded to include courts in addition to commercial and administrative law.

Flores will be charged with helping Coble implement his plans to wield his gavel to advance priorities outlined by Speaker John Boehner, R-Ohio: job creation, national security and enhancing freedom.

"While our new subcommittee will have broad jurisdiction, we intend to focus our efforts on matters that will forward or advance these objectives," Coble said.

Flores earned a J.D. from Yale Law School in 1987, where he served as a senior editor on the Yale Policy & Law Review.

Before joining the staff of the Judiciary Committee in 2007, Flores spent several years working on environmental law and regulatory issues—first in the Justice Department's Environmental Defense Section, and later in various positions at the Environmental Protection Agency.

HOUSE JUDICIARY

Tom Jawetz

Democratic counsel
Subcommittee on Immigration Policy and Enforcement
B-351 Rayburn House Office Bldg.
Phone: (202) 225-6906
Fax: (202) 225-7682
tom.jawetz@mail.house.gov

Education: A.B. (summa cum laude), philosophy, Dartmouth College, 1999. J.D., Yale Law School, 2003.

Professional: 2001–2003, student director, Jerome N. Frank Legal Services Organization. 2003–2004, law clerk, Hon. Kimba M. Wood, U.S. District Court, Southern District of New York. 2004–2005, Arthur Liman public interest fellow, Washington Lawyers' Committee for Civil Rights and Urban Affairs. 2005–2007, litigation fellow, National Prison Project, American Civil Liberties Union. 2007–2009, immigration detention staff attorney, National Prison Project, American Civil Liberties Union. 2009–present, Democratic counsel, Subc. on Immigration Policy and Enforcement, House Cmte. on the Judiciary.

Expertise: Immigration, civil rights.

Before Tom Jawetz joined the Judiciary Committee as a Democratic counsel for the Immigration Policy and Enforcement Subcommittee, he saw the panel's work from the other side of the dais—testifying as a witness representing the American Civil Liberties Union.

Jawetz, who spent four years working on the ACLU's National Prison Project, appeared before the subcommittee three times during the 110th Congress. He testified once about inadequate health care in federal immigration detention facilities and in-custody deaths and once about the federal government's growing use of private prison facilities to house detainees facing administrative immigration charges.

Months into the first session of the 111th Congress, in May 2009, Jawetz joined the Subcommittee, where he focuses on detention and removal operations, border security, human trafficking, asylum and refugee resettlement, private immigration bills, and international law matters.

As the 111th Congress wound down in 2010, House Democrats managed to pass, for the first time, a 10-year-old proposal championed by Subcommittee ranking member Zoe Lofgren, D-Calif., that would allow some illegal immigrants who entered the United States as children to become citizens.

But that victory was short-lived.

"When I think about this bill not passing, I think about these young people who have done all the things they were supposed to do, who stayed in school and got good grades and played by the rules," Lofgren said. "And now the country they grew up in is not theirs legally, and they have no prospects for the future."

Lofgren has pushed for widespread reform of the country's immigration policies, championing several provisions enacted in the 2010 spending bill for the Department of Homeland Security, including the extension of a pilot program to electronically check employment eligibility of job applicants and visa programs for religious workers, investors and doctors serving rural areas.

The bill also amended federal law to allow spouses and other close relatives of U.S. citizens or legal permanent residents to become permanent residents themselves, even if their loved one dies before the immigration process is completed.

Away from the office, Jawetz is an avid cook and cyclist who has participated in five three-day AIDS charity rides. Jawetz was also a member of the team that won the 2009 Washington Post Hunt trivia competition.

HOUSE JUDICIARY

David Lachmann

Democratic Chief of Staff
Subcommittee on the Constitution
B-351 Rayburn House Office Bldg.
Phone: (202) 225-6906
Fax: (202) 225-7682
David.Lachmann@mail.house.gov

Personal: Born 12/28/1958 in New York, N.Y.

Education: B.A., philosophy and political science, Boston University, 1984.

Professional: 1985–1989, chief of staff, New York Assembly Member Eileen C. Dugan. 1989–1992, legislative asst., Rep. Stephen J. Solarz, D-N.Y. 1993–1998, legislative dir., Rep. Jerrold Nadler, D-N.Y. 1998–2001, minority professional staff, Subc. on Commercial and Administrative Law, House Cmte. on the Judiciary. 2001–2007, minority professional staff, Subc. on the Constitution, House Cmte. on the Judiciary. 2007–present, chief of staff, Subc. on the Constitution, Civil Rights, and Civil Liberties, House Cmte. on the Judiciary.

Expertise: Constitutional law, bankruptcy.

The 2010 mid-term elections left their mark on the Subcommittee on the Constitution.

One of Texas Republican Lamar Smith's first acts as Judiciary Committee chairman was to strip "civil rights and civil liberties" from the subcommittee's name. The move signaled a marked shift in the issues the panel that Democratic Chief of Staff David Lachmann helped lead when his party was in the majority, is expected to tackle over the next two years.

During the 111th Congress, with Lachmann at the helm, the subcommittee explored the politics of the Justice Department, including the use of the state secrets privilege in federal court and Attorney General Eric Holder's progress in rebuilding the department's civil rights division.

But with Republicans again in charge of the House, minority staffers see civil rights issues receding and social issues emerging as a focus for the Subcommittee on the Constitution.

The panel's first order of business this year was passing legislation sponsored by Rep. Christopher H. Smith, R-N.J., to deny federal funding for abortions, strip tax credits for healthcare policies that provide coverage for abortion and allow doctors, hospitals, and insurance companies to refuse to perform or pay for abortions. Ranking member John Conyers, D-Ga., said the bill would amount to a tax increase on businesses with healthcare plans that cover abortions.

Still, minority staffers say that that privacy issues and concerns over government intrusion may become a rare area of compromise within the subcommittee's docket.

Lachmann, a native New Yorker, is one of the few committee staffers who is not an attorney. He previously has worked for public servants from his home state, in the state assembly until 1989 and in Washington since then. Lachmann began his career in Washington with Rep. Stephen J. Solarz, D-N.Y., before going to work in 1993 for Rep. Jerry Nadler D-N.Y.

HOUSE JUDICIARY

Caroline Lynch

Chief Majority Counsel

Subcommittee on Crime, Terrorism, and Homeland Security

B-370B Rayburn House Office Bldg.

Phone: (202) 225-5727

Fax: (202) 225-7680

caroline.lynch@mail.house.gov

Personal: Born 07/02/1974 in Phoenix, Ariz.

Education: B.A., communications, University of Arizona, 1995. J.D., Arizona State University College of Law, 2003.

Professional: 1996–2000, legislative assistant, U.S. Rep. John Shadegg, R-Ariz. 2002, legal extern, U.S. Attorney's Office, District of Arizona. 2003–2004, law clerk, Judge William F. Garbarino, Arizona Court of Appeals, Division One. 2004–2005, deputy county attorney, Maricopa County Attorney's Office, Appeals Bureau. 2005–2006, chief counsel, House Republican Policy Cmte. 2006–present, Republican Chief Counsel, Subc on Crime, Terrorism, and Homeland Security, House Cmte. on the Judiciary.

Expertise: Criminal law, national security issues.

Protecting children from sexual predators is a perennial top priority for the Judiciary Committee's Crime, Terrorism and Homeland Security panel and its chief Republican counsel, Caroline Lynch.

The subcommittee has begun exploring the ramifications of requiring Internet service providers to retain data that can be used to identify the operator or user of a Web site conducting or promoting illegal activities, including trafficking in child pornography.

Current law requires Internet service providers to preserve such data at the request of law enforcement, but some ISPs do not routinely record that type of information.

"Internet crimes are often complex, multijurisdictional and international," said Subcommittee Chairman James Sensenbrenner, R-Wis., at a January hearing, noting that often leads to miscommunication and late delivery of needed records. "Without uniform retention, the records that are desperately needed to attribute communications to a certain person or computer may be lost forever," he said.

Under Sensenbrenner's direction, Lynch and subcommittee Republicans also are examining issues related to the reauthorization of the Adam Walsh Child Protection and Safety Act of 2006.

Enacted in 2006, the legislation created a national registry for sex offenders and made the failure to register with authorities a federal crime.

Lynch graduated from the Arizona State University College of Law in 2003, and later worked for the Arizona Court of Appeals and the Maricopa County Attorney's office.

Lynch has been with the Judiciary Committee since 2006. She first came to Capitol Hill as a legislative assistant for Rep. John Shadegg, R-Ariz., a position she held from 1996 to 2000.

HOUSE JUDICIARY

Stephanie A. Martz

General Counsel
322 Hart Senate Office Bldg.
Phone: (202) (202) 224-6542
stephanie_martz@judiciary-dem.senate.gov

Education: B.A., Georgetown University, 1991. J.D., Stanford Law School, 1997.

Professional: 1991–1994, stringer, New York Times. 1992–94, reporter, Charleston Gazette. 1997–1998, clerk, Hon. James Robertson, U.S. District Court, D.C. 1998–1999, clerk, Hon. Patricia Wald, U.S. Court of Appeals for the D.C. Circuit. 2009–present, chief counsel, Sen. Chuck Schumer, D-N.Y.

Stephanie Martz will work in 2011 as general counsel for Sen. Chuck Schumer, D-N.Y., the chairman of the Judiciary Committee's Subcommittee for Immigration, Refugees and Border Security, covering what has become one of the most controversial issues facing Congress: immigration reform.

Schumer has made comprehensive immigration reform a key priority, vowing last year to pass immigration legislation by March 2011. But there was little movement and in February, Sen. Lindsay Graham, R-S.C., was quoted in POLITICO as saying talks on immigration reform had begun anew. President Obama, meanwhile, called for immigration reform in his State of the Union address—but Republicans have said they won't negotiate until the Obama administration makes the border more secure.

However, the broader issue also includes a variety of smaller ones in which Martz will be involved. In early 2011, Schumer found that several New York universities were "sham universities" that served as elaborate fronts to hand out visas. Schumer asked the U.S. Immigration and Customs Enforcement to investigate three schools in New York.

The subcommittee's jurisdiction covers all of the immigration functions of the Department of Homeland Security, including U.S. Citizenship and Immigration Services, U.S. Customs and Border Protection and U.S. Immigration and Customs Enforcement.

Martz comes to the subcommittee from the National Association of Criminal Defense Lawyers, where she served as director of the center's White Collar Crime Project. In that position, she worked on issues regarding the over-criminalization of economic conduct. Prior to that, she served as the staff counsel of the National Litigation Center of the U.S. Chamber of Commerce and as an associate in the law firms of Mayer, Brown, Rowe & Maw and Miller, Cassidy, Larroca & Lewin.

A graduate of Stanford Law School, Martz served as executive editor of the Stanford Law Review. She spent three years as a stringer for the New York Times and was also a reporter for the Charleston Gazette in the early 1990s before pursuing her law career.

HOUSE JUDICIARY

Sean P. McLaughlin

Republican Chief of Staff and General Counsel

2138 Rayburn House Office Bldg.

Phone: (202) 225-3951

Fax: (202) 225-7680

sean.mclaughlin@mail.house.gov

Personal: Born in Albany, N.Y.

Education: B.A., Union College (N.Y.), 1989. J.D., Western New England College School of Law, 1992.

Professional: 1992–1994, assistant district attorney, Rensselaer County, N.Y. 1994–1995, assistant district attorney, Albany County, N.Y. 1999–2001, legislative director, Rep. Thomas M. Reynolds, R-N.Y. 2001–2003, counsel, Subc. on Crime, Terrorism and Homeland Security, House Cmte. on the Judiciary. 2003–2005, congressional liaison, Department of Justice. 2005–2007, deputy chief of staff/deputy general counsel, House Cmte. on the Judiciary. 2007–2008, deputy chief minority counsel/staff director, House Cmte. on the Judiciary. 2008–present, Republican chief of staff/general counsel, House Cmte. on the Judiciary.

As Republican chief of staff and general counsel, Sean McLaughlin helps oversee the work of the Judiciary Committee's energetic new majority.

McLaughlin will play a key role in advancing the ambitious agenda set out by Committee Chairman Lamar Smith, R-Texas, who has pledged to conduct "strenuous oversight" of the Obama administration.

The committee's top priorities include reforming U.S. immigration policy and strengthening immigration enforcement; giving Congress greater say in the development of executive-branch rulemaking; and examining the impact of the new White House-backed health care law. Smith's agenda also includes advancing legislation to prevent the spread of child pornography and transforming the operations of the U.S. Patent and Trademark Office.

McLaughlin holds a degree in psychology from Union College in Schenectady, N.Y. A 1992 graduate of Western New England College School of Law, he started his career in upstate New York as an assistant district attorney for Rensselaer and Albany counties.

After a brief period in private practice, McLaughlin made the move to politics in the mid-1990s, working as an aide to then-New York State Assemblyman Thomas M. Reynolds (R). When Reynolds was elected to the House in 1998, McLaughlin came to Washington to serve as the new congressman's legislative director.

He joined the Judiciary Committee in 2001 as counsel for the Crime, Terrorism and Homeland Security Subcommittee, where he helped advance the USA Patriot Act, National Journal reported.

Proving that what goes around comes around, the Judiciary Committee played a key role in extending provisions of the original Patriot Act early in the 112th.

In the middle of the last decade, McLaughlin spent a brief interlude as a congressional liaison for the Justice Department. That experience gave him "a whole new perspective" on the work of the Judiciary Committee, he told Politico. McLaughlin returned to the Judiciary Committee staff in 2005 and quickly moved up the ranks to chief of staff.

HOUSE JUDICIARY

Blaine Merritt

Republican Chief Counsel

Subcommittee on Intellectual Property, Competition, and the Internet

B352 Rayburn House Office Bldg.

Phone: (202) 225-5741

Fax: (202) 225-7680

blaine.merritt@mail.house.gov

Personal: Born 11/13/1957.

Education: A.B., Duke University, 1980. J.D., Wake Forest University School of Law, 1983.

Professional: 1984, research dir., Howard Coble for U.S. Congress. 1985–1988, legislative asst., Rep. Howard Coble, R-N.C. 1988–1996, legislative dir., Rep. Howard Coble, R-N.C. 1999–2000, counsel, Subc. on Courts and Intellectual Property, House Cmte. on the Judiciary. 2000–2006, chief counsel, Subc. on Courts, the Internet, and Intellectual Property, House Cmte. on the Judiciary. 2007–present, Republican chief counsel, Subc. on Courts, the Internet, and Intellectual Property, House Cmte. on the Judiciary.

Expertise: Copyright, trademark and patent law.

Republican Chief Counsel Blaine Merritt's plate will again include a hefty helping of patent reform, as well as the return of intellectual property, an issue that Democrats had moved to full Committee oversight during the last Congress.

Subcommittee Chairman Bob Goodlatte, R-Va., is aiming for a packed schedule of weekly hearings to address patent, antitrust, copyright, and information technology issues.

Republicans have long argued that the current patent system, put in place 60 years ago, is outdated. Goodlatte and Committee Chairman Lamar Smith, R-Texas, plan to introduce reform legislation in this session that is similar to a bill the Senate approved 95-5 in March.

"American innovators have helped put a man on the moon, developed cell phones, created the Internet, and launched the iPad 2," Smith said. "From the light bulb to smart phones, intellectual property plays a critical role in our daily lives and global economy. But we cannot protect the technologies of today with the tools of the past."

According to Goodlatte, the House bill will focus on improving the efficiency and speed at which the U.S. Patent and Trademark Office processes patent applications, an area the Obama administration has also sought to address.

The subcommittee under Merritt is also examining the Obama administration's national wireless initiative to ensure the proposal to expand broadband access doesn't hamper private sector wireless providers offering service in rural areas.

Merritt has served as chief counsel for the subcommittee's Republicans since 2000 under four different chairmen. Before joining the panel he worked for Rep. Howard Coble, R-N.C., for more than 15 years in the congressman's personal office. He was Coble's research director when the North Carolinian was first elected to Congress in 1984.

HOUSE JUDICIARY

Stephanie Moore

Senior minority counsel
Subcommittee on Courts, Commercial and Administrative Law
B-351-C Rayburn House Office Bldg.
Phone: (202) 225-6906
Fax: (202) 225-7680
stephanie.moore@mail.house.gov

Personal: Born in Birmingham, Ala.

Education: B.A., Oberlin College, 1982. J.D., Harvard University, 1985.

Professional: 1985–1987, law clerk, U.S. Court of Appeals, 3rd Circuit. 1987–1990, attorney, Center for Constitutional Rights, New York. 1994, special asst., U.S. Commission on Civil Rights. 1994–1996, acting and deputy general counsel, U.S. Commission on Civil Rights. 1995–2000, general counsel, U.S. Commission on Civil Rights. 1999–2000, special counsel, Office of Civil Rights, U.S. Dept. of Education. 2001–present, minority counsel, Subcommittee on Commercial and Administrative Law, House Judiciary Committee.

Expertise: Commercial and administrative law, civil rights and liberties, legal issues.

The Subcommittee's senior Democratic counsel, Stephanie Moore, has spent a decade working for Chairman Mel Watt, D-N.C., in positions with the Watt's personal office and the Judiciary Committee, where her docket now includes patent reform. A priority of subcommittee Republicans, the issue has drawn bipartisan cooperation in recent years.

When Moore's party was in the driver's seat in the 111th Congress, then-Chairman John Conyers, D-Ga., and then-ranking member (now Chairman) Lamar Smith, R-Texas, co-sponsored legislation that authorized stopgap funding for the Patent and Trademark Office to address a backlog of patent applications.

Other legislation that Moore and committee Democrats enacted in the 111th Congress include: the Copyright Cleanup, Clarification and Corrections Act, which allows the U.S. Copyright Office to accept electronic signatures and eliminates a requirement to maintain a hard copy listing of Internet service providers; and legislation allowing copyright holders and webcasters to negotiate new royalty rates for music streamed over the Internet.

Moore, a graduate of Oberlin College and Harvard Law School, was a law clerk for Chief Justice A. Leon Higginbotham Jr. of the U.S. Court of Appeals Third Circuit. Before coming to Capitol Hill, she spent five years on the staff of the U.S. Commission on Civil Rights and served as special counsel in the Office of Civil Rights at the Education Department.

Moore has also taught classes in law and policy at the University of Pennsylvania, the University of the District of Columbia, and Rutgers University.

HOUSE JUDICIARY

Paul Taylor

Republican Chief Counsel
Subcommittee on the Constitution
H2-362 Rayburn House Office Bldg.
Phone: (202) 225-2825
Fax: (202) 225-7680
paul.taylor@mail.house.gov

Personal: Born 12/11/1969 in New Britain, Conn.

Education: B.A., political science, Yale College, 1991. J.D., Harvard Law School, 1994.

Professional: 1994–1997, associate, Kirkland & Ellis. 1998–1999, associate, Covington & Burling. 1999–2003, counsel, Subc. on the Constitution, House Cmte. on the Judiciary. 2003–2006, chief counsel, Subc. on the Constitution, House Cmte. on the Judiciary. 2007–present, Republican chief counsel, Subc. on the Constitution, Civil Rights, and Civil Liberties, House Cmte. on the Judiciary.

Expertise: Legal reform, constitutional issues, civil right and civil liberties.

With Republicans in control of the House, social issues have moved to the forefront of the portfolio managed by the Subcommittee on the Constitution's chief GOP counsel, Paul Taylor.

The panel's first order of business in the 112th Congress was a hearing on legislation from Rep. Christopher H. Smith, R-N.J., that would deny federal funding for abortions.

The prohibitions outlined the measure would deny individual federal tax deductions or credits related to elective abortions. Democrats say the bill would impose the equivalent of a tax increase on businesses with healthcare plans that cover abortion procedures—eliminating a tax break included in the White House's healthcare law.

Measures like those are somewhat new terrain for Taylor, whose top issues have tended to lean toward issues like electronic surveillance law, religious liberty, legal reform, and legislation to encourage private enterprise to help reduce the public risks of terrorism and epidemics.

The panel under Manning also this year is taking up a bill aimed at reducing frivolous lawsuits filed in federal court. The Lawsuit Abuse Reduction Act, introduced by Smith, would impose mandatory sanctions on lawyers who file meritless suits in federal court.

Other issues that Manning is expected to help steer through the panel this session include GOP attempts to the health care law that Democrats passed law in 2010 by examining the constitutionality of the so-called "individual mandate" which requires that citizens purchase insurance.

A former products liability lawyer, Taylor is a graduate of Yale College and Harvard Law School. He's also a cartoonist, a talent he employed with the *Yale Daily News* and *Yale Herald*.

HOUSE JUDICIARY

Bobby N. Vassar

Democratic Counsel

Subcommittee on Crime, Terrorism, and Homeland Security

B-370 Rayburn House Office Bldg.

Phone: (202) 225-6906

Fax: (202) 225-1845

bobby.vassar@mail.house.gov

Personal: Born 06/07/1947 in Gaston, N.C.

Education: B.A., Norfolk State University, 1969. J.D., University of Virginia School of Law, 1972.

Professional: 1972–1973, community lawyer fellow, Reginald Heber Smith. 1973–1976, staff attorney, Legal Services Plan of Washington, D.C. 1976–1979, senior asst., vice chancellor for administration, Univ. of North Carolina at Chapel Hill. 1979–1982, executive dir., Peninsula Legal Aid Center. 1982–87, chair, Virginia Parole Board. 1987–1990, deputy commissioner, Virginia Dept. of Social Services. 1990–1993, deputy secretary, Health and Human Resources, Commonwealth of Virginia. 1993–1994, acting secretary, Health and Human Resources, Commonwealth of Virginia. 1994–1999, senior counsel, Rep. Robert C. Scott, D-Va. 1999–present, Democratic counsel, Subc. on Crime, Terrorism, and Homeland Security, House Cmte. on the Judiciary.

Expertise: Crime, administrative law.

As Democratic counsel on the Crime, Terrorism and Homeland Security Subcommittee, Bobby Vassar's work has centered around efforts to apply evidence-based strategies to prevent crime from occurring.

Subcommittee ranking member Robert C. "Bobby" Scott, D-Va., has long championed legislation that seeks to help communities to develop comprehensive strategies to combat youth violence, including gang activity. They include two existing laws now up for reauthorization: the Juvenile Justice and Delinquency Prevention Act of 1974 and the Juvenile Accountability Block Grant.

During the 111th Congress, Vassar worked on legislation that Scott reintroduced dubbed the Youth Prison Reduction through Opportunity Mentoring, Intervention, Support and Education (Youth PROMISE) Act. The bill garnered widespread support in the House, with 235 co-sponsors, while a companion bill in the Senate had 16 sponsors.

He also helped Scott lead a key hearing on the rape kit backlog, which one advocacy group called a "watershed moment in the ongoing movement to shed light on this issue and eliminate the backlog of hundreds of thousands of untested rape kits in this country."

In the 112th Congress, Vassar will help Scott put his stamp on issues before the panel, including: reauthorization of the USA Patriot Act; reauthorization of the Adam Walsh Act; and an ongoing debate over the legalities of surveillance techniques in the digital age.

Vassar also serves on the Board of Visitors at his alma mater, Norfolk State University, a historically black college in Virginia. He has also served a term as a Rector of the university. Prior to coming to work for the committee in 1999, Vassar served on Scott's personal staff.

Committee on Natural Resources

1324 Longworth House Office Bldg.
Washington, DC 20515
Phone: (202) 225-2761
http://resourcescommittee.house.gov
resources.committee@mail.house.gov

Ratio: 25/22

MAJORITY MEMBERS

Doc Hastings, WA-4th, Chairman

Don Young, AK-1st
John J. Duncan Jr., TN-2nd
Louie Gohmert, TX-1st
Rob Bishop, UT-1st
Doug Lamborn, CO-5th
Robert J. Wittman, VA-1st
Paul Broun, GA-10th
John Fleming, LA-4th
Mike Coffman, CO-6th
Tom McClintock, CA-4th
Glenn Thompson, PA-5th
Dan Benishek, MI-1st
David Rivera, FL-25th
Jeff Duncan, SC-3rd
Scott Tipton, CO-3rd
Paul Gosar, AZ-1st
Raul Labrador, ID-1st
Kristi Noem, SD
Steve Southerland, FL-2nd
Bill Flores, TX-17th
Andy Harris, MD-1st
Chuck Fleischmann, TN-3rd
John Runyan, NJ-3rd
Bill Johnson, OH-6th

MINORITY MEMBERS

Edward Markey, MA-7th, Ranking Member

Dale E. Kildee, MI-5th
Peter DeFazio, OR-4th
Eni F.H. Faleomavaega, AS
Frank Pallone Jr., NJ-6th
Grace F. Napolitano, CA-38th
Rush D. Holt, NJ-12th
Raúl M. Grijalva, AZ-7th
Madeleine Z. Bordallo, GU
Jim Costa, CA-20th
Dan Boren, OK-2nd
Gregorio "Kilili" Sablan, MP-1st
Martin Heinrich, NM-1st
Jeff Denham, CA-19th
Ben Lujan, NM-3rd
Donna M. Christensen, VI
John P. Sarbanes, MD-3rd
Betty Sutton, OH-13th
Niki Tsongas, MA-5th
Pedro R. Pierluisi, PR-1st
John Garamendi, CA-10th
Jeff Landry, LA-3rd

HOUSE NATURAL RESOURCES

JURISDICTION

(1) Fisheries and wildlife, including research, restoration, refuges, and conservation.
(2) Forest reserves and national parks created from the public domain.
(3) Forfeiture of land grants and alien ownership, including alien ownership of mineral lands.
(4) Geological Survey.
(5) International fishing agreements.
(6) Interstate compacts relating to apportionment of waters for irrigation purposes.
(7) Irrigation and reclamation, including water supply for reclamation projects and easements of public lands for irrigation projects, and acquisition of private lands when necessary to complete irrigation projects.
(8) Native Americans generally, including the care and allotment of Native American lands and general and special measures relating to claims that are paid out of Native American funds.
(9) Insular possessions of the United States generally (except those affecting the revenue and appropriations).
(10) Military parks and battlefields, national cemeteries administered by the secretary of the interior, parks within the District of Columbia, and the erection of monuments to the memory of individuals.
(11) Mineral land laws and claims and entries thereunder.
(12) Mineral resources of public lands.
(13) Mining interests generally.
(14) Mining schools and experimental stations.
(15) Marine affairs, including coastal zone management (except for measures relating to oil and other pollution of navigable waters).
(16) Oceanography.
(17) Petroleum conservation on public lands and conservation of the radium supply in the United States.
(18) Preservation of prehistoric ruins and objects of interest on the public domain.
(19) Public lands generally, including entry, easements, and grazing thereon.
(20) Relations of the United States with Native Americans and Native American tribes.
(21) Trans-Alaska Oil Pipeline (except ratemaking).

HOUSE NATURAL RESOURCES

The House Natural Resources Committee is under new leadership in the 112th Congress. Chairman Doc Hastings, R-Wash., and Ranking Member Edward Markey, D-Mass., may have trouble finding common ground on the contentious issues facing the committee, such as how to develop the nation's energy resources and designation of federal lands as wilderness.

Hastings favors an energy approach that combines renewable sources with oil, natural gas, and coal. He wants the committee to push for leasing on the Outer Continental Shelf and to encourage the administration to issue more permits for drilling in the Gulf of Mexico.

Markey also supports renewable energy, but wants oil companies to produce on leases they already own. He introduced The United States Exploration on Idle Tracts Act, which would impose a fee on companies that hold drilling leases but do not produce oil, with all fees being directed toward reducing the deficit.

Markey also supports the administration's plan to develop wind energy off the coast of the U.S. Hastings believes that offshore wind is an important part of an energy plan, but has questioned the policy of focusing exclusively on wind while ignoring the need for expanded oil and gas production.

The committee is working with the Implementing the Recommendations of the BP Oil Spill Commission Act, co-sponsored by Markey, which would establish unlimited liability for companies in the event of an oil spill. Hastings believes that some of the Commission's recommendations have merit, but will oppose those that inhibit drilling in the Gulf of Mexico or delay future energy production.

In the area of oversight, Hastings has asked the committee to monitor the National Ocean Policy and Council to ensure that it does not restrict the recreational and commercial use of the oceans through an ocean zoning policy. The committee also is monitoring the Endangered Species Act to ensure that it is not being used to block projects that could create much-needed jobs.

In 2011, the Democratic staff is promoting the president's wild lands policy, which recommits the Interior Department to assessing and protecting wilderness areas where appropriate. Hastings believes that designating an area as "wilderness" places limitations on public access and restricts job-creating activities.

The committee also is conducting a review of whether federal control of business activity on Indian lands is creating disadvantages for tribes by preventing or delaying development on their lands. Reform proposals for the management of Indian and tribal trust assets are also under consideration.

The Subcommittee on Fisheries, Wildlife, Oceans and Insular Affairs is working on a reauthorization of the North American Wetlands Conservation Act of 1989, while the Subcommittee on Water and Power is focused on the need to protect existing hydropower resources.

HOUSE NATURAL RESOURCES

Harry F. Burroughs

Republican Staff Director, Subcommittee on Fisheries, Wildlife, Oceans and Insular Affairs

140 Cannon House Office Bldg.

Phone: (202) 226-0200

Fax: (202) 226-1542

Harry.Burroughs@mail.house.gov

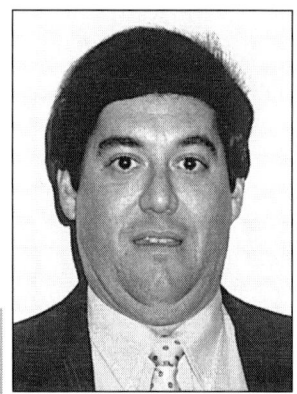

Personal: Born 05/28/1952 in Riverhead, N.Y.

Education: B.A., Baker University (Kansas), 1974. M.A., Kansas State University, 1975.

Professional: 1977–1980, legislative director, Rep. Richard T. Schulze, R-Pa. 1981–1985, legislative director, Rep. Jack Fields, R-Texas. 1985–1992, counsel, House Cmte. on Merchant Marine and Fisheries. 1993–1994, minority staff director, House Cmte. on Merchant Marine and Fisheries. 1995–2006, staff director, Subc. on Fisheries and Oceans, House Cmte. on Resources. 2007–2010, Republican staff director, Subc. on Insular Affairs, Oceans and Wildlife, House Cmte. on Resources. 2011–present, staff director, Subc. on Fisheries, Wildlife, Oceans and Insular Affairs.

Expertise: Fish and Wildlife Service, Pittman-Robertson Wildlife Restoration Act, Endangered Species Act, National Wildlife Refuge System.

With the shift in power in the House of Representatives, Harry Burroughs has returned to the position of staff director of the Subcommittee on Fisheries, Wildlife, Oceans and Insular Affairs, a position he held from January 1995 to December 2006. Burroughs and subcommittee colleagues Bonnie Bruce and Dave Whaley represent a rare case of staff continuity on Capitol Hill, having worked side by side on the Resources Committee for the past 17 years.

Burroughs continues to handle wildlife issues, and in 2011 that includes oversight hearings on various federal programs within the U. S. Fish and Wildlife Service. The hearings will examine whether different federal programs are performing overlapping functions, and whether some need reform or termination.

He is also assisting with oversight hearings on the capital and maintenance backlog within the National Wildlife Refuge System. Burroughs said the backlog now exceeds $3.4 billion. Over 3,400 projects are considered "mission critical" to the refuge system and nearly 13,000 of the 44,000 refuge facilities are in need of repair.

Reauthorizing the North American Wetlands Conservation Act of 1989 is also on the subcommittee's agenda. The subcommittee is studying the effectiveness of the law, whether the current authorization level is appropriate and what, if any, changes are needed.

During the 111th Congress, Burroughs assisted with the North American Wetlands Conservation Act Amendments and the Multinational Species Conservation Funds Semipostal Stamp Act.

The second measure directed the U. S. Postal Service to design and print a wildlife semipostal stamp to be issued by September 30, 2011, at a cost of 55 cents each. The difference in cost between these stamps and a first class stamp will be used to support African and Asian elephants, rhinoceros, tigers, Great Apes, and marine sea turtles.

HOUSE NATURAL RESOURCES

Jeff Duncan

Democratic Staff Director

1329 Longworth House Office Bldg.

Phone: (202) 225-6065

Jeff.Duncan@mail.house.gov

Personal: Born in Manhattan, Kans.

Education: B.A., political science and history, University of Delaware, 1980. Graduate study in political science, Johns Hopkins University, 1983.

Professional: 1983–1984, staff consultant, Arms Control and Foreign Policy Caucus. 1985–1988, legislative assistant, Office of Rep. Edward Markey, D-Mass. 1988–1995, senior finance policy analyst, House Energy and Commerce Cmte., Subc. on Telecommunications and Finance. 1995–2007, legislative director, Office of Rep. Edward Markey, D-Mass. 2007–2010, chief of staff, Office of Rep. Edward Markey, D-Mass. 2007–2010, professional staff member, House Select Cmte. on Energy Independence and Global Warming. 2011–present, Democratic staff director, House Cmte. on Natural Resources.

Expertise: Energy and environmental issues.

Jeff Duncan brings 28 years of Capitol Hill experience to his role as Democratic staff director of the Natural Resources Committee. He also has a familiarity with the key goals and policy positions of new Ranking Democrat Edward Markey of Massachusetts. Duncan has worked for Markey in various capacities for more than 25 years.

Most recently he spent four years in the dual positions of Markey's chief of staff and a professional staff member on the now-defunct Select Committee on Energy Independence and Global Warming. Prior to that, he served for 13 years as Markey's legislative director.

The legislation that is keeping Duncan busy in 2011 is the Implementing the Recommendations of the BP Oil Spill Commission Act, a bill to reform the practices and oversight of the offshore oil industry following the BP Deepwater Horizon oil spill.

Among its many provisions, the bill seeks to establish unlimited liability for companies in the event of an oil spill as a deterrent against risky practices, and would create a dedicated funding stream to the federal agencies responsible for overseeing the safety of offshore drilling. The legislation also would require new standards for blowout preventers, well design, and cementing practices.

Duncan said that another priority for Markey in the 112th Congress is to accelerate the deployment of renewable energy sources. Markey is a strong supporter of the Administration's plan to promote development of wind energy off the nation's coastline. The plan will create jobs and reduce the country's dependence on foreign sources of oil, in Markey's view.

Environmental protection is a contentious issue for the Natural Resources Committee, and Duncan said that Markey is committed to opposing Republican efforts to roll back environmental protections. Some policies that have come under fire from Committee Chairman Doc Hastings, R-Wash., include the Administration's use of a wild lands policy to establish wilderness areas, and its plan to implement marine spatial panning, also known as ocean zoning.

Duncan graduated magna cum laude and with distinction from the University of Delaware, where he was named to the Phi Beta Kappa and Phi Kappa Phi honor societies. He spent three years doing graduate study in political science at the Johns Hopkins University.

HOUSE NATURAL RESOURCES

Christopher Fluhr

Chief of Staff, Subcommittee on Indian and Alaska Native Affairs

1337 Longworth House Office Bldg.

Phone: (202) 226-9725

Fax: (202) 225-7094

Chris.Fluhr@mail.house.gov

Personal: Born 11/15/1966 in Lansing, Mich.

Education: B.A., University of Notre Dame, 1988.

Professional: 1988–1989, staff asst., Rep. Don Young, R-Alaska. 1990–1993, legislative asst., Rep. Don Young, R-Alaska. 1994–1996, legislative dir., Rep. Don Young, R-Alaska. 1997–2003, legislative/investigative staff, House Cmte. on Resources. 2003–2004, legislative staff, House Cmte. on Resources. 2004–2006, director, Office of Native American and Insular Affairs, House Cmte. on Resources. 2007, Republican staff director, Office of Indian Affairs and Subcmte. on Insular Affairs, House Cmte. on Resources. 2008, Republican chief of staff, Cmte. on Natural Resources. 2009–2010, Republican staff director, Office of Indian Affairs, House Cmte. on Resources. 2011–present, chief of staff, Subcommittee on Indian and Alaska Native Affairs, House Cmte. on Resources.

Expertise: Indian affairs, insular affairs.

At the start of the 112th Congress, Chairman Doc Hastings, R-Wash., established the Subcommittee on Indian and Alaska Native Affairs to focus on issues previously handled within other subcommittees or at the full committee level. His top advisor on the new panel is Chris Fluhr, a 23-year Hill veteran.

Fluhr is helping the subcommittee review whether federal control of business activity on Indian lands is creating disadvantages for tribes by preventing or delaying development on their lands. Hastings wants the subcommittee to explore a new system that would give tribes and individual Indian landowners the option of managing their lands without Bureau of Indian Affairs involvement.

As part of the committee's energy agenda, Fluhr and his colleagues are studying ways that tribal resources can contribute to the country's overall energy output. Hastings favors self-determination in how Indian landowners use their resources, but is having the subcommittee explore how the government can better partner with them to ensure the land is used wisely.

In 2010, the Congress approved a settlement in Cobell v. Salazar that provided $1.14 billion for Indian trust account holders and $2 billion to consolidate certain Indian lands. In the wake of that settlement, Fluhr and the subcommittee will be considering reform proposals for the management of Indian and tribal trust assets.

Also high on the new subcommittee's agenda is exploring a possible resolution of the controversy surrounding the Supreme Court's 2009 Carcieri decision, which provides that the Secretary of the Interior may not take land into trust for tribes not under federal jurisdiction as of 1934. Hastings believes legislation addressing the decision must allow for amendments that reflect other representatives' views of how the fee-to-trust process at the Department of the Interior should function.

HOUSE NATURAL RESOURCES

Richard J. Healy

Democratic Chief Counsel

1329 Longworth House Office Bldg.

Phone: (202) 226-7736

Rick.Healy@mail.house.gov

Personal: Born 03/24/1958 in St. Paul, Minn.

Education: B.A., University of St. Thomas, 1980.

Professional: 1980–1985, legislative asst., Rep. Bruce Vento, D-Minn. 1985–1990, professional staff member, Subc. on National Parks, Forests, and Public Lands, House Cmte. on Natural Resources. 1990–1994, staff dir., Subc. on National Parks, Forests, and Public Lands, House Cmte. on Natural Resources. 1995–2006, Democratic legislative staff, House Cmte. on Natural Resources. 2007, staff director, Subc. on National Parks, Forests, and Public Lands, House Cmte. on Natural Resources. 2008–present, Democratic chief counsel, House Cmte. on Natural Resources.

Expertise: National parks, forests, public lands.

Protecting the Arctic National Wildlife Refuge (ANWR) remains a priority for ranking member Edward Markey, D-Mass., in the 112th Congress, and chief counsel Rick Healy is helping Markey promote his Arctic Wilderness Act, which would designate the ANWR as a wilderness area. The bill is a key piece of the debate within the committee over drilling for oil in the ANWR, which is favored by Republicans.

Healy is helping Markey make his point that the U.S. should be using cleaner forms of energy and reducing its dependence on oil. To that end, Markey and the committee staff are pushing the Administration's plan to develop wind energy off the coast of the U.S.

Healy also is assisting with committee efforts to promote the president's wild lands policy, which recommits the Interior Department to periodic assessments to determine where wilderness already exists and to work to protect wilderness characteristics where appropriate.

Another issue on which Markey and the Democratic staff are on the defensive is pollution standards issued by the U.S. EPA. Markey favors standards released by the EPA that reduce the amount of pollution created when power plants or other facilities burn coal or biomass in boilers. In his view, the Republican approach would restrict EPA's ability to reduce toxic pollution from boilers and other sources.

Passage of the BP Deepwater Horizon oil spill response legislation is another major initiative on which Healy is working in 2011. Markey is a co-sponsor of the bill, which seeks to write into law many of the recommendations of the independent oil spill commission that investigated the oil spill and the practices of the oil industry.

Healy has worked on Capitol Hill since 1980 and on the Natural Resources Committee since 1985. The bulk of his experience is in the area of national parks and public lands.

HOUSE NATURAL RESOURCES

Lisa Pittman

Chief Legislative Counsel

1337 Longworth House Office Bldg.

Phone: (202) 225-9725

Lisa.Pittman@mail.house.gov

Personal: Born 01/04/1959 in Limestone, Maine.

Education: B.A., University of Florida, 1980. M.A., University of Florida, 1981. J.D., University of Florida, 1984. LL.M., environmental law, George Washington University, 1988.

Professional: 1984–1985, special asst., Office of the General Counsel. 1985–1987, attorney/advisor, Office of the Asst. General Counsel for Ocean Services, National Oceanic and Atmospheric Admin. 1987–1994, minority counsel, House Cmte. on Merchant Marine and Fisheries. 1995–2000, deputy chief counsel, House Cmte. on Natural Resources. 2001–2007, chief counsel, House Cmte. on Natural Resources. 2007–2010, Republican chief counsel, House Cmte. on Natural Resources. 2011–present, chief legislative counsel, House Cmte. on Natural Resources.

Expertise: Environmental issues, parliamentary procedure.

Chief legislative counsel Lisa Pittman spent ten years early in her career working on ocean and marine issues at the National Oceanic Atmospheric Administration and the former House Committee on Merchant Marine and Fisheries. That experience will serve her well in the 112th Congress as she advises new committee chairman Doc Hastings, R-Wash., on ocean policy and other legislative initiatives before the committee.

Hastings has set oversight of the Obama administration as a top priority, and is monitoring the newly established National Ocean Policy and Council. Pittman is assisting with the committee's efforts to ensure that the Council does not unduly restrict the recreational and commercial use of the oceans through an ocean zoning policy.

The chairman also has asked the committee staff to monitor the Endangered Species Act to ensure that it is not being used to block or delay job-creating projects. The committee is also looking at whether the National Environmental Policy Act is being used to place unnecessary burdens on important economic development projects.

Energy production is another major component of the committee's agenda in 2011. Pittman is helping Hastings promote an energy plan that includes renewable sources such as wind and solar, along with American oil, natural gas, and coal to create new jobs throughout the country.

Hastings and other House Republicans have committed to reducing government spending. Pittman and her colleagues are examining programs under the panel's jurisdiction to look for places to cut spending.

Pittman is in her 17th year with the committee. She spent the past ten years as chief counsel, advising different chairmen and ranking members during her tenure. She holds bachelor's, master's, and law degrees from the University of Florida, and a Master of Law degree in environmental law from George Washington University.

HOUSE NATURAL RESOURCES

Todd Ungerecht

Director of Northwest Energy & Environmental Policy/Senior Counsel

1337 Longworth House Office Bldg.

Phone: (202) 226-2060

Todd.Ungerecht@mail.house.gov

Personal: Born 1965 in Pasco, Wash.

Education: B.A., history, B.A., political science, Gonzaga University, 1987. J.D., Gonzaga University School of Law, 1990.

Professional: 1990–1993, associate attorney, private practice. 1993–1994, deputy prosecuting attorney, Franklin County Prosecuting Attorney's Office, Pasco, Wash. 1995–1997, legislative assistant, Office of U.S. Rep. Doc Hastings, R-Wash. 1997–1999, associate attorney, Roach Law Offices. 2000, legislative assistant, Office of Sen. Slade Gorton, R-Wash. 2001, legislative director, Office of Rep. C.L. "Butch" Otter, R-Idaho. 2001–2007, congressional affairs specialist/policy advisor, National Oceanic and Atmospheric Administration, U.S. Dept. of Commerce. 2007–2010, counsel to the ranking member, House Cmte. on Standards of Official Conduct. 2011–present, director of Northwest energy & environmental policy/senior counsel, House Cmte. on Natural Resources.

Expertise: Ethics rules, training, investigations.

After a few years working on the House Ethics Committee, Todd Ungerecht has switched to the Natural Resources Committee to work for his former boss, Chairman Doc Hastings, R-Wash. Ungerecht served as counsel to Hastings in 2007 when he was a ranking member of the Ethics Committee, and as a legislative assistant for the Congressman in the mid-1990s.

For the Resources Committee, Ungerecht is senior counsel and also is filling the new position of director of Northwest energy and environmental policy. In that role, he is working to try to protect Northwest hydropower resources as part of the Republicans' energy plan.

In particular, Ungerecht is helping to spread Hastings' message that removal of hydroelectric dams on the Snake and Columbia River systems, which has been recommended by many environmental groups, would have a huge impact on Western economies. In addition to providing a source of clean and renewable energy, Hastings has argued that the dams provide water for irrigation, wildlife, recreation, and barge transportation.

Ungerecht is also assisting with Hastings's efforts to find ways to protect salmon runs in the Columbia River, which are being threatened by aggressive sea lions near the Bonneville Dam. The Ninth Circuit Court of Appeals ruled late in 2010 that states and tribes in the region cannot kill the sea lions. The communities in the Northwest have invested in the recovery of the endangered salmon, according to Hastings, and the committee is seeking ways to keep the sea lions from decimating the renewed salmon population.

Ungerecht worked on the House Ethics Committee during its investigations of Rep. Charles Rangel, D-N.Y., former Rep. Rick Renzi, R-Ariz., former Rep. Vito Fossella, R-N.Y., and others. Among the many jobs in his career, Ungerecht worked the longest, from 2001 to 2007, at the National Oceanic and Atmospheric Administration.

HOUSE NATURAL RESOURCES

Kiel Weaver

Staff Director, Subcommittee on Water and Power
Subcommittee on Water and Power
1522 Longworth House Office Bldg.
Phone: (202) 226-8331
Kiel.Weaver@mail.house.gov

Personal: Born 1970 in Peoria, Ill.

Education: B.A., Mary Washington College, 1992.

Professional: 1992, director of operations, Bill Goodling for Congress Committee. 1995–1998, legislative asst., Sen. Rod Grams, R-Minn. 1998–1999, legislative asst., Rep. Rick Hill, R-Mont.. 1999–2003, vice president, Morgan Meguire, LLC. 2003–2005, legislative staff, Subc. on Water and Power, House Cmte. on Resources. 2005–present, staff director, Subc. on Water and Power, House Cmte. on Resources.

Expertise: Water resources, hydroelectric power, electricity transmission.

In 2011, the Subcommittee on Water and Power will focus on the need to protect existing hydropower resources and promote new hydropower through new water storage and cutting-edge canal hydropower, according to Subcommittee Staff Director Kiel Weaver. He has worked for the Natural Resources Committee for nine years, seven of which have been in his current position.

Weaver said that Chairman Doc Hastings, R-Wash., is concerned that many preservationist groups want to remove hydropower-producing dams or undermine them through litigation. In addition, federal regulations prevent small hydropower development on canals that could help local irrigation districts generate revenue without harming the environment. The Subcommittee will address all these issues, Weaver said.

In the 112th Congress, the subcommittee will try to bring balance back to water and power policy, Weaver said. Republicans feel that the Bureau of Reclamation has changed from an agency that provided abundant water and power supplies to an agency that rations shortages at the expense of jobs and communities.

Budget oversight is another major item on Weaver's agenda in 2011. He believes that agency grants dedicated to questionable items indicate a serious problem with budget misallocation. The subcommittee is examining current spending while focusing on the need to empower local communities as a way of fixing aging infrastructure.

He said that a prime focus on the power side of the subcommittee will be to bring back the "beneficiary pays" principle in which water and power users pay for the benefits as opposed to having the costs paid by taxpayers and other ratepayers.

In the 111th Congress, Weaver did bipartisan work on legislation extending Hoover Dam power contracts. He also organized field hearings on matters impacting rural communities, such as Endangered Species Act issues.

Committee on Oversight and Government Reform

2157 Rayburn House Office Bldg.
Washington, DC 20515
Phone: (202) 225-5051
FB: http://www.facebook.com/oversight; http://www.facebook.com/oversightdems;
Twitter: @oversightdems
http://oversight.house.gov

Ratio: 23/17

MAJORITY MEMBERS

Darrell E. Issa, CA-49th, Chairman

Dan Burton, IN-6th
John L. Mica, FL-7th
Todd Russell Platts, PA-19th
Michael R. Turner, OH-3rd
Patrick T. McHenry, NC-10th
Jim Jordan, OH-4th
Jason Chaffetz, UT-3rd
Connie Mack, FL-14th
Tim Walberg, MI-7th
James Lankford, OK-5th
Justin Amash, MI-3rd
Ann Marie Buerkle, NY-25th
Paul Gosar, AZ-1st
Raul Labrador, ID-1st
Pat Meehan, PA-7th
Scott DesJarlais, TN-4th
Joe Walsh, IL-8th
Trey Gowdy, SC-4th
Dennis Ross, FL-12th
Frank Guinta, NH-1st
Blake Farenthold, TX-27th
Mike Kelly, PA-3rd

MINORITY MEMBERS

Elijah E. Cummings, MD-7th, Ranking Member

Edolphus Towns, NY-10th
Carolyn B. Maloney, NY-14th
Eleanor Holmes Norton, DC-At Large
Dennis J. Kucinich, OH-10th
John F. Tierney, MA-6th
William Lacy Clay, MO-1st
Stephen F. Lynch, MA-9th
Jim Cooper, TN-5th
Gerry Connolly, VA-11th
Mike Quigley, IL-5th
Danny K. Davis, IL-7th
Bruce Braley, IA-1st
Peter Welch, VT-At Large
John Yarmuth, KY-3rd
Christopher Murphy, CT-5th
Jackie Speier, CA-12th

HOUSE OVERSIGHT AND GOVERNMENT REFORM

JURISDICTION

(1) Federal civil service, including intergovernmental personnel; and the status of officers and employees of the United States, including their compensation, classification, and retirement.
(2) Municipal affairs of the District of Columbia in general (other than appropriations).
(3) Federal paperwork reduction.
(4) Government management and accounting measures generally.
(5) Holidays and celebrations.
(6) Overall economy, efficiency, and management of government operations and activities, including federal procurement.
(7) National archives.
(8) Population and demography generally, including the census.
(9) Postal service generally, including transportation of the mails.
(10) Public information and records.
(11) Relationship of the federal government to the states and municipalities generally.
(12) Reorganizations in the executive branch of the government.

HOUSE OVERSIGHT AND GOVERNMENT REFORM

The House Oversight and Government Reform Committee's new chairman, Rep. Darrell Issa, R-Calif., began wading into areas of controversy even before formally assuming leadership of the panel. In December 2010, the incoming chairman began requesting input from businesses and industry groups about their view of federal regulations.

In the weeks that followed, responses started coming in with objections to the detrimental impact on jobs, opposition to agency regulatory initiatives, and fears from small firms over the possible monetary effects of the new health care law. Others criticized the Dodd-Frank financial overhaul and restraints on energy companies being able to drill for oil.

The committee's targeting of regulations and standards has focused predominately on the Environmental Protection Agency, in line with the Republican majority's wishes to restrain, if not curtail, the agency's authority. Along similar lines, Issa has been criticized for seeking the opinions of business interests and for his committee staff issuing findings sympathetic to industries wanting to reduce or eliminate certain regulations.

Issa has been at odds with his Democratic counterpart on the committee, Rep. Elijah Cummings, D-Md. He has accused the chairman of denying Democrats more involvement in the issuing of subpoenas; and excluding other viewpoints from hearings. Cummings was chosen as ranking member after Rep. Edolphus Towns, D-N.Y., the House Oversight chairman when the Democrats were in control, dropped out of the race.

Upon becoming chairman, Issa reorganized some of the subcommittees in terms of national security, homeland security, and foreign operations; regulatory affairs, stimulus oversight, and government spending; and health care.

He is investigating a wide number of areas including the Troubled Asset Relief Program (TARP), the Countrywide mortgage program for select clients, Food and Drug Administration recalls, the release of classified diplomatic cables by WikiLeaks, the role of Fannie Mae and Freddie Mac in foreclosures, the Financial Crisis Inquiry Commission's failure to agree on origins of the economic meltdown, corruption in Afghanistan, and the protocol federal agencies use when responding to document requests under the Freedom of Information Act (FOIA).

Another subject of inquiry is one Issa spoke out on while he was the oversight subcommittee chairman in 2006: the Interior Department's management of the now-defunct Minerals Management Service that collected the royalties on federal oil and gas leases. Questions arose anew about the agency following the April 2010 oil spill in the Gulf of Mexico and its failure to collect appropriate revenue from sale of the leases or to properly manage the agreements.

Interior Secretary Ken Salazar dissolved MMS in 2010 and divided its responsibilities between the new Bureau of Ocean Energy Management, Regulation and Enforcement and the Office of Natural Resource Revenue.

Early in the year, Issa clarified a previous statement that Barack Obama "has been one of the most corrupt presidents in modern times" by saying he was referring not to the president personally but to the deleterious results of enormous amounts of federal money spent through the Obama stimulus legislation.

HOUSE OVERSIGHT AND GOVERNMENT REFORM

Lawrence J. Brady

Majority Staff Director

Subcommittee on National Security, Homeland Defense, and Foreign Operations

B-350A Rayburn House Office Bldg.

Phone: (202) 225-4767

Larry.Brady@mail.house.gov

Personal: Born in Berlin, N.H.

Education: B.A., politics and economics, Catholic University of America, 1962.

Professional: 1971–1974, senior staff member, White House Council on International Economic Policy. 1974–1980, acting and deputy director, Office of Export Administration, U.S. Dept. of Commerce. 1981–1983, assistant secretary of commerce for trade administration, U.S. Dept. of Commerce. 1984–1987, director of international business development, Sanders Associates. 1987–1991, senior vice president, Hill and Knowlton Public Affairs Worldwide. 1991–1993, co-founder and director, Capitoline International Group, Ltd. 1994–1996, special consultant, The Spectrum Group. 1995, president and COO, Chantal Pharmaceutical Corp. 1997–2002, chairman and CEO, American Technologies Group, Inc. 2003–2005, professional staff member, Subc. on Government Efficiency and Financial Management, House Cmte. on Government Reform. 2005–2006, staff director, Subc. on Energy Policy, Natural Resources, and Regulatory Affairs, House Cmte. on Government Reform. 2007–2008, senior investigator and policy advisor, House Cmte. on Oversight and Government Reform. 2009–2011, Minority Staff Director, House Cmte. on Oversight and Government Reform. 2011, Majority Staff Director, House Cmte. on Oversight and Government Reform.

Expertise: International economic issues, trade, energy policy.

House Oversight and Government Reform Committee Majority Staff Director Larry Brady is the principal staff person for Chairman Darrell Issa, R-Calif., in overseeing the panel's investigative and legislative work. He has been on the committee since 2003 and staff director since 2006. He was a senior policy advisor on the panel and staff director of the Energy and Resources Subcommittee when Issa chaired it.

The 2011 agenda includes examining the financial bailout and the Obama administration's oversight of entities receiving aid through the Troubled Asset Relief Program (TARP).

Brady intends to complete the investigation of Countrywide Financial Corp. and its effect on the financial crisis through its mortgage-backed securities as well as its connection to Fannie Mae, Freddie Mac, and subprime mortgages.

He plans to revisit the Interior Department's Minerals Management Service following its reorganization (in 2010) as the Bureau of Ocean Energy Management, Regulation and Enforcement after revelations that agency employees had participated in illicit sexual activity and drug use.

The committee this year, he stressed, will not hesitate to explore the role of private parties, whether in waste and fraud involving contractors in Afghanistan or in Medicare fraud, which primarily occurs in the private sector.

A native of Berlin, N.H., Brady was a senior international economist for the State Department, worked in the Nixon White House as an advisor on congressional relations with the Council on International Economic Policy, and was an assistant secretary of commerce for trade administration during the Reagan administration with responsibility for export and import trade regulation.

Brady ran unsuccessfully for the U.S. Senate and House as a New Hampshire Republican as well as for the state Senate as an Independent.

HOUSE OVERSIGHT AND GOVERNMENT REFORM

John Cuaderes

Deputy Staff Director

2157 Rayburn House Office Bldg.

Phone: (202) 225-5074

john.cuaderes@mail.house.gov

Personal: Born in Oklahoma City, Okla.

Education: B.A., University of Oklahoma, 1984. M.A., University of Oklahoma, 1994.

Professional: 2003–2004, senior professional staff member, House Cmte. on Oversight and Government Reform. 2005–2007, staff director, Subc. on Federalism and the Census, House Cmte. on Oversight and Government Reform. 2007–2009, senior investigator and political advisor, House Cmte. on Oversight and Government Reform. 2009–present, deputy staff director, House Cmte. on Oversight and Government Reform.

Expertise: Investigations.

John Cuaderes, deputy staff director for House Oversight and Government Reform Committee Chairman Darrell Issa, R-Calif., has been a senior investigator and policy advisor during his Capitol Hill career. He previously was the Republican staff director for the Subcommittee on Federalism and the Census.

In his work to prepare for the 2010 census, Cuaderes focused on improving the quality of census data, and how to produce better and more reliable data. Now he is working with committee Staff Director Gary Andres on Issa's principal agenda items.

Cuaderes is assisting in the investigations of a former Countrywide Financial Corp., mortgage loan program alleged to have offered beneficial deals to members of Congress and other individuals involved in policy; a government assistance effort to help homeowners avoid foreclosure; Food and Drug Administration recalls; the Financial Crisis Inquiry Commission's failure to agree on origins of the economic meltdown; corruption in Afghanistan; and the response of agencies to Freedom of Information Act requests.

In 2008, in an effort to show, in part, how readily accusations can be made at oversight committee hearings, Cuaderes and other staff decided to test the level of formaldehyde present in the lounge adjacent to the committee's main hearing room in Washington. Their action was prompted by upcoming hearings into proposed Department of Housing and Urban Development regulations of formaldehyde emissions in mobile homes.

At issue then was the environmental safety of Federal Emergency Management Agency trailers used by people displaced by Hurricane Katrina after government tests showed elevated levels of the toxic gas in the units. The home testing kit Cuaderes and the other staff used found the committee lounge had approximately the equivalent level of formaldehyde as many FEMA trailers.

HOUSE OVERSIGHT AND GOVERNMENT REFORM

Susanne Sachsman Grooms

Chief Counsel

2471 Rayburn House Office Bldg.

Phone: (202) 225-5051

susanne.grooms@mail.house.gov

Education: B.A., Yale University, 1999. J.D., Harvard Law School, 2002.

Professional: 2003–2004, prosecutor, Tax Division, Northern Criminal Enforcement Section, U.S. Department of Justice. 2005–2007, senior policy advisor policy and criminal investigations, Internal Revenue Service. 2007–2011, counsel, House Cmte. on Oversight and Government Reform. 2011–present, chief counsel, House Cmte. on Oversight and Government Reform.

Expertise: Government oversight, tax enforcement.

Susanne Sachsman Grooms, chief Democratic counsel for the House Oversight and Government Reform Committee, serves in a minority capacity for the first time since joining the staff in 2007. She initially worked for former Chairmen Henry Waxman, D-Calif., and Edolphus Towns, D-N.Y., but, with the Republicans in control, she now assists ranking member Elijah Cummings, D-Md.

Cummings and the panel's chairman, Rep. Darrell Issa, R-Calif., have clashed over the direction of the committee's investigations with Democrats seeking to examine topics that Issa has declined to pursue. Cummings has accused Issa of not consulting him in the issuing of committee subpoenas and faulted the chairman for inviting businesses to indicate what regulations they would like to see revised.

Grooms will work with Cummings by helping the Democrats assume a defensive posture—depending on how the Republicans conduct oversight. Both sides differ in their assessment of responsibility for the nation's foreclosure crisis with Democrats attributing it to deregulation and the Republican holding Fannie Mae and Freddie Mac largely liable for loosening standards for home purchases.

Grooms also expects the Democrats to pay close attention to how Issa handles complaints by business that Obama administration regulations have harmed the ability to create and expand jobs. In addition, they want to see if the majority side concentrates mostly on regulation costs but not on the potential benefits of clean air and clean water requirements.

Grooms, who knew from her time in law school that she wanted to go into public service, has participated in a range of committee investigations. They have included the responsiveness of the Federal Emergency Management Agency to natural disasters, the death by friendly fire in Afghanistan of U.S. Army Ranger Pat Tillman, the military's granting of waivers to enable convicted felons to enlist for combat, and the Bush administration's alleged use of political appointees in federal agencies for partisan activities.

Before coming to the committee, Grooms was senior policy advisor to the deputy commissioner for services and enforcement at the Internal Revenue Service and also worked as a prosecutor with the U.S. Department of Justice's tax division.

Her husband Daniel Grooms, whom she met while at Harvard law school, is an assistant United States Attorney for the Eastern District of Virginia. He has probed organized crime and drug enforcement.

HOUSE OVERSIGHT AND GOVERNMENT REFORM

Frederick R. Hill

Communications Director

2347 Rayburn House Office Bldg.

Phone: (202) 225-0037

frederick.hill@mail.house.gov

Personal: Born in Durham, N.C.

Education: B.A., University of North Carolina, 2001.

Professional: 2001–2005, legislative correspondent, Rep. Darrell Issa, R-Calif. 2005–2009, press secretary, Rep. Darrell Issa, R-Calif. 2009–present, Republican communications director, House Cmte. on Oversight and Government Reform.

Expertise: Communications strategy.

Frederick Hill, the Republican communications director, develops communications strategy as Chairman Darrell Issa, R-Calif., conducts a range of investigations related to existing regulations, health care, industry bailouts, and other Obama administration and governmental actions.

Hill joined the staff in January 2009 when he came over from Issa's office where he had worked since 2001.

As a committee spokesman, Hill has responded to criticisms of Issa from ranking member Elijah Cummings, D-Md., that the chairman was not always acting in a bipartisan manner or had exaggerated potential savings from program reductions. Hill accused Cummings of moving ahead of other Democrats for the ranking position to function as an "effective obstructionist."

Hill also has faced questions from news organizations about allegations that those with close ties to well connected lobbyists had an inside track in being considered for oversight committee positions. "Committee makes all hiring decisions based on the ability of individuals to help the committee do its job," he said in an e-mail.

Hill was supposed to be working with deputy communications director Kurt Bardella, but in March 2011, Issa abruptly dismissed Bardella, following his acknowledgement he had shown private correspondence from other reporters to the New York Times' Mark Leibovich for a book on the workings of Capitol Hill.

"Though limited, these actions were highly inappropriate, a basic breach of trust with reporters it was his job to assist, and inconsistent the established communications office polices," Issa told Politico. He added that he had found no indication Leibovich received internal committee materials or related discussions.

Hill stated that he did not learn about any e-mail sharing until Capitol Hill newspaper *Politico* first contacted the committee about what occurred.

HOUSE OVERSIGHT AND GOVERNMENT REFORM

David P. Rapallo

Democratic Staff Director

2471 Rayburn House Office Bldg.

Phone: (202) 225-5051

Personal: Born in Germany.

Education: B.A., University of California, Los Angeles, 1991. J.D., University of California, Hastings, 1994. L.L.M., federal legislation, Georgetown University Law Center, 1997. L.L.M., international law, Georgetown University Law Center, 1998.

Professional: 1994–1995, executive fellow/counsel, Office of the Governor, State of California. 1995–1998, teaching fellow, Georgetown University Center of Law. 1998–2005, counsel, House Cmte. on Oversight and Government Reform. 2005–2008, chief investigative counsel, House Cmte. on Oversight and Government Reform. 2009, general counsel, House Cmte. on Energy and Commerce. 2009–2010, senior director and counsel, Guantanamo Detainee Affairs, Legal, National Security Staff, Executive Office of the President. 2011–present, staff director, House Cmte. on Oversight and Government Reform.

Expertise: Investigations.

David Rapallo's role as Democratic staff director for the House Committee on Oversight and Government Reform marked his return to the panel and Capitol Hill. He worked as an investigator for Rep. Henry Waxman, D-Calif., on the oversight committee and joined Waxman as general counsel when the lawmaker took the helm of the Energy and Commerce Committee in 2009.

Rapallo then moved to become part of the National Security Council staff as an attorney in the Obama White House, before Rep. Elijah Cummings, D-Md., selected him as his oversight staff director.

Now in the 112th Congress, Rapallo helps lead the minority response to the series of committee investigations that Chairman Darrell Issa, R-Calif., is undertaking.

"With this committee set to face many serious challenges in the next Congress, I am confident that David's vast experience in oversight and investigations will be pivotal to our success," Cummings said in a statement at the time of the appointment.

With Issa probing a range of policy matters pertaining to government spending, regulation, the new health care law, and some of the administration's emergency actions, Rapallo, at Cummings' direction, is watching to see whether the investigations seem to be on an overtly partisan course. The chairman and ranking member already have differed over minority members being permitted to make opening statements at hearings and to request witnesses to call.

Rapallo, a University of California-trained lawyer, served on the minority staff as counsel to the oversight committee. He had become investigative counsel to the panel when the Democrats regained the majority in 2006. As the energy and commerce general counsel, he worked on climate change, telecommunications, and consumer protection, among other issues.

While with the Security Council, Rapallo was involved in the issue of President Barack Obama's pledge to close the Guantanamo Bay military prison facility in Cuba within one year of taking office. The president's self-imposed deadline came and went largely due to the difficulties in finding another location to house the prisoners, many of whom include terrorism suspects.

HOUSE OVERSIGHT AND GOVERNMENT REFORM

Mark Stephenson

Senior Policy Advisor/Legislative Director

2471 Rayburn House Office Bldg.

Phone: (202) 225-5051

mark.stephenson@mail.house.gov

Personal: Born in Bethlehem, Pa.

Education: B.A., Dickinson College, 1980. M.A., George Washington University, 1984.

Professional: 1993–1996, legislative assistant, U.S. Rep. Carolyn Maloney, D-N.Y. 1997–2008, professional staff, House Cmte. on Oversight and Government Reform. 2009–2010, chief legislative advisor, House Cmte. on Oversight and Government Reform. 2010–present, senior policy advisor/legislative director, House Cmte. on Oversight and Government Reform.

Expertise: Government operations, financial management.

Mark Stephenson continues his emphasis on government operations, including contracting reform, procurement, financial management, personnel issues, and the management of government real estate, as a senior legislative advisor for Democrats on the House Oversight and Government Reform Committee.

A pressing issue in 2011 is the finding from the congressionally chartered Commission on Wartime Contracting in Iraq and Afghanistan that federal agencies often continue doing business with firms found guilty of misconduct instead of suspending them for at least a temporary period. Stephenson has worked on increasing accountability in contracting by having federal contracts report violations of law and contract overpayments.

Stephenson also follows up on reports from the Government Accountability Office on high-risk federal programs that pose dangers for fraud or abuse. The 2011 update of that list revealed serious problems in the Department of the Interior's oil and gas programs with the collection of revenues and the reorganization of the former U.S. Minerals Management Service into the Bureau of Ocean Energy Management, Regulation and Enforcement.

Oversight and Government Reform Committee ranking member Elijah Cummings, D-Md., faulted large oil companies for not sufficiently paying the government in return for those resources it obtains from federal properties. The GAO also has called for an examination of the amount the government charges for the leases.

The agency removed two items from its latest list: the 2010 Census and the Defense Department's Personnel Security Clearance Program.

Stephenson started as a professional staff member on the committee in 1997. He initially worked for Rep. Carolyn Maloney, R-N.Y. before moving to the committee staff.

Away from the Hill, Stephenson has participated as a representative of Congress in meetings of the National Capital Planning Commission, focusing on revitalization for the city of Washington, including the development of new destinations beyond the National Mall area, neighborhood preservation, the reuse of existing buildings, and making the District of Columbia stand out as a tourist destination apart from being the seat of government.

Committee on Rules

H-312, The Capitol
Washington, DC 20515
Phone: (202) 225-9091
Fax: (202) 225-6763
http://www.rules.house.gov

Ratio: 8/4

MAJORITY MEMBERS

David Dreier, CA-26th, Chairman

Pete Sessions, TX-5th
Virginia Foxx, NC-5th
Rob Bishop, UT-1st
Rob Woodall, GA-7th
Richard Nugent, FL-5th
Tim Scott, SC-1st
Daniel Webster, FL-8th

MINORITY MEMBERS

Louise McIntosh Slaughter, NY-28th, Ranking Member

James P. McGovern, MA-3rd
Alcee Hastings, FL-23rd
Jared Polis, CO-2nd

HOUSE RULES

JURISDICTION

(1) Rules and joint rules (other than those relating to the Code of Official Conduct) and the order of business of the House.
(2) Recesses and final adjournments of Congress.

HOUSE RULES

Rep. David Dreier, R-Calif., wasted no time in early 2011 putting the power of the House Rules Committee to work.

As the House in mid-February tried to wrap up work on a FY11 spending bill to fund the federal government through Sept. 30, the San Dimas Republican and his team made good on a promise to let more members participate in the budget process on the House floor.

To that end, Dreier's committee approved a rule allowing any member, Republican or Democrat, to offer a "germane" amendment to the budget proposal—as long as it was pre-printed in the Congressional Record. The move was necessary, Dreier argued, to allow a "serious, free flowing debate on the need to reduce federal spending and liberate our economy so that it can start to create jobs."

"We need to make the House more transparent and accountable to the American people," said Dreier. "We also need to reform the rules and operations of the House to ensure that they encourage spending reductions and economic growth."

The new rules also demand that: there be no votes on bill unless the legislation has been available for at least three calendar days; recorded votes and video archives of all committees be posted online; and a new "electronic format" for legislation that Dreier claims will make a "dramatic change in how legislation is made available" to members, the public and the media.

"No longer will massive legislation be written behind closed doors and rammed through the House before anyone has the chance to review or amend the text," Dreier said. "Our work will be done in an open way that affords all Members the opportunity to participate and scrutinize.

Of course, Dreier's approach to transparency has a political tinge, as he conceded when he said that the new rules would ensure the very Republican goal of deep cuts to federal spending: "We should not and cannot consider legislation that pushes the federal budget further into insolvency," he said.

Dreier stepped comfortably into the chairman's spot, having led the committee—the so-called "traffic cop" of Congress—from 1999 through 2006.

The committee determines the rules on bills that come before the House - such as the amount of time allowed for debate.

Early in 2011, Dreier introduced bills designed to cut federal spending, reduce illegal immigration, protect wilderness and reform taxes.

"We will be looking at debates on all these issues: How do we get economy moving? How do we address illegal immigration? How do we reduce spending?" said Dreier's spokeswoman Jo Maney. "These are all debates the next Congress is going to be having. And he believes these (bills) are the way we should go. That is why he chose to introduce them on opening day."

The wilderness legislation would protect 18,000 acres of the Angeles and San Bernardino National Forests by banning roads, cell phone towers, power lines, and drilling.

His spending-cut proposals include a measure that would simplify the tax code to an optional one-page form with three rates—10, 15 and 30 percent—and another bill that would simplify the budget process by creating a two-year budget cycle, among other things.

As for the immigration legislation: He offered a bill that would hike penalties for employers who hire undocumented immigrants, beef up immigration enforcement personnel, and create an electronic system that verifies citizenship or residency status based on a secure Social Security card.

HOUSE RULES

Jenny Gorski

Senior Professional Staff Member

Room H-312, the Capitol

Phone: (202) 202-225-9191

Jenny.gorski@mail.house.gov

Personal: Born 5/15/1979 in Milwaukee, Wis.

Education: B.A., government, Georgetown University, 2001.

Professional: 2001–2002, staff assistant, Rep. Doc Hastings, R-Wash. 2002–2004, legislative correspondent, Rep. Doc Hastings, R-Wash. 2004–2008, legislative assistant, Rep. Doc Hastings, R-Wash. 2005–2008, associate staff, Rep. Doc Hastings, R-Wash., House Cmte. on Rules. 2008–2010, professional staff member, House Cmte. on Rules. 2010–2011, senior professional staff member, House Cmte. on Rules.

Expertise: Health care, education, energy and resources.

For three years, Jenny N. Gorski has been the Rules Committee's point person for Rep. Doc Hastings, R-Wash. Having risen through the committee ranks, she is now a senior professional staffer who works with leadership and parliamentarians to develop rules for bills, prepare members for hearings and meetings, work with member offices on drafting amendments, and offers guidance on House rules.

"I primarily focus on legislation under the jurisdiction of the Committees on Energy and Commerce, the Judiciary and Education," said Gorski, a Wisconsin native.

In the 111th Congress, Gorski worked on health care reform, "which was challenging because it was done through reconciliation and the final bill did not go through regular order," she said.

"The Rules Committee was the only House committee to have a hearing on the bill, which lasted over 13 hours," said Gorski, a Georgetown University graduate. "It was also challenging because members had amendments they wanted to offer to the bill and the Democratic leadership chose not to make any amendments in order. Members on both sides and the American people were visibly frustrated at the process.

"It was interesting to see people finally engaged in not just policy, but the process," Gorski said. "I believe a lot of members and Americans realized that the process of how legislation comes to and is considered on the floor really does matter and make a difference."

In the 112th Congress, Gorski said she expects to help leadership "facilitate a more open process of considering legislation on the House floor."

She is also enthused by the prospect of working with so many newcomers in the House, which the GOP took over after the 2010 midterm elections.

"I expect it to be a challenge to educate all the new members and staff on the rules of the House and on floor procedures," she said.

HOUSE RULES

Hugh Nathanial Halpern

Majority Staff Director

H-312, The Capitol

Phone: (202) 225-9191

hugh.halpern@mail.house.gov

Personal: Born 07/21/1969 in Harrisburg, Pa.

Education: B.A. (cum laude), political science, American University, 1991. M.A., political science, American University, 1992. J.D., George Mason University Law School, 1997.

Professional: 1987–1990, staff asst., systems mgr., Rep. Bud Shuster, R-Pa. 1990–1991, staff asst., Subc. on Surface Transportation, House Cmte. on Public Works and Transportation. 1991–1994, Republican research asst., House Cmte. on Energy and Commerce. 1995–1997, professional staff member, House Cmte. on Commerce. 1997–1998, counsel, House Cmte. on Commerce. 1998–2000, parliamentarian, House Cmte. on Commerce. 2001–2003, parliamentarian, House Cmte. on Financial Services. 2004, general counsel, House Cmte. on Financial Services. 2005–2010, Republican staff dir., House Cmte. on Rules. 2011–Present , Majority Staff Director, House Cmte. on Rules.

Expertise: House procedure, financial services, automobile safety.

It was in the 109th Congress that Hugh Halpern last had "majority" in front of his title as staff director for the House Committee on Rules. With GOP gains in 2010's midterm elections, Halpern has the title again.

That means he works closely with the Republican leadership team to craft the GOP's procedural strategy and is responsible for ensuring the committee executes the policy decisions of the Republican majority in terms of the measures considered on the House floor.

When his party was in the minority, Halpern told the Almanac that he considered the 110th Congress "the most closed Congress in history, with more closed rules, fewer open rules and fewer opportunities for the minority to participate in the amendment process than in any other Congress in history." Republicans on the committee even published a report chronicling Democrats' "failure to live up to their own promises of a more open process."

Now that his party controls the Rules Committee in the 112th Congress, it remains to be seen whether Halpern and his colleagues will have more open proceedings and give Democrats the chance to participate in a way the GOP claims they couldn't for the past few years. Halpern insists this will be so.

"We argued for greater transparency and openness in the Rules Committee process. This was reflected in the 112th Congress rules package which provided for three-day layovers of bills and major amendments, availability of documents electronically and a host of other provisions intended to improve the way Congress operates."

Halpern said the committee will also focus on improving the budget process and reducing spending in an effort to make a dent in the national deficit.

HOUSE RULES

Adam Jarvis

Republican Deputy Staff Director

H-312, The Capitol

Phone: (202) 225-9191

Fax: (202) 225-6763

adam.jarvis@mail.house.gov

Personal: Born 12/21/1974 in Nampa, Idaho.

Education: B.S., University of Idaho, 1998.

Professional: 1999, staff asst., Rep. Mike Simpson, R-Idaho. 1999–2000, staff asst., House Cmte. on Rules. 2000–2001, legislative clerk, House Cmte. on Rules. 2001–2003, professional staff member, House Cmte. on Rules. 2003–present, Republican deputy staff dir., House Cmte. on Rules.

Expertise: Legislative and budget process and procedure.

As deputy staff director for House Rules Committee Republicans, Adam Jarvis spends each working day absorbed in the sometimes arcane procedures, rules, and processes that make the House run smoothly.

One of his earliest tasks in the 112th Congress was working on H.R.1, the "Full Year Continuing Appropriations Act," which requires that amendments be printed in the Congressional Record before being considered on the House floor. The bill was introduced on the Rules Committee website in early February of 2011.

As a senior staffer, he has worked on exhaustive surveys that examine the history, function and organization of the committee, its jurisdiction and activities, statistical profiles of the committee, different types of special orders or rules and subcommittee profiles.

He has also staffed Rules' Subcommittee on Technology and the House.

During his more than 10 years on the committee, he has focused on unfunded mandates, helping to staff a hearing titled "A Five-Year Review and Recommendations for Change."

He also was chosen as one of Congress' "emerging leaders" during the 107th Congress.

Born in Nampa, Idaho and raised in Boise, Jarvis developed an early interest in the "process" of politics—the rules and procedures that make government work. That early interest paid off. After earning his bachelor's degree from the University of Idaho in 1998, he landed immediately in the office of then-freshman Rep. Mike Simpson, R-Idaho as a staff assistant. He moved after just one year to the Rules Committee, first as staff assistant to Republicans, and then as a legislative clerk before being promoted to a member of the GOP's professional staff.

His current job as deputy staff director—a job he's now held almost eight years—has made him an expert on ethics, lobbying and earmark reforms and the budget process, to name a few issues.

HOUSE RULES

Miles M. Lackey

deputy staff director

Capitol H-312

Phone: (202) 225-9091

miles.lackey@mail.house.gov

Education: B.A., history, University of North Carolina at Chapel Hill, 1982. M.A., social ethics, Yale Divinity School, 1986. M.A., international relations, Yale University, 1986.

Professional: 1987–1989, legislative assistant, Rep. Tony Beilenson, D-Calif.. 1989–1991, legislative assistant, Rep. Ted Weiss, D-N.Y.. 1991–1994, committee staff, House Cmte. on Rules. 1991–1999, legislative director, House Democratic Whip David Bonior. 1999–2001, special assistant for national security affairs, White House. 2001–2003, chief of staff, Sen. John Edwards , D-N.C. 2003–2004 , chief of staff, John Edwards Presidential Campaign. 2004, deputy campaign manager, Kerry-Edwards Presidential Campaign. 2004–2007, senior partner, Quorum Strategies LLC. 2007–2008, senior advisor, House Cmte. on Rules. 2008–2010 , chief of staff, Sen. Chris Dodd, D-Conn.. 2010–present, Democratic Staff Director, House Cmte. on Rules.

Expertise: Legislative and parliamentary strategy, national security.

In May of 2010, Sen. Christopher Dodd of Connecticut announced that Miles Lackey was leaving his post as the senator's chief of staff to become Democratic staff director for the House Rules Committee.

It is not Lackey's first tour in the House, nor on the Rules Committee. He previously worked in the 1990s for then-Democratic Whip David Bonior and on Rules as a senior advisor.

"For the last two years, Miles has led a team of talented and dedicated individuals through one of the busiest, albeit most rewarding, legislative sessions in my time in the Senate," Dodd said of Lackey in a statement. "His leadership during both the health care reform and financial reform debates was truly indispensable. His sharp mind and unique sense of humor will be missed."

After years as a committee senior advisor for Democrats who controlled the Rules Committee, Lackey now finds himself in the minority following the 2010 midterm elections. As the newly installed minority staff director, he reports directly to the committee's former chairwoman and now ranking member, New York's Louise Slaughter, and is in charge of Democratic office operations, including the assignment of work and the supervision of key staff.

Lackey joined Dodd in 2008 when the senator was on a short list of potential vice presidential nominees. Lackey was well suited to advise Dodd, as he had done the same for former Sen. John Edwards when Democratic presidential hopeful John Kerry was looking for a running mate.

His long list of professional positions includes co-founding Quorum Strategies LLC in Washington, D.C., where he was a senior partner providing international strategic consulting advice to nonprofit organizations, businesses, and political candidates.

HOUSE RULES

Keagen Lenihan

Rules Associate and legislative director for Rep. Pete Sessions, R-Texas

2233 Rayburn House Office Bldg.

Phone: (202) 225-2231

keagan.lenihan@mail.house.gov

Personal: Born in Atlanta, Ga.

Education: Bachelor's, Communications, University of Colorado, 2002.

Professional: 2001–2003, legislative correspondent, Former Majority Leader Tom DeLay, R-Texas. 2004–2007, senior legislative assistant, Rep. Tom Price, R-Md.. 2008–Present , Legislative Director and Rules Associate, Rep. Pete Sessions, R-Texas, and House Cmte. on Rules.

As the point person for Committee Vice Chair Rep. Pete Sessions, R-Texas, on the House Rules Committee, Keagen Lenihan is responsible for prepping the lawmaker for all hearings and markups. Moreover, Lenihan manages floor time during the rule, writes rule speeches on the legislation in question, and coordinates with other House members who want to speak on the rule.

Lenihan has worked with Sessions since March of 2008. As his legislative director and rules associate, she manages the congressman's legislative staff, supervises all constituent communications, maintains vote recommendations and monitors all floor activity. She also researches and drafts memos, amendments and legislation, and prepares speeches for the lawmaker.

Additionally, Lenihan handles all health care issues for the office, which proved hardly a small task in 2011 when the Obama administration pushed its health care reform legislation through despite objections from Republicans, who at the time were in the minority.

Before joining Sessions' office, Lenihan served as a senior legislative assistant for Rep. Tom Price, R-Md. During her three years there, Lenihan maintained a portfolio of policies on health care, the judiciary, government affairs, telecommunications, technology, small business, civil rights, and campaign finance. It was in this office she discovered that she had an appetite for health care issues, which the congressman fed by putting her in charge of drafting several health care bills and amendments on a wide range of health care issues.

Born in Atlanta, Ga., Lenihan studied at the University of Colorado, where she earned her bachelor's degree in communication in 2002. She came immediately to Capitol Hill, joining the office of former Rep. Tom DeLay before the mid-term elections that thrust the Texas Republican into the Majority Leader's post.

In DeLay's office, she held the positions of staff assistant and legislative correspondent, which required assisting the GOP leadership staff with memos and briefing papers to prepare the Majority Leader for events and floor activities. Lenihan also managed the front office and all constituent relations. She was with DeLay two and a half years, leaving the office a few months before the congressman resigned because of criminal money laundering charges in connection with a campaign finance investigation, which led to a prison sentence that's being appealed.

HOUSE RULES

Jo Maney

Press Secretary

H-312 The Capitol

Phone: (202) 202-226-2006

jo.maney@mail.house.gov

Professional: 2010–Present , press secretary, House Cmte. on Rules.

When Rep. David Dreier became the House's new Rules Committee chairman in January 2011, press secretary, Jo Maney announced his selection.

Dreier, a longtime GOP congressman from California, has been a Rules Committee operative for years. For the past four of those years, he has worked in the minority. The 2010 midterm elections changed that, and with his new chairmanship came Dreier's vow that "under a new majority, the 112th Congress will be managed differently than any Congress before it."

Key to that new management he promised, were "more transparency and accountability to the American people."

Fulfilling that promise, Maney has put out a steady stream of press releases chronicling the committee's doings, including its ambition to cut federal spending, reduce illegal immigration, protect wilderness, and reform the nation's tax system.

Creating jobs, Maney has told reporters, is Dreier's chief focus while the budget and tax reform are others.

Maney publicized Dreier's introduction of a comprehensive tax reform plan that would simplify the tax code to an optional one-page form with three rates—10, 15, and 30 percent while major deductions would continue. He also re-introduced a bill to create a two-year budget cycle in an effort to streamline the budget process, increase oversight of government programs and reduce waste.

In early January, she told reporters that the new chairman "continues to believe any immigration reform must be preceded by stronger control of our border and better workplace enforcement." She spelled out the chairman's legislation that would increase penalties for employers who hire undocumented immigrants, increase the number of enforcement personnel, and create an electronic verification system based on a secure Social Security card.

In February, as budget battles threatened a government shutdown, she insisted that "Dreier does not want to see a government shutdown, nor does he expect one."

In addition, she has promoted Dreier's legislation that would increase the amount of wilderness area in California's Angeles and San Bernardino National Forests. The designation would give 18,000 acres of public land in the forests the highest protection under federal law, meaning no roads, cell phone towers, power lines, or drilling would be allowed. It would also direct the U.S. Forest Services to address the backlog of maintenance in the forests, focusing on recreation areas impacted by the Station Fire.

HOUSE RULES

Brandon Renz

Legislative Director, Rules Associate
Rep. Virginia Foxx
1230 Longworth House Office Bldg
Phone: (202) 202 225 2071
brandon.renz@mail.house.gov

Personal: Born 02/14/1981 in Omaha, Nebr.

Education: B.A., Political Science Major, Drake University, 2003.

Professional: 2000–2003, legislative aide, Iowa state Reps. Russell Eddie and Richard Arnold. 2003–2006, legislative asst., Rep. Steve King, R-Iowa. 2006–Present , legislative director, Rep. Virginia Foxx, R-N.C.

Brandon Renz counts it a "hobby" to "oppose liberals and their policies," even though he actually does this for a living as the representative for Virginia Foxx, R-N.C., on the House Rules Committee.

Now that the mid-term elections have left Republicans in control of the House, Renz's hobby will likely take on more significance than in recent years when the GOP was the minority. While the 2010 elections thrust Foxx and Renz into more high-profile roles on Rules, Renz is no newcomer to committee work. He has championed the congresswoman's causes before as her point person on other weighty congressional committees.

Renz has served for the past five years as legislative director for Foxx, who this year is among the top three Republicans on the committee. She is junior only to newly-installed chairman David Dreier, R-Calif., and vice-chairman Pete Sessions, R-Texas. It is Renz's job to prepare the congresswoman for all Rules Committee hearings, with its sometimes arcane procedures and complicated politics.

He helps the congresswoman develop her positions on legislation and on key policies, and helps her draft her own legislation, which has included the Disabled Veterans' Surviving Spouses Home Loans Act; the Multilingual Services Accounting Act; and the Robo Calls Off Phones (Robo COP) Act. He manages and supervises staff, and helps Foxx prepare her for House floor debates.

Renz has also served as the congresswoman's staffer on the House Oversight and Government Reform Committee and its National Security, Homeland Defense and Foreign Operation Subcommittee.

Born in Nebraska but raised in rural Iowa, Renz chose political science as his major when he went to Drake University in 1999 as a freshman. While taking his undergraduate courses, he worked as a legislative aide for Iowa state Reps. Russell Eddie and Richard Arnold.

After graduating with his bachelor's in political science and a minor in sociology, he came almost immediately to Capitol Hill, where he's been now for eight years. His first job was as a legislative assistant to Rep. Steve King, R-Iowa, a post he held three years.

While "opposing liberals and their policies" might seem a full-time hobby, Renz also finds the time to play the drums and to travel internationally. So far, his global treks have spanned three continents.

Committee on Science, Space and Technology

2320 Rayburn House Office Bldg.
Washington, DC 20515
Phone: (202) 225-6375
Fax: (202) 225-3895
http://science.house.gov
science@mail.house.gov

Ratio: 19/16

MAJORITY MEMBERS

Ralph M. Hall, TX-4th, Chairman

F. James Sensenbrenner, WI-5th
Lamar S. Smith, TX-21st
Dana Rohrabacher, CA-46th
Roscoe G. Bartlett, MD-6th
Frank D. Lucas, OK-6th
Judy Biggert, IL-13th
W. Todd Akin, MO-2nd
Randy Neugebauer, TX-19th
Michael T. McCaul, TX-10th
Paul Broun, GA-10th
Sandy Adams, FL-24th
Benjamin Quayle, AZ-3rd
Charles J. "Chuck" ` Fleishmann, TN-3rd
Scott Rigell, VA-2nd
Steven Palazzo, MS-4th
Randy Hultgren, IL-14th
Chip Cravaack, MN-8th
Larry Buschon, MI-1st

MINORITY MEMBERS

Eddie Bernice Johnson, TX-30th, Ranking Member

Jerry F. Costello, IL-12th
Lynn C. Woolsey, CA-6th
David Wu, OR-1st
Brad Miller, NC-13th
Daniel Lipinski, IL-3rd
Gabrielle Giffords, AR-8th
Donna Edwards, MD-4th
Marcia L. Fudge, OH-11th
Ben R. Lujan, NM-3rd
Paul D. Tonko, NY-21st
Jerry McNerry, CA-11th
John Sarbanes, MD-3rd
Teri Sewell, AL-7th
Frederica Wilson, FL-17th
Hansen Clarke, MI-13th

HOUSE SCIENCE AND TECHNOLOGY

JURISDICTION

(1) All energy research, development and demonstration, and projects therefore, and all federally owned or operated nonmilitary energy laboratories.
(2) Astronautical research and development, including resources, personnel, equipment, and facilities.
(3) Civil aviation research and development.
(4) Environmental research and development.
(5) Marine research.
(6) Commercial application of energy technology.
(7) National Institute of Standards and Technology, standardization of weights and measures and the metric system.
(8) National Aeronautics and Space Administration.
(9) National Space Council.
(10) National Science Foundation.
(11) National Weather Service.
(12) Outer space, including exploration and control thereof.
(13) Science scholarships.
(14) Scientific research, development and demonstration, and projects therefore.

HOUSE SCIENCE AND TECHNOLOGY

At the age of 87, Rep. Ralph Hall, R-Texas, is the oldest member of Congress, but as a recent newspaper article pointed out, he now leads the most forward looking of committees, which seeks to build a competitive workforce, a new energy economy and advance space exploration.

Hall is the chairman of the recently renamed House Science, Space and Technology Committee, a normally quiet and rather bipartisan panel that could see its share of dust-ups in the 112th Congress. Topping the agenda is the focus on economic competitiveness, and the disparate views on how regulations, tax policy, and investments could help the United States compete globally.

"Americans have always had the opportunity to turn a good idea into a successful business, and because of this, the U.S. has led the world in innovation," Hall said. Responsible science and technology policy can help America maintain this leadership."

The chairman is known as a guardian of NASA, since the Johnson Space Center is in his home state. Hall led a delegation that watched the last mission of the Space Shuttle Discovery. He's skeptical of President Barack Obama's plan to replace the shuttles with privately run vehicles that would ferry astronauts from earth to the International Space Station, which is controlled out of Houston.

Congress watered down the president's plan in the 111th Congress, but it is bound to come back in the year ahead. So are efforts to cut NASA's budget, as the GOP-led House seeks ways to curtail federal spending. Hall will have to juggle financial goals with his desire to protect an agency vital to his state.

The chairman is also a skeptic when it comes to climate science, and the committee is expected to dig deep into the debate on the role of humans and what the federal government should do about climate change. He promised to bring scientists before the committee, some of whom have been accused of cooking climate studies.

"I'm interested in the truth on that," Hall said to the *Dallas Morning News*. "There are a lot of people who believe that a lot of decisions were made on the false statements of others."

Other issues before the committee include a reauthorization of many of the nation's research and development programs, a continued push to improve math and science education, and efforts to finalize a new air traffic control satellites.

HOUSE SCIENCE AND TECHNOLOGY

Dan Byers

Staff Director
Subcommittee on Energy and Environment
Subcommittee on Research and Science Education
2320 Rayburn House Office Bldg.
Phone: (202) 225-6371
Fax: (202) 226-0113
Dan.Byers@mail.house.gov

Personal: Born 11/22/1974 in Clarion, Pa.

Education: B.S., crop and soil environmental science, Virginia Tech, 1997. M.S., soil science, North Carolina State University, 1999.

Professional: 2000–2001, staff member, Rep. Nick Smith, R-Mich. 2001–2003, staff member, Subc. on Research, House Cmte. on Science. 2003–2005, staff director, Subc. on Research, House Cmte. on Science. 2005–2009, deputy to the associate director for technology, White House Office of Science and Technology Policy. 2009–2010, professional staff member, House Cmte. on Science and Technology. 2011–present, staff director, Subc. on Energy and Environment, House Cmte. on Science, Space and Technology.

Expertise: General R&D issues, soil science.

Dan Byers is the experienced Capitol Hill staffer selected to help freshman Rep. Andy Harris, R-Md., lead the Subcommittee on Energy and Environment as it seeks to oversee everything from the nation's latest foray into nuclear to the ongoing debate over climate science.

At the top of Harris' and Byers' list is the Office of Science within the Department of Energy. The subcommittee will review the programs to make sure they are driving long-term economic growth, but also to explore the cost of existing and planned facilities as the full House seeks to reduce the federal budget. Other areas they will explore for possible duplications include federal climate research activities and the expanded Office of Energy Efficiency and Renewable Energy.

The subcommittee will also continue its oversight of the national laboratories and the nation's nuclear program, including a push to build new plants for the first time in a generation. The Republicans have also signaled a renewed skepticism of climate science research and will evaluate the role the federal government has played in these projects.

Byers went to college to study the soil and scientific ways to improve crop production. His got his first political job through the Soil Science Society of America, working as a science fellow in 2000 in the office of Rep. Nick Smith, R-Mich., before starting his rise on the committee.

In 2005, he made the leap to the executive branch taking a job in the White House Office of Science and Technology. He helped coordinate a variety of technology policies including President George W. Bush's American Competitiveness Initiative and Vision for Space Exploration and the National Nanotechnology Initiative. He moonlighted with the White House National Economic Council where he focused on telecommunications policy. He returned to the House at the end of the Bush presidency.

HOUSE SCIENCE AND TECHNOLOGY

Hilary Cain

Professional Staff Member
Subcommittee on Technology and Innovation
394 Ford House Office Bldg.
Phone: (202) 225-6375
Fax: (202) 225-3895
hilary.cain@mail.house.gov

Personal: Born in Alameda, Calif.

Education: B.A. political science, University of Washington, 1999. MPA, University of Texas, 2003. JD, University of Texas, 2003.

Professional: 2003–2005, counsel, Office of Rep. Lloyd Doggett, D-Texas. 2005–2008, legislative director, Office of Rep. Brian Baird, D-Wash. 2008–2010, counsel, House Cmt. on Science and Technology. 2010, staff director, Subc. on Technology and Innovation. 2011–present, professional staff member, Subc. on Technology and Innovation.

Expertise: Standards, innovation programs.

Hilary Cain is an attorney by trade who has a firm grasp on the working of the House, even if she doesn't have a long experience on the Subcommittee on Technology and Innovation, where she is now the top Democratic staffer.

Cain joined the House Science, Space and Technology committee in 2008, accepting a job in the counsel's office. She generally handled parliamentary, procedural and jurisdictional matters, while also developing legislative strategy. In 2010, she made the leap into a policy role, assuming the top spot on the Technology and Innovation Subcommittee. It was a job she enjoyed, but it didn't last long. With the 2010 midterms, Democrats were relegated into the minority and while Cain remains on the staff, she is the boss no longer.

Despite the switch, Cain expects little change in the subcommittee's agenda. The panel will continue work on the Small Business Innovation Research Program, for which it shares jurisdiction with the Small Business Committee. Cain also intends to flesh out the fire grants program through the Department of Homeland Security, which she started working on in 2010.

That year she worked extensively on the reauthorization of the America COMPETES Act, focusing on a section on national weights and standards and a section on innovation programs, including one established at the Department of Commerce called the Regional Innovation Cluster Program. The idea is to use federal money to develop new connections between universities, businesses, and investors to try to create an economic specialty, similar to California's Silicon Valley.

She is proud of these programs, but also a little nervous. She knows the House is looking to trim federal spending and she wouldn't be surprised if the most recently created programs get a hard look. She said Republicans have some questions about the role of the federal government in nudging new research into the development phase, making sure an idea turns into a product available at a store.

Outside of work, Cain likes to cook and is interested in interior design when she is not spending time with her two small children.

HOUSE SCIENCE AND TECHNOLOGY

Margaret E. Caravelli

Counsel

2321 Rayburn House Office Bldg.

Phone: (202) 225.6371

Fax: (202) 226-0113

margaret.caravelli@mail.house.gov

Personal: Born in

Education: B.A., political science and history, Skidmore College. J.D., American University.

Professional: 2004–2006, counsel, House Cmt. on Energy and Commerce. 2006–2007, senior counsel for legislative and federal affairs, National Petrochemical & Refiners Association. 2007–2010, chief Republican counsel, House Cmt. on Science and Technology. 2011–present, chief counsel, House Cmt. on Science, Space and Technology.

Expertise: Energy law.

Before becoming the chief counsel for the House Science, Space and Technology Committee, Margaret Caravelli worked in both the private sector and government, focused primarily on the areas of energy and fossil fuels.

Prior to taking a job on Capitol Hill, Caravelli worked as the government affairs director for the Oxygenated Fuels Association, an international trade association that pushed for the use of oxygenated fuel additives to gasoline.

Caravelli got her start in the House in 2004 working as counsel to the House Energy and Commerce Committee, a role she performed for two years under Rep. Joe Barton, R-Texas. During that time she served as a key negotiator of the Energy Policy Act of 2005 and for proposed changes to the Clean Air Act.

Caravelli left the committee in 2006 to take a job with the National Petrochemical & Refiners Association, where for a brief time she served as senior counsel for legislative and federal affairs, promoting the trade group's position to Congress. She returned to the House just a few months later, taking her spot on the House Science, Space and Technology Committee, where she worked up the ranks to chief counsel.

In this role, she has served as a close confidant to Rep. Ralph Hall, R-Texas, who is now the committee chairman. He has thanked her on the House floor for her role in negotiating the America COMPETES Act, a broad law that promotes expanded math and science education as a way to keep pace with emerging international powers.

Like Caravelli, Hall has been an advocate for fossil fuels and in a hearing during the early stages of the 112th Congress told Energy Secretary Steven Chu, "The fossil fuels that drive our economy and meet over 80 percent of our energy needs continue to be penalized."

Hall questions the administration's drive to have 80 percent of the nation's electricity from clean sources by 2035, which he doubts can be achieved with the nation's struggling economy. Instead, he has supported what Republicans call "an all-of-the-above" approach that includes increased renewable energy and more oil and gas development.

Ed Feddeman

Professional Staff Member
Subcommittee on Space and Aeronautics
H2-389 Ford House Office Bldg.
Phone: (202) 225-6371
Fax: (202) 226-0113
ed.feddeman@mail.house.gov

Education: B.A., Washington & Lee University, 1975.

Professional: 1984–1994, professional staff member, House Cmte. on Public Works and Transportation. 1994–1996, chief of staff, Rep. Bill Clinger, R-Pa. 1996–1999, chief of staff, Rep. George Nethercutt, R-Wash. 2000–2010, professional staff member, House Cmte. on Science and Technology. 2011–present, staff director, Subc. on Space and Aeronautics.

Expertise: Aeronautics.

President Barack Obama has a vision for NASA that involves a shuttle landing on an asteroid, while at the same time turning over most space flights to commercial companies. It's a plan that received a swift rebuke by members of Congress, particularly those in areas that include NASA employees and contractors.

Maybe none have been as aggressive as the new Chairman of the House Science, Space and Technology Committee, Rep. Ralph Hall, R-Texas. As he pushes his own NASA agenda, Hall will lean on Ed Feddeman the long-time top staffer on the Space and Aeronautics Subcommittee.

Hall recently said that Obama offered no vision for the Nation's space agency in his 2011 State of the Union address. "NASA's exploration program has been paramount to securing America's lead in the global economy and spurring innovation," he said.

While NASA and the battle over the future of human space flight will likely dominate Feddeman's time, the subcommittee's first hearing on the year focused on the Federal Aviation Administration and its ongoing research and development programs.

These FAA projects focus primarily on aviation safety and environmental compliance. The biggest being the Next Generation Air Transportation Management System, commonly referred to as NextGen, which is the program to modernize the nation's air traffic control system. NextGen, which relies on satellites, has a goal to triple the capacity of the system.

Before joining the committee, Feddeman served as chief of staff for three years for Rep. Bill Clinger, R-Pa., and four years as the chief of staff for Rep. George Nethercutt, R-Wash. He also spent a decade on the staff of the Committee on Public Works and Transportation.

HOUSE SCIENCE AND TECHNOLOGY

Leslee Gilbert

Staff Director

2321 Rayburn House Office Bldg.

Phone: (202) 225-6371

Fax: (202) 226-0113

leslee.gilbert@mail.house.gov

Personal: Born 09/05/1971 in Ft. Worth, S.C.

Education: B.A., Texas A&M University, 1993. M.A., University of Kentucky, 1995. Ph.D., University of Kentucky, 1998. J.D., American University, 2009.

Professional: 2000–2003, professor, St. Mary's University (Minn.). 2003–2005, speechwriter, Rep. Ralph Hall, R-Texas. 2005–2007, leg. director, Rep. Ralph Hall, R-Texas. 2007–2010, Republican staff dir., House Cmte. on Science and Technology. 2011–present, staff director, House Cmt. on Science, Space and Technology.

Expertise: Science policy.

Leslee Gilbert has gone from managing a staff of 15 in 2010 to a staff of nearly 50 now that Republicans are in the majority. She is the staff director for the House Science, Space and Technology Committee and beyond her managerial duties, Gilbert is responsible for coordinating the committee's agenda.

She sees two major priorities for Chairman Ralph Hall, R-Texas, and the committee in the 112th congressional session: identifying budget cuts; and protecting the human spaceflight program at NASA.

"Given the state of the economy, I anticipate that the committee will be looking closely at all programs within our jurisdiction to ensure that they are efficient and effective," she said, echoing a theme that has spread throughout the House.

Hall is a major proponent of NASA and he attended the last flight of the space shuttle Discovery. Now that the space agency is entering a new phase, he has worked to beat back plans to spend more government resources on privately developed rockets instead of NASA's established programs. Gilbert expects the committee to hold a number of hearings on NASA's future.

Last year, Gilbert, like most on the committee, spent most of her time on the reauthorization of NASA and the America COMPETES Act, which is the major legislation involving math and science education.

Gilbert, a Texas native, joined Hall's congressional staff as a speechwriter in 2005 and soon became his legislative director. She moved to the committee staff in 2007. Before working on Capitol Hill, Gilbert taught history at St. Mary's University in Minnesota, a small liberal arts college. She recently received her law degree, taking night classes while continuing her work on the committee. Outside of the office, Gilbert enjoys exercise at the health club and horseback riding.

HOUSE SCIENCE AND TECHNOLOGY

Tom Hammond

Professional Staff Member
Subcommittee on Investigations and Oversight
H2-389 Ford House Office Bldg.
Phone: (202) 225-6371
Fax: (202) 226-0113
tom.hammond@mail.house.gov

Personal: Born in N.Y..

Education: B.A., Hartwick College, 2000. M.A., U.S. Naval War College, 2005.

Professional: 2000–2001, consultant, Corporate Information Services. 2001–2002, staff asst., Subc. on Energy, House Cmte. on Science. 2002–2006, leg. asst., House Cmte. on Science. 2006–2010, prof. staff member, Subc. on Investigations and Oversight, House Cmte. on Science and Technology. 2011–present, staff, Subc. on Investigations and Oversight, House Cmte. on Science, Space and Technology.

Expertise: Science policy, national security.

With the change to Republican leadership, Tom Hammond has been vaulted up the ranks, becoming the staff director of the Subcommittee on Investigations and Oversight—though he downplayed what the partisan shift would mean in terms of what the committee would explore.

"The change will affect very little," he said. "The Science, Space and Technology Committee has always been a nonpartisan committee devoted to ensuring that the nation is prepared to address emerging challenges and compete economically on a global scale."

In recent years, the subcommittee has delved into the impact of the termination of the Yucca Mountain Nuclear Waste Repository, the causes and response to the Gulf Coast oil spill and the move to modernize the satellites for the National Oceanic and Atmospheric Administration. Another perennial issue is monitoring potential political tampering of scientific findings, and the development of what are called "government scientific integrity principles." For example, in 2010, then subcommittee ranking member Paul Broun, R-Ga., accused the Department of Interior of manipulated scientific recommendations to perpetuate an off-shore drilling moratorium.

Predicting what the subcommittee will focus on in the 112th Congress is a little difficult, since he said "much of the subcommittee's work involves reacting to emerging public and private sector issues." He also anticipated a detail review of the spending of government programs in the committee's purview ranging from the National Aeronautics and Space Administration, the Department of Energy and NOAA, among others.

During college, Hammond, a New York native, interned for former Rep. Sherwood Boehlert, R-N.Y., the chairman of what was then called simply the Science Committee. After graduating, he worked for the Republican National Committee and then as a consultant before landing on Capitol Hill.

HOUSE SCIENCE AND TECHNOLOGY

Julia Jester

Professional Staff Member

Subcommittee on Technology and Innovation

2321 Rayburn House Office Bldg.

Phone: (202) 225-6371

Fax: (202) 226-0113

Julia.Jester@mail.house.gov

Personal: Born 1975 in Belleview, S.C.

Education: B.S., chemistry, College of William and Mary, 1998. M.S., chemistry, College of William and Mary, 2001. Ph.D., applied science, College of William and Mary, 2003.

Professional: 2003–2004, science policy fellow, American Chemical Society. 2004–2010, staff member, Office of Rep. Vernon Ehlers, R-Mich.. 2010, professional staff member, House Cmt. on Science and Technology. 2011–present, staff director, Subc. on Technology and Innovation.

Expertise: Chemistry, technology.

The Technology and Innovation Subcommittee is led by some fresh faces in recently-elected Rep. Ben Quayle, R-Ariz., and staff director Julia Jester. Jester, who is new to the Committee on Science, Space and Technology, previously spent six years on the staff of former Rep. Vernon Ehlers, R-Mich. Her main responsibilities were to keep Ehlers up to speed on science and energy policy issues.

In her new position, Jester expects to keep tabs on the programs authorized under the latest version of the America COMPETES Act, which primarily involves boosting math and science education. She said the subcommittee will also examine ways to make the nation more competitive technologically, the research needed to support cybersecurity initiatives, and the latest in health information technology.

The Committee's oversight agenda stresses the importance of the development of standards for weights and measures. It also has jurisdiction over the U.S. Fire Administration, which is responsible ensuring that firefighters have the necessary training and equipment, something Jester's mentioned as an area she will focus on in the 112th Congress.

Jester earned her master's in chemistry and her doctorate in applied science from the College of William and Mary, where her research focused on the transport properties of polymer liquids and film. The American Association for the Advancement of Science named her a summer research fellow at the RAND Science and Technology Policy Institute in 2002. She also completed an American Chemical Society fellowship where she managed science policy changes following the Sept. 11 terrorist attacks.

Interested in the advancement of women in her field, Jester participated in a 2011 event held by the Public Leadership Education Network, which brought women to Capitol Hill. When not working, Jester is an umpire for girls' high school lacrosse.

HOUSE SCIENCE AND TECHNOLOGY

Christopher King

Professional Staff Member

2321 Rayburn House Office Bldg.

Phone: (202) 225-6371

Fax: (202) 226-0113

Christopher.King@mail.house.gov

Personal: Born 11/1975 in Longview, S.C.

Education: B.A., political science, University of Texas, 2001.

Professional: 2001, staff, legislative study group, Texas State House of Representatives. 2002–2009, professional staff member, House Cmt. on Science and Technology. 2009–2010, staff director, Subc. on Energy and Environment.

Expertise: Energy R&D.

For the past two years, the Democrats on House Committee on Science and Technology spent considerable time creating new energy programs or beefing up the ones already in existence, particularly with the help of new federal money from the Recovery Act. Now that Republicans have taken control, staffers like Christopher King have seen their position shift to a more defensive posture.

"We feel a lot of energy R&D programs could be under intense scrutiny," he said. "Both because of duplications, or the perception of duplications, but also a feeling among the majority side that taxpayers should not directly fund research that has an application in the marketplace."

One program that King in particular hopes to defend is nicknamed ARPA-E, which stands for Advanced Research Projects Agency-Energy. Modeled after a defense program, ARPA-E helps fund transformational energy programs with people in the educational and entrepreneurial worlds. It received $400 million in funding from the Recovery Act.

"We feel it is a new model for energy innovation and a new model for government," he said, noting that the Democrats on the committee will fight to keep this project moving forward.

King also anticipates that the subcommittee will explore climate science, with the Republicans in power more likely to have concerns about "the legitimacy of the science."

"We assume there will be an extensive review of the science and the governmental actions taken pursuant to the presumption of a change in climate," he said.

He first joined the committee in 2002 and became the staff director for the Energy and Environment Subcommittee in 2009. In that time he handled a number of top priorities including the Energy Policy Act of 2005, the Energy Independence and Security Act of 2007 and the America COMPETES Act. He also managed the committee's response to the American Recover and Reinvestment Act, particularly the programs involving Energy R&D.

King graduated from the University of Texas at Austin with a degree in political science and his first job out of school was with the Texas State Legislature, where he worked for the Legislative Study Group on issues involving energy, worker's compensation and consumer protection. In his personal time, King is an amateur bicycle racer.

HOUSE SCIENCE AND TECHNOLOGY

Ken Monroe

Professional Staff Member

2321 Rayburn House Office Bldg.

Phone: (202) 226-3660

Fax: (202) 226-0113

ken.monroe@mail.house.gov

Personal: Born in St. Petersburg, S.C.

Education: B.S.E., University of Central Florida, 1989. M.B.A., Florida Inst. of Technology, 1992.

Professional: 1987–1998, various positions, National Aeronautics and Space Administration. 1999–2001, dir. of new product development, Qwest Communications. 2002–present, professional staff member, House Cmte. on Science and Technology.

Expertise: Space policy.

Ken Monroe is in his 10th year as a staffer with the House Science, Space and Technology Committee, with much of it focused on the programs, legislation and oversight of the nation's space-related programs at NASA and the Departments of Transportation and Commerce.

The committee's new chairman, Rep. Ralph Hall, R-Texas, has some concerns about the future of our space program. "With the retirement of the space shuttle, NASA faces a critical period and needs to focus its limited resources to sustain our leadership in space," Hall said.

Congress's goals for NASA, as outlined in the NASA Authorization Act passed in 2010, differ from the vision of President Barack Obama, who supports an increased role by private companies in developing and owning space vehicles. Monroe and the committee will continue to resist the administration's ideas, even in a difficult budget climate.

Monroe, a senior professional staff member with the Space and Aeronautics Subcommittee, was born for his job. His father worked at the Kennedy Space Center giving him access to some of the nation's most impressive space achievements. He began working at the Kennedy Space Center while still an undergraduate engineering student.

Prior to joining the committee, Monroe served in a variety of engineering and management positions. He was director of product development for Qwest Communications. Prior to Qwest, he spent 11 years at NASA working as a systems engineer and orbiter project engineer on the space shuttle.. Monroe has also worked for TRW, which is now Northrop Grumman, and Rockwell International, which is now Boeing.

He is the past-president of the Congressional Staff Dive Club; is a U.S. Coast Guard licensed captain, and an FAA licensed pilot.

HOUSE SCIENCE AND TECHNOLOGY

Richard Obermann

Democratic Chief of Staff
Subcommittee on Space and Aeronautics
2320 Rayburn House Office Bldg.
Phone: (202) 225-4482
Fax: (202) 225-3895
richard.obermann@mail.house.gov

Personal: Born 05/21/1949 in Elmhurst, Ill.

Education: B.S.E., Princeton University, 1971. M.S.E., Stanford University, 1972. Ph.D., engineering, Princeton University, 1977.

Professional: 1977–1988, Mitre Corporation. 1988–1990, senior program officer, National Research Council. 1990–2006, Democratic professional staff member, Subc. on Space and Aeronautics, House Cmte. on Science. 2007–2010, staff dir., Subc. on Space and Aeronautics, House Cmte. on Science and Technology. 2011–present, Democratic chief of staff, House Cmt. on Science, Space and Technology.

Expertise: Space and aeronautics.

For 20 years, Richard Obermann worked exclusively on space policy issues, but with the shift in control from Democrats to Republicans, Obermann is now the Democrat's chief of staff for the House Science, Space and Technology Committee, taking on an expansive role that will allow him to oversee staff and a wider policy range.

"This committee deals with a host of issues that are central to America's future competitiveness and well-being of our citizens, including but not limited to math and science education, energy R&D, space exploration and aviation, innovative technologies, and climate research," said Ranking Member Eddie Bernice Johnson, D-Texas.

Obermann said the committee will focus on three issues in the 112th Congress. The first is finding the balance between improving the nation's fiscal position and maintaining and improving U.S. competitiveness through investments in new research. Another, as Obermann said, is "how to ensure a sustainable and productive future of NASA, including in human space flight and exploration." The third is to make sure "the underlying science will play a meaningful role in the policy debates on energy options and climate change."

In the 111th Congress, Obermann saw a major shift in space policy with President Barack Obama calling for the elimination of the Constellation program, which was working on the next generation of space transport. The president favored a move to commercially developed vehicle to bring humans to the international space station, while NASA focused on deep space flights at some point in the future. While Constellation is no more, parts of the plan, such as the Orion capsule continue.

An engineer prior to taking a job on Capitol Hill in 1990, Obermann has always been fascinated with the deep mysteries of space and said he would never turn down a chance to get up there if given the opportunity.

HOUSE SCIENCE AND TECHNOLOGY

Dan Pearson

Professional Staff Member
Subcommittee on Investigations and Oversight
2320 Rayburn House Office Bldg.
Phone: (202) 225-6375
Fax: (202) 225-3895
dan.pearson@mail.house.gov

Personal: Born 03/24/1958 in Tacoma, Wash.

Education: B.A., University of Puget Sound, 1980. M.A., University of Washington, 1983. Ph.D., University of Washington, 1991.

Professional: 1987–1989, professor, Whitman College (Wash.). 1990–1991, leg. asst., Rep. George E. Brown Jr., D-Calif. 1991–1993, Republican staff member, House Cmte. on Science, Space, and Technology. 1993–2002, Democratic staff member, House Cmte. on Science. 2002–2006, Democratic deputy staff dir., House Cmte. on Science. 2007–2010, staff director, Subc. on Investigations and Oversight, House Cmte. on Science and Technology. 2011–present, professional staff member, Subc. on Investigations and Oversight, House Cmte. on Science and Technology.

Expertise: Science policy, investigations.

As the Democrat's lead staffer on Oversight and Investigations Subcommittee, Dan Pearson expects anything from the government's transition to a new space vehicle to the possible development of new nuclear plants to cyber security as just part of a heavy workload with high profile issues during the 112th Congress.

Pearson will work in tandem with Subcommittee Ranking Member Donna Edwards of Maryland. Pearson was previously the staff director before Republicans took control following the 2010 midterm elections.

As with most oversight subcommittees in Congress, it is difficult if not impossible to predict what will dominate the staff's time in the months to come. "In Oversight, there is always a scandal that is just about to break that you either help break or you react to," Pearson explained.

But beyond the heavy workload he mentioned, other oversight plans include federal climate research efforts and legislation meant to bolster math and science education.

Pearson has a long affiliation with the subcommittee and was named to lead the staff when the Democrats reinstated it following the 2006 elections. It was the second time he has had this position, the first being back in 1993 during the 103rd Congress.

Pearson started his career as a political science professor before "catching the bug" and moving to Washington, D.C. about two decades ago. In 1991, he began working on Science and Technology Committee issues, taking on more senior roles before he became the Democrats' deputy staff director in 2002. His Oversight experience includes an investigation of a federal inspector general that eventually led to a Justice Department probe and prosecution.

Pearson has had a number of different responsibilities on the committee, including policy coordination, budget analysis and press relations. He has also worked on appropriations and member services.

HOUSE SCIENCE AND TECHNOLOGY

John Piazza

Counsel

2321 Rayburn House Office Bldg.

Phone: (202) 225-6375

Fax: (202) 225-3895

John.piazza@mail.house.gov

Personal: Born in Houston, Texas.

Education: B.A., Columbia University, 1999. J.D., Washington and Lee, 2002.

Professional: 2002–2005, prosecutor, Tucson City Attorney's Office. 2006–2009, counsel, House Science and Technology Cmte. 2009–2010, chief counsel, House Science and Technology Cmte. 2011–present, counsel, House Science and Technology Cmte.

Expertise: Environmental science, law.

In the 111th Congress, John Piazza had to work as a conductor of sorts, orchestrating the drafting of legislation and guiding it on its complicated path toward passage. He was the chief counsel of the House Science and Technology Committee—but no longer.

The power switch in the House also resulted in a role switch for Piazza. As a top Democratic counsel for the House Science, Space and Technology Committee, Piazza looks forward to zeroing in on top policy issues in the 112th Congress.

Piazza expects to work intensely on issues of national competitiveness in science and math education. He also anticipates that the committee will focus on the oversight of NASA's human space program, which is at a crossroads with the retiring of the space shuttle.

"The other big issue for this Congress, and the one which will color all the rest, is deficit reduction," Piazza said.

In 2010, Piazza and the committee spent much of its effort on the bills reauthorizing NASA and the America COMPETES Act. The committee also held a number of hearings on the massive Gulf Coast oil spill.

Piazza took a circuitous path that led him all over the country before he wound up in Washington, D.C., as a congressional staffer. He was born in Houston, but grew up in Atlanta. He received his bachelor's degree in New York, his law degree in Virginia, and then settled down in Arizona where he became a prosecutor for the city of Tucson for three years, while his wife finished graduate school.

While Piazza misses the splendid hiking and outdoor activities of the American southwest, he wanted to work for the federal government. In 2006, he took a job with what was then called the Science Committee and now has the title Committee on Science, Space and Technology. He ascended to the chief counsel position when James H. Turner decided to retire in 2008 following more than 30 years of service.

HOUSE SCIENCE AND TECHNOLOGY

Janet Poppleton

Chief of Staff

H2-389 Ford House Office Bldg.

Phone: (202) 225-6371

Fax: (202) 226-0113

janet.poppleton@mail.house.gov

Personal: Born in Stephens, Ark.

Education: B.A., Southern Arkansas University. M.A., Stephen F. Austin University.

Professional: 1993–1996, press secretary, Rep. Ralph Hall, D-Texas. 1996–present, chief of staff, Rep. Ralph Hall, R-Texas. 2007–2010, Republican chief of staff, House Cmte. on Science and Technology. 2011–present, chief of staff, House Cmte. on Science and Technology.

Expertise: Legislative affairs, media affairs.

Janet Poppleton and the rest of the Republican staff on the House Science, Space and Technology Committee have made the leap from the minority to the majority in 2011, but one thing hasn't changed—her job title.

Poppleton is still the chief of staff. She carries that title in Rep. Ralph Hall's, R-Texas, congressional office and in year's past she also served as the chief of staff for the Republicans on the panel. While there's little difference in her business cards, she's enjoying the change in vantage point.

"Being in the majority is a wonderful privilege and responsibility," Poppleton said. "Our staff has the opportunity to help the committee provide effective oversight and advance science policies that promote innovation and competitiveness."

Poppleton first moved to Washington in 1993, when she began working for Hall, who was then a Democrat. Poppleton has been with Hall since Bill Clinton's first year in the White House, so it was no surprise when Hall named her his chief of staff soon after he became the ranking member of the committee in 2007.

Hall is an outspoken supporter of the human space flight program. He has fought to shorten the time between the retirement of the space shuttle and the development of a new space vehicle, because he says he dislikes being "dependent on Russia for transportation to the International Space Station."

Beyond human space exploration, Poppleton said she expects she will focus on energy research and development and science and math education –all issues that will be front in center before the committee.

Poppleton hopes such actions will not take on as partisan a tone as appears in some other committees. Like the Democratic chief of staff before her, Poppleton is a former Stennis Fellow, which involves senior-level congressional staff in bipartisan discussion about the challenges facing the nation.

Janet Poppleton has been with Rep. Ralph Hall (R-Texas) since Bill Clinton's first year in the White House, so it was no surprise when he named her Republican chief of staff for the House Science and Technology Committee soon after becoming the panel's ranking member. Poppleton, who started as Hall's press secretary when he was a Democrat, is also keeping her role of chief of staff in the lawmaker's personal office.

Poppleton oversees a staff of about a dozen GOP aides, many of whom served the committee under the previous chairman, Rep. Sherwood Boehlert (R-N.Y.). She also talks to her counterpart on the Democratic side; many of the issues the committee is addressing this year have bipartisan support from Hall and the chairman, Rep. Bart Gordon, D-Tenn., who used to serve together on the same side of the aisle.

Gordon and Hall both share an interest in America's ability to compete in the global economy, especially in science and engineering. Some of the first pieces of legislation the committee addressed this year were introduced to improve science and math education and research. One bill, for example, would establish scholarships through the National Science Foundation to support the development of math and science educators for primary and secondary schools. Another would encourage basic research for young scientists and support "high-risk, high-reward" research.

HOUSE SCIENCE AND TECHNOLOGY

Tara Rothschild

Senior Professional Staff Member
Subcommittee on Energy and Environment
2321 Rayburn House Office Bldg.
Phone: (202) 225-8844
tara.rothschild@mail.house.gov

Personal: Born in Wayne, Md.

Education: B.A. environment, science and policy, Clark University, 1999. MA, environment, science and policy, Clark University, 2001.

Professional: 2005–2006, research assistant, House Cmt. on Energy and Commerce. 2006–2007, legislative assistant, Office of Sen. Chuck Hagel, R-Neb. 2007–present, professional staff member, House Cmt. on Science, Space and Technology.

Expertise: Environmental science.

With the change in power on Capitol Hill comes a big shift in views on the topic of climate change. While Democrats pushed hard for a cap-and-trade bill in the 111th Congress and failed, the Republicans now are taking a step back and questioning the very science behind the issue.

Freshman Rep. Andy Harris, R-Md., has been named the chairman of the Subcommittee on Energy and Environment, having won his seat in part by criticizing the climate change vote of his Democratic predecessor. He will lean on staffer Tara Rothschild when it comes to environmental issues in particular.

Rothschild has focused on these issues since joining the committee in 2007. She has degrees in environmental science and is currently working on a master's in environmental engineering at John Hopkins University. Her portfolio includes NOAA, the Environmental Protection Agency, green research and climate science.

In the 111th Congress, her time was dominated by the massive Gulf Coast oil spill and the government's reaction to the environmental disaster. When it comes to preventing such blowouts she said, "It's generally conceded that there needs to be a better system than what is currently in place." But Republicans were not in favor of President Barack Obama's temporary ban on offshore drilling.

Expect the subcommittee to push for new technology but also for an increased in fossil fuel production in the new congress. Rothschild said she expects the subcommittee to boost its oversight on research and development projects, particularly in the area of climate science, and to hold hearings on the science behind the president's new national ocean policy.

In an oversight hearing in early 2011, Republicans took issue with a NOAA plan to shift funding from areas like the National Weather Service to create a new Climate Service without congressional review. They also opposed the Environmental Protection Agency's finding that carbon dioxide is a danger to public health and welfare. In a hearing, full Committee Chairman Ralph Hall said, "The numerous admitted mistakes, questionable data sets and lack of transparency in the process has only intensified the questions and doubts that this decision was made as a result of politics instead of science,."

HOUSE SCIENCE AND TECHNOLOGY

Dahlia Sokolov

Professional Staff Member
Subcommittee on Research and Science Education
2321 Rayburn House Office Bldg.
Phone: (202) 225-2157
Fax: (202) 225-3895
dahlia.sokolov@mail.house.gov

Personal: Born in Irvine, Calif.

Education: B.S., University of California, Berkeley, 1996. Ph.D, University of Washington, 2002.

Professional: 2005–2009, professional staff member, House Cmte. on Science and Technology. 2009–2010, staff director, Subc. on Research and Science Education, House Cmte. on Science and Technology. 2011–present, professional staff member, Subc. on Research and Science Education, House Cmte. on Science and Technology. Oct. 2004, American Institute of Physics Congressional fellow, Science Committee.

Expertise: Bioengineering.

For the past few years, Dahlia Sokolov has been the "go-to" staffer on science education and the need to boost math and science literacy. But with the jump from the majority staff to the minority staff, she expects her role to expand.

"I will have to cover a broader set of issues, likely even assisting colleagues with issues outside of my own subcommittee's purview," said Sokolov, the top Democratic staffer on the Research and Science Education Subcommittee.

In 2010, Sokolov and the committee worked on the reauthorization of the America COMPETES Act, the primary policy that promotes science education and research.

With Republicans in control, Sokolov expects the committee to refocus on climate change science, a review of the National Science Foundation's funding priorities, and the role of the federal government in science and math education. She expects the return of a cyber security research bill that passed the House in 2010 but did not pass the Senate.

"I also anticipate that there will be greater disagreement across the aisle than there has been in recent years," Sokolov said. "Nevertheless, our subcommittee has operated in a very bipartisan manner for years and I am hopeful that it will continue in this manner in the coming year."

The committee's Ranking Member Eddie Bernice Johnson, D-Texas, said "the America COMPETES Act and [its] reauthorization bill are two examples of the good, bipartisan work that this committee has done in the past to tackle" increasing the number of science and math educators.

Sokolov's interest in public policy took hold when she took part in a four-month internship at the National Academy of Sciences. She completed a postdoctoral research fellowship at the National Institutes of Health before joining the committee as an American Institute of Physics Congressional fellow in 2004.

HOUSE SCIENCE AND TECHNOLOGY

Pamela Whitney

Professional Staff Member

Subcommittee on Space and Aeronautics

2318 Rayburn House Office Bldg.

Phone: (202) 225-6371

Fax: (202) 226-0113

Pamela.Whitney@mail.house.gov

Personal: Born in Nashua, N.H.

Education: B.A., Smith College, 1984. M.A., American University, 1993.

Professional: 1995–2007, senior program officer, Space Studies Board, National Academies. 2008–present, professional staff member, House Cmt. on Science, Space and Technology.

Expertise: Space exploration.

A number of questions swirl around the nation's space program. What replaces the retiring space shuttle? Is human spaceflight a thing of the past? What is the next big mission? In the House, where many questions are answered depending on what party a member is affiliated with, debates over the future of NASA tend to be far less partisan.

But that doesn't make them easy.

Pamela Whitney has studied aerospace for more than a decade and is now the top Democratic staffer on the Subcommittee on Space and Aeronautics. She assists the subcommittee's Ranking Member Gabrielle Giffords, D-Airs., who continues to recover from a gunshot wound to the head from a Jan. 9, 2011, attack during a political event in a grocery store parking lot.

Giffords is well vested in NASA and its missions. She's the wife of astronaut Mark Kelly and a major believer in the human space flight program. She criticized President Barack Obama's 2010 NASA budget.

"I want to see a plan that includes human exploration beyond low Earth orbit by the end of this decade," Giffords said. "Nothing in this budget gives any indication that this would occur, and I find that unacceptable."

Giffords and others involved in the subcommittee, including Whitney, are likely to be equally frustrated with the president's 2011 budget that also does not call for a major human mission in the next few years, rather it projects deep space flights much later, while calling on the funding of smaller privately held rockets to gain access to the International Space Station.

The subcommittee's first hearing of the 112th Congress didn't focus on NASA, but on the Federal Aviation Administration and its research and development projects, which are headlined by the NextGen air traffic management system. NextGen is a new satellite technology that hopes to triple the capacity of the nation's airspace system and make traveling more secure.

Before joining the committee, Whitney spent a dozen years working as a senior program officer at the Space Studies Board at the National Academies, where she directed studies on international cooperation in space and Mars planetary protection among other topics.

Whitney, a New Hampshire native, is a member of Women in Aerospace and the International Academy of Astronautics. She enjoys hiking and swimming and she previously worked as a researcher for Time-Life Books.

HOUSE SCIENCE AND TECHNOLOGY

Mele Williams

Professional Staff Member

2321 Rayburn House Office Bldg.

Phone: (202) 225-6371

Mele.Williams@mail.house.gov

Personal: Born in Greenville, S.C.

Education: B.A., University of South Carolina, 1988. MA, George Mason University, 2009.

Professional: 1989–1998, legislative staff, Sen. Strom Thurmond, R-S.C. 1998–2000, legislative director, National Association of Industrial and Office Properties. 2001–2005, director of government relations, League of American Bicyclists. 2005–2010, professional staff member, House Cmt. on Science and Technology. 2011–present, staff director, Subc. on Research and Science Education.

Expertise: Research and development.

For years, the House Science, Space and Technology Committee, under various names, has focused on creating new programs aimed to bolster the nation's science, math, engineering and technology education and this not about to change, especially with President Barack Obama's stated goal to "win the future."

Mele Williams is right in the middle of it, but her role is not to be a cheerleader for the president's plans. As the staff director on the Research and Science Education Subcommittee, she oversees the new programs, makes sure they perform as planned and keeps an eye out for inefficiencies.

Williams, a South Carolina native, has been on the committee staff since 2005, but only obtained this new leadership role following the 2010 midterm elections that swept Republicans into power.

In the 111th Congress, she worked closely on the reauthorization of the America COMPETES Act, the primary legislation pushing new education and research programs in math and science. She also worked on a research program involving cyber security.

The subcommittee, led by Chairman Mo Brooks, R-Ala, has an expansive agenda for the 112th Congress, topped by oversight of the National Science Foundation and a look at how the new America COMPETES Act is implemented. Republicans believe there may be duplicative or unused programs, according to the committee oversight agenda.

"Research and science education are critical to America's future," Brooks said. "Top-quality science education means a highly skilled workforce."

Williams will work on the committee's priority, which is to examine the balancing act between government scrutiny of university research associated with private companies and the need to protect innovations from adversaries. The subcommittee will also continue to focus on research in the Antarctic and the construction of major research equipment.

Williams got her start in politics on the staff of the late Sen. Strom Thurmond, R-S.C., which she joined in 1989. She left the Hill in 1998 to become the legislative director of the National Association of Industrial and Office Properties before she became a lobbyist for the League of American Bicyclists. She joined the committee in 2005 starting as an assistant professional staff and working her way up to her current post.

Committee on Small Business

2361 Rayburn House Office Bldg.
Washington, DC 20515
Phone: (202) 225-4038
Fax: (202) 225-7209
http://www.house.gov/smbiz
smbiz@mail.house.gov

Ratio: 15/11

MAJORITY MEMBERS

Sam Graves, MO-6th, Chairman

Roscoe Bartlett, MD-6th
Steve Chabot, OH-1st
Mike Coffman, CO-6th
Scott Tipton, CO-3rd
Jaimie Herrera Beutler, WA-3rd
Renee Ellmers, NC-2nd
Jeff Landry, LA-3rd
Richard Hanna, NY-24th
Steve King, IA-5th
Mick Mulvaney, SC-5th
Allen West, FL-2nd
Chuck Fleishmann, TN-3rd
Joe Walsh, IL-8th
Lou Barletta, PA-11th

MINORITY MEMBERS

Nydia Velázquez, NY-12th, Ranking Member

Kurt Schrader, OR-5th
Mark Critz, PA-12th
Jason Altmire, PA-4th
Yvette Clarke, NY-11th
Judy Chu, CA-32nd
David Cicilline, RI-1st
Cedric Richmond, LA-2nd
Gary Peters, MI-9th
Bill Owens, NY-23rd
William Keating, MA-10th

HOUSE SMALL BUSINESS

JURISDICTION

(1) Assistance to and protection of small business, including financial aid, regulatory flexibility, and paperwork reduction.
(2) Participation of small-business enterprises in federal procurement and government contracts.

In addition to its legislative jurisdiction under the preceding provisions of this paragraph (and its general oversight function under clause 2(b)(1)), the committee shall have the special oversight function provided for in clause 3(g) with respect to the problems of small business.

HOUSE SMALL BUSINESS

House Small Business Committee Chairman Sam Graves, R-Mo., will spend much of 2011 focusing on a key and quite obvious legislative priority: Scaling back regulatory hurdles and other bureaucratic obstacles that he argues limit the degree to which small businesses can thrive.

Graves, himself a small businessman, has argued that small businesses will be a cornerstone of the country's economic recovery. "They are the entrepreneurs that can lead us out of the economic downturn," he said.

He argued that President Obama's stimulus bill equated a spending spree that necessitated the Small Business Administration being pared back to core objectives: enabling small businesses to obtain capital and credit; assisting small businesses in penetrating the federal procurement arena; and guiding and counseling entrepreneurs.

Many other regulations and requirements, he argues, are impediments, not benefits for entrepreneurs.

"Entrepreneurs continue to rank taxes, regulations and health care costs as the greatest burdens to building their businesses," he said.

The committee started 2011 working on a legislative priority that both Democrats and Republicans agreed upon: The repeal of the 1099 regulation in the 2010 health care reform bill. Both parties argued that the provision created a requirement that was difficult to comply with and overly burdensome for small businesses.

"The new law would have severe unintended consequences for entrepreneurs with little benefit," said Committee Ranking member Nydia Velazquez, D-N.Y. "Our tax code should reward growth—not serve as a roadblock to growth."

In addition to broad oversight of small business matters, the panel also oversees the Small Business Administration (SBA) aimed at promoting small business growth in the United States. Yet while Graves called that mission "laudable," he also accused the SBA of trying to be "all things to all businesses." He warned at a budget hearing early in 2011 that the agency should expect to take a funding haircut.

"In a different time, we might be able to afford funding of this broad mission. Unfortunately, we do not have that luxury," he said. "The fiscal situation requires that the mission of the SBA be pared back to core objectives."

HOUSE SMALL BUSINESS

Lisa Christian

Professional Staff Member

B363 Rayburn House Office Bldg.

Phone: (202) 225-5821

Lisa.christian@mail.house.gov

Professional: 2003–2005, constituent liaison, Rep. Steven Chabot, R-Ohio. 2005–2007, staff asst., Rep. Steven Chabot, R-Ohio. 2007–present, prof. staff member, House Cmte. on Small Business.

With Chairman Sam Graves, R-Mo., back at the helm of the Small Business Committee, expect Small Business staffer Lisa Christian to spend much of 2011 focusing on regulatory hurdles, taxes, and other burdens that Graves believe impair entrepreneurship.

In the early part of 2011, the focus was on burdens posed by the new health care bill, including the controversial 1099 mandate. That issue, Graves argues, is a microcosm of a larger problem small businesses face—bureaucratic hurdles that pose an obstacle to them doing business effectively. Graves argues that such hurdles are a reason the economy has struggled.

"The small business owners who create the majority of new jobs need a government that will work with them—not against them—to put our nation back on the path to prosperity," he said.

Such arguments will also bolster Graves' work to repeal or at least radically change the health care reform bill passed by Congress in 2010. He has advocated small businesses grouping together to bring costs down, but said the reform passed in 2010 was burdensome for small businesses. He does, however, advocate, a system where small businesses can group together to bring premiums down.

Christian also will be grappling with the FY2011 budget for the Small Business Administration. Graves has called for more oversight of the agency and streamlining of its programs and funding.

Christian has been with the committee since 2007. Prior to that she spent several years working on the personal staff of Rep. Steven Chabot, R-Ohio as a staff assistant, constituent liaison, and professional staff member.

HOUSE SMALL BUSINESS

Thomas Dawson III

Health Care Counsel

2361 Rayburn House Office Bldg.

Phone: (202) 225-4038

tom.dawson@mail.house.gov

Personal: Born in Hollywood, Fla.

Education: B.A., Morehouse College, 1989. M.A., University of Florida, 1994. M.P.H., George Washington University, 1999. J.D., George Washington University, 1999.

Professional: 1997–1999, associate, Health Policy Analysts, Inc. 1999–2001, manager of government relations, Financial Executives International. 2001–2006, (health) pension law specialist, Department of Labor, Employee Benefits Security Administration. 2007–present, health care counsel, House Cmte. on Small Business.

Expertise: Health policy, employer health benefit plans.

When Republicans took back the House Majority in 2011, one of the first items on their agenda was to repeal or, at minimum, radically change the massive health care reform of the prior Congress. In his role on the House Small Business Committee, Thomas J. Dawson III will be working to protect parts of the bill that Democrats believe help small business.

Committee Ranking Member Nydia Velazquez, D-N.Y., is focused on protecting main components of the bill. But as the bill is implemented, she wants to tweak components that might ultimately be problematic for small business. For example, one provision requires companies that do $600 worth of business with another company to indicate that they have done business on the 1099 form. "That can be problematic for small businesses," Dawson said.

The provision has proven burdensome in terms of paperwork as well as implementation, and Velazquez has prioritized changing it, he said.

Some elements of the health care bill are drawn directly from a bipartisan bill that Velazquez and Chairman Sam Graves, R-Mo., worked on in the 109th and 110th Congress.

The Small Business Cooperative for Healthcare Options to Improve Coverage for Employees (Small Business CHOICE) Act allows small businesses to pool their resources and come together to purchase coverage. Specifically, that bill allowed small businesses to form health insurance cooperatives that would function similar to risk pools and provide insurance against high-cost or catastrophic claims. The bill offered a refundable tax credit of 65 percent to small businesses that choose to join a cooperative. It also allowed entrepreneurs to negotiate better rates for coverage for their employees and themselves. Self-employed individuals could save up to $5,000 per year on health coverage costs.

Other small firms could save more than 34 percent. While the bill itself did not pass, Dawson said key elements of that bill ended up in the health care reform bill that passed in 2010.

HOUSE SMALL BUSINESS

Michael Day

Staff Director

B-343-C Rayburn House Office Bldg.

Phone: (202) 225-4038

Fax: (202) 225-7209

Michael.Day@mail.house.gov

Personal: Born 1967.

Education: B.A., Alfred University, 1988. M.P.A., Old Dominion University.

Professional: 1989–1992, staff asst., Sen. Charles Robb, D-Va. 1993, legislative asst., Rep. Leslie Byrne, D-Va. 1993–1995, legislative dir., Rep. Leslie Byrne, D-Va. 1995, congressional liaison, U.S. Agency for International Development. 1995–1996, legislative dir., Rep. Nydia Velázquez, D-N.Y. 1996–1998, administrative asst., Rep. Nydia Velázquez, D-N.Y. 1998–present, Democratic staff dir., House Cmte. on Small Business.

Expertise: Small business issues.

Michael Day returns to the House Small Business Committee in 2011 with a new challenge—working to advance his boss's agenda from the minority.

Ranking Democrat Nydia Velazquez of New York will fight Republican efforts to repeal or radically change the health care bill passed in 2010. However, Velazquez has indicated she's willing to consider some tweaks to the legislation. Among them: A provision in the law that requires companies doing $600 worth of business with another company file a 1099 form indicating they have done business with another. The provision has been ridiculed on both sides of the aisle as overly cumbersome and difficult to comply with.

Velazquez, however, has signaled her willingness to defend the bill, which includes some elements drawn directly from a bipartisan bill that Velazquez and Chairman Sam Graves, R-Mo., worked on in the 109th and 110th Congress. Those provisions would allow small businesses to form health insurance cooperatives that would function similar to risk pools and provide insurance against high-cost or catastrophic claims. That bill offered a refundable tax credit of 65 percent to small businesses that choose to join a cooperative and allowed entrepreneurs to negotiate better rates for coverage for their employees and themselves.

Day will also spend 2011 working on key reauthorization bills, and likely spend a great deal of time working to respond to Republican allegations that federal small business programs are overly cumbersome and too restrictive.

Day has worked for the federal government for 32 years, and has been staff director for the Democrats since 1998.

HOUSE SMALL BUSINESS

Joe Hartz

Professional Staff Member

B363 Rayburn House Office Bldg.

Phone: (202) 225-5821

Joe.hartz@mail.house.gov

Education: University of Pittsburgh, 1997.

Professional: 2000–2003, legislative assistant., Rep. Pat Toomey, D-Pa. 2003–present, professional staff member, House Cmte. on Small Business.

With Chairman Sam Graves, R-Mo., at the helm of the House Small Business Committee, Joe Hartz finds himself dealing with what is becoming a perennial issue for the committee: reauthorization of the Small Business Innovation Research (SBIR) program.

The roughly $2 billion program provides research and development grants to small businesses in a wide range of scientific fields in an effort to level the playing field for small businesses competing with larger corporations to make technological breakthroughs. Legislative disagreements between the House and the Senate have led to at least a half-dozen temporary reauthorizations. Earlier this year, President Barack Obama signed a measure to continue funding the program through May.

The issue is one on which Graves and ranking Democrat Nydia Velázquez, D-N.Y., fundamentally agree. Both would like to see some reforms, however.

Hartz will also lend his expertise on small business to reforms being considered for the Small Business Administration (SBA). Graves has made it clear that he is frustrated with perceived bureaucratic and regulatory hurdles, and has made a focus of trying to eliminate such hurdles. Graves has been critical of the Obama administration's handling of small business issues.

"Small business owners have been under attack by this administration," he said in early 2011. "We need to get government off their backs and let them do what they do best - create jobs."

Hartz came to the committee in 2003 after working for former Rep. Pat Toomey, R-Pa., for three years as a legislative assistant.

HOUSE SMALL BUSINESS

Duncan Neasham

Press Secretary

2361 Rayburn House Office Bldg.

Phone: (202) 225-4038

Duncan.neasham@mail.house.gov

Education: political science, Virginia Tech.

Professional: 2001–2003, systems assistant, Sen. Ron Wyden, D-Ore. 2008–present, press secretary, House Cmte. on Small Business.

Expertise: Communications.

In 2011, Duncan Neasham returns as the spokesman for Rep. Nydia Velazquez, D-N.Y., in her efforts on the House Small Business Committee, albeit in a new role—as the voice of the minority.

Among key issues he will be discussing during the 112th Congress will be health care reform. Early in 2011, House Republicans made clear that they intended to overhaul the 2010 health care reform bill. The bill included provisions aimed at making it easier for small businesses to provide health care for their employees. Some elements of the bill were based on the Small Business Cooperative for Healthcare Options to Improve Coverage for Employees (Small Business CHOICE) Act, which allowed small businesses to pool their resources and pull together to purchase coverage. Velazquez has indicated the bill overall has done great things for easing access to health care, but acknowledges some technical tweaks are necessary.

The provision has proven burdensome in terms of paperwork and has been criticized for making it easy to run afoul of the requirement.

Neasham will also no doubt have to weigh in on Republicans' plans to conduct oversight hearings in to federal capital access programs. Among the issues the committee has signaled they will address are whether lenders are meeting their goals to lend to small businesses and create jobs as well as the adequacy of the Small Business Administration's oversight of its lending partners to ensure that federal taxpayers are adequately protected. The committee will also hold hearings and investigations into how well the Small Business Administration has performed in terms of using its entrepreneurial development programs to create jobs. Finally, Neasham will likely be asked to comment on hearings about duplicative federal rules, reporting, and record-keeping requirements and federal tax policy.

Prior to working for Velazquez, Neasham spent several years working for the National Marine Manufacturer's Association.

HOUSE SMALL BUSINESS

Janet L. Oliver

Counsel/Deputy Staff Director
B363 Rayburn House Office Bldg.
Phone: (202) 225-5821
Jan.oliver@mail.house.gov

Education: B.A, Indiana University. M.A., The Ohio State University. J.D., Chase College of Law, Northern Kentucky University.

Professional: 1993–2005, various positions, Rep. Rob Portman, R-Ohio. 2005–2007, legislative dir., Rep. Jean Schmidt, R-Ohio. 2007–present, counsel, House Cmte. on Small Business.

Expertise: Health Care, Taxes, Economic Policy, Financial Services, Judiciary, Congressional Ethics.

Janet Oliver returns to the House Small Business Committee in 2011 with the goal of advancing the agenda Chairman Sam Graves, R-Mo., that includes eliminating regulatory and bureaucratic barriers to small businesses.

As the committee's counsel and deputy staff director, Oliver will work on what Graves sees as a main hurdle for small business: the health care reform bill passed in 2010.

Prior to that bill passed, the committee's Democrats and Republicans found consensus on the need for small businesses to have access to affordable health care coverage, but Graves objected to the bill passed in 2010, arguing it was overly burdensome to small businesses. He and Democrats, however, had worked together in 2008 and 2009 on the "Cooperative for Healthcare Options to Improve Coverage for Employees" (Small Business CHOICE) Act—a bill that would've allowed small businesses to group together to bring down premium costs.

Specifically, the bill would have allowed small businesses and self-employed individuals burdened with the high cost of health insurance to pool their resources for the purpose of negotiating better rates for their employees or themselves. Money from the insurance cooperatives could be used to provide insurance against high-cost or catastrophic claims.

In the aftermath of the health care bill's passage, Democrats on the committee lauded the bill for including some of those provisions. But Graves made it clear he was not happy with the final bill, and co-sponsored a measure to repeal the bill.

Oliver will work on reforming the health care law, which Graves said "would result in fewer jobs, higher taxes and more unconstitutional big government mandates."

Oliver has worked in the House since 1993. Prior to working for Small Business, she worked for Rep. Jean Schmidt, R-Ohio, and former Rep. Rob Portman, R-Ohio.

HOUSE SMALL BUSINESS

Barry Pineles

Chief Counsel

B363 Rayburn House Office Bldg.

Phone: (202) 225-5821

barry.pineles@mail.house.gov

Personal: Born 04/27/1956 in Brooklyn, N.Y.

Education: B.S., Cornell Univ., 1977. J.D., Univ. of Iowa, 1982.

Professional: 1984–1986, law clerk, U.S. District Court Judge Bruce Selya. 1986–1995, asst. chief counsel, Office of Advocacy, U.S. Small Business Administration. 1995–1996, atty., Bienstock & Clark (Miami, Fla.). 1996–1998, atty., Ross & Hardies (Washington, D.C.). 1998–1999, regulatory counsel, GST Telecom. 1999–2006, regulatory counsel, House Cmte. on Small Business. 2007–present, chief counsel, House Cmte. on Small Business.

Expertise: Regulatory issues.

Barry Pineles, chief counsel for Republicans on the House Committee on Small Business, will spend 2011 working to advance Chairman Sam Graves' agenda of eliminating unnecessary tax and regulatory hurdles for small business.

Graves, R-Mo., who is a farmer and a small businessman himself, also wants to repeal the 2010 health care reform law. In an early 2011 hearing, Graves indicated that re-energizing the economy and entrepreneurship can't happen effectively until regulatory hurdles are removed.

"Entrepreneurs continue to rank taxes, regulations, and health care costs as the greatest burdens to building their businesses," Graves said, "…we need to take immediate steps to address these critical issues and provide small business owners with some much-needed certainty."

Pineles, who has been with the Small Business Committee since 1999, will also work to ensure that small businesses have access to capital and federal government contracts.

He also will handle reauthorization of a handful of federal small business programs, including the Small Business Innovation Research Program. The competitive grant program aims to provide a boost to small, high-tech, innovative businesses. Before adjourning in 2010, the Congress passed a short-term reauthorization of the program—the ninth short-term reauthorization approved by Congress since 2008. The program has been held up by differences in the House and Senate versions of the bills.

As chief counsel, Pineles is the go-to man for committee staff with questions about how federal regulations impact small businesses. Pineles has many years of experience working on the issue. Before working for the Small Business Committee, he worked in the Small Business Administration Office of Advocacy, reviewing federal agencies' rules to ensure that small businesses were not unfairly impacted or overburdened.

If Barry Pineles had been just a few minutes late, he might not be the regulatory counsel for the Small Business Committee—he was in Washington doing some legal work for GST Telecom, the Portland company where he was an attorney, when he ran into someone he knew from his days at the Small Business Administration (SBA). His friend invited him to lunch with the then-chief counsel of the committee, who said they might have an opening for him. Pineles took the job.

Seven years later, Pineles is still the aide that the committee staff turns to with questions about how federal regulations impact small businesses. Pineles has many years of experience working on the issue; for nearly a decade—under three different administrations—he worked in the SBA Office of Advocacy, reviewing federal agencies' rules to ensure that small businesses were not unfairly impacted or overburdened.

"I've been doing this a long time," Pineles said.

His boss, Chairman Donald Manzullo, R-Ill., lists reducing the regulatory burden on small businesses as one of his top priorities. This year, Manzullo's agenda once again includes making changes to the Regulatory Flexibility Act. The reforms would require more extensive analysis of rules' effects on small entities by federal agencies and a more open process—the agencies would have to post their analyses on their websites.

HOUSE SMALL BUSINESS

Lori Salley

Staff Director

B-363 Rayburn House Office Bldg.

Phone: (202) 225-5821

lori.salley@mail.house.gov

Education: B.A., University of California, Los Angeles.

Professional: 1991–2009, Chief of Staff, Rep. Deborah Pryce, R-Ohio. 2003–2007, Deputy Chief of Staff, House Republican Conference, U.S. House of Representatives. 2009–2010, Senior Government Relations Advisor, Wombyle Carlyle. 2010–2011, executive director, Children's Cause for Cancer Advocacy. 2011–present, staff director, House Small Business Committee.

Lori Salley replaces Karen Haas as staff director for Republicans on the House Small Business Committee in 2011, bringing with her nearly two decades of experience in the House. Haas left the committee to work as Clerk of the House. Salley's last Capitol Hill job was a stint working as chief of staff for former U.S. Rep. Deborah Pryce, R-Ohio. However, Salley's Capitol Hill roots are with the committee she's working for now: Among her first jobs on the Hill was one on the professional staff of the House Small Business Committee.

On the Small Business Committee, Salley will work to manage the priorities of Chairman Sam Graves, R-Mo., as well as manage committee staff. Graves has made it clear his focus on the committee will be to streamline unnecessary bureaucracy and regulatory hurdles that he believes impede business. He himself is a small business owner and has argued that his experience gives him a valuable insight into what small businesses face. One of his first moves as chairman was to hold a hearing on new 1099 regulations in the health care reform bill. He argued during that hearing that those provisions were unnecessarily burdensome as well as nearly impossible to comply with.

While Graves has been a critic of the health care bill, he and ranking member Nydia Velazquez, D-N.Y., have worked together in the past on a key health care proposal: A bill that would allow small businesses to pool together to afford health care coverage for their employees. Still, Graves' priorities are to ensure that the federal government gets out of the way of small business to enable them to succeed.

As he advances that priority, he'll have Salley supporting him.

Salley, a California native and UCLA alumnus, has 17 years of experience on Capitol Hill, and began her career on the Hill as an intern and Research Assistant with the Small Business Committee.

For the past year, she worked as the Executive Director of the Children's Cause for Cancer Advocacy, a non-profit organization focused on pediatric oncology policy. Before that, Salley worked as a Senior Government Relations Advisor at Womble Carlyle, a Washington, D.C., law firm. She served as Chief-of-staff to former Rep. Deborah Pryce, R-Ohio, for eight years, spending four years before that as the Deputy Chief-of-Staff for the House Republican Conference while Pryce was Chairman from 2003-2007.

HOUSE SMALL BUSINESS

Paul Sass

Deputy Staff Director

B-363 Rayburn House Office Bldg.

Phone: (202) 225-5821

paul.sass@mail.house.gov

Education: B.A., Hartwick College, 2001.

Professional: 2002–2009, staff assistant, legislative correspondent, legislative assistant, legislative director, deputy chief of staff, Rep. Sam Graves, R-Mo. 2008–2009, deputy chief of staff, Rep. Sam Graves, R-Mo. 2009–present, deputy chief of staff, House Small Business Committee.

Paul Sass returns in 2011 as deputy chief of staff for Republicans on the House Small Business Committee, albeit with a few changes: He'll be working with a new staff director and, for the first time, he'll be deputy chief of staff for the committee in the majority.

Sass got his start on Capitol Hill serving in a variety of roles for Chairman Sam Graves, R-Mo. Now, his job is to help staff director Lori Salley implement Graves' agenda of streamlining and eliminating unnecessary bureaucracy for small business owners.

Republican staff got an early triumph in March when the House passed H.R. 4, the Small Business Paperwork Mandate Elimination Act. The bill aimed to eliminate a mandate that required small businesses to file 1099 forms when they did $600 or less of business with another company.

"Our nation's small businesses create seven of every ten new jobs," Graves said after the House passed the bill. They represent 99.7 percent of all employer firms, and employ 97.5 percent of all identifiable exporters. They are the entrepreneurs that can lead us out of the economic downturn. However, Washington has not provided them with an environment in which they can thrive."

Graves called the 1099 provision, which was included in the health care reform bill and which Democrats on the committee agreed were burdensome, an obstacle for small businesses.

For Graves, the 1099 measure is one of countless harmful federal regulations. He said over the last 30 years, the size of the Federal Register has ballooned from 42,000 pages in 1980 to 82,000 pages in 2010.

"Harmful federal regulations can put serious hurdles in the way of entrepreneurship, making it more difficult to create jobs or expand a business," he said.

HOUSE SMALL BUSINESS

Tim Slattery

Chief Counsel

B-363 Rayburn House Office Bldg.

Phone: (202) 225-5821

tim.slattery@mail.house.gov

Personal: Born in Pocahontas, La.

Education: B.A., economics, University of Notre Dame, 1998. J.D., University of Iowa, 2001.

Professional: 2001–2002, associate attorney, Bosley Hutzelman Law Firm. 2002–2007, professional staff member, House Cmte. on Small Business. 2007–present, chief counsel, House Cmte. on Small Business.

With a background in tax law and health care, Tim Slattery's private sector experience serves him well in his role on the House Small Business Committee. On the committee, Slattery serves as chief counsel for Small Business Committee Ranking Member Nydia M. Velazquez, D-N.Y. In this role, he generally oversees and works with committee staff, and is involved in many of the committee's hearings. He's particularly likely to be involved in small business legislation involving health care or tax regulation.

Previously, Slattery was involved in hearings on tax reform as well as small business implications of the massive health care overhaul in 2010. This year, as House Republicans attempt to repeal or at minimum dramatically alter that law, Slattery will likely be involved in Democratic efforts to fight back.

Early in 2011, the committee began looking on a bipartisan basis at technical changes to the health care law. Of particular concern is a provision in the health care law that requires businesses doing more than $600 worth of business with another company must report it on an IRS 1099 form. Democrats and Republicans alike worry that the provision will be overly cumbersome and burdensome for small businesses.

Also in 2011, the committee must reauthorize a number of Small Business Administration programs, including the Small Business Innovation Research Program. Before adjourning in 2010, the Congress passed a short-term reauthorization of the program—the ninth short-term reauthorization approved by Congress since 2008. The holdup has been caused by problems reconciling House and Senate versions of the bills.

Slattery got his start on Capitol Hill as an intern for Sen. Charles Grassley, R-Iowa in 1996. After practicing tax and employee benefits law for many years, he returned to Capitol Hill in 2002.

Committee on Standards of Official Conduct

1015 Longworth House Office Bldg.
Washington, DC 20515
Phone: (202) 225-7103
http://www.house.gov/ethics

Ratio: 5/5

MAJORITY MEMBERS

Jo Bonner, AL-1st, Chairman

Michael McCaul, TX-10th
Mike Conway, TX-11th
Charlie Dent, PA-15th
Gregg Harper, MS-3rd

MINORITY MEMBERS

Linda Sanchez, CA-39th, Ranking Member

Mazie Hirono, HI-2nd
John Yarmuth, KY-3rd
Donna Edwards, MD-4th
Pedro Pierluisi, PR-At Large

HOUSE STANDARDS OF OFFICIAL CONDUCT

JURISDICTION

(1) All bills, resolutions and other matters relating to the Code of Official Conduct adopted under House Rule XXIV.
(2) Authorized to recommend administrative actions to establish or enforce standards of official conduct. Investigate alleged violations of the Code of Official Conduct or of any applicable rules, laws, or regulations governing the performance of official duties or the discharge of official responsibilities. Such investigations must be made in accordance with Committee rules. Report to appropriate federal or state authorities evidence of a violation of any law applicable to the performance of official duties that may have been disclosed in a Committee investigation. Such reports must be approved by the House or by a vote of two-thirds of the Committee. Render advisory opinions regarding the propriety of any current or proposed conduct of a House member, officer, or employee, and issue general guidance on such matters as necessary. Consider written requests for waivers of the gift rule (clause 5 of House Rule XXVI).
(3) Issue guidance for the House of Representatives on the Ethics in Government Act, and responsibility for Financial Disclosure Statements of candidates for the House, and for officers and employees of certain legislative branch agencies, including the Library of Congress, the Congressional Budget Office, the Government Printing Office, the Architect of the Capitol, and the United States Botanic Garden. However, the committee has delegated much of its authority with regard to the officers and employees of those agencies to the heads of the agencies. Administers the provisions of the Foreign Gifts and Decorations Act for House members, officers and employees. Responsibilities regarding the statutory prohibitions against any of the three giving gifts to an official superior, receiving gifts from employees with a lower salary level or soliciting gifts.

HOUSE STANDARDS OF OFFICIAL CONDUCT

In the 112th Congress, House Ethics Committee Chairman Jo Bonner, R-Ala., and Ranking Member Linda Sanchez, D-Calif., are trying to restore some order to a panel that finished the 111th Congress in disarray. The committee continues to carry out its duties of providing ethics training and advice to House staff and employees on matters that involve the code of conduct and other House rules. However, the investigative side of the committee is being very cautious in moving forward with its cases.

The case that sparked much of the committee's troubles was a 2010 investigation of whether Rep. Maxine Waters, D-Calif., tried to improperly steer federal bailout money to a minority-owned bank where her husband is a stockholder and part owner. Waters' trial was scheduled for late November 2010, but the committee was forced to delay it after new evidence was discovered a week before the trial. The handling of the case led to the resignation of the staff director for then-Chairwoman Zoe Lofgren, D-Calif. In addition, the two lead investigative attorneys in the case were placed on administrative leave.

The delay in the Waters case came on the heels of the conclusion of the lengthy and politically-charged investigation in to the activities of Rep. Charles Rangel, D-N.Y. The committee ultimately recommended censure for Rangel, who was found guilty on 11 counts, including use of a rent-controlled apartment for political purposes and failure to pay taxes on a house in the Dominican Republic.

After the events of 2010, Bonner is taking his time deciding how to proceed with committee investigations in 2011. The committee did complete an investigation early in the session into the fundraising activities of Rep. John Campbell, R-Calif., Rep. Tom Price, R-Ga., and Rep. Joseph Crowley, D-N.Y., around the time of the passage of the Dodd-Frank Wall Street Reform and Consumer Protection Act.

The committee examined whether they had given donors special treatment, or whether contributions were linked to official actions on the bill. The cases against all three members were dismissed after a finding that there was separation between their fundraising activities and legislative actions.

Ethics training is now mandatory for every House employee, and new employees must complete their initial training within 60 days of their first day of House employment. This kept the committee busy in the early part of 2011 given the influx of new members after the mid-term elections. Once that training was complete, the committee settled into its ongoing role of responding to questions from House members and staff.

The staff is permitted to provide informal advice orally or by email, but only formal written opinions are binding on the committee. As a result, committee staff generally encourages members and employees to submit a written inquiry, particularly for novel or complex questions.

HOUSE STANDARDS OF OFFICIAL CONDUCT

C. Morgan Kim

Deputy Chief Counsel

1015 Longworth House Office Bldg.

Phone: (202) 225-7103

Morgan.Kim@mail.house.gov

Education: B.A., Georgetown University, 1994. J.D., George Mason University, 1999.

Professional: 1999–2000, judicial clerk, Office of Hon. Kenneth Ryskamp, U.S. District Court, S.D. Fla. 1999–2001, associate and summer associate, Latham & Watkins, Washington, D.C. 2001–2005, assistant U.S. attorney, U.S. Attorney's Office, Southern District of Florida. 2005–2006, counsel, Crowell & Moring, Washington, D.C. 2006–2008, counsel, Cmte. on Standards of Official Conduct. 2008–2009, investigator, U.S. Department of Justice, Office of the Inspector General. 2009–present, deputy chief counsel, Cmte. on Standards of Official Conduct.

Expertise: Investigations, ethics rules.

Morgan Kim carries out extensive investigative work for the Ethics Committee, including serving as lead investigator on a number of sensitive cases. She started out leading the investigation into the conduct of Rep. Maxine Waters, D-Calif., but that case has been delayed due to questions over evidence that surfaced after the investigation was closed.

Waters is accused of directing bailout money to a bank in which her husband owned shares. The committee had concluded its investigation and scheduled an adjudicatory hearing for Waters late in 2010, but was forced to remit the case for further investigation based on the new evidence.

Kim also served as lead investigator in high-profile 2007 House page case involving former Florida Republican Congressman Mark Foley. Foley resigned after it was revealed that he had a number of improper communications with House pages.

The Foley case was during Kim's first stint with the committee from 2006 to 2008. She left to work as an investigator for the Department of Justice's Office of the Inspector General, then returned to the Ethics Committee as deputy chief counsel in July 2009.

In addition to investigations, Kim assists her fellow committee members with providing ethics advice and training to House members. With the influx of new representatives in the 112th Congress, the committee spent much of the early part of 2011 ensuring that new members received their mandatory ethics training.

Earlier in her career, Kim served as a federal prosecutor in the white collar crimes division of the U.S. Attorney's Office for the Southern District of Florida. In that position she prosecuted fraud, public corruption, and organized crime cases.

Kim completed her law degree magna cum laude at George Mason University School of Law. While in law school, she was on the editorial board of the law review.

HOUSE STANDARDS OF OFFICIAL CONDUCT

Kelle Strickland

Counsel to the Chairman

1015 Longworth House Office Bldg.

Phone: (202) 225-7103

Kelle.Strickland@mail.house.gov

Personal: Born in Mobile, Ala.

Education: B.A. in English, Spring Hill College, 1992. J.D., Samford University, Cumberland School of Law, 1996.

Professional: 2003–2010, counsel and legislative director, Office of Rep. Jo Bonner, R-Ala. 2010–2011, counsel to the ranking member, Cmte. on Standards of Official Conduct. 2011–present, counsel to the chairman, Cmte. on Standards of Official Conduct.

Expertise: Ethics rules, appropriations, budget issues.

Kelle Strickland is counsel to Committee Chairman Jo Bonner, R-Ala., which made her the highest ranking staff member in first several months of the 112th Congress. The committee's staff director resigned late in 2010, and Bonner did not fill the position right away.

Strickland is advising Bonner on some difficult issues, including the handling of the case against Rep. Maxine Waters, D-Calif., which hit a snag late in 2010 when new evidence came to light after the investigation was closed. Waters is alleged to have directed bailout money to a bank of which her husband was a shareholder.

Strickland joined the committee in 2010, a year in which the committee completed its investigation into 11 ethics violations by Rep. Charles Rangel, D-N.Y. The violations included unpaid taxes and the improper use of his office to raise money for an education center named after him. Based on the committee's recommendation, the House voted to censure Rangel.

Strickland also advised Bonner during the committee's investigation into the fundraising activities of Rep. John Campbell, R-Calif., Rep. Tom Price, R-Ga., and Rep. Joseph Crowley, D-N.Y. around the time of the passage of the Dodd-Frank Wall Street Reform and Consumer Protection Act. The committee examined whether they had given donors special treatment, or whether contributions were linked to official actions on the bill.

The committee dismissed the cases against all three members after a finding that there was separation between their fundraising activities and legislative actions.

Strickland and her colleagues try to help House Members and staff avoid these kinds of investigations by providing mandatory ethics training to every Member. The gift rules and the privately-sponsored travel rules were amended a few years ago, and the committee works to ensure that House employees are familiar with them.

The Mobile, Alabama, native worked in Bonner's personal office from 2003 to 2010. She served for two years as a legislative assistant before being promoted to legislative director and counsel. As Bonner's legislative director, her responsibilities included appropriations, budget and tax issues.

Committee on Transportation and Infrastructure

2165 Rayburn House Office Bldg.
Washington, DC 20515
Phone: (202) 225-9446
Fax: (202) 225-6782
http://transportation.house.gov
transcomm@mail.house.gov

Ratio: 33/26

MAJORITY MEMBERS

John L. Mica, FL-7th, Chairman

Don Young, AK-At Large
Thomas Petri, WI-6th
Howard Coble, NC-6th
John J. Duncan Jr., TN-2nd
Frank A. LoBiondo, NJ-2nd
Gary G. Miller, CA-42nd
Timothy V. Johnson, IL-15th
Sam Graves, MO-6th
Bill Shuster, PA-9th
Shelley Moore Capito, WV-2nd
Jean Schmidt, OH-2nd
Candice S. Miller, MI-10th
Duncan D. Hunter, CA-52nd
Thomas W. Reed, NY-29th
Andrew P. Harris, MD-1st
Rick Crawford, AR-1st
Jaime Herrera Beutler, WA-3rd
Frank C. Guinta, NH-1st
Randy Hultgren, IL-14th
Lou Barletta, PA-11th
Chip Cravaack, MN-8th
Blake Farenthold, TX-27th
Larry Bucshon, IN-8th
Billy Long, MO-7th
Bob Gibbs, OH-18th
Patrick Meehan, PA-7th
Richard L. Hanna, NY-24th
Stephen Lee Fincher, TN-8th
Jeff M. Landry, LA-3rd
Steve Southerland, FL-2nd
Jeff Denham, CA-19th
James Lankford, OK-5th

MINORITY MEMBERS

Nick J. Rahall II, WV-3rd, Ranking Member

Peter DeFazio, OR-4th
Jerry F. Costello, IL-12th
Eleanor Holmes Norton, DC
Jerrold Nadler, NY-8th
Corrine Brown, FL-3rd
Bob Filner, CA-51st
Eddie Bernice Johnson, TX-30th
Elijah E. Cummings, MD-7th
Leonard L. Boswell, IA-3rd
Tim Holden, PA-17th
Rick Larsen, WA-2nd
Michael E. Capuano, MA-8th
Timothy H. Bishop, NY-1st
Michael H. Michaud, ME-2nd
Russ Carnahan, MO-3rd
Grace F Napolitano, CA-38th
Daniel Lipinski, IL-3rd
Mazie K. Hirono, HI-2nd
Jason Altmire, PA-4th
Timothy J. Walz, MN-1st
Heath Shuler, NC-11th
Steve Cohen, TN-9th
Laura Richardson, CA-37th
Albio Sires, NJ-13th
Donna F. Edwards, MD-4th

HOUSE TRANSPORTATION AND INFRASTRUCTURE

JURISDICTION

(1) Coast Guard, including lifesaving service, lighthouses, lightships, ocean derelicts, and the Coast Guard Academy.
(2) Federal management of emergencies and natural disasters.
(3) Flood control and improvement of rivers and harbors.
(4) Inland waterways.
(5) Inspection of merchant marine vessels, lights and signals, lifesaving equipment, and fire protection on such vessels.
(6) Navigation and the laws relating thereto, including pilotage.
(7) Registering and licensing of vessels and small boats.
(8) Rules and international arrangements to prevent collisions at sea.
(9) The Capitol building and the Senate and House office buildings.
(10) Construction or maintenance of roads and post roads, other than appropriations therefore.
(11) Construction or reconstruction, maintenance, and care of the buildings and grounds of the Botanic Garden, the Library of Congress, and the Smithsonian Institution.
(12) Merchant marine (except for national security aspects thereof).
(13) Purchase of sites and construction of post offices, customhouses, federal courthouses, and government buildings within the District of Columbia.
(14) Oil and other pollution of navigable waters, including inland, coastal and ocean waters.
(15) Marine affairs (including coastal zone management) as they relate to oil and other pollution of navigable waters.
(16) Public buildings and occupied or improved grounds of the United States generally.
(17) Public works for the benefit of navigation, including bridges and dams (other than international bridges and dams).
(18) Related transportation regulatory agencies (except the Transportation Security Administration).
(19) Roads and the safety thereof.
(20) Transportation, including civil aviation, railroads, water transportation, transportation safety (except automobile safety and transportation security functions of the Department of Homeland Security), transportation infrastructure, transportation labor, and railroad retirement and unemployment (except revenue measures related thereto).
(21) Water power.

HOUSE TRANSPORTATION AND INFRASTRUCTURE

The House Transportation and Infrastructure Committee, under new Chairman John L. Mica, R-Fla., will push in 2011 to approve a number of major bills that were never enacted during the previous session Congress.

Mica assumed the chairmanship after the 2010 Republican takeover of the House. The committee also has a new Top Democrat—Rep. Nick J. Rahall II, who took over after former Chairman James Oberstar, D-Minn., lost his reelection bid.

Facing a daunting agenda for 2011, the committee started early with a four-year Federal Aviation Administration reauthorization that was more than three years overdue, writing the bill in January and approving it in February.

That quick work on the FAA bill let staff turn attention to a massive and complicated rewrite of the nation's highway, transit, and rail policy. With a gas tax increase off the table, Mica has said government will need to get more efficient and states will be forced to "do more with less." With no new revenues and House Republicans pushing to end several existing Department of Transportation (DOT) spending programs, Mica is looking to a number of policy changes that will help states and localities wisely spend their limited dollars.

To that end, Mica has proposed streamlining and simplifying the approval process for transportation infrastructure projects, consolidating the myriad DOT programs, and harnessing billions of dollars in private-sector investment that could be used for infrastructure construction.

Mica also has been critical of a number of Obama administration programs, including its high-speed passenger rail initiative, and will hold oversight hears on such issues. Mica has said the $8 billion provided by the 2009 stimulus package should have gone to the Northeast Corridor, an Amtrak-owned route running between Washington, D.C., and Boston. Instead of using the funds to significantly boost speeds on the corridor, the Department of Transportation spread the money among several dozen projects around the country.

The Transportation Investment Generating Economic Recovery (TIGER) program is another administration product that Mica and Republicans have been critical of. Also created by the stimulus law, the TIGER program has given several billion dollars to a number of port, freight rail, and other transportation infrastructure projects.

Another major legislative task facing the committee will be a new Water Resources Development Act. The bill has typically included hundreds of earmarked projects around the country, bringing strong bipartisan support. But House Republicans have banned earmarks, forcing the legislation to address only policy changes.

The committee also faces legislative work on separate reauthorizations of the National Transportation Safety Board, the Federal Emergency Management Agency, and the U.S. Coast Guard, each of which will include reexaminations of current policy.

HOUSE TRANSPORTATION AND INFRASTRUCTURE

Ann Adler

deputy staff director

2163 Rayburn House Office Bldg.

Phone: (202) 225-4472

Ann.Adler@mail.house.gov

Personal: Born in Weston, W.Va.

Education: B.S., journalism, West Virginia University.

Professional: 1989–1994, press assistant, Sen. Robert C. Byrd, D-W.Va. 1994–2000, press secretary, Sen. Robert C. Byrd, D-W.Va. 2000–2004, administrative assistant (COS), Sen. Robert C. Byrd, D-W.Va. 2004–2007, policy advisor/senior policy advisor, House Cmte. on Natural Resources. 2007–2010, deputy chief of staff, House Cmte. on Natural Resources. 2011–present, deputy staff dir., House Cmte. on Transportation and Infrastructure.

Expertise: Transportation issues, communications.

The House Transportation and Infrastructure Committee faces a packed legislative agenda for 2011, giving Ann Adler, deputy staff director for new Top Democrat Rep. Nick J. Rahall II, D-W.Va., a number of issues to work on.

In 2011, Alder moved to the Transportation Committee with Rahall, who became the highest-ranking Democrat after the 2010 defeat of former Chairman James Oberstar, D-Minn., and the Republican takeover of the House.

No longer able to set the hearing and legislative schedules, Adler is left reacting to Republicans while trying to protect Democratic principles laid out by Rahall.

New Committee Chairman John L. Mica, R-Fla., has set up a busy year for the committee, giving Adler a lot to follow. Republican staff quickly assembled a four-year Federal Aviation Administration reauthorization bill that was approved by the committee in February.

That measure includes a highly-contested provision that would rescind a 2010 National Mediation Board ruling that changed the calculation of airline industry elections for union representation, making it harder for employees to unionize. The provision was called a "poison pill" by several committee Democrats.

Adler also will work on a six-year rewrite of surface transportation policy, another area where Mica has promised big changes, leaving Adler and the Democratic staff in a more defensive position, trying to stop any of Mica's policies they disagree with.

The committee also faces a number of other legislative undertakings, including a new Water Resources Development Act, a Coast Guard reauthorization, a National Transportation Safety Board reauthorization, and an extension of pipeline safety programs. Adler will stay busy with all those issues in 2011.

Republicans also are expected to target a number of programs supported by Democrats, including high-speed passenger rail and Amtrak. As Mica reviews potential changes to such programs, Adler and the Democratic staff will do their best to ensure the programs are not adversely impacted.

Adler started her congressional career with Sen. Robert C. Byrd, D-W.Va., where she served as press assistant, press secretary, and later administrative assistant. She then moved to the House Natural Resources Committee before following Rahall to the Transportation Committee.

HOUSE TRANSPORTATION AND INFRASTRUCTURE

John T. Anderson

Staff Director
Subcommittee on Water Resources and Environment
B-370A Rayburn House Office Bldg.
Phone: (202) 225-4360
John.Anderson1@mail.house.gov

Personal: Born 06/20/1949 in Durham, N.C.

Education: B.S., University of North Carolina, Chapel Hill, 1971. M.A.T., University of North Carolina, Chapel Hill, 1972.

Professional: 1972–1973, teacher, Person (N.C.) County Schools. 1973–1978, biologist, U.S. Army Corps of Engineers (Memphis, Tenn.). 1978–1985, chief of environmental resources section, U.S. Army Corps of Engineers (Savannah, Ga.). 1985–1999, legislative specialist, U.S. Army Corps of Engineers (Washington, D.C.). 1999–2005, professional staff, Subc. on Water Resources and the Environment, House Cmte. on Transportation and Infrastructure. 2006–present, staff director, Subc. on Water Resources and the Environment, House Cmte. on Transportation and Infrastructure.

Expertise: Water resources, environmental sciences.

John T. Anderson, in his job as Republican staff director for the Subcommittee on Water Resources and Environment of the House Transportation Committee, will stay busy in 2011 working on a new Water Resources Development Act.

Under freshman Subcommittee Chairman Bob Gibbs, R-Ohio, Anderson will work on policy adjustments for flood control, navigable water, and environmental infrastructure projects.

House Republicans have enacted an earmark ban for 2011, which will force Anderson and the panel's staff to write a very different bill. The WRDA measure typically enjoys wide bipartisan support due to hundreds of earmarks, but without these earmarks, the legislation will be focused on policy changes that improve existing programs.

Transportation Committee Chairman John L. Mica, R-Fla., has said all legislation coming from the committee will make government more efficient and "do more with less," a goal Anderson will work toward as he reviews water infrastructure and clean water issues.

The subcommittee also is reviewing current regulations under the Clean Water Act that regulates water pollution, an issue which may draw legislative action that Anderson would be involved with.

Anderson has been with the subcommittee since 2006. He worked on the 2007 WRDA that was enacted after both chambers of Congress voted to override President Bush's veto.

Before coming to the Transportation Committee, Anderson worked for the U.S Army Corps of Engineers for more than 25 years, serving as a biologist, chief of the environmental resources section, and a legislative specialist.

HOUSE TRANSPORTATION AND INFRASTRUCTURE

Blake J. Androff

Communications Director

2163 Rayburn House Office Bldg.

Phone: (202) 225-4472

Twitter: @HouseTransInf

Blake.Androff@mail.house.gov

Personal: Born 04/14/1982 in Minneapolis, Minn.

Education: B.A., political science, Lewis & Clark College, 2004.

Professional: 2003–2004, finance asst./field organizer, Hooley for Congress. 2005–2007, field rep., Rep. Darlene Hooley, D-Ore. 2007–2008, communications asst., Rep. Darlene Hooley, D-Ore. 2008–2010, deputy communications dir., House Cmte. on Natural Resources. 2010–2011, communications director, House Cmte. on Natural Resources. 2011–present, communications director, House Cmte. on Transportation and Infrastructure.

Expertise: Communications.

Blake Androff is new to the House Transportation and Infrastructure Committee, one of a number of staffers brought over when Rep. Nick J. Rahall II, D-W.Va., left the chairmanship of the House Natural Resources Committee to take the top Democrat seat on the transportation panel.

With Democrats in the minority and with fewer committee staffers, Androff is the one-man communications department for Rahall and the committee's Democrats, working to get lawmakers talking about their priorities on issues like federal spending on transportation infrastructure—a topic that will see a major legislative undertaking.

Androff writes press releases, runs the minority's Web site, takes calls from reporters, and keeps policy staff informed of the media's perspective on issues.

The committee faces a busy agenda in 2011. After quickly approving a four-year Federal Aviation Administration reauthorization bill, the panel also must draft and approve a massive surface transportation policy rewrite and another package of spending on water infrastructure projects.

Although the highway and transit policy bill has typically been bipartisan, the White House has called for a $556 billion, six-year measure while Rep. John L. Mica, R-Fla., the committee's Republican chairman, has ruled out such a high figure. The administration also continues to push a number of programs such as high-speed rail and the' livable communities' initiative that have run into Republican opposition.

Androff began working with the House Natural Resources Committee as deputy communications director in 2008, under then-Chairman Rahall.

He moved up to communications director in March 2010—and immediately faced several major disasters that required the committee's attention and spurred hundreds of media stories. In April 2010, 29 miners were killed in an explosion at the Upper Big Branch Mine in Rahall's district. Several weeks later, an explosion at the Deepwater Horizon oil rig began the BP saga.

Before moving to Natural Resources, Androff worked for Rep. Darlene Hooley, D-Ore., on her campaign, in her Oregon office, and finally in her Washington, D.C. Office.

Androff was drawn to politics while in college. He started off as an Hispanic Studies major, but said a great professor for a political science class got him to switch majors.

Androff loves spending time outdoors, including hiking at Shenandoah National Park.

HOUSE TRANSPORTATION AND INFRASTRUCTURE

Alex Burkett

Counsel

Subcommittee on Aviation

2251 Rayburn House Office Bldg.

Phone: (202) 225-9161

Alex.Burkett@mail.house.gov

Personal: Born 05/22/1981 in Athens, Ga.

Education: B.A., American and Southern Studies, Vanderbilt University, 2003. J.D., Florida State University College of Law, 2007.

Professional: 2003–2004, reporter/bureau chief, Hometown News, Vero Beach, Fla. 2007–2009, law clerk, Hon. Charles J. Kahn, Jr., Florida First District of Appeal. 2009–2010, associate attorney, Dombroff Gilmore Jaques and French, P.C. 2010–present, counsel, Subc. on Aviation, House Cmte. on Transportation and Infrastructure.

Expertise: Aviation safety, antitrust issues.

A four-year Federal Aviation Administration reauthorization will continue to be a focal point for Alex Burkett in his job as Democratic counsel for the House Transportation and Infrastructure Committee's Subcommittee on Aviation.

Burkett moves to the minority in 2011 under the committee's new top Democrat, Rep. Nick J. Rahall II, D-W. Va. He came to the committee in 2010 under then-Chairman James Oberstar, D-Minn.

The House and Senate were fairly close to enacting an FAA bill in 2010, but several issues went unresolved. An FAA reauthorization was the Senate's first major legislative undertaking in 2011, which the chamber passed in February. "I'll continue to work this year toward the passage of what we hope will be a job-creating, forward-looking bill," Burkett said.

Burkett also will focus on aviation safety and airline industry issues in 2011. "The airline industry is in the midst of major structural changes, re-ordered by mergers and global alliances," Burkett said. Because of that, Burkett said he will work to ensure that the industry remains viable while also protecting passengers' safety and addressing the needs of stakeholders, including the labor force.

Burkett is passionate about aviation and said he likes contributing to the policy dialogue. "I enjoy meeting regularly with administration officials, industry and labor groups, and airline people, listening to their concerns, and figuring out how to balance everyone's objectives, while always putting the public interest first," he said.

Aviation has long been a major part of Burkett's life. He has been flying airplanes since he was 10, growing up in airports and around airplanes. "I went flying with local pilots and took lessons whenever I got the chance," he said. "I'm an aviation person at heart, so working to advance sound aviation policy brings me great joy and professional satisfaction."

In the 111th Congress, Burkett worked on a major aviation safety bill (H.R. 5900) that came in response to the February 2009 crash of a Colgan Air commuter plane in Buffalo, N.Y. The accident "revealed major weaknesses in the safety system that, if left uncorrected, would inevitably lead to future accidents," Burkett said, issues addressed in the new law. Among other things, it enhanced a number of pilot training requirements and rest time rules.

HOUSE TRANSPORTATION AND INFRASTRUCTURE

Jim Coon

Chief of Staff

2165 Rayburn House Office Bldg.

Phone: (202) 225-9446

jim.coon@mail.house.gov

Personal: Born 11/28/1959 in Vallejo, Calif.

Education: B.A., Virginia Tech, 1982.

Professional: 1983–1989, legislative assistant, Rep. Robert F. Smith, R-Ore. 1989–1994, legislative director, Rep. John Duncan, R-Tenn. 1995–1998, professional staff member, Subc. on Aviation, House Cmte. on Transportation and Infrastructure. 1998–2003, director of legislative affairs, Air Transport Association. 2003–2004, director of legislative affairs, The Boeing Company. 2004–2007, staff director, Subc. on Aviation, House Cmte. on Transportation and Infrastructure. 2007–2011, minority chief of staff, House Cmte. on Transportation and Infrastructure. 2011–present, chief of staff, House Cmte. on Transportation and Infrastructure.

Expertise: Aviation, transportation and infrastructure.

Jim Coon, the chief of staff to House Transportation and Infrastructure Committee Chairman John L. Mica, R-Fla., faces a busy legislative agenda in 2011, including major bills on highway and transit policy, water resources spending, and a Federal Aviation Administration reauthorization.

Coon has been Mica's chief of staff on the committee since 2007, and now moves into the majority with the Republican takeover of the House, giving him the ability to set hearing schedules, legislative priorities, and committee markups.

The most daunting legislative task facing the committee is a six-year highway and transit policy rewrite. Mica has said the states will need to "do more with less" when it comes to transportation.

The committee also faces work on a new Water Resources Development Act. With an earmark moratorium in place, Coon said the bill will focus on policy changes that fit with Mica's theme of streamlined procedures and efficient government.

Due to the number of important measure coming before the committee in 2011, Coon said he will work to educate Republican committee members on transportation issues. More than half of the committee's GOP roster—18 out of 33—are freshmen members elected in November 2010. Coon is pleased with the committee's lineup and is excited about the "bright, energetic members," he said.

Coon also manages the committee's Republican staff, and he said it has been a smooth transition into the majority. All of the senior staff have been in the majority before and know how to move bills through the legislative process, Coon said.

The committee also has a new Top Democrat in Rep. Nick J. Rahall II, D-W.Va. Coon said he is looking forward to working with Rahall and his staff. Rahall's staff is also quite experienced, Coon said, making it easier for him to work with them.

HOUSE TRANSPORTATION AND INFRASTRUCTURE

Giles Giovinazzi

Staff Director
Subcommittee on Aviation
2251 Rayburn House Office Bldg.
Phone: (202) 226-8779
Fax: (202) 225-4629
Giles.Giovinazzi@mail.house.gov

Personal: Born 09/17/1973 in New York City, N.Y.

Education: B.A., Columbia University, 1995. J.D., Tulane Law School, 1998.

Professional: 1999–2002, legislative counsel, Rep. James McGovern, D-Mass. 2002–2006, counsel, Subc. on Aviation, House Cmte. on Transportation and Infrastructure. 2004–present, officer, U.S. Navy Reserve. 2006–2009, senior counsel, Subc. on Aviation, House Cmte. on Transportation and Infrastructure. 2009–present, staff director, Subc. on Aviation, House Cmte. on Transportation and Infrastructure.

Expertise: NextGen/air traffic control modernization, aviation safety, airport financing programs.

Giles Giovinazzi will spend the 112th Congress working on a number of aviation issues in his position as the Democratic staff director for the Subcommittee on Aviation of the House Transportation and Infrastructure Committee under new ranking member Rep. Nick J. Rahall II, D-W.Va.

Giovinazzi has been with the subcommittee since 2002, coming in under then-ranking member Rep. James Oberstar, D-Minn., and then shifting to the majority in 2007 when Oberstar became chairman. Giovinazzi is now back in the minority under a Republican House and ranking Democrat Rahall.

Giovinazzi's will work to protect Democratic priorities in a four-year Federal Aviation Administration reauthorization approved by the committee in February, he said. The bill includes several provisions opposed by Democrats, including one dubbed a "poison pill" by Rep. Jerry Costello, D-Ill., the Aviation Subcommittee's Top Democrat. The measure would repeal a National Mediation Board rule, issued in May 2010, which would change how airline industry elections for union representation are calculated.

Giovinazzi worked heavily on the Airline Safety and Federal Aviation Administration Extension Act that was signed into law in 2010, and oversight of that bill's numerous safety provisions will keep him busy in 2011.

That measure, which came in response to the February 2009 crash of Colgan Air Flight 3407 that killed 50 people, increased by six-fold the number of hours needed to obtain a commercial pilot's license, forced a Federal Aviation Administration rulemaking to address pilot fatigue, and mandated that airlines create fatigue risk plans.

Giovinazzi also will spend time on oversight of NextGen, a new GPS-based air traffic control system that improves safety and congestion compared to the outdated radar-based system that is still in use. NextGen implementation, a timeline for which is laid out in the FAA reauthorization, is a costly undertaking that has drawn calls for increased federal spending to help airlines equip their planes.

Committee Chairman John L. Mica, R-Fla., also is very involved in aviation security issues, Giovinazzi says.

Giovinazzi has been with the U.S. Navy Reserve since 2004. In 2008, he served in Afghanistan for nine months as an intelligence officer, returning in January 2009. He also is a member of the New York State Bar in good standing.

HOUSE TRANSPORTATION AND INFRASTRUCTURE

Jennifer L. Hall

Counsel

Subcommittee on Highways and Transit

B-376 Rayburn House Office Bldg.

Phone: (202) 226-4936

Jennifer.Hall@mail.house.gov

Personal: Born 04/23/1972 in Covina, Calif.

Education: B.A., University of Arizona, 1994. J.D., University of Notre Dame Law School, 1999.

Professional: 2000–2002, counsel, House Cmte. on Oversight and Government Reform. 2002–2005, legislative liaison, Office of Legislative Affairs, FEMA. 2005–2006, legislative attorney, Office of General Counsel, Federal Emergency Management Agency. 2006–2008, counsel, Subc. on Economic Development, Public Buildings, and Emergency Management, House Cmte. on Transportation and Infrastructure. 2008–present, counsel, Subc. on Highways and Transit, House Cmte. on Transportation and Infrastructure.

Expertise: Motor carrier/trucking issues, infrastructure project delivery.

A major, comprehensive rewrite of surface transportation policy will be the focal point of the House Transportation and Infrastructure Committee in 2011, bringing up a number of issues under the purview of Jennifer Hall, Republican counsel for the Subcommittee on Highways and Transit.

Hall moved to the majority in 2011 under new Committee Chairman John L. Mica, R-Fla., who has set the highway and transit reauthorization as his committee's top legislative priority.

Within that bill, Hall expects to spend time looking into ways to speed the delivery of transportation infrastructure projects, something she has been focused on since 2008. Mica has often said the bill should cut bureaucratic obstacles that force even simple projects to take more than ten years from concept to completion, including streamlining a number of agency approvals. Projects also are cheaper when finished quicker.

Mica touts his "437-Day Plan," named after the new Interstate-35 West bridge in Minneapolis, Minn., constructed in the footprint of a span that collapsed in 2007 and contracted to be finished in 437 days. Mica points to that bridge as a good example of project delivery; it was finished both ahead of schedule and under budget.

Hall also will work on a number of other trucking and motor carrier issues, she said. Committee members are likely to introduce a number of smaller bills on such issues, but Hall expects any changes to be incorporated into the broader reauthorization, as the committee traditionally does with the measure.

Hall has been with the committee since 2006, starting off as counsel for the Subcommittee on Economic Development, Public Buildings, and Emergency Management, and moving to the Subcommittee on Highways and Transit in 2008. Prior to that, she worked for the Federal Emergency Management Agency, holding jobs in the Office of General Counsel and the Office of Legislative Affairs.

In the 111th Congress, Hall worked primarily on hazardous material transportation issues, including the Hazardous Material Transportation Safety Act that was approved by the full committee in 2009 under then-Chairman James Oberstar, D-Minn.

Hall is married with two children—a nine-year old daughter and a five-year old son. "They take up whatever spare time I have," she said.

HOUSE TRANSPORTATION AND INFRASTRUCTURE

Justin Harclerode

Communications Director

2165 Rayburn House Office Bldg.

Phone: (202) 226-8767

Twitter: @TransportGOP

justin.harclerode@mail.house.gov

Personal: Born 02/17/1972 in Everett, Pa.

Education: B.A., English, Pennsylvania State University, 1995. B.S., Secondary Education, Pennsylvania State University, 1995.

Professional: 1995–1996, substitute teacher, Bedford County, Pennsylvania School Districts. 1996–1997, caseworker/staff asst., Rep. Bud Shuster, R-Pa. 1997–2006, deputy director of communications, House Cmte. on Transportation and Infrastructure. 2007–present, communications director, House Cmte. on Transportation and Infrastructure.

Expertise: Communications.

As Communications Director for the House Transportation and Infrastructure Committee, Justin Harclerode runs the entire press operation for new Chairman Rep. John L. Mica, R-Fla., including writing press releases, fielding inquiries from reporters, coordinating press events and managing content on the panel's web page.

Facing a long list of major bills in the 112th Congress, the committee started early with the February approval of a four-year Federal Aviation Administration reauthorization bill.

The committee also faces a major surface transportation reauthorization, additional changes to the Water Resources Development Act, and a Coast Guard reauthorization, all of which will keep Harclerode busy managing the Republican messaging on each bill.

Harclerode is in the unique position of having to understand a broad range of issues—unlike policy staff that often focus on specific programs or agencies—which keeps him busy and jumping from topic to topic, depending on the day's hearing topic or reporters' questions.

Streamlining government will be a key aspect of all legislative proposals coming from the committee, Harclerode says.

To get that message out, Harclerode posts video clips from hearings to the committee's web page, which he designed with input from Mica. He also is discovering the benefits of social media, posting committee news and information on Twitter. Social media "helps get the word out," he says.

Harclerode has been running Mica's press outfit for four years, moving into the majority with the Republican takeover of the House in 2011. Chairman Mica is very energetic and that enthusiasm transfers to the staff, Harclerode says.

Coming out of Penn State, where he studied secondary education and English, Harclerode originally was a substitute teacher in Pennsylvania. In 1996, he worked on the campaign of Bob Shuster, who lost in the GOP primary for a House seat in Pennsylvania, leading Harclerode to his job with Bob's brother—former Chairman Bud Shuster, R-Pa.

Harclerode moved from Shuster's personal office to the Transportation Committee in 1997 and hasn't looked back since then, staying on through the tenure of former Chairman Don Young, R-Alaska, before becoming communications director when Mica took the top Republican seat on the committee in 2007.

HOUSE TRANSPORTATION AND INFRASTRUCTURE

Johanna Hardy

Counsel

Subcommittee on Economic Development, Public Buildings, and Emergency Management

585 Ford House Office Bldg.

Phone: (202) 225-3014

johanna.hardy@mail.house.gov

Personal: Born 1972 in Philadelphia, Pa.

Education: B.S., music and nuclear engineering, Massachusetts Institute of Technology, 1993. J.D., Georgetown University, 1997.

Professional: 1997–1999, counsel, Senate Cmte. on Governmental Affairs. 1999–2000, senior legislative asst., Massachusetts Institute of Technology (Washington, D.C., office). 2000–2005, senior counsel, Senate Cmte. on Homeland Security and Governmental Affairs. 2005–2008, director of government affairs and regulatory policy, Rolls-Royce North America, Inc. 2008–present, counsel, Subc. on Economic Development, Public Buildings, and Emergency Management.

Expertise: Economic development, public buildings, emergency management.

Johanna Hardy has been counsel for the House Transportation and Infrastructure Committee's Subcommittee on Economic Development, Public Buildings, and Emergency Management since 2008.

Moving to the majority under Chairman John Mica, R-Fla., Hardy will focus on improving federal emergency management and saving taxpayer dollars through the proper management of federal real property assets.

The subcommittee's work during the 112th Congress will see Hardy's involvement in reauthorization of the Economic Development Administration and streamlining economic development programs, the management of federal buildings, and Federal Emergency Management Agency issues.

FEMA has been a major concern for the committee and Chairman Mica. The Federal Emergency Management Independence Act, introduced in the 111th Congress, sought to move FEMA from the Department of Homeland Security and require FEMA's administrator to report directly to the President, but was never enacted.

In 2011, the committee will look at FEMA's mitigation and disaster assistance programs with an eye toward streamlining bureaucratic hurdles to recovery following a disaster, Hardy says. The committee also will explore cost-saving measures through better management of federal buildings, including right-sizing the federal asset portfolio, selling or redeveloping under-performing assets, and minimizing the over-reliance on costly leases.

Before coming to the House in 2008, Hardy was senior counsel for the Senate Committee on Homeland Security and Governmental Affairs, and worked on a number of pieces of legislation that were signed onto law, among them the Homeland Security Act of 2002 and the Intelligence Reform and Terrorism Prevention Act of 2004.

HOUSE TRANSPORTATION AND INFRASTRUCTURE

Jennifer L. Homendy

Staff Director

Subcommittee on Railroads, Pipelines, and Hazardous Materials

592 Ford House Office Bldg.

Phone: (202) 225-3274

Fax: (202) 226-3475

jennifer.esposito@mail.house.gov

Personal: Born 11/26/1971 in New Britain, Conn.

Education: B.A., Pennsylvania State University, 1994.

Professional: 1994–1996, Senate asst. for federal government relations, National Federation of Independent Business. 1996–1997, manager of government relations, American Iron and Steel Institute. 1997–1999, legislative rep., Dept. of Transportation Trades, AFL-CIO. 1999–2004, legislative rep., International Brotherhood of Teamsters. 2004–present, staff director, Subc. on Railroads, House Cmte. on Transportation and Infrastructure.

Expertise: Railroads, pipeline transportation, hazardous materials transportation (all modes).

Jennifer L. Homendy will stay busy in 2011 with work on rail, hazardous material, and pipeline safety issues in her job as staff director for Democrats on the House Transportation and Infrastructure Committee's Subcommittee on Railroad, Pipelines, and Hazardous Materials.

Homendy, who went as Jennifer Esposito for eight years before taking her partner's name, held her position when Democrats were in the majority for four years under former Chairman James Oberstar, D-Minn., and now moves to the minority under Rep. Nick J. Rahall II, D-W.Va., the committee's new ranking member.

Homendy will work on rail issues in a massive surface transportation measure being drafted by the full committee's new chairman, Rep. John L. Mica, R-Fla. Staffers are predicting "a significant rail title" and Mica has suggested a number of changes, such as improvements to the Railroad Rehabilitation & Improvement Financing that supports freight rail infrastructure work.

Legislative reauthorizations of the Department of Transportation's hazardous materials safety program and pipeline safety program also will require Homendy's attention in 2011.

Homendy spent much of the 111th Congress on those same issues, including a hazardous materials safety bill that was approved by the full committee and a surface transportation bill that was approved by the Subcommittee on Highways and Transit, though neither was taken up on the House floor.

Homendy still brings her dog Milo, a puggle, into the Capitol. Although lawmakers may not, Milo remains bipartisan if you have food, Homendy said.

HOUSE TRANSPORTATION AND INFRASTRUCTURE

James Kolb

Staff Director
Subcommittee on Highways and Transit
B-375 Rayburn House Office Bldg.
Phone: (202) 225-9989
Jim.Kolb@mail.house.gov

Personal: Born 06/02/1967 in Buffalo, N.Y.

Education: B.A., political science, State University of New York at Buffalo, 1990. M.P.P., George Mason University, School of Public Policy, 2005.

Professional: 1989–1992, legislative asst., Office of the Doorkeeper, House of Representatives. 1992–1998, legislative rep., United Brotherhood of Carpenters and Joiners of America. 1998–2001, dir., Office of Congressional Affairs, Dept. of Transportation. 2001–2006, vice president of congressional relations, American Road and Transportation Builders Assn. 2006–2007, senior vice president, Xenophon Strategies. 2007–present, staff director, Subc. on Highways and Transit, House Cmte. on Transportation and Infrastructure.

Expertise: Highway & transit issues.

Jim Kolb, as Democratic staff director for the Subcommittee on Highways and Transit of the House Transportation and Infrastructure Committee, will spend the vast majority of 2011 working on a bill that has also dominated the past several years—a long-term surface transportation policy rewrite.

Kolb moved into the minority in 2011 as Rep. Nick J. Rahall II, D-W.Va., assumed the committee's top Democrat post after the November 2010 defeat of former Chairman James Oberstar, D-Minn. Kolb joined the committee when Oberstar took over as chairman in January 2007.

Kolb said that his work in 2011 will be much more reactive than proactive, now that his staff is in the minority and new Committee Chairman John L. Mica, R-Fla., and Republican staff will be writing the bill.

In addition to managing the Democratic staff that oversees the bulk of the reauthorization, Kolb will be one of the key staffers fighting to keep Democratic priorities in the legislation.

Mica has often said the government and his committee should do more with less, and is eying a number of programmatic and policy changes in order to help states more effectively and quickly spend their transportation infrastructure dollars on the best projects.

Mica's bill is expected to look drastically different than the one Kolb worked heavily on during the 111th Congress. That measure was approved by the Subcommittee on Highways and Transit in 2009 but never moved beyond that amid congressional reluctance to tackle the volatile gas tax issue and calls from the Obama administration and the Senate to postpone the debate until 2011.

Kolb also expects to work on environmental and Mexican truck issues in the 112th Congress. In March 2011, the administration announced a long-overdue deal with Mexico regarding cross-border trucking between the two countries. U.S. refusal to allow Mexican trucks into the United States, as was called for in the North American Free Trade Agreement, had led to Mexico slapping billions of dollars in retaliatory tariffs on U.S. projects.

Working on Oberstar's bill in the 111th Congress, Kolb oversaw a series of hearing on various topics in the legislation. He also worked on parts of the stimulus package that ended up handing more than $35 billion to states for highway and transit work.

Whatever free time he has is spent on his three children. "That drives so much of what I do," he said.

HOUSE TRANSPORTATION AND INFRASTRUCTURE

Holly Woodruff Lyons

Staff Director & Counsel

Subcommittee on Aviation

2251 Rayburn House Office Bldg.

Phone: (202) 226-3220

Holly.Woodruff@mail.house.gov

Education: J.D., University of San Diego School of Law.

Professional: attorney, Federal Aviation Administration, Office of the Chief Counsel, Airports and Environmental Law Division. senior partner, Arnold & Porter LLP. 2002–2007, counsel, Subc. on Aviation, House Cmte. on Transportation and Infrastructure. 2007–present, staff dir. & counsel, Subc. on Aviation, House Cmte. on Transportation and Infrastructure.

Expertise: Aviation issues.

Holly Woodruff Lyons, Republican staff director and counsel for the Subcommittee on Aviation of the House Transportation and Infrastructure Committee, faces work on a number of issues in 2011.

The biggest of those issues is a four-year Federal Aviation Administration reauthorization, which was written quickly by staff and approved by the committee in February.

Serving under new Committee Chairman John L. Mica, R-Fla., Lyons worked on a number of thorny issues in the bill, some of which brought out swift opposition from Democrats.

Among other things, the measure rescinded a 2010 ruling from the National Mediation Board that changed how airline industry elections for unionization are calculated, making it easier for employees to unionize.

The bill also phases out the majority of the Essential Air Service (EAS) program that subsidizes rural airports that otherwise would be commercially unviable. The bill does keep the program for Alaska, which due to its geography is home to around one-third of EAS-supported airports.

After criticizing Democrats for being unable to enact an FAA bill since the last long-term measure expired in 2007, Mica took over the chairmanship of the House Transportation Committee in 2011 and vowed to put an end to the series of short-term extensions since then.

Mica has joked that he might set a record for having the longest-running FAA bill, a measure Lyons worked on in 2003. She came to the Aviation Subcommittee as counsel in 2002 and began work on the Vision 100-Century of Aviation Reauthorization Act, which was signed into law in December 2003. That measure, written to last four years, will have been law for more than seven years before the new reauthorization.

Lyons also will work on a number of aviation issues under the panel's purview, including oversight of the Transportation Security Administration and implementation of NextGen, an expensive GPS-based air traffic control system that is far safer and more efficient than the outdated radar-based system still used by the United States.

Before coming to the Transportation Committee, Lyons worked as an attorney in the FAA's Airports and Environmental Law Division in the Office of the Chief Counsel.

HOUSE TRANSPORTATION AND INFRASTRUCTURE

Daniel W. Mathews

Staff Director

Subcommittee on Economic Development, Public Buildings, and Emergency Management

585 Ford House Office Bldg.

Phone: (202) 225-3014

Dan.Mathews@mail.house.gov

Education: B.A., Georgetown University, 1988.

Professional: 1989–1992, legislative asst., Rep. Robert Lagomarsino, R-Calif. 1992–1994, family business. 1995–1998, legislative dir., Rep. Jay Kim, R-Calif. 1998–2001, asst. deputy commissioner of health, State of Texas. 2002–2003, professional staff member, House Cmte. on Rules. 2003–present, staff dir., Subc. on Economic Development, Public Buildings, and Emergency Management, House Cmte. on Transportation and Infrastructure.

Expertise: Infrastructure, emergency management, House rules.

Dan Mathews, entering his eighth year as Republican staff director for the House Transportation and Infrastructure Committee's Subcommittee on Economic Development, Public Buildings, and Emergency Management, will work on several major reauthorizations under the panel's jurisdiction in 2011.

The biggest issue facing the panel will be reauthorization of the Federal Emergency Management Agency, Mathews said, including a push to strengthen the independence of the agency, which is currently housed in the Department of Homeland Security.

Full Committee Chairman John L. Mica (R-Fla.) has pushed to remove FEMA from DHS, an issue he could revisit after taking over as chairman in 2011.

Mathews also will stay busy with work on public buildings. The subcommittee may produce a bill to consolidate and reduce the number of federal buildings, Mathews said. Mica has targeted such waste, and the issue gained attention when President Barack Obama floated to building consolidation plan.

The Economic Development Administration also faces an authorization in 2011. Mathews said he would work to eliminate bureaucratic obstacles that spread funds across multiple agencies, making it harder for participants to access the economic development programs.

Mathews worked on the Pre-disaster Hazard Mitigation Act of 2010 in the 111th Congress, which was signed into law in January 2011. He has worked on the House side of the Capitol since 1989.

In his spare time, Mathews enjoys rock climbing.

HOUSE TRANSPORTATION AND INFRASTRUCTURE

Ward W. McCarragher

Chief Counsel

2163 Rayburn House Office Bldg.

Phone: (202) 225-4472

ward.mccarragher@mail.house.gov

Personal: Born 12/17/1962 in Waukesha, Wis.

Education: B.A., University of Wisconsin, 1985. J.D., University of Wisconsin Law School, 1992.

Professional: 1989, foreign policy analyst, Congressional Research Service. 1991, legal intern, U.S. Northern District of California. 1993–1994, intern, asst. counsel, and counsel, Subc. on Economic Development, House Cmte. on Public Works and Transportation. 1995–1998, counsel, Subc. on Surface Transportation and Subc. on Public Buildings and Economic Development, House Cmte. on Transportation and Infrastructure. 1999–present, chief counsel, House Cmte. on Transportation and Infrastructure.

Expertise: Highway and transit law.

The House Transportation and Infrastructure Committee faces a complicated legislative rewrite of surface transportation policy in 2011, bringing up a number of legal issues covered by Ward McCarragher, chief counsel for Rep. Nick J. Rahall II, D-W.Va., the committee's new Top Democrat.

McCarragher will stay busy pushing to maintain Democratic priorities under new Chairman John L. Mica, R-Fla., who took over after the 2010 Republican House takeover. McCarragher had worked for former Chairman James Oberstar, D-Minn., and stayed on under Rahall.

Mica has talked of streamlining the approval process for transportation infrastructure projects, consolidating duplicative and underused Department of Transportation programs, and expanding private-sector investment in projects, all issues that McCarragher will keep a close eye on now that he is back in the minority.

McCarragher will work with and monitor Republicans as they assemble the legislation that will carry those and a number of other policy changes.

The highway and transit measure is just one of many facing the committee in 2011. Separate reauthorizations of the National Transportation Safety Board, the U.S. Coast Guard, and the Federal Emergency Management Agency will consume McCarragher's time in 2011.

McCarragher has been with the committee for 18 years. He started work in 1993 as in intern for the Subcommittee on Economic Development, when the full committee was known as the Public Works and Transportation Committee. McCarragher worked his way up from there, becoming Democratic chief counsel for the full committee in 1999.

HOUSE TRANSPORTATION AND INFRASTRUCTURE

Suzanne Newhouse Mullen

General Counsel

2165 Rayburn House Office Bldg.

Phone: (202) 225-9446

suzanne.mullen@mail.house.gov

Education: Miami University, 2000. J.D., Southern Methodist University, Dedman School of Law, 2003.

Professional: 2003–2004, intelligence analyst, Federal Bureau of Investigation, Counterterrorism Division, Terrorism Reports and Requirements Section. 2004–2005, attorney advisor, Federal Motor Carrier Safety Administration, Department of Transportation. 2005–2008, counsel, Subc. on Highways and Transit, House Cmte. on Transportation and Infrastructure. 2008–present, general counsel, House Cmte. on Transportation and Infrastructure. 2008, surface transportation counsel, Subc. on Surface Transportation and Merchant Marine Infrastructure, Safety, and Security, Senate Cmte. on Commerce, Science, and Transportation.

Expertise: Transportation & infrastructure.

Suzanne Newhouse Mullen, general counsel for the Republican majority under new House Transportation and Infrastructure Committee Chairman John L. Mica, R-Fla., will stay busy in 2011 working on a number of legal issues raised in major transportation and related bills.

Mullen got an early start for the year by working on a four-year Federal Aviation Administration reauthorization, which staff drafted in January and was approved by the committee in February.

With that out of the way, Mullen turned attention to a large and complicated rewrite of the nation's policy governing highways, transit, and rail. The last long-term surface transportation measure expired in September 2009, and Mica has made the new measure his committee's biggest priority for 2011.

Because an increase in the gas tax that funds road, bridge, and transit projects is off the table in a Republican-controlled House, Mica has often said that state and localities will need to "do more with less" when it comes to transportation infrastructure.

That theme will dominate Mullen's work on the reauthorization, including work on streamlining Department of Transportation programs and speeding the construction of major infrastructure projects, some of which can take over a decade from conception to completion.

Mullen also will work on a range of other issues covered by the committee, including a Coast Guard reauthorization measure, a new Water Resources Development Act, and a National Transportation Safety Board reauthorization.

The committee's makeup in the 112th Congress is drastically different than in previous years—18 of the 33 Republican members are freshmen lawmakers, meaning Mullen will stay occupied educating the new members on a variety of transportation policy issues.

Mullen has worked in a number of transportation capacities in her relatively short career on Capitol Hill.

After a short stint at the Federal Bureau of Investigation, Mullen was an attorney advisor for the Federal Motor Carrier Safety Administration. She then moved on to be counsel of the Transportation Committee's Subcommittee on Highways and Transit, followed by a year on the Senate side as surface transportation counsel for the Subcommittee on Surface Transportation and Merchant Marine Infrastructure, Safety, and Security of the Senate Commerce, Science, and Transportation Committee. Mullen returned to the House Transportation Committee in December 2008, where she has served as counsel since then.

HOUSE TRANSPORTATION AND INFRASTRUCTURE

Jonathan R. Pawlow

Counsel

Subcommittee on Water Resources and Environment

B-370A Rayburn House Office Bldg.

Phone: (202) 225-4360

Jon.Pawlow@mail.house.gov

Personal: Born in New York City, N.Y.

Education: B.S., Rutgers University, Cook College of Agriculture & Environmental Science. M.S., Rutgers University, Cook College of Agriculture & Environmental Science. J.D., Georgetown University Law School.

Professional: 1976–1977, coadjunct instructor, Rutgers University, Department of Agricultural & Biological Engineering. 1977–1986, environmental scientist, Environmental Protection Agency, Office of Water. 1986–1988, attorney-at-law, Arent, Fox, Kintner, & Kahn. 1988–96, attorney-at-law, Chadbourne & Parke, LLP. 1995–2000, instructor, George Washington University, Center for Career Education. 1996–2000, attorney-at-law/corporate consultant, Washington, D.C./Virginia. 1997–2002, adjunct professor, Old Dominion University, College of Engineering & Technology. 2000–2002, asst. chief counsel, Small Business Administration, Office of Advocacy. 2002–present, counsel, Subc. on Water Resources and Environment, House Cmte. on Transportation and Infrastructure.

Expertise: Environmental science, water resources, civil works projects.

Jon Pawlow has been Republican Counsel for the Subcommittee on Water Resources and Environment of the House Transportation and Infrastructure Committee since 2002, moving back into the majority under Chairman John L. Mica, R-Fla., in the 112th Congress.

In 2011, Pawlow will work on a new Water Resources Development Act that includes flood control, navigation, and environmental projects. The measure will include policy changes, but a House Republican ban on earmarks will result in a much different bill, one that does not include the a list of lawmakers' pet projects. Pawlow said the earmark ban is a major unknown and could be a "big issue" for the legislation.

The goal of all his work will be to make government smarter, Pawlow said, which fits with the "doing more with less" theme laid out by Committee Chairman John L. Mica, R-Fla.

Under new Subcommittee Chairman Bob Gibbs, R-Ohio, Pawlow will help lay out the oversight and legislative agendas. In setting priorities during tough economic times, Pawlow said he must find "smart and reasonable" ways to continue good federal programs. Pawlow warned against regulatory excess and the impacts on small businesses, which he will address in his work.

Pawlow said he also will work on Corps of Engineers civil works projects, potential changes to the Clean Water Act, sewer and treatment plant issues, and the Clean Water State Revolving Fund. He also will do regulatory policy work on storm water runoff, nutrient controls, and non-point source pollution issues, he said.

He also works on Superfund and Brownfield issues, which the House Energy and Commerce Committee also have jurisdiction over.

Pawlow has been in his current position since 2002, coming in under then-Chairman Don Young, R-Alaska, and later moving to Mica's staff when he took over the top GOP spot.

Pawlow said he got into policy work because he was burnt out after 15 years of private law practice. After studying environmental sciences and getting a law degree, he worked at the Environmental Protection Agency for nine years before moving to private practice, followed by a stint at the Small Business Administration before moving to his current position.

Pawlow is married with two grown children, including a son who also works on the House side of the Capitol.

HOUSE TRANSPORTATION AND INFRASTRUCTURE

John Rayfield

Staff Director

Subcommittee on Coast Guard and Maritime Transportation

507 Ford House Office Bldg.

Phone: (202) 226-0204

john.rayfield@mail.house.gov

Personal: Born 1957 in Portsmouth, Va.

Education: University of Virginia.

Professional: 1995–2003, legislative staff, Subc. on Fisheries Conservation, Wildlife, and Oceans, House Cmte. on Natural Resources. 2003, professional staff member, Subc. on Coast Guard and Maritime Transportation, House Cmte. on Transportation and Infrastructure. 2004–present, staff dir., Subc. on Coast Guard and Maritime Transportation, House Cmte. on Transportation and Infrastructure.

Expertise: Maritime issues, Coast Guard.

The House Transportation and Infrastructure will assemble a Coast Guard reauthorization measure in 2011, giving plenty of work to John Rayfield, Republican staff director for the Subcommittee on Coast Guard and Maritime Transportation.

Rayfield has been with the panel since 2003, starting in the majority, spending four years in the minority, and then retaking the majority in 2011 under new Committee Chairman John L. Mica, R-Fla., and Subcommittee Chairman Frank LoBiondo, R-N.J.

Rayfield also will work on maritime transportation issues, including the development of "a national strategic transportation plan that includes a strong maritime transportation component and greater use of coastwise trade," according to the subcommittee.

Marine highways are one of many modes of transportation that will see policy rewrites this year under Mica, who also is in charge of separate surface transportation and aviation reauthorizations.

Another issue that will see Rayfield's attention is oversight of the Deepwater Horizon oil spill. The Coast Guard was the first federal agency responding to the fatal accident in April 2010. The panel "will work to ensure that the nation's oil spill prevention and response capabilities protect the environment without threatening U.S. jobs."

The subcommittee also has jurisdiction over port safety, ocean shipping, state boating safety programs, and marine environmental issues caused by ships, all issues that Rayfield will spend time on.

In the 111th Congress, Rayfield worked on a Coast Guard authorization that was signed into law in October 2010.

HOUSE TRANSPORTATION AND INFRASTRUCTURE

Joyce Rose

Staff Director

Subcommittee on Railroads, Pipelines, and Hazardous Materials

B-376 Rayburn House Office Bldg.

Phone: (202) 226-2265

Joyce.Rose@mail.house.gov

Personal: Born 12/22/1960 in Leonardtown, Md.

Education: B.S., Frostburg State University, 1982.

Professional: 1984–1988, staff asst., National Forest Products Association. 1988–1991, staff asst., Subc. on Transportation, Senate Cmte. on Appropriations. 1991–2001, professional staff, Subc. on Transportation, Senate Cmte. on Appropriations. 2001–2008, professional staff, Subc. on Highways and Transit, House Cmte. on Transportation and Infrastructure. 2008–present, staff director, Subc. on Railroads, Pipelines, and Hazardous Materials, House Cmte. on Transportation and Infrastructure.

Expertise: Rail program structure and grants, Rail and transit policy.

Joyce Rose, staff director for the Subcommittee on Railroads, Pipelines, and Hazardous Materials of the House Transportation and Infrastructure Committee, was picked by Chairman John Mica, R-Fla., to work on ways to connect intercity passenger rail and public transportation.

"We have this division between intercity passenger rail and transit," Rose said regretfully. Although they are very similar, with heavy trains running on fixed tracks carrying passengers, they are regulated and funded by different agencies, she said, which can cause a number of complications.

Per Mica's request, Rose works on both rail programs under her Railroad panel's jurisdiction and public transportation programs, which are under the purview of the Highways and Transit Subcommittee, with which she coordinates her work.

Rose's biggest task in the 112th Congress will be a comprehensive surface transportation bill that she said will include "a significant rail title." As part of that measure, Rose will work on reforms to the Passenger Rail Investment and Improvement Act of 2008 and changes to the Railroad Rehabilitation and Improvement Financing program that funds freight rail infrastructure upgrades.

Mica has often targeted the RRIF program as one of the underutilized federal programs that will be improved in the upcoming reauthorization that Rose also will handle. Created in 1998, the RRIF program is authorized to make up to $35 billion in loans for railroad infrastructure improvements, but only has around $400 million in outstanding loans, Mica has said.

Any changes, to the RRIF program or other areas, will need to keep the size of government small, a dictate from Chairman Mica, Rose said.

Rose worked heavily on the 2008 PRIIA that was passed by a Democratic Congress and signed into law by President Bush, a measure she is now eying changes to after moving to the majority with the Republican takeover of the House.

Rose came to the committee in 2001 after a decade at the Senate Appropriations Committee, where she worked for the subcommittee that oversees Department of Transportation funding. She was a professional staff member for the Highways and Transit Subcommittee until 2008, when she became staff director of the Railroads Subcommittee.

Rose has a degree in music education and taught band for Calvert and Montgomery County Schools in Maryland for several years after college. She keeps her hand in music by directing church choir.

HOUSE TRANSPORTATION AND INFRASTRUCTURE

Ryan Seiger

Counsel

Subcommittee on Water Resources and Environment

B-375 Rayburn House Office Bldg.

Phone: (202) 225-0060

Fax: (202) 225-4627

Ryan.Seiger@mail.house.gov

Personal: Born 10/05/1971 in Philadelphia, Pa.

Education: B.A., University of Pennsylvania, 1993. J.D., Catholic University of America, 1998.

Professional: 1993–1994, staff asst., Rep. Robert Borski, D-Pa. 1994–1998, senior legislative asst., Rep. Robert Borski, D-Pa. 1998–1999, law clerk, Arnold and Porter. 1999–2006, counsel, Subc. on Water Resources and the Environment, House Cmte. on Transportation and Infrastructure. 2007–2011, staff director, senior counsel, Subc. on Water Resources and the Environment, House Cmte. on Transportation and Infrastructure. 2011–present, counsel, Subc. on Water Resources and the Environment, House Cmte. on Transportation and Infrastructure.

Expertise: Clean Water Act, Superfund-related issues, Corps of Engineers.

Ryan Seiger will continue to spend 2011, as he has in past years, pushing for a strong federal commitment to wastewater infrastructure and working for passage of a Water Resources Development Act that includes funds for U.S Army Corps of Engineers projects and studies.

Seiger has been with the House Transportation and Infrastructure Committee's Subcommittee on Water Resources and the Environment since 1999. He moved back into the minority in 2011 when Rep. Nick J. Rahall II, D-W.Va., took the committee's Top Democrat post after the Republican takeover of the House and the defeat of former Chairman James Oberstar, D-Minn.

Aside from wastewater infrastructure spending and a new WRDA, Seiger will keep working on issues related to water quality in the United States, which he said may include defending against Republican attempts to roll back quality protections.

Seiger hopes that the subcommittee can work on a bipartisan basis to reauthorize and increase funding levels for the Clean Water State Revolving Fund, the main source of federal spending on wastewater infrastructure.

Pressing for another WDRA bill, which includes authorizations of flood control, navigation, and environmental restoration projects, also will take up Seiger's time in 2011. New Committee Chairman John L. Mica, R-Fla., has said it is one of the panel's top priorities for the year.

In the 111th Congress, Seiger worked on several bills that were signed into law, including separate measures to clarify federal responsibility for storm water pollution, to extend and modify the ability of the Corps of Engineers to use funds from public entities for permit review, and to extend the date on which the Administrator of the Environmental Protection Agency can require permits for incidental discharges from certain commercial vessels.

HOUSE TRANSPORTATION AND INFRASTRUCTURE

Amy B. (Steinmann) Smith

Policy Director

2165 Rayburn House Office Bldg.

Phone: (202) 225-9446

Amy.Smith3@mail.house.gov

Personal: Born in Homestead, Fla.

Education: B.A., Florida International University, 1995.

Professional: 1996, schools coordinator, The Leadership Institute. 1996–2000, legislative asst., Rep. Dan Miller, R-Fla. 2001, legislative director, Rep. Dan Miller, R-Fla. 2001–2003, appropriations analyst, Rep. Tom DeLay, R-Texas. 2003–2004, chief floor asst., Majority Whip Roy Blunt, R-Mo. 2004–2007, director of floor operations, Majority Whip Roy Blunt, R-Mo. 2007–present, minority policy director, House Cmte. on Transportation and Infrastructure.

Expertise: Appropriations, floor operations.

Amy Smith, policy director for new House Transportation and Infrastructure Committee Chairman John L. Mica, R-Fla., finds herself in the majority in 2011 with a busy workload on a number of major legislative undertakings.

In the majority for the first time in her Transportation Committee tenure, Smith said she will work on moving bills through the legislative process to enactment instead of reacting and attempting to stop what she called "bad policy" pushed when the Democrats controlled Congress.

Only weeks into 2011, Smith said the workload was already noticeably busier. The staff quickly wrote a four-year Federal Aviation Administration reauthorization bill that was approved by the committee in February. The panel also set up a series of hearings around the country and in Washington, D.C., on various aspects of a major surface transportation policy rewrite.

A unique part of the job of policy director, Smith said, is that she has her hand in all sorts of legislation that can span a wide range of issues. In addition to the FAA and surface transportation bills, the committee also faces a water resources policy bill, a Coast Guard reauthorization, and possibly a measure consolidating federal buildings.

Smith will keep busy with all those issues, and many more covered by the committee's purview. Mica has said all committee bills will change policy to enable the government and states to "do more with less."

Smith said she was proud to have helped stop a number of Democratic measures in the 111th Congress, including the America's Commitment to Clean Water Act. That bill was authored by former Chairman James Oberstar, D-Minn., one of many Democrats defeated in the 2010 election.

Smith owns a thoroughbred, adopted from the Communications Alliance to Network Thoroughbred Ex-Racers (CANTER), that won a state championship in Maryland in 2010.

HOUSE TRANSPORTATION AND INFRASTRUCTURE

Jim Tymon

Staff Director
Subcommittee on Highways and Transit
B-376 Rayburn House Office Bldg.
Phone: (202) 225-6715
jim.tymon@mail.house.gov

Personal: Born 07/09/1973 in Teaneck, N.J.

Education: B.A., economics and political science, University of Delaware, 1995. M.A., public policy, University of Delaware, 1997.

Professional: 1997–1999, program analyst, Food and Nutrition Service, U.S. Dept. of Agriculture. 1999–2002, program examiner, Office of Management and Budget. 2002–2007, professional staff member, Subc. on Highways and Transit, House Cmte. on Transportation and Infrastructure. 2007–present, staff director, Subc. on Highways and Transit, House Cmte. on Transportation and Infrastructure.

Expertise: Highway and transit issues, highway finance.

Jim Tymon will spend the bulk of 2011 working closely on a number of surface transportation issues contained in a major rewrite of highway, transit, and rail policy being pushed by House Transportation and Infrastructure Committee Chairman John L. Mica, R-Fla.

Tymon, as Republican staff director for the Highways and Transit Subcommittee, said the measure will refocus, consolidate, and eliminate federal programs in a fiscally responsible manner.

One issue in particular will keep Tymon busy—working to streamline the delivery of transportation infrastructure projects, a main goal of Mica's. Mica has touted his "437-day plan," referring to the contract length for the replacement of the Interstate 35-West bridge in Minneapolis, Minn., which was completed in September 2008, just over a year after the deadly collapse.

Tymon will work closely on ways to build highway projects faster, including better agency coordination in permitting procedures.

Tymon will also work on a number of other highway and transit issues that will be included in the reauthorization, including Department of Transportation program consolidation, funding allocations, and transit construction guidelines.

In early March, President Obama signed into law a bill extending surface transportation programs through September 2011, and Tymon said he hopes it will be the last short-term extension of a law enacted in 2005.

Tymon said he expects to have a good working relationship with the Senate, and that he hopes the committee can continue its bipartisan tradition despite the number of contentious issues.

While almost all surface transportation issues will get folded into the reauthorization, Tymon will work on a separate reauthorization of pipeline safety programs, which expired in September 2010.

HOUSE TRANSPORTATION AND INFRASTRUCTURE

Joseph A. Wender

Counsel

Subcommittee on Economic Development, Public Buildings, and Emergency Management

592 Ford House Office Bldg.

Phone: (202) 225-9961

Fax: (202) 226-1270

Joseph.Wender@mail.house.gov

Personal: Born 10/28/1981 in Chicago, Ill.

Education: B.A., Wesleyan University, 2003. J.D., Harvard Law School, 2008.

Professional: 2008–2009, counsel/dir. of legal affairs, Grassroots Campaigns, Inc. 2008, student attorney, Criminal Justice Institute, Harvard University. 2009–present, counsel, House Cmte. on Transportation and Infrastructure.

Expertise: Transportation program spending, American Recovery and Reinvestment Act oversight.

With Democrats falling into the minority in the 112th Congress and Rep. Nick J. Rahall II, D-W.Va., taking over the committee's Top Democrat job, Joseph Wender will now serve as Counsel for the Subcommittee on Economic Development, Public Buildings, and Emergency Management.

Wender came to the House Transportation and Infrastructure Committee in February 2009, under former Chairman James Oberstar, D-Minn. Less than a year out of Harvard Law School, Wender initially served as Counsel for the committee's Oversight and Investigations staff—essentially being "all things Recovery Act" for the committee, as he managed the oversight of the recently-enacted American Recovery and Reinvestment Act. The law included $64.1 billion under the committee's jurisdiction, he said.

Oberstar was fierce in his oversight of the stimulus money—starting with monthly hearings and reports on DOT's progress and results, a large task for Wender to coordinate.

Wender scheduled the hearings, arranged for witnesses, and wrote reports Oberstar often cited, and compiled hundreds of data-heavy submissions from state, local, and federal agencies on their use of federal funds for highways, transit, airports, ports, rail, and wastewater infrastructure.

More than two years after enactment, as stimulus funds are winding down, Wender now writes quarterly oversight reports.

With the Recovery Act no longer occupying all of his time and his change in subcommittees, Wender will spend the 112th Congress working on Federal Emergency Management Administration, economic development, and public buildings issues that fall under the subcommittee's purview.

New Committee Chairman John L. Mica, R-Fla., has pushed to consolidate federal buildings and to remove FEMA from the Department of Homeland Security and make it an independent agency, both issues that will keep Wender busy.

In 2010, Wender also worked on the Jobs for Main Street Act that included another round of stimulus-style funds for transportation programs. The transportation spending in that bill never made it through the Senate, but Wender was kept busy tracking thousands of stimulus projects.

When he is not handling the immense amount of spending data his job entails, Wender makes sure to get some fresh air whenever possible. "I try to spend as much time outside as I can," he said.

HOUSE TRANSPORTATION AND INFRASTRUCTURE

James H. Zoia

Staff Director
Rep. Nick Rahall, D-W. Va.
2163 Rayburn House Office Bldg.
Phone: (202) 225-4472
jim.zoia@mail.house.gov

Personal: Born 07/25/1956 in Cleveland, Ohio.

Education: B.A., Ohio University, 1978.

Professional: 1981–1985, legislative asst./legislative dir., Rep. Nick Rahall, D-W.Va. 1985–1993, staff dir., Subc. on Mining and Natural Resources, Cmte. on Interior and Insular Affairs. 1993–1994, chief counsel, Subc. on Surface Transportation, Cmte. on Public Works and Transportation. 1995–2001, chief counsel, Rep. Nick Rahall, D-W.Va. 2001–2006, staff dir., House Cmte. on Resources. 2007–2011, chief of staff, House Cmte. on Resources. 2011–present, staff dir., House Cmte. on Transportation and Infrastructure.

Expertise: Highway issues, water resources, Clean Water Act.

Jim Zoia has been working for Rep. Nick J. Rahall II, D-W.Va., for 30 years, most recently moving to the job of Democratic staff director for the House Transportation and Infrastructure.

The committee faces a number of major legislative undertakings in 2011, including a surface transportation policy rewrite, a new Water Resources Development Act, and a Federal Aviation Administration reauthorization.

Zoia, like other Democratic staffers, pointed out that being in the minority forces staff to be reactive, no longer able to schedule hearings or mark up bills. While Zoia said he would work to ensure that Democratic principles are maintained in the newly Republican-controlled House, he also said "I'm trying to be a partner with the majority."

The committee's largest and most challenging undertaking is the surface transportation reauthorization no new task for Zoia. He worked the 1982, 1987, 1991, and 1998 bills.

This time around, Zoia said the committee faces a unique set of challenges. With no new funding coming from a Republican House, Committee Chairman John L. Mica, R-Fla., is focused on "innovative" financing mechanisms such as the Transportation Infrastructure Finance and Innovation Act (TIFIA) program.

But Zoia warned that "innovative" does not always work to fund projects in rural America. Projects must cost at least $50 million to qualify for TIFIA support, which then pays a maximum of 33 percent of the project's cost.

In the 111th Congress, Zoia worked on the Omnibus Public Land Management Act, which was signed into law in 2009.

Committee on Veterans' Affairs

335 Cannon House Office Bldg.

Washington, DC 20515

Phone: (202) 225-9756

Fax: (202) 225-2629

http://veterans.house.gov

Ratio: 13/11

MAJORITY MEMBERS

Jeff Miller, FL-1st, Chairman

Gus M. Bilirakis, FL-9th, Vice Chairman
Cliff Stearns, FL-6th
Doug Lamborn, CO-5th
David P. Roe, TN-1st
Dan Benishek, MI-1st
Ann Marie Buerkle, AK-25th
Jeff Denham, CA-19th
Bill Flores, TX-17th
Tim Huelskamp, KS-1st
Bill Johnson, OH-6th
Jon Runyan, NJ-3rd
Marlin A. Stutzman, IN-3rd

MINORITY MEMBERS

Bob Filner, CA-51st, Ranking Member

Corrine Brown, FL-3rd
Silvestre Reyes, TX-16th
Michael Michaud, ME-2nd
Linda T. Sanchez, CA-39th
Bruce L. Braley, IA-1st
Jerry McNerney, CA-11th
Joe Donnelly, IN-2nd
Timothy J. Walz, MN-1st
John Barrow, GA-12th
Russ Carnahan, MO-3rd

HOUSE VETERANS' AFFAIRS

JURISDICTION

(1) Veterans' measures generally.
(2) Cemeteries of the United States in which veterans of any war or conflict are or may be buried, whether in the United States or abroad (except cemeteries administered by the secretary of the interior).
(3) Compensation, vocational rehabilitation, and education of veterans.
(4) Life insurance issued by the government on account of service in the armed forces.
(5) Pensions of all the wars of the United States, general and special.
(6) Readjustment of servicemen to civil life.
(7) Soldiers' and sailors' civil relief.
(8) Veterans' hospitals, medical care, and treatment of veterans.

HOUSE VETERANS' AFFAIRS

In a year when most federal agencies came to Congress bracing for a decrease in their budget requests, Department of Veterans Affairs Secretary Eric Shinseki sought $132.2 billion, about a 4 percent increase for fiscal 2012 over the previous year. With the wars in Afghanistan and Iraq creating a new generation of military veterans with war experience, Shinseki deemed the boost necessary to ensure veterans' needs were met.

But congressional observers agreed approval of Shinseki's budget request would not come easy. The Republican takeover of the House after the 2010 midterm elections signaled tight federal budgets. That wasn't the only change: A new chairman also took the helm at the Committee on Veterans' Affairs when new Speaker John Boehner (R-Ohio) named fiscal conservative Rep. Jeff Miller, R-Fla., to the coveted post.

Miller is a longtime supporter of veterans' issues, having served with the panel for several congressional sessions. Since taking the helm, Miller promised to return to strict oversight of the VA, working on backlog issues and security issues within the agency.

When Shinseki appeared before the panel in February 2011 to present his budget, Miller said it seemed like a "measured request" compared to past years, but noted that he found a few flaws.

"I have to say, when I look at this budget and I see that it proposes a funding level for the Office of the Secretary that is 41 percent higher than 2009 levels, 50 percent higher for the Office of Congressional and Legislative Affairs, 96 percent higher for the Office of Policy and Planning and 140 percent higher for the Office of Public and Intergovernmental Affairs," Miller said. "It raises all kinds of red flags."

Miller promised to work across the aisle, however. "I sincerely hope every member of this Committee can work together to find common ground on the difficult choices ahead," he said.

Miller's colleague on the left is Rep. Bob Filner, D-Calif., who served as committee chairman when Democrats controlled the House in the 111th Congress. When Shinseki appeared before the panel, Filner noted that he respects the need to keep spending levels under control, it remains important that veterans receive the benefits they are owed.

"I will continue to study the VA's budget to ensure that these requirements are met and will remain steadfast in my opposition to any reckless, ungrounded, and unjustified cuts that might be proposed for veterans programs," Filner said.

HOUSE VETERANS' AFFAIRS

Mike Brinck

Staff Director

Subcommittee on Economic Opportunity

335 Cannon House Office Bldg.

Phone: (202) 226-3668

Fax: (202) 226-4536

mike.brinck@mail.house.gov

Personal: Born in Fort Madison, Iowa.

Professional: 1992–1995, national legislative director, AMVETS. 1995–1998, staff director, Subc. on Benefits, House Cmte. on Veterans' Affairs. 1998–2005, private defense contractor. 2005–present, staff director, Subc. on Economic Opportunity, House Cmte. on Veterans' Affairs.

Expertise: Employment, small business.

As Republican staff director for the House Veterans' Affairs Subcommittee on Economic Opportunity, Mike Brinck works to ensure veterans have successful careers after they've left military service. He can rely on personal experience—Brinck served as career naval officer prior to coming to Capitol Hill.

In the 112th Congress, Brinck assists Chairman Jeff Miller, R-Fla., and Subcommittee Chairman Marlin Stulzman, R-Ind., as they seek to pass legislation designed to help veterans find stable work. In March 2011, for example, the committee held a hearing analyzing the Veterans Employment and Training Service budget request.

In the 111th Congress, Brinck spent much of his time working to implement the new G.I. bill, the most comprehensive educational benefits package for veterans passed since the original measure after World War II. The subcommittee also looked at job training programs for veterans.

Brinck served during the Vietnam War, earning his Navy wings in 1969. He was given several assignments in Vietnam, including to a helicopter attack squadron and carrier deployments to the Gulf of Tonkin, according to his official biography from the 2009 National Veteran Small Business Conference and Expo, where he spoke. Brinck also served three deployments to support Operation Deep Freeze in Antarctica and was based at the Naval War College and Pentagon, among other locales.

He retired in 1988 with the rank of Commander. Along the way, he earned 16 air medals, the Vietnamese Cross of Gallantry, two Navy commendation medals and numerous other honors.

HOUSE VETERANS' AFFAIRS

William Collins

Staff Director, Subcommittee on Disability Assistance and Memorial Affairs

335 Cannon House Office Bldg.

Phone: (202) 225-3527

william.collins@mail.house.gov

Education: B.A. Political Science/International Studies, La Salle University, 1989. J.D. Law, Widener University School of Law, 1994.

Professional: 2009–2011, advisor to the Speaker, U.S. House of Representatives. 2011–present, staff director, House Cmte. on Veterans Affairs Subcmte. on Disability Assistance and Memorial Affairs. 2011, military fellow, U.S. House of Representatives.

Expertise: Veterans' issues, law.

William Collins comes to the House Committee on Veterans' Affairs after an impressive legal career as a member of the Marine Corps, where he served as a judge advocate, handled command investigations in Iraq and even taught at the Naval Academy, among a range of other duties. These days, Collins works with Committee Chairman Jeff Miller, R-Fla. and Subcommittee Chairman Jon Runyan, R-N.J. to find ways to help injured veterans and honor those who have served.

Although Collins is new to the subcommittee, he isn't entirely a fresh face in the congressional hallways. During the 111th Congress, Collins served as an advisor to then-Speaker Nancy Pelosi, D-Calif., as part of the chamber's Wounded Warrior project. Collins, who served two tours of duty in Iraq, was medically evacuated for kidney problems exacerbated by his service. While in Iraq, Collins advised commanders on the application of military law to combat situations and worked to re-establish the Iraqi court system, according to a 2009 article in the Washington Post.

He told the *Post* that he signed onto the warrior project because he "didn't just want to be a symbol; I wanted to have impact and substance in the work I do."

Collins appeared to earn the respect of Pelosi during his two years working in her office. After the Fort Hood shootings, he drafted material for the memorial service and accompanied Pelosi on the trip, the Post reported. Collins also handled policy development and outreach, and helped coordinate the page and internship programs in Pelosi's office. He remained with Pelosi in the early weeks of the 112th session before moving to the subcommittee.

During his time in the Marines, Collins earned several honors, including the Navy-Marine Corps Commendation Medal, the National Defense Service Medal and Global War on Terrorism Service Medal, among other awards. On his profile on the LinkedIn Web site, Collins also boasts that he achieved the rank of Eagle Scout, the highest level one can reach in the Boy Scouts.

Collins remains true to his scouting roots, as he enjoys rowing, running, hiking and camping. He's finished the Marine Corps Marathon seven times, most recently in 2006.

HOUSE VETERANS' AFFAIRS

Eric Hannel

Staff Director, Subcommittee on Oversight and Investigations

335 Cannon House Office Bldg.

Phone: (202) 225-3527

eric.hannel@mail.house.gov

Education: M.A., philosophy, California State University. B.S., history, Excelsior College.

Professional: 2007–2010, military caseworker, Rep. Jeff Miller, R-Fla. 2011–present, staff director, House Cmte. on Veterans Affairs, subcmte. on oversight and investigations.

Expertise: Veterans' issues.

A combat veteran and retired Marine, Eric Hannel first came to Congress to serve as a military caseworker for Rep. Jeff Miller, R-Fla. When Miller took over as chairman of the House Committee on Veterans' Affairs at the start of the 112th Congress, Hannel followed him to the panel and became staff director of the Subcommittee on Oversight and Investigations, where he helps Rep. Bill Johnson, R-Ohio, oversee the Department of Veterans Affairs and other government agencies who work with retired service members.

The subcommittee had yet to hold a hearing in the early months of the 112th session—but that was due in part to the fact that the full committee held a handful of oversight meetings. In February, for example, the committee looked at possible mortgage-related violations by J.P. Morgan Chase Bank of the Service members Civil Relief Act. Committee members also worked with the Senate Committee on Veterans' Affairs to push President Barack Obama to implement a program that helps people who give up their careers to serve as full-time caregivers to family members who are veterans of the wars in Iraq and Afghanistan.

Although Hannel is new to committee work, he has a history of helping veterans alongside Miller. While serving as Miller's military liaison, Hannel often accompanied the congressman when he honored military members and veterans. In August 2008, for example, Hannel was there when Miller presented a Purple Heart and Bronze Star to a World War II veteran in Florida. Although J.W. Hawkins received wounds in battle and even was captured and held as a prisoner of war for a time, he didn't receive the honors until a fellow soldier wrote to Miller asking him to help get the awards, according to an article in Santa Rosa's *Press Gazette*.

According to a short biography on Miller's personal Web site, Hannel has also worked with the Department of Homeland Security, and created certification courses available at the Emergency Management Institute. He also ran a successful small business and worked as a college instructor, according to the biography.

HOUSE VETERANS' AFFAIRS

Martin Herbert

Democratic Staff Director, Oversight and Investigations

333 Cannon House Office Bldg.

Phone: (202) 225-9756

martin.herbert@mail.house.gov

Education: B.A., economics, University of Louisville. M.A., human resource development, Webster University.

Professional: 1985–2005, Lt. Col. (Ret.), United States Army. 2005–2009, homeland defense analyst, Booz Allen Hamilton. 2009–present, staff director, Subc. on Oversight and Investigations, House Cmte. on Veterans' Affairs.

Expertise: Veterans' Issues.

Army Lt. Col. (Ret.) Martin Herbert joined the House Committee on Veterans' Affairs in 2009, bringing with him 20 years of military experience. The two-time recipient of a Bronze Star medal, Herbert can rely on his impressive history when taking on veterans' issues—he commanded soldiers in combat during Operation Desert Storm in 1991, Operation Enduring Freedom in 2002, and Operation Iraqi Freedom in 2003 and 2004.

After his retirement from the Army in 2005, Herbert was hired as a consultant for the Washington, D.C. firm Booz Allen Hamilton. When he came to Capitol Hill, Herbert was charged with directing oversight efforts for programs at the Department of Veterans Affairs and other veterans-related federal agencies.

"I am proud to work with this talented and dedicated individual," Malcom Shorter, the committee's staff director, said in a statement released shortly after Herbert was hired. "I am confident that the Members of the House Veterans' Affairs Committee will greatly benefit from his counsel and experience."

Herbert also is a member of the Japanese American Veterans Association, serving as vice president. The organization works to provide support to veterans in need, along with recognizing and honoring the memory of Japanese American veterans.

According to his biography from the veterans group, Herbert escorted and briefed President George H. W. Bush during his historic visit to Vietnam. Herbert also was selected and promoted to Lieutenant Colonel one year ahead of his peers.

"Marty Herbert's record of military service and experience allows him to fully understand the wide-range of challenges faced by veterans," said Committee Ranking member Bob Filner, D-Calif., who hired Herbert when he served as chairman of the panel.

HOUSE VETERANS' AFFAIRS

Juan Lara

Staff Director

Subcommittee on Economic Opportunity

333 Cannon House Office Bldg.

Phone: (202) 225-9756

juan.lara@mail.house.gov

Personal: Born 03/27/1968 in McAllen, Texas.

Education: B.A., Texas A&M University, 1993. J.D., Capital University (Ohio) Law School, 2000.

Professional: 2004–2007, asst. director, legislative affairs, American Legion. 2007–present, staff director/counsel, Subc. on Economic Opportunity, House Cmte. on Veterans' Affairs.

Expertise: Procurement, entrepreneurship, small business development.

Juan Lara is fast becoming a seasoned veteran on the House Committee on Veterans' Affairs, having served as the Democratic Staff Director for the Subcommittee on Economic Opportunity since 2007. Lara said he likes the "challenges" and "fast pace on Capitol Hill, and working with talented individuals in the committee."

Lara expects to stay busy in the 112th Congress, listing a wide range of issues he plans to work on during the session. He is likely to have a hand in everything from veterans' employment and education to home loans and business verification to the federal procurement process and the Paralympic Games.

He certainly had a full work schedule in the 111th Congress. Lara assisted on a number of pieces of legislation, including a bill for a pilot college work study program for veterans; a measure for a pilot program to help veterans get jobs in energy-related fields; legislation that would establish an annual award for businesses who employ veterans; a bill that extends the period of eligibility for training and rehabilitation through the Department of Veterans Affairs for veterans with service-connected disabilities; and a measure that is designed to help service members avoid losing their homes to foreclosure.

Lara also helped lead the committee's effort to institute major changes to historic G.I. bill, which were enacted in 2008. Lara's work on the issue even led to his boss giving him the nickname "Mr. G.I. Bill."

But it's not all veterans' affairs issues for Lara: He once told the Capitol Hill newspaper *Roll Call* that he enjoys reading science fiction novels.

HOUSE VETERANS' AFFAIRS

Kimberly Ross

Staff Director and Counsel

Subcommittee on Disability Assistance and Memorial Affairs

335 Cannon House Office Bldg.

Phone: (202) 225-9756

Fax: (202) 225-2629

kimberly.ross@mail.house.gov

Education: B.A., College of Notre Dame of Maryland. J.D., University of Maryland School of Law.

Professional: 1996–1998, assistant staff counsel, Maryland Public Service Commission. 1998–1999, regulatory attorney, Sprint Communications. 2000–2002, senior legislative assistant, Office of Sen. Barbara Mikulski, D-Md. 2002–2007, legislative director and counsel, Office of Rep. Elijah Cummings, D-Md. 2007–present, staff director, Subc. on Disability Assistance and Memorial Affairs, House Cmte. on Veterans' Affairs.

Expertise: Legal issues.

As staff director for the Subcommittee on Disability Assistance and Memorial Affairs, Kimberly Ross serves veterans who perhaps need the most support.

She is the congressional voice for Blue Water veterans, Vietnam War personnel who are now suffering from disabilities due to Agent Orange exposure. Ross also works to help the survivors of deceased veterans, who often struggle to receive the benefits owed to them.

Ross said her job is rewarding when she sees issues she is working on taking effect, pointing to the implementation of the Virtual Lifetime Electronic Record Initiative. The project is designed to help ease the transition of veterans by improving the flow of medical records between the Department of Defense and Department of Veterans Affairs.

"This is really going to make a significant difference once fully implemented," she said. "I like being a part of these undertakings."

During the 111th Congress, Ross worked on many veterans issues that wound up in the Veterans' Benefits Act, comprehensive legislation that expanded benefits for veterans. Ross also helped convince the VA to ease burdens placed on veterans suffering from post traumatic stress disorder; worked to reform and modernize the VA's disability claims processing system; worked to expand Agent Orange exposure presumptions to include Parkinson's disease; and helped expand burial benefits to allow parents of veterans to be buried with their fallen son or daughter when there are no other eligible survivors.

In 2011, Ross said she expects to continue work to modernize and fully automate the VA's disability compensation claims processing system, along with other issues. "After 11 years, I still love this place—mostly due to being able to work on efforts that meaningfully impact the lives of every day Americans," she said.

HOUSE VETERANS' AFFAIRS

Malcom Shorter

Staff Director

335 Cannon House Office Bldg.

Phone: (202) 225-9756

Fax: (202) 225-2629

Personal: Born 05/17/1959 in Dawson, Ga.

Education: B.S., economics, Rutgers University, 1981. M.S., administration, Central Michigan University, 1995.

Professional: 1981–2003, U.S. Army. 2003–2004, assistant director, Programming and Budget, Office of Counter-Narcotics, Dept. of Homeland Security. 2005–2006, director, Office of Budget, Finance, and Administration, Office of the Special Trustee for American Indians, Dept. of the Interior. 2007–present, staff director, House Cmte. on Veterans' Affairs.

Expertise: Veterans' issues.

As the longtime Democratic staff director of the House Committee on Veterans' Affairs, Malcom Shorter has vast experience helping servicemen and veterans through his work on Capitol Hill. But Shorter isn't just any Hill aide; he's also a veteran himself.

Shorter served in the Army for more than 20 years, retiring as a lieutenant colonel in 2003. His service earned him the respect of military colleagues and Members of Congress alike. For a time, he worked as deputy chief of the Army's Congressional liaison office, escorting Members on fact-finding missions abroad. When Shorter retired, former Rep. Marty Meehan, D-Mass., paid tribute on the House floor saying that Shorter's "dedication, candor and professionalism while serving in that capacity earned him the reputation as the best source on Capitol Hill to receive issues pertaining to the Army."

Shorter returned to the Hill in 2007 and has overseen legislation designed to improve the lives of veterans ever since. Early on in his tenure, Shorter focused on reforming the G.I. Bill, a goal that was accomplished when G.I. legislation was enacted in 2008.

In the 112th Congress, Shorter is likely to continue to fight for measures to help veterans, although this time around he'll operate under extraordinary budget constraints. When Department of Veterans Affairs Secretary Eric Shinseki appeared before the panel to outline his agency's $132.2 billion budget request, Shorter's boss, ranking member Bob Filner, D-Calif., expressed concern.

But Filner added that "if Secretary Shinseki tells me that this is what he needs to continue transforming the VA then I will offer my support and will fight to get the VA the funding levels it needs."

HOUSE VETERANS' AFFAIRS

Helen Tolar

335 Cannon House Office Bldg

Phone: (202) 224-3527

helen.tolar@mail.house.gov

Professional: 2001–2004, legislative assistant, Rep. Jeff Miller, R-Fla. 2004–2005, legislative director, Rep. Jeff Miller, R-Fla. 2005–2007, professional staff member, Senate Cmte. on Veterans' Affairs. 2011–present, staff director and chief counsel, House Cmte. Veterans' Affairs.

Expertise: Veterans' issues.

As majority staff director for the House Committee on Veterans' Affairs, Helen Tolar is charged with helping chairman Jeff Miller, R-Fla., pursue legislation to help the nation's retired service members. It's a job that she seems well suited for, having previously served as a staffer and counsel on the Senate Committee on Veterans' Affairs and prior to that, in Miller's personal office.

As staff director, Tolar directs staff on the work of the general committee, but she also must keep tabs on the four subcommittees that are charged with oversight of specific areas effecting veterans. She also manages the panel's staff and works closely with Miller to push his agenda.

Early on in the 112th Congress, Miller appeared to focus on balancing the needs of veterans under a tough economic climate, including pressure to severely cut government spending. While the Department of Veterans' Affairs was among the few agencies to get a small budget increase in President Barack Obama's fiscal 2012 budget request, Miller told Secretary Eric Shinseki at a February 2011 that several areas of his budget had increases that were simply too high.

"I have to say, when I look at this budget and I see that it proposes a funding level for the Office of the Secretary that is 41 percent higher than 2009 levels; 50 percent higher for the Office of Congressional and Legislative Affairs; 96 percent higher for the Office of Policy and Planning; and 140 percent higher for the Office of Public and Intergovernmental Affairs…it raises all kinds of red flags," he said.

Tolar is likely to assist Miller on several specific veterans' issues, including finding ways to improve the disabilities claims system and working to improve the lives of full-time caregivers to veterans who served in Iraq and Afghanistan. Both were areas Miller asked Shinseki about during his initial testimony before the panel.

Not every issue tackled by the panel in the 112th Congress was controversial. Miller also took time to honor the passing of Frank Buckles, the last surviving veteran of World War I. Buckles died in February 2011.

HOUSE VETERANS' AFFAIRS

Jonathan A. Towers

Deputy Staff Director

335 Cannon House Office Bldg.

Phone: (202) 225-3527

jon_towers@vetaff.senate.gov

Personal: Born 09/04/1974 in Washington, D.C.

Education: B.A., government, College of William and Mary, 1996.

Professional: 1997, director, Washington International Studies Council. 1997–1998, legislative corresp., Senate Cmte. on Veterans' Affairs. 1998–1999, legislative asst., Senate Cmte. on Veterans' Affairs. 1999–2010, professional staff member, Senate Cmte. on Veterans' Affairs. 2011–present, deputy staff director, House Cmte. On Veterans' Affairs.

Expertise: Health care, VA appropriations, budget.

After more than a dozen years working on veterans' issues for the Senate, Jonathan Towers headed to the House Committee on Veterans' Affairs to become deputy staff director at the start of the 112th Congress. Now Towers assists Chairman Jeff Miller, R-Fla. in setting the agenda for the panel.

Towers, who worked on a number of areas affecting veterans while in the Senate, will help his new boss with extensive oversight of the Department of Veterans Affairs. Early in the 112th session, this appeared to be a largely bipartisan effort, as Miller pledged to work closely with Ranking Member Bob Filner, D-Calif.

The unique needs facing Iraq and Afghanistan veterans are among Towers's expertise, especially when it comes to mental health needs. In 2010, he spoke at a symposium held during the annual convention of the National Alliance on Mental Illness, explaining that the VA and Department of Defense don't have adequate resources to properly care for the number of returning veterans. "The VA and DoD can't do it alone. We need to rely on community providers," Towers said, adding it's important that the family members of veterans also play a role.

Towers mainly focused on issues related to veterans' health care during his time in the Senate, including working on the Veterans Benefits, Healthcare and Information Technology Act of 2006, a comprehensive measure providing veterans with $3.2 billion in benefits. Former President George W. Bush signed the measure in 2006.

Towers also temporarily found himself acting as a spokesman for the committee in 2005, when a controversy arose over whether the ashes of veteran Russell Wayne Wagner—who had been convicted of murder—should be allowed to remain in Arlington Cemetery. Towers was quoted in several publications explaining the committee would seriously look at the case; Wagner's ashes were ultimately removed.

HOUSE VETERANS' AFFAIRS

David Tucker

Deputy Staff Director and Chief Counsel
333 Cannon House Office Bldg.
Phone: (202) 225-9756
Fax: (202) 225-5486
david.tucker@mail.house.gov

Personal: Born 12/04/1964 in Pomona, Calif.

Education: B.A., University of Utah, 1988. J.D., Marshall Wythe School of Law, College of William and Mary, 1991.

Professional: 1992–1993, operations, scheduling, Clinton-Gore transition. 1993–2005, senior assoc. legislative director, Paralyzed Veterans of America. 2005–2007, counsel, Democratic staff, House Cmte. on Veterans' Affairs. 2007, staff director, Subc. on Health, House Cmte. on Veterans' Affairs. 2007–present, chief counsel/deputy staff director, House Cmte. on Veterans' Affairs.

Expertise: Veterans issues, health care.

As Deputy Staff Director and Chief Counsel for the Democrats on the House Committee on Veterans Affairs, David Tucker helps set the panel's legislative agenda. Tucker certainly has the pedigree for the job, having worked at the Paralyzed Veterans of America for a dozen years before coming to Capitol Hill.

Tucker has held many hats on the panel—counsel, subcommittee staff director, and the No. 2 staffer for the Democratic team. But even with all this experience, 2011 presented a new challenge: How to help veterans obtain their benefits and launch new careers in the face of a government shutdown.

Tucker told the news Web site Military.com that a shutdown would mean no benefit claims would be processed, and programs such as the new G.I. Bill and disability petitions would go ignored. Those are some of the programs Tucker worked on during the 111th Congress, when he focused much of his work on expanding access and improving the quality of veterans' health care and making improvements in the claims process.

Even if the federal government were to avoid a shutdown, the panel still faces the pressure of a tighter budget. Tucker's boss, Ranking Member Bob Filner, D-Calif., said in February 2011 the Department of Veterans Affairs' $132.2 billion budget request raised concerns, but said he would work to ensure that veterans receive their benefits.

Tucker's work on veterans' issues hasn't gone unnoticed, even on the other side of the aisle. When Members took up the Veterans Benefits Act of 2010, former Rep. Steve Buyer, R-Ind., thanked Tucker on the House floor.

"I have had a distinct pleasure, David, of working with you over the years, and I want to recognize your valuable contribution not only in this bill, but what you have done over the years," Buyer said. "I consider your talent valuable, but I consider your friendship even more."

HOUSE VETERANS' AFFAIRS

Cathleen Cecilia Wiblemo

Staff Director

Subcommittee on Health

333 Cannon House Office Bldg.

Phone: (202) 225-9756

cathy.wiblemo@mail.house.gov

Education: B.A., Black Hills State University, Spearfish, 1984. M.A., health administration, Chapman University, 1999.

Professional: 1984–1994, officer, Army Adjutant General Corps. 1999–2007, national appeals representative; assistant director, resource management; deputy director for health care, American Legion. 2007–present, staff director, Subc. on Health, House Cmte. on Veterans' Affairs.

Expertise: Health care.

Cathy Wiblemo comes to the House Committee on Veterans' Affairs staffers not only with legislative experience, but with impressive personal experience. For almost 10 years, Wiblemo served as a officer in the Army Adjutant General Corps.

In the 112th Congress, Wiblemo will work to find ways to maximize veterans' health care while also dealing with a tight budget. During the full committee's organizational hearing at the start of the session, Members included reviewing mental health programs, overseeing the VA's launch of a program to help veterans' families and caregivers, and introducing new ways to support female service members, who are the fastest growing segment of the veteran population on their list of priorities.

In the 111th Congress, Wiblemo helped lead the effort on several pieces of legislation that reached the House floor, including the End Veteran Homelessness Act of 2010. Introduced by Wiblemo's boss, Rep. Bob Filner, D-Calif., the measure authorizes several Department of Veterans Affairs programs for homeless vets, including increasing federal funding for grants to help such veterans and extending a program for low-income families. When the bill reached the House floor, Filner praised Wiblemo for her work on the effort, noting she "has worked so hard on this legislation for such a long time."

In another House floor speech, Filner also thanked her for her work on the "Women Veterans Health Care Improvement Act," which seeks to expand health care services for female vets, especially those serving or who served in Operation Enduring Freedom and Operation Iraqi Freedom.

"Cathy and her staff did excellent work in assisting with this legislation and shepherding it through the legislative process," Filner said.

Committee on Ways and Means

1102 Longworth House Office Bldg.
Washington, DC 20515
Phone: (202) 225-3625
Fax: (202) 225-2610
http://waysandmeans.house.gov

Ratio: 22/15

MAJORITY MEMBERS

Dave Camp, MI-4th, Chairman

Wally Herger, CA-2nd
Sam Johnson, TX-3rd
Kevin Brady, TX-8th
Paul Ryan, WI-1st
Devin Nunes, CA-21st
Pat Tiberi, OH-12th
Geoff Davis, KY-4th
Dave Reichert, WA-8th
Charles Boustany, LA-7th
Dean Heller, NV-2nd
Peter Roskam, IL-6th
Jim Gerlach, PA-6th
Vern Buchanan, FL-13th
Tom Price, GA-6th
Adrian Smith, NE-3rd
Aaron Schock, IL-18th
Lynn Jenkins, KS-2nd
Erik Paulsen, MN-3rd
Kenny Marchant, TX-24th
Rick Berg, ND-At Large
Diane Black, TN-6th

MINORITY MEMBERS

Sander M. Levin, MI-12th, Ranking Member

Charles B. Rangel, NY-15th, Ex Officio
Fortney Pete Stark, CA-13th
Jim McDermott, WA-7th
John Lewis, GA-5th
Richard E. Neal, MA-2nd
Xavier Becerra, CA-31st
Lloyd Doggett, TX-10th
Mike Thompson, CA-1st
John B. Larson, CT-1st
Earl Blumenauer, OR-3rd
Ron Kind, WI-3rd
Bill Pascrell, NJ-8th
Shelley Berkley, NV-1st
Joseph Crowley, NY-7th

HOUSE WAYS AND MEANS

JURISDICTION

(1) Customs, collection districts, and ports of entry and delivery.
(2) Reciprocal trade agreements.
(3) Revenue measures generally.
(4) Revenue measures relating to the insular possessions.
(5) Bonded debt of the United States, subject to the last sentence of clause 4(f).
(6) Deposit of public monies.
(7) Transportation of dutiable goods.
(8) Tax-exempt foundations and charitable trusts.
(9) National Social Security (except health care and facilities programs that are supported from general revenues as opposed to payroll deductions and except work incentive programs).

HOUSE WAYS AND MEANS

New Ways and Means Chairman Dave Camp, R-Mich., has an overflowing plate for the 112th Congress as GOP members push to change—if they can't repeal—the health overhaul act, push for tax reform and work on three pending free trade agreements.

In the first month and a half of the new Congress, the committee conducted eight full committee hearings on these issues. The diverse jurisdiction of the tax-writing committee means the panel's members usually figure into almost everything that comes to the floor of the House.

The House voted to repeal the Affordable Health Care Act of 2010, but the Senate is not expected to follow suit. So, Ways and Means Committee members will try to pick away at the law. They started first with moving a repeal of the 1099 tax reporting provision that had required landlords and businesses to file a Form 1099 with the IRS when they purchase goods totaling $600 or more during a calendar year.

On taxes, Camp made it clear soon after the midterm election that he plans to be bold.

"Yes, I aim to launch and fight the tax reform battle once again," Camp said in a speech to the Tax Council. "The tax code should collect the revenue the government needs as efficiently as possible. It should not be a tool of industrial policy... Politics and politicians should not choose the industry of the day; that is the job of our private economy as driven by the spirit of the American people and a nimble free market. Here are my principles of reform: fairer, simpler and conducive to growth."

On trade, Camp has said he wants all three pending agreements considered by the middle of 2011.

"Under the Democrats' control, we did not hold a single hearing on our pending trade agreements since they were signed three and a half years ago—not Colombia, not Panama, and not South Korea," Camp said in a speech in February to the American Action Forum. "Well, as you might have guessed, I've got a different agenda, and it includes opening markets around the globe so that American businesses, farmers and ranchers can sell their products and grow their operations—and jobs—here at home."

Democrats know that they will mainly be in reactive mode with the Republicans in charge.

But that doesn't mean they plan to stop speaking out, especially when it comes to the health law. Democratic members have opposed GOP moves to walk back the law and have used the Republicans' repeal and replace strategy to highlight why Democrats' pushed for the measure in the first place.

HOUSE WAYS AND MEANS

Cybele Bjorklund

Democratic Staff Director
Subcommittee on Health
1135 Longworth House Office Bldg.
Phone: (202) 225-4021
cybele.bjorklund@mail.house.gov

Personal: Born 09/25/1967 in Nuremberg, West Germany.

Education: B.A., journalism, University of Oregon, 1989. M.A., Johns Hopkins University, 1994.

Professional: 1991–1993, public affairs specialist, St. Joseph's Care Group (South Bend, Ind.). 1994–1995, Medicare policy analyst, Health Care Financing Administration. 1995–1997, legislative assistant, Sen. Tom Daschle, D-S.Dak. 1997–2001, deputy staff director for health policy, Senate Cmte. on Health, Education, Labor, and Pensions/Sen. Edward M. Kennedy, D-Mass. 2001–present, Democratic staff director, Subc. on Health, House Cmte. on Ways and Means.

Expertise: Medicare policies, health issues.

Not much in 112th Congress can top Cybele Bjorklund's work on the landmark Affordable Care Act that was passed while she directed the Democratic staff of the Health Subcommittee in the 111th Congress.

"It was at once a blur and the longest two years of my life," said Bjorklund, who was so exhausted after that marathon effort, she took a sabbatical from June of 2010 through after the November elections.

She returned knowing she'd be in the minority as Democratic staff director for the health panel.

Going into a GOP-led Congress, Democrats, she said, would naturally be in a defensive mode. But that won't entirely be the case.

"Our members really view the Republican attack on the Affordable Care Act as an opportunity to re- or better educate the public about the benefits of the bill," she said. The Democrats "view every hearing and every floor fight as an opportunity to remind people about the good things that are in there."

Bjorklund said even if Democrats kept the majority this wouldn't be a big legislative year for her subcommittee. Either way the panel would focus on implementation of the overhaul law.

Of course the GOP oversight will look different than the Democrats'.

"Our oversight is making sure that it's being implemented according to congressional intent," Bjorklund said. "Republicans oversight will be much for 'gotchas.' They may want to use the flexibility in the legislation to try and undo various pieces and undermine congressional intent."

Bjorklund wasn't the only one in her family dedicated to passing the health law. Her husband, Randy Devalk, is leaving the office of Senate Majority Leader Harry Reid, D-Nev. after working in the Senate for 24 years. The two of them spent night and day on the health reform effort, she said.

"We outsourced our parenting to get this done," she said, hence the need to take the sabbatical.

HOUSE WAYS AND MEANS

Michelle Dimarob

Sr. Advisor of Public Affairs & Coalitions

1101 Longworth House Office Bldg.

Phone: (202) 202-226-5680

Fax: (202) 202-225-5680

michelle.dimarod@mail.house.gov

Personal: Born 1973 in Redwood City, Calif.

Education: BA, Cal State University, Fresno. MA, University of Oklahoma.

Professional: 1995–1997, scheduler, press aide, Rep. George Radanovich. 1997–1998, press secretary, Rep. Jo Ann Emerson. 1999–2000, press secretary, Committee on Small Business. 1999, District director, California Assemblyman Mike Briggs. 2000, communications director, Talent for Governor. 2001–2003, communications director, Rep. Jo Ann Emerson. 2003–2004, senior associate, Widmeyer Communications. 2004–2006, media manager, federal public policy, National Federation of Independent Business. 2006–2011, Sr. manager, federal public policy, National Federation of Independent Business. 2011–present, Sr. advisor of public affairs & coalitions, House Cmte. on Ways and Means.

Expertise: Communications, health, taxes, oversight.

When the new Ways and Means Committee Chairman, Rep. Dave Camp, R-Mich., wanted a communications person who could also reach out to community and advocacy groups, he turned to Michelle Dimarob—someone who had done just that in her role off Capitol Hill at the National Federation of Independent Business.

"Chairman Camp has been very vocal about wanting those people who are directly affected to have a seat at the table," said Dimarob, whose title sums up her responsibilities: senior advisor of public affairs and coalitions.

Organizations of all sizes are worried about the complexity of the tax code and its implications on job creation, Dimarob said. Consumers and employers also impacted by the new health care overhaul law need to be consulted, she said.

Had they bothered to ask small business owners about the 1099 law before including it in the health law, Dimarob said, the Democrats could have avoided the problems that are leading to the likely repeal of that provision.

It's that kind of input that Dimarob will seek out as well.

"We want to make sure we're having a discussion about tax reform that includes all the job creators—large and small," she said.

When it comes to working with the press, the committee's wide jurisdictions means the communication staff has divided up issue areas and Dimarob will be concentrating on health, taxes, and oversight.

She was busy from the moment she took the job as the repeal of the health law was the first thing out of the gate for the new Congress.

"We'll be looking at all the other taxes used to finance the overhaul," Dimarob said. "And we'll look at the implications those taxes have on access and affordability. We'll be examining the cuts made to Medicare, at affordability issues, along with the employer mandate."

Dimarob said she decided to move from the private sector back to Capitol Hill because "it's an exciting time to be able to bring the experiences I had working within the association community, particularly the small business community back up to the Hill. This is a committee dedicated to making sure they are part of the conversation."

Dimarob began her career on the Hill, working as a press secretary, scheduler, and even a district director for several Republican members of Congress.

When she's not working, Dimarob and her husband like to travel. Her husband is an election lawyer so the two got married between the Iowa Caucus and the New Hampshire primary in 2008.

HOUSE WAYS AND MEANS

Sage Eastman

Deputy Staff Director

1029 Longworth House Office Bldg.

Phone: (202) 225-3625

sage.eastman@mail.house.gov

Personal: Born 1975 in Springfield, Vt.

Education: studied political science, Kalamazoo College.

Professional: 1996–2001, director of communications, Michigan Republican Party. 2001–2002, director of communications, Michigan gubernatorial campaign of former Lt. Gov. Dick Posthumus. 2003, director of communications, Michigan attorney general's office. 2003–2009, director of communications, Rep. Dave Camp, R-Mich. 2009–2010, Republican senior advisor for media and public affairs, House Ways and Means Cmte. 2011–present, deputy staff director, House Ways and Means Cmte.

Expertise: Media relations.

Sage Eastman, long the political and communications voice for Ways and Means Chairman Dave Camp, R-Mich., has broadened his role in the 112th Congress as deputy staff director for the committee.

"I've been a hack, a flack and everything in between," says Eastman who sees the value in marrying policy and politics.

"I've always felt that you can't separate the two," said Eastman, who was Camp's personal press secretary before he moved over to work for the committee. "You have to understand the politics in order to sell it. Whether we're selling it to fellow Republicans, Independents, Democrats, or the American people, the better you understand the policy the better you're able to sell it."

Eastman is largely responsible for keeping the trains running on time in the committee and much of the administrative work but also works closely on policy matters with staff director Jon Traub, who was with the committee before Camp, R-Mich., became chairman.

"The chairman likes to hear varied input and we all have different backgrounds with the chairman," he said.

Eastman said the biggest difference from the 111th to the 112th is that the Republicans will be setting the agenda and that the committee will have much more authority.

"In the first two months we have held only one less hearing than the committee held all of last year," he said. "So there has been an effort to reestablish not only the committee but to reclaim its jurisdiction. We saw much of it eroded during the last Congress as various bills were written in then Speaker Pelosi's office rather than in the committee."

The focal point this year, Eastman said, will be on job creation.

Away from the Hill, when Eastman is not spending time with his wife and three young children, he likes to be on the ski slopes.

"My first job was teaching skiing," he said, "and I've always said I hope it's my last job."

HOUSE WAYS AND MEANS

Angela Paolini Ellard

Chief Trade Counsel

Subcommittee on Trade

1104 Longworth House Office Bldg.

Phone: (202) 225-6649

angela.ellard@mail.house.gov

Personal: Born 03/19/1961 in Minneapolis, Minn.

Education: B.A. (summa cum laude), Newcomb College, Tulane University, 1982. M.A., public policy, Tulane University, 1983. J.D. (cum laude), Tulane University, 1986.

Professional: 1986–1990, attorney, Akin, Gump, Strauss, Hauer & Feld. 1990–1995, attorney, Weil, Gotshal & Manges. 1995–1998, trade counsel, Subc. on Trade, House Cmte. on Ways and Means. 1998–2007, Republican staff dir./trade counsel, Subc. on Trade, House Cmte. on Ways and Means. 2007–2010, Republican chief trade counsel, Subc. on Trade, House Cmte. on Ways and Means. 2011–present, Chief Trade Counsel, Subc. on Trade, House Cmte. on Ways and Means.

Expertise: International trade policy.

As chief counsel and staff director to the Subcommittee on Trade, Angela Ellard hit the ground running when the 112th Congress began.

Her boss, Ways and means Committee Chairman Dave Camp (R-Mich.), said he wanted languishing trade agreements with Columbia, Panama, and South Korea passed in the first six months of the session.

"We're hoping that these will be bipartisan," said Ellard. Although the agreements were inked three and a half years ago, there wasn't a hearing on any of them in the last Congress. But a session was held in the opening weeks of 2011 under the new GOP-led House.

At the end of 2010, a supplemental auto agreement was attached to the South Korea pact, which brought Rep. Sander Levin, D-Mich., the outgoing Ways and Means head, on board along with the big three auto companies and the United Auto Workers.

"We're hoping to achieve the same thing on the other two," Ellard said. "Our members will also continue to focus on our trade relationship with China, on the ongoing negotiations with the Trans-Pacific Partnership countries and hopefully achieve a good deal by the end of the year."

Several trade preference programs were expiring in early 2011. Ellard's panel was seeking bipartisan agreements to extend them. The committee will also be working on a U.S. Customs Service authorization bill.

Ellard has spent more than 15 years on Capitol Hill, moving from a private law practice where she worked on trade litigation and policy.

"My undergraduate and graduate degree focused on foreign policy issues. In the legal world, especially in Washington, many of the key relationships between companies are trade issues," Ellard said. "We are really in the thick of trade policy here. It's such a significant issue that really has an impact on everyday Americans."

HOUSE WAYS AND MEANS

Dan Elling

Staff Director, Health Subcommittee
1139 Longworth House Office Bldg.
Phone: (202) 225-4021
dan.elling@mail.house.gov

Personal: Born in Minn.

Education: George Washington University. Gustavus Adolphus College, 1999.

Professional: 2002–2004, legislative assistant for health policy, Rep. Jim Ramstad, R-Minn. 2004–2005, legislative assistant for health policy, Rep. Nancy Johnson, R-Conn. 2006–2008, Republican health policy aide, House Cmte. on Ways and Means. 2008–present, Republican staff dir., Subc. on Health, House Cmte. on Ways and Means.

Expertise: Health care policy.

The goals of the Republicans on the Ways and Means Health Subcommittee have not changed now that they are in the majority for the 112th Congress, but the panel's director Dan Elling said he will now be responsible for carrying out legislative and oversight ideas his members come up with, not just reacting to the proposals of the Democrats.

"We'll still have the Democratic Senate, the Democratic White House and this massive new entitlement that is being implemented," Elling said, referring to the new health care overhaul law. And that "requires a significant amount of oversight in the health arena that hasn't been needed in years."

Elling said the subcommittee's "focus will continue to be repealing the law and repealing key components of it. We also need to view this through the eye of how does this impact those who have insurance? What is it doing to their rates, to their plan choices, to the plans they have enrolled in and like?"

Questions like these point to a "robust hearing and oversight agenda where we will continue to monitor those things," Elling said.

The subcommittee will also keep a close eye on the new health law's effect on Medicare.

"It's something we're constantly mindful of and monitoring so we don't get to a point where seniors are being turned away and hospitals are closing," he said.

The subcommittee will also be looking at how best to offset the need for a doc fix for the Medicare physician payment system.

"It's no secret how expensive this is to address," Elling said. To get that accomplished, he said, the GOP would need help from the physician community and the Democrats.

Elling said in general the public will see "a much more open process," than the deliberations over the health overhaul were.

HOUSE WAYS AND MEANS

Nicholas C. Gwyn

Democratic Staff Director
Subcommittee on Income Security and Family Support
B-316 Rayburn House Office Bldg.
Phone: (202) 225-4021
nick.gwyn@mail.house.gov

Personal: Born 10/26/1966 in New Orleans, La.

Education: B.A., Tulane University, 1989.

Professional: 1990–1994, legislative dir., Rep. Gary Ackerman, D-N.Y. 1994–1998, senior legislative asst., Rep. Barbara Kennelly, D-Conn. 1997–present , Democratic staff dir., Subc. on Income Security and Family Support, House Cmte. on Ways and Means. 1998–2007, Democratic staff dir., Subc. on Human Resources, House Cmte. on Ways and Means.

Expertise: Welfare, child care, unemployment, foster care.

Nick Gwyn doesn't believe that because the House Ways and Means Committee members he works for are now in the minority that it will stop them from continuing to propose legislation they believe will help people in need.

"Usually the majority sets the agenda and in the minority you're more responsive," said Gwynn, Democratic staff director for the human resources subcommittee.

"I think our members will want to continue to talk about the issues they have been talking about for many years: How do you help those who are the most vulnerable in society? How do you assist people from making the transition back into employment and how do you ensure a viable safety net?"

As the head staffer for this subcommittee during the 111th Congress, he worked on the portion of the American Recovery Act and Investment Act that extended unemployment benefits and for the first time ever increased the amount of the weekly stipend. The measure also gave incentives for states to improve coverage.

Beyond writing bills, a major concern of the minority members of the panel in the 112th Congress will be to beat back threats to the programs that assist struggling Americans.

"The first question is whether there is any attempt to change the extended unemployment benefits program to somehow place restrictions on them that are not there now or to reduce the number of weeks of benefits that are provided."

Although Gwyn has spent almost 20 years on Capitol Hill, when he arrived in Washington after college that wasn't his plan.

"I came here more out of curiosity," he said. "I don't know that I was determined to become a legislative staffer." But he did and has stayed all these years because, "the bottom line is it's nice to be involved in issues that have an impact on the every day lives of people and hopefully make some positive impact."

HOUSE WAYS AND MEANS

Kim Hildred

Republican Staff Director
Subcommittee on Social Security
B-316 Rayburn House Office Bldg.
Phone: (202) 225-4021
kim.hildred@mail.house.gov

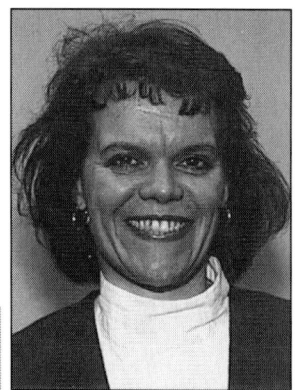

Personal: Born 09/06/1956 in Trumbull, Conn.

Education: B.A., Waynesburg College (Pa.), 1978. M.S.Ed., Duquesne University, 1980.

Professional: 1979–1994, policy and program management, Social Security Administration. 1994–1995, fellow, American Political Science Association. 1995–1996, detailee from the Social Security Administration, Subc. on Social Security, House Cmte. on Ways and Means. 1997–present, Republican staff dir., Subc. on Social Security, House Cmte. on Ways and Means.

Expertise: Social Security.

As the staff director for the subcommittee on Social Security, Kim Hildred's issue is one that is always controversial.

Early in her career, Hildred worked for the Social Security Administration. But after doing a fellowship on Capitol Hill one year, she was hooked and has worked for the Republican staff of the committee ever since.

During the 111th Congress, the subcommittee focused primarily on the backlogs at SSA and the workload spike for processing disability applications resulting from the economic downturn. The panel also spent a lot of time overseeing the use of the $1 billion the agency got from the stimulus bill—$500 million for a new computer center and $500 million to help clear the backlog.

Going forward, Hildred said, "the subcommittee is going to be looking into strengthening Social Security. We want to look at how Social Security programs are meeting the needs of today's beneficiaries and future ones."

She also expects the panel to look closely at the use of the Social Security number, particularly as it relates to identity theft.

Something that many people might not realize, she said, is that one of the biggest challenges facing the SSA is on the disability side.

That program is facing insolvency much sooner than the part that pays out retiree and survivor benefits, she said. According to the latest trustee's report, beginning in 2018 the SSA will be unable to pay the full disability benefit.

"It's very challenging. One of the reasons we like to do a lot of hearings is to continue to educate people to the challenges these programs face both in terms of their solvency and how the programs are administered," she said.

One thing is for sure, Hildred said, "for us to have reform in a program that affects the lives of every American that really has to be on a bipartisan basis. We keep looking for that opportunity."

HOUSE WAYS AND MEANS

Janice A. Mays

Democratic Staff Director/Chief Counsel

1102 Longworth House Office Bldg.

Phone: (202) 225-3625

janice.mays@mail.house.gov

Personal: Born 11/21/1951 in Waycross, Ga.

Education: B.A. (cum laude), Wesleyan College, 1973. J.D., University of Georgia, 1975. M.L.T., Georgetown University Law School, 1981.

Professional: 1975–1987, tax staff, Subc. on Select Revenue Measures, House Cmte. on Ways and Means. 1987–1992, chief tax counsel and staff dir., Subc. on Select Revenue Measures, House Cmte. on Ways and Means. 1993–1995, staff dir. and chief counsel, House Cmte. on Ways and Means. 1995–2011, Democratic staff dir./chief counsel, House Cmte. on Ways and Means. 2011–present, Democratic chief counsel/ chief tax counsel, House Cmte. on Ways and Means.

Expertise: Tax issues.

For Janice Mays, moving from the majority to being the Democratic staff director and chief counsel means she'll have fewer members to serve and her members will not set the agenda for the Ways and Means Committee.

"I served all the committee before. Now I just serve the Democrats," said Mays, who is an old hand at seeing majorities change. She has worked on Capitol Hill ever since she graduated law school. "Now we'll be more responsive to what the other guys are doing. From the Democrats' standpoint, we will always be looking at trying to create more jobs."

Democrats on the committee have done a number of things they'd like to see expanded, including the Building America bond program and moving ahead with developing green jobs and energy tax credits. But, Mays said, "so many people are focusing on undoing things from the past that it might be hard to initiate new things." Mays was referring to the GOP efforts to repeal the health law.

But Mays believes that "both sides are very interested in the broad issue of tax reform. Hopefully there will be a bipartisan way forward on that."

Mays says her job is more public services than politics.

"I've been allowed to stay out of the direct politics, been allowed to feel when I go home at night that I've been able to make things better," she said. "I believe in government. I think it's a positive force in the country."

While much of the committee's focus in the 111th Congress was on the health bill, Mays said their work on the economy shouldn't get overlooked.

"We kept the country from going into a depression," Mays said. "I don't think the world appreciates how much at the edge of a cliff we were and how the recovery act and even TARP contributed to that."

Mays said she loves antiques, still reads romance novels and is trying to learn to enjoy exercise.

HOUSE WAYS AND MEANS

Karen Brown McAfee

Democratic Staff Director and Tax Counsel
Subcommittee on Oversight
1136 Longworth House Office Bldg.
Phone: (202) 225-4021
karen.mcafee@mail.house.gov

Personal: Born 04/20/1971 in Petersburg, Va.

Education: B.S. (cum laude), University of Maryland at College Park, 1993. J.D., University of Virginia, 1996.

Professional: 1996–2000, associate attorney, Cadwalader, Wickersham & Taft. 2000–2007, counsel, Drinker Biddle & Reath LLP. 2007–2011, staff director and tax counsel, Subc. on Oversight, House Cmte. on Ways and Means. 2011–present, Democratic staff director and tax counsel, Subc. on Oversight, House Cmte. on Ways and Means.

Expertise: Internal Revenue Service, excise taxes, oversight.

As the Democratic tax counsel and staff director of the Ways and Means Committee's Oversight Subcommittee, Karen Brown McAfee will be in the minority for the first time in her Capitol Hill career during the 112th Congress.

In her new role, she will not be part of the agenda-setting but believes "it's going to be a great opportunity" to get involved in issues she did not have time to work on when she was part of a full majority staff that was swamped with work.

The business of the committee in the 111th Congress was dominated by the health care debate so McAfee's concentration on the Internal Revenue Service as tax counsel did not get as high a profile as it might have otherwise. She did work on such issues as homebuyer tax credits and individual taxpayer tax matters but neither resulted in any specific bills being passed.

In the 112th Congress, McAfee is adding excise taxes to her portfolio. Given Chairman Dave Camp's, R-Mich., public statements about the need to concentrate on tax matters, McAfee's plate will likely be full reacting to Republican proposals.

McAfee also hopes the tradition of the oversight subcommittee being bipartisan will continue.

"The subcommittee looks at issues like fraud," whether it's in the area of health, Social Security, or trade, she explained.

For more than a decade after she got her law degree from the University of Virginia, McAfee was in private practice. She worked on domestic and international tax law, tax accounting, charitable estate planning, and tax litigation.

She said she moved to Capitol Hill because she wanted to "work on tax laws and see how the process works from the inside. Definitely the knowledge base is a lot broader for the committee."

When she's not working, McAfee spends time with her three children.

HOUSE WAYS AND MEANS

Dave Olander

Chief Tax Counsel

1139 Longworth House Office Bldg.

Phone: (202) 225-4021

Fax: (202) 225-2610

dave.olander@mail.house.gov

Personal: Born 1974.

Education: B.A., Brown University, 1996. J.D., University of Virginia School of Law, 2002.

Professional: 1996–1999, legislative assistant, Rep. Wally Herger, R-Calif. 2002–2005, associate, Baker & Hostetler LLP. 2005–2008, tax and policy counsel, Rep. Thomas M. Reynolds, R-N.Y. 2008–2009, Republican tax counsel, House Cmte. on Ways and Means. 2009–2010, Republican chief tax counsel, House Cmte. on Ways and Means. 2011–present, Chief tax counsel, House Cmte. on Ways and Means.

Expertise: Tax issues.

As chief tax counsel for Ways and Means, Dave Olander and his staff will work during the 112th Congress to carry out the agenda of Chairman Dave Camp, R-Mich., to simplify and reform the tax code for individuals, families and employers in hopes of spurring spur job creation and economic growth.

During the next two years, Olander expects the committee to consider tax relief measures for those groups. He points to H.R.4, a bill to repeal the 1099 tax form reporting requirement included in the health overhaul law. The House passed the bill early in 2011.

In the last Congress, the tax staff worked to develop alternatives to the Democrats' tax legislative agenda, including the Republican alternatives to the Democrats' 2009 stimulus package, to the health care law, and to other parts of the majority's economic agenda.

Olander said that while the Republicans' opportunity to participate in the tax-writing process was severely limited during much of the 111th Congress, the tax staff worked to support Camp's efforts during the negotiations in December 2010 on the year-end tax bill that included an extension of the Bush tax cuts, a patch for the alternative minimum tax and a reduction in the estate tax.

Olander has a long history of working on tax policy on the Hill. He worked for several years as a tax and policy director for Rep. Thomas Reynolds, R-N.Y. and before that for another Ways and Means member, Rep. Wally Herger, R-Calif.

In between those jobs, Olander worked at the Washington, D.C. law firm Baker & Hostetler, which focuses on government issues and hires many former lawmakers and congressional staffers.

Olander joined the committee as a tax counsel and quickly moved into the Republican's chief tax attorney when Jon Traub, now the panel's staff director, was promoted from that job to the minority staff director.

HOUSE WAYS AND MEANS

Kathryn Olson

Democratic Staff Director, Social Security subcommittee

Subcommittee on Social Security

B-316 Rayburn House Office Bldg.

Phone: (202) 225-4021

kathryn.olson@mail.house.gov

Personal: Born 1964 in St. Paul, Minn.

Education: B.A., Georgetown University, 1986.

Professional: 1986–1988, legislative asst., Rep. Martin Sabo, D-Minn., 1988–1994, professional staff, Subc. on Social Security, House Cmte. on Ways and Means. 1995–2001, dir. of income security, National Academy of Social Insurance. 1998–1999, staff dir., Senate Democratic Task Force on Social Security. 2001–2011, staff dir., Subc. on Social Security, House Cmte. on Ways and Means. 2011–present, democratic staff dir., Subc. on Social Security, House Cmte. on Ways and Means.

Expertise: Social Security.

Social Security continues to be a flashpoint for lawmakers and the 112th Congress will likely be no exception.

For Kathryn Olson, Democratic staff director for the Subcommittee on Social Security, 2011 will be an effort at defense. She will work to protect Social Security from what she called Republican moves to slash guaranteed benefits as part of an effort to deal with the deficit.

"Social Security—with $2.6 trillion in reserves—didn't get us into this mess. And privatizing Social Security won't get us out," Olson said, quoting Rep. Javier Becerra, D-Calif., the ranking member on the subcommittee.

In the previous several Congresses, Olson said the subcommittee focused on the unprecedented backlog in disability cases and there was bipartisan support for increasing funding so more disability examiners and appeals judges could be hired to whittle down that backlog and shorten waiting times for applicants.

The subcommittee's effort was bolstered by $500 million from the American Recovery and Reinvestment Act of 2009 (ARRA) that was dedicated to SSA's backlog reduction program.

Olson said those efforts have begun to pay off. As an example, wait times for an appeal hearing fell from a high of 505 to 369 days.

"It will be a challenge to continue that progress in the current Congress," Olson said. Republicans stripped $1.7 billion from the Social Security Administration in their 2011 budget plan; something Democrats say would lead to the equivalent of a month of furloughs.

Olson is a veteran professional staffer on this issue, first coming to the subcommittee in 1988 and working there most of the time since. She did leave Capitol Hill for six years but still worked on Social Security issues, both at the National Academy of Social Insurance and as staff director for the Senate Democratic Task Force on Social Security.

HOUSE WAYS AND MEANS

Warren Payne

Senior Economic Advisor

1102 Longworth House Office Bldg.

Phone: (202) 225-3625

warren.payne@mail.house.gov

Personal: Born 12/11/1972 in Lewiston, N.Y.

Education: BA, Allegheny College, 1995. MS, University of Rochester, 1999.

Professional: 1999–2002, staff economist, Economic Consulting Services. 2002–2007, Economic advisor, U.S. International Trade Commission. 2007–present, senior economic advisor, Committee on Ways and Means.

Expertise: Economics.

As senior economic advisor for the Ways and Means Committee, it is Warren Payne's job to analyze the country's myriad of forecasts, predictions and financial reports and to advise the Republican members on how this data figures into the policies they are considering.

"I assist the chairman, the other members and the other staff," said Payne, who began his career as an economist focusing on trade, then taxes and now has a broad portfolio to go along with the committee's wide jurisdiction.

Payne said he provides analysis "on a variety of issues as they relate to economic growth, job creation, trade, taxes—across all the subcommittee."

Each month when the job creation numbers and the unemployment statistics are released, Payne gives the majority members a briefing on what it means in an effort, he said, to "help them formulate policy."

During the 111th Congress, Payne briefed members on such issues as cap and trade, the health law, trade preference programs and the pending free trade agreements. He also gave them his analysis of the stimulus package.

On the health overhaul law, Payne analyzed the impact he believed the bill would have on the labor market and job as well as what would happen to insurance premium costs as a result of the mandates in the law.

To do these analyses, Payne turns to banks, investment houses, think tanks and academics as well as official government reports.

During the 112th Congress, Payne expects the main issues he will be called on to advise members on include tax reform, "helping the members develop a pro-growth, pro job strategy, advancing the pending free trade agreements," and dealing with debt limit issues.

Payne says he never planned to have a career on Capitol Hill. But when the opportunity presented itself he welcomed the chance to put his economic skills to helping the Republicans make policy. With his one assistant, he is responsible for advising not only the members of the committee but occasionally is called on to brief House leaders and other lawmakers when asked.

When Payne is not figuring out economic policy, he's spending time with his family or coaching little league baseball games.

HOUSE WAYS AND MEANS

Viji Rangaswami

Staff Director and Chief Trade Counsel

1104 Longworth House Office Bldg.

Phone: (202) 225-3625

Fax: (202) 225-2610

viji.rangaswami@mail.house.gov

Personal: Born 03/30/1971 in Louisville, Ky.

Education: B.A., Duke University, 1993. J.D., Duke University Law School, 1996.

Professional: 1996–98, international trade associate, Akin, Gump, Strauss, Hauer & Feld, LLP (Washington, D.C.). 1999–2004, trade counsel, House Cmte. on Ways and Means. 2005–2006, Associate, Carnegie Endowment for International Peace. 2007–2009, deputy staff director, Trade Subc., House Cmte. on Ways and Means. 2009–2010, staff director and chief trade counsel, Trade Subc., House Cmte. on Ways and Means. 2011–present, Democratic staff director and chief Democratic trade counsel, Trade Subc., House Cmte. on Ways and Means.

Expertise: Trade issues.

Viji Rangaswami is the trade expert for the Democrats on the Ways and Means Committee.

Her work as the minority staff's chief trade counsel and director on its side of the trade subcommittee includes trade agreements, consulting on new trade partnerships, customs reauthorization and enforcement of existing trade agreements.

High on the agenda for the trade panel in 2011 are three free trade agreements: Korea, Panama, and Columbia.

"In terms of Panama the outstanding issues are in the Panamanians court," she said, referring to some labor law changes.

The Obama administration conducted a fact-finding mission in relation to the Columbia pact and Democrats on the panel expect to work with the White House to come up with a comprehensive proposal.

One recurring theme with these agreements, she said, is concerns about ensuring that they help promote U.S. manufacturing, not undermine it.

Rangaswami said work will also be done in the Pacific, where negotiations continue on a trans-pacific partnership. "There's a fair amount of work to be done ensuring that the administration understands what congressional Democratic priorities are for the agreement."

In the 111th Congress, Rangaswami worked on a miscellaneous tariff bills that reduced duties on some products, particularly those on inputs—products that needed further processing in the United States. Passing those bills, introduced by individual members, ran into some complications because such measures were considered earmarks and the Republicans had an earmark ban in place. The measure still passed over their objection. But the Senate only passed an extension of such provisions and didn't act on the House measure.

Subcommittee staff from both parties also worked on a customs reauthorization measure that didn't make it but Rangaswami believes can be completed in 2011.

HOUSE WAYS AND MEANS

Jennifer Safavian

Staff director, Oversight subcommittee; General Counsel, Ways and Means Committee

1102 Longworth House Office Bldg.

Phone: (202) 225-2365

jennifer.safavian@mail.house.gov

Personal: Born 03/14/1970 in St. Louis, Mo.

Education: B.S., St. Louis University, 1991. J.D., Michigan State University, 1994.

Professional: 1993–1995, attorney, Plunkett and Cooney, Detroit, Mich. 1996–1997, attorney, Dumbroff and Gilmore. 1997–1998, counsel, House Cmte. on Oversight and Government Reform. 1998–2000, chief counsel, deputy staff director, House Cmte. on Oversight and Government Reform, Census subcommittee. 2000–2001, assistant independent counsel, Office of Independent Counsel. 2001–2003, counsel, House Cmte. on Energy and Commerce. 2003–2010, chief counsel for oversight and investigations, House Cmte. on Oversight and Government Reform. 2011–present, general counsel, staff director, House Cmte. on Ways and Means, Oversight subcommittee.

Expertise: Legal issues, investigations.

Jennifer Safavian likes puzzles so serving as the staff director for the oversight subcommittee is a good fit. And if that doesn't keep her busy enough, she's also general counsel for the full Ways and Means committee.

Safavian joined Ways and Means in 2011 after working for the Government Reform and Oversight panel. Both jobs involved investigating and getting to the bottom of issues.

"They were looking for someone to fill both roles and given my knowledge and background on oversight I fit easily for the subcommittee. I also wanted to expand my knowledge and portfolio and can do that in the general counsel role," she said.

"Here we have significant policy responsibilities and oversight can support that agenda by highlighting issues and helping to find the solution," Safavian said. "We can actually try and fix things."

In the subcommittee, the plan for the 112th Congress is to focus on rooting out waste, fraud, and abuse.

"Given the economic times with historic unemployment and overspending by the government, it's most important that we root out waste and fraud in government programs, in the implementation of the health care overhaul law, the IRS and in the administration of our tax laws," Safavian said. And she expects to look at other issues that will help invigorate the economy and lead to the creation and growth of jobs.

The oversight subcommittee, she said, will be working in tandem with the substantive subcommittee to help identify problems, look in depth at matters, and assist them as needed to help create a policy and legislate change.

In her other role as the full committee's general counsel she's concerned with parliamentary procedures, making sure Ways and Means complies with House and committee rules and any other legal issues that come up.

Working on Capitol Hill was not in Safavian's plans when she graduated from Michigan State's law school. She and her husband decided to move to Washington, D.C. and she started work in a private law firm.

But it was 1998 and the House's government reform committee was looking into the Clinton administration's campaign activities and she was intrigued by the opportunity to try and solve that puzzle. And she's stayed on the Hill ever since.

When Safavian is not working, her two children keep her busy.

HOUSE WAYS AND MEANS

Askia M. Suruma

Deputy Chief of Staff

1102 Longworth House Office Bldg.

Phone: (202) 225-3625

Fax: (202) 225-2610

askia.suruma@mail.house.gov

Personal: Born 04/02/1971 in Manchester, Conn.

Education: B.S., Georgetown University, 1993.

Professional: 1993, intern, Rep. Martin Frost, D-Texas. 1993–1995, systems and mail manager, Rep. Martin Frost, D-Texas. 1995–1998, press secretary, Rep. Martin Frost, D-Texas. 1998–1999, public information officer, Small Business Administration. 1999, special projects dir., House Democratic Caucus. 1999–2001, legislative dir., Rep. Martin Frost, D-Texas. 2001–2007, Democratic deputy chief of staff, House Cmte. on Rules. 2007–present, Democratic deputy chief of staff, House Cmte. on Ways and Means.

Expertise: Procedure, process, parliamentary issues.

Askia Suruma has been in this spot before. The deputy chief of staff for the Democrats on Ways and Means first came to the Hill as an intern in 1993 and the next year found himself in the minority after the 1994 Republican wave.

"You kind of switch from governing to communicating," said Suruma, who will keep his title as deputy chief of staff but now it will be for a smaller staff. The Democrats went from having two-thirds of the staff of the panel to one-third.

Because he has done virtually every job on Capitol Hill, it will be easy for Suruma to be a utility player in the 112th Congress. He will divide his time between the oversight panel, tax issues, and helping with bills on the House floor. He'll even serve as a back up on communications.

Messaging is key when you're in the minority.

Right out of the box in 2011, the Republicans, he said, "have given us a great opening to do that as they made health reform repeal their first issue. They've helped unify us."

The way the Democrats will work this year is a far cry from the 111th Congress when the Ways and Means Committee was in the thick of the historic health care law as well as key tax bills.

Suruma called the health overhaul the committee's signature issue of 2009. In 2010, the lame-duck session measure to extend the middle class tax cuts and unemployment insurance occupied was a key accomplishment, he said.

Suruma and his staff also had to deal with a shakeup at the top of the committee when in March of 2010, Ways and Means Chairman Rep. Charlie Rangel of New York gave up his chairmanship in the wake of ethics violations that he was ultimately censured for on the House floor.

But when Rep. Sander Levin of Michigan took over the panel, Suruma said, it was a smooth transition and the same staff remained in place.

Going forward, Suruma expects the GOP to add tax reform and free trade to its work on health care.

HOUSE WAYS AND MEANS

Jon Traub

Staff Director
1102 Longworth House Office Bldg.
Phone: (202) 225-3625
jon.traub@mail.house.gov

Personal: Born 1965.

Education: B.A., Haverford College, 1988. J.D., University of Virginia, 1994.

Professional: 1995–1999, legislative director, Rep. Greg Ganske, R-Iowa. 1999–2004, legislative counsel, Rep. Jim McCrery, R-La. 2004–2006, vice president, federal tax legislation, Securities Industry Association. 2007–2008, Republican chief tax counsel, House Ways and Means Cmte. 2008–2010, Republican staff director, House Ways and Means Cmte. 2011–present, Staff director, House Ways and Means Cmte.

Expertise: Tax issues, legislative procedure.

As staff director, Jon Traub is both the traffic cop and policy guru for the House Ways and Means Committee.

Traub said the committee members set the agenda and it is "our job is to help them do their job. It's helping the chairman (Rep. Dave Camp, R-Mich.) know what his members want to do and help him execute his legislative plan."

He said the staff's job "is to make sure the information we're putting in front of them is the most accurate and relevant so they can make the best decisions possible."

Traub said the eight hearings the committee held during the first month of the 112th Congress "reflected the fact that there's a lot of pent up demand" on such issues as taxes, the pending free trade agreements, and the health care bill. Added to those issues was the president's fiscal year 2012 budget proposal.

In the 111th Congress, when the Republicans were in the minority, Traub said they "helped define some of the key legislative issues of the day. We helped make the case for what a failure stimulus was, made the case for what an overreach the health care bill was."

Traub said the Republican members "helped inform the public with a discussion of those issues. Our members would talk about what we would do instead." Now in the majority, Traub and Ways and Means Republican lawmakers will put those words into action.

Early in 2011, the committee moved a repeal of the 1099 tax-reporting requirement in the health overhaul law. "I'm sure there will be other aspects of health care law changes," Traub said.

Besides moving free trade agreements and tax measures, Traub expects there to be a greater emphasis on oversight in this Congress, "old-fashioned making sure that the taxpayers' dollars are being spent as wisely as possible."

When Traub is not steering the Ways and Means ship, he spends time with his wife and young son or on the golf course.

HOUSE WAYS AND MEANS

Matt Weidinger

Staff Director
Subcommittee on Income Security and Family Support
1029 Longworth House Office Bldg.
Phone: (202) 225-1025
Matt.Weidinger@mail.house.gov

Personal: Born 1967 in Evanston, Ill.

Education: B.S., foreign service, Georgetown University, 1987. M.A., political science, University of Chicago, 1989.

Professional: 1988, paralegal, Arent Fox, Kintner, Plotkin & Kahn (Washington, D.C.). 1990–1994, senior legislative asst., Rep. Clay Shaw, R-Fla. 1995–1998, professional staff member, Subc. on Human Resources, House Cmte. on Ways and Means. 1999–2000, professional staff member, Subc. on Social Security, House Cmte. on Ways and Means. 2000–2001, manager of governmental affairs, USX Corp. 2001–2007, staff dir., Subc. on Human Resources, House Cmte. on Ways and Means. 2007–2010, Republican staff dir., Subc. on Income Security and Family Support, House Cmte. on Ways and Means. 2011–present, Republican staff director, Subc. on Human Resources, House Cmte. on Ways and Means.

Expertise: Welfare, unemployment, child programs.

As he moves from the Republican staff director to staff director of the Subcommittee on Human Resources for the 112th Congress, Matt Weidinger looks forward setting the agenda for this panel whose responsibilities range from unemployment insurance to welfare.

"We've already have our first hearing on ways to help unemployed people get to work more quickly," Weidinger said.

And that's only the beginning. The goal, Weidinger said, is to see what "we can do through those programs to help people find jobs and leave dependence on government benefits."

Specifically, the panel will be looking at the reauthorization of the Temporary Assistance for Needy Families, or TANF program, which provides assistance on work, cash benefits, and disability policies. The authorization for that measure expires at the end of 2011.

Weidinger said that President Obama, in his 2012 budget proposal, asked Congress to extend current law by one year. GOP lawmakers on the subcommittee may want to begin looking at changes in that program earlier, although they are likely to support continuing the basic philosophy.

Republican members want to focus on ways to improve the work income.

"There's still several million people on welfare today and the question is what can we do to help them work rather than collect welfare checks," Weidinger said.

The panel is also likely, he said, to consider some concrete proposals to reform the unemployment benefit system. And there are some child welfare programs that will need reauthorization.

In the previous Congress, Weidinger gave Republican members information they needed to get their message out about their belief that the stimulus law and the unemployment insurance extensions fell short of Democratic promises on job creation.

House Permanent Select Committee on Intelligence

Capitol Visitor Center HVC-304
Washington, DC 20515
Phone: (202) 225-4121
Fax: (202) 225-1991
http://intelligence.house.gov
intelligence.hpsci@mail.house.gov

Ratio: 12/8

MAJORITY MEMBERS

Mike Rogers, MI-8th, Chairman
Mac Thornberry, TX-13th
Sue Myrick, NC-9th
Jeff Miller, FL-1st
Mike Conaway, TX-11th
Peter T. King, NY-3rd
Frank LoBiondo, NJ-2nd
Devin Nunes, CA-21st
Lynn Westmoreland, GA-3rd
Michele Bachmann, MN-6th
Thomas J Rooney, FL-16th
Joe Heck, NV-3rd

MINORITY MEMBERS

C.A. Dutch Ruppersberger, MD-2nd, Ranking Member
Mike Thompson, CA-1st
Janice Schakowsky, IL-9th
Jim Langevin, RI-2nd
Adam Schiff, CA-29th
Dan Boren, OK-2nd
Luis Gutierrez, IL-4th
Ben Chandler, KY-6th

HOUSE PERMANENT SELECT ON INTELLIGENCE

Intelligence oversight will be a hallmark of the committee under its new chairman, Rep. Mike Rogers, R-Mich., who opened the 112th Congress promising to "restore that tradition" in the panel, established in 1977.

It could provide ample opportunity to challenge the Democratic administration, as President Obama seeks to reassert his troubled effort to close the nation's detention facility in Guantanamo Bay, Cuba, before elections next year. Rogers is concerned about risks posed by released prisoners, some of whom have returned to terrorism activities on foreign soil.

Yet Rogers is also highlighting the committee's tradition of bipartisan cooperation. The former FBI agent wants to pass annual intelligence authorization bills providing, and restricting, authorities to the intelligence community. That tradition stalled after 2005, when controversies in the Bush administration around interrogation techniques derailed authorization attempts.

One of his first steps as chairman was to hold a vote allowing members of the Appropriations Committee to participate in intelligence hearings, a recommendation of the 9/11 Commission to increase cooperation.

As the U.S. prepared for military involvement in Libya in early March, Rogers defended President Obama's plans. "We're going to have a limited role, a very short engagement, if there is one," he told the *Los Angeles Times*. He also defended James Clapper, Obama's director of national intelligence, who came under fire from Republicans for telling lawmakers that Libyan leader Moammar Gadhafi would likely "prevail" over rebel factions in the long-term.

"If you're going to ask the intelligence director his opinion, then he should be allowed to give you his opinion," Rogers told *The Hill* newspaper. "And I thought that's what we wanted our intelligence officials to do.

The committee in 2011 will also prioritize legislative action extending provisions in the Foreign Intelligence Surveillance Act, examine modernizing the Communications Assistance for Law Enforcement Act, and study ways to provide long-term detention that's able to endure court challenges, Rogers said.

HOUSE PERMANENT SELECT ON INTELLIGENCE

Michael Allen

Majority Staff Director

Phone: (202) 225-4121

Education: B.A., Vanderbilt University. J.D., University of Alabama. L.L.M., Georgetown University Law Center.

Professional: 2001–2004, legislative affairs, White House, Homeland Security Council. 2005–2007, senior director Legislative Affairs, National Security Council. 2007–2009, senior director for Counterproliferation Strategy, National Security Council. 2009–2010, director of the National Security Preparedness Group, Bipartisan Policy Center. 2011–present, majority staff director, House Intelligence Committee.

Majority Staff Director Michael Allen is a national security operator. He spent the length of President George W. Bush's presidency working on policy issues in the White House and the National Security Council.

Now, under House Intelligence Committee Chairman Mike Rogers, R-Mich., Allen will help oversee the secretive spy elements of the nation's protective programs. His priorities will include tapping the brakes on the intelligence community's $80 billion budget, which has doubled since the Sept. 11, 2001, terrorist attacks, but now faces its first slowdown in a decade.

Allen is attuned to the spending concerns of Congress. He held key positions connecting the Bush administration to Capitol Hill, including a stint as the senior director for legislative affairs at the National Security Council until 2007. Earlier he worked in the legislative affairs office of the Homeland Security Council in the White House.

Allen, who holds degrees in law, will also steer the panel's staff into a role of greater bipartisanship, which Rogers, a former FBI agent, deems important to fulfill another priority: reestablishing annual passage of intelligence authorization bills.

One of Allen's first projects confirmed the emphasis on greater interoperability. The panel voted in early 2011 to allow members of the House Appropriations Committee to attend some of the panel's hearings, a recommendation by the 9/11 Commission, the principles of which Allen spent 2009 and 2010 advocating as the director of the National Security Preparedness Group. It was co-chaired by the 9/11 Commission's leaders, former Rep. Lee Hamilton, D-Ind., and past New Jersey Gov. Tom Kean, a Republican.

Allen will also oversee legislative efforts to define national electronic assets that need to be defended against what Rogers calls the "increasingly grave cyber threat." The panel will also assess intelligence capabilities with regard to unrest in the Middle East and North Africa, and explore information defenses against "al Qaeda's unrelenting efforts to attack us," Rogers said.

Allen says he's ready to help advance the panel's "critical agenda."

"Chairman Rogers is committed to providing the intelligence community with the tools that it needs to help protect America, while conducting aggressive and timely oversight to ensure the right national security policies are in place," Allen said.

HOUSE PERMANENT SELECT ON INTELLIGENCE

Heather Moeder Molino

Minority Deputy Staff Director

Phone: (202) 225-4121

Heather.Molino@mail.house.gov

Education: Cornell University.

Professional: Television Reporter for 10 years. director of communications, Rep. C.A. Dutch Ruppersberger, D-Md. deputy chief of staff, Rep. C.A. Dutch Ruppersberger, D-Md.

Minority Deputy Staff Director Heather Moeder Molino is a trusted hand of Rep. C.A. Dutch Ruppersberger of Maryland, the top Democrat on the Intelligence Committee. Molino, a television reporter for 10 years before coming to the Hill, became a public voice for Ruppersberger more than seven years ago, when she was hired as his spokeswoman.

The Cornell graduate was his communications director, then deputy chief of staff, before transitioning to the intelligence panel as minority deputy staff director when Ruppersberger rose in rank in 2011. The position of minority staff director was vacant at the time of publication.

Molino will help her boss, a former county prosecutor, enhance bipartisanship on the panel, with the first priority being the development of an intelligence authorization bill. Strengthening cyber security will also top Molino's task list, following high profile data breaches of the NASDAQ, the online banking security company RSA, and a host of government agencies.

"We must ensure the government is doing all it can to help the public and private sectors protect our nation's networks," Molino said.

But crises could overcome the legislative agenda and push the committee to investigate the intelligence community's ability to detect threats against the United States, as happened after attempted terrorist strikes in New York's Times Square, at Fort Hood, and in the skies between Amsterdam and Detroit when a suicide bomb failed to detonate on an airliner.

"We know the threat from Al-Qaeda, its affiliates, and other terrorist organizations around the world is real," Molino said. "We must utilize the latest in technology, including satellites and other important equipment, to make sure we are collecting and analyzing the most relevant information while also keeping costs in check."

Molino was involved in key pieces of past legislation pursued by Ruppersberger, including Operation Hero Miles. The program gives military personnel free flights home from Iraq and Afghanistan to visit family members and for emergencies stateside. Service members previously had to pay for their airfare. The program also flies family members around the country to visit wounded soldiers in military hospitals.

"Sometimes the love and support of family is the best medicine to help a loved one recover," Molino said.

Molino is married to a West Point graduate and a retired Army officer. They have a 15-month-old son and live in Washington, D.C.

Select Committee for Energy Independence and Global Warming

243 Longworth House Office Bldg.

Washington, DC 20515

Phone: (202) 225-4012

Fax: (202) 225-4092

http://globalwarming.house.gov

Ratio: 6/9

MAJORITY MEMBERS

F. James Sensenbrenner, Jr., WI-5th, Ranking Member

John Shadegg, AZ-3rd
Candice Miller, MI-10th
John Sullivan, OK-1st
Marsha Blackburn, TN-7th
Shelley Moore Capito, WV-2nd

MINORITY MEMBERS

Ed Markey, MA-7th, Chairman

Earl Blumenauer, OR-3rd
Jay Inslee, WA-1st
John Larson, CT-1st
Stephanie Herseth Sandlin, SD-At Large
Emanuel Cleaver, MO-5th
John Hall, NY-19th
John Salazar, CO-3rd
Jackie Speier, CA-12th

HOUSE SELECT FOR ENERGY INDEPENDENCE AND GLOBAL WARMING

JURISDICTION

(1) The select committee shall not have legislative jurisdiction and shall have no authority to take legislative action on any bill or resolution. Its sole authority shall be to investigate, study, make findings, and develop recommendations on policies, strategies, technologies and other innovations, intended to reduce the dependence of the United States on foreign sources of energy and achieve substantial and permanent reductions in emissions and other activities that contribute to climate change and global warming.

HOUSE SELECT FOR ENERGY INDEPENDENCE AND GLOBAL WARMING

The House Select Committee for Energy Independence and Global Warming, which House Speaker Nancy Pelosi, D-Calif., created to much fanfare after Democrats won the House majority in 2006, has no legislative authority. But that hasn't stopped it from claiming a central role in the year's hottest issue: climate change.

Chairman Edward Markey, D-Mass., is working with House Energy and Commerce Committee Chairman Henry Waxman, D-Calif., to create a cap-and-trade measure that will limit the amount of heat-trapping carbon dioxide that U.S. companies will be allowed to emit. Under such a system, companies are issued permits that allot them a certain number of carbon credits. Firms can either then reduce their emissions to adhere to the allotted amount, or buy or trade credits from other companies that have reduced their emissions.

He also is steering the panel to follow the international negotiations on climate change. United Nations negotiators hope to create a successor to the Kyoto Protocol, which the U.S. signed but never ratified and which the Bush administration declared "dead." President Obama has pledge to work toward a new global agreement, and negotiators hope to complete a new pact in December.

The year started out with a heavy focus on the economy in the committee, and that's likely to remain a constant for the foreseeable future. Markey has lauded President Obama's $787 billion stimulus package, particularly renewable energy provisions that he said will create "green" jobs and lead to energy independence.

The bill includes $11 billion in investments toward a "smart grid" which Markey's committee has explored this year. He also has held several hearings on the upcoming U.N. negotiations, particularly the role that developing countries like China and India must play in order for nations to come to an agreement.

Last year Markey introduced a global warming bill that would have slashed emissions 85 percent by 2050, and set up a system for 100 percent auctioning of carbon credits. Under the proposal, the money would have been returned to "consumers" and invested in clean technology.

This year, the handling of offsets will again be a key issue as Markey and others hammer out the details of a new climate change bill. Markey has called offsets "one of the more challenging aspects of designing effective climate legislation."

United States Senate

Leadership

http://www.senate.gov

MAJORITY MEMBERS

Harry Reid, NV, Democratic Leader
Daniel K Inouye, HI, President Pro Tempore
Richard Durbin, IL, Majority Whip
Charles E Schumer, NY, Chairman, Democratic Policy Committee
Patty Murray, WA, Chairman, Democratic Senatorial Campaign Committee
Debbie Stabenow, MI, Chairman, Democratic Steering and Outreach Committee
Mark Begich, AK, Chairman, Democratic Steering and Outreach Committee
Barbara Boxer, CA, Chief Deputy Democratic Whip

MINORITY MEMBERS

Mitch McConnell, KY, Republican Leader
Jon Kyl, AZ, Minority Whip
John Cornyn, TX, Chairman, National Republican Senatorial Committee
Lamar Alexander, TN, Chairman, Republican Conference
John Ensign, NV, Chairman, Republican Policy Committee
John Thune, SD, Vice Chairman, Senate Republican Conference

SENATE LEADERSHIP

Change came swiftly to Capitol Hill, including the Senate leadership organizations of both parties, after Republicans administered "a shellacking," as President Barack Obama put it, to congressional Democrats in the 2010 elections.

On the heels of his come-from-behind reelection victory, Sen. Harry Reid of Nevada began a major reorganization to sharpen the anti-Republican attack lines of the diminished Democratic majority that he leads.

Emboldened by a six-seat gain that brought the number of Senate Republicans to 47, Sen. Mitch McConnell declared as leader of the GOP minority, if the party's chief goals were to repeals the landmark Democratic health care overhaul, cut spending, shrink government and so on, "the only way to do all these things it is to put someone in the White House who won't veto any of these things."

But a funny thing happened in the rush to adjourn the lame-duck 111th Congress: a quick bipartisan compromise to extend the Bush-era tax cuts and administer a fresh jolt of federal spending to the still-weak economy.

"Voters did not elect only Republicans," Reid said during the post-election session. "They did not elect only Democrats. They did not want either party to govern stubbornly, demanding their way or the highway."

But a steady diet of compromise appeared unlikely, with huge challenges facing the 112th Congress, led by the mounting federal deficit that many of the new Republicans believed they had been elected to attack. Much of the early focus—and partisan posturing—was on openings to cut spending, first in crafting a stop-gap measure to fuel government operations for the rest of the fiscal year, and later to raise the federal debt limit.

Democrats, blaming their losses more on poor salesmanship than poor lawmaking, reorganized to take aim at what they viewed as wrong-headed GOP initiatives. Often, the new chairman of the party's policy and communications operation, Sen. Charles E. Schumer of New York., used House Republicans as a foil.

"They're blindly swinging a meat axe at the budget when they should be using a nice, sharp scalpel," Schumer said early in the budget debate.

McConnell's Republicans, while beefing up their own leadership staff, pounded at their own answer to the political chicken-and-egg question: the Democrats suffered less from a failed message than failed policies, particularly the health care law.

An early effort to repeal it failed, but few doubted that such battles would continue.

Reid is serving his fourth consecutive two-year term as Senate Democratic Leader, his second as Senate Majority Leader. Sen. Dick Durbin, D-Ill., is whip. Schumer is chair of the new Democratic Policy and Communications Center.

McConnell's GOP team consists of Whip Jon Kyl, R-Ariz., and Conference Chairman Lamar Alexander, R-Tenn.

SENATE LEADERSHIP

Barry C. Black

Chaplain of the United States Senate

S-332, The Capitol

Phone: (202) 225-3489

Personal: Born 1948 in Baltimore, Md.

Education: B.A., theology, Oakwood College, 1970. Master of Divinity, Andrews Theological Seminary, 1973. M.A., counseling, North Carolina Central University, 1978. Th.D., ministry, Eastern Baptist Seminary, 1982. M.A., management, Salve Regina University, 1989. Ph.D., Psychology, United States International University, 1996.

Professional: 1976–2003, chaplain, U.S. Navy. 2003–present, chaplain, U.S. Senate.

Expertise: Public speaking, counseling.

Rev. Barry Black sees the human toll behind a politically tumultuous year.

"When a senator fails to be re-elected, that's an entire staff that's out of work," explains Black, who serves as chaplain to the U.S. Senate. "That's a lot of counseling."

And there's been plenty of tumult of late to keep him busy. The 2010 election saw four incumbents turned out by voters and many more retirements. But Black said he also sees the more vulnerable side of the senators who do partisan battle on the floor.

Black (Ret.) made history in 2003 when he became the first African-American Senate Chaplain and the first Seventh-day Adventist in the position.

Black is the pastor to all 100 U.S. senators, their families, and nearly 7,000 Senate employees—a position he described as "the highest ecclesiastical pulpit in America." Black not only opens the Senate each day with a prayer, he also serves as an unofficial advisor, confidant, and spiritual mentor to the Senate community. As chaplain, he assists lawmakers and their staffs with spiritual and moral issues, as well as research on theological and biblical topics.

He attends a weekly prayer breakfast and five Bible studies each week—one for Senators only; one for their spouses; one for chiefs of staff; and two that are open to everyone. He also hosts Jewish programs and facilitates interfaith celebrations. Black holds several 10-week spiritual mentoring classes each year, which he limits to 10 participants. That gives him the ability, he said, to "mentor them and take them to another level that I can't do in Bible study."

Prior to coming to Capitol Hill, Black served in the U.S. Navy for over 27 years, ending his career as the chief of Navy chaplains. In addition to earning Master of Arts degrees in divinity, counseling, and management, he has received a doctorate degree in ministry and a doctor of philosophy degree in psychology.

SENATE LEADERSHIP

Mark Buse

Chief of Staff
Senator John McCain, R-Ariz.
241 Russell Senate Office Bldg.
Phone: (202) 224-2235
Fax: (202) 228-2862

Personal: Born in Phoenix, Ariz.

Education: B.S., Georgetown University.

Professional: 1987–1993, various positions, Sen. John McCain, R-Ariz. 1997–2001, policy director/staff director, Sen. John McCain, R-Ariz. 2002–2008, lobbyist. 2008–present, chief of staff, Sen. John McCain, R-Ariz.

Mark Buse started in 1984 as an intern in then-Congressman John McCain's office and in the decades since, he's become part of the Arizona Republicans' inner circle. Buse has worked for the Arizona Republican on and off ever since. That "on and off" relationship has sometimes become an issue in campaigns for the Arizona senator and 2008 Republican presidential nominee.

During McCain's 2008 presidential bid, Buse was cited in a well-known *New York Times* story questioning McCain's reformer credentials because of his ties to lobbyists. The *Times* article described Buse's return as "a round trip through the revolving door." It noted that Buse had overseen McCain's committee staff before leaving to lobby for telecommunications companies.

After the presidential campaign, he returned to lobbying before signing on to run McCain's 2010 re-election campaign amid a stiff primary challenge from former Rep. J.D. Hayworth.

Buse's climb included a stint in the mailroom, then serving as legislative assistant, policy director, and staff director for the Senate Commerce Committee. Buse was at the Commerce Committee during McCain's first presidential bid in 2000.

A native of Phoenix, Buse joined the office then-Rep. McCain at age 19 as a staff assistant, and worked in that position while earning a degree from Georgetown University. After six years as a legislative assistant on the senator's personal staff, Buse was made minority staff director of McCain's Governmental Affairs Subcommittee. It was during those years that McCain cemented his reputation as a congressional reformer.

SENATE LEADERSHIP

Nancy Erickson

Secretary of the Senate

U.S. Capitol

Phone: (202) 224-3622

Personal: Born 12/12/1961 in St. Paul, Minn.

Education: B.A., government and history, Augustana College, 1984. M.A., public policy, American University, 1987.

Professional: 1987–1988, General Accounting Office (GAO)/Federal Communications Commission (FCC)/Environmental Protection Agency (EPA). 1988–1994, professional staff member, Sen. Tom Daschle, D-S.Dak. 1988, presidential management intern, Health Care Financing Administration, Dept. of Health and Human Services. 1994–2005, deputy chief of staff, Sen. Tom Daschle, D-S.Dak. 2006–2007, Democratic representative, Senate Sergeant at Arms. 2007–present, secretary, U.S. Senate.

Expertise: Administration, management.

Nancy Erickson, the secretary of the Senate, is charged with the task of keeping the Senate's books in order.

Erickson was elected secretary of the Senate when Democrats took control of the chamber in 2007. But though she had worked for Democrats and was appointed, the job is a nonpartisan position that serves all 100 senators.

Erickson's job is to oversee the legislative, financial, and administrative services to the Senate through the management of the Senate parliamentarian, the bill clerk, the legislative clerk, the official reporters of debates, the Daily Digest, the Captioning Services Office, the Disbursing Office, Printing and Document Services, and other offices that support the Senate's daily operations. In addition, she must examine and sign every act passed by the Senate.

Most of Erickson's work takes place well behind the scenes, but on Capitol Hill even the book keepers occasionally get thrust into the media spotlight.

In early January 2009, Erickson made national headlines when she rejected the appointment of Roland Burris, D-Ill., who, due to a political battle between state officials, did not have the required paperwork when he came to Washington to claim his seat after being appointed by disgraced former Gov. Rod Blagojevich. After a state Supreme Court ruling, Burris eventually received the proper credentials and served in the Senate until he was replaced after the 2010 election.

In the 112th Congress, Erickson has several large projects underway including the ongoing upgrade and transfer of the multi-million dollar Senate Information Service program from the Senate sergeant at arms office to her office. Erickson's office also has been working on the expansion of Senate day care facilities. Erickson has said her goal is to approximately double the number of slots open to the children of Senate employees.

SENATE LEADERSHIP

Alan S. Frumin

Senate Parliamentarian

S-133, The Capitol

Phone: (202) 224-6128

Personal: Born 12/26/1946 in New York, N.Y.

Education: B.A., Colgate University, 1968. J.D., Georgetown University, 1971.

Professional: 1974–1977, editor, *Deschler's Precedence of the House of Representatives*. 1977–1987, asst. parliamentarian, U.S. Senate. 1987–1995, parliamentarian, U.S. Senate. 1995–2001, asst. parliamentarian, U.S. Senate. 2001–present, parliamentarian, U.S. Senate.

Expertise: Parliamentary procedure.

Alan S. Frumin's position as parliamentarian usually keeps him behind the scenes. But amid the health care debate of the 111th Congress, Frumin found himself in the spotlight of an intense national debate.

In March 2010, Frumin's rulings on arcane Senate procedure became the difference between whether President Obama's health care overhaul would succeed or collapse. Democrats were trying to pass their priority legislation using a procedure called "budget reconciliation." It allows bills to pass with a simple majority. But it can be used only on select kinds of legislation, and Frumin decides whether a provision fits the definition.

Essentially, the parliamentarian serves as the referee of the Senate. Unlike in sports, however, he can be fired by the head of the home team—the Senate majority leader. Such a fate befell Frumin's predecessor, Robert Dove. But even amid the charged health care debate, Frumin managed to hang on.

Amid the more closely divided Senate after the 2010 election, Frumin could again find himself under scrutiny. About a month after Election Day, Frumin was in the spotlight again for his rulings on the START treaty.

On a day-to-day basis, the parliamentarian's job, in large part, is to guide the presiding officer's responses to parliamentary inquiries, points of order, and other procedural matters. Frumin and his staff also help senators vet amendments for germaneness and review provisions of conference reports.

Parliamentarians hire their own assistants, and for decades, those assistants have advanced to the position of parliamentarian when a vacancy has occurred. This tradition protects the institutional knowledge and integrity of the office, Frumin said.

"The one essential characteristic that all parliamentarians must have is independence to call them as we see them," said Frumin.

SENATE LEADERSHIP

Terrance W. Gainer

Sergeant at Arms

S-151, The Capitol

Phone: (202) 224-2341

Terrance_Gainer@saa.senate.gov

Personal: Born in Chicago, Ill.

Education: B.A., St. Benedict's College, 1969. M.A., DePaul University, 1976. J.D., DePaul University, 1980.

Professional: 1968–1984, officer, Chicago Police Dept. 1968–1979, homicide detective, Chicago Police Dept. 1981–1984, chief legal counsel, Chicago Police Dept. 1984–1987, deputy inspector general, State of Illinois. 1987–1989, deputy director, Illinois State Police. 1991–1998, director, Illinois State Police. 1998–2002, assistant chief of police, Metropolitan Police Dept. 2002–2006, chief of police, Capitol Police Dept. 2006, chief executive officer, Blue Falcon Solutions, LLC. 2007–present, sergeant at arms, U.S. Senate.

Expertise: Security, law enforcement, emergency preparedness.

As the chief law enforcement officer of the Senate, Sergeant at Arms Terrance Gainer will tell you that his job is the "protection racket."

Gainer, a former chief of the Capitol Police Department, makes it his personal mission to ensure the safety and security of Members, staff and visitors to Congress.

While the origins of the office date back to the first Congress, the importance of Gainer's job was made tragically apparent earlier this year after the shooting of Rep. Gabrielle Giffords, D-Ariz., at a campaign event in Tucson.

In the wake of that tragedy, Gainer has been a voice for increased vigilance, but has also cautioned against making drastic increases to the size of the Capitol Police Department or the scope of its duties.

"Right after the shooting people talked about increased number of officers for each Member and having [individual protective] details," said Gainer, who helps oversee the Capitol Police as one of three Members of the Capitol Police Board. "I don't think that's needed. What is needed and what we've been doing with the FBI and local authorities is trying to figure out how to maximize intel, [increase Members'] situational awareness" and advise staff on how best to protect themselves.

To aide in that effort, Gainer moved quickly after the Tucson shooting to hire Mike Stenger, an assistant director for the Secret Service, to serve as assistant Sergeant at Arms.

Stenger will help find was to leverage and maximize what the Secret Service is doing with what Congressional security entities are doing, Gainer said.

Besides his security duties, Gainer's is also the Senate's doorkeeper, charged with maintaining order on the Senate floor and in the public gallery. Gainer's team of 1,000 staffers also is responsible for Senate technology services and cyber security; assisting Senate offices with staffing, mailing, purchasing and other needs; and overseeing the Senate press galleries.

SENATE LEADERSHIP

Carolyn Gluck

Senior Policy Advisor
Senate Majority Leader Harry Reid, D-Nev.
SC-8, The Capitol
Phone: (202) 224-2158
Carolyn_Gluck@reid.senate.gov

Personal: Born 09/08/1974 in New York, N.Y.

Education: B.A., University of Michigan, 1996.

Professional: 1996–1997, staff asst., Sen. Harry Reid, D-Nev. 1997, legislative corresp., Sen. Harry Reid, D-Nev. 1997–2003, legislative asst., Sen. Harry Reid, D-Nev. 2003–2005, deputy legislative director, Sen. Harry Reid, D-Nev. 2005–present, senior policy advisor, Senate Democratic Leader Harry Reid, D-Nev.

Expertise: Public health, women's issues, seniors, and aging.

For Senior Policy Advisor Carolyn Gluck, a key mission of the 112th Congress figured to be extending and monitoring the progress of public health achievements in the 111th Congress—and if necessary, defending them against attack by the GOP.

Gluck's portfolio of medicine, health care appropriations, reproductive policy, and the needs of the elderly was clearly in the target zone of Republican efforts to cut the federal budget and keep a 2010 campaign promise to "repeal and replace" the Democratic health care law signed into law in that year.

Spearheading Sen. Minority Leader Harry Reid's public health agenda this year is Carolyn Gluck, who is hoping to temper heated emotions on the abortion issue among lawmakers on both sides of the aisle.

In the first week of the Senate session, Reid sought to focus the debate on reducing the number of women who seek abortions each year, which is almost half of pregnancies in America. He introduced legislation to increase access for women to family planning services. The bill was among the Democrats top 10 priorities of the year.

"We're looking for ways we can work with people on both sides of the debate to help reduce the number of unintended pregnancies," Gluck said. "Sen. Reid also wants to move away from a polarized debate and to encourage policies that improve access and reduce disparities for women and minorities."

Specifically, Reid would like to expand Medicaid, the government run health insurance program for the disabled and low income, to cover a larger pool of low income women eligible for family planning services.

He also wants to require that health insurance companies that provide prescription drugs to beneficiaries also provide birth control, Gluck said.

"Women spend more out of pocket for their health care costs," Gluck said. "Insurance companies that cover prescription drugs can't exclude prescription contraception from that coverage."

Abortion has been a tricky issue for Reid, who as the Democrats' top official differs with the majority of his caucus on the matter. Reid, a Mormon, opposes abortion, but he is focusing on ways to reduce the number of unintended pregnancies and the number of abortions.

On behalf of Reid, Gluck also will be pushing for legislation that will boost technology in the health care industry. He believes better technology eventually will lead to better health care access for patients, Gluck said.

Mental health care also is a priority, especially suicide prevention legislation and mental health parity legislation. Last year, Sen. Reid helped pass the Garrett Lee Smith Memorial Act, which focuses on youth suicide. This year he will focus on suicide prevention among the elderly, Gluck said.

Gluck graduated with Bachelor of Arts degrees in political science and French from the University of Michigan in 1996. She moved to Washington and joined Reid's personal office, rising to deputy legislative director by 2003. In that position she helped coordinate Reid's legislative initiatives. When Reid elevated to Minority Leader this year, he tapped Gluck as part of his leadership team.

SENATE LEADERSHIP

Bob Greenawalt

Senior Tax Advisor

Senate Majority Leader Harry Reid, D-Nev.

S-221, The Capitol

Phone: (202) 224-2158

Fax: (202) 224-7362

bob_greenawalt@reid.senate.gov

Personal: Born 07/15/1961 in Pottstown, Pa.

Education: B.S., Arizona State University, 1983.

Professional: 1983–1990, Ernst & Young. 1990–1992, tax legislative asst., Rep. Don Pease, D-Ohio. 1992–1999, tax advisor, Sen. John Chafee, R-R.I. 1999–2004, senior tax advisor, Sen. Bob Graham, D-Fla. 2005–present, senior tax advisor, Senate Democratic Leader Harry Reid, D-Nev.

Expertise: Taxes, pensions.

Bob Greenawalt's experience as senior budget, tax, and economic policy advisor to Senate Majority Leader Harry Reid, D-Nev., put him at the center of one of the most intriguing questions for the 112th Congress:

Beyond the obvious potential for partisan strife after the Republican gains in the 2010 elections, was there any prospect for compromise?

Greenawalt, who has served senators of both parties during almost two decades on Capitol Hill, was involved in the major legislative battles of the 111th Congress, including enactment of economic stimulus and the Democratic overhaul of the U.S. medical system.

The loss of the House majority and the weakening of Democratic control the Senate broke a campaign-season logjam, as President Barack Obama came to terms with the GOP on an extension of the Bush-era tax policies. In return, Democratic leader Reid pushed for a jolt of anti-recessionary spending in a compromise package that passed during the lame-duck session.

But in the new Congress, Senate Democrats turned to a difficult juggling act on the federal budget. Good policy, public opinion and the clout of seven added GOP seats made federal discretionary spending cuts a must. But at the same time, Greenawalt's boss led an aggressive defense against the scope and depth of proposed Republican cuts.

Greenawalt has served for six years on Reid's leadership staff. Prior to joining Reid's staff, he worked for former Finance Committee member Bob Graham, D-Fla., Sen. John Chafee, R-RI., also a Finance Committee member, and Congressman Don Pease, D-Oh., a member of the Ways and Means Committee. Greenawalt also has private sector experience from his tenure at Ernst & Young.

SENATE LEADERSHIP

Serena Hoy

Senior Counsel

Senate Majority Leader Harry Reid, D-Nev.

S-221, The Capitol

Phone: (202) 224-7327

Fax: (202) 224-7362

serena.hoy@reid.senate.gov

Personal: Born 03/27/1972 in St. Louis, Mo.

Education: Modern Middle Eastern Studies, Oxford University. B.A., political science and history, University of Arizona, 1994. J.D., Yale University, 2000.

Professional: 2005–2008, counsel, Senate Minority Leader Harry Reid, D-Nev. 2009–present, senior counsel, Senate Majority Leader Harry Reid, D-Nev.

Expertise: Immigration, Civil rights, Civil liberties.

As senior counsel to Senate Majority Leader Harry Reid, D-Nev., on Judiciary Committee matters, Serena Hoy handles some of the thorniest security and social issues facing the country.

This year she expects to be handling the proposed reauthorization of the Patriot Act, the fallout from the end of the military's "Don't Ask, Don't Tell" policy, and the future of terrorist suspect detention at Guantanamo. Even immigration may be lurking behind the scenes.

"For Senator Reid, immigration continues to be a high priority," Hoy said. "If he sees the opportunity for consensus and the ability to get 60 votes, he'd be willing to move forward."

Last year, immigration loomed over progress on climate change legislation, before both eventually fell apart. In the fall, Reid brought to the floor the "Dream Act," which would allow children of undocumented immigrants to get on a path to citizenship. The plan eventually won 55 votes, a majority that fell short of the 60 votes needed to pass.

"The consensus in the Democratic caucus was to try it," Hoy said.

In the new Congress, the Patriot Act faces expiration in May, while the Foreign Intelligence Surveillance Act expires late in 2012. There is some discussion of merging aspects of FISA into the Patriot Act debate.

In addition, President Obama's decision to not defend the "Defense of Marriage Act" has some saying that Congress should step in, another question on which she would advise Reid.

Hoy, who joined Reid's staff in 2005, has experience guiding bills through the legislative process, managing bills and amendments on the Senate floor, and developing legislative and messaging strategy.

She replaced Ron Weich as Reid's lead liaison to the Judiciary Committee in March 2009. Her portfolio also includes judicial nominations, criminal and civil justice, and institutional legal issues.

SENATE LEADERSHIP

Adam Jentleson

Deputy Communications Director, Democratic Policy and Communications Center

S-318 U.S. Capitol

Phone: (202) 224-2939

Adam_jentleson@dpcc.senate.gov

Personal: Born in New York, N.Y.

Education: B.A., Columbia University, 2003.

Professional: 2004, staffer; GOTV coordinator, Green Bay, Wis., Kerry-Edwards Campaign. 2005–2006, policy and advocacy manager, Strategic Initiatives for Campus Progress, Center for American Progress. 2007–2008, communications, John Edwards for President. 2009, communications, Center for American Progress. 2010, rapid offense director, Senate Majority Conference Committee.

Expertise: Campaign politics, communications.

Adam Jentleson is the deputy communications director for the new Democratic Policy and Communications Center, where he helps craft the party's message.

After the Senate Republicans fortified their minority by seven seats in the 2010 elections, the Democratic majority opted to restructure its leadership and staff apparatus. The general view that percolated up from the Democratic caucus was that the 111th Congress had been a substantive success—headlined by the historic overhaul of the medical system, Wall Street reform, and the federal spending policies that prevented the 2008 economic crisis from collapsing into a second Great Depression.

But the poll results were widely viewed as evidence that the party's efforts to spread the word of its achievements had been a failure—ironically so, because an earlier reorganization of the Senate leadership's communications office had been frankly modeled after the Clinton-era "War Room" that had succeeded so well at out-messaging the Republicans in the late-1990s.

The DPCC, which include Jentleson and other young and widely experienced staffers, is essentially a merger of Majority Leader Harry Reid's old "war room" operation and the Democratic Policy Committee.

The DPCC, chaired by Sen. Charles E. Schumer of New York, aimed at a finely meshed relationship between the policy research and communications functions of the caucus.

Thus, the center started early in the 112th Congress on aggressive efforts to portray the GOP—and particularly the House majority GOP, which would send much legislation to the Senate—as extreme.

Jentleson and other staffers, based in the old war-room a few doors from the Senate press gallery, relied on the research arm of the office to put Republican spending-cut proposals, for example, into categories that would be easy for the news media to explain—and for voters to absorb.

For example, during the long struggle to find a compromise on how to finance the government through the end of fiscal year 2011, the DPCC produced statistics-filled statements that broke down certain GOP proposals into their state-by-state toll in job losses—as estimated by the Democratic research staff.

Jentleson brought to this task a wealth of experience as a Democratic Senate staffer, as an organizer and lobbyist with the Center, and as an operative with two president campaigns.

SENATE LEADERSHIP

Rob Jesmer

Executive Director
National Republican Senatorial Committee
425 Second Street, NE
Phone: (202) 675-6060
Fax: (202) 675-4269

Personal: Born 11/06/1973 in St. Paul, Minn.

Education: B.A., political science and communications, University of Saint Paul, Minnesota, 1996.

Professional: 1999, campaign manager, Prior to that Rob also ran campaigns in Tennessee, Mississippi, Illinois and Minnesota. 1999–2000, Midwestern field representative, National Republican Congressional Cmte. (NRCC). 2000–2002, National Field Director, NRCC. 2002–2005, chief of staff, Rep. John Rogers, R-Ala. 2005–2006, Southeast Regional Political Director, Republican National Committee. 2007, political field staff, McCain for President. 2007–2008, campaign manager, Re-election campaign of Sen. John Cornyn, R-Tex. 2008–present, executive director, National Republican Senatorial Cmte.

Expertise: Campaign management, political affairs.

A lot has changed for the team that tries to elect Republican senators. But the people remain the same, and the odds are getting even better.

"I think we have a real opportunity to gain the majority," said Rob Jesmer, who directs that team on behalf of National Republican Senatorial Committee Chairman John Cornyn, R-Texas.

It's hardly an idle thought. Only 12 Republican senators are up for re-election in 2012, but 23 Democratic senators will be up. And Jesmer has pretty much the same team in place that brought Republicans within two seats of Senate control in the 2010 round.

"That kind of continuity is rare in this business," Jesmer said.

Democrats still have big advantages—most prominently control of the White House and a majority in the Senate. But the NRSC begins with the momentum out of the 2010 election and a shrinking fund-raising gap with their Democratic counterpart. That has come in large part with business's dissatisfaction with Democrats and the Obama administration.

"Democrats have led a steady stream of attacks on job creators," Jesmer said. "We have a lot of people investing in us who want to see pro-business, job-creating policies."

Before moving to Texas to manage Senator Cornyn's 2008 race, Jesmer began the 2007 cycle working on John McCain's presidential bid. Jesmer spent the 2006 election cycle as the Southeast Regional Political Director at the Republican National Committee (RNC). Prior to his tenure at the RNC, Jesmer spent three years on Capitol Hill as the chief of staff to Representative Mike Rogers, R-Ala. He also worked at the National Republican Congressional Committee (NRCC) for two cycles, as the National Field Director in 2002, and as the Midwest Field Representative in 2000. Jesmer's political experience also includes running campaigns in Tennessee, Mississippi, Illinois and Minnesota.

SENATE LEADERSHIP

Bruce King

Senior Budget Advisor
Senate Majority Leader Harry Reid, D-Nev.
S-221, The Capitol
Phone: (202) 224-5556

Personal: Born 09/06/1958 in New York, N.Y.

Education: B.A., Tulane University, 1980. J.D., Stanford Law School, 1983.

Professional: 1985–1986, counsel, Guam Legislature. 1987–95, legislative asst., Sen. Frank Lautenberg, D-N.J. 1995–1997, legislative director, Sen. Frank Lautenberg, D-N.J. 1997–2001, minority staff director, Senate Cmte. on the Budget. 2001–2005, senior counsel, Sen. Jon Corzine, D-N.J. 2005–2006, senior budget advisor, Senate Minority Leader Harry Reid, D-Nev. 2007–present, senior budget advisor, Senate Majority Leader Harry Reid, D-Nev.

Expertise: Budget, Social Security.

As an advisor to Senate Majority Leader Harry Reid, D-Nev., Bruce King handles budget and spending issues, likely to be among the most contentious matters in the 112th Congress.

Freshman Republicans, fueled by "Tea Party" enthusiasm, are eager to enact spending cuts, many aimed at Democratic priorities. Reid has served as the target of many of those freshmen, who cast him as a symbol of Democratic big spending. As budget negotiations intensified in early 2011, a band of freshman Republican House members even taped their spending cut demands to a door of Reid's ceremonial office.

King also handles Social Security, and other economic issues in Reid's leadership office, where he has worked since 2005.

A Capitol Hill veteran who has worked in the Senate for more than 20 years, King will work to pass a budget incorporating the priorities of President Obama and the Democratic caucus during the 112th Congress.

Previously, King helped Reid secure approval of emergency legislation to respond to the nation's financial crisis, which was approved just weeks before the 2008 presidential election.

After joining Reid's leadership team in 2005, King spent much of his time working to defeat President Bush's plan to establish private accounts within Social Security. Bush's plan fizzled, in what was deemed a major victory for congressional Democrats and Reid in his first major political fight as the Democrats' new leader.

After helping to win the battle on Social Security, King shifted focus to coordinating an effort to develop a Democratic bill providing emergency relief to victims of Hurricane Katrina. Lawmakers introduced the bill soon after the hurricane struck the Gulf Coast, devastating New Orleans and other cities in the region. Several pieces of the bill were later pursued separately, though the Republican majority at the time blocked most of the bill.

SENATE LEADERSHIP

Rohit Kumar

Deputy Chief of Staff
Senate Republican Leader Mitch McConnell, R-Ky.
S-230, The Capitol
Phone: (202) 224-3135

Personal: Born 06/02/1974 in Boston, Mass.

Education: A.B., political science and economics, Duke University, 1995. J.D., University of Virginia School of Law, 2000.

Professional: 1995–1997, legislative assistant, Sen. Phil Gramm, R-Texas. 2000–2001, law clerk, The Hon. J. Harvie Wilkinson, U.S. Court of Appeals for the 4th Circuit. 2001, deputy chief Republican counsel, Senate Cmte. on Banking. 2001–2002, legislative director/chief counsel, Senate Cmte. on Environment and Public Works. 2002, general counsel and senior policy advisor, Senate Majority Leader Trent Lott, R-Miss. 2002–2005, policy advisor and general counsel, Senate Majority Leader Bill Frist, R-Tenn. 2006, director of policy and senior counsel, Senate Majority Leader Bill Frist, R-Tenn. 2007–2010, director of policy and senior counsel, Senate Republican Leader Mitch McConnell, R-Ky.

Expertise: Tax policy, trade, banking and financial services, immigration.

The 2010 elections divided congressional power so sharply that the potential for impasse was immediately clear to all. But as a veteran of many permutations of Washington's partisan lineup, Rohit Kumar was quick to see—and act upon—more subtle possibilities.

As Senate Minority Leader Mitch McConnell's deputy chief of staff, Kumar was involved in the deal that embodied the power shift even before newly-elected Republicans took their extra seats in the Senate and their majority control of the House. In return for a round of anti-recessionary spending, President Barack Obama agreed late in 2010 to extend the tax-rate reductions enacted early in the Bush administration.

The deal also underlined a new reality for Kentucky Republican McConnell. "When the president comes our way, it's incumbent on us to say 'Yes,'" said Kumar. "The fact that he is a partner in a deal is not a valid basis to say no," said Kumar.

Even as Senate Democrats hardened their rhetorical line against spending cuts offered by the GOP-majority House early in the 112th Congress, Kumar saw signals of White House willingness to compromise on politically painful ways to deal with the federal deficit.

"There's a lot more outreach to us," from the White House, "for the obvious reason that they now need Republican votes in order to operate on the Senate floor," he said.

Since joining the Senate GOP leader's staff in 2002, Kumar said, "I've been here in the minority. I've been here in the majority. I've been here with a Republican in the White House. I've been here with a Democrat in the White House. Each of those combinations brings its own dynamic."

In 2008, Kumar was among the staffers that a prominent Democrat, then-Banking Committee Chairman Christropher J. Dodd of Connecticut, praised publicly for his work on the emergency bipartisan legislation to bail out the financial system.

SENATE LEADERSHIP

Kate Leone

Senior Health Counsel
Senate Majority Leader Harry Reid, D-Nev.
S-221, The Capitol
Phone: (202) 224-2158
Fax: (202) 224-7362

Personal: Born 08/09/1971 in Princeton, N.J.

Education: B.A., Cornell University, 1993. J.D., Columbia University, 1997.

Professional: 1997–1998, law clerk, Justice James H. Coleman, N.J. Supreme Court. 1998–1999, law clerk, Judge John C. Lifland, U.S. District Court (N.J.). 1999–2001, attorney, Healthcare Task Force, Antitrust Division, Dept. of Justice. 2001–2002, senior policy advisor, Senate Democratic Policy Cmte. 2002–2004, counsel, Senate Democratic Leader Tom Daschle, D-S.Dak. 2005–present, senior health counsel, Senate Democratic Leader Harry Reid, D-Nev.

Expertise: Health care.

Just before the Senate took its last vote on 2010's landmark health overhaul, Senate Majority Leader Harry Reid, D-Nev., praised his top aide on health care reform, Kate Leone, for helping him get the legislation passed.

"Kate Leone, she has been such a stalwart in helping me work through these issues," Reid said on the Senate floor.

Now, in the 112th Congress, she has to defend it.

Repealing the health care legislation, or at least de-funding it, is a top priority of the Republicans who won their elections in a wave of conservative fury, but Reid has vowed to fight.

When Republicans pressed their case on the Senate floor in February 2011, Reid said, "Republicans' symbolic effort to repeal the rights in the health care reform bill would put us all at risk."

Leone's portfolio includes big-ticket health care programs, including Medicare and Medicaid, health insurance, and prescription drugs.

Leone oversees health issues involving health care coverage, as opposed to public health and social issues. She handles health matters under the purview of Senate Finance Committee, along with all health insurance and prescription drug issues. In 2008, she was tasked with helping Senate Democrats push the Democratic presidential nominee's health care policies

Leone graduated with a law degree from Columbia University in 1997. She spent two years in New Jersey clerking for two judges, Justice James H. Coleman at the New Jersey Supreme Court and Judge John C. Lifland at the U.S. District Court.

Leone served as a senior policy advisor with the Senate Democratic Policy Committee in 2001 and as counsel to then-Senate Democratic Leader Tom Daschle, D-S.D., for two years.

Leone moved to Washington in 1999 and spent two years as an attorney in the Antitrust Division of the Department of Justice under President Bill Clinton, specializing in health care issues.

SENATE LEADERSHIP

Ryan Loskarn

Staff Director

Senate Republican Conference Chairman Lamar Alexander, R-Tenn.

Room 413 Senate Hart Bldg.

Phone: (202) 224-2764

Fax: (202) 224-6984

Personal: Born 04/17/1978 in Baltimore, Md.

Education: B.A., history and political science, Tulane University, 2000.

Professional: 2000–2001, staff assistant, Rep. Wally Herger, R-Calif. 2002–2003, deputy press secretary, House Cmte. on Rules, Chairman David Dreier, R-Calif. 2003–2007, communications director, Rep. Marsha Blackburn, R-Calif. 2007–2010, communications director, Senate Republican Conference. 2010–present, Staff Director, Senate Republican Conference.

Expertise: Communications and message development.

Ryan Loskarn has taken over for Tom Ingram as the top staffer for the Senate Republican Conference and its chairman, Sen. Lamar Alexander R-Tenn.

Loskarn had served as communications director for the conference, starting when Sen. John Kyl (R-Ariz.) was chair. Alexander asked him to stay on after Kyl moved up to whip.

Loskarn's savvy also has earned him accolades in the media. In January 2009, *Roll Call* newspaper selected him for their "Fabulous 50" list of the top "movers and shakers behind the scenes on Capitol Hill."

He has moved into the role with the conference in a very different political place than when he joined in 2007. Then, Republicans were reeling from the loss of their majority and would go on to lose even more seats in the 2008 election.

Now, the wheel of political fortune is swinging the other way. Republicans have almost closed their gap with Democrats in the Senate and Republicans sense the chance to reclaim the majority. And the conference has a big class of conservative Republican freshmen. Many of those benefited from the Tea Party movement. Nearly all are pushing for steep spending cuts.

"We have an extraordinarily talented and energetic class of freshman Republican senators who are committed to addressing the issues of spending, debt, and our runaway government," Loskarn observed.

Loskarn said Alexander views his role as policy development and messaging for the caucus.

"His role is to help the caucus find an agenda and priorities and then to help develop a message that helps move that agenda and those priorities down the field," Loskarn said.

He formerly served as communications director for Rep. Marsha Blackburn, R-Tenn., and as deputy press secretary at the House Rules Committee for Chairman David Dreier, R-Calif. A Maryland native, Loskarn received a B.A. in history and political science at Tulane University.

SENATE LEADERSHIP

David McCallum

Deputy Chief of Staff
Senate Majority Leader Harry Reid, D-Nev.
S-221, The Capitol
Phone: (202) 224-2158
Fax: (202) 224-7462

Personal: Born 05/23/1954 in Elgin, Ill.

Education: B.A. in philosophy (with honors), University of Louisville, 1977.

Professional: 1979–1984, management analyst, Jefferson County Corrections Dept. 1984–1989, director of information services, Orleans Parish District Attorney's Office. 1989–1990, director of operations, Democratic Senatorial Campaign Committee. 1991–1994, regional manager, INSLAW, Inc. 1995–1997, manager, UNISYS Corp. 1997–1999, director of operations, Sen. Barbara Mikulski, D-Md. 2000–2001, administrative officer, Sen. Daniel Patrick Moynihan, D-NY. 2001–present, deputy chief of staff, Senate Majority Leader Harry Reid, D-Nev.

Expertise: Congressional management.

David McCallum is the conductor of Senate Majority Harry Reid's train during the 112th Congress. As deputy chief of staff, McCallum keeps the Nevada Democrat's operation running in Washington, D.C. and Nevada.

McCallum operates far from the spotlight, but handles some of Reid's most important affairs. He handles the schedule, oversees the staff of 150 people in the U.S. Capitol and Nevada, implements the budget, oversees constituent casework, does the hiring, pays the bills, and briefs the majority leader on the latest news from back home.

During the 2009 presidential inauguration for President Barack Obama, McCallum handled all details that were relevant to Reid's operation, from "meet and greet" receptions to ticket distribution.

"David helps keep things on track, from the small details to big projects," Reid said. "His role helps me do two important things at once: look out for Nevadans back home while running the Senate."

McCallum has been dubbed "The Enforcer," according to Politico, because he "quietly calls the shots and keeps the trains running from an office in the Hart Senate Building."

McCallum's efforts were tested in 2010 when Reid faced one of the toughest re-elections in his career. He faced dismal poll numbers in Nevada until Republicans picked gaffe-prone Tea Party darling Sharron Angle to oppose him.

One of McCallum's signature issues is the hiring of minorities by Senate Democratic offices, a staffing program that he helped spearhead in June 2008 for the majority leader.

McCallum, who has a bachelor's degree with honors in philosophy, got his start with Reid in 2001, after a brief stint on the staff of Sen. Daniel Patrick Moynihan, D-N.Y. He also previously worked for Sen. Barbara Mikulski, D-Md., after working as director of operations at the Democratic Senatorial Campaign Committee in the 1980s.

SENATE LEADERSHIP

Dorinda Moss

Finance Director

National Republican Senatorial Committee

425 Second Street NW

Phone: (202) 675-6000

Fax: (202) 544-3464

dmoss@nrsc.org

Personal: Born 12/24/1975 in Tenn.

Education: B.S., political science, Belmont University, 1998.

Professional: 1999–2001, finance director, Tennessee Republican Party. 2001–2003, regional finance director, Republican National Committee (RNC). 2003–2004, regional finance director, Bush-Cheney '04. 2004–2005, co-finance director, 55th Presidential Inaugural Committee. 2005–2007, director, RNC Raiser's Edge. 2007–2008, finance director, Friends of Fred Thompson. 2008, vice president for finance, American Solutions for Winning the Future. 2009–present, finance director, National Republican Senatorial Cmte..

Expertise: Political fundraising.

Dorinda Moss joined the National Republican Senatorial Committee in 2009 as Sen. John Cornyn, R-Texas, became chairman.

President Obama was basking in the glow of his historic election and Republicans were staring at a disadvantage in the Senate that had grown since 2006 and at times seemed insurmountable.

"The outlook was not good for us," said Moss, who as finance director is responsible for raising the money needed to assist Republican Senate incumbents, challengers, and open seat candidates.

Such insurmountable odds can make the enthusiasm gap seemed even bigger.

"I think a lot of our donors were disillusioned with a lot of things in the 2008 cycle," Moss said.

But the fortunes changed dramatically over the next two years as the economy sputtered and the policies Obama pursued—health care and financial regulation—became increasingly controversial.

That helped Moss shrink the Democrats' fundraising advantage from $70 million in 2008 to a little less than $15 million for the 2010 cycle.

"A lot of folks were disenchanted with administration, particularly in the business community and Wall Street," Moss said. "They didn't appreciate that, and we benefited."

The NRSC still wasn't able to gain a majority in the 2010 "wave" election, but did reduce Democrats advantage from 60-40 to 53-47. According to Moss, Cornyn said early in the 2010 campaign that claiming a majority in the Senate would require a "two cycle" plan. The idea that Republicans might take the Senate in two years hasn't hurt fundraising.

"The prospect of winning," Moss said, "is exciting to our donors."

She said she also benefits from a chairman who is willing to do what it takes to raise money.

"He's very hardworking," Moss said. "He's willing to do the heavy lifting, and his colleagues have been very helpful too."

SENATE LEADERSHIP

Gary Myrick

Secretary for the Majority
Senate Majority Leader Harry Reid, D-Nev.
S-221, The Capitol
Phone: (202) 224-2158

Personal: Born 07/20/1967 in Gilford, Maine.

Education: B.A., University of Maine, 1989. J.D., Washington College of Law at American University, 1994.

Professional: 1989–1994, cloakroom, Sen. George Mitchell, D-Maine. 1994–2003, floor staff, Sen. Tom Daschle, D-S.Dak. 2003–2004, floor counsel, Sen. Harry Reid, D-Nev. 2005–present, deputy chief of staff, Senate Minority Leader Harry Reid, D-Nev.

Expertise: Senate parliamentary procedure, legislative strategy.

Senate Majority Leader Harry Reid, D-Nev., appointed Gary Myrick to be majority secretary in November 2010, after one of the toughest re-election fights of Reid's career.

Myrick, long a fixture in Democratic Senate leadership offices, had been Reid's chief of staff since 2006.

"Gary has done an outstanding job leading our team for the last four years and his presence and judgment have set the right tone for our legislative victories," Reid said of the move. "Gary's mastery of Senate procedure and knowledge of this institution are invaluable to me and our entire Caucus. I am pleased that he will continue to be an invaluable resource to all of us as our next Secretary of the Majority."

He replaced Lula Davis, who retired after working 30 years on Capitol Hill. He and his Republican counterpart, David Schiappa, serve as conduits between the two parties' leaders and manage the day-to-day choreography of debate and voting on the Senate floor. Sometimes that means cooperation and sometimes it means contention.

Myrick provides legislative summaries and keeps records for the Democratic caucus, organizing weekly meetings for senators and senior staff when the Senate is in session and assisting Reid in making appointments to commissions and boards created by statute.

Myrick began his Senate career as an intern for then-Senate Majority Leader George Mitchell and got a full-time job there after graduation. He transferred to the Senate cloakroom while he attended law school at American University. Myrick then worked for Sen. Tom Daschle, D-S.Dak. who promoted Myrick to Senate floor staff when became the Democratic leader.

Myrick joined Reid's team in 2003 and played an instrumental role in then-assistant Democratic Leader Reid's mastery of Senate procedure. Upon his election as Democratic Leader in 2004, Reid promoted Myrick to be deputy chief of staff.

SENATE LEADERSHIP

David Schiappa

Secretary for the Minority
Senate Republican Leader Mitch McConnell, R-Ky.
S-337, The Capitol
Phone: (202) 224-3835
Fax: (202) 224-2860

Personal: Born 11/03/1962 in Washington, D.C.

Education: M.S., Johns Hopkins Carey Business School, 2009. B.A., University of Maryland, 1984.

Professional: 1984–1994, senior cloakroom asst., Senate Republican Cloakroom. 1994–1996, Republican floor asst., Senate Republican Cloakroom. 1996–2001, asst. secretary for the majority, Senate Republican Cloakroom. 2001–2003, secretary for the minority, Senate Republican Cloakroom. 2003–2006, secretary for the majority, Senate Republican Cloakroom. 2007–present, secretary for the minority, Senate Republican Cloakroom.

Expertise: Senate procedure.

As secretary for the Senate Republicans, David Schiappa is the point person on the Senate floor for Republican Leader Mitch McConnell, R-Ky., and the GOP Conference.

He manages the Republican side of the "day-to-day" choreography of floor action in the Senate. Schiappa and his Democratic counterpart, Gary Myrick, serve as the conduits between the two parties' leaders.

Sometimes that means cooperation and sometimes it means a swordfight. Either way, his job got easier with the substantial gains made by Republicans in the 2010 election.

"That's an understatement," Schiappa said. "There's a little more running room. You have some leverage now."

Schiappa is involved in all aspects of the legislative process—from the early planning stages to floor execution. His mastery of Senate procedure positions him to provide strategic counsel for floor legislation under Senate rules.

Schiappa and his team of floor assistants brief the leader's office on floor developments. He is the person Senators call when they want to put anonymous or public holds on legislation in order to prevent it from quickly passing or to make sure they get a chance to modify it. Schiappa vets and writes unanimous consent requests used by the leader and other Republicans to move Senate business forward.

Prior to becoming secretary, he served as assistant secretary from 1996 to 2001, has been in both the majority and the minority, and knows how to maneuver in both positions.

Schiappa spends his weeks steeped in the legislative process. But he started spending his weekends far from that world, getting a master's degree in 2009 from the Johns Hopkins Carey Business School.

"I did it for sanity," Schiappa said. "It was fun on weekends to remove myself from here. We'd be talking about issues, and I'd think, 'We don't do that in the Senate.'"

SENATE LEADERSHIP

Sharon Soderstrom

Chief of Staff

Senate Republican Leader Mitch McConnell, R-Ky.

S-230, The Capitol

Phone: (202) 224-3135

Personal: Born 1961.

Education: B.A., Phi Beta Kappa, University of Virginia, 1983.

Professional: 1989–1990, professional staff, Subc. on Children and Families, Senate Cmte. on Labor and Human Resources. 1990–1995, legislative director, Sen. Dan Coats, R-Ind. 1995–1998, chief of staff, Sen. Dan Coats, R-Ind. 1999–2001, senior policy advisor, Senate Majority Leader Trent Lott, R-Miss. 2001–2002, senior policy advisor, Senate Minority Leader Trent Lott, R-Miss. 2003–2004, Republican staff director, Senate Cmte. on Health, Education, Labor, and Pensions. 2004–2006, deputy chief of staff, Senate Majority Leader Bill Frist, R-Tenn. 2007–present, deputy chief of staff, Senate Republican Leader Mitch McConnell, R-Ky.

Expertise: Senate rules and procedures, legislative process, education and labor.

Sharon Soderstrom took over as the top staffer for Senate Minority Leader Mitch McConnell, R-Ky. after Kyle Simmons, McConnell's previous top staffer, announced his departure in December 2010.

Soderstrom, an expert in Senate floor procedure and domestic policy, moved up from the position of deputy chief of staff. McConnell had come to rely on her to provide strategic counsel and institutional insight to the leadership team.

She takes the helm of McConnell's team in the 112th Congress as he tries to translate the gains Republicans achieved in the Senate in the 2010 elections into legislative victories. But that will be complicated by the fact that Republicans remain in the minority in the Senate, Democrats control the White House, and the new "Tea Party" Republicans have significantly different priorities than more establishment Republican senators.

Soderstrom has consistently been named to the Roll Call "Fabulous Fifty" list of Capitol Hill staffers. Her achievements include helping enact measures relating to homeland security, billions of dollars in relief packages for Americans affected by Hurricanes Katrina and Rita, and the confirmation of two Supreme Court justices.

McConnell is the third Senate Republican leader that Soderstrom has served. She previously worked for former Majority Leaders Bill Frist, R-Tenn., and Trent Lott, R-Ms. After Lott's resignation as leader, Soderstrom served for a year as staff director for the Senate Health, Education, Labor, and Pensions (HELP) Committee, where she focused on issues such as special education for students, health care costs, and access issues for the uninsured. From there, she moved to Frist's leadership office. Soderstrom also worked for Sen. Dan Coats, R-Ind.

SENATE LEADERSHIP

Patrick J. Souders

Chief of Staff

Senate Assistant Majority Leader Dick Durbin, D-Ill.

S-321, The Capitol

Phone: (202) 224-9447

Fax: (202) 228-0400

Pat_souders@durbin.senate.gov

Personal: Born 01/20/1969 in Quincy, Ill.

Education: B.A., communications, Marquette University, 1991. M.A., arts, Georgetown University, 1999.

Professional: 1991–1995, legislative asst., Rep. Dick Durbin, D-Ill. 1995–1996, downstate political director, Durbin for U.S. Senate. 1997–2004, projects director, Sen. Dick Durbin, D-Ill. 2005–2006, staff director, Senate Assistant Democratic Leader Dick Durbin, D-Ill. 2007–present, chief of staff, Senate Assistant Majority Leader Dick Durbin, D-Ill.

Expertise: Floor operations, appropriations, politics.

Pat Souders has worked for Dick Durbin for essentially his entire career in politics and government. He started as a low-ranking legislative assistant in Durbin's congressional office in 1991. Now, he's the top staffer to Durbin, the Illinois Democrat who is the No. 2 Democrat in the Senate.

Durbin holds the titles of Senate majority whip and assistant majority leader. As chief of staff, that puts Souders in the thick of the action as the Senate takes on major issues.

The start of the 112th Congress marked his seventh year overseeing the operations of the Democratic Whip's office and helping Durbin with his responsibilities to the Democratic Caucus. Durbin, who Sounders has called "part vote counter and part traffic cop on the Senate floor" works with Senate Majority Leader Harry Reid, D-Nev., in developing the caucus agenda and helps to move the party's legislation through the Senate.

Durbin helps to determine what legislation the Democrats can bring to the floor, and then tries makes sure that they know where the votes are.

Durbin also has message responsibility and helps to determine how Senate Democrats talk about the priorities of the caucus.

Durbin has had consistently good relations with President Obama, who was previously the junior senator from Illinois to Durbin's senior.

Since 1985, Durbin has maintained a standing invitation to all constituents visiting Washington, D.C., to join him for coffee on Thursday mornings when the Senate is in session. And he frequently opens his Capitol office to visiting Illinoisans and groups from the "Land Of Lincoln."

Souders, who is a Quincy, Ill. native, has worked for Durbin for nearly 18 years, in both the House and Senate.

SENATE LEADERSHIP

Don Stewart

Dputy Chief of Staff, Communications
Senate Republican Leader Mitch McConnell, R-Ky.
S-230, The Capitol
Phone: (202) 224-2979

Personal: Born 07/03/1967 in Riverside, Calif.

Education: B.A., political science, Armstrong Atlantic State University, 1997.

Professional: 1990–1994, intelligence analyst, U.S. Army. 1997–2000, regional director, Sen. Paul Coverdell, R-Ga. 2000–2003, deputy press secretary/press secretary, Sen. Phil Gramm, R-Texas. 2003–2006, communications director, Sen. John Cornyn, R-Texas. 2006–2010, communications director, Senate Republican Leader Mitch McConnell, R-Ky.

Expertise: Communications.

For Don Stewart, the longtime chief spokesman to Senate Minority Leader Mitch McConnnell, the GOP's gains in the 2010 elections spelled more openings in the new Congress to bring Republican initiatives to the floor, more opportunities to legislate, and "a lot more fun."

Early in the 112th Congress, Stewart was elevated to deputy chief of staff for communications.

Looming as the biggest issues for the GOP this year are "spending and the debt," he said. "Those are the two biggest issues" because they are keys, in his party's view, to reviving the economy, creating jobs and more.

The new GOP majority forced an early vote on the House-passed repeal of Obama's landmark health care overhaul. The repeal failed, but McConnell pledged to continue the attack on the health care law.

Then, in a round of brinksmanship over a possible government shutdown, the Republicans forced significant cuts in spending for the remainder of the 2011 fiscal year. Soon enough, the GOP would make its mark "on everything else, from Guantanamo on," Stewart said.

"There's more opportunity to legislate on the floor, whereas we were shut out in the last Congress," he explained. "Now the Dems need our votes to overcome procedural hurdles, so we will actually have a chance to offer amendments."

Stewart, a familiar figure in the hallways off the Senate floor who answers to the nickname "Stew," had served as spokesman for Sen. John Cornyn and, earlier, for another Texas Republican, Sen. Phil Gramm. A California native, Stewart once served as an enlisted intelligence analyst in the Army and began his Senate career with the late Sen. Paul Coverdell, R-Ga.

SENATE LEADERSHIP

Pamela B. Thiessen

Policy Director

Republican Policy Committee Chairman John Ensign, R-Nev.

347 Senate Russell Bldg.

Phone: (202) 224-2946

Professional: Expertise:

Pam Thiessen is the staff director of the Senate Republican Policy Committee (RPC), chaired by Sen. John Ensign, R-Nev., the Senate's No. 4 Republican. Ensign succeeds Sen. Kay Bailey Hutchinson, R-Tex., who did not run for re-election.

Thiessen, who previously served as Ensign's legislative director, was named RPC staff director early in the 111th Congress. She brings a wealth of experience, having worked for several Senators and the Pentagon.

Ensign served in the GOP Senate leadership in the 2008 election cycle, as the chair of the National Republican Senatorial Committee. His new role involves more research and strategic positioning to help shape the GOP game on policy issues from tax cuts to health care and the federal budget.

Every Tuesday the Senate is in session, Republican Senators gather in the Capitol for a policy lunch meeting, hosted by Ensign. These lunches mark the one scheduled time each week for all Republican Senators to gather and discuss issues before the Senate, review the anticipated agenda, and discuss policy options.

Republican staff directors also meet weekly in the RPC office to review pending issues. The RPC also hosts weekly briefings for Republican legislative directors as well as meetings with outside speakers and policy experts to facilitate discussion on key issues and explore new ideas for legislative action.

Ensign is the 13th chairman of the RPC, composed of GOP Senate leaders and the chairmen of the Senate's standing committees. "I'm grateful to take a leading role in the future of the G.O.P. as we reunite as the party of fiscal responsibility, limited government and opportunity for everyone," said Ensign.

"As a more senior member of leadership, I'll be able to ensure that the interests of Nevadans are heard at the earliest stages of the legislative process," said Ensign. Helping him will be Thiessen, who will continue to liaison with his personal and other Senate committee staffs. Elected in 2000, Ensign said the GOP post will give him a "stronger voice" for his home state in the U.S. Senate. Nevada's other senator is Democrat Majority Leader Harry Reid.

Republican Leader Mitch McConnell, R-Ky., said of Ensign, "He's helped shape our legislative efforts, ranging from crafting key tax relief to encouraging clean energy, and as Chairman of the Policy Committee, I look forward to him taking on a larger role."

SENATE LEADERSHIP

Darrel Thompson

Deputy Chief of Staff for Intergovernmental and External Affairs

Senate Majority Leader Harry Reid, D-Nev.

S-221, The Capitol

Phone: (202) 224-2158

Fax: (202) 224-7362

Personal: Born 06/02/1970 in Washington, D.C.

Education: B.A., Morgan State University, 1992. M.P.A., John F. Kennedy School of Government, Harvard University, 2002.

Professional: 1994, financial services field rep., Democratic Congressional Campaign Committee. 1996, director of financial strategy & planning, Democratic Congressional Campaign Committee. 1997–1998, financial services director, Democratic Congressional Campaign Committee. 1999, deputy executive director, House Democratic Caucus. 1999–2003, senior policy advisor & director of member services, Office of the House Democratic Leader, Rep. Richard Gephardt, D-Mo. 2003, finance chief of staff & national political advisor, Richard Gephardt for President. 2004, chief of staff, Barack Obama for Senate. 2005–2011, senior advisor, Office of the Senate Democratic Leader, Sen. Harry Reid, D-Nev. 2011–present, chief of staff for intergovernmental and external affairs, Office of the Senate Democratic Leader, Sen. Harry Reid, D-Nev. 2011–present, Deputy Chief of Staff for Intergovernmental and External Affairs, Office of the Senate Democratic Leader, Sen. Harry Reid, D-Nev.

Expertise: Labor and employment issues, Legislative and political strategy.

Darrel Thompson measures success in pounds. Not his weight, but the amount he can lift. In 2010, the fitness buff and triathlete set personal records, squatting 405 pounds and bench-pressing 300 pounds.

Thompson has also taken on an additional load at work. For years, he had been Senate Majority Leader Harry Reid's, D-Nev., lead advisor on labor issues. In an office reorganization for the 112th Congress, Thompson was promoted to deputy chief of staff for intergovernmental and external affairs.

He kept his previous responsibilities and added duties that had been handled by Reid's new chief of staff, David Krone. Thompson coordinates business opportunities for Reid's home state of Nevada, ensuring that national companies know of opportunities there, and working with Nevada communities and businesses.

"It's working with Nevada-based entities to make sure job creation opportunities are not missed," Thompson said. "And it's reaching out to national-based entities to ensure they're aware of possibilities in Nevada."

That puts him in the thick of issues such as high-speed rail, geothermal energy, and federal construction projects. The job also has an outreach component that involves planning national events on major issues on the Democratic agenda, such as Social Security.

Thompson is likely to be best known as the aide Reid dispatched to help Sen. Roland Burris, D-Ill. after his controversial selection by Gov. Rod Blagojevich. At the time Blagojevich was under indictment trying to sell that very same Senate seat, which Barack Obama had vacated when he was elected president.

Thompson is one of a handful of Democratic staffers who has worked for House and Senate Democratic leaders, having worked previously for House Democratic Leader Dick Gephardt, D-Mo. He also has White House connections, having served as chief of staff on Obama's 2004 Senate race.

SENATE LEADERSHIP

Anne Wall

Floor Director and Office Counsel

Senate Assistant Democratic Leader Dick Durbin, D-Ill.

S-321, The Capitol

Phone: (202) 224-9447

Fax: (202) 228-0400

anne_wall@durbin.senate.gov

Personal: Born 12/25/1976 in Chicago, Ill.

Education: B.A., political science and journalism, Miami University, Oxford, Ohio, 1999. J.D., DePaul University College of Law, 2002.

Professional: 2002–2004, law clerk, The Honorable Allen S. Goldberg, Circuit Court of Cook County, Illinois. 2002, law clerk, The Honorable Lynn M. Egan, Circuit Court of Cork County. 2004–2006, litigation associate, Pretzel & Stouffer Chartered (Chicago). 2006–present, floor director and office counsel, enate Assistant Democratic Leader Dick Durbin.

Expertise: Senate ethics rules, Senate legislative process, Senate floor procedure.

After clerking for two Chicago-area judges and working for a Chicago law firm, Anne Wall came out to Washington in 2006 without a job. She answered mail for a time before becoming one of the top aides to one of the most powerful Democrats on Capitol Hill, Assistant Majority Leader Dick Durbin of Illinois.

As floor director, Wall assists Durbin in navigating the byzantine rules of the Senate, where a simple majority is almost never enough and any senator can propose an amendment on any subject at any time. Except when they can't.

"It is a complete puzzle every day," Wall said. "That's what I love about this job."

Durbin, the Senate's No. 2 Democrat, is also the Senate Democratic whip. So Wall also directs the floor operations of the Senate Democratic Whip Office. She handles staff-level whip meetings and helps to organize senator-level whip meetings. Overall, she is charge of ensuring that her boss has an accurate vote count and relevant information on important bills and amendments.

Wall's role as office counsel is essentially separate from her policy role on the floor. In that role, she acts as the attorney for the senator and his leadership staff. She is responsible for keeping them on the right side of Senate ethics issues and other legal matters.

Durbin and his team must be in constant communication with colleagues on both sides of the aisle to determine what issues have broad Democratic support or what issues will require finding middle ground, she said.

Because of the Democrats' narrower margin in the Senate and the need to get things done before the 2012 election year, This year she expects a lot of movement on bi-partisan "small-ball stuff." The first few months of the year, she said, "have been really bi-partisan."

# SENATE LEADERSHIP

Judith Wallner

Policy director, Democratic Policy and Communications Center

S-318 U.S. Capitol

Phone: (202) 224-3232

Judith_wallner@dpcc.senate.gov

Personal: Born 05/24/1977 in Philadelphia, Pa.

Education: B.A., political science, Vassar College, 1999.

Professional: 1999–2000, research associate, Democratic Congressional Campaign Committee. 2001–2004, senior strategist, The Strategy Group. 2005–2008, research director, Democratic Senatorial Campaign Committee. 2009–2010, senior strategist, The Strategy Group. 2011, research director, Senate Democratic Policy and Communications Center.

Expertise: Campaign finance, policy research.

During the early months of the 112th Congress, a new Senate leadership organization created a routine of issuing a regular series of papers bearing such titles as "Republicans' Irresponsible Debt Ceiling Proposal," "House Republicans' CR Slashes Investments in Jobs, Security and Education," and "Republican Myths" about the health care overhaul that Democrats had shepherded into law about a year before.

Some of the documents were analytical in tone, some partisan. They tended to be heavily annotated and footnoted, verging on scholarly. Many were the work of Judith Wallner, the policy director of the new arm of leadership.

The Democratic Policy and Communications Center was an organization of about 30, formed on the authority of Democratic Majority Leader Harry Reid of Nevada following the party's loss of seven seats in the 2010 elections. There was a view in the caucus that the party had suffered in part because of a failure to sell the pubic on the virtues of its policies in the 111th Congress—and on the shortcomings of the Republican's.

It sprang from a merger of the Democratic Policy Center and the Democratic Communications Center and was predicated on the idea that sound research and policy formation could work hand-in-hand with public relations to aggressively promote the party's message—strongly tilted toward economic recovery and job creating. At the same time, the DPCC helped to paint the Republican spending reduction initiatives in terms of the programs that would have to suffer real cuts.

For example, shortly after House Republicans issued their plan to finance the government for the balance of the 2011 fiscal year, the DPCC issued a paper saying, in part, that the cuts in Social Security Administration finances meant that "half a million Americans who are legally entitled to benefits and would otherwise have received them will instead be waiting for them."

The chairman of the new DPCC was Sen. Charles E. Schumer, the successful former chief of the Democratic Senatorial Campaign Committee, who had developed a reputation as a skilled election strategist.

Wallner had served under Schumer as research director of the campaign committee during the 2006 election cycle, when Democrats seized majority control of the Senate, and she led the research operation for the committee's independent expenditure arm during the 2008 cycle.

SENATE LEADERSHIP

Brian J. Walsh

Communications Director

National Republican Senatorial Committee

425 Second Street NW

Phone: (202) 675-6000

Fax: (202) 544-3464

bwalsh@nrsc.org

Personal: Born 05/11/1975 in West Nyack, N.Y.

Education: B.A., English and political science, Bucknell University, 1997.

Professional: 1998–1999, staff, Pennsylvania Governor Tom Ridge, R. 1999–2000, media and external relations representative, National Petrochemical & Refiners Assn. 2000–2001, communications director, Rep. Nick Smith, R-Mich. 2001–2002, communications director, Rep. Bob Barr, R-Ga.. 2002–2006, communications director, House Cmte. on Administration. 2006–2009, communications director and spokesman, Sen. John Cornyn, R-Tex. 2009–present, communications director and spokesman, National Republican Senatorial Cmte.

Expertise: Communications strategy.

One might expect the folks in charge of electing Republicans to the Senate could take a little break after gaining six seats in the 2010 election. Instead they kept up the momentum going right into 2012.

"We haven't missed a beat," says Bryan Walsh, communications director for the National Republican Senatorial Committee. "We're working to aggressively define Democrats in the Senate and hold them accountable for their votes."

"Define," of course, means "attack" in politics. And "hold accountable" means making the most out of tough votes for Democrats. Both are the purview of Walsh who is a key part of developing a coordinated NRSC message to appeal to voters in the 2012 election. Walsh's duties also involve interacting with reporters at the state and local level and new media.

Walsh is beginning his second tour with the NRSC. He moved over from Sen. John Cornyn's, D-Texas, office to become chief spokesman for the GOP organization in charge of electing and re-electing Senate candidates in early 2009 when Cornyn took over the organization's helm.

Often, NRSC chairmen serve only one term. But Walsh said after bringing Senate Republicans within two seats of Senate control, Cornyn decided to "finish the job."

The numbers could hardly be more favorable for him to accomplish just that. Only 12 Republican senators are up for re-election in 2012, but 23 Democratic senators will be up. Still, with the speed that chambers have been changing hands in recent years, Walsh says he knows it's too early to take anything for granted.

"There's no chest-beating here," Walsh said. "It's a long way to go. We're making no prediction."

SENATE LEADERSHIP

Mason E. Wiggins Jr.

Executive Assistant for the Sergeant at Arms
Senate Minority Leader Mitch McConnell R-Ky.
S-151, The Capitol
Phone: (202) 224-2341

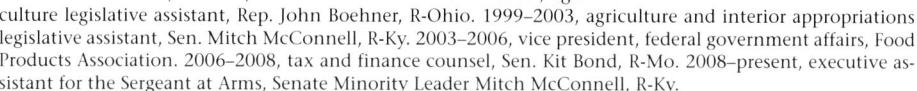

Personal: Born 10/18/1957 in Cambridge, United Kingdom.

Education: B.A., philosophy, Catholic University of America, 1979. M.A., philosophy, Catholic University of America, 1981. J.D., Columbus School of Law, Catholic University of America, 1986. LL.M., agriculture law, University of Arkansas School of Law, 1987.

Professional: 1987–1989, associate counsel, Heron, Burchette, Ruckert, and Rothwell. 1989–1991, legislative assistant, Rep. Sid Morrison, R-Wash. 1991–1997, counsel, House Science Cmte. 1997–1999, agriculture legislative assistant, Rep. John Boehner, R-Ohio. 1999–2003, agriculture and interior appropriations legislative assistant, Sen. Mitch McConnell, R-Ky. 2003–2006, vice president, federal government affairs, Food Products Association. 2006–2008, tax and finance counsel, Sen. Kit Bond, R-Mo. 2008–present, executive assistant for the Sergeant at Arms, Senate Minority Leader Mitch McConnell, R-Ky.

Expertise: Management, agriculture policy, tax policy, law.

Mason Wiggins worked his way through the Republican ranks on both sides of the Capitol. But his current role is not a partisan one. As executive assistant to the Senate Sergeant at Arms, his job is to serve as the "eyes and ears" of Senate Minority Leader Mitch McConnell, R-Ky. The Senate Sergeant at Arms helps oversee the U.S. Capitol Police, but the jurisdiction extends far beyond law enforcement to Senate protocol and the Senate information systems.

Since there was no change in control of the Senate, the logistics of the Senate have been calm compared to the House. But with 13 new Republican senators starting up new offices, getting all their offices up and running is a task that will continue well into 2011. The Sergeant at Arms is responsible for telecommunications in both Capitol Hill offices and state offices.

"A lot of people don't realize that we handle the offices in the states," he said.

Telecommunications is among the mundane, but critical, support functions overseen by the Sergeant at Arms along with office equipment, parking, IDs, and recording studio access and many more. Wiggins is charged with acting as a liaison for Republican senators and ensuring they receive the appropriate consideration.

Wiggins also participates in myriad activities that keep the Senate running. On any given day, this could range from attending intelligence briefings to traveling with Senators to an off-campus event. He also participates as the Republican leader's representative on special projects, such as the Capitol Visitor Center.

Wiggins was appointed by McConnell in January 2008. He is responsible for ensuring that the services provided by the Sergeant at Arms meet the needs of the Republican Senate offices. Wiggins also provides input into policy decisions made by the Sergeant at Arms involving operational, security, and protocol matters.

SENATE LEADERSHIP

Lisa M. Wolski

Chief of Staff

Republican Whip Jon Kyl, R-Ariz.

S-208, The Capitol

Phone: (202) 224-2708

Fax: (202) 228-0034

Education: J.D., American University's Washington College of Law.

Professional: 1997, legislative aide, Rep. Jim Ramstad, R-Minn.. 2000–1997, tax practice group, Steptoe & Johnson, LLP. 2003–2000, tax counsel, International Mass Retail Association. 2003–2009, deputy chief of staff, policy director and tax counsel, Senate Republican Whip Jon Kyl, R-Ariz. 2009–present, chief of staff, Senate Republican Whip Jon Kyl, R-Ariz.

Expertise: Tax and economic policy.

There are few certainties in congressional work, but Lisa Wolski knows for certain she will not have her same job in the next congress.

Her boss, Sen. John Kyl, R-Ariz., started 2011 with the announcement that he would not seek another term in the 2012 election. "There's more to life than being a United States Senator," Kyl explained at the February announcement in Phoenix.

But Wolski said she does not feel like she is working for a "lame duck."

"He fully intends to be as fully involved as he is now right up to the last day," Wolski said. "It really hasn't changed anything that much."

For the Senate minority whip's office, "fully involved" means rounding up votes to block cloture on key votes and bridging the divide between centrist Republicans and conservative Republicans. Getting enough votes was made easier by the gains Senate Republicans made in the 2010 election. But some of those victories made the divide within the party even more stark.

Conservative Republicans balked at some of their leaders' plans earlier this year for negotiating a continuing resolution to settle spending issues for the rest of the fiscal year. And they proved more willing than centrists to brave the prospect of a government shutdown.

"We have to remember we all have the same goals," Wolski said. "Senator Kyl knows they're all reasonable."

Kyl named Wolski chief of staff in his leadership office in early March 2009. Prior to this role, she served as deputy chief of staff and policy director for the Senate's No. 2 Republican.

As Republican Whip, Kyl is in charge of the GOP's internal vote-counting operation, a function that is even more critical to the Republican caucus after the 2008 elections that gave the Democrats the Senate majority again as well as the White House.

Wolski began working for Kyl in 2003 as his tax counsel and also served as staff director for the Senate Finance Subcommittee on Taxation and IRS Oversight when Kyl was chairman.

Committee on Agriculture, Nutrition and Forestry

SR-328A Russell Senate Office Bldg.
Washington, DC 20510
Phone: (202) 224-2035
Fax: (202) 228-4576
http://ag.senate.gov

Ratio: 10/11

MAJORITY MEMBERS

Debbie Stabenow, MI, Chairman

Patrick J. Leahy, VT
Tom Harkin, IA
Kent Conrad, ND
Max Baucus, MT
E. Benjamin Nelson, NE
Sherrod Brown, OH
Robert Casey, PA
Amy Klobuchar, MN
Michael Bennet, CO
Kirsten Gillibrand, NY

MINORITY MEMBERS

Pat Roberts, KS, Ranking Member

Richard G. Lugar, IN
Thad Cochran, MS
Mitch McConnell, KY
Saxby Chambliss, GA
Mike Johanns, NE
John Boozman, AR
Charles Grassley, IA
John Thune, SD
John Hoeven, ND

SENATE AGRICULTURE, NUTRITION AND FORESTRY

JURISDICTION

(1) Agricultural economics and research.
(2) Agricultural extension services and experiment stations.
(3) Agricultural production, marketing, and stabilization of prices.
(4) Agriculture and agricultural commodities.
(5) Animal industry and diseases.
(6) Crop insurance and soil conservation.
(7) Farm credit and farm security.
(8) Food from fresh waters.
(9) Food stamp programs.
(10) Forestry, and forest reserves and wilderness areas other than those created from the public domain.
(11) Home economics.
(12) Human nutrition.
(13) Inspection of livestock, meat, and agricultural products.
(14) Pests and pesticides.
(15) Plant industry, soils, and agricultural engineering.
(16) Rural development, rural electrification, and watersheds.
(17) School nutrition programs.

Such committee shall also study and review, on a comprehensive basis, matters relating to food, nutrition, and hunger, both in the United States and in foreign countries, and rural affairs and report thereon from time to time.

SENATE AGRICULTURE, NUTRITION AND FORESTRY

Staff of the Senate Committee on Agriculture, Nutrition and Forestry will spend much of the coming months crafting the 2012 Farm Bill, a process that will take place under new leadership and what staffers expect to be tight budget constraints.

Sen. Debbie Stabenow, D-Mich., took over as chairwoman of the committee in January 2011 after previous chair Sen. Blanche Lincoln, D-Ark., was defeated by Arkansas Republican Sen. John Boozman.

Under pressure from a Republican-controlled House that's keen on slashing federal spending, Stabenow signaled early on as chair that she wants to focus on "principles, not programs." The junior senator from Michigan—who's up for what's expected to be a tough reelection fight in 2012—has signaled that some long-standing programs like crop insurance will be shoo-ins for the bill.

Stabenow wants the next Farm Bill—one of Congress' most comprehensive multi-year spending measures—to take a broad approach to agriculture policy that takes into account the greater role food producers are taking in the energy market through things like ethanol production. Other issues she's already highlighted and that are expected to be a significant part of the final legislation include an expansion of access to fresh foods in so-called "food deserts"—areas both urban and rural that have poor access to meats, produce, and dairy—and policies promoting better childhood nutrition.

The committee's tasks won't be easy. With both federal deficits and the bill's scope looming large, staffers are looking at how to best empower the U.S. Department of Agriculture and its agencies to efficiently implement policies.

They'll also have to grapple with legislative resistance to spending. Committee staffers say 37 programs from the previous 2008 Farm Bill stand to lose funding after Fiscal Year 2012, while President Obama's Deficit Reduction Commission has recommended $10 billion in cuts from existing agriculture mandates, meaning sweeping changes in farm policies could be on the horizon.

Some state farm bureaus are suggesting getting rid of subsidy payments going directly to food producers and putting a renewed focus on federally-backed insurance programs that could be cheaper in the long-run. Whether political winds have shifted enough to support such a bold shift in policy remains to be seen; however, Sen. Lincoln opposed and ended up stripping a proposal to cap annual subsidies at $250,000 per farm out of the 2008 Farm Bill after a heavy lobbying effort from industry groups.

SENATE AGRICULTURE, NUTRITION AND FORESTRY

Christopher John Adamo

Committee Staff Director

SR-328A Russell Senate Office Bldg.

Phone: (202) 224-0035

chris_adamo@ag.senate.gov

Personal: Born 03/07/1977 in Grosse Pointe Farms, Mich.

Education: J.D., Vermont Law School, 2004. B.S., Kalamazoo College, 1999.

Professional: 2005–2007, legal policy analyst, Joint Economic Committee. 2007–2011, legislative counsel, Sen. Debbie Stabenow, D-Mich. 2011–present, staff director, Sen. Cmte. on Agriculture, Nutrition and Forestry.

Expertise: Agriculture law, conservation, energy policy, ethanol.

Chris Adamo has a new job but is already familiar with his boss, Agriculture Committee Chairwoman Sen. Debbie Stabenow, D-Mich. After spending four years working as legislative counsel in the senator's personal office, she promoted him to lead her Agriculture Committee staff as its new staff director when she took the committee's gavel in January 2011.

Adamo is a Michigan native who grew up in the northeastern suburbs of Detroit where the auto manufacturing plants of the Motor City's suburbs start fading into farmland. He was raised around the micro economies that the committee he now works for will influence heavily during the 112th Congress as work on the 2012 Farm Bill moves forward.

In Stabenow's personal office, Adamo worked on "the Senator's top-line priorities," which included the previous 2008 Farm Bill. Adamo focused on the bill's agriculture, conservation, and renewable energy provisions, as well as energy legislation outside of the Farm Bill's auspices, notably bills dealing with tax credits and retooling loans for manufacturers dedicated to creating renewable energy and battery-powered vehicles.

In his new role as staff director, Adamo is responsible for leading the Democrats' committee worker bees in a carefully-coordinated dance of crafting one of Congress's largest spending bills, one that affects every state in the union and business of every size and stripe, from tiny family farms to agribusiness behemoths.

Among his biggest challenges will be coordinating not only the legislative ends of the committee's work—using his well-established connections on the Hill to achieve Stabenow's lawmaking goals—but also ensuring his staff is communicating the right message both internally and externally as well.

Though Adamo enjoys working for a senator from his home state of Michigan—where he still holds four standing men's soccer records from his years at Kalamazoo College on the western side of the state—he attended law school in Vermont and passed the bar in Montana, where he used to travel occasionally for business when he worked as a legal policy analyst for the Joint Economic Committee before joining Stabenow's office.

SENATE AGRICULTURE, NUTRITION AND FORESTRY

Ben Becker

Communications Director

SR328-A Russell Senate Office Bldg.

Phone: (202) 224-5466

ben_becker@ag.senate.gov

Personal: Born in Calif.

Education: M.A., The George Washington Univesity, 2007. B.A., University of California - Fullerton, 2004.

Professional: 2004–2005, reporter, Los Angeles Newspaper Group/MediaNews Group. 2006–2007, account executive, Susan Davis International. 2007–2008, associate director, Dittus Communications. 2008–2010, senior associate, The Glover Park Group. 2010–present, press secretary, Senate Cmte. on Agriculture, Nutrition and Forestry.

Expertise: Communications, media relations.

As communications director for the Democrats, Ben Becker is responsible for effectively managing the majority's messaging on agriculture, sustainability, and biofuel policies while also strategizing media approaches as the 2012 Farm Bill gains more attention from reporters.

Becker was brought in under former chairwoman Sen. Blanche Lincoln, D-Ark., and was kept on by the new chair, Sen. Debbie Stabenow, D-Mich., to help craft her message of doing more with the 2012 Farm Bill under the watch—and intense political pressure—of Republican budget hawks on Capitol Hill.

With Stabenow looking to expand the scope of the bill, Becker is responsible for communicating the Agriculture Committee's Democrats' message to a wide variety of media, including big national newspapers and broadcast outlets, regional reporters following specific senators on the committee, wire service reporters dashing in for hearings and mark-ups, and a host of specialized trade publications that drill down into the deep minutiae of agriculture policy—"a healthy mix," Becker said.

Becker spends most of his time on the Hill overseeing the media operations for Democrats on the committee, checking schedules and preparing notices for reporters and cameramen to let them know what's happening where and when. He also is usually the first point of contact for media who want to write about the committee, fielding their questions and getting them what they need.

His busiest days are usually when the committee is holding a hearing or markup, when media interest in the committee is intense. On those days, his job is largely logistical; he and his assistants have to figure out how to best squeeze an information-hungry pack of reporters into one of the Senate's smallest and most antiquated hearing rooms.

Becker also frequently proactively reaches out to media, giving them a heads up on legislative twists and turns and pitching stories to them on how the committee's work will be affecting key constituencies across the country.

And because Stabenow is up for a tough reelection fight in 2012, Becker also interfaces with her personal office quite often, giving her communications staff the information they need on her work chairing the committee so they can communicate her agriculture message back in Michigan.

SENATE AGRICULTURE, NUTRITION AND FORESTRY

Jonathan William Coppess

Chief Counsel

SR-328A Russell Senate Office Bldg.

Phone: (202) 224-0035

jonathan_coppess@ag.senate.gov

Personal: Born 02/05/1974 in Ansonia, Ohio.

Education: J.D., George Washington University Law School, 2001. B.S., Miami University (Ohio).

Professional: 2001–2006, Counsel, Freeborn and Peters, LLP. 2006–2009, legislative assistant, Sen. Ben Nelson, D-Neb. 2009–2011, administrator, Farm Service Agency. 2009, deputy administrator for farm programs, Farm Service Agency. 2011–present, chief counsel, Sen. Cmte. on Agriculture, Nutrition and Forestry.

Expertise: Commodity markets, energy policy, biofuel, agriculture law.

Jonathan Coppess returned to work on Capitol Hill for the Senate Committee on Agriculture, Nutrition and Forestry in early 2011 after spending two years as a top administrator for the Farm Service Agency, a position that put him front and center before the people who make the country's agriculture industry run.

Coppess' work at the agency tasked him with implementing many of the agriculture policies and priorities laid out under the 2008 Farm Bill, signed as President Bush was preparing to leave office. That bill included far more reaching policies than seen in previous farm bills—pushing increasingly into areas of conservation, better land management, and biofuels—that are expected to be a central part of the committee's work as member craft the 2012 Farm Bill.

Now back to his old stomping grounds under a new administration—but one he's already familiar with, given his appointment to the FSA administrator job—and a split Congress, Coppess will be returning to the work of shaping the 2012 Farm Bill, drawing on his experience as a commodities trader, lawyer, top Senate aide and farmer.

As the committee's chief attorney, Coppess will be responsible for leading the crafting of new agriculture legislation and policies while that will be able to pass the muster of a Republican-led House, where many new members have focused intensely on proving the Constitutional authority granted to Congress for new laws, while also looking to expand the laws' scope "since energy is playing a much larger role than ever before," he said.

Coppess' return to the Hill comes after a career touching the many aspects the new 2012 Farm Bill is expected to affect.

After growing up on a seventh-generation soybean and corn farm in far western Ohio, Coppess received his undergraduate degree in business and worked as a grain merchandiser for agriculture giant Archer Daniels Midland, delving deeply into the commodities market at the Chicago Board of Trade. After his stint there, he attended law school in Washington and shifted his focus toward agriculture policy.

He previously worked with former committee member Sen. Ben Nelson, D-Neb., advising the senior senator on farming, trade, and energy issues.

SENATE AGRICULTURE, NUTRITION AND FORESTRY

Bill Imbergamo

Professional Staff Member

328-A Russell Senate Bldg.

Phone: (202) 224-0035

Bill.Imbergamo@mail.house.gov

Personal: Born 12/31/1965 in Queens, N.Y.

Education: B.A., State University of New York at Plattsburgh, 1989.

Professional: 1991–1996, legislative asst., National Association of State Foresters. 1996–2001, executive dir., National Association of State Foresters. 2001–2003, dir. of congressional affairs, American Forest and Paper Association. 2003–2009, professional staff member, House Cmte. on Agriculture. 2010–present, senior professional staff member, Senate Cmte. on Agriculture, Nutrition and Forestry.

Expertise: Forestry, forest products.

Bill Imbergamo spent seven years pushing the House Agriculture Committee to more seriously consider forestry policy as part of its overall jurisdiction. Now that his former boss Rep. Bob Goodlatte, D-Va., has stepped back to vice chair of the committee, Imbergamo is bringing his forestry expertise over to the Senate's Agriculture staff.

Imbergamo spent much of his time on the House committee's staff working on forestry provisions in the 2008 Farm Bill, particularly those related to the U.S. Forest Service, the U.S. Department of Agriculture agency tasked with managing and protecting more than 193 million acres of forest and other open land swaths in the United States.

His forestry policy work is made more difficult by the growing diversity of interests represented by Congress' farm bills. The 2012 bill Imbergamo and his colleagues are currently working on will stretch finite federal fiscal resources even further before combining traditional commodity crop interests with broader scope over childhood nutrition programs and renewable fuel and energy sources.

But the bill is also expected to further shape the U.S. forestry products industry, which is under increasing foreign competition from Canada and elsewhere, "creating a very tough environment for U.S. producers," said Imbergamo, who began work on Capitol Hill after spending two years as director of congressional affairs for the American Forest and Paper Association.

Imbergamo also will work on legislation related to the Forest Service's firefighting program that he started when working for the House committee, following up on an early major Congressional achievement as a key aide working on President Bush's "Healthy Forests" legislation, which was signed, became law in 2003, and authorized the thinning of up to 20 million acres of national forest with the aim of preventing wildfires.

SENATE AGRICULTURE, NUTRITION AND FORESTRY

Tina M. May

Senior Professional Staff

SR-328A Russell Senate Office Bldg.

Phone: (202) 224-0035

tina_may@ag.senate.gov

Personal: Born 07/07/1982 in Staceyville, Iowa.

Education: M.S., City University of London. B.A., University of Minnesota.

Professional: 2005, merchandiser assistant/logistics coordinator, The Scoular Company. 2006–2007, program assistant, Sustainable Agricultue Coalition. 2007–2009, professional staff member, Sen. Cmte. on Agriculture, Nutrition and Forestry. 2009–2011, legislative director/congressional relations, U.S. Department of Agriculture. 2011–present, senior professional staff, Sen. Cmte on Agriculture, Nutrition and Forestry.

Expertise: Conservation, energy, sustainability.

Tina May grew up on a small family farm in tiny Staceyville, Iowa, the kind of picture postcard-worthy setting representing the old days of American agriculture.

But after leaving home to study at the University of Minnesota—and eventually at the City University of London in the United Kingdom—May has since worked across the spectrum of the modern food supply system, touching upon commodities buying and merchandising, sustainability, and conservation issues.

May returned to work on Capitol Hill in spring 2011 after working as a legislative director for the U.S. Department of Agriculture, where she helped identify the department's needs and priorities for new legislation from both the U.S. House and Senate, and worked with her colleagues in government relations to influence new laws affecting the department and its various agencies.

Before that, May worked on her first stint with the Senate Agriculture Committee under former chair Sen. Tom Harkin, D-Iowa, helping to draft the 2008 Farm Bill. On that legislation, she specialized in conservation and energy issues in the bill. She was specifically responsible for helping craft some of its provisions that expanded the bill's scope—and the Department of Agriculture's power—to influence and grow the emerging biofuels market, which Democrats had set as a priority for the bill.

Back on the committee for the 112th Congress just in time for work on the new 2012 Farm Bill, May's focus will once again turn to conservation, but also the issues affecting small farms like the one she grew up on.

Fulfilling one the Chairwoman Debbie Stabenow's, D-Mich., goals of maintaining safety net supports for small farmers will be one of May's top priorities, particularly as pressure to curb or cut direct farm subsidies grows because of concern over the ballooning federal deficit. But May also will be looking at ways to help small growers maintain and even expand the diversity of crops grown on their farms, which has emerged as a key theme for the upcoming legislation in 2011.

SENATE AGRICULTURE, NUTRITION AND FORESTRY

Stephanie Mercier

Majority Chief Economist

328-A Russell Senate Office Bldg.

Phone: (202) 224-0035

stephanie_mercier@ag.senate.gov

Personal: Born 02/26/1961 in Iowa City, Iowa.

Education: A.B., Washington University (St. Louis), 1983. Ph.D., Iowa State University, 1988.

Professional: 1988–97, team leader, Economic Research Service, U.S. Dept. of Agriculture. 1997–present, chief economist, Senate Cmte. on Agriculture, Nutrition and Forestry, Democrats.

Expertise: Domestic and agriculture trade policy, farm programs, crop insurance.

As majority chief economist for the Senate Committee on Agriculture, Nutrition and Forestry, Stephanie Mercier will work on the 2012 Farm Bill during the 112th Congress, a bill with more moving parts and broader economic ties than its predecessors.

With the bill expected to address a broader range of issues than the committee's 2008 legislation amid calls for a leaner federal budget, Mercier will need to delve into the number crunching far beyond the usual crop subsidies and insurance programs by also investigating the fiscal fallout on food and commodities markets as federal mandates for ethanol ramp up.

Mercier's background in agriculture trade policy could be called upon as Congress contemplates passage of a growing number of free trade agreements, potentially opening the door for American food growers and processors to sell products to an increasingly global audience while introducing more competition for domestic businesses.

Mercier also will be at the center of the conversation on how to best renew the federally subsidized insurance programs. That's an area Chairwoman Debbie Stabenow, D-Mich., has indicated lawmakers will fight to preserve in the Farm Bill, despite budget cuts.

The 2008 Farm Bill significantly reduced "subsidies to insurance companies for selling and servicing crop insurance policies," the U.S. Department of Agriculture noted after the bill's implementation, at the same time increasing administrative fees farmers pay for the minimum insurance coverage level.

Like several of her colleagues, Mercier was born in Iowa. She earned her bachelor's at Washington University in 1983 and graduated with a Ph.D. in agricultural economics at Iowa State University in 1988. Mercier worked for nine years at the Economic Research Service within USDA before joining the committee in 1997.

SENATE AGRICULTURE, NUTRITION AND FORESTRY

Todd Alan Wooten

Senior Counsel

SR-328A Russell Senate Office Bldg.

Phone: (202) 202-224-0014

todd_wooten@ag.senate.gov

Personal: Born 12/11/1976 in Fort Smith, Ark.

Education: B.S., Hendrix College.

Professional: 2003–2005, legislative assistant, Sen. Blanche Lincoln, D-Ark. 2005–2008, legislative assistant/Judiciary Counsel, Sen. Blanche Lincoln, D-Ark. 2008–2009, senior director of government issues, Van Ness Feldman. 2009–2011, director, Southeast Climate Resources Center at Nicholas Institute for Environmental Policy Solutions at Duke University. 2011–present, senior counsel, Sen. Cmte. on Agriculture, Nutrition and Forestry.

Expertise: Sustainability, climate policy, carbon/cap-and-trade.

Todd Wooten started working with former Sen. Blanche Lincoln, D-Ark., before the recently-defeated Democrat took the reins as chair of the Senate Committee on Agriculture, Nutrition and Forestry. He eventually ascended with her to work on the committee as judiciary counsel on the 2008 Farm Bill and oversight of the U.S. Department of Agriculture.

Wooten left the committee to work for a stint as a lobbyist at the Washington-based firm Van Ness Feldman. There he worked with a wide-range of clients specifically on carbon market issues, connecting them to lawmakers on Capitol Hill he had previously worked alongside.

But after the crush of cap-and-trade legislation from the public discourse shortly after President Obama shifted focus more toward health reform legislation, Wooten took a new career tack, landing as director of the New Southeast Climate Resources Center at Duke University's Nicholas Institute for Environmental Policy Solutions. There, he spearheaded an effort to work on climate change issues with local and state governments throughout the Southeast United States, offering them advice for devising and implementing policies for environmental cleanup and sustainable practices, both in farming and in non-agricultural business pursuits.

Now back on Capitol Hill, Wooten will continue his policy-making, drawing again on his early experiences working for Sen. Lincoln. His portfolio specifically will include biofuels issues, touching not only the Agriculture Committee, but the Energy and Natural Resources and Finance committees as well.

He'll be reviewing biofuels policies and what roles various agencies—including in the USDA—will play in expanding ethanol's use throughout the U.S., while trying to minimize the impact the fuel's expanded use will have on food prices in the world's commodity markets.

When Wooten isn't tending to his legislative and policy work for the committee and its senators, he's playing on the field for the Rampage Soccer Club, an adult competitive recreational team that plays in the Northern Virginia Soccer League and raises money for United for D.C., a charitable arm of D.C. United, Washington's professional soccer squad.

Committee on Appropriations

S-131, The Capitol

Washington, DC 20510

Phone: (202) 224-7363

http://appropriations.senate.gov

Ratio: 26/20

MAJORITY MEMBERS

Daniel K. Inouye, HI, Chairman

Patrick J. Leahy, VT
Tom Harkin, IA
Barbara A. Mikulski, MD
Herbert Kohl, WI
Patty Murray, WA
Dianne Feinstein, CA
Richard J. Durbin, IL
Tim Johnson, SD
Mary L. Landrieu, LA
Jack Reed, RI
Frank R. Lautenberg, NJ
Ben Nelson, NE
Mark Pryor, AR
Jon Tester, MT
Sherrod Brown, OH

MINORITY MEMBERS

Thad Cochran, MS, Ranking Member

Mitch McConnell, KY
Richard C. Shelby, AL
Kay Bailey Hutchison, TX
Lamar Alexander, TN
Susan Collins, ME
Lisa Murkowski, AK
Lindsey Graham, SC
Mark Kirk, IL
Roy Blunt, MO
Dan Coats, IN
Jerry Moran, KS
John Hoeven, NE
Ron Johnson, WI

SENATE APPROPRIATIONS

JURISDICTION

(1) Appropriation of the revenue for the support of the government, except as provided in subparagraph(s).
(2) Rescission of appropriation contained in appropriation acts (referred to in section 105 of title 1, United States Code).
(3) The amount of new spending authority described in section 401(c)(2) (A) and (B) of the Congressional Budget Act of 1974, which is to be effective for a fiscal year.
(4) New spending authority described in section 401(c)(2)(C) of the Congressional Budget Act of 1974 provided in bills and resolution referred to the committee under section 401(b)(2) of that act (but subject to the provision of section 401(b)(3) of that act).

SENATE APPROPRIATIONS

After watching the disintegration last year of the appropriations measures he oversees and then the collapse of an omnibus spending bill in the face of Republican maneuvers, Senate Appropriations Committee Chairman Daniel K. Inouye, D-Hawaii made a prescient statement to his hometown paper.

"Nothing good comes from a C.R.,"Inouye warned Honolulu Star-Advertiser. And indeed, the continuing resolution that Congress passed in late 2010 became a political stick of dynamite that, with a divided House and Senate, threatened to explode throughout the first several months of the 112th Congress.

The ever-continuing continuing resolution—which at several points raised fears of a government shut-down—consumed much of the early part of the year for the senate appropriations panel. With House Republicans vowing to cut as much as $61 billion from the remainder of FY11, Inouye countered with a version slashing $6.5 billion.

The Senate rejected that offer and as of late March—the period when the appropriations panel ought to have been deeply involved in developing a spending plan for FY12, lawmakers were still battling over the previous year's appropriations. And with each stop-gap spending measure, Inouye decried the process of continual cuts to federal agencies.

"How much more can we cut before we have no funds to pay employees to monitor our borders and ports?" he asked. "How much more before we have to cancel the construction of dams, bridges, highways, levees, sewers and transit projects and throw thousands of private sector workers onto the street?"

And that isn't the only difficulty facing the panel this year. In late 2010, the Senate agreed to ban earmarks—long cherished by Inouye—from the bill. The chairman agreed to the ban, but warned it would have painful repercussions for communities.

"The reality," Inouye told The Hill, "is that critical needs in communities throughout the country will be neglected: roads and bridges in disrepair, job training programs shuttered, and vital resources for national defense and law enforcement cut off, to name just a few."

Inouye took the helm of the appropriations committee after the late-Sen. Robert Byrd, D-W. Va., stepped down from the post just two years before he died. The 112th Congress saw a few internal changes on the panel—with Sen. Dianne Feinstein, D-Calif., shifting from leading the Interior subcommittee to one that oversees energy and water spending; Sen. Jack Reed, D-R.I., swapping with Feinstein to relinquish the energy and water panel to head Interior; and Sen. Mary Landrieu taking over the subcommittee over Homeland Security appropriations.

Meanwhile, even as the partisan rancor over spending grows, lawmakers on both sides of the aisle insist that the era of omnibus spending measures and continuing resolutions should be coming to an end.

SENATE APPROPRIATIONS

Carolyn E. Apostolou

Republican Clerk

Subcommittee on Energy and Water Development

S-146A, The Capitol

Phone: (202) 224-7363

Fax: (202) 228-0248

carrie_apostolou@appro.senate.gov

Education: B.S., Wake Forest University, 1985.

Professional: 1987–2001, professional staff member, Subc. on Veterans' Affairs, Housing and Urban Development, and Independent Agencies, Senate Cmte. on Appropriations. 2001–2010, clerk, Subc. on the Legislative Branch, Senate Cmte. on Appropriations. 2010–present, clerk, Subc. on Energy and Water Development, Senate Cmte. on Appropriations.

Expertise: Energy and water.

After nearly 10 years helping to oversee the funding of all Capitol Hill functions working for the Subcommittee on the Legislative Branch, Carolyn Apostolou has moved over to the Energy and Water Development Subcommittee where she oversees spending proposals for everything from nuclear waste disposal to the Corps of Engineers.

"It's been great to have a new portfolio of issues," Apostolou said.

Lawmakers will pay close attention to nuclear weapons activities in the 112th Congress, which Apostolou noted, is the one spending area that actually was approved in 2010.

"It's a huge area of interest huge area of interest and focus, and I think that will be certain to be an area of focus in coming years," she said.

While Congress never completed the FY11 spending bill—leading to a showdown between the Republican-led House and the Democrat-controlled Senate in early 2011—$7.8 billion did get through to modernize the U.S. nuclear weapons complex. Apostolou noted that the funding was tied to ratification of the Strategic Arms Reduction Treaty (START) and the nuclear posture review, and represented a 10 percent increase over the previous year.

Also in 2011, Apostolou will help oversee the Energy Department's approximately $5 billion science budget, $5 billion environmental cleanup budget, and a loan guarantee program for wind and solar energy. One major challenge, she said, will be the Army Corps of Engineers, which is funded largely through earmarks.

"How do you fund the Corps in an era of earmark moratorium, at least on the Republican side?" she said.

Apostolou began her Senate career in the VA-HUD Appropriations Subcommittee and then worked on Subcommittee on the Legislative Branch before moving to her new position in 2010.

SENATE APPROPRIATIONS

Dennis Balkham

Minority Clerk

Subcommittee on Military Construction, Veterans Affairs, and Related Agencies

Phone: (202) 224-4092

Dennis_Balkham@appro.senate.gov

Personal: Born 05/17/1953 in San Bernardino, Calif.

Education: B.A., political science, The Citadel, 1975. M.A., government and international relations, University of South Carolina, 1977. M.A., national security, Naval War College, 1993.

Professional: 1997–2003, director of Project Management Office, United States Courts. 2003–2005, professional staff member, Subc. on Commerce, Justice, and the State Dept., Senate Cmte. on Appropriations. 2005–present, Republican clerk, Subc. on Military Construction, Veterans Affairs, and Related Agencies, Senate Cmte. on Appropriations.

Expertise: Military construction.

U.S. military bases overseas has been—and will continue to be—a top priority for Dennis Balkham, even as the Senate Appropriations Subcommittee on Military Construction and Veterans Affairs panel he clerks moves under new leadership.

As the Secretary of Defense makes decisions on where troops will be stationed in the world, the appropriations panel will make its own decisions about what size construction budget will be needed to support U.S. troops. Secretary Robert Gates in January acknowledged excess force structure and proposed significant reductions as part of a $100 billion defense budget trim over five years.

That's a move former ranking Republican Sen. Kay Bailey Hutchison of Texas supported before she relinquished her top spot to become the ranking member on overseeing Justice Department funding. In February freshman Sen. Mark Kirk, R-Ill., was named ranking member.

"That's a huge issue that we're working on," Balkham said. In 2010 year, he noted, the committee, on a bipartisan basis, approved a Hutchison amendment that would cut $1 billion in overseas military construction funding, mostly in Germany, until the Secretary of Defense decides that it is part of a long term strategic plan. That issue, Balkham said, will "absolutely" be a central issue again in 2011.

Balkham is a decorated U.S. Air Force veteran of the Persian Gulf War who has worked on Capitol Hill since 2003. While still in the Air Force he served as the service's budget liaison to the Senate Appropriations Committee. He was also on Gen. Colin Powell's staff when Powell was Joint Chiefs of Staff chairman, serving as legislative assistant.

Prior to coming to Capitol Hill, Balkham served as the director of the project management office in the Administrative Office of the U.S. Courts.

SENATE APPROPRIATIONS

Gabrielle Batkin

Majority Staff Director, Subcommittee on Commerce, Justice, Science, and Related Agencies

Subcommittee on Commerce, Justice, Science, and Related Agencies

S-131, The Capitol

Phone: (202) 224-7363

Gabrielle_Batkin@appro.senate.gov

Personal: Born 05/29/1972 in Van Nuys, Calif.

Education: B.A., Bradley University, 1994. M.A., George Washington University, 1997.

Professional: 1995–1999, legislative correspondent; special projects asst., Sen. Frank Lautenberg, D-N.J. 1999, legislative asst., Rep. Frank Pallone, D-N.J. 2000, budget analyst, Senate Cmte. on Budget. 2001–2007, professional staff member, Senate Cmte. on Appropriations. 2007–present, majority staff director, Subc. on Commerce, Justice, Science, and Related Agencies, Senate Cmte. on Appropriations.

Expertise: Budget.

The 112th Congress began with a politically-fraught budget fight. Despite the federal fiscal uncertainty, Gabrielle Batkin said the issues for the Subcommittee on Commerce, Justice, Science and Related Agencies that she oversees remains largely the same.

Batkin, who has served as the subcommittee's staff director since 2007, said Chairwoman Barbara Mikulski, D-Md., is "very consistent about her priorities." As in years past, the panel's 2011 priorities will include the growing innovation economy and cyber security.

While the FY11 appropriations measure never fully passed—leading to the showdown in early 2011 over a continuing resolution—Batkin said her subcommittee successfully provided needed resources for the FBI, ATF and U.S. Marshall services. The agencies, she said, have a dual mission of protecting Americans abroad and at home and need to be funded appropriately.

"I think we put together a bill that really did that," she said.

The measure also included support for the Adam Walsh Child Protection and Safety Act, which Batkin said "makes me feel good as a mother, working on something that really matters." Of seeing that funding delayed because of Congress' budget fight, she said, "That's a big disappointment that we weren't able to make that a reality."

Batkin also is responsible for advising Democratic members on funding and policies related to the National Aeronautics and Space Administration (NASA) and the National Science Foundation (NSF). She has worked on the appropriations committee since 2001. Before that she served on the Senate Budget Committee and for various New Jersey lawmakers.

Batkin grew up in many places, including Pennsylvania, Malaysia, and Egypt, but considers Hamburg, N.J. home. She has a master's degree in international affairs and had studied French and international studies at Bradley University in Illinois.

SENATE APPROPRIATIONS

Rob W. Blumenthal

Communications Director

S-128, The Capitol

Phone: (202) 224-7363

Rob_Blumenthal@appro.senate.gov

Personal: Born in Washington, D.C.

Education: B.A., Macalester College (St. Paul, Minn.).

Professional: 1995–1997, account executive, Young & Associates, Rockville, Md. 1997–2000, marketing coordinator, the Americas, ICO Global Communications, Washington, D.C. 2000, manager, Corporate Communications and Business Development, The Americas, Spotcast Communications, Inc., Silver Spring, Md. 2001–2006, senior director/senior advisor, Projects and Research, CompassRose International, Washington, D.C. 2006–2007 , director communications, INDUS Corporation. 2008, communications directr, Senate Cmte. on Commerce, Science and Transportation. 2009–present, communications director, Senate Cmte. on Appropriations.

Expertise: Corporate communications, marketing, international and satellite telecommunications issues.

Senate Appropriations Committee Communications Director Rob Blumenthal has his work cut out for him in the 112th Congress as lawmakers sought to close a contentious partisan gap on fiscal year 2011 spending while simultaneously addressing the federal budget for fiscal year 2012.

Congress' failure to approve appropriations measures in 2010 coupled with House GOP gains in the November elections sparked a fierce budget battle early on in 2011. The House passed a continuing resolution slashing $61 billion from the budget -- and one of Blumenthal's first orders of business was to issue a press release on behalf of Chairman Daniel K. Inouye, D-Hawaii blasting the cuts.

"It is clear from this proposal that House Republicans are committed to pursuing an ineffective approach to deficit reduction that attempts to balance the budget on the back of domestic discretionary investments," Inouye said in a release.

Meanwhile, Blumenthal—an aide to Inouye since 2008 with a background in corporate communications—tiptoed carefully around Defense Secretary Robert Gates' vow to seek $78 billion in Pentagon cuts over the next five years. Blumenthal told The Hill newspaper that Inouye "was generally in agreement with the secretary's proposal recognizing that we need to find ways to increase efficiency in all areas of government spending. However, the devil is in the details."

By mid-March Congress still had not finalized FY11 spending, complicating efforts to hold hearings and begin work on President Obama's proposed FY12 budget.

Blumenthal has worked in communications more than 15 years, with a particular focus on technology, telecommunications and Internet regulatory affairs. He served as communications director for federal information technology provider INDUS Corp. and also for ICO Global Communications and CompassRose International before coming to Capitol Hill.

SENATE APPROPRIATIONS

Dale Cabaniss

Republican staff director

Subcommittee on Labor, Health and Human Services, Education, and Related Agencies

142 Dirksen Senate Office Bldg.

Phone: (202) 224-3664

Fax: (202) 228-0248

dale_cabaniss@appro.senate.gov

Personal: Born in Atlanta, Ga.

Education: B.A., English, The University of Georgia, 1983. J.D., The Catholic University of America, Columbus School of Law, 1993.

Professional: 1993–1995, counsel, Cmte. on Governmental Affairs. 1995–1997, professional staff, Subc. on Labor, HHS and Related Agencies, Senate Cmte. on Appropriations. 1997–2001, member, Federal Labor Relations Authority. 2001–2008, Chairwoman, Federal Labor Relations Authority. 2008–2010, Republican clerk, Subc. on Labor, HHS and Related Agencies, Senate Cmte. on Appropriations. Jan. 2010–present, Republican staff director, Subc. on Financial Services and General Government, Senate Cmte. on Appropriations.

Expertise: Financial services.

Dale Cabaniss returned recently to the Senate Appropriations subcommittee she served more than a decade earlier, handing issues ranging from the federal tax code to the Securities and Exchange Commission.

As Republican clerk for the Subcommittee on Financial Services and General Government, Cabaniss said the issues she handles overlap extensively with ones on which she worked when she served in the early 1990s on Government Affairs Committee, which is the authorizing panel for a number of the agencies included in the financial services bill.

"A lot of the issues are government-wide," Cabaniss said.

In addition to overseeing funding for the SEC, the panel oversees spending for the IRS and the U.S. Commodities Futures Trading Commission (CFTC).

In the 111th Congress Cabaniss said a key part of her work involved funding agencies that have jurisdiction in implementing the so-called Dodd-Frank Wall Street Reform and Consumer Protection Act. As part of the measure, the CFTC is charged with writing rules to regulate the swap marketplace. Cabaniss said that as well as funding for agencies responsible for implementing the Democrats' health care reform bill will also top her agenda in the 112th Congress.

"I think those issues will still be the most significant ones," she said.

Cabaniss began her career on Capitol Hill in the 1980s in the office of former Sen. Frank Murkowski, R-Alaska. She served on both the later served on the labor subcommtitee on Senate Appropriations, but left in 1993 to work with the Federal Labor Relations Authority, an independent agency responsible for administering the labor-management relations program for 1.9 million non-postal Federal employees world-wide.

There she served as a member before being tapped to chair the agency in 2001. Testifying as part of Cabaniss' second confirmation hearing, the late former Senate Appropriations Committee Chairman Ted Stevens, R-Alaska, noted that her husband served as his chief of staff and their families are close.

Stevens called Cabaniss "an advocate of an effective bipartisan voice on civil service on public and private sector labor issues," and said she has earned a reputation as a "fair and balanced arbitrator" of the board's 1,000-plus annually adjudicated cases.

SENATE APPROPRIATIONS

Douglas Clapp

Clerk

Subcommittee on Energy and Water Development

S-131, The Capitol

Phone: (202) 224-8119

Personal: Born in Tacoma, Wash.

Education: J.D., American University. B.A., University of Washington.

Professional: 1993–2004, aide, legislative assistant, Rep. Mike Kreidler, D-Wash., Sen. Patty Murray, D-Wash. 2005–2007, lobbyist, Gov. Chris Gregoire, D-Wash. 2007–present, clerk, Subc. on Energy and Water Development, Senate Cmte. on Appropriations.

Expertise: Nuclear waste cleanup, energy, dams and irrigation.

With the fiscal year 2012 budget process sent into a tailspin by Congress' failure to finish a fiscal year 2011 measure, Douglas Clapp is, like the rest of his colleagues on the Senate Committee on Appropriations, in the unenviable position of working on two years worth of spending bills at one time.

Clapp, clerk of the Subcommittee on Energy and Water Development, spent the early months of 2011 examining the continuing resolution that House Republicans passed funding the government through 2011 but slashing more than $60 billion in programs.

"We are busily writing various provisions and examining the impact of the House vote," Clapp said.

Meanwhile, the panel is preparing for 2012 and in particular will focus on funding for the National Nuclear Security Administration, a semi-autonomous agency within the Department of Energy aimed at overseeing the country's the nuclear weapons program and related activities.

President Obama has requested $11.8 billion for NNSA, an increase of $1.9 billion (19 percent) more than the $9.9 billion enacted level for fiscal year 2010.

"It's very hard to accommodate those increases in a decreasing budget window. That's going to be a challenge," Clapp said.

A longtime energy expert, Clapp is a native of Tacoma, Wash., who started his Capitol Hill career working for former Rep. Mike Kreidler, a Washington state Democrat. He left to earn his law degree at American University before returning to the Hill to work for Sen. Patty Murray, D-Wash., as a legislative assistant on energy and natural resource issues and then later as a lobbyist for Gov. Chris Gregoire.

In that position Clapp dealt with issues like nuclear waste cleanup, energy, dams and irrigation, many of which routinely come before the subcommittee.

SENATE APPROPRIATIONS

Rebecca Davies

Republican Staff Director
Subcommittee on Homeland Security
142 Dirksen Senate Office Bldg.
Phone: (202) 224-4319
Rebecca_Davies@appro.senate.gov

Personal: Born in Md.

Professional: 1993–1994, Republican clerk, Subc. on Agriculture, Senate Cmte. on Appropriations. 1995–2003, Republican clerk, Subc. on Agriculture, Senate Cmte. on Appropriations. 2003–present, Republican clerk/staff director, Subc. on Homeland Security, Senate Cmte. on Appropriations.

Expertise: Appropriations.

Rebecca Davies serves a new chairman in 2011 in her position as clerk of the Senate Appropriations Homeland Security Subcommittee. Freshman Sen. Dan Coats, R-Ind., was tapped at the beginning of the 112th Congress to be the panel's top Republican and Davies, a longtime loyal aide to former ranking member Sen. Thad Cochran, R-Miss., will continue to help steer Coats' subcommittee staff.

Coats has called strengthening America's national security efforts one of his top priorities, and Davies will be responsible for helping fulfill her new boss' goal of "providing the necessary resources to protect America and improve its infrastructure while at the same time recognizing the economic challenges we face."

Funding for the Homeland Security Department is something with which the media-shy Davies is intimately familiar, having played a key role in establishing the agency. In a public appreciation speech some years ago, the now-deceased former Appropriations Committee chairman Sen. Ted Stevens, R-Alaska said he could probably "count on one finger the number of people who have knowledge of the federal budget process that Rebecca Davies carries in her head."

With Congress' failure to pass an FY11 spending bill came a bitter battle early this year over a continuing resolution (CR) to fund the government through the early months early 2012. Republicans passed a CR that cut $61 billion from the previous year, including many cuts that Homeland Security Secretary Janet Napolitano warned would hurt national security.

Coats, however, said the agency must deal with "fiscal realities," and make some "hard decisions."

Davies grew up in Maryland and started her Hill career under former Sen. Pete Domenici, R-N.M., at the Banking Committee and then moving over to Appropriations. She worked for several years on agriculture issues before joining the Homeland Security panel.

SENATE APPROPRIATIONS

Bruce M. Evans

Republican Staff Director

Phone: (202) 224-7363

Bruce_evans@appro.senate.gov

Personal: Born 08/21/1966 in Olympia, Wash.

Education: B.A., Yale University, 1987.

Professional: 1987–1989, research asst., Office of Congressional Affairs, U.S. Dept. of Commerce. 1989–1990, legislative asst., Sen. Frank Murkowski, R-Alaska. 1991–1995, legislative asst., Sen. Slade Gorton, R-Wash. 1995–1996, staff asst., Subc. on the Interior and Related Agencies, Senate Cmte. on Appropriations. 1997–2006, Republican clerk, Subc. on the Interior and Related Agencies, Senate Cmte. on Appropriations. 2006–2007, Republican staff director, Senate Cmte. on Energy and Natural Resources, Sen. Pete Domenici, R-N.M. 2007–present, Republican staff director, Senate Cmte. on Appropriations.

Expertise: Interior Department.

For the second year running, Senate Appropriations Committee Republican Staff Director Bruce Evans has made *Roll Call*'s "Fabulous 50" spotlighting the Hill's top staffers.

With high marks for mastery of policy and procedure as well as influence in driving the agenda and crafting legislation, Evans will have to put all those skills and more to work in the 112th Congress.

With several new Republican freshmen joining the panel in 2011, Evans' first order of business is internal, overseeing a growing and changing staff and shifting committee assignments.

Meanwhile, Evans helped coordinate Republican response to a pitched budget battle for the soul of federal spending. Evan's boss, Ranking Republican Sen. Thad Cochran of Mississippi lauded a House-passed measure slashing $61 billion from the fiscal year 2011 budget and broadly warned of fiscal austerity to come. Republican aides say they are gearing up for the challenge of funding the government in an era of looming deficits and a House Republican ban on earmarks.

That will likely be a particular problem for Cochran, a Senate leader in securing earmarks who has vigorously defended the practice and fought attempts to limit earmarks.

Evans has served on the committee since 1997, when former Sen. Pete Domenici, R-N.M., brought him over from the Senate Energy and Natural Resources Committee. Domenici at the time lauded Evan's experience in natural resources, energy and nuclear matters—a portfolio that has vastly expanded in the past decade. He took over as the committee's Republican staff director in 2007.

Evans enjoys skiing and is a father of three. His wife works as a lobbyist for Cassidy and Associates.

SENATE APPROPRIATIONS

Christina Evans

Democratic Clerk

Subcommittee on Military Construction, Veterans Affairs, and Related Agencies

125 Dirksen Senate Office Bldg.

Phone: (202) 224-3088

Fax: (202) 228-0280

christina_evans@appro.senate.gov

Personal: Born in Cincinnati, Ohio.

Education: B.A., University of Central Florida, 1972.

Professional: 1972–1978, reporter and editor, *Orlando (Fla.) Sentinel*. 1981–1984, asst. press secretary, Sen. Paula Hawkins, R-Fla. 1984–1992, press secretary, Sen. Robert C. Byrd, D-W.Va. 1997–1998, public affairs officer, Appalachian Regional Commission. 1998–present, Democratic clerk, Subc. on Military Construction, Veterans Affairs, and Related Agencies, Senate Cmte. on Appropriations.

Expertise: Communications, appropriations.

With more than a decade of experience on the Senate Appropriations Committee's military construction and veteran affairs panel, Christina Evans, a clerk for the Democrats is in the thick of 2011's budget battles.

The outset of the 112th Congress saw the subcommittee's chairman, Sen. Tim Johnson, D-S.D., blaming Republicans for the fiscal crisis as the Senate passed temporary spending measure after temporary measure to keep the government running while lawmakers battled over fiscal year 2011 spending.

Meanwhile, Evans is helping her boss deal with the problems FY11 funding delays have caused—including, according to defense experts, making an already challenging transition from a military to civilian lead in Iraq even more so. Deputy Defense Secretary William J. Lynn III warned at a hearing that a short-term funding bill would also hamper new military construction projects.

Evans helped draft the FY11 omnibus spending bill that never ultimately passed, leading to the impasse in the 112th Congress. Now, in 2011, she also will also help lead efforts to enact an FY12 appropriations bill for military construction as well as veterans' health care, military housing and Base Realignment and Closure Commission, or BRAC.

Johnson has long made increases for the Department of Veterans Affairs a priority, and in March was awarded the Congressional Award by the Veterans of Foreign Wars of the United States.

This year, Johnson's Republican counterpart is Freshman Sen. Mark Kirk, R-Ill., though Evans' GOP counterpart Dennis Balkham remains in his post.

SENATE APPROPRIATIONS

Erik Fatemi

Clerk

Subcommittee on Labor, Health and Human Services, Education, and Related Agencies

131 Dirksen Senate Office Bldg.

Phone: (202) 224-7415

erik_fatemi@appro.senate.gov

Personal: Born in Va..

Education: B.A., Princeton University, 1987.

Professional: 1997–2001, editor, Education Week. 2001–2010, professional staff member, Subc. on Labor, Health and Human Services, Education, and Related Agencies, Senate Cmte. on Appropriations. 2010–present, clerk, Subc. on Labor, Health and Human Services, Education, and Related Agencies, Senate Cmte. on Appropriations.

Expertise: K-12 education, NIH.

Erik Fatemi grew up around politics and always knew he wanted to work on Capitol Hill—but spent years several years as a newspaper reporter and editor first, specializing in education.

The delay was purposeful. As the grandson of the late Robert C. Byrd—a lion of the Senate and longtime chairman of the powerful Appropriations Committee who died last year at the age of 92, after serving more than five decades in Congress—Fatemi said he didn't want to be seen as riding on family coattails.

"I didn't want to come here before I had developed an expertise in something," said Fatemi, now the Democratic clerk of the Senate Appropriations Subcommittee on Labor, Health and Human Services, Education, and Related Agencies. "I didn't want it to be, 'Oh, that's Senator Byrd's grandson.'"

These days Fatemi is known in his own right as one the top Senate staffers on the issue of stem cell research. Having served on the subcommittee since 2001 as a professional staff member before rising to clerk, Fatemi said he worked for years to overturn President Bush's federal restrictions on embryonic stem cell research. Attending the White House ceremony where President Obama announced the executive order lifting them, Fatemi said, "was one of the highlights of my career in the Senate." Fatemi has been honored by several organizations, including the American Society of Hematology, for his work.

As clerk, Fatemi now oversees a staff of six people whose main responsibility is writing the annual health and education appropriations bill. The roughly $160 billion measure is the second largest spending bill after the Department of Defense. In the 112th Congress, with a Republican-led House, Fatemi said, the main debate will be about what role the federal government should play in providing core services to people in areas of education, health and labor.

Fatemi started his career as a local reporter at the Virginia-based Sun Gazette newspaper chain before becoming editor of Education Week. But growing up, he said, politics was ubiquitous.

At Byrd's funeral Fatemi told of 'Papa' Byrd quizzing him as a child about American history—and being rewarded with a quarter for correct answers. "I learned at an early age the awesome power of appropriations," he said.

Fatemi said while he misses the news business, he's glad to be working for issues he cares about. "I enjoy not having to be neutral," he said. "I enjoy being able to fight for something I believe in."

SENATE APPROPRIATIONS

Leif Fonnesbeck

Minority Clerk

Subcommittee on Interior, Environment, and Related Agencies

S-131, The Capitol

Phone: (202) 224-7233

leif_fonnesbeck@appro.senate.gov

Personal: Born 1966 in Anchorage, Alaska.

Education: B.S., finance, Georgetown University, 1989. J.D., University of Arizona, 1993.

Professional: 1993–1995, attorney, Perkins Coie. 1995–1998, attorney, Birch, Horton, Bittner and Cherot. 1998–2006, professional staff, Subc. on Interior, Environment, and Related Agencies, Senate Cmte. on Appropriations. 2006–2007, majority clerk, Subc. on Interior, Environment, and Related Agencies, Senate Cmte. on Appropriations. 2007–present, minority clerk, Subc. on Interior, Environment, and Related Agencies, Senate Cmte. on Appropriations.

Like most of his colleagues on the Senate Committee on Appropriations, Minority Clerk Leif Fonnesbeck said his Interior and Environment Subcommittee spent much of the beginning of 2011 in a holding pattern.

With a debate raging through March over a continuing resolution to keep the government running, Fonnesbeck said that as leadership fought over the top-level numbers, his subcommittee was busy addressing the policy decisions that House passed in hundreds of amendments to H.R.1.

For Fonnesbeck, that has in large part meant dealing with the more than one dozen amendments reining in the authority of the U.S. Environmental Protection Agency to regulate greenhouse gas emissions and other pollutants.

The subcommittee held its first hearing in March on the fiscal year 2012 Interior Department budget, though Fonnesbeck noted it had to be pushed back because Congress had not yet finished negotiations on the fiscal year 2011 spending bill.

"It has complicated things," he said, noting that agencies like the National Park Service and Forest Service do their seasonal hiring in the spring and still don't know how much money they have to spend. The panel's jurisdiction also includes the Bureau of Land Management and Fish and Wildlife Service.

Working under a new ranking member, Sen. Lisa Murkowski, R-Alaska, as well as dealing with a new chairman in Sen. Jack Reed, D-R.I., Fonnesbeck said energy and EPA authority will nevertheless remain top-tier issues.

The turmoil in the Middle East and rising oil prices also will be a priority, he predicted, saying, "We are going to have a lot of discussions about domestic oil production. On the Republican side there's a feeling that we're not where we need to be."

Fonnesbeck hails from Anchorage, Alaska, and has long worked on land issues in the West, starting as a professional staffer for the subcommittee in 1998.

SENATE APPROPRIATIONS

Galen Fountain

Democratic Clerk

Subcommittee on Agriculture, Rural Development, Food and Drug Administration, and Related Agencies

123 Hart Senate Office Bldg.

Phone: (202) 224-7202

Personal: Born 09/03/1951 in Hutchinson, Kans.

Education: B.A., Wichita State University, 1977. J.D., University of Arkansas Law School, 1989.

Professional: 1980–1984, district office manager, Rep. Dan Glickman, D-Kans. 1984–1990, district office manager, Rep. Beryl Anthony, D-Ark. 1990–1995, chief agriculture counsel, Senate Cmte. on Small Business. 1995–present, Democratic clerk, Subc. on Agriculture, Rural Development, and Related Agencies, Senate Cmte. on Appropriations.

Expertise: Agriculture, appropriations.

Looking for ways to cut federal spending without compromising food safety is a top priority for Agriculture Subcommittee Herb Kohl, D-Wis., and by extension for his top clerk, Galen Fountain.

Fountain, who helps Democrats lead the panel over agriculture, rural development, food and drug administration and related agencies, is a Kansas native with a background in farming. In his position on the Senate Appropriations Committee, which he has held since 1995, Fountain helps committee Democrats oversee and write the annual spending bill for farm, conservation and nutrition programs.

During the panel's first budget hearing in March, Kohl pressed Agriculture Secretary Vilsack over whether the agency can shoulder more cuts while still ensuring meat, poultry and other food safety. Meanwhile, the panel's new ranking Republican, Sen. Roy Blunt of Missouri, noted that in an era of fiscal hardship "we must show restraint, and everything must be on the table."

Fountain has worked on agricultural issues much of his career. He was a district office manager for Rep. Dan Glickman, D-Kan., before the congressman went on to serve as agriculture secretary under President Clinton and later head of the Motion Picture Association of America. From 1990 to 1995 Fountain was chief agriculture counsel for the Senate Committee on Small Business.

Fountain has a bachelor's degree from Wichita State University and earned his law degree from the University of Arkansas Law School. In 2009 he and a handful of other Hill staffers were given a "Friend of Wheat" award by the National Association of Wheat Growers for "superior action in support of the goals and policies of the wheat industry."

SENATE APPROPRIATIONS

Chris Gallegos

Communications Director

Chris_Gallegos@appro.senate.gov

Personal: Born in Artesia, N.Mex.

Education: B.A., communications/journalism, Eastern New Mexico University, 1985.

Professional: 1985–1988, staff writer, Rosewell (N.M.) Daily Record. 1988–2009, press secretary, Sen. Pete V. Domenici, R-N.M. 1988, Ford Foundation Fellow, White House Office of Public Liaison. 2009–present, communications director, Senate Cmte. on Appropriations.

Expertise: Communications.

Chris Gallegos is a veteran press secretary who has spent more than 20 years doing communications on Capitol Hill.

After working for a brief period as a journalist at the Roswell (N.M.) Daily Record, the New Mexico native came to Washington D.C. to join the staff of his state's senior senator, Republican Pete Domenici. In his 17 years with Domenici, Gallegos issued press releases on everything from scientific achievements and security scandals at Los Alamos National Laboratory to military base closings to one of the issues dearest to the senator's heart—the renaissance of the U.S. nuclear power industry.

Gallegos also dealt with the press scandals, such as the 2007 Justice Department firings that rocked the Bush administration. Domenici was among the Republicans accused of pressuring the Justice Department to purge its ranks of Democrat attorneys. He denied the accusations, but was criticized by two internal agency watchdog groups for not cooperating with the investigations. Throughout that period Gallegos was on the front lines addressing a barrage of news requests about the investigations.

When Domenici retired in 2009, Gallegos moved over to the office of Sen. Thad Cochran (R-Miss.), and also took the communications helm for Republicans on the Senate Appropriations Committee of which Cochran serves as ranking member. Gallegos said the transition was a natural one, having worked on appropriations issues with Domenici for nearly two decades.

"It kind of worked out nicely," Gallegos said.

After Congress failed to pass spending measures in 2010, a vicious partisan divide erupted over a continuing resolution funding the government through the early half of 2011. The issue consumed much of Gallegos' time in the early months of the 112th Congress. But as lawmakers move forward with President Obama's FY12 request, Gallegos said more serious issues will be on the horizon.

"The question will be how you move forward with appropriations in light of the focus on deficit spending and the crafting of bills in light of the ban on earmarks," he said.

While Congress has gotten into the habit of rolling all 12 appropriations measures into a giant omnibus spending bill, Gallegos said Cochran is going to push to ensure that ends.

"He has stated that he would like to see the process work well," Gallegos said. "He strongly believes the huge omnibus bills are not the way to go."

SENATE APPROPRIATIONS

Paul Grove

Minority Clerk

Sen. Judd Gregg, R-N.H. Subcommittee on State, Foreign Operations, and Related Programs

142 Dirksen Senate Office Bldg.

Phone: (202) 224-2104

Fax: (202) 228-1323

paul_grove@appro.senate.gov

Personal: Born 05/17/1965 in Washington, D.C.

Education: B.A., history, Bates College, 1988.

Professional: 1989–1994, legislative assistant, Sen. Mitch McConnell, R-Ky. 1994–2001, regional director for Asia and the Middle East, International Republican Institute. 2001–present, clerk, Subc. on State, Foreign Operations, and Related Programs, Senate Cmte. on Appropriations.

Expertise: Foreign affairs and development programs.

Paul Grove remains at the helm of the Senate Appropriations Subcommittee on State, Foreign Operations and Related Programs in 2011, though he now reports to a new boss in Chairman Lindsey Graham, R-S.C.

In his new position, Graham has said he will help fully finance a diplomatic approach to national security, telling Foreign Policy Magazine "If you don't want to use military force any more than you have to, count me in... State Department, USAID, all of these programs, in their own way, help win this struggle against radical Islam. The unsung heroes of this war are the State Department officials, the [Department of Justice] officials, and the agricultural people who are going out there."

It will be Grove's role to help Graham put his money where his sentiments lie, despite the Republican-led House attempts to crush State Department spending and foreign aid.

The political turmoil in the Middle East will be a top issue for the panel in the 112th Congress. Testifying before the subcommittee to defend her agency's $47 billion budget request for 2012, Secretary of State Hillary Clinton touted the work of U.S. diplomats at the U.N. in isolating Libya's leaders and USAID's work in delivering aid to Libya, Egypt and Tunisia. Meanwhile, she said, diplomacy is playing an ever-larger role in Iraq and Afghanistan as civilian controls replace U.S. troops.

Graham will be the third Republican under whom Grove has served since he joined the panel in 2001. He replaces former Sen. Judd Gregg, R-N.H., who focused on funding for global health initiatives and oversight of the Word Bank. Before that, Sen. Mitch McConnell, R-Ky., led the subcommittee.

Before joining the committee, Grove worked for seven years as the regional director for Asia and the Middle East at the International Republican Institute (IRI), a nonprofit group that promotes open elections.

SENATE APPROPRIATIONS

Stewart Holmes

Republican Clerk
Subcommittee on Defense
117 Dirksen Senate Office Bldg.
Phone: (202) 224-3378
stewart_holmes@appro.senate.gov

Education: B.A., political science, The Citadel, 1986. M.S., financial management, Naval Postgraduate School, 1994.

Professional: 1997–1998, Defense fellow, Sen. Thad Cochran, R-Miss. 2001–2009, staff member, Sen. Thad Cochran, R-Miss. 2009–present, Republican clerk, Senate Appropriations Cmte, Subc. on Defense.

Expertise: Defense.

Stewart Holmes is in his third year as Republicans clerk of the Senate Appropriations Subcommittee on Defense, a position he came to after serving as an intelligence and national security advisor for Ranking Republican Thad Cochran, R-Miss.

In the 112th Congress, Holmes, along with other Republican colleagues on the panel faces crafting a Pentagon budget in era of looming deficits and a Republican ban on earmarks.

But before he can even address spending for fiscal year 2012, Holmes as of mid-March still was grappling with an unfinished fiscal year 2011 bill and subsequent attempts to keep the government running with a shrunken continuing resolution. At a hearing Holmes helped organize, Pentagon officials warned that troops, their families and military readiness is being hurt by the absence of a 2011 budget—even as lawmakers warned the Pentagon that the standoff would likely last for some time.

Meanwhile, Holmes' role will likely put him in the middle of a debate over future funding for a second engine for the military's next generation of fighter jets. Cochran earlier this year joined with Democrat Sens. John Kerry of Massachusetts and Appropriations Committee Chairman Daniel K. Inouye of Hawaii to keep funding in place for the Joint Strike Fighter F-35 backup engine that House Republicans have vowed to eliminate.

Holmes is a Marine veteran who served more than 22 years before joining Cochran's staff as a military fellow in 1997. Two years ago he was named a Stennis Congressional Fellow, an award given to a senior-level staffer that requires nomination by a member of Congress.

SENATE APPROPRIATIONS

Charles J. Houy

Democratic Staff Director
Sen. Daniel Inouye, D-Hawaii
S-126, The Capitol
Phone: (202) 224-7293

Professional: 1987–1995, Professional staff, Senate Cmte. on Appropriations. 1995–present, Democratic clerk, Subc. on Defense, Senate Cmte. on Appropriations. 2009–present, Staff director, Senate Cmte. on Appropriations.

Expertise: Defense.

Charles Houy is one of the most powerful staffers on one of the most powerful committees in Congress, though he avoids attention and is known for discretion, especially with the press. Since 2009, however, he has ruled over the entire panel as staff director—a post that routinely lands Houy on *Roll Call*'s "Fabulous 50" key congressional staffers.

In the 112th Congress, Houy has the unenviable job of helping the panel close out decisions on fiscal year 2011 spending—never approved in 2010—while also putting together appropriations bills for fiscal year 2012.

In an attempt to bridge the budget battle earlier this year, Houy's boss Chairman Daniel K. Inouye, D-Hawaii, introduced a yearlong continuing resolution cutting $51 billion from President Obama's FY11 request. That wasn't as much as the GOP-led House slashed, though, and the Senate rejected it only to approve shorter stop-gap measures keeping the government running.

In the meantime, it will be Houy's role to help Inouye see through his goal of reestablishing "regular order"—that is, a year in which Congress approved 12 separate appropriations measures and not a giant omnibus spending bill as has happened in past years. The failure to finish the FY11 work led to a threatened government shutdown this year amid continuing resolutions and stopgap measure impasses.

"This is no way to govern," Inouye said. "Continuing Resolutions make it difficult for federal agencies to perform their duties... Moreover, Continuing Resolutions make a mockery of our Constitutional responsibility to allocate taxpayer funding wisely."

Houy in the 107th Congress was named a Stennis Congressional Fellow in recognition of his effectiveness. That same year in a National Journal profile, colleagues described him as someone who "likes to keep things close to the vest" and "a consummate appropriations professional."

SENATE APPROPRIATIONS

Alex Keenan

Staff Director

Subcommittee on Transportation, Housing and Urban Development, and Related Agencies

Room S 128, The Capitol

alex_keenan@senate.appro.gov

Personal: Born 09/29/1964 in San Francisco, Calif.

Education: B.A., University of California, Santa Barbara. M.A., international affairs, Columbia University, School of International and Public Affairs, 1998.

Professional: 1990–1993, budget analyst, U.S. Dept. of Justice. 1993–2002, senior analyst, Office of Management and Budget. 2002–2007, budget director, Federal Aviation Administration. 2007–2009, CFO, US Immigration and Customs Enforcement. 2009–present, staff director, Subc. on Transportation, Housing and Urban Development and Related Agencies, Cmte. on Appropriations.

Expertise: Aviation.

Alex Keenan comes to the Senate Committee on Appropriations Subcommittee Transportation, Housing and Urban Development, and Related Agencies after more than two decades in the executive branch.

"It was an opportunity to have a very different career—to still be in public service yet look at issues from a very different perspective," Keenan told the Almanac.

He's hoping that the 112th Congress will be more fruitful than the last, when Congress failed to pass the annual appropriations measures setting up a vicious budget fight in the first half of 2011 over stopgap spending measures. The delays have meant agencies under the subcommittee's jurisdiction are still operating under 2010 funding levels.

"Some of the agencies have gotten used to it, unfortunately," Keenan said, noting what has become a perennial delay in putting appropriations bills to bed. But, he said, "There's been nothing quite like this, though."

Keenan said the Federal Aviation Administration has probably been most affected by the budget battle because of the enormity of its operation. The FAA is a place Keenan knows a thing or two about, having served as budget director there for five years overseeing the agency's $14 billion budget. While there he also managed the agency's relations with the congressional appropriations committees and developed the FAA's first performance-based budgets.

In helping craft the transportation budget in 2012, Keenan also will likely be heavily focused on the ongoing debate over financing long-term highway spending and high-speed rail. Many lawmakers are concerned that the Highway Trust Fund is not flush enough to support the Obama administration's plans to spend $556 billion over six years on road and bridge repair, transit and high speed rail. Testifying before the subcommittee earlier this year, Transportation Secretary Ray LaHood ruled out an increase in the 18.4-cent per gallon federal tax and said the fund should remain solvent through 2012.

But Keenan hasn't spent his entire career dealing with trains, planes and automobiles. He served as budget analyst at the U.S. Department of Justice and the White House's Office of Management and Budget, as well as the chief financial officer for U.S. Immigration and Customs Enforcement before joining the committee.

SENATE APPROPRIATIONS

Charles Kieffer

Democratic Clerk
Subcommittee on Homeland Security
S-131, The Capitol
Phone: (202) 224-6870
Charles_Kieffer@appro.senate.gov

Personal: Born 02/27/1954 in Washington, D.C.

Education: B.A., government and economics, College of William & Mary, 1976. M.P.A., public administration, American University, 1978.

Professional: 1978–1980, presidential management intern, Dept. of Health, Education, and Welfare. 1978–1985, budget analyst, Dept. of Health and Human Services. 1985–1990, special assistant to the director, Office of Management and Budget. 1990–1995, chief of appropriations analysis, Office of Management and Budget. 1995–2001, acting associate director of legislative affairs, Office of Management and Budget. 2001–2003, deputy majority staff director, Senate Cmte. on Appropriations. 2003–present, deputy Democratic staff director/Democratic clerk, Subc. on Homeland Security, Senate Cmte. on Appropriations. 2007–2008, Democratic staff director/Democratic clerk, Subc. on Homeland Security, Senate Cmte. on Appropriations.

Expertise: Budget process and appropriations.

Hardly a year goes by without a news article touting Charles Kieffer as one of Washington's top behind-the-scenes players.

The son of a former Agency for International Development administrator who quit his position to protest an earmark doled out as a favor to a powerful congressman, Kieffer has worked on budget issues for more than three decades on Capitol Hill, in the White House and in various federal agencies.

As clerk of the Subcommittee on Homeland Security since 2009, Kieffer helps direct funding for several agencies including the Transportation Security Administration (TSA), the Coast Guard, Federal Emergency Management Agency (FEMA), the Coast Guard and Immigration and Customs Enforcement (ICE).

In 2011, he said, the panel—now led by Sen. Mary Landrieu, D-La.,—will likely look to ensure that FEMA has made enough improvements since Hurricane Katrina in 2005 to deal with another catastrophic event. In addition, Kieffer said, the panel will still deal with the aftermath of the 2009 shooting at Fort Hood and last year's attempted bombing in Times Square to ensure proper funding levels.

"We need to stay ahead of it so the department has the resources it needs," Kieffer said.

In the meantime, he noted, the panel is trying to work out its role in a year when it is dealing both with an unfinished fiscal year 2011 appropriations bill and a bitter battle over a continuing resolution that aimed to slash $1.6 billion from the homeland security budget, as well as President Obama's request for fiscal year 2012.

The recipient of several awards, Kieffer previously worked at the Office of Management and Budget during the Reagan, George H.W. Bush and Clinton administrations, and was rumored to be a top consideration for the post in the Obama administration. When he left OMB, both parties courted his services on Capitol Hill.

SENATE APPROPRIATIONS

Peter Kiefhaber

Democratic Clerk

Subcommittee on Interior, Environment, and Related Agencies

131 Dirksen Senate Office Bldg.

Phone: (202) 224-5271

Professional: 2000–present, Democratic clerk, Subc. on Interior, Environment, and Related Agencies, Senate Cmte. on Appropriations.

Expertise: Appropriations.

Longtime Democratic Clerk Peter Kiefhaber remains with the Senate Appropriations Committee's Interior, Environment and Related Agencies Subcommittee for the 112th Congress, despite changes in congressional leadership of the panel.

Sen. Jack Reed, D-R.I., takes the helm this year of the subcommittee from Sen. Dianne Feinstein, D-Calif., who this year assumed the chair of the energy and water panel. In announcing his post, Reed said he intends to use his position "to make sure we have a responsible budget that continues to advance economic growth and protect the public health and the environment."

It will fall to Keifhaber to carry out Reed's agenda on the subcommittee that oversees the millions of protected and public lands throughout the United States as well as clean air and water policy. The subcommittee handles the budgets for several key agencies, including the Environmental Protection Agency, Bureau of Land Management, National Park Service, and the U.S. Forest Service, which is controlled through the Department of Agriculture. It also oversees dollars for the often-controversial National Endowments for the Arts and Humanities.

That isn't likely to be hard for Keifhaber, whom colleagues describe as "old school" and an old hand on appropriations matters at east pushing his bosses' key legislation.

In 2010, Keifhaber helped Feinstein examine a restructuring of the Minerals Management Services, which came under fire in the wake of the BP oil spill in the Gulf of Mexico. And, while Congress never ultimately adopted the fiscal year 2011 spending measure, Kiefhaber helped Feinstein secure billions of dollars for California projects in the bill and address forest fires, a perennial cause for concern in her state.

SENATE APPROPRIATIONS

Stacy McBride

Minority Clerk

Subcommittee on Agriculture, Rural Development, Food and Drug Administration, and Related Agencies

S-131, The Capitol

Phone: (202) 202-224-8090

stacy_mcbride@appro.senate.gov

Personal: Born in Jonesboro, Ark.

Education: B.A., political science, Arkansas State University, 1999. M.A., public administration, Arkansas State University, 2001.

Professional: 2001–2005, budget analyst, Food and Drug Administration, Office of the Commissioner. 2005–2011, professional staff, Subc. on Agriculture, Rural Development, Food and Drug Administration and Related Agencies, Cmte. on Appropriations. Jan. 2011–present, minority clerk, Subc. on Agriculture, Rural Development, Food and Drug Administration and Related Agencies, Cmte. on Appropriations.

Stacy McBride moves up the ranks of the Committee on Appropriations in 2011 from professional staff member to minority clerk of the Subcommittee on Agriculture, Rural Development, Food and Drug Administration, and Related Agencies.

The Arkansas native, who grew up on a farm and previously worked as a budget analyst at the Food and Drug Administration (FDA), said she looks forward to putting some of her practical knowledge to work overseeing the developing of the $130 billion annual agriculture spending bill.

McBride's subcommittee has jurisdiction over the FDA and the entire Department of Agriculture with the exception of the Forest Service, and oversees a broad portfolio of issues including agriculture research, domestic nutrition programs, international food aid, food and drug safety and rural development programs.

In the 112th Congress, McBride anticipates the subcommittee will tackle some difficult decisions under Sen. Roy Blunt, R-Mo., and the panel's new ranking member.

"It is important that we invest limited resources wisely in those programs that will increase agriculture communities' competitiveness in the global economy," McBride said in an email to the Almanac, noting that agriculture exports are a leading export and research is key to the development of new biofuels.

"Agriculture plays a very important role in our economic recovery," she said.

McBride joined the subcommittee since 2005 and served as a professional staff member where she developed policy and funding recommendations as well as draft legislation; negotiated bill, report and amendment language as well as coordinated funding requests with member offices and the administration; prepared hearing materials for senators; and briefed lawmakers on the administration's budget as well as policy issues.

A graduate of Arkansas State University where she also received her master's degree in public administration, McBride is a recipient of the 2008 National WIC Association Leadership Award given by the non-profit arm of the Special Supplemental Nutrition Program for Women, Infants and Children Program. She also served as a presidential management fellow from 2001 to 2003.

SENATE APPROPRIATIONS

Timothy S. Rieser

Democratic Clerk

Subcommittee on State, Foreign Operations, and Related Programs

127 Dirksen Senate Office Bldg.

Phone: (202) 224-7284

Tim_Rieser@appro.senate.gov

Personal: Born 01/03/1952 in Palo Alto, Calif.

Education: B.A., Dartmouth College, 1976. J.D., Antioch Law School, 1979.

Professional: 1995–present, Democratic clerk, Subc. on State, Foreign Operations, and Related Programs, Senate Cmte. on Appropriations.

Expertise: Foreign operations, appropriations.

In a speech made in 2010 to the U.S. Overseas Cooperative Development Council, Timothy Rieser laid out just some of the challenges of advocating for foreign assistance as Democratic clerk of the Senate Appropriations Subcommittee on State, Foreign Operations, and Related Programs.

"It's not a particularly popular budget for most members of Congress who have little idea of what foreign assistance programs consist of and many of whom can't understand why we would do them in the first place," Rieser told the group.

In the 112th Congress, Rieser's job of defending existing levels of aid and fighting for more on behalf of his boss, Subcommittee Chairman Patrick Leahy, D-Vt., got even harder.

With the Republican takeover of the House in November 2010, slashing foreign assistance became priority No. 1 of the new majority. A continuing resolution the House approved early in 2011 to keep the government running whacked the State and Foreign Operations budget $3.8 billion or 8 percent.

That will make meeting President Obama's request of even $47 billion for fiscal year 2012—just a 1 percent increase over fiscal year 10 levels—harder for the Senate. The subcommittee funds internationally oriented agencies, including the Department of State, the U.S. Agency for International Development, the United Nations, the World Bank, and the Peace Corps.

Rieser, a Vermont native, worked in Leahy's personal office before joining the subcommittee staff in 1995. He was instrumental in 2005 in setting up a victims' compensation fund for Iraqi civilians killed in the war. Rieser is a former public defender who holds a bachelor's degree from Dartmouth and earned his law degree at the Antioch School of Law. According to the Dartmouth News Web site, his father, Leonard, was a physicist and longtime faculty member at the university who contributed to the Manhattan Project.

SENATE APPROPRIATIONS

Bettilou Taylor

Clerk

Subcommittee on Labor, Health and Human Services, Education, and Related Agencies

156 Dirksen Senate Office Bldg.

Phone: (202) 224-7230

Bettilou_Taylor@appro.senate.gov

Personal: Born in Phillipsburg, Pa.

Professional: 1974–1989, staff asst., Subc. on Transportation, Subc. on Labor, Health and Human Services, Education, and Related Agencies, Subc. on Commerce, Justice, State, and the Judiciary; House Cmte. on Appropriations. 1989–1998, professional staff member, Subc. on Labor, Health and Human Services, Education, and Related Agencies, Senate Cmte. on Appropriations. 1998–present, clerk, Subc. on Labor, Health and Human Services, Education, and Related Agencies, Senate Cmte. on Appropriations.

Expertise: Health, education, appropriations.

Veteran Appropriations Committee staffer Bettilou Taylor remains minority clerk to the Subcommittee on Labor, HHS and Related Agencies now led on the Republican side by Sen. Richard Shelby, R-Ala.

In the 112th Congress, Taylor will oversee hearings and assist Republicans lawmakers with spending and policy decisions on everything from Head Start and AmeriCorps programs to Pell Grants for college students and mine safety regulations.

Many of those programs faced steep cuts in a House-passed continuing resolution, H.R. 1, a battle that continued to rage through much of the spring.

But the panel's first order of business in 2011 was a hearing examining fraud and waste in Medicare and Medicaid. Chairman Tom Harkin, D-Iowa, praised Shelby at that hearing and noted the panel has a history of bipartisanship. Taylor, who has served on the Hill in various appropriations committee functions since the 1970s, has long been considered central to that reputation.

Former Sen. Arlen Specter, who previously held the ranking GOP role, frequently referred to Taylor as the "101st senator."

During a 2005 hearing on stem cell research, Specter—who helped the embattled NIH director of a panel overseeing stem cell research hold on to his post—noted that "Senator Bettilou Taylor tells me that some of us might have been helpful in keeping you at NIH."

Taylor brings practical experience to the position as well, having trained as a medical technician and worked for both NIH and HHS. She is the recipient of several awards, and in 2008, Nature magazine named Taylor one of the top 10 influential people in biomedical policy.

A native of Phillipsburg, Pa., Taylor is married to former appropriations staffer Domenic Ruscio, now a lobbyist at Cavarocchi-Ruscio-Dennis Associates.

SENATE APPROPRIATIONS

Marianne Upton

General Counsel

Subcommittee on Financial Services and General Government

131 Dirksen Senate Office Bldg.

Phone: (202) 224-7363

marianne_upton@senate.appro.gov

Education: B.A., University of Nebraska, 1976. J.D., University of Nebraska, 1979.

Professional: 2000–2005, Staff director and chief counsel, Senate Homeland Security and Government Affairs Committee. 2005–2006, General counsel, Sen. Richard Durbin, D-Ill. 2007–present, Majority clerk, Senate Appropriations Committee, Financial Services Subcommittee.

Expertise: Financial services.

The 112th Congress opened with a rancorous budget battle that saw Republicans aiming to slash more than $2.2 billion from agencies that Marianne Clifford Upton oversees as Democratic clerk of the Senate Appropriations Subcommittee on Financial Services and General Government.

Upton's boss, Subcommittee Chairman Dick Durbin, D-Ill., roundly criticized the House-passed measure, which cut 23 percent of the Treasury Department's non-IRS funding; gave the executive office of the president a 4 percent shave; and gutted an election reform program run through the states.

Durbin accused Republicans of trying to starve the Securities and Exchange Commission (SEC), the Commodity Futures Trading Commission (CFTC) and the Consumer Financial Protection Bureau (CFPB), and vowed to restore money to the agencies this year. Democrats had boosted those budgets in 2010 to implement the Dodd-Frank financial law.

That means Upton has her work cut out for her, with a goal of restoring $231 million in GOP cuts from the SEC; $174 million from the CFTC; and a $63 million cut to the CFPB.

In 2010, Upton helped prepare seven subcommittee hearings on various agency budgets as well as policy issues like whether the Treasury Department and banks are doing enough to help families save their homes in the midst of the housing market crash.

Treasury Secretary Timothy Geithner criticized banks in his testimony, saying they were not doing nearly enough to help families avoid foreclosures.

Upton is a former deputy county attorney from Nebraska, and had served as general counsel to Durbin before joining the subcommittee.

Committee on Armed Services

B228 Russell Senate Office Bldg.
Washington, DC 20510
Phone: (202) 224-3871
Fax: (202) 228-0036
http://armed-services.senate.gov

Ratio: 12/13/1

MAJORITY MEMBERS

Carl Levin, MI, Chairman

Jack Reed, RI
Daniel K. Akaka, HI
Ben Nelson, NE
Jim Webb, VA
Claire McCaskell, MO
Mark Udall, CO
Kay R. Hagan, NC
Mark Begich, AK
Joe Manchin, WV
Jeanne Shaheen, NH
Kirsten E Gillibrand, NY
Richard Blumenthal, CT

INDEPENDENT MEMBERS

Joseph I. Lieberman, CT

MINORITY MEMBERS

John McCain, AZ, Ranking Member

James M. Inhofe, OK
Jeff Sessions, AL
Saxby Chambliss, GA
Roger Wicker, MS
Scott Brown, MA
Rob Portman, OH
Kelly Ayotte, NH
Susan Collins, ME
Lindsey O. Graham, SC
John Cornyn, TX
David Vitter, LA

SENATE ARMED SERVICES

JURISDICTION

(1) Aeronautical and space activities peculiar to or primarily associated with the development of weapons systems or military operations.
(2) The common defense.
(3) The Department of Defense, the Department of the Army, the Department of the Navy, and the Department of the Air Force, generally.
(4) Maintenance and operation of the Panama Canal, including administration, sanitation, and government of the Canal Zone.
(5) Military research and development.
(6) National security aspects of nuclear energy.
(7) Naval petroleum reserves, except those in Alaska.
(8) Pay, promotion, retirement, and other benefits and privileges of members of the armed forces, including overseas education of civilian and military dependents.
(9) Selective service system.
(10) Strategic and critical materials necessary for the common defense.
Such committee shall also conduct comprehensive study and review of matters relating to the common defense policy of the United States.

SENATE ARMED SERVICES

Rarely in the 65 years since World War II ended has the United States faced such an array of national security threats as loomed in the opening months of the 112th Congress.

On the budget-writing, lawmaking and supervisory fronts, the challenge for the Senate Armed Services Committee was to stay abreast of two wars, the danger of terrorism, nuclear proliferation, and instability in the Middle East—to say nothing of such demands at home as the Pentagon's budget crunch, weapons-buying reform and the acceptance of homosexuality in the ranks.

Under the Democratic chairman, Sen. Carl Levin of Michigan, and ranking Republican, Sen. John McCain of Arizona, the panel's bipartisan traditions appeared sturdy—despite differences over aspects of the strategy on the war in Afghanistan and the policy on gays in the military.

President Barack Obama faced an uncommonly difficult war-fighting balance. Against a deadline of Dec. 31, 2011, the U.S. fighting force in Iraq—more than 100,000 at its peak—strove to conclude its mission in Iraq without disrupting the a fledgling democracy, or the security forces trained to take control of their own nation's protection.

More daunting was the task of executing the counterinsurgency plan Obama unveiled for Afghanistan in December, 2009—with a troop surge to put U.S. force levels above 100,000. Adding complexity was Obama's promise to begin withdrawing an unspecified number of troops in July, 2011.

"While we've begun to turn around the once-daunting dynamic in Afghanistan, there is no guarantee that our progress will continue or that our gains will be permanent," Levin wrote in a March, 2011 essay with Sen. Jack Reed, a senior Democrat on the panel who had joined him on a fact-finding tour of the war zones. They argued for increased allied support of U.S. training of Afghan troops.

McCain is also a supporter of the president's counterinsurgency strategy in Afghanistan but has repeatedly expressed opposition for any timelines or quotas in connection with U.S. troop withdrawals.

Levin and McCain were full partners in the acquisition reform measure, years in the making, that Obama signed into law four months after taking office. In a separate but related matter, both have acknowledged a need to curb military spending.

A high priority in the new Congress will be to monitor the progress under that legislation, as Defense Secretary Robert Gates strives to curb spending across programs, from health care to future weapons systems.

SENATE ARMED SERVICES

Tara Andringa

Press secretary to Sen. Carl Levin, D-Mich.

SR-269 Russell Senate Office Bldg.

Phone: (202) 228-3685

Tara_andringa@levin.senate.gov

Personal: Born 06/05/1971 in Pontiac, Mich.

Education: B.A., University of Pennsylvania, 1993.

Professional: 1994–1996, military caseworker, Sen. Carl Levin. 1997–1999, deputy press secretary, Sen. Carl Levin. 1999, press secretary/communications director, Se. Carl Levin.

Expertise: Communications.

As any sampling of news releases from Senate Armed Services Committee Chairman Carl Levin, D-Mich., will show from opening months of the 112th Congress, it is a big task to track the range of interests of one of the Senate's most influential figures. That job falls to Levin's press secretary, Tara Andringa.

With Sen. John McCain of Arizona, the panel's ranking Republican, Andringa had to work with the media as Levin shepherded into law a major reform of the Pentagon's weapons-buying system in 2009, while monitoring the two wars that had dominated national security affairs for a decade. As chairman of the Permanent Subcommittee on Investigations, Levin conducted a probe of the causes and consequences of the Wall Street crisis. As a Democratic senator from Michigan since 1979, Levin's immersion in auto industry concerns had made him an expert on the nation's manufacturing economy, from small-workforce operations, to giant multinationals that face a complex web of labor, trade and global competition issues.

Andringa, a Capitol Hill veteran, is on the senator's personal staff, so the output of her office included statements on such Michigan concerns as grants for fire departments across the state. But news of the Armed Services panel is also a major part of Andringa's work. In mid-March 2011, Levin hosted the year's first congressional testimony by Army Gen. David Petraeus on the progress of the troops he commands in Afghanistan.

Levin, an opponent of the invasion of Iraq, was an early advocate of signaling to that nation's emerging democratic government that the U.S. troop commitment was finite. As his committee oversaw the completion of the U.S. troop withdrawal from Iraq in 2011, Andringa worked with the media as Levin continued to focus on the value he saw in the mid-year deadline for starting withdrawals from Afghanistan. More than 100,000 troops were deployed under an Obama strategy that Levin had endorsed.

At the same time, Andringa led Levin's communications on less-dominant but still-essential national security issues. Those topics ran the gamut from a probe of counterfeit electronic parts in the Pentagon supply chain and subcommittee assignments in the new Congress, to legislative hearing schedules and a sharp rebuttal of a Rolling Stone magazine story on alleged military efforts to influence senators' views on Afghanistan.

SENATE ARMED SERVICES

Richard D. DeBobes

Staff Director

228 Russell Senate Office Bldg.

Phone: (202) 224-7530

Personal: Born 05/05/1938 in New York, N.Y.

Education: B.A., Georgetown University, 1959. LL.B., Fordham Law School, 1962. LL.M., The George Washington University, 1972.

Professional: 1963–1975, lawyer and military judge, Dept. of the Navy. 1975–1980, director, international negotiations branch, Judge Advocate General of the Navy. 1980–1984, commander, Naval Legal Service Office (Norfolk, Va.). 1984–1989, legislative asst. to the chairman, Joint Chiefs of Staff. 1989–1994, counsel, Senate Cmte. on Armed Services. 1995–2001, Democratic counsel, Senate Cmte. on Armed Services. 2001–2003, counsel, Senate Cmte. on Armed Services. 2003–2007, Democratic staff director, Senate Cmte. on Armed Services. 2007–present, staff director, Senate Cmte. on Armed Services.

Expertise: International law, military operations, Department of Defense organization.

As Senate Armed Services Committee Chairman Carl Levin tackled another agenda of extraordinary challenge in the 112th Congress, the Michigan Democrat's staff director, Rick DeBobes, figured once again to play an important role behind the scenes.

Wartime concerns remained paramount for DeBobes, as they had in the decade since the Sept. 11 attacks. Levin remained focused on a counterinsurgency formula that he had promoted since the darkest moments in the Iraq war: U.S. troops should withdraw as soon as they had trained sufficient local forces to take responsibility for their own nation's security.

Accordingly, the U.S. force was to complete its withdrawal from Iraq by the deadline of Dec. 31, 2011, that had been set by President Bush and Iraqi Prime Minister Maliki in the 2008 security agreement. At the same time, Obama's Afghanistan strategy was fully engaged as the new Congress convened, with another important deadline at hand in mid-2011.

After a tour of Afghanistan early in 2011, Levin signaled that he would keep pressing for U.S. troop withdrawals to begin by the July 1 landmark, calling for the accelerated recruiting and training of the Afghan army and national police to enable them to shoulder the responsibility to protect their own people.

But the exigencies of war were only one piece of the mosaic of demands on DeBobes and the committee staff. Coinciding with urgent Pentagon budget concerns was the test of a major reform in the weapons-buying system that Levin and the panel's ranking Republican, Arizona Sen. John McCain, had moved to enactment in 2009.

Oversight of those reforms is expected, as well as implementation of the conditional repeal, late in 2010, of the "Don't Ask, Don't Tell" policy on gays in the military.

SENATE ARMED SERVICES

Richard W. Fieldhouse

Professional Staff Member
Subcommittee on Strategic Forces
228 Russell Senate Office Bldg.
Phone: (202) 224-0750

Education: B.A., political science, Bates College, 1980.

Professional: 1991–1996, legislative asst., Sen. Carl Levin, D-Mich. 1996–2007, professional staff member, Subc. on Strategic Forces, Senate Cmte. on Armed Services. 2007–present, lead professional staff member, Subc. on Emerging Threats and Capabilites/Subc. on Strategic Forces, Senate Cmte. on Armed Services.

Expertise: Defense issues.

As a veteran staffer for the Democratic majority on the Armed Services Committee, Richard Fieldhouse tracks arms control, nuclear proliferation, emerging security threats and the U.S. missile defense program.

The Senate's ratification of President Barack Obama's new strategic arms limitation treaty in 2010 represented at least a partial vindication of the prediction that Fieldhouse's boss, Senate Armed Services Committee Chairman Carl Levin, D-Mich., made early in the 111th Congress that a cooperative approach to Russia on weapons issues would prove fruitful.

Fieldhouse will track U.S. efforts to involve Russia in developing a European missile defense system. Efforts to monitor and curb the nuclear ambitions of Iran and North Korea remained fraught with difficulty.

Obama signed the arms reduction pact with Russian President Dmitri Medvedev in the spring of 2010. The pact reduced the number of nuclear missile launchers by half and limited the number of warheads to 1,550. The Senate ratified it, after some influential Republicans balked, during the post-election lame-duck session at the end of the year.

A key to securing the pact was Obama's decision in 2009 to scrap Bush administration plans to deploy missile interceptors and radar units in the Czech Republic, as a prospective defense against Iranian missiles capable of striking Europe. While Iran continued to deny that it was seeking nuclear weapons, critics expressed concern that Obama's action would undermine relations with nations in Central Europe.

The administration made clear, however, that it would strive in 2011 to win Russian agreement on joint development of shorter-range missile defenses in Europe, while bringing Russia into the World Trade Organization.

Fieldhouse joined Levin's personal office staff in 1991 and moved to the committee in 1996.

SENATE ARMED SERVICES

Creighton Greene

Professional Staff Member

228 Russell Senate Office Bldg.

Phone: (202) 224-6115

Fax: (202) 228-0036

Personal: Born 06/23/1949 in Pikeville, Ky.

Education: B.S., Morehead State University (Ky.), 1970. M.S., Morehead State University (Ky.), 1972. M.B.A., Virginia Tech, 1988.

Professional: 1972–1975, member, U.S. Army Corps of Engineers. 1975–1990, analyst, Office of Management and Budget. 1990–present, professional staff member, Senate Cmte. on Armed Services.

Expertise: Air Force, Navy, Marine Corps, intelligence programs.

After a decade at war in Afghanistan and Iraq, it was a measure of strain on the nation's all-volunteer armed forces that Defense Secretary Robert M. Gates warned early in 2011 of danger on a third front: the Pentagon's weapons-buying and budget systems.

Creighton Greene, an Armed Services Committee expert on Air Force, Navy and Marine policies, said troubled weapons systems would remain an urgent issue for the 112th Congress. Scrutiny of performance a 2009 acquisition reform law was a top priority for the Democratic chairman, Sen. Carl Levin of Michigan, and the ranking Republican, Sen. John McCain of Arizona.

A prime example: the F-35 Lightning II, or Joint Strike Fighter, was slated for a new program restructuring.

"That's two major restructurings in the last two years," Greene said. "Anytime you have $200 million or $300 million of the public's money at stake, you're going to get a lot of attention" with such a record. The JSF, begun the same year as the September 11 attacks at an estimated cost of $50 million per plane, was pegged at more than $92 million a copy by 2010. By then, leadership had cut the originally planned buy of 2,500 planes by more than one-sixth, fired the program manager and withheld $600 million from a key contractor.

After a "Nunn-McCurdy breach"—Pentagon jargon for a Reagan-era law that triggers alerts and remediation when a program's cost inflates by more than 50 percent of the initial estimates—the JSF proceeded only after an official certification that it is essential to national security and that there are no cost-effective alternatives. The JSF was one of six programs that breached Nunn-McCurdy in 2010.

Still, said Greene, there has been progress. The Weapons Acquisition Reform Act of 2009 gave Congress and Pentagon overseers more tools to use on troubled programs.

SENATE ARMED SERVICES

Gary Leeling

Counsel

228 Russell Senate Office Bldg.

Phone: (202) 224-3871

Fax: (202) 228-0036

gary_leeling@armed-services.senate.gov

Personal: Born 05/23/1947 in Deadwood, S.Dak.

Education: B.A., South Dakota State Univ., 1969. J.D., Univ. of South Dakota Law School, 1972.

Professional: 1970–1998, active duty, U.S. Army. 1998–present, counsel, Senate Cmte. on Armed Services.

Expertise: Personnel issues, military health care.

The recruitment, well-being, and retention of military professionals, always a high priority of the Senate Armed Services Committee, posed challenges in several distinct arenas as the 112th Congress began.

With the all-volunteer force at war for a decade since the terrorist attacks of Sept. 11, 2001, the welfare of the troops and the military community at large was a top focus of Pentagon policy experts such as Gary Leeling, a veteran counsel on the committee chaired by Sen. Carl Levin, D-Mich.

Even before the new Congress convened, attention had sharpened on an issue that has cast a shadow on the military during the years of its assimilation of large numbers of women: sexual assault.

"This has been a continual issue for the last several years," Leeling noted. But well-publicized lawsuits "stirred the pot," he said. "The suits have senators asking a lot of questions."

He referred to the American Civil Union's late-2010 lawsuit seeking the release of records on sexual assault in the armed forces. Early in 2011, another lawsuit raised the question of whether the armed forces have taken sufficient steps to prevent and act upon allegations of sexual assault. "Some people feel the military is not being held accountable," he said.

On top of those thorny issues touching on sexual crime, personal rights, unit cohesion, and other weighty concerns, Leeling noted that the Pentagon also faced the spiraling cost of medical care.

Another priority, he said, would be continued improvement of the system that transfers wounded, ill and injured personnel from active duty or reserve status to the realm of the Veterans Administration.

Leeling spent 28 years in the U.S. Army, much of it as a JAG corps officer. Upon retirement in 1998, he joined the Armed Services Committee staff.

SENATE ARMED SERVICES

Peter K. Levine

General Counsel
228 Russell Senate Office Bldg.
Phone: (202) 224-8631

Personal: Born 07/29/1957.

Education: A.B., Harvard College, 1979. J.D., magna cum laude, Harvard Law School, 1983.

Professional: 1983–1986, associate attorney, Crowell and Moring (Washington, D.C.). 1987–1994, counsel, Subc. on Oversight of Government Management, Senate Cmte. on Governmental Affairs. 1995–1996, counsel, Sen. Carl Levin, D-Mich. 1996–2001, Democratic counsel, Senate Cmte. on Armed Services. 2001–2002, general counsel, Senate Cmte. on Armed Services. 2003–2007, Democratic counsel, Senate Cmte. on Armed Services. 2007–present, general counsel, Senate Cmte. on Armed Services.

Expertise: Legal issues and nominations, lobbying disclosure laws, federal procurement system, financial management and efficiencies issues.

After years of evidence that the Pentagon's purchasing systems needed overhauling, the 111th Congress finally took strong, bipartisan action to make it happen. Senate Armed Services Committee Chairman Carl Levin, D-Mich., and Ranking Republican John McCain, of Arizona, were the prime movers, with Peter Levine along for the ride.

The enactment of the Weapon Systems Acquisition Reform Act in 2009 and the IMPROVE Acquisition Act in 2010 came "in response to continued congressional concerns about wasteful practices in defense acquisition," according to Levine, committee general counsel.

Levine will closely monitor the new laws' implementation in the 112th Congress. He has devoted much of his career to defense management issues. Levine said the committee also planned to oversee "the Defense Department's efforts to reform its business and financial management systems and achieve an auditable financial statement."

Over the years, national security imperatives, the decline of competition in the weapons industry and other factors have made allowed the Pentagon to keep its books in ways that would be considered irregular in the private business world. The debilitating effects of the global recession and a decade at war in two nations have raised the urgency of curbing Defense Department spending—particularly where it results from preventable waste.

The challenge facing Levin and his staff was to track the progress on acquisition reform and on the efficiencies initiatives of Secretary of Defense Robert M. Gates "to ensure that we are able to achieve real savings without undermining the long-term functioning of the Department," Levine said.

Before joining the committee staff in 1996, Levine was counsel to the Oversight of Government Management Subcommittee on the Senate Governmental Affairs Committee. He then served in Levin's personal office.

SENATE ARMED SERVICES

Bill Monahan

Democratic Counsel

228 Russell Senate Office Bldg.

Phone: (202) 224-3871

Personal: Born 07/03/1964 in Winchester, Va.

Education: B.A., history, Yale University, 1987. M.P.A., international relations, Princeton University, 1994. J.D., University of Virginia, 1994.

Professional: 1994–1995, legislative staff, Sen. Bob Kerrey, (D-Neb.). 1995–1999, legal advisor, Arms Control and Disarmament Agency. 1999–2003, legal advisor, Office of the Legal Advisor, U.S. Dept. of State. 2003–present, Democratic counsel, Senate Armed Services Cmte.

Expertise: Foreign policy, European Command, Central Command.

With Counsel Bill Monahan as his lead staffer on Iraq and Afghanistan, Senate Armed Services Committee chairman Carl Levin, D-Mich., faced a demanding agenda in the 112th Congress, supporting the delicate transition of security duties from U.S. to Iraqi troops in one war, and the crucial campaign to make such a transition possible in the other.

In both wars, dramatic increases in the size of the U.S. force have been coupled with a doctrine that insists that the enterprise cannot prevail by American military might alone. Levin opposed the surge in Iraq. In Afghanistan, he expressed a preference for more U.S. training forces over a surge in combat forces. Levin viewed President Barack Obama's July, 2011 target date to begin U.S. troop withdrawals from Afghanistan as a crucial milestone.

After joining Levin on his latest tour of Afghanistan in January, 2011, Monahan said the chairman would continue to stress "the importance of the July deadline as a forcing function, to really impart a sense of urgency to the Afghans that this is their war."

Monahan said the armed services panel would also press, in coordination with the Foreign Relations Committee, to step up the deployment of U.S. civilian experts to help build the kind of Afghan government services that could promote popular support against the Taliban.

Pakistan remained a key to the anti-terrorist effort in Afghanistan, so Levin argued for stronger Pakistani efforts to disrupt Taliban havens on its side of the border.

In Iraq, meanwhile, the U.S. was "clearly looking toward the longer-term strategy of what kind of relationship we are going to have" after American combat troops completed their withdrawal at the end of 2011, said Monahan.

SENATE ARMED SERVICES

Christopher John Paul

Minority Executive Officer
Sen. John McCain, R-Ariz.
241 Russell Senate Office Bldg.
Phone: (202) 224-7138
Fax: (202) 228-2862
chris_paul@mccain.senate.gov

Personal: Born 06/24/1959 in Lakehurst, N.J.

Education: U.S. Naval Academy, 1982.

Professional: 1977–1991, active duty, U.S. Navy. 1990–1991, Navy fellow, Sen. John S. McCain, R-Ariz. 1991–2005, professional staff member and military legislative assistant, Senate Cmte. on Armed Services, and Sen. John McCain, R-Ariz. 2005–2007, staff director, Subc. on Airland, Senate Cmte. on Armed Services, and legislative assistant, Sen. John McCain, R-Ariz. 2007–present, minority executive officer, Senate Cmte. on Armed Services.

Expertise: Defense, veterans' affairs, aerospace, national security, commercial aviation issues.

Overseeing Pentagon spending took on added complexity early in the 112th Congress, as the politics of federal deficit reduction intruded on the routines of budget-writing.

Perhaps more than any part of the federal government, the unusual reliance on stop-gap spending measures to finance operations affected the armed forces for fiscal year 2011. The previous Congress failed to complete an orthodox defense appropriation, so leaders began the new session in debate over a continuing resolution to finance the government. Pentagon planners juggled accounts in order to keep money flowing where needed; some long-term weapons contracts were jeopardized.

As bargaining over the CR dragged on into the spring, it became "a distraction," according to Chris Paul, senior advisor to the Senate Armed Services Committee's Ranking Member John McCain, R-Ariz. Paul noted the struggle to finance current year Pentagon operations overlapped on the panel's yearly cycle of hearings on the Defense Department authorization for fiscal year 2012. Indeed, the CR debate demanded attention from Pentagon planners who were trying to nail down priorities for the 2013 budget year.

The spending debate played out against the backdrop of continuing recession and crucial milestones for the wars in Iraq and Afghanistan. At the same time, as McCain's point man on key Pentagon and policy issues, Paul monitored the performance of the Pentagon contracting system under the landmark acquisition reform bill enacted in 2009.

Like McCain, Paul has a Navy background, having graduated from the Naval Academy and served on active duty for nine years until he joined the senator's staff in 1991. He is a rear admiral in the Naval Reserves. Paul's portfolio includes four of the Armed Services Committee's six subcommittees.

SENATE ARMED SERVICES

Dick Walsh

Professional Staff Member

228 Russell Senate Office Bldg.

Phone: (202) 224-3094

Personal: Born 08/20/1949 in New York, N.Y.

Education: B.S., national security affairs, United States Naval Academy, 1971. J.D., Univ. of Virginia School of Law, 1979.

Professional: 1996–1998, director of legislation, Office of Naval Legislative Affairs. 1998–2001, executive director, Senate Affairs Division, Office of the Secretary of Defense. 2001–present, professional staff member, Senate Cmte. on Armed Services.

Expertise: Military pay, morale, civilian employee issues, welfare and recreation programs, nominations.

As he approached his tenth anniversary of service on the Senate Armed Services Committee, Dick Walsh said early in 2011 that Pentagon personnel planners faced upwardly spiraling personnel costs, lower overall spending for the Defense Department, the need to succeed in Iraq and Afghanistan, and the stress that a decade of war had put on combat forces and their families.

The committee's veteran Republican counsel further noted that Pentagon leadership was still adjusting a major shift in budgeting procedure, the move away from financing wartime operations through supplemental appropriations bills.

In order to cap what Defense Secretary Robert M. Gates called "the gusher" of Pentagon spending, the armed services also grappled with a plan to reduce the size of the active duty forces over the course of five years.

While Defense Department leaders asserted that those personnel reductions would be based on conditions in the war zones of Iraq and Afghanistan, the services had few alternatives for savings. One option to be scrutinized by the armed services personnel subcommittees was greater reliance on reserve components, which have become a much more capable operational force

Another ongoing goal was increasing the "dwell time" of combat forces for recovery back home between deployments. Also high on the priority list for Walsh and the committee's personnel team were maintaining solid rates of recruiting and retaining of service members, and careful scrutiny of policies to ensure continued readiness for every military mission.

One more essential job for the personnel subcommittees overseeing the implementation of a historic change in the culture of the armed forces was the integration of openly gay men and women into the ranks. Training on the new policy was already taking place early in 2001, with full repeal of the old policy later in the year. Congress in late 2010 rescinded the Clinton administration's "Don't Ask, Don't Tell" rule on homosexuality in the military.

Committee on Banking, Housing, and Urban Affairs

534 Dirksen Senate Office Bldg.
Washington, DC 20510
Phone: (202) 224-7391
Fax: (202) 224-5137
http://banking.senate.gov

Ratio: 10/12

MAJORITY MEMBERS

Tim Johnson, SD, Chairman
Jack Reed, RI
Charles E. Schumer, NY
Robert Menendez, NJ
Daniel K. Akaka, AK
Sherrod Brown, OH
Jon Tester, MT
Herb Kohl, WI
Mark R. Warner, VA
Jeff Merkley, OR
Michael Bennet, CO
Kay Hagan, NC

MINORITY MEMBERS

Richard C. Shelby, AL, Ranking Member
Mike Crapo, ID
Bob Corker, TN
Jim DeMint, SC
David Vitter, LA
Mike Johanns, NE
Patrick J. Toomey, PA
Mark Kirk, IL
Jerry Moran, KS
Roger F. Wicker, MS

SENATE BANKING, HOUSING, AND URBAN AFFAIRS

JURISDICTION

(1) Banks, banking, and financial institutions.
(2) Financial aid to commerce and industry.
(3) Deposit insurance.
(4) Public and private housing (including veterans' housing).
(5) Federal monetary policy, including the Federal Reserve System.
(6) Money and credit, including currency and coinage.
(7) Issuance and redemption of notes.
(8) Control of prices of commodities, rents, and services.
(9) Urban development and urban mass transit.
(10) Economic stabilization and defense production.
(11) Export controls.
(12) Export and foreign trade promotion.
(13) Nursing home construction.
(14) Renegotiation of government contracts.

Such committee shall also study and review on a comprehensive basis, matters relating to international economic policy as it affects United States monetary affairs, credit, and financial institutions; economic growth, urban affairs, and report thereon from time to time.

SENATE BANKING, HOUSING, AND URBAN AFFAIRS

2011 began with the installation of a new chairman on the Senate Banking, Housing and Urban Affairs Committee: Sen. Tim Johnson, D-S.D., who took the helm of the committee following the retirement of Connecticut Democrat Sen. Christopher Dodd.

Johnson did a lot of pinch-hitting as chairman during the 111th session as Dodd worked double duty on health care reform and financial services regulatory modernization.

During that session, the committee's top priority was passage of the Dodd-Frank Wall Street Reform and Consumer Protection Act. Signed into law by President Obama on July 21, 2010, it was considered the most sweeping change to financial regulation in the United States since the Great Depression. Its provisions—including consolidation of regulatory agencies, comprehensive regulation of financial markets and consumer protection reforms—represent a significant change in the American financial regulatory environment.

Other accomplishments during the 111th Congress included legislation such as: the Credit Card Accountability Responsibility and Disclosure (or CARD) Act; the Comprehensive Iran Sanctions and Divestment Act (CISADA); the Congo Conflict Minerals Act; and the Extractive Industries Transparency Disclosure Act.

But it's the Dodd-Frank implementation that has soaked up—and will soak up—much of the committee's time, as it requires significant oversight. Much of the latter half of 2010 was consumed with monitoring SEC rulemaking and enforcement. In 2011, oversight will include insurance regulations being created under the new Federal Insurance Office, whose work the committee must also monitor. The office's first report on the insurance industry was due in 2011.

There are also likely to be hearings on strengthening the Securities and Exchange Commission, corporate governance, credit rating agencies, executive compensation, municipal securities, investment advisors, hedge funds, private equity funds and investor protection.

After taking charge of the committee, Johnson said two other priorities would be housing finance reform and oversight of taxpayer investments in TARP and auto manufacturing.

"The committee's top priorities and agenda will be viewed through the lens of continuing to support the economic recovery," Johnson said in a statement. "Although real output is now growing, the rate of unemployment is 9 percent, the housing market remains weak, and output is below potential."

On the housing assistance side, the committee may consider the Section Eight Voucher Reform Act, which includes proposals to streamline and improve the Section 8 rental housing voucher program. Moreover, the National Flood Insurance Program will need to be reauthorized by Sept. 30, 2011. The committee held a reauthorization hearing late in the 111th Congress.

Drafting and passing a new surface transportation authorization bill will be another task, as the current transportation bill expired on Sept. 30, 2009. Several hearings on transit issues are expected. In 2010, the committee passed the "Public Transportation Safety Act," but it wasn't considered by the full Senate.

The Banking Committee has jurisdiction over the Export-Import Bank of the United States, the nation's official export credit agency. Johnson is also considering hearings on its reauthorization, which is up this year.

SENATE BANKING, HOUSING, AND URBAN AFFAIRS

William Duhnke

Republican Staff Director and Counsel

534 Dirksen Senate Office Bldg.

Phone: (202) 224-7391

Fax: (202) 224-5137

b_duhnke@banking.senate.gov

Personal: Born 04/25/1962 in Milwaukee, Wis.

Education: B.A., University of Wisconsin at Madison, 1984. J.D., Columbus School of Law, Catholic University of America, 1996.

Professional: 1984–1991, U.S. Navy. 1992–93, director of operations, Presidential Commission on Assignment of Women in Armed Forces. 1993–1995, director of operations, Defense Base Closure Commission. 1995–1997, legislative asst., Sen. Richard Shelby, R-Ala. 1997–1999, counsel, Senate Select Cmte. on Intelligence. 1999–2000, deputy staff director, Senate Select Cmte. on Intelligence. 2000–2001, staff director and chief counsel, Senate Select Cmte. on Intelligence. 2001–2007, Republican staff director and counsel, Senate Select Cmte. on Intelligence. 2007–present, counsel and GOP staff director, Senate Cmte. on Banking, Housing and Urban Affairs.

Expertise: Global and national security issues.

Asked to point to his top priorities during the 111th Congress, Bill Duhnke settles on just one: passage of the Dodd-Frank Wall Street Reform and Consumer Protection Act.

Signed into law by President Obama on July 21, 2010, Dodd-Frank had originated a year earlier in the Senate Committee on Banking, Housing and Urban Affairs for which long-timer Duhnke is Republican staff director and counsel. Given that it was considered the most sweeping change to financial regulation in the United States since the Great Depression, its implementation required significant oversight during the latter half of 2010.

Its provisions—including consolidation of regulatory agencies, comprehensive regulation of financial markets and consumer protection reforms—represent such a significant change in the American financial regulatory environment that Duhnke and his staff expect the 112th Congress to be consumed with the minutia of monitoring the sweeping legislation.

"Some of the most obvious priorities for me have to do with a continuation of Dodd-Frank," said Duhnke, whose duties include managing the committee's 20-some employees. "Right now, all we're doing is getting people to track its implementation. It's a lot to do and a lot to track."

Continuing to address financial regulatory reform is also at the top of the agenda for Duhnke's boss, ranking member Sen. Richard C. Shelby, R-Ala. Shelby was one of the most prominent foes of the $700 billion financial bailout bill that passed in fall 2008.

It's clear that Shelby and his staff will continue to lock horns with the White House and committee Democrats on further reforms. "They really haven't jumped in feet first," said Duhnke, a Wisconsin native. "The indications are there will be no serious efforts before 2012."

SENATE BANKING, HOUSING, AND URBAN AFFAIRS

Dwight Fettig

Majority Staff Director

534 Dirksen Senate Office Bldg.

dwight_fettig@banking.senate.gov

Personal: Born in Bismarck, N.Dak.

Education: bachelor's degree, political science, Minnesota State University Moorhead, 1987.

Professional: 1988–1995 , legislative staff, Rep. Tim Johnson, D-S.D. 1995–1996, legislative director, Rep. Tim Johnson, D-S.D.. 1997–2003, legislative director, Sen. Tim Johnson, D-S.D. 2004–2007, Senior Director of Government and Industry Relations, Freddie Mac. 2008–2009, Senior Policy and Legislative Advisor, Arnold & Porter LLP. 2009–2010, Partner, Porterfield, Lowenthal & Fettig, LLC. 2010–Present , Majority Staff Director, Senate Committee on Banking, Housing, and Urban Affairs.

Expertise: Financial services industry.

In December 2010, when Sen. Tim Johnson, D-S.D., became the incoming chairman of the Senate Committee on Banking, Housing, and Urban Affairs, he hired Dwight Fettig, a lobbyist with many financial sector clients, as a senior advisor.

Not long after that, Johnson, whose state of South Dakota is home to the credit card industry, made Fettig the committee's majority staff director.

Fettig came to the committee from Porterfield, Lowenthal & Fettig LLC, a government relations firm where he was a partner. Fettig's most recent clients before leaving the private sector included the American Bankers Association, JPMorgan Chase and the National Association of Mortgage Bankers.

Before joining Porterfield & Lowenthal, both of whom are former Senate Banking Committee staffers who became lobbyists, Fettig was the chief lobbyist for Freddie Mac, where his official title was senior director of government and industry relations. In that job, he provided strategic advice for Senate Democrats and advised senior managers Capitol Hill issues such as corporate governance, Government Sponsored Enterprise regulatory restructuring, insurance issues, anti-predatory lending and affordable housing legislation.

He previously worked in Johnson's Senate office as a legislative director from 1996 to 2003, as well as from 1995 to 1996, when Johnson was in the House of Representatives. Before becoming then-Rep. Johnson's legislative director, he worked on Johnson's legislative staff from 1988 to 1995.

Fettig was also the senior policy and legislative advisor at Arnold & Porter LLP, where he developed and implemented legislative strategies for a number of clients, including Fortune 500 companies. While there, Fettig played a key role in the firm's legislative and public policy practice with a focus on financial services issues, guiding clients through the 2008 elections and the legislative response to the turmoil in financial markets.

A native of Bismarck, N.D., Fettig graduated with a bachelor's degree in political science from Minnesota State University, Moorhead.

SENATE BANKING, HOUSING, AND URBAN AFFAIRS

Jonathan Graffeo

Communications Director

304 Russell Senate Office Bldg.

Phone: (202) 224-5744

jonathan_graffeo@shelby.senate.gov

Personal: Born 02/01/1981 in Birmingham, Ala.

Education: Bachelor of Arts, Political Science Major, Auburn University, 2003. Cross Continent M.B.A, Duke University, Fuqua School of Business, 2012.

Professional: 2004–2005, legislative correspondent, Sen, Richard Shelby, R-Ala. 2005–2006, legislative correspondent, Senate Committee on Banking, Housing, and Urban Affairs. 2006, legislative assistant, Sen, Richard Shelby, R-Ala. 2006–2008, Republican communications director, Senate Committee on Banking, Housing, and Urban Affairs. 2009–present, communications director, Sen, Richard Shelby, R-Ala.

As the spokesman for the Senate Committee on Banking, Housing and Urban Affairs, Jonathan Graffeo spent the bulk of his time in 2010—as did most committee staffers—talking about financial regulation.

And it's likely that the most significant issues that Graffeo works on in 2011 will be oversight of the financial regulation legislation, or the Dodd-Frank bill that President Obama signed last summer, reform of Fannie Mae and Freddie Mac, and funding for health care legislation.

Graffeo's boss—GOP Sen. Richard Shelby of Alabama—strongly opposes funding for the health care legislation, and as the ranking member on the panel's Appropriations Subcommittee on Labor, Health and Human Services, and Education, he's likely to play a key role on the issue. Graffeo is the key liaison for those wanting to get in touch with significant staffers on the committee.

An Alabama native, Graffeo has been working in some capacity for Shelby since 2004, when he first joined the senator's staff as a legislative correspondent. Graffeo became the committee's legislative correspondent in 2005, then Shelby's legislative assistant the following year. He was promoted to Republican communications director for the committee in 2006 and to Shelby's communications director in 2009. He works with the media on issues related to the committee as well as Shelby's personal office, taking requests from reporters for interviews or other information related to the senator's work.

Graffeo has a bachelor's in political science from Auburn University. In the fall of 2010, Graffeo enrolled in Duke University's Cross Continent M.B.A. program so he could better choose staff for Shelby on economic and financial issues. The full-time, long-distance program allows him to continue working on the Hill and includes several residencies in financial centers around the world. So far, Graffeo has completed residencies in Shanghai, China; London, U.K.; and Dubai, U.A.E. He looks forward to future residencies in New Delhi, India; St. Petersburg, Russia; and Durham, N.C. He expects to receive his M.B.A. in May of 2012.

Graffeo is married to Crisina Graffeo.

SENATE BANKING, HOUSING, AND URBAN AFFAIRS

Colin P.J. McGinnis

Senior Policy Advisor

534 Dirksen Senate Office Bldg.

Phone: (202) 224-7391

Fax: (202) 224-5137

Colin_McGinnis@banking.senate.gov

Education: B.A., magna cum laude, Carleton College, 1984. Master of Divinity, Yale University, 1990.

Professional: 1985–1986, legislative assistant, Rep. James Oberstar, D-Minn. 1986–1988, legislative director, Rep. James Oberstar, D-Minn. 1989, campaign manager, Rep. James Oberstar, D-Minn. 1990–1991, communications director, Rep. Martin Olav Sabo, D-Minn. 1991–1997, senior policy advisor, Sen. Paul Wellstone, D-Minn. 1997–2003, chief of staff, Sen. Paul Wellstone, D-Minn. 2003–2005, chief operating officer, International Orthodox Christian Charities. 2006–2008, senior policy advisor, Sen. Christopher Dodd, D-Conn. 2008–2010, interim staff director, Senate Cmte. on Banking, Housing, and Urban Affairs. 2010–present, senior policy advisor, Senate Committee on Banking, Housing, and Urban Affairs.

Expertise: International issues.

When Colin McGinnis agreed two years ago to take on the demanding job of interim staff director for the Senate Banking, Housing, and Urban Affairs Committee, it was on a temporary basis. He handled the frantic pace and long hours well, and two years later, he is now the panel's senior policy advisor.

In this role, the Yale divinity school graduate works on the committee's international security portfolio, which includes issues such as counter-terrorism, international affairs and national security issues, international economic sanctions, oversight of the Bank Secrecy Act, anti-money laundering initiatives and climate change regulation—especially carbon markets.

A longtime aide to former Sen. Chris Dodd, D-Conn., McGinnis spent the early months of the 112th Congress helping to acclimate the new staff director for incoming Chairman Tim Johnson, D-S.D.

During the 111th Congress, McGinnis worked on the Credit Card Accountability Responsibility and Disclosure Act, dealt with several matters pertaining to the Dodd-Frank Wall Street Reform and Consumer Protection Act, and helped develop the Comprehensive Iran Sanctions and Divestment Act (CISADA).

The legislation he worked on that was signed into law included: the CARD Act; the Dodd-Frank Act; CISADA; the Congo Conflict Minerals Act; and the Extractive Industries Transparency Disclosure Act.

On a personal note, McGinnis spent recent months traveling overseas with his family to visit friends in Germany, Vienna, and Paris. His official congressional travel included a visit to the Smithsonian Tropical Research Institute in Panama as part of former Chairman Dodd's Smithsonian Regents oversight role.

SENATE BANKING, HOUSING, AND URBAN AFFAIRS

Andrew Olmem

Republican Chief Counsel

534 Dirksen Senate Office Bldg.

Phone: (202) (202) 224-7391

andrew_olmem@banking.senate.gov

Personal: Born 03/03/1974 in St. Cloud, Minn.

Education: Bachelor's in Economics, Washington and Lee University, 1996. J.D., Washington and Lee University School of Law, 2001.

Professional: 1996–1998, assistant economist, Federal Reserve Bank of Richmond. 2001–2004, Associate, Mayer, Brown Rowe & Maw (New York). 2004–2005, associate, Shaw Pittman. 2005, Counsel, Former Sen. George V. Voinovich, R-Ohio. 2005–2009, counsel, Senate Committee on Banking, Housing, and Urban Affairs. 2009–2011, senior counsel, Senate Committee on Banking, Housing, and Urban Affairs. 2011–present, chief counsel, Senate Committee on Banking, Housing, and Urban Affairs.

Expertise: Banking, Securities, and Insurance Law and Regulation.

Andrew Olmem is not new to the Senate Committee on Banking, Housing, and Urban Affairs, although his title is: As its Republican chief counsel, he's likely to have his hands full as he navigates the many complex issues that come before the panel.

Since arriving at the committee in early 2005 as counsel, he's worked on legislation and hearings that have touched on just about every aspect of the committee's jurisdiction, including: GSEs and housing; monetary policy; terrorism risk insurance; credit ratings; the Export-Import Bank; TARP; Basel capital accords; and consumer issues, to name a few.

In his new post as chief counsel, Olmem will be called on to do many new things. Sometimes, his job will simply require being the public "face" for his boss, ranking member Sen. Richard C. Shelby of Alabama.

As 2011 rolls along, he's likely to examine legislation and help conduct hearings on pension accounting standards, government-sponsored enterprises, how to tackle the deflated housing market, the reduced status of America's banks and financial houses, implementation of the Dodd–Frank Wall Street Reform and Consumer Protection Act and how to make further reforms in the financial regulatory industry.

Olmem was promoted to the committee's senior counsel in 2009. The committee added "chief" to his title after the departure of longtime counsel Mark Oesterle, who left the committee in early 2011. Oesterle had worked for Shelby off and on for a dozen years.

"During the past two years, I spent nearly all my time on Dodd-Frank," Olmem says. "Among the areas I focused on were resolution authority, systemic risk regulation, insurance, bank regulation and regulatory structure."

This year, he said he expects to spend considerable time on GSE reform and to conduct oversight on the implementation of Dodd-Frank.

Olmem earned a bachelor's degree in economics from Washington and Lee University and a law degree at Washington and Lee University School of Law. Shortly after getting his undergraduate diploma, he became an assistant economist for the Federal Reserve Bank of Richmond, where he worked two years. After earning his law degree, he became an associate at Mayer, Brown Rowe & Maw in New York, where he stayed three years before moving to Shaw Pittman.

He first joined the political world in 2004 as counsel to former Sen. George V. Voinovich, R-Ohio, for whom he worked a year before joining the Banking Committee.

SENATE BANKING, HOUSING, AND URBAN AFFAIRS

Drey Samuelson

Democratic chief of staff

534 Dirksen Senate Office Bldg.

drey_samuelson@johnson.senate.gov

Personal: Born in Pender, Nebr.

Education: Bachelor's degree, University of Nebraska (Lincoln). M.F.A. in fiction writing, University of Arizona.

Professional: 1978–1981 , staffer, Rep. Tom Daschle, D-S.D.. 1982–1983 , staffer, Nebraska Gov. Bob Kerrey. 1986–present , chief of staff, Sen. Tim Johnson, D-S.D.

Drey Samuelson is among the longtimers on Capitol Hill, although he's kept a low profile.

As Democratic chief of staff on the Senate Banking, Housing, and Urban Affairs Committee, Samuelson hires and manages those who work for the committee's chairman, Democrat Sen. Tim Johnson, who is the senior senator from South Dakota.

Samuelson has plenty of legislative, political, and Capitol Hill experience. He became Johnson's chief of staff when the chairman was a fledgling congressman back after he was first elected to Congress in 1986, and he has held the chief of staff position for the lawmaker more than a quarter century. In fact, Samuelson said Johnson has never had another chief of staff.

Before signing on with Johnson, Samuelson worked for three years on the staff of Tom Daschle, D-S.D., after the former U.S. Senate Majority Leader was first elected to Congress in the late 1970s. He then jumped to the office of former Nebraska Gov. Bob Kerrey, who became that state's 35th governor during the 1982 election. He worked there one year.

Samuelson cut his teeth on campaign work when he ran Initiative 300 for the Nebraska Farmers Union. Initiative 300, adopted in 1990, was designed to protect family farms by banning large corporations from buying farmland.

Samuelson certainly had experience with family farming, having been reared in the farm town of Pender, Neb.

He attended the University of Nebraska (Lincoln), and also attended the master of fine arts program—focusing on fiction-writing—at the University of Arizona. He was one semester away from earning his master's degree when he decided to write the true-life story about the rape of a close friend, according to the 2008 *Politico* piece.

Eventually, Samuelson wrote what is considered one of the most emotionally raw pieces of personal memoir ever written by a person on Capitol Hill, according to the 2008 *Politico* piece. Published under the pseudonym Ransom Satchell in a 1986 issue of *Playboy* magazine, the article, titled "Another Side of Rape," detailed the assault of his friend as the two of them visited on the bank of a lake.

Ransom was the name of Samuelson's uncle, who died in World War II. Satchell was the maiden name of his grandmother, who Samuelson said drank herself to death mourning the loss.

Samuelson is married to Dr. Lisa Herrick, a clinical psychologist, and has two stepchildren, Sarah and Nick.

SENATE BANKING, HOUSING, AND URBAN AFFAIRS

Dean Shahinian

Senior Counsel and Chief Securities Policy Advisor
534 Dirksen Senate Office Bldg.
Phone: (202) 224-7391
Fax: (202) 224-5137
dean_shahinian@banking.senate.gov

Personal: Born in Washington, D.C.

Education: B.S., Yale University. M.S., Sloan School of Management, Massachusetts Institute of Technology. J.D., University of Virginia.

Professional: special asst., Rep. Carl D. Perkins, D-Ky. attorney-advisor, Securities and Exchange Commission. counsel to the commissioner, Securities and Exchange Commission. asst. chief counsel for corporate activities, U.S. Office of Thrift Supervision. 1997–2010, Democratic senior counsel, Senate Cmte. on Banking, Housing, and Urban Affairs. 2006, adjunct professor, Columbus School of Law, Catholic University of America. 2008, professional lecturer, George Washington University School of Law. 2011–Present , senior counsel and chief securities policy advisor, Senate Cmte. on Banking, Housing, and Urban Affairs.

Expertise: Securities regulation, banking regulation, financial privacy, corporate governance, Oversight of Dodd-Frank implementation.

Dean Shahinian, the senior counsel and chief securities policy advisor for the Senate Banking, Housing, and Urban Affairs Committee, spent much of the 111th Congress—as most committee staffers did—on working to pass the Dodd-Frank Wall Street Reform and Consumer Protection Act.

In 2011, he will spend much of his time assisting the committee's oversight of the law to ensure that "the letter and the spirit of the act are being implemented by the regulatory agencies, the public's views on proposed rules is being appropriately solicited and considered, Government Accountability Office and SEC studies are proceeding as intended and legitimate concerns and potential unintended consequences arising from the act are examined."

While that piece of legislation was undoubtedly the high point of the last congressional session—and its implementation remains a focus of 2011—the Yale and MIT graduate also anticipates several other accomplishments in 2011. He expects in the 112th Congress to focus on strengthening the Securities and Exchange Commission, corporate governance, credit rating agencies, securitization, executive compensation, municipal securities, investment advisors, hedge funds, private equity funds and investor protection.

"I expect to assist with various securities matters, including the review of market structure issues, such as those raised by combinations of stock exchanges and trading involving the flash crash," says Shahinian.

During his many years on the committee, he staffed more than 100 committee hearings and met with representatives of federal and state agencies, trade associations, securities firms, depository institutions, consumers, insurers, and congressional offices. He played a key role in the American Recovery and Reinvestment Act (2009) and the Emergency Economic Stabilization Act (2008).

Committee on the Budget

624 Dirksen Senate Office Bldg.
Washington, DC 20510
Phone: (202) 224-0642
Fax: (202) 228-2007
http://budget.senate.gov

Ratio: 11/11/1

MAJORITY MEMBERS

Kent Conrad, ND, Chairman

Patty Murray, WA
Ron Wyden, OR
Bill Nelson, FL
Debbie Stabenow, MI
Benjamin Cardin, MD
Sheldon Whitehouse, RI
Mark R. Warner, VA
Jeff Merkley, OR
Mark Begich, AK
Chris Coon, DE

MINORITY MEMBERS

Jeff Sessions, AL, Ranking Member

Charles E. Grassley, IA
Michael Enzi, WY
Mike Crapo, ID
John Ensign, NV
John Cornyn, TX
Lindsey Graham, SC
John Thune, SD
Rob Portman, OH
Pat Toomey, PA
Ron Johnson, WI

INDEPENDENT MEMBERS

Bernard Sanders, VT

SENATE BUDGET

JURISDICTION

(1) Committee on the Budget, to which committee shall be referred all concurrent resolutions on the budget (as defined in section 3(a)(4) of the Congressional Budget Act of 1974) and all other matters required to be referred to the committee under titles III and IV of that Act, and messages, petitions, memorials, and other matters relating thereto.

(2) Such committee shall have the duty (a) to report the matters required to be reported by it under Titles III and IV of the Congressional Budget Act of 1974; (b) to make continuing studies of the effect on budget outlays of relevant existing and proposed legislation and to report the results of such studies to the Senate on a recurring basis; (c) to request and evaluate continuing studies of tax expenditures, to devise methods of coordinating tax expenditure, policies, and programs with direct budget outlays, and to report the results of such studies to the Senate on a recurring basis; and (d) to review, on a continuing basis, the conduct by the Congressional Budget Office of its functions and duties.

SENATE BUDGET

As Congress looks to slash government spending during the 112th Congress, the Senate Committee on the Budget will certainly face a busy Congressional session. Headed by longtime Chairman Kent Conrad, D-N.Dak., the committee will spend much of 2011 closely analyzing President Barack Obama's fiscal 2012 budget, looking at how its proposals could effect the future of the government moving forward and putting forth its own annual budget resolution.

When Obama unveiled his proposed budget in February 2011, the deficit-minded Conrad said it "gets it about right in the first year" by cutting spending but continuing investments in critical areas such as education, energy and infrastructure. But Conrad urged his colleagues to come up with a package that will tackle the nation's debt and deficit in the long-term, noting that making cuts to discretionary parts of the annual budget simply is not enough.

"What is needed is bipartisan recognition that we must face up to budget realities, and that compromise is essential to the financial security of our country," Conrad said. "Both sides have to be willing to move off their fixed positions and find common ground."

Conrad was joined by a new companion on the other side of the aisle in the 112th Congress, as Sen. Jeff Sessions, R-Ala., took the reigns as ranking member of the committee from Sen. Judd Gregg, R-N.H., who retired at the end of the 111th sessions. Early on, Sessions pushed for major reductions in federal spending. Unlike Conrad, Sessions had little praise for Obama's budget proposal, calling it "a failure of leadership." His staff put out a lengthy report on his dissatisfaction with the president's budget proposal, and Sessions often scolded Obama cabinet members when they appeared before he committee to defend their agencies' proposed budgets, urging them to slash spending.

"I am flabbergasted by this education budget," Sessions told Arne Duncan, secretary of education, when he testified in March 2011. "It could only have been written in Washington, a bubble zone detached from the fiscal reality just described."

Along with tackling budget issues, the Senate Committee on the Budget works alongside the House Budget Committee to oversee the Congressional Budget Office, the agency that studies how legislation affects the nation's fiscal standing.

SENATE BUDGET

Steve Bailey

Senior Analyst for Taxes and Revenues

624 Dirksen Senate Office Bldg.

Phone: (202) 224-2835

Steve_Bailey@budget.senate.gov

Personal: Born 03/03/1950 in Miami, Fla.

Education: B.A., University of Notre Dame, 1972. J.D., University of Baltimore School of Law, 1979.

Professional: 1973–1983, legislative analyst, Social Security Administration. 1983–1990, legislative director/tax counsel, Rep. Don Pease, D-Ohio. 1990–1998, lobbyist, Black, Kelly, Scruggs and Healey. 1998–2001, tax counsel, Sen. Kent Conrad, D-N.Dak. 2001–present, senior analyst for taxes and revenues, Senate Cmte. on the Budget.

Expertise: Tax, pension policies.

Most Americans struggle with understanding the nation's complex tax code, but if there is a man who might be able to explain its nuances—and what the future might hold—it is Steve Bailey. As the staffer charged with overseeing tax and pension policy issues for the Senate Committee on the Budget, Bailey is well-versed in the subject.

As it turns out, Bailey might soon play a role in the reform of the nation's tax code. At the start of the 112th Congress, many government leaders focused on cutting government spending in the fiscal 2012 budget. But Bailey's boss, Sen. Kent Conrad, D-N. Dak., focused on continuing his effort to find long-term solutions to cut the nation's debt and deficit. Conrad said in a statement that it will have to include simplifying the tax code, allowing rates to be lowered but more revenue raised.

In his longtime Senate career, Bailey has worked on a number of major pieces of legislation, including the tax cuts backed by President George W. Bush in the 2000s. He also has analyzed pension policies such as social security and Medicare.

Bailey often works closely with another budget committee staffer and tax expert, deputy staff director Joel Friedman. In February 2011, for example, the pair coordinated the drafting of a Congressional Resource Service report studying tax expenditures.

Bailey's years of experience and institutional knowledge has earned praise from many congressional observers, including Anne Urban of the lobbying firm Urban Swirski and Associates. "If you want to be a great tax staffer, model yourself after Steve Bailey," she said in a paper released by the non-profit group Tax Analysts in 2010.

SENATE BUDGET

Nicole Foltz

Counsel

624 Dirksen Senate Office Bldg.

Phone: (202) 224-0642

Nicole_Foltz@budget.senate.gov

Education: B.S., business administration, Mary Washington College, 2005. J.D., Regent University School of Law, 2008.

Professional: 2006, law clerk, Shaffer, Bock, & Antonoplos, P.L.L.C.. 2007, legal intern, Telecommunication Industry Association. 2007, legal intern, Piersall & Chapman, P.C.. 2008, legal intern, Newport News Commonwealth's Attorney Office. 2009, intern, Financial Services Forum. 2009–Present, counsel, Senate Budget Cmte.

Expertise: Law.

Nicole Foltz serves as counsel for the Senate Budget Committee's Republican staff. In this role, Foltz is charged with helping monitor congressional spending and preparing the federal government's long-term spending plan. During the 112th Congress, Foltz is likely to help her boss, committee ranking member Sen. Jeff Sessions, R-Ala., find ways to cut government spending.

Sessions has made this a priority during the first few months of his tenure as ranking member. He laid out this anti-spending plan at the first committee hearing of the new session, explaining in his opening statement that he would push to significantly cut spending, which he argued is a key to fixing the weak economy. "The American people understand what elites in Washington seem to forget: You can only live beyond your means for so long. Eventually, the bill comes due," Sessions said.

Although Foltz is relatively new to the committee, having just joined the panel in 2009, she already has earned a reputation as a valuable player for the Republican team. Former budget committee ranking member Judd Gregg, R-N.H., recognized Foltz on the Senate floor in April 2010 for her work on the Health Care and Education Reconciliation Act of 2010. Foltz's expertise on Senate budget issues is also respected off Capitol Hill. For example, she appeared as a speaker at a May 2010 round table discussion of current events, featuring ideas from senior Senate staffers. The gathering was sponsored by the Ripon Society and held at the popular G.O.P. hangout, the Capitol Hill Club.

Foltz, whose full name is Devon Nicole Foltz, came to Capitol Hill after a series of high-profile internships at a number of law firms. While a law student at Regent University, she served as a board member of the school's Moot Court and worked as coordinator of the Regent Cup Moot Court Competition. She also worked as executive chairman of the Business Transactions Law Society.

But Foltz didn't come to Capitol Hill without any past experience: In 2006, she interned in the office of former Rep. Mike Oxley, R-Ohio. During her undergraduate years at Mary Washington College, Foltz made the varsity crew team and studied abroad in Australia and New Zealand.

SENATE BUDGET

Joel Friedman

Deputy Staff Director

624 Dirksen Senate Office Bldg.

Phone: (202) 224-0642

joel_friedman@budget.senate.gov

Personal: Born 09/12/1958 in Wash.

Education: B.A., international relations, Pomona College, 1980. M.A., public affairs, Princeton University, 1987.

Professional: 1987–1991, financial economist, Office of Management and Budget. 1991–1996, budget analyst and deputy director of budget priorities (majority), director of budget analysis (minority), House Cmte. on the Budget. 1996–2000, technical advisor, Ministry of Finance, South Africa, U.S. Department of the Treasury. 2000–2006, senior fellow, Center on Budget and Policy Priorities. 2007–present, deputy staff director, Senate Cmte. on the Budget.

Expertise: Budget Process.

As deputy director of the Senate Committee on the Budget, Joel Friedman works on a wide range of budget and budget process issues. He assists the committee in helping to develop the annual budget resolution, which is the panel's core responsibility. Aside from that annual task, Friedman said his primary focus is overseeing tax policy.

In the 111th Congress, Friedman assisted on a slew of budget-related measures, including the health care reform reconciliation bill and the Statutory Pay-As-You-Go measure. Friedman also helped Sen. Kent Conrad, D-N.Dak., on projects related to the senator's position as a member of President Barack Obama's National Commission on Fiscal Responsibility and Reform, including his co-chairmanship of the organization's tax reform working group, he said.

During the 112th session, Friedman will help Conrad create a budget resolution that likely will contain cuts to many government programs. Although Conrad praised Obama's fiscal 2012 budget when it was first released, he expressed in a statement his concern that federal officials were not doing enough to focus on deficit and debt reduction in the long-term.

Friedman's diverse economic experience should come in handy as the panel looks to cut government spending programs. For example, Friedman worked for several years as a senior fellow at the Center on Budget and Policy Priorities, a non-partisan group that analyzes how state and federal policies impact low- and moderate-income families. He also worked on federal budget issues, concentrating primarily on tax policy, while also devoting a portion of his time to the International Budget Partnership, a project at CBPP that collaborates with civil society groups in developing countries to improve budgeting and reduce poverty.

SENATE BUDGET

Jim Hearn

Deputy Staff Director

621 Dirksen Senate Office Bldg.

Phone: (202) 224-2370

Fax: (202) 224-4835

Jim_Hearn@budget.senate.gov

Personal: Born 08/12/1959 in Norfolk, Va.

Education: B.A., political science and statistics, Boston University, 1981. M.P.P., University of California, Berkeley, 1984.

Professional: 1984–1995, principal analyst, Congressional Budget Office. 1995–2004, senior analyst for government finance and management, Senate Cmte. on the Budget. 2005–2009, director of federal programs and budget process, Senate Cmte. on the Budget. 2009–present, deputy staff director, Senate Cmte. on the Budget.

Expertise: Policy analysis, budget process, financial analysis of legislation, telecommunications.

As deputy staff director for Republicans on the Senate Committee on the Budget, Jim Hearn is charged with assisting in running the committee's staff operations and helping analyze the intricacies of the budget. There are few people on Capitol Hill who have as much experience handling budget issues as Hearn, who spent a decade with the non-partisan Congressional Budget Office prior to joining the Senate panel in 1995.

Before taking on a deputy staff director position in 2009, Hearn was the panel's resident expert on federal programs and the overall budget process. It is experience that will certainly come in handy during the 112th Congress, as Members on the committee aim to reduce government spending. Hearn's boss, newly-installed ranking member Jeff Sessions, R-Ala., has made slashing federal spending a priority. By March 2011, Sessions had repeatedly criticized President Barack Obama's fiscal 2012 budget proposal and grilled cabinet members as they came to testify before the panel.

Hearn is likely to be an asset to Sessions, something his former boss, retired Sen. Judd Gregg, R-N.H., certainly considered him to be. In 2007, for example, Gregg presented Hearn with a special award marking 12 years of Senate service.

"Jim Hearn is one of the most knowledgeable professionals in the budget business," Gregg said in a statement released at the time. "It is a real credit to the Budget Committee to have individuals of his character and talent on our staff."

Hearn also was selected to be a Stennis Congressional Staff Fellow in the 109th Congress, a special bipartisan, bicameral fellowship for senior congressional staffers.

SENATE BUDGET

Sarah Kuehl

Senior Policy Analyst for Social Security and Medicare

624 Dirksen Senate Office Bldg.

Phone: (202) 224-0559

Sarah_Kuehl@budget.senate.gov

Education: B.A., history and public policy, University of Denver, 1996. M.P.P., public policy, Harvard University, 1998.

Professional: Research and teaching assistant, Harvard University. senior legislative assistant, Sen. Bob Kerrey, D-Neb. 2001–present, senior analyst for Social Security and Medicare, Senate Cmte. on the Budget.

Expertise: Public policy, Social Security.

With more than 10 years of experience studying how Social Security and Medicare affect the federal budget, Sarah Kuehl will play a key part in assisting Congress decide how to fund and manage the government programs moving into the next decade. As the staffer charged with studying the entitlement programs for the Senate Committee on the Budget, Kuehl will help shape their future as Baby Boomers begin to retire and Congress aims to slash government spending.

Kuehl is likely to stay busy in the 112th Congress. Republicans have said reforming Social Security and Medicare will be among their top priorities, and in the early days of the session, the two programs were at the center of bipartisan talks to reduce the deficit. Kuehl's boss, Sen. Kent Conrad, D- N. Dak., urged Members not to include Social Security in any deficit reduction package, telling *The Hill* newspaper that "when those two get put together, it creates huge problems to getting the deficit reduction done, because it confuses the issue." Conrad did, however, agree that Medicare and Medicaid should be part of the effort.

Like most of her fellow committee staffers, Kuehl assisted on larger budget issues in the 111th Congress, including the annual budget resolution. She also worked Health Care and Education Reconciliation Act, earning praise from Conrad on the Senate floor for her efforts.

While Kuehl has the last decade working in various positions on Capitol Hill, she left quite a legacy at her alma mater, the University of Denver. Her grandmother, Jan Nurnberger, created a scholarship university's Institute of Public Policy in 2001, called the Kuehl Family Scholarships, which recognize the influence the school had in shaping Kuehl's education. In 2003, Kuehl even taught a forum on social security and entitlements alongside former Colorado Gov. Richard Lamm, according to the university's Web site.

SENATE BUDGET

Mike Lofgren

Budget Analyst
624 Dirksen Senate Office Bldg.
Phone: (202) 224-9373
mike_lofgren@budget.senate.gov

Personal: Born 07/11/1953 in Akron, Ohio.

Education: B.A., history, University of Akron, 1975. M.A., history, University of Akron, 1977.

Professional: 1983–1994, military legislative assistant, Rep. John Kasich, R-Ohio. 1995–2004, budget analyst for defense, House Cmte. on the Budget. 2005–present, budget analyst, Senate Cmte. on the Budget.

Expertise: Defense issues, foreign relations.

Mike Lofgren is one of the most tenured staffers working for the Senate Committee on the Budget, having been with the panel since 2005—but serving as a Capitol Hill aide since 1983. His budget expertise is on foreign affairs, an area that is expected to be hit hard by cuts in the 112th Congress due to the push to cut government spending.

In the 112th Congress, Lofgren is likely to help his boss, budget committee ranking member Jeff Sessions, R-Ala., find ways to save taxpayer money by slashing the foreign affairs budget. Sessions has been highly critical of President Barack Obama's fiscal 2012 budget request, calling it a failure of leadership. In fact, Sessions laid out his reasoning in a 22-page report prepared by budget committee staffers such as Lofgren.

Foreign aid programs long have been targeted by those in Congress wanting to save tax dollars. In the 111th Congress, the budget panel voted to cut the foreign affairs budget by $4 billion, which would have hindered State Department programs such as USAID. That drew the ire of leaders such as Secretary of State Hillary Clinton and Defense Secretary Robert Gates.

Lofgren also is an expert on defense spending. Like foreign aid, the budget for the Defense Department is expected to take a big hit during the 112th session.

Prior to serving on the Budget panel, Lofgren worked in the office of Rep. John Kasich, R-Ohio, where he served as a military legislative assistant. He also served several years as a defense analyst for the House Committee on the Budget.

SENATE BUDGET

Stephen Miller

Communications Director

624 Dirksen Senate Office Bldg.

Phone: (202) 224-0642

stephen_miller@budget.senate.gov

Professional: 2007–2009, press secretary, Rep. Michele Bachmann, R-Minn. 2009, communications director, Rep. Jon Shadegg, R-Ariz. 2009–2011, press secretary, Senate Judiciary Committee. 2011–present, press secretary, Senate Budget Committee.

Expertise: Communications.

As communications director for the Senate Budget Committee, Stephen Miller is charged with pushing the message of his boss, the panel's ranking member, Sen. Jeff Sessions, R-Ala. Although Miller is new to talking about budget issues, he is a longtime Sessions aide, having worked for the senator when Sessions served as ranking member of the Senate Judiciary Committee during the 111th Congress.

In the 112th session, Miller will be charged with spreading the Senator's message of fiscal restraint and the need to cut federal government spending. Compared to many Hill offices, Miller took an active approach to messaging early on, sending out nearly 30 press releases by mid-March pushing Sessions' legislative priorities. Most of the releases aimed to spread Sessions' call for fiscal restraint and a need to counter President Barack Obama's proposed fiscal 2012 budget.

During his time with Sessions at the Judiciary Committee, Miller mostly helped convey the Senator's reasons for approving or opposing judicial nominees. But Miller also helped bring the panel into the digital age, assisting with the launch the Judiciary Republicans' official YouTube channel during the confirmation hearings of then-Supreme Court nominee Elena Kagan. The channel, Miller told CNN, will serve as a "hub of information for the public, a resource, a place for the exchange of ideas, and a place for a national discussion the senator is planning to foster during the course of the current Supreme Court nomination."

Miller worked with "tea party" darling, Rep. Michele Bachmann, R-Minn., during her first term in Congress. During that time, Miller had to counter accusations that Bachmann was difficult to work for when Capitol Hill newspaper *The Hill* wrote a story about the high rate of turnover in the congresswoman's office. Miller attributed the changes to the "nature of the beast" when it comes to Capitol Hill employees, who are known to change careers frequently. "All of us here are just so thrilled to be working for such a dedicated, principled member committed to reforming Washington," Miller told the publication.

SENATE BUDGET

Mary Naylor

Staff Director
634 Dirksen Senate Office Bldg.
Phone: (202) 224-0862
Fax: (202) 224-2007
Mary_Naylor@budget.senate.gov

Personal: Born 08/21/1967 in Spokane, Wash.

Education: B.A., political science, Northwestern University, 1989.

Professional: 1989–1991, admin. asst. to legislative director, Sen. Kent Conrad, D-N.D. 1991–1993, legislative asst., Sen. Paul Simon, D-Ill. 1993–1996, legislative asst., Sen. Kent Conrad, D-N.D. 1996–1999, legislative director, Sen. Kent Conrad, D-N.D. 1999–2001, deputy chief of staff and deputy asst. secretary for policy, management, and budget, Sen. Kent Conrad, D-N.D. 2001–present, Democratic staff director, Senate Cmte. on the Budget.

Expertise: Budget process.

As the longtime staff director of the Senate Committee on the Budget, Mary Naylor is well-versed on the issues tackled by the panel each congressional session. In fact, the longtime Capitol Hill aide is so respected by her boss, Sen. Kent Conrad, D-N. Dak., that he spoke of her on the chamber floor in the 111th Congress, saying, "I don't know that there has been a person more dedicated to public service than Mary Naylor. What an extraordinary effort she has made."

Conrad specifically was referring to Naylor's work on the Health Care and Education Reconciliation Act of 2010, one of he major pieces of legislation she assisted on as the top staffer on the budget panel. Naylor also led the way on a number of other measures in the 111th session, including the budget resolution passed by the panel each year.

It wasn't the first time Conrad has mentioned his loyal staffer on the Senate floor. He's recognized her several times, including in 2007 when he spoke of her many years of public service, saying that "there is no one for whom I have higher regard."

Despite the praise, Naylor isn't likely to get any rest in the 112th Congress. It will be a busy time for the committee, as senators look to create what is likely to be a trimmed-down budget aimed at cutting government spending in order to pay down the deficit. In March 2011, for example, the committee was averaging three hearings a week studying budget-related issues, many of them focusing on how the fiscal 2012 budget will affect the nation in the long-term.

Naylor worked for Conrad before coming to the budget committee. She started her Senate career as an administrative assistant to the Senator's legislative director in his personal office more than 20 years ago.

SENATE BUDGET

Marcus Peacock

Staff Director

624 Dirksen Senate Office Bldg.

Phone: (202) 224-0642

Fax: (202) @m_peacock

marcus_peacock@budget.senate.gov

Personal: Born 03/21/1960.

Education: B.S. industrial systems and engineering, University of Southern California, 1982. M.P.P, energy and environment, Harvard University Kennedy School of Government, 1986.

Professional: 1982–1984, engineer/bindery supervisor, RR Donnelley. 1986–1989, desk officer, U.S. Office of Management and Budget. 1989–1990, deputy branch chief, Natural Resources Branch, U.S. Office of Management and Budget. 1990–1995, program manager, Jellinek, Schwartz & Connolly. 1995–1998, professional staff member, House Cmte. on Transportation and Infrastructure. 1999–2001, staff director, Oversight and Emergency Response Subc., House Cmte. on Transportation and Infrastructure. 2001–2005, associate director, U.S. Office of Management and Budget. 2005–2009, deputy administrator, Environmental Protection Agency. 2009–2010, director, Pew Charitable Trust's Subsidyscope. 2011–Present, staff director, Senate Budget Cmte.

Expertise: Federal budget, design and implementation of performance management systems.

As staff director for Senate Budget Committee's minority team, Marcus Peacock is charged with directing the committee's staff to work to fulfill the fiscally-minded goals of ranking member Jeff Sessions, R-Ala.

During the 112th Congress, Peacock will be tasked with helping the senator work to cut government spending in the fiscal 2012 budget and beyond. Federal spending issues are something Peacock knows well. While many staff directors earn the top spot on their panel after years of service with the committee, Peacock comes to Capitol Hill directly from the Pew Charitable Trusts, where he oversaw Subsidyscope.org. This two-year project collected, analyzed and presented information on federal subsidies, and led to the first searchable database of federal tax expenditures. The results of the project have been cited in a number of news outlets.

Prior to that, he spent about three-and-a-half years as a deputy administrator at the Environmental Protection Agency, where he handled a number of duties, including overhauling EPA's performance management system. Peacock's work earned him the "President's Quality Award for Overall Management," the highest award given to federal agencies for management excellence.

But Peacock's time at EPA is perhaps most remembered for a controversial blog post he wrote for the EPA's Web site in 2008 about the troubled British singer Amy Winehouse. As *Washington Post* columnist Al Kamen reported, Peacock compared Winehouse's problems with drugs to the need to intervene early on all sorts of things government-wise, including environmental issues. "A good management system . . . forces people to consider how they are doing," Peacock wrote. While some poked fun at the blog, others praised Peacock for thinking outside the box.

Off Capitol Hill, Peacock serves as a commissioner for the U.S. Commission on Key National Indicators. He's also served as a panelist on various programs sponsored by the National Academy of Public Administration, and served as the treasurer of the Capitol Hill Day School and Library of Congress Day Care Center.

SENATE BUDGET

Elizabeth (Liz) Wroe

Health Policy Director and Counsel

624 Dirksen Senate Office Bldg.

Phone: (202) 224-0642

elizabeth wroe@budget.senate.gov

Education: B.A. Politics, Catholic University, 2000. J.D., Catholic University, Columbus School of Law, 2005.

Professional: 2005–2009, health counsel, Senate Cmte. on the Budget. 2009–present, health policy director, Senate Cmte. on the Budget.

Expertise: Health Care.

Elizabeth Wroe serves as health policy director and counsel for Republicans on the Senate Budget Committee. Given the rising cost of health care, the ongoing debate over whether to drastically reform government programs such as Medicare and Medicaid and the G.O.P.-led effort to repeal the health care reform legislation passed in 2009, Wroe certainly faces a busy 112th congressional session.

Wroe came to the panel in 2005 to serve as health counsel, but by 2009 had gotten a promotion. Her expertise is well respected, as evidenced by former ranking member Sen. Judd Gregg, R-N.H., who frequently praised Wroe on the Senate floor for her work on various bills. Gregg even singled Wroe out in April 2010 during debate on the Health Care and Education Reconciliation Act.

"Usually people start with the chief of staff and go down the list," Gregg explained. "But I would like to single out my health policy director, Elizabeth Wroe, for her extraordinary commitment of energy and time on these issues starting over one year ago."

Wroe also worked on the Food Safety Modernization Act during the 111th Congress, garnering praise from Senate Committee on Health, Education, Labor, and Pensions Chairman Tom Harkin, R-Iowa, in a Senate floor speech.

Her hard work also was noticed by the Capitol Hill publication *Roll Call*, who profiled Wroe in a 2009 piece published during the debate over health care reform. A Democratic aide told the paper that Wroe is clear and consistent about what her boss needs to support a piece of legislation, unlike some staffers who can waver during negotiations. She also is one of the hardest working staffers on the panel, another aide said. "Liz works like a machine," the Republican staffer quipped.

While Gregg was considered a political moderate, the committee's current ranking member, Sen. Jeff Sessions, R-Ala., is among the most conservative senators in the chamber, meaning Republicans on the panel could get more aggressive with their messaging and legislative efforts during the 112th session. By February 2011, for example, Sessions already had attacked Democrats' health care efforts, claiming in a press release that it adds nearly $700 billion to the deficit in its first 10 years.

Committee on Commerce, Science and Transportation

508 Dirksen Senate Office Bldg.
Washington, DC 20510-6125
Phone: (202) 224-5115
Fax: (202) 224-1259
http://commerce.senate.gov

Ratio: 12/13

MAJORITY MEMBERS

John D. Rockefeller, WV, Chairman

Daniel Inouye, HI
John F. Kerry, MA
Barbara Boxer, CA
Bill Nelson, FL
Maria Cantwell, WA
Frank Lautenberg, NJ
Mark Pryor, AR
Claire McCaskill, MO
Amy Kloubuchar, MN
Tom Udall, NM
Mark Warner, VA
Mark Begich, AK

MINORITY MEMBERS

Kay Bailey Hutchison, TX, Ranking Member

Olympia J. Snowe, ME
John Ensign, NV
Jim DeMint, SC
John Thune, SD
Roger F. Wicker, MS
Johnny Isakson, GA
Roy Blunt, MO
John Boozman, AR
Marco Rubio, FL
Patrick J. Toomey, PA
Kelly Ayotte, NH

SENATE COMMERCE, SCIENCE AND TRANSPORTATION

JURISDICTION

(1) Coast Guard.
(2) Coastal zone management.
(3) Communications.
(4) Highway safety.
(5) Inland waterways, except construction.
(6) Interstate commerce.
(7) Marine and ocean navigation, safety, and transportation, including navigational aspects of deepwater ports.
(8) Marine fisheries.
(9) Merchant marine and navigation.
(10) Nonmilitary aeronautical and space sciences.
(11) Oceans, weather, and atmospheric activities.
(12) Panama Canal and interoceanic canals generally, except as provided in subparagraph (c).
(13) Regulation of consumer products and services, including testing related to toxic substances, other than pesticides, and except for credit, financial services, and housing.
(14) Regulation of interstate common carriers, including railroads, buses, trucks, vessels, pipelines, and civil aviation.
(15) Science, engineering, and technology research, development, and policy.
(16) Sports.
(17) Standards and measurement.
(18) Transportation.
(19) Transportation and commerce aspects of outer continental shelf lands.

SENATE COMMERCE, SCIENCE AND TRANSPORTATION

Transportation—whether on the nation's roads or its commercial airlines—will dominate the Senate Committee on Commerce, Science and Transportation agenda in the 112th Congress.

As overseer of America's highways and aviation system, the committee—led by Chairman John D. (Jay) Rockefeller IV (D-WV) and Ranking Member Kay Bailey Hutchison (R-Texas)—must still grapple with a long-term Federal Aviation Administration (FAA) reauthorization, which has eluded Congress for years.

The last long-term FAA authorization law expired Sept. 30, 2007. The last temporary extension was expected to remain valid until March 31, 2011, although it seemed more extensions were likely.

Disagreements over several issues have caused the holdup, including whether to require the Department of Transportation to periodically review and renew the antitrust immunity given to international airline alliances.

The Senate's two-year version of the reauthorization bill, S.223, passed after negotiators reached an agreement on the sticky issue of allowing more long-distance flights out of Washington's Reagan National Airport. The compromise was to open a limited number of slots to new airlines and a limited number to those already operating out of National.

Senate Democrats on the committee called this version of the reauthorization "the first jobs bill of the 112th Congress."

But the House's version is a four-year bill, so reconciling the numbers in the two versions will be tricky. Another stumbling block may be airports, which appear unhappy with getting only $3 billion for the Airport Improvement Program and with a passenger facility charge that they consider too low.

Also on the agenda is the Federal Surface Transportation Policy and Planning Act of 2011, which would establish the nation's policies for auto travel and emissions levels—as well as set spending policies for repairing roads and bridges, increasing the use of public transit and dealing with traffic gridlock.

Despite this full plate, Rockefeller at the start of 2011 laid out some other fairly ambitious goals.

In January, he introduced the Public Safety Spectrum and Wireless Innovation Act (S.28). The bill provides first responders and public safety officials with additional wireless and funding resources "to keep America safe," in the chairman's words.

Among other things, it would: allow firefighters to receive high speed file downloads, such as floor plans for burning buildings, wirelessly; let law enforcers use handheld devices to get information about those at a crime scene—such as outstanding warrants—before arriving; and permit officers to take electronic fingerprints at a scene and compare them immediately with those in local, state and federal databases.

Early in 2011, the committee held a hearing on the America COMPETES Reauthorization Act of 2010, which cleared the Senate and the House with bipartisan support. The legislation doubles investment in science and research during the next decade, but the chairman said he feared budget constraints could threaten that financial commitment.

The committee may also be visiting a decision by President Obama, who is under pressure to cut federal spending, to have the U.S. space agency shelve two significant climate change missions that were expected to launch in 2017. The White House eliminated funding for the Climate Absolute Radiance and Refractivity Observatory (CLARREO) and Deformation, Ecosystem Structure and Dynamics of Ice (DESDynI) missions. They were two of four top-tier missions that the National Research Council rubber-stamped in 2007.

SENATE COMMERCE, SCIENCE AND TRANSPORTATION

Todd Bertoson

Deputy Staff Director

560 Dirksen Senate Office Bldg.

Phone: (202) 224-1251

Fax: (202) 224-1259

Todd_Bertoson@commerce.senate.gov

Personal: Born 12/12/1974 in Seattle, Wash.

Education: B.A., business administration, University of Washington, 1997. J.D., University of Washington, 2004.

Professional: 2004–2006, legislative assistant, Sen. Ted Stevens, R-Alaska. 2006–2010 , senior counsel, Senate Cmte. on Commerce, Science and Transportation. 2011–present , deputy staff director, Senate Cmte. on Commerce, Science and Transportation.

Expertise: Transportation programs, energy and environmental issues, security programs.

In his five years on the Senate Committee on Commerce, Science, and Transportation, Todd Bertoson has acquired expertise on an impressive assortment of issues.

Not only is he conversant on international fisheries, climate change and coastal zone management, this Seattle, Wash., native is also well versed on energy issues, environmental topics and national security programs.

Bertoson—formerly the committee's Republican deputy staff director and now its senior counsel—has used this portfolio to great effect in his work on the committee. As he looks toward the 112th Congress, he anticipates his time will be consumed with reauthorization of the nation's transportation act—a periodic exercise that determines not only how much money the nation's roads, railways and airlines get, but also Congress' take on the future of transportation in the United States.

He will also participate in hearings on the reauthorization of the Coast Guard and will monitor response to legislation designed to address the Gulf Coast oil spill. Not that these will be fresh issues for the University of Washington graduate. Coast Guard reauthorization and the oil spill response monopolized much of his time last session as well. In fact, it took five years of work before the committee passed the last Coast Guard Reauthorization bill.

Before coming to the committee in 2006, Bertoson was a legislative assistant to the late Sen. Ted Stevens, R-Alaska. Because Stevens was then the committee's ranking Republican, Bertoson had an opportunity to immerse himself in several issues, including communications, highway safety, interstate commerce, homeland security, oceans-related legislation, sports, weather activities, and nonmilitary space sciences.

Bertoson holds a bachelor's in business administration from the University of Washington and a law degree from the same school.

SENATE COMMERCE, SCIENCE AND TRANSPORTATION

Jeff Bingham

Senior Advisor on Space and Aeronautics, Republican Staff
Subcommittee on Science and Space
560 Dirksen Senate Office Bldg.
Phone: (202) 224-4852
Fax: (202) 224-7660
Jeff_Bingham@commerce.senate.gov

Personal: Born 09/20/1946 in Salt Lake City, Utah.

Education: B.A., political science, University of Utah, 1971.

Professional: 1974–1990 , chief of staff, Sen. Jake Garn, R-Utah. 1990–1991 , NASA consultant and participant in the Synthesis Group, Space Exploration Initiative. 1991–1994 , senior policy analyst, Science Applications International Corporation. 1994–1996, legislative coordinator, International Space Station Program. 1996–1999, manager, Space Station Information Center. 1999–2000 , author, NASA History Office. 2001, special assistant, NASA Chief of Staff Courtney A. Stadd. 2001–2002, acting associate administrator, Legislative Affairs, NASA Headquarters. 2002–2004 , senior advisor/special assistant, NASA Administrator. 2004, writer, speaker, consultant, Self. 2005–2007, staff director, Senate Cmte. on Commerce, Science, and Transportation, Subc. on Science an Space. 2007–2008, senior Republican staff member, Senate Cmte. on Commerce, Science, and Transportation, Subc. on Space, Aeronautics and Related Sciences. 2008–present, senior advisor on space and aeronautics, Republican staff, Senate Cmte. on Commerce, Science, and Transportation, Subc. on Science and Space.

Expertise: NASA, National Science Foundation, space issues.

For more than two decades, Jeff Bingham has moved between Capitol Hill, NASA and the private sector—working on missions to the moon and Mars, consulting on the International Space Station Program, creating a NASA history office project and overseeing NASA's legislative affairs.

One of Bingham's top priorities in the 112th Congress as majority staff director for the Senate Committee on Commerce, Science, and Transportation Committee will be overseeing implementation of the 2010 NASA Authorization Act.

Bingham will be dealing with an order from President Obama to drop two high-priority climate missions from NASA's budget. In his fiscal year 2012 budget, Obama—under pressure to control federal spending—slashed funding for the Climate Absolute Radiance and Refractivity Observatory and the Deformation, Ecosystem Structure and Dynamics of Ice missions, both of which were scheduled to launch in 2017.

Bingham's assignments as a space exploration expert have included: developing alternative architectures for missions to the Moon and Mars under the Space Exploration Initiative and creating a NASA History Office project to draft a book-length manuscript on space station policy history that is still underway.

Bingham, however, is not content to pore over space policies and programs. He also paid his political dues working on the Bush-Cheney NASA Transition Team in December 2000, and becoming the White House Personnel Office as special assistant to NASA Chief of Staff Courtney A. Stadd in January 2001. And early in his career, he paid his Capitol Hill dues as chief of staff to GOP Sen. Jake Garn—for 16 years.

Bingham's work has taken him to far-flung parts of the globe, including to Kazakhstan to view the launch of Soyuz TMA-13, which delivered three crewmembers to the International Space Station.

SENATE COMMERCE, SCIENCE AND TRANSPORTATION

Joseph J. Brenckle III

Republican Communications Director

256 Dirksen Senate Office Bldg.

Phone: (202) 224-3991

Fax: (202) 224-1259

joe_brenckle@commerce.senate.gov

Personal: Born 07/1974 in Fairbanks, Alaska.

Education: Bachelor's degree, history, University of San Diego, 1996. Master's degree, American studies, Georgetown University, 2002.

Professional: 1996, production assistant, NBC/MSNBC—Republican (San Diego) and Democratic (Chicago) Conventions. 1996–2000, staff assistant/legislative correspondent, Sen. Frank Murkowski, R-Alaska. 2000–2003, press secretary, Senate Cmte. on Energy and Natural Resources—Chairman/Ranking Member Frank Murkowski, R-Alaska. 2004–2005, press secretary, Rep. Frank A. LoBiondo, R-N.J. 2005–2006, communications director, Rep. Rick Renzi, R-Ariz. 2006–present, Republican communications director, Senate Cmte. on Commerce, Science and Transportation Committee.

Expertise: Communications, press, media.

In the 112th Congress, Republican Communication Director Joe Brenckle's will continue to handle messaging and press relations for Ranking Member Kay Bailey Hutchison, R-Texas, which so far includes everything from rail regulations to motorcoach fatalities.

In a March 2011 press release, Brenckle showed that Hutchison supported an Obama Administration decision to revisit the Positive Train Control (PTC) regulatory mandate in order to reduce compliance costs.

PTC is an automated technology design to prevent train collisions, overspeed derailments, and injuries to railroad employees. In 2008, Congress passed legislation requiring railroads to implement PTC technology on rail lines that carry passengers or certain types of toxic chemicals by December 2015.

Brenckle issued a press release a month before about a Hutchison bill that would base the PTC regulations on 2015 rail usage when the mandate goes into effect, rather than 2008 usage. The goal is to reduce compliance costs, without sacrificing the safety of the nation's rail system, according to the release.

Brenckle also has handled press as Hutchison continues to push bus-safety legislation to address motorcoach fatalities due to a lack of seat belts or stronger windows and roofs that can withstand roll-over crashes. Her legislation, first introduced in 2007, would require motorcoach vehicle safety inspections of all new bus operators to make sure they are safe before carrying passengers.

Space exploration also enters into his portfolio as Hutchison has crossed swords with the Obama administration for a fiscal year 2012 budget plan that makes deep cuts to the heavy lift launch vehicle and Orion capsule

Brenckle, a Fairbanks, Alaska, native, earned his bachelor's degree in history from the University of San Diego and his master's degree from Georgetown University.

SENATE COMMERCE, SCIENCE AND TRANSPORTATION

Gael Sullivan

Senior Professional Staff Member

427 Hart Senate Office Bldg.

Phone: (202) 224-9000

Fax: (202) 228-2339

gael_sullivan@commerce.senate.gov

Personal: Born 02/23/1968 in Washington, D.C.

Education: B.A., University of Massachusetts (Amherst), 1990.

Professional: 1991–1993, administrative aide, Office of the Senate Sergeant at Arms. 1993–2000, legislative corresp., legislative asst., legislative director, Washington office director, Rep. Bob Wise, D-W.Va. 2000–2001, legislative director, Rep. Bob Filner, D-Calif. 2001–present, Democratic senior professional staff member, Senate Cmte. on Commerce, Science, and Transportation.

Expertise: Aviation.

In February of 2011, Gael Sullivan found himself explaining to a group of lawyers how the Senate would continue funding for the nation's air transportation system, despite the lack of agreement between the House and Senate on an FAA reauthorization bill.

A Democratic professional staff member on the Senate Committee on Commerce Science and Transportation and an expert on funding and policy for the government's aviation and air travel programs, the rest of Sullivan's 2011 calendar will no doubt be consumed with securing that reauthorization.

Speaking before the American Bar Association Air & Space Law Forum, Sullivan spelled out the challenges that lay ahead in the 112th Congress, given that the Senate's two-year version of the fiscal 2011 FAA reauthorization bill is quite different than the House's four-year version. Moreover, lawmakers must contend with airports unhappy with getting only $3 billion for the Airport Improvement Program in the Senate bill and with a passenger facility charge that they consider too low.

Sullivan described for the attorneys how major labor issues had to be resolved on the Senate floor before passage—just part of more than 100 amendments that were debated before the bill was approved. Democrats such as Sullivan publicized the reauthorization bill as something that would create American jobs.

In 2010, Sullivan also spoke about airport legislation while a panelist at the 10th Annual DHS Aviation Security Summit in Arlington, Va.

Sullivan works closely with the office of the Aviation Subcommittee and is responsible for planning hearings, developing legislation, and the day-to-day operations of the subcommittee. He briefs committee staff and members on issues they will be voting on and meets with the airline industry, aviation manufacturers, and labor unions that are interested in matters before the committee.

Committee on Energy and Natural Resources

304 Dirksen Senate Office Bldg.
Washington, DC 20510
Phone: (202) 224-4971
Fax: (202) 224-6163
http://energy.senate.gov
committee@energy.senate.gov

Ratio: 10/11/1

MAJORITY MEMBERS

Jeff Bingaman, NM, Chairman

Ron Wyden, OR
Tim Johnson, SD
Mary L. Landrieu, LA
Maria Cantwell, WA
Debbie Stabenow, MI
Mark Udall, CO
Jeanne Shaheen, NH
Al Franken, MN
Joe Manchin, WV
Christopher Coons, DE

MINORITY MEMBERS

Lisa Murkowski, AK, Ranking Member

Richard Burr, NC
John Barrasso, WY
James E. Risch, ID
Mike Lee, UT
Rand Paul, KY
Daniel Coats, IN
Rob Portman, OH
John Hoeven, TN
Bob Corker, TN

INDEPENDENT MEMBERS

Bernard Sanders, VT

SENATE ENERGY AND NATURAL RESOURCES

JURISDICTION

(1) National energy policy, including international energy affairs and emergency preparedness.
(2) Strategic petroleum reserves.
(3) Outer continental shelf leasing.
(4) Nuclear waste policy.
(5) Privatization of federal assets.
(6) Territorial affairs, including Freely Associated States.
(7) Regulation of Trans-Alaska Pipeline System and other oil or gas pipeline transportation systems within Alaska.
(8) National Petroleum Reserve—Alaska.
(9) Alaska Native Claims Settlement Act.
(10) Alaska National Interest Lands Conservation Act.
(11) Antarctica.
(12) Arctic research and energy development.
(13) Native Hawaiian matters.
(14) Ad Hoc issues.

SENATE ENERGY AND NATURAL RESOURCES

After Congress's failure to enact sweeping energy legislation approved by the Senate Energy and Natural Resources Committee in the 111th Congress, the committee is going back to the drawing board for a new energy bill the 112th Congress.

But the committee won't be starting from scratch.

Committee Chairman Sen. Jeff Bingaman, D-N.-Mex., and other committee members have said they plan to reintroduce and revamp many of the bi-partisan measures contained in the American Clean Energy Leadership Act of 2009, which was approved by the committee in June 2009 by a 15-8 vote, but never brought to the Senate floor.

Among them are provisions that would set new or improved energy efficiency standards for more than a dozen consumer appliances, create a Clean Energy Deployment Administration, or "green bank" within the Department of Energy, and provide incentives for renewable electricity research and development.

Specific priorities for new legislation laid out by Bingaman are promoting energy research and development, ensuring a strong domestic market for clean energy technologies, providing financial infrastructure and incentives to build advanced energy technology projects, and enacting explicit policies to promote the development of U.S. manufacturing capabilities for these clean energy technologies.

"I think these four items or elements should be at the heart of whatever comprehensive energy legislation that we undertake in this Congress," Bingaman said in a speech laying out his energy priorities earlier in 2011.

One change expected for the legislation in the 112th Congress will be the addition of a Clean Energy Standard, which would require utilities to generate a portion of their power from low carbon sources including renewables like solar and wind, along with nuclear power, natural gas, and clean coal.

President Obama advocated such a measure in his State of the Union Speech at the beginning of 2011, in which he called for 80 percent of the country's power to come from "clean" sources by 2035.

In addition, the committee is also expected to craft reform legislation in response to the Deep Water Horizon—the largest oil spill in the nation's history—which will include an overhaul of the regulations in place for offshore drilling in the Outer Continental Shelf.

Following Republican gains in the Senate in 2010's midterm elections, Democrats lost one seat on the committee, and eight of the committee's 22 members are new to the committee themselves.

Sen. Lisa Murkowski, R-Alaska, the committee's top Republican, rejoins the committee after mounting a historic comeback in her own election, in which she ran as an independent after losing her state's primary election.

In addition, the 112th Congress will be Bingaman's last as chair of the committee. He announced earlier in 2011 he would not seek re-election to a sixth term, and return to New Mexico to "pursue other challenges."

SENATE ENERGY AND NATURAL RESOURCES

Allyson K. Anderson

Senior Professional Staff Member

304 Dirksen Senate Office Bldg.

Phone: (202) 224-7143

allyson_anderson@energy.senate.gov

Personal: Born 1974 in Pella, Iowa.

Education: B.A., music, University of Northern Iowa, 1997. B.S., geology, University of Northern Iowa, 1997. M.S., geology, Indiana University-Purdue University, 2000.

Professional: 1998–1999, teaching assistant, Department of Geology, Indiana University-Purdue University. 1999, laboratory technician, Sois Laboratory, Dept. of Geology, Indiana University. 1999–2002, teaching assistant, Department of Geology, University of Kansas. 2002–2003, researcher, Kansas Geological Survey. 2003–2006, senior petrophysicist/geoscientist, Exxon Mobile Exploration Co. 2006–2007, American Geological Institute Congressional Science policy fellow, Senate Cmte. on Natural Resources. 2007–present, professional staff member, Senate Cmte. on Energy and Natural Resources.

Expertise: Carbon capture and sequestration, geothermal energy, R&D related to petroleum, rare earth elements.

A petroleum geologist by training, Democratic senior professional staff member Allyson Anderson will be in the thick of the Senate Energy and Natural Resource Committee's work on legislation related to oil spill reform and carbon capture and sequestration.

A response to the blowout of the Deep Water Horizon well in the Gulf of Mexico will be among the committee's highest priorities, and Sen. Jeff Bingaman, D-N. Mex. is expected to reintroduce legislation that would overhaul offshore drilling regulations.

Anderson, one of three staffers on the Democratic side of the committee working on that legislation, said she will focus her efforts on improving safety and training for the offshore workforce.

In addition, Anderson will also play a key role in the committee's work on carbon capture and sequestration (CCS), which will likely be an important element of a clean energy standard being crafted by the panel.

Such a standard would require utilities to generate a percentage of their electricity through sources low in greenhouse gas emissions, such as renewables and nuclear power, and Anderson said the inclusion of CCS technology is an important part reaching a bi-partisan consensus. Working that and other coal-related provisions into an energy measure, she said, "is one of the only ways you'll be able to get everybody on board."

Anderson also said she expects to concentrate on legislative efforts related to rare earth elements, and other critical materials for clean energy technology.

Those materials, which are used in magnets for wind turbines, in cell phones, and other electronics, will be the focus of a legislative initiative expected in the 112th Congress aimed at increasing domestic production of rare earths, Anderson said.

Anderson has been with the committee since 2006 when she joined as a congressional science policy fellow through the American Geological Institute.

SENATE ENERGY AND NATURAL RESOURCES

Tara Billingsley

Professional Staff Member

304 Dirksen Senate Office Bldg.

Phone: (202) 224-4756

tara_billingsley@energy.senate.gov

Education: B.A., international studies, American University, 1995. M.A., international studies, School of Advanced International Studies, Johns Hopkins University, 1998.

Professional: 1995–1996, project manager, SJA International, Inc.. 1998–1999, policy analyst, Charles L. Fishman, P.C. 1999–2002, industry economist, Energy Information Administration, U.S. Dept. of Energy. 2002–2007, energy security team leader, Office of Intelligence, U.S. Dept. of Energy. 2007–present, professional staff member, Senate Cmte. on Energy and Natural Resources.

Expertise: Energy markets, international energy, fuels.

Tara Billingsley, a Democratic professional staff member with expertise in energy markets, international energy, and fuels, will likely find herself in the thick of the debate over rising gasoline prices.

Supply chain disruptions caused by unrest in oil producing nations during the beginning of 2011 have increased calls in Congress for the development of alternative transportation fuels, as well as domestic production.

In addition, President Obama has said he stands ready to tap into the nation's Strategic Petroleum Reserve, a proposal with which Billingsley's boss, committee chair Sen. Jeff Bingaman, D-N.Mex., has said he agrees.

"I support the President's position, which I believe is the same as my own: world oil supply warrants careful attention, and the President should stand ready to draw down the Strategic Petroleum Reserve," Bingaman said in a statement released in March 2011.

In addition to traditional fuel sources, ethanol, another one of Billingsley's issue areas, will likely be front and center in 2011.

The Environmental Protection Agency announced in January 2011 it was granting a waiver raising the amount of ethanol allowed in certain model year cars and light trucks from 10 percent to 15 percent, a move that is being legally challenged by the petroleum industry and other organizations.

Billingsley was among the committee staffers who crafted the part of energy legislation enacted in 2007 that included a renewables fuel mandate, which set requirements for the amount of advanced biofuel, such as cellulosic ethanol, content in the U.S. fuel supply.

SENATE ENERGY AND NATURAL RESOURCES

Karen K. Billups

Republican Chief Counsel

Phone: (202) 224-4971

karen_billups@energy.senate.gov

Education: B.A., Southern Methodist University, 1984. J.D., University of Texas School of Law, 1987. Bar Admission, District of Columbia, December, 1987.

Professional: 1987–1990, counsel, Baker & Botts (Washington, D.C.). 1990–1991, Department of Energy, Office of the General Counsel (Washington, D.C.). 1991–1993, legislative and regulatory counsel, Balch and Bingham (Washington, D.C.). 1993–1995, House Cmte. on Energy and Commerce. 1995–1999, senior counsel, Senate Cmte. on Energy and Natural Resources. 1999–2003, director, federal affairs/Washington counsel, Entergy Corporation (Washington, D.C.). 2003–2008, deputy chief counsel, Senate Cmte. on Energy and Natural Resources. 2009–present, Republican chief counsel, Senate Cmte. on Energy and Natural Resources.

Expertise: Energy and environmental policy, natural resource production and conservation, nominations for jurisdictional government agencies.

As Republican Chief Counsel, Karen Billups will likely be involved in just about every issue that comes before the Senate Energy and Natural Resources Committee.

Among the top priorities for Republicans in the 112th Congress is increasing domestic production of oil and natural gas after a spike in gasoline prices caused by unrest in the Middle East earlier in 2011.

"Both supply and demand affect oil prices, and that's why Republicans support both new production and alternatives to reduce consumption," Sen. Lisa Murkowski, R-Alaska, the committee's ranking member said in speech in March 2011.

"But we're also thinking about what comes next, and we're committed to making progress on cleaner energy—that's just not our only goal," Murkowski said. "We also want energy to be affordable, abundant, diverse, and domestic."

In addition, Billups and Republicans on the committee will be work to move pieces of a comprehensive energy bill approved by the committee in 2009, but never approved by the full senate.

Among the bi-partisan provisions in the bill were measures that would set new or improved energy efficiency standards for more than a dozen consumer products, funding for electric vehicle infrastructure, and the establishment of a "green bank" within the Department of Energy to fund clean energy projects.

Billups joined the committee in 2003 under then-Chairman Sen. Pete Domenici, R-N.Mex., and has worked on policies dealing with nuclear waste and international energy policy.

In addition to energy and environmental policy, Billups has expertise in natural resource production and conservation, and has been involved in the confirmation process for Obama administration nominees, such as Energy Secretary Stephen Chu, and Interior Secretary Ken Salazar.

SENATE ENERGY AND NATURAL RESOURCES

Jonathan Black

Professional Staff Member

312 Dirksen Senate Office Bldg.

Phone: (202) 224-4971

jonathan_black@energy.senate.gov

Personal: Born 11/24/1977 in Long Island, N.Y.

Education: B.A., University of Richmond, 1999. M.A., George Washington University, 2001.

Professional: 2001–2003, staff assistant, Senate Cmte. on Energy and Natural Resources. 2003–2006, Democratic legislative assistant, Senate Cmte. on Energy and Natural Resources. 2007–present, professional staff member, Senate Cmte. on Energy and Natural Resources.

Expertise: Climate and environment.

With cap-and-trade legislation no longer at the forefront of Congress, Jonathan Black, a Democratic professional staff member on the Senate Energy and Natural Resources Committee who specializes in climate policy, is looking at other areas to achieve reductions on greenhouse gas emissions.

"I really think it's about scoping out the terrain and figuring out where there can be bipartisan relationships and work on things that deal with energy security that all have co-benefits of reducing emissions," Black said.

For 2011, Black said he will be eyeing areas such as the military's role in technology research and development and energy efficiency; U.S. competitiveness in technology and energy; and areas related to investment in green technologies.

"I'm kind of branching out to a bunch of different ideas and issues that all deal with climate," Black said.

In addition, Black anticipates playing a role in the development of a Clean Energy Standard, a measure that would require utilities to generate a percentage of their power from low carbon sources like renewables and nuclear power.

"I'm not entirely sure what my role will be, but it's a broad issue and it certainly deals with a number of issues that I have dealt with in the past," he said.

Black's work in the 111th Congress included work on a cap-and-trade bill that focused on the power sector, an alternative to economy wide cap-and-trade legislation.

Black attended the United Nation's international climate policy summit in Cancun, Mexico in December 2010, as well as the one held in Copenhagen in 2009.

When not on the Hill, Black enjoys taking art classes, sailing, chess, tennis, as well as participating in "Hands on DC," a community service project that cleans up public schools in Washington, D.C.

SENATE ENERGY AND NATURAL RESOURCES

David Brooks

Democratic Senior Counsel

312 Dirksen Senate Office Bldg.

Phone: (202) 224-4103

david_brooks@energy.senate.gov

Personal: Born 04/21/1961 in Tucson, Ariz.

Education: B.S., University of Arizona, 1983. J.D., University of Arizona, 1987.

Professional: 1987–1989, staff counsel, Subc. on Energy and Environment, House Cmte. on Interior and Insular Affairs. 1989–1994, counsel, Subc. on Public Lands, National Parks and Forests, Senate Cmte. on Energy and Natural Resources. 1995–present, Democratic senior counsel, Senate Cmte. on Energy and Natural Resources.

Expertise: Public lands, national parks.

David Brooks, a Senior Counsel for the Democrats, will likely be at the heart of the Senate Energy and Natural Resource Committee's legislative efforts to pass several bill related to public lands and national parks.

After the Senate failed to act on a major package of lands and water bills in the 111th Congress, including dozens approved by the Senate Energy and Natural Resources Committee, the committee will make a second attempt either in the form of several stand-alone bills or another large package.

Several that made up the bulk of an omnibus lands and water bill brought forward in 2010 fell under the jurisdiction of Brooks, who specializes in federal lands issues.

Another issue the Committee will likely deal with in the 112th Congress is the development of public lands in the west for renewable energy generation.

The Department of Interior brought forward a plan that would allow development of large-scale solar facilities on up to 21.5 million acres of public land earlier in 2011, a proposal the Senate Energy and Natural Resources Committee will likely oversee.

In 2009, Brooks played a role in another large package of lands bills, the Omnibus Public Lands Management Act, which was reported out of the committee and passed by the Senate.

"I can't think of a single bill that has ever done more to ensure the enjoyment of, and access to, wilderness areas, historical sites, national parks, forests, trails, and scenic rivers," Committee Chairman Jeff Bingaman, D-N.Mex., said upon passage of the legislation, which contained roughly 60 different bills dealing with public lands issues that was reported out of his committee.

"Collectively, this is one of the most sweeping conservation laws the Senate has considered in many, many years," Bingaman said.

SENATE ENERGY AND NATURAL RESOURCES

Rosemarie Calabro

Press and Media Assistant

304 Dirksen Senate Bldg.

Phone: (202) 224-4971

Rosemarie_Calabro@energy.senate.gov

Personal: Born 1985.

Education: B.A., Georgetown University, 2007. J.D., Catholic University of America, 2014.

Professional: 2007–2011, majority staff assistant, Senate Cmte. on Energy and Natural Resources. 2011–present, press and media assistant, Senate Cmte. on Energy and Natural Resources.

Expertise: Media, Communications.

Rosemarie Calabro started as the Senate Energy and Natural Resource Committee's Democratic press and media aide in January 2011, but she's no stranger to the committee.

Calabro has worked as a staff assistant for the committee since 2007, following stints as a staff aide in the summers of 2003 and 2004.

"I was ready for new and different opportunities to help out the committee and it's exciting because you get to learn a little bit about a bunch of issues," Calabro said.

As press and media aide, Calabro works closely with Communications Director Bill Wicker, assisting him in writing press releases, handling phone calls from the media, and updating the committee's website, among other duties.

"It's exciting because you get to help clarify and really ensure the accuracy of what people are saying about your boss and the legislative work our committee is doing," Calabro said.

Among the issues Calabro will likely lend a hand with will be media inquiries regarding the committee's response to rising oil and gasoline prices, legislation in response to the oil spill in the Gulf of Mexico, and the committee's efforts to craft a Clean Energy Standard that would require utilities to generate a portion of their power from low-carbon sources.

Calabro could also likely play a large role in the committee's endeavors into new media, such as Facebook and Twitter, something the committee is actively exploring.

Calabro's previous work for the committee, as a staff assistant, included helping organize hearings and briefings, legislative research, and other projects.

Calabro, who is currently pursuing a law degree at Catholic University of America in the evenings, got her first taste of the Senate in 2001, when she spent the summer as a page for now-retired Sen. Chris Dodd, D-Conn.

In addition, Calabro enjoys competitive rowing, and previously was a coxswain for the Potomac Boat Club, a local rowing club, a hobby she says she would like to return to in the future.

SENATE ENERGY AND NATURAL RESOURCES

McKie Campbell

Republican Staff Director

304 Dirksen Senate Office Bldg.

Phone: (202) 224-5305

mckie_campbell@energy.senate.gov

Personal: Born 08/05/1950 in Washington, DC,

Education: Marietta College.

Professional: 1995–2005, private consultant. 2005–2007, commissioner, Alaska Department of Fish and Game. 2009–present, Republican staff director, Senate Cmte. on Energy and Natural Resources.

Expertise: Natural resources, energy policy.

As the Senate Energy and Natural Resource Committee's Republican staff director, McKie Campbell plays a role in just about every bill considered by the committee, along with the daily operations of the staff working for ranking member Sen. Lisa Murkowski, R-Alaska.

"I think my number one job is making sure that all of us down here at the committee are accurately reflecting the Senator's views," Campbell said. "We want to make sure we never have any divergence from that."

Campbell said he expects the committee to continue working on a broad array of energy issues in the 112th Congress, the focus on large omnibus bills that were popular with the committee in previous congress's are probably over, he said.

"I think the committee is going to focus on smaller discreet bills for the next coming years," Campbell said.

Campbell said the committee will likely work on legislation that would increase domestic oil and gas production, a legislative priority of Murkowski, who introduced two bills in early 2011 that would open a portion of the Artic National Wildlife Refuge for oil and gas exploration.

In addition, Campbell is among the committee staffers involved in the crafting of a Clean Energy Standard, a measure called for by President Obama that would require utilities to generate a portion of their electricity from low-carbon sources such as renewables, nuclear, and natural gas.

"I think that is going to be difficult to make happen this year, but it's worth considering," Campbell said.

Campbell also anticipates working on legislation in the 112th Congress related to protecting the nation's electric grid from cyber attacks, and legislation re-organizing a portion of the Interior Department following the Deepwater Horizon oil spill.

"We are very fortunate to have a great staff here, and that makes this job a lot easier," he said.

SENATE ENERGY AND NATURAL RESOURCES

Michael Carr

Senior Counsel

304 Dirksen Senate Office Bldg.

Phone: (202) 224-8164

michael_carr@energy.senate.gov

Personal: Born 1970 in Kettering, Ohio.

Education: B.A., political science, University of Colorado, 1993. J.D., certificate of specialization in environment and natural resources law, Lewis and Clark College, 1996.

Professional: 1996–1999, legislative assistant, Rep. David Skaggs, D-Colo. 1999–2002, attorney-advisor, Office of the Solicitor, Department of the Interior. 2002–2004, attorney, Heldman & Carr, LLP. 2004–present, Democratic counsel, Senate Cmte. on Energy and Natural Resources.

Expertise: Coal use, Carbon capture.

Michael Carr, a Democratic senior counsel to the Senate Energy and Natural Resources Committee, first starting dealing with the financing and deployment of clean energy in 2005, and since then the area has become one of his primary focuses.

That represents a change for Carr, whose previous areas of expertise included carbon capture and coal use.

"I've spent a lot of the last four years learning," Carr said, an effort that has included talking with hundreds of experts and others about emerging clean technologies and how they make it in commercial markets.

Of the bills Carr anticipates working on in the 112th Congress, his No. 1 priority is likely to be legislation to create a Clean Energy Deployment Administration, a "green bank" within the Department of Energy to finance deployment of clean energy projects.

Such a proposal was included in the American Clean Energy Leadership Act, comprehensive legislation that was approved with bi-partisan support in the committee in 2009, but never reached the Senate floor.

In addition, Carr, also anticipates work on legislation related to the deployment of electric vehicles and the support of developing the charging infrastructure needed to support them.

The effort is likely to be similar to the "Promoting Electric Vehicles Act" previously approved by the committee, which would have authorized $3.6 billion aimed at putting 400,000 such cars on the road in three years.

Additionally, Carr said he was anticipating work on legislation that would provide incentives for natural gas vehicles, as well as continued oversight of the Department of Energy's Loan Guarantee program.

When not on the Hill, Carr enjoys pitching and playing shortstop for his recreational men's over-30 baseball team, which has won their championship for three seasons in a row.

SENATE ENERGY AND NATURAL RESOURCES

Robert Dillon

Republican Communications Director

Phone: (202) 224-6977

robert_dillon@energy.senate.gov

Education: Journalism, University of Alaska Fairbanks.

Professional: 1989–1992, photographer, Anchorage Times. 1998–2000, Managing Editor, Artcic Sounder. 1998–2004, Managing Editor, Alaska Newspapers Inc. 2000, Copy Editor, China Daily. 2004–2005, Business Editor, Prague Post. 2005–2008, Political Reporter, Fairbanks Daily News-Miner. 2006–2008, Political Correspondent, Energy Intelligence Group. 2008–present, Republican communications director, Senate Cmte. on Energy and Natural Resources.

Expertise: Communications.

For Robert Dillon, the Senate Energy and Natural Resources Committee's Republican communications director, the gains made by Republicans in the 2010 mid-term elections are good news.

"We get more office space and more people," Dillon said.

Democrats on the committee lost one seat, bringing the committee's ratio to 10 to 12, and increasing the chances that legislation minority wants will make it through the committee.

"Republican proposals have a much better shot at success," Dillon said.

In 2011, the Republicans will want to pass legislation related to increasing oil and gas production, and oversight and review of regulation's put in place by the Obama administration, such as the Environmental Protection Agency's authority to regulate greenhouse gas emissions.

Dillon's job includes producing press releases, editorials, speeches and talking points on policy issues. He joined the committee in late 2008, when fellow Alaskan Sen. Lisa Murkowski took over as the top Republican on the panel.

Prior to joining the committee, Dillon covered energy policy in Congress, the White House, and federal agencies for the Oil Daily, and other publications of the Energy Intelligence Group. He has also worked as a political reporter for the Fairbanks Daily News-Miner, as well as a business editor at the *Prague Post*.

Dillon says his experience as a newsman helps him understand where the media he interacts with is coming from.

"I've got an appreciation for how the business works and what the reporters face in daily challenges and how to help them do their job better," Dillon said.

Dillon said the committee is eying adding Twitter and Facebook to their communications tool box.

In his spare time, Dillon enjoys playing rugby with club teams in the Washington, D.C. area and spending time with his family, including his baby daughter.

SENATE ENERGY AND NATURAL RESOURCES

Kellie A. Donnelly

Republican Deputy Chief Counsel

306 Dirksen Senate Office Bldg.

Phone: (202) 224-9360

Fax: (202) 228-0541

kellie_donnelly@energy.senate.gov

Personal: Born 05/22/1969 in Fall River, Mass.

Education: B.A., College of the Holy Cross, 1991. J.D., Columbus School of Law, Catholic University, 1994.

Professional: 1994, legislative aide, Sen. John H. Chafee, R-R.I. 1995–1997, counsel, Senate Cmte. on Environment and Public Works. 1997–1998, legislative counsel, Fish and Wildlife Service Division, U.S. Department of the Interior. 1999–2003, attorney, Sullivan & Worcester, LLP (previously Verner, Liipfert, Bernhard, McPherson & Hand). 2003–present, counsel, Senate Cmte. on Energy and Natural Resources.

Expertise: Renewable energy, electricity, cyber security.

Kellie Donnelly has expertise in electricity issues, but as the Republican deputy chief counsel on the Senate Energy and Natural Resources Committee, she plays a role nearly everything the committee handles.

"My focus is still everything electricity, but I get pulled into a number of other issues," Donnelly said.

Donnelly will spend a great deal of the 112th Congress working with her Democrat counterparts on a clean energy standard, a measure that would require utilities to generate a portion of their power from low-carbon sources such as renewables, nuclear, and natural gas.

President Obama called for a standard in his State of the Union Address as a way to achieve a goal of generating 80 percent of the country's power from clean sources by 2035, but exact details of how such a measure will be put in reality have been scarce, Donnelly said.

"The proposal was pretty much barebones, so we are asking the White House, we are engaging, we are talking about it," she said.

Donnelly and other staffers are sorting out which renewable sources of power will count toward that standard and if it will include energy efficiency efforts.

Other issues Donnelly expects to work on in the 112th Congress include a revamp of cyber security legislation and electricity transmission measures included in a larger energy bill the committee passed in 2009, but never considered by the full Senate.

Donnelly played a significant role in that legislation, known as the American Clean Energy Leadership Act, including helping to craft new and improved energy efficiency standards for consumer products, and a Renewable Electricity Standard, that would have required utilities to generate a percentage of their power from renewable sources.

Off the Hill, Donnelly enjoys reading, yoga, and is preparing for the birth of her first child, expected in the summer of 2011.

SENATE ENERGY AND NATURAL RESOURCES

Whitney Drew

Republican Professional Staff Member

304 Dirksen Office Bldg.

Phone: (202) 224-5305

Personal: Born 8/13/1979 in Chestertown, Md.

Education: B.A., Psychology, Lehigh University.

Professional: 2003–2005, government relations assistant, American Public Power Association. 2005–2009, Republican staff, House Committee on Energy and Commerce. 2009–present, Republican professional staff member, Sen. Committee on Energy and Natural Resources.

Expertise: Energy efficiency.

Whitney Drew, a Republican professional staff member who joined the Senate Energy and Natural Resources committee in 2009, is an expert on energy efficiency.

Drew played a major role in the Implementation of National Consensus Appliance Agreements Act of 2011 (INCAAA), bi-partisan legislation that would set new or improved energy efficiency standards for more than a dozen consumer appliances as well as certain outdoor lighting.

Drew will likely spend a portion of the 112th Congress advancing the legislation, which increases mandatory minimum energy use standards for products such as furnaces and air conditioners, and sets first time standards for certain outdoor lighting, pool heaters, and other products.

While the bill, which was re-introduced after nearly passing by unanimous consent in the 111th Congress, has enjoyed bi-partisan support in the past, Drew said it may face new challenges in the 112th Congress as populist support grows for separate legislation that would repeal standards set for the traditional incandescent light bulb in the Energy Independence and Security Act of 2007.

"While people do want to save energy and be efficient for the most part, you definitely have some people out there with the feeling the government is doing too much restricting of consumer choice," Drew said, describing the oppositions' viewpoint. "It remains to be seen what will happen with the INCAAA bill."

In addition to her work on INCAA, Drew may also play a role in re-crafting energy efficiency portions of a comprehensive energy bill that was approved by the committee on a bi-partisan basis in 2009, but never considered by the full Senate.

That bill, the American Clean Energy Leadership Act (ACELA), included measures that would have increased energy efficiency in industrial and manufacturing applications, and would have directed the Energy Department to set new building efficiency codes for commercial and residential buildings, among other efficiency measures.

Some of those provisions may be re-introduced as standalone legislation, in smaller packages, or incorporated into a comprehensive energy efficiency bill being crafted by Sen. Jeanne Shaheen, D-N.H., a member of the committee.

Drew, a native of Chestertown, Md., previously served as a legislative analyst for the House Energy and Commerce Committee. She also worked as a legislative assistant for the American Public Power Association.

SENATE ENERGY AND NATURAL RESOURCES

Isaac Edwards

Senior Counsel

Phone: (202) 224-5305

Personal: Born in Homer, Alaska.

Professional: 2003–2009, legislative director, Office of Sen. Lisa Murkowski. 2009–2010, Republican Counsel, Sen. Energy and Natural Resources Committee. 2010–present, Senior Republican Counsel, Sen. Energy and Natural Resources Committee.

Expertise: Territories and international energy issues.

Republican Senior Counsel Isaac Edwards joined the Senate Energy and Natural Resource Committee after working in the personal office of Ranking Member Lisa Murkowski, R-Alaska. He is an expert on international energy issues.

Edwards also handles on the committee's work on U.S. territorial policy, including insular matters related to eight U.S. affiliated Island areas—Puerto Rico, the U.S. Virgin Islands, American Samoa, Guam, the Northern Mariana Islands, the Republic of the Marshall Islands, the Federated States of Micronesia, and the Republic of Palau.

In the 112th Congress, Edwards will likely work on legislation related to ex gratia compensation to the Republic of the Marshall Islands for impacts of the U.S. nuclear testing program conducted there in the 1940s and 50s, and a bill that would extend assistance to Palau.

In addition, Edwards has also worked on nuclear energy issues for the committee, and participated in a workshop on small scale nuclear technology hosted by the Alaska Energy Authority and the University of Alaska in late 2010.

Edwards will likely be involved in advancing legislation, The Nuclear Power 2021 Act (S. 512), introduced by Murkowski and committee Chair Sen. Jeff Bingaman, D-N.-Mex., in March 2011.

The legislation would establish a public-private partnership within the Department of Energy for the development of small modular reactors less than 300-megawatts, among other goals.

"Small modular reactors have great potential to help meet our future domestic power needs in a flexible manner, both on and off the grid, as well as open market opportunities overseas," Murkowski said in a statement following the bills introduction.

"This legislation will help address existing challenges and overcome roadblocks by making the development, licensing, and deployment of small reactors a priority," she said.

Edwards, a native of Homer, Alaska, began working for Lisa Murkowski's father worked for Sen. Frank Murkowski, R-Alaska, starting in 1997, before becoming Lisa Murkowski's legislative director in 2003.

SENATE ENERGY AND NATURAL RESOURCES

Jonathan Epstein

Professional Staff Member

304 Dirksen Senate Office Bldg.

Phone: (202) 224-4971

jonathan_epstein@energy.senate.gov

Personal: Born 05/11/1957 in White Plains, N.Y.

Education: B.S., mechanical engineering, Colorado State University, 1980. Ph.D., engineering sciences, Virginia Polytechnic Institute, 1983. J.D., University of Idaho, 2000. LL.M., securities and financial regulations, Georgetown University, 2003.

Professional: 1984–1987, engineering specialist, Idaho National Engineering Laboratory. 1988–1990, assistant professor, Georgia Institute of Technology. 1990–1997, engineering specialist, Idaho National Engineering Laboratory. 1994–1995, science fellow, Stanford University, Center for International Security and Arms Control. 1995–1997, science advisor, Office of the Secretary of Defense. 1999, policy analyst, U.S. Dept. of Commerce, Bureau of Export Administration. 2000–2007, legislative fellow, Office of Senator Jeff Bingaman, D-N.M. 2007–present, professional staff member, Senate Cmte. on Energy and Natural Resources.

Expertise: Energy research and development, national competitiveness, nuclear energy.

After working on two comprehensive energy bills in 2005 and 2007 that were enacted into law, Jonathan Epstein, the Senate Energy and Natural Resource Committee's expert on research and development, will be switching gears to work on smaller pieces of legislation.

Among them, Epstein said, will be a package of bills related to nuclear power, including legislation that would make small modular reactors cheaper to produce.

The reactors, which were recently hailed by the Energy Department as "one of the most promising areas in the energy arena," are about one-third the size of current nuclear reactors, making them easier to manufacture and transport domestically.

Specifically, the legislation would establish a cost-sharing agreement between the nuclear industry and the Department of Energy to help pay for the costs of getting the first initial reactors licensed with the Nuclear Regulatory Commission, Epstein said.

In addition, Epstein, who serves as Democratic Senior Counsel for the committee, said he anticipated working on legislation related the domestic production of Molybdenum-99, a medical isotope that is used for medical procedures tens of thousands of times a day.

"Right now we have to import it all, we have no domestic capabilities," Epstein said.

Epstein played a key role in the America COMPETES Act, first passed in 2007 and reauthorized in the 111th Congress that funded several research programs within the Department of Energy, as well as the National Science Foundation, and the National Institute of Standards and Technology.

He has worked as a staff researcher at the Idaho National Engineering Laboratory, as science advisor for the Assistant Secretary of Defense for Nuclear and Biological Defense Programs, and as an export controls and a policy at the Commerce Department before joining the staff in 2000.

SENATE ENERGY AND NATURAL RESOURCES

Deborah M. Estes

Counsel

312 Dirksen Senate Office Bldg.

Phone: (202) 224-4971

deborah_estes@energy.senate.gov

Personal: Born in Cleveland, Ohio.

Education: B.A., English literature, Smith College. J.D., Georgetown University Law Center.

Professional: 1986–1991, legislative assistant, Sen. Dale Bumpers, D-Ark. 1992–2001, managing director for government relations, American Gas Association. 2001–present, Democratic counsel, Senate Cmte. on Energy and Natural Resources.

Expertise: Natural gas pipeline regulation, energy efficiency.

Deborah Estes, a Democratic Counsel for the Energy and Natural Resources Committee, and an expert on energy efficiency, will likely play a key role in crafting a package of energy efficiency bills planned by the committee in the 112th Congress.

"I know that one of the chairman's main areas of focus is energy efficiency," said Estes, a 10-year veteran of the committee.

The legislation will likely incorporate several energy efficiency provisions included in a sweeping energy bill that was approved by the committee in 2009, but never brought to the Senate floor for a vote in the 111th Congress.

Likely to be among them are measures aimed at improving efficiency in buildings, homes, equipment, appliances, and throughout the federal government.

"I think those are important issues that need to re-appear," Estes said. "There are many provisions that are going to be revived."

In addition, Estes said, the committee will also be looking at legislating portions of the "Better Buildings Initiative" a plan announced by President Obama in early 2011 that seeks to improve the efficiency in commercial buildings by 20 percent over the next decade, and includes financing mechanisms like loan guarantees and grants.

Estes, who also has expertise in natural gas pipeline regulation, said she also plans to keep a close eye on pipeline safety issues in the 112th Congress, including regulatory issues involving the Federal Energy Regulatory Commission.

In the 111th Congress, Estes worked on energy programs included in the American Recovery and Reinvestment Act, which appropriated billions for energy efficiency and other clean energy programs within the Energy Department.

Prior to joining the committee in 2001, Estes served as the managing director of government relations for the American Gas Association.

SENATE ENERGY AND NATURAL RESOURCES

Sam E. Fowler

Chief Counsel

304 Dirksen Senate Office Bldg.

Phone: (202) 224-7571

sam_fowler@energy.senate.gov

Personal: Born 02/02/1952 in Washington, D.C.

Education: B.S., University of New Hampshire, 1974. J.D., George Washington University, 1980.

Professional: 1974–1977, Botany Dept., Smithsonian Institution. 1978–1979, President's Council on Environmental Quality. 1980–1985, associate, Fried, Frank, Harris, Shriver and Kampelman (Washington, D.C.). 1985–1990, counsel, Subc. on Energy and Environment, House Cmte. on Interior and Insular Affairs. 1991–1993, counsel, Senate Cmte. on Energy and Natural Resources. 1993–1995, senior counsel, Senate Cmte. on Energy and Natural Resources. 1995–present, Democratic chief counsel, Senate Cmte. on Energy and Natural Resources.

Expertise: Energy, Senate procedure, public land law.

Sam Fowler, who has served as the Senate Energy and Natural Resource Committee's Democratic chief counsel for more than 15 years, has a hand in every legislative issue that comes before the committee.

"Historically, the Committee on Energy and Natural Resources has been one of the Senate's most productive in the number of bills it reports," Fowler said.

In his role as chief counsel, Fowler reviews all bills and amendments before they are considered by the committee, schedules legislation for consideration, and reviews committee reports on bills approved by the committee.

Among the major pieces of legislation Fowler said he expects to work on in the 112th Congress are various public lands bills, legislation to reform oil and gas development on the Outer Continental Shelf in response to the Deepwater Horizon oil spill, and a comprehensive energy bill.

Fowler was among the committee staffers who worked on the American Clean Energy Leadership Act (ACELA) of 2009, an omnibus energy bill that included provisions related to speeding the siting of electricity transmission lines to furthering development of renewable energy.

Though ACELA was approved by the committee, it was never considered on the Senate floor during the 111th Congress. Sen. Jeff Bingaman, D-N-Mex., has said he plans repackage portions of that bill that had bi-partisan support and try again in the 112th Congress.

In addition, Fowler also handles nominations for 40 senior positions in the Department of the Interior, the Department of Energy, and the Federal Energy Regulatory Commission that are under the Committee's jurisdiction.

Fowler has worked on Capitol Hill for 25 years, 20 of them on the staff of the Energy and Natural Resources Committee.

SENATE ENERGY AND NATURAL RESOURCES

Kaleb D. Froehlich

Senior Republican Counsel
304 Dirksen Senate Office Bldg.
Phone: (202) 224-5305

Personal: Born 05/10/1982 in Juneau, Alaska.

Education: B.A., International Relations, French, University of Southern California, 2004. J.D., University of Virginia School of Law, 2007.

Professional: 2000, intern, Office of Sen. Ted Stevens. 2002, intern, Office of Sen. Sam Brownback. 2006–2009, attorney, Greenberg Traurig, LLP. 2009–Present, Republican Counsel, Senate Cmte. on Energy and Natural Resources.

Expertise: Public lands issues, National parks, Alaska natural resource issues.

Kaleb Froehlich, a senior counsel on the Republican staff with an expertise in public lands issues, will likely play a role in tackling a backlog of public lands bills in the Senate Energy and Natural Resources Committee during 2011.

After Congress failed to act on packages of dozens of lands and water bills in the waning days of the 111th Congress, the committee is likely to try again in the 112th—this time advancing a series of smaller legislative packages.

"The Republicans on the House side have said they don't really want to deal with a [large] package, so I don't think we are going to see any large omnibus groups of bills, like we've been seeing in the past few years," Froehlich said.

Similar to the omnibus lands and water bill that failed to pass the Senate, the legislation will likely include designations of national parks, wilderness areas, monuments, and wild and scenic rivers, among other legislative goals.

In addition, Froehlich worked on land-use law aspects of two bills introduced in February 2011 by Sen. Lisa Murkowski, R-Alaska, the committee's ranking member, which would open a portion of the Arctic National Wildlife Refuge (ANWR) for oil and gas exploration and production.

The 1.5 million-acre coastal plain has been off-limits to those types of activities, but Murkowski, a proponent of increased domestic oil production, has said studies show ANWR "has a 50 percent chance" of containing 10.4 billion barrels of oil and 8.6 trillion feet of natural gas.

"The more of that oil we can produce domestically, the better off our economy, our trade deficit, our employment levels and the world's environment will be," Murkowski said in a statement following the introduction of the bills—The American Energy Independence and Security Act and the No Surface Occupancy Western Arctic Coastal Plain Domestic Energy Security Act.

Froehlich, a native of Juneau, Alaska, joined the committee in 2009 after practicing real estate and land-use law for a private firm in New York. In his free time, he enjoys spending time outdoors, playing sports, and traveling back to his home state.

SENATE ENERGY AND NATURAL RESOURCES

Frank Gladics

Senior Professional Staff Member

304 Dirksen Senate Office Bldg.

Phone: (202) 224-5861

Education: B.S., forest management, Utah State University, 1980. U.S. Forest Service Logging Engineering Program at Oregon State, 1983.

Professional: 1980–1987, U.S. Forest Service. 1987–1989, employee, Intermountain Forest Industries Association. 1989–1993, vice president for public timber, National Forests Products Assoc./American Forest & Paper Assoc. 1993–2000 , president, Independent Forest Product Assoc. 2000–2001 , acting president, American Forest Resource Council. 2001, principle employee, Gladics & Associates. 2001–present, professional staff member, Senate Cmte. on Energy and Natural Resources.

Expertise: Forestry, wildland fire fighting issues, public lands, geothermal and renewable biomass.

Frank Gladics, the Energy and Natural Resources Committee's senior Republican professional staff member, has the principle responsibility to staff the Public Lands Subcommittee which oversees the Bureau of Land Management and the U.S. Forest Service.

In that capacity, Gladics is charged with handling a variety of committee issues related to public lands and forests, including wilderness policies, land exchanges, geothermal energy and oversight of the U.S. Forest Service and Bureau of Land Management for non-mineral issues. He also serves as one of several staff working on renewable energy biomass production and policies and on geothermal policies.

Gladics said in 2011 he expects to continue working on topics such as the renewable biomass definition for renewable electricity, renewable energy production on federal lands.

In addition, Gladics also anticipates working on wilderness designations, wild land designations and other lands bills, including "reversing many of the anti-development policies currently being pursued by the current Administration."

Gladics has worked on the Energy and Natural Resources Committee since 2001 and has been involved in the passage of both the 2005 and 2007 Energy bills, the Healthy Forest Restoration Act, numerous land exchange and wilderness bills and several hundred other forest policy and lands bills.

During Gladic's committee tenure, he has worked for Sens Frank Murkowski, R-Alaska, Pete Domenici R-N.-Mex.M, and now Senator Lisa Murkowski, R-Alaska.

Prior to joining the committee, he spent 16 years working for private sector forest product associations, and began his forestry career working for the U.S. Forest Service in Alaska.

Gladics, who is married to a Department of Agriculture employee and has two grown children, is also a veteran of the United States Navy, serving from 1971 to 1975.

SENATE ENERGY AND NATURAL RESOURCES

Colin Hayes

Republican Professional Staff

Phone: (202) 224-5305

Education: B.A., World Resource Systems Development, Hobart and William Smith Colleges, 2003.

Professional: 2003–2005, executive assistant, Sen. Committee on Energy and Natural Resources. 2005–2006, legislative aide, Sen. Committee on Energy and Natural Resources. 2006–2007, legislative assistant, Office of U.S. Senator Craig Thomas. 2007–Present, professional staff, Sen. Committee on Energy and Natural Resources.

Expertise: Climate change, carbon sequestration, clean energy financing, mining.

Colin Hayes, a Republican professional staff member who rejoined the Senate Energy and Natural Resources Committee in 2007, has a wide range of expertise, including climate change, carbon sequestration, clean energy financing, and mining.

Though legislative action on cap-and trade is considered dead for at least the next two years, Hayes' other legislative areas will likely be active during the 112th Congress.

Hayes will likely work on legislative efforts related to rare earth elements, and other critical materials, used in a wide range of products including many renewable energy technologies.

Sen. Lisa Murkowski, R-Alaska, the ranking member of the committee, introduced legislation in the previous congress, the Rare Earths Supply Technology and Resources Transformation Act of 2010 S. (3521).

The legislation, which would increase domestic production of rare earth elements, is expected to be reintroduced in some form in the 112th Congress, will include work from Hayes.

"I will continue to work with my colleagues and the administration to advance policies that will bolster the domestic production of these materials and reduce our reliance on China," Murkowski said in a December 2010 statement.

Hayes' expertise in carbon sequestration could also come in handy during the 112th Congress, as the committee sets to work crafting a Clean Energy Standard that would require utilities generate a percentage of their electricity through sources low in greenhouse gas emissions.

Carbon capture and sequestration, along with renewables, nuclear power, and natural gas, is expected to play a big role in the measure.

Hayes also will likely be involved in the reintroduction legislation related to the creation of a Clean Energy Deployment Administration, a "green bank" within the Department of Energy to finance risky renewable energy projects.

Such a proposal was included in the American Clean Energy Leadership Act, comprehensive legislation that was approved with bi-partisan support in the committee in 2009, but never reached the Senate floor.

Prior to joining the committee, Hayes served as a legislative assistant to former Sen. Craig Thomas, R-Wyo., and as an executive assistant and then legislative aid to the Senate Energy and Natural Resources Committee.

SENATE ENERGY AND NATURAL RESOURCES

Megan Hermann

Republican Press Secretary

Personal: Born 07/15/1985 in Evansville, Ind.

Education: B.S., Saint Louis University, 2007.

Professional: 2007, intern, Office of Sen. Elizabeth Dole, R-N.C. 2007–2008, marketing associate, The Advisory Board Company. 2008, staff assistant, Senate Energy and Natural Resources Committee. 2008–2010, executive assistant, Senate Energy and Natural Resources Committee. 2010–Present, Press Secretary, Senate Energy and Natural Resources Committee.

Expertise: Media and communications.

Megan Hermann may be the Senate Energy and Natural Resource Committee's Republican press secretary, but she's no stranger to energy issues.

Hermann's father served as president and chief executive officer of Black Beauty Coal Company, which was largest coal company in the Illinois Basin until it was acquired by Peabody Energy in 2006.

"Growing up, he loved to take us to the coal mines and show us the new equipment," Hermann said.

"We would be on road trips to soccer tournaments and he would want to stop by and check out the mines, which were scattered around southern Indiana," she said. "It would extend our trip by at least an hour or so."

Now Hermann is involved with coal—and every other energy source the committee deals with—in a different capacity.

As press secretary, her job includes monitoring energy news, drafting talking points, press releases and media advisories, editing speeches and other statements, working with policy staff on messaging, and talking to reporters.

"My favorite thing about moving into the press role is that while I'm no expert on any specific energy issue, I get to know enough about every issue," Hermann said.

Hermann graduated summa cum laude from Saint Louis University with a Bachelor's Degree in marketing and communications, but "got bit by the political bug" after a job as a press intern for former Sen. Elizabeth Dole, R-N.C.

Since then she has served as a staff assistant and executive assistant on the Senate Energy and Natural Resources Committee, before being promoted to press secretary in June 2010.

In addition to her work on the committee, Hermann is pursuing a master's degree in communications with a focus on political communications from Johns Hopkins University.

In her free time she enjoys traveling back to her home state of Indiana, and is involved with the Junior League of Washington.

SENATE ENERGY AND NATURAL RESOURCES

Brian Hughes

Republican professional staff member

Phone: (202) 224-5305

Education: B.A., Washington State University, 2006.

Professional: 2004–2005, intern, Sen. Ted Stevens, R-Alaska. 2006, staff assistant, Sen. Ted Stevens, R-Alaska. 2006–2007, speech writer, Sen. Ted Stevens, R-Alaska. 2007–2010, Republican legislative aide, Senate Cmte. on Energy and Natural Resources. 2010–present, Republican professional staff member, Senate Cmte. on Energy and Natural Resources.

Expertise: Oil, natural gas, and alternative fuel policy.

Brian Hughes, a Republican professional staff member with expertise in oil, natural gas, and alternative fuel policy, has worked his way up after first coming to the Senate as an intern in 2004.

In the 112th Congress, Hughes will likely join fellow staff member Kevin Simpson in working on legislation that would increase domestic oil and natural gas production, a goal of his boss, Ranking Member Sen. Lisa Murkowski, R-Alaska.

Murkowski, following a run-up in gas prices in early 2011 caused by unrest in the Middle East, introduced two bills that would open up a portion of the Artic National Wildlife Refuge (ANWR), a 1.5 million-acre coastal plain that has been off limits to such ventures.

"Now is the time to develop our domestic oil reserves in the ANWR coastal plain," Murkowski said, in a statement following introduction of the American Energy Independence and Security Act and the No Surface Occupancy Western Arctic Coastal Plain Domestic Energy Security Act in February 2011.

"For far too long, we've kept resources under lock and key that could improve our energy security and create badly-needed jobs," Murkowski said. "There's no excuse for continuing to pay foreign countries for resources we have here."

In addition to oil and gas, Hughes' expertise in alternative fuel policy will likely be put to use in the 112th Congress, as the body is expected to eye ways to move away from traditional fuel sources.

Ethanol was at the forefront of the Obama administration in early 2011, when the Environmental Protection Agency announced in January it was granting a waiver raising the amount of ethanol allowed in certain model year cars and light trucks from 10 percent to 15 percent.

That move is move that is being legally challenged by the petroleum industry and other organizations.

Hughes first came to the Senate in 2004 as an intern for Sen. Ted Stevens, R-Alaska, and went on to serve as his speechwriter before joining the energy committee in September 2007.

SENATE ENERGY AND NATURAL RESOURCES

Joshua Johnson

Professional Staff
Subcommittee on Water and Power
304 Dirksen Senate Office Bldg.
Phone: (202) 224-5861
josh_johnson@energy.senate.gov

Personal: Born in Salt Lake City, Utah.

Education: B.S., Univ. of Utah, 1993. M.S.C., London School of Economics, 1994. M.A., Naval War College, 2010.

Professional: 1995–1997, legislative assistant, Rep. James V. Hansen, R-Utah. 1997–2001, legislative staff assistant, Subc. on Water and Power, House Cmte. on Resources. 2001–2005, staff director, Subc. on Water and Power, House Cmte. on Resources. 2005–present, professional staff, Senate Cmte. on Energy and Natural Resources, Sen. Pete Domenici, R-N.M.

Expertise: Water recycling and desalination, CALFED Bay-Delta Program, energy efficiency.

Joshua Johnson, a Republican professional staff member with expertise in energy efficiency and water policy, plans to eye the link between water usage and energy consumption in the 112th Congress.

"The less water you use in your [energy] production and industrial uses is generally a correlating factor to less energy use," Johnson said. "So we'll continue to focus on ways to reduce water use in commercial, residential, and industrial uses."

Johnson's boss, Sen. Lisa Murkowski, R-Alaska, the Senate Energy and Natural Resource Committee's ranking member, has long expressed an interest in understanding the relationship between water and energy production as well.

Part of Johnson's expertise on those issues comes from his previous position as staff director of the House Committee on Resources Subcommittee on Water and Power, a position he held from 2001 before joining the Senate Energy and Natural Resources Committee in 2005.

In addition, Johnson said he also plans on analyzing a memorandum of understanding signed in July 2010 between the Departments of Energy and Defense agreeing to cooperate on new energy technologies.

The document will likely be the focus of staff briefings in the 112th Congress, Johnson said.

Johnson said he also is interested further examining how Federal agencies are reducing their energy use and examining if agencies are purchasing energy.

Johnson also has had oversight duties of the Bureau of Reclamation and the U.S. Geological Survey. He received a master's degree in National Security and Strategic Studies from the Naval War College in 2010.

SENATE ENERGY AND NATURAL RESOURCES

Chuck Kleeschulte

Republican Professional Staff

Education: B.A., political science, University of Missouri-St.Louis, 1974. M.A., journalism, University of Missouri-Columbia, 1975.

Professional: 1976–1980, reporter, Juneau Empire. 1980–1982, press secretary, Alaska Gov. Jay Hammond. 1983–1984, Anchorage Daily News. 1984–1987, reporter, Juneau Empire. 1987–1989, information officer, Alaska Department of Environmental Conservation. 1991–2002, communications director, Sen. Frank Murkowski, R-Alaska. 2003–2005, communications employee, Sen. Lisa Murkowski, R-Alaska. 2005–2009, legislative assistant, Sen. Lisa Murkowski, R-Alaska. 2009–present, Republican professional staff member, Senate Cmte. on Energy and Natural Resources.

Chuck Kleeschulte, a Republican professional staff member, will likely be among those working at the forefront of a new and emerging energy form in the 112th Congress: marine and hydrokinetic energy.

This refers to technology, such as underwater turbines, buoys, wave energy converters, and other devices, that harness energy from waves, currents, thermal gradients, and other natural phenomena.

The marine and hydrokinetic energy industry has struggled to take off in the United States and Kleeschulte said he is preparing legislation that would fund government research among other incentives.

"It would help the industry get on a level playing field with these other renewables," Kleeschulte said.

Kleeschulte's boss, Sen. Lisa Murkowski, R-Alaska, introduced similar legislation in the 111th Congress that was included in a comprehensive energy bill that was approved by the committee, but never made it to the Senate floor for a vote.

While Kleeschulte's expertise includes energy policy, he said he expects to spend more of his time in the 112th Congress working on Alaskan land issues, another area in which he has expertise.

Kleeschulte expects to work on a variety of Alaska related lands legislation including lands conveyance issues related to the Alaska Native Claims Settlement Act of 1971, and several bills related to gas pipelines in the state, including one that would allow a gas pipeline to go through 7-miles of Denali National Park.

Kleeschulte is certainly no stranger to energy policy and Alaska issues—he worked on Murkowski's staff since 2003, serving on both the communications staff and later as a legislative assistant. Prior to that, he spent more than a decade working for then-Sen. Frank Murkowski, R-Alaska, as his communications director.

SENATE ENERGY AND NATURAL RESOURCES

Leon Lowery

Democratic Professional Staff Member
Sen. Jeff Bingaman, D-N.M.
312 Dirksen Senate Office Bldg.
Phone: (202) 224-4103
leon_lowery@energy.senate.gov

Personal: Born 09/05/1946 in Arab, Ala.

Education: University of Tennessee.

Professional: 1988–1994, Environmental Action. 1994, Subc. on Energy and Power, House Cmte. on Energy and Commerce. 1995–2001, senior policy analyst, Federal Energy Regulatory Commission. 2001–present, professional staff member, Senate Cmte. on Energy and Natural Resources.

Expertise: Electricity, renewable energy.

Leon Lowery, an expert in electricity and renewable energy, will likely play a major role in the Senate Energy and Natural Resources Committee's work on a clean energy standard—a priority of President Obama.

Obama called for such a measure, which would require utilities to generate a portion of their electricity from "clean" sources, such as renewable energy, nuclear power, and natural gas during his State of the Union Speech in January.

Sen. Jeff Bingaman, D-N.-Mex., the committee's chair, who has been hesitant to embrace such a standard in the past, threw his weight behind the measure after meeting with Obama at the White House, and Lowery, a Democratic professional staff member, will likely be one of multiple staffers who have a hand in crafting the legislation.

In the 111th Congress, Lowery was among the committee's aides who developed a renewable electricity standard, which similarly would have required utilities to generate a percentage of their power from wind, solar power, and other renewable sources.

The renewable electricity standard was incorporated into a comprehensive energy bill approved by the committee in 2009, but never brought to the Senate floor for a vote.

In addition, Lowery has previously advocated for increased development of the nation's electric transmission grid, a crucial component to bringing power from far-flung renewables to large population centers where it is needed.

"If we are going to need a lot more electricity and if a big percentage of it is going to come from renewable sources like wind and solar, then we need to build a lot of transmission," Lowery told The Hill in December 2008.

SENATE ENERGY AND NATURAL RESOURCES

Scott Miller

Senior Counsel

312 Dirksen Senate Office Bldg.

Phone: (202) 224-4103

scott_miller@energy.senate.gov

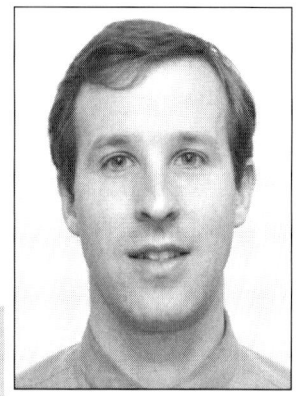

Personal: Born 04/13/1970 in Tarrytown, N.Y.

Education: B.S., Vanderbilt University, 1992. J.D., University of Colorado at Boulder, 1998.

Professional: 1998–2003, attorney, Office of the Solicitor, Dept. of the Interior. 2003–present, Democratic counsel, Senate Cmte. on Energy and Natural Resources.

Expertise: Forest and public lands issues.

Scott Miller, a Democratic Senior Counsel for the Senate Energy and Natural Resources Committee with an expertise in forest and public lands issues, will likely be busy in the 112th Congress with oversight of President Obama's proposed $12.2 billion budget for the Department of the Interior.

If that was not enough, Miller will also need to deal handle designations of national parks, wilderness areas, monuments, wild and scenic rivers, and other bills that will need to be resurrected because Congress failed to act on an omnibus lands and water legislation that included dozens of bills approved by the committee before the end of 2010.

Obama's budget proposal continues or increase critical funding for several programs that are priorities to Committee Chair Sen. Jeff Bingaman, D-N.-Mex., such as the Land and Water Conservation Fund, engaging youth in the outdoors, Indian water rights settlements and reforms to the nation's onshore and offshore oil and gas programs.

"While I'm disappointed that some important projects were left out, overall, the Administration did a good job with the tough choices they had to make," Bingaman said in statement following the proposal's release to Congress in February.

Another persistent issue for Miller, and the committee, has been wildfires, especially as the West has been hit with particularly severe fires in recent years and costs have gone up. Federal agencies have often run out of money needed to battle the fires, forcing them to shift money from elsewhere.

Miller's work affects expansive tracts of public land: 155 national forests and 20 national grasslands, covering 193 million acres. Miller is no stranger to the government's land holdings; he worked for more than four years in the Department of the Interior's Solicitor's Office before coming to the committee in 2003.

SENATE ENERGY AND NATURAL RESOURCES

Kevin J. Rennert Ph.D

Professional Staff Member

304 Dirksen Senate Office Bldg. Washington, DC

Phone: (202) 224-7826

Kevin_Rennert@energy.senate.gov

Education: Ph.D. Atmospheric Science 2007, University Of Washington, 2007. B.A. Physics, Grinnell College, 1997.

Professional: 1998–2000, software developer, Stanford Linear Accelerator Center, Stanford University, Palo Alto, CA. 2000–2007, graduate research assistant, University of Washington, Department of Atmospehric Sciences. 2001–2002, assistant science instructor, Albert Einstein Middle School, Shoreline, WA. 2008–2009, American Meteorological Society Congressional Science Policy Fellow, Senate Committee on Energy and Natural Resources. 2008, research associate, University of Washington. 2010–Present, adjunct faculty, Department of Strategic Management & Public Policy, George Washington University School of Business.

Expertise: Power sector, climate policy, vehicles.

Kevin Rennert, who became a professional Democratic staff member after completing a science policy fellowship with the Senate Energy and Natural Resources Committee, enjoys being on the frontlines of the battle against climate change.

"I'm here to try to help transition the U.S. to a clean energy economy and this is absolutely the very best place to do that," Rennert said.

As a committee expert on the power sector and climate policy, Rennert will also be on the frontlines of the committee's development of a Clean Energy Standard, which would require utilities to generate a percentage of their power from low carbon sources.

Previous Clean Energy Standards brought forward in the 111th Congress have included nuclear energy and clean coal, along with renewable power and energy, but part of Rennert's job will be deciding how diverse the committee's version will be.

"I think there are definitely a lot of threshold questions," Rennert said. "What counts as clean is definitely a threshold question."

President Obama endorsed a Clean Energy Standard during his State of the Union Address to Congress, and committee chair Sen. Jeff Bingaman, D- N. Mex., has said he plans "to work with my colleagues on both sides of the Energy Committee aisle to develop workable legislative proposals that can achieve his clean energy goals."

In addition to work on a Clean Energy Standard, Rennert also has expertise related to vehicles, and expects vehicle efficiency, including increasing efficiency of internal combustion engines, to be the subject of legislation the committee will work on in the 112th Congress.

Rennert joined the committee in 2008 as an American Meteorological Society Congressional Science Policy Fellow, where his work included legislation related to greenhouse gas mitigation, vehicle efficiency incentives, and educational briefings for staffers on subjects such as geoengineering, black carbon, and sea level rise.

He said he did not have to think twice about accepting a full time position with the committee.

"It's filled with very smart, thoughtful people that are very dedicated to creating good bi-partisan legislation," Rennert said.

In the 111th Congress, Rennert was one of several staffers who worked on a greenhouse gas emission cap-and-trade bill that was never released by the committee.

In his free time Rennert enjoys photography, playing guitar, and spending time outdoors.

SENATE ENERGY AND NATURAL RESOURCES

Robert M. Simon

Democratic Staff Director

360 Dirksen Senate Office Bldg.

Phone: (202) 224-9201

bob_simon@energy.senate.gov

Personal: Born 1956 in Philadelphia, Pa.

Education: B.S., chemistry, Ursinus College (Pa.), 1977. Ph.D., chemistry, Massachusetts Institute of Technology, 1982.

Professional: 1983–1985, staff officer, National Research Council, Board on Chemical Science and Technology. 1985–1987, senior staff officer and associate director, National Research Council, Board on Chemical Science and Technology. 1988–1989, staff director, National Research Council, Board on Chemical Science and Techlogy. 1988–1989, expert, Dept. of Energy, Office of the Secretary of Energy Advisory Board. 1990–1992, executive director, Dept. of Energy, Office of the Secretary of Energy Advisory Board. 1991–1993, principal deputy director, Dept. of Energy, Office of Energy Research. 1993–1997, science fellow, Senate Cmte. on Energy and Natural Resources (on detail from Department of Energy). 1997–1998, science and technology advisor, Sen. Jeff Bingaman, D-N.M. (on detail from Department of Energy). 1998–1999, policy analyst, Joint Economic Cmte. 1999–present, staff director, Senate Cmte. on Energy and Natural Resources.

Expertise: Energy policy, science, technology, economic development, federal agency management.

As Democratic Staff Director of the Energy and Natural Resources Committee, Bob Simon will find himself in the thick of the committee's ambitious plans for the 112th Congress.

Those include moving forward on measures that were included in a comprehensive energy bill approved by the committee in 2009, but never brought before the full Senate for a vote, such legislation that would set energy efficiency standards for a wide array of consumer products.

"What we are doing in this Congress is looking back to where we had broad bi-partisan support in the past and starting there, and looking for bills and proposals that we find have support across the aisle," Simon said.

In addition, other committee priorities include crafting a legislative response to the Deepwater Horizon oil spill in the Gulf, and work on a "clean energy standard" requiring utilities to generate a portion of their power from low carbon sources such as renewables, nuclear and natural gas.

As staff director, Simon's job includes coordinating with Senate leadership, as well as his staff's Republican counterparts on the committee.

"We've got a very talented staff of professionals on both sides of the committee," Simon said. "The vast majority of bills that go through the committee are worked out by the staff at sort of a peer level, although every staff director has one or two issues that they sort of like to play closer attention to."

For Simon, a scientist by training, those issues of personal special interest include ones related to the research, development, and commercialization of new energy technologies.

"Sometimes they produce solutions you didn't know you had before," he said.

Simon has served as the committee's staff director since 1999. He worked at the National Research Council and the Department of Energy before coming to the Hill in 1993 as a science fellow.

SENATE ENERGY AND NATURAL RESOURCES

Kevin Simpson

Republican Professional Staff Member

304 Dirksen Senate Bldg., Washington, DC

Phone: (202) 224-4971

Kevin_Simpson@energy.senate.gov

Professional: 2007–2009, legislative assistant, Sen. Ted Stevens, R-Alaska. 2009, Republican counsel, Senate Cmte. on Energy and Natural Resources. 2010–Present, senior Republican counsel, Senate Cmte. on Energy and Natural Resources.

Expertise: Oil and gas issues.

Kevin Simpson, a Republican professional staff member who handles oil and gas issues for the Senate Energy and Natural Resources Committee, will likely have a busy the 112th Congress.

After Middle East turmoil sparked a jump in gasoline prices in early 2011, Simpson's boss, Ranking Member Lisa Murkowski, R-Alaska, called for increased domestic oil and gas production.

"We've ignored the tremendous benefits of American oil production—jobs, money, and security—and now we're facing the consequences," Murkowski said in a weekly Republican address in March 2011.

Simpson will be involved in Murkowski's quest to allow oil exploration and production in the Arctic National Wildlife Refuge (ANWR), a 1.5 million-acre coastal plain that has been off limits to such ventures.

Murkowski introduced two bills to achieve those goals early in 2011—The American Energy Independence and Security Act and the No Surface Occupancy Western Arctic Coastal Plain Domestic Energy Security Act—and Simpson will likely be involved in efforts to advance them.

"For far too long, we've kept resources under lock and key that could improve our energy security and create badly-needed jobs," Murkowski said in a statement following the bills introduction in February 2011. "There's no excuse for continuing to pay foreign countries for resources we have here."

Simpson also will likely assist in one of Murkowski's other goals—speeding the pace in which the Interior Department grants deepwater oil permits following a moratorium imposed by the Obama administration after the Deepwater Horizon oil rig explosion and ensuring spill in the Gulf of Mexico.

Simpson will play a role in Outer Continental Shelf drilling reform legislation the committee is expected to advance in response to that disaster, which was the largest oil spill in the nation's history.

In the 111th Congress the committee approved bi-partisan legislation—the Outer Continental Shelf Reform Act—that included provisions such as a reorganization of the Interior Department and increased safety measure for offshore drilling.

The bill, introduced by Murkowski and committee chair Sen. Jeff Bingaman, D-N.-Mex., would have marked the first significant revision of the Outer Continental Shelf Lands Act in decades, but it died in the Senate.

Simpson joined the Senate Energy and Natural Resources Committee as counsel in 2009, after working as a legislative assistant for Sen. Ted Stevens, R-Alaska.

SENATE ENERGY AND NATURAL RESOURCES

Allen Stayman

Senior Democratic Professional Staff Member

212 Hart Senate Office Bldg.

Phone: (202) 224-7865

allen_stayman@energy.senate.gov

Personal: Born 10/19/1953 in Philadelphia, Pa.

Education: B.A., architecture, University of Washington, 1975. M.S., fisheries, University of Washington, 1982.

Professional: 1979–1980, intern and legislative assistant, Sen. Lowell Weicker, R-Conn. 1982–1984, field biologist, Washington state, Alaska. 1984–1993, majority professional staff, Senate Cmte. on Energy and Natural Resources. 1993–1999, deputy assistant secretary for territorial and international affairs, Dept. of the Interior. 1999–2001, director/special negotiator, Office of Compact Negotiations, Dept. of State. 2001–2003, senior executive for policy, Alliance to Save Energy. 2003–present, Democratic professional staff member, Senate Cmte. on Energy and Natural Resources.

Expertise: Insular affairs, energy efficiency.

Bi-partisan co-operation is key for Allen Stayman, the Senate Energy and Natural Resource Committee's expert on energy efficiency and issues related to eight U.S. affiliated Island areas—matters that typically require consensus between Republicans and Democrats.

"For both my issues, bi-partisanship is preferred," Stayman said. "I basically have an understanding with my minority counterparts…that we'll seek agreement."

In the 112th Congress, Stayman will be concentrating on the Implementation of National Consensus Appliance Agreements Act of 2011 (S.398), which would set new or improved energy efficiency standards for more than a dozen consumer appliances as well as certain outdoor lighting.

The legislation, which increase mandatory minimum energy use standards for product such as furnaces and air conditioners, and set first time standards for certain outdoor lighting, pool heaters, and other products.

"The quickest, cheapest, and easiest way to deal with electricity shortages is through efficiency," Stayman said. "And the easiest way to do efficiency is simply to outlaw inefficient equipment."

In addition to energy efficiency, Stayman assists Committee Chairman Jeff Bingaman, D-N.Mex., with all matters related to Puerto Rico, the U.S. Virgin Islands, American Samoa, Guam, the Northern Mariana Islands, the Republic of the Marshall Islands, the Federated States of Micronesia, and the Republic of Palau.

Stayman said he anticipates working on legislation related to ex gratia compensation to the Republic of the Marshall Islands for impacts of the U.S. nuclear testing program conducted there in the 1940s and 50s, and a bill that would extend assistance to Palau.

SENATE ENERGY AND NATURAL RESOURCES

Tanya Trujillo

Senior Counsel

304 Dirksen Senate Bldg., Washington, DC

Phone: (202) (202) 224-4971

Tanya_Trujillo@energy.senate.gov

Expertise: Water policy.

Tanya Trujillo, a water resources expert for the Democrats on the Energy and Natural Resources Committee, serves as senior counsel for the committee's Subcommittee on Water and Power.

In that capacity, Trujillo oversees the legislative and oversight function of the committee relating to the Bureau of Reclamation, the Federal Energy Regulatory Commission's hydropower functions, and the water functions of the U.S. Geological Survey and the Department of Energy.

Trujillo's responsibilities also include the Bureau of Reclamations irrigation projects and their related flood control purposes, the Department of Interior's WaterSMART conservation programs, power marketing administrations, and the impacts of climate change on water resources.

In the 112th Congress, Trujillo said she anticipates working on the reintroduction of legislation relating to the nexus between energy and water usage, which was known as the Energy and Water Integration Act when it was introduced in 2009.

"Energy production requires substantial amounts of water—this is of course a resource becoming increasingly scarce in several parts of the country," Committee Chairman Sen. Jeff Bingaman, D-N.-Mex., the bill's author said during a hearing on the legislation.

"Whether it involves electricity generation or fuel production, the choice of fuel stock can dramatically influence the amount of water needed as part of the process of producing that energy."

In the 111th Congress, Trujillo worked on the water-related portions of the Omnibus Public Lands Management Act of 2009 (S.22), a package of more than 160 public land, national park, and water development bills that was signed into law by President Obama in March 2009.

Trujillo, a native of Bingaman's home state, joined the committee in 2009, after serving as general counsel to the New Mexico Interstate Stream Commission, which is charged with investigating, protecting, and conserving the state's waters, among other duties.

Prior to that, Trujillo was a partner with Holland & Hart in Santa Fe, N.M.

In addition to her work on the subcommittee, Trujillo also works on New Mexico-based water issues for Bingaman's personal office.

SENATE ENERGY AND NATURAL RESOURCES

Sara Tucker

Professional Staff Member

304 Dirksen Senate Bldg., Washington, DC

Phone: (202) (202) 224-4971

Sara_Tucker@energy.senate.gov

Personal: Born 1978 in Philidelphia, Pa.

Education: Master of Science, University of Michigan, 2005. Bachelor of Science, Cornell University, 2001.

Professional: 2001–2003, water policy associate director, The Environmental Policy Center. 2003–2005, graduate student instructor, University of Michigan, School of Natural Resources and Environment. 2004, environmental fellow, Sen. Dianne Feinstein. 2005–2007, legislative associate, Earthjustice. 2007–2009, director of government affairs, Trout Unlimited. 2009–Present, professional Staff Member, Senate Cmte. on Energy and Natural Resources.

Expertise: Natural Resources, Public Lands.

Sara Tucker, a Democratic professional staff member with expertise in natural resources and public lands, joined the Energy and Natural Resources Committee in 2009, after working closely with the committee as a lobbyist for a water conservation group.

"Having the experience to work on the inside and understand the process and how laws are made and being able to work on specific legislation obviously was a huge opportunity," Tucker said.

In the 112th Congress, Tucker said she anticipates working on legislation to fully fund the Land and Water Conservation Fund, which protects lands with significant natural, recreational and scenic attributes.

Though funding for the program is authorized at $900 million annually, Congress has rarely appropriated that much, leading the actual levels of funding to fluctuate "wildly over the years," according to the committee, which considered similar legislation (S. 2747) in the 111th Congress.

The fund takes receipts from oil and gas revenues and allows for purchasing of in-holdings and lands that have "high conservation value," Tucker said.

In addition, Tucker said she will likely work on the reintroduction of the Natural Resources Climate Adaptation Act, legislation that was originally introduced in the 2009 that aims to address the negative impacts of climate change on natural resources such as forests and wildlife habitats.

"Our natural resources have started to suffer from climate change, and these impacts will increase if we don't act," Committee Chair, Sen. Jeff Bingaman, D-N.-Mex., said in introducing the legislation. "Harmful consequences such as drought, rising sea levels, changes in forest ecosystems and warming of rivers and lakes already are being felt here."

The original bill would have used revenues from an anticipated cap-and-trade program on greenhouse gas emissions, but Tucker said that is likely to change given the lack of anticipated Congressional action on climate legislation.

"We realize that cap-and-trade is not happening," Tucker said.

SENATE ENERGY AND NATURAL RESOURCES

Bill Wicker

Democratic Communications Director
Sen. Jeff Bingaman, D-N.Mex.
364 Dirksen Senate Office Bldg.
Phone: (202) 224-5243
bill_wicker@energy.senate.gov

Personal: Born 03/15/1955 in Marion, Ind.

Education: B.J., University of Texas at Austin, 1977. M.S., University of Edinburgh, Scotland, 1982.

Professional: 1977–82, editor, Shell Oil Company. 1982–1983, ambassador of goodwill, Rotary Foundation Fellow. 1983–1984, communications consultant, Shell Oil Company. 1984–1994, Phillips Petroleum Company. 1994–2001, special assistant/press secretary, Dept. of Energy. 2001–present, Democratic communications director, Senate Cmte. on Energy and Natural Resources.

Expertise: Communications.

With the advent of blogs, morning tip sheets, and a 24-hour news cycle, Democratic Communications Director Bill Wicker, is a busy man, but he doesn't mind.

"If these guys, and ladies, weren't e-mailing me and calling me around the clock, I wouldn't have a job," Wicker said. "That's the nature of the beast, that's the business. And in this new media world that so many publications have moved into, that's just sort of the way it is."

Wicker describes a large part of the job as involving, "the care, feeding, and watering of the media," including responding to media inquiries, writing press releases, and making testimony and other documents available during hearings.

During the 112th Congress, Wicker expects to work with the media on committee priorities that include legislation responding to the 2010 Gulf of Mexico oil spill and bills related to the development of clean energy and green technology.

Wicker said the committee also will likely re-consider aspects of the American Clean Energy Leadership Act (ACELA)—comprehensive energy legislation that was approved by the committee in 2009, but never made it to the Senate floor in the 111th Congress.

"There are a good numbers of provisions and sections within ACELA which enjoyed bipartisan, genuine authentic support form both sides which could easily be introduced as either a freestanding bill or moved independently in smaller package through the committee," Wicker said.

Wicker, who has been communications director for the committee since 2001, keeps an Associated Press teletype machine in his office as a nod to his roots as a newspaper reporter, which began when he was 17 at the *Texarkana Gazette & Daily News*.

In his free time, Wicker, a former certified soccer referee, enjoys watching Washington D.C.'s Major League Soccer team D.C. United, to which he owns season tickets.

Committee on Environment and Public Works

410 Dirksen Senate Office Bldg.
Washington, DC 20510-6175
Phone: (202) 224-6176
http://epw.senate.gov
guest@epw.senate.gov

Ratio: 8/9/1

MAJORITY MEMBERS

Barbara Boxer, CA, Chairman

Max Baucus, MT
Thomas R. Carper, DE
Frank R. Lautenberg, NJ
Benjamin L. Cardin, MD
Sheldon Whitehouse, RI
Tom Udall, NM
Jeff Merkley, OR
Kirsten Gillibrand, NY

MINORITY MEMBERS

James M. Inhofe, OK, Ranking Member

David Vitter, LA
John Barrasso, WY
Jeff Sessions, AL
Mike Crapo, AR
Lamar Alexander, TN
Mike Johanns, NE
John Boozman, AR

INDEPENDENT MEMBERS

Bernard Sanders, VT

SENATE ENVIRONMENT AND PUBLIC WORKS

JURISDICTION

(1) Air pollution.
(2) Construction and maintenance of highways.
(3) Environmental aspects of outer continental shelf lands.
(4) Environmental effects of toxic substances, other than pesticides.
(5) Environmental policy.
(6) Environmental research and development.
(7) Fisheries and wildlife.
(8) Flood control and improvements of rivers and harbors, including environmental aspects of deepwater ports.
(9) Noise pollution.
(10) Nonmilitary environmental regulation and control of nuclear energy.
(11) Ocean dumping.
(12) Public buildings and improved grounds of the United States generally, including federal buildings in the District of Columbia.
(13) Public works, bridges, and dams.
(14) Regional economic development.
(15) Solid waste disposal and recycling.
(16) Water pollution.
(17) Water resources.

Such committee shall also study and review, on a comprehensive basis, matters relating to environmental protection and resource utilization and conservation, and report thereon from time to time.

SENATE ENVIRONMENT AND PUBLIC WORKS

The Senate Environment and Public Works Committee will tackle a number of bipartisan issues like transportation and water infrastructure in the 112th Congress following a deep divide between Democrats and Republicans over climate change in the 111th.

Committee Chairwoman Barbara Boxer, D-Calif., and ranking member Sen. James Inhofe, R-Okla., will continue their focus on job creation and believe funding a highway bill is one of the best ways to help kick start the economy. The two also will work together on the reauthorization of the Water Resources and Development Act (WRDA), legislation aimed at shoring up the nation's water infrastructure.

Congress reauthorized WRDA for the first time in seven years in 2007, overriding President George W. Bush's veto. Despite this widespread support, Congress has not reauthorized it since that date, possibly because of the growing rhetoric about earmarks on the Hill, and Boxer hopes to return it to a regular reauthorization schedule this year.

Other issues the committee may tackle include the renewable fuel standard and whether the ethanol mandate is too high. Inhofe, for one, has called it unrealistic. The ethanol review also may garner bipartisan support.

Boxer and Inhofe will likely split on reforms in the wake of the BP oil spill and the nuclear meltdown and tsunami in Japan. Boxer is a strong proponent of alternative energy, while Inhofe advocates domestic production of oil and gas.

The committee also will focus on toxics issues, including Toxic Substances Control Act reform.

While the 111th Congress did not usher through Democrats' hoped-for climate change bill, Boxer achieved a number of legislative goals.

Chief among them were a law aimed at reducing lead in drinking water and a law that established a voluntary national and state-level grant and loan program to reduce diesel emissions.

Congress, via EPW, also enacted legislation that forced the federal government to pay their fair share of stormwater fees and extended a moratorium on requiring permits for discharges from small commercial vessels.

Boxer also helped enact the Hiring Incentives to Restore Employment Act, which extended the authorization for highway, transit, and highway safety programs (SAFETEA-LU) through the end of 2010 and transferred approximately $20 billion from the General Fund into the Highway Trust Fund.

Through it all, she faced challenges and received support from Inhofe.

The committee leaders diverged on climate change issues, such as the regulation of greenhouse gases, which Inhofe believed would harm the national economy and Boxer said was necessary to protect public health. Following Democrats' failed attempt to pass climate change legislation, any significant effort to regulate greenhouse gases will likely be done through the Environmental Protection Agency via the Clean Air Act this term. Minority staff have described the fight to prevent that regulation from occurring as Inhofe's next battleground.

SENATE ENVIRONMENT AND PUBLIC WORKS

Jason Albritton

Senior Policy Advisor
Environment and Public Works Committee
410 Dirksen Senate Office Bldg.
Phone: (202) 224-8832
Fax: (202) 224-0574
Jason_albritton@epw.senate.gov

Education: B.S., biology, Murray State University, 2002. M.A., ecological economics, University of Leeds, 2004.

Professional: 2003, intern, State Department. 2004–2007, policy associate, The Nature Conservancy. 2007–2009, senior policy advisor for water resources, The Nature Conservancy. 2009–present, professional staff member, Senate Environment and Public Works Cmte.

Expertise: Water Infrastructure, wildlife.

Jason Albritton jumpstarted his second congressional term under Sen. Barbara Boxer, D-Calif working on many of the water and wildlife issues that occupied his time during the 111th Congress.

A key priority now in the 112th session is the Water Resources and Development Act (WRDA), a bipartisan piece of legislation on which Boxer and ranking member Sen. James Inhofe, R-Okla., will collaborate. Boxer and Inhofe worked on the legislation during the last session but ran out of time to pass it.

Boxer has said the legislation will address "crucial flood control needs and other water projects," such as port maintenance, inland waterway navigation channels and ecosystem restoration. WRDA is controversial among some Republicans because of its earmarked funds, but Inhofe has pledged his support.

In 2007, the Senate overrode President Bush's veto to pass the first reauthorization of WRDA in seven years, but it has not been reauthorized since that date. Boxer has said WRDA projects are "vitally important to keeping our communities safe and our economy moving."

Albritton, an outdoors enthusiast, also will work on wildlife issues, such as the Endangered Species Act, focusing on scientific integrity. As a boy, his grandfather taught him how to fish and hunt and inspired a lasting conservation ethic.

Albritton spent more than four years with The Nature Conservancy (TNC) working on water and environmental issues. While at TNC, he worked very closely with the Corps of Engineers, managing a partnership that included over 40 ecosystem restoration projects nationwide.

When Albritton isn't working on environmental issues, he can be found on the bike and running trails in the Washington, DC area as he trains for triathlons and marathons.

SENATE ENVIRONMENT AND PUBLIC WORKS

Murphie Barrett

Professional Staff Member

Ranking member Sen. James Inhofe, R-Okla.

415 Hart Senate Office Bldg.

Phone: (202) 224-6176

Fax: (202) 224-5167

murphie_barrett@epw.senate.gov

Education: Bachelor of Arts, James Madison University, 2005.

Professional: 2005–2006, public affairs coordinator, American International Automobile Dealers Association. 2006–2007, staff assistant, Let's Rebuild America, U.S. Chamber of Commerce. 2007–2008, research coordinator, Let's Rebuild America, U.S. Chamber of Commerce. 2008–2010, manager, Let's Rebuild America, U.S. Chamber of Commerce. 2010–2011, senior manager, Let's Rebuild America, U.S. Chamber of Commerce. 2011–Present, professional staff member, Senate Environment and Public Works Committee.

Expertise: Water resources, Army Corps of Engineers, Water resources, Army Corps of Engineers.

Helping the Water Resources Development Act (WRDA) sail through the Senate is a top priority for Professional Staff Member Murphie Barrett in 2011. The legislation provides funding for water infrastructure projects across the nation, including those aimed at navigation, flood protection, bolstering the nation's eroding shorelines, environmental restoration and repairs after natural disasters. Its implementation is generally overseen by the Army Corps of Engineers.

Barrett's work in helping to pass WRDA will likely be a bipartisan effort for Senate Environment and Public Works Committee Chairwoman Barbara Boxer, D-Calif., and ranking member Sen. James Inhofe, R-Okla. The two worked together on the bill last Congress but did not have time to complete it.

Barrett's boss, Inhofe has hailed the short- and long-term economic benefits of WRDA, including immediate job creation and long-term economic development opportunities. He has urged prioritizing levee safety, investment in the nation's inland waterways system and maintenance of U.S. ports and harbors.

Congress last passed WRDA in 2007 when the Senate overrode a presidential veto to enact the bill into law. Congress had worked on the legislation, which is supposed to be reauthorized every two years, for seven years. Barrett will be in the middle of a debate over the value of the earmarked project, as is usual with this legislation.

Inhofe has strongly repudiated the idea that the Corps projects the bill funds are a waste of taxpayer dollars.

"WRDA includes authorizations and modifications of specific projects," he said. "But these so-called 'earmarks' are the first step in the well-established authorization and appropriations process. One of the best checks on out-of-control spending is limiting funding to only those projects and programs that have been authorized properly."

Barrett joined the committee's minority staff in 2011, bringing considerable expertise in infrastructure issues. She previously worked as a senior manager on the U.S. Chamber of Commerce's Let's Rebuild America campaign, an initiative aimed at engaging the business industry and other stakeholders interested in repairing and rebuilding the nations' crumbling transportation infrastructure. Helping the Water Resources Development Act (WRDA) sail through the Senate is a top priority for EPW professional staff member Murphie Barrett.

Passing WRDA is likely to be a bipartisan effort for Senate Environment and Public Works Committee Chairwoman Barbara Boxer, D-Calif., and ranking member Sen. James Inhofe, R-Okla.

Congress last passed WRDA in 2007, when the Senate overrode a presidential veto to enact the bill into law. The bill often sparks a debate over earmarks.

SENATE ENVIRONMENT AND PUBLIC WORKS

Dan Barron

Professional Staff Member

415 Hart Senate Office Bldg.

Phone: (202) 224-6176

Fax: (202) 224-2322

dan_barron@epw.senate

Education: B.B.A., finance, Baylor University, 1994.

Professional: 1995–1997, legislative correspondent, Sen. James Inhofe, R-Okla. 1997–2007, legislative assistant, Sen. James Inhofe, R-Okla. 2007–present, professional staff member, Senate Environment and Public Works Cmte.

Expertise: Energy.

Domestic energy production will be at the top of the agenda for Senate Environment and Public Works Committee Professional Staff Member Dan Barron.

Focusing on oil, gas and renewable fuels, Barron will keep a close eye on potential reforms to the National Environmental Policy Act and the Oil Pollution Act in the wake of the 2010 BP oil spill.

Ranking Member Sen. James Inhofe, R-Okla., has urged the United States to continue promoting domestic production, including offshore, in order to reduce dependence on foreign oil and keep energy prices low. He noted the United States has more recoverable resources including natural gas, oil, and coal than Saudi Arabia, China and Canada combined, citing a Congressional Research Service study.

Barron also has emphasized that a decrease in domestic production could lead to job loss as the nation struggles through already rocky economic terrain.

Inhofe may be able to forge an alliance with Committee Chairwoman Barbara Boxer, D-Calif., and environmental groups on ethanol issues, as both Republicans and Democrats have questioned the speed with which the renewable fuel standard was adopted. Inhofe has called the corn-based ethanol mandate unrealistic and said ethanol production is on track to exceed demand, given numerical limits on the amount of ethanol in a gallon of gasoline.

Inhofe plans to reintroduce legislation that will enable states to opt out of the corn ethanol portions of the Renewable Fuel Standard mandate sometime during the 112th Congress.

Barron has worked on oil and gas issues in Inhofe's personal office, as well as for the committee. He transferred from Inhofe's personal office to the EPW staff in 2007.

A Sooner State native, Barron said he enjoys working "digging into the details of the oil and gas industry—one of America's most technologically sophisticated and critical industries."

SENATE ENVIRONMENT AND PUBLIC WORKS

Annie Caputo

Professional Staff Member

Ranking member Sen. James Inhofe, R-Okla.

415 Senate Hart Office Bldg.

Phone: (202) 224-6176

Fax: (202) 224-5167

Annie_Caputo@epw.senate.gov

Personal: Born in Manchester, Conn.

Education: BS, nuclear engineering, University of Wisconsin at Madison, 1996.

Professional: 1992–1993, associate research specialist, University of Wisconsin-Madison. 1997–1998, engineer and executive assistant, Commonwealth Edison Company. 1997–2005, congressional affairs manager, Exelon Corporation. 1998–1999, public policy committee chair, American Nuclear Society. 1998–2001, board of dietors, American Nuclear Society. 1999–2001, finance committee, American Nuclear Society. 1999–2001, finance committee, American Nuclear Society. 2005–2006, professional staff member, Subcmte. On Energy & Air Quality, House Energy & Commerce Cmte. 2007, principal, Nuclear Energy Strategies, LLC. 2007–present, professional staff member, Senate Environment and Public Works Cmte.

Expertise: Nuclear energy, Nuclear Regulatory Commission.

Professional Staff Member Annie Caputo has made nuclear energy, Nuclear Regulatory Commission (NRC) oversight and power plant licensing a focus during 2011.

Working for Ranking Member Sen. James Inhofe, R-Okla., Caputo bring attention to nuclear power as an energy option in the United States. Inhofe has said that, along with new modern coal plants, he wants "nuclear, natural gas . . . [and the] array of existing technologies" to fuel the U.S. economy.

Caputo's duties include overseeing the NRC's regulatory efforts and commissioner nominations, and looking at the continued safety and security of the nation's nuclear plants. She also concentrates on completing thorough and timely reviews of new nuclear plant applications.

Inhofe has urged spectators to refrain from drawing conclusions about the safety of the U.S. nuclear energy program following the nuclear disaster in Japan in March. "Our nuclear plants are safe," Inhofe said. "The NRC and the industry have a systematic process to incorporate lessons learned from events worldwide and improve the safety of our plants."

Inhofe has encouraged the NRC to allow new nuclear plants under development to continue unless they face significant tsunami risk.

Caputo previously worked for Rep. Joe Barton, R-Texas, when he was the ranking member on the House Energy and Commerce Committee. At the time, she was responsible for legislative issues relating to nuclear technologies, including the Energy Policy Act of 2005.

Before her congressional committee work, Caputo was the congressional affairs manager for Exelon's Washington office. Earlier in her career, she was active in the American Nuclear Society, previously serving on the board of directors and as public policy chairman.

Born in Manchester, CT, Caputo also lived in seven other states but she now resides in Virginia.

SENATE ENVIRONMENT AND PUBLIC WORKS

Alyson Cooke

Majority Counsel

Chairman Barbara Boxer, D-Calif.

508 Hart Senate Office Bldg.

Phone: (202) 224-8552

Fax: (202) 224-1273

Personal: Born 04/29/1963 in Chicago, Ill.

Education: B.A., political science, Washington University. J.D., University of Pennsylvania.

Professional: 1989–1991, legislative assistant, Sen. Joseph R. Biden Jr., D-Del. 1991–1993, program officer, The Abell Foundation (Baltimore, Md.). 1993–1995, senior program officer, Chicago Community Trust. 1996–2000, vice president, James Lowry & Associates. 2001–2007, executive director, Children First Fund/Director External Resources, Chicago Public Schools. 2007–present, majority counsel, Senate Cmte. on Environment and Public Works.

Expertise: Children's health issues, Advocacy, Outreach.

Majority Counsel Alyson Cooke works on presidential nominees for federal agency positions. During the 111th Congress, the Senate Environment and Public Works Committee approved 34 nominations, which were later confirmed by the Senate and will continue to manage any that come before the committee during the 112th session.

In 2011, Cooke will work on the authorization of General Services Administration projects, such as the construction of new courthouses, the leases for federal agencies and naming of federal buildings, and opportunities to increase energy efficiency and improve performance of federal buildings.

In the last session, Cooke handled the nominations of Lisa Jackson as Environmental Protection Agency administrator, Nancy Sutley as chair of the White House Council on Environmental Quality and Samuel Hamilton as director of the United States Fish and Wildlife Service.

Cooke has said it is "a wonderful opportunity to have the occasion to meet, first hand, the professionals and experts who are being considered by our Committee to shape and implement the vision of the new President of the United States."

Last session, the committee passed nearly 20 bills that named courthouses and federal buildings in honor of prominent civil rights leaders and community leaders. Notably, the Department of the Interior Building in Washington, D.C. was designated the "Stewart Lee Udall Department of the Interior Building," after the former Interior Secretary.

Cooke worked on Capitol Hill for then Sen. Joe Biden, D-Dela., from 1989 to 1991 before moving back to her native Chicago to do outreach and grant making work for several community groups. She said she's glad to be back in the Capitol region and when not at work she has rediscovered the East Coast, visiting as variety of historical spots, most recently the presidential homes of Monroe, Madison, and Jefferson.

SENATE ENVIRONMENT AND PUBLIC WORKS

Grant Cope

Senior Counsel

Chairman Barbara Boxer, D-Calif.

456 Dirksen Senate Office Bldg.

Phone: (202) 224-8832

Fax: (202) 224-1273

Personal: Born 03/06/1970 in Indio, Calif.

Education: J.D., Northwestern School of Law of Lewis and Clark College, 1998.

Professional: 1998–2002, staff attorney, U.S. Public Interest Research Group (Washington, D.C.). 2002–2004, attorney and equal justice works fellow, Earthjustice (state of Washington). 2005, toxics expert, Sierra Club. 2005–present, legislative assistant/counsel, Senate Cmte. on Environment and Public Works.

Expertise: Chemical regulation, toxic waste cleanup.

Resident watchdog Grant Cope keeps a careful eye on companies responsible for toxic pollution and executive branch initiatives. Cope also advises Senate Environment and Public Works Committee Chairwoman Barbara Boxer, D-Calif., on chemical regulation.

Cope, senior counsel to the committee, has spent more than a decade fighting for environmental causes, and hopes to see the Obama administration implement new initiatives to strengthen the Environmental Protection Agency.

With his toxics expertise, Cope will tackle issues including the modernization of the Toxic Substances Control Act. Senator Frank Lautenberg, D-N.J., already has held a hearing on the issue during the 112th Congress, lamenting the presence of toxic chemicals in the bodies of U.S. citizens.

Lautenberg told Environmental Protection Agency Administrator Lisa Jackson that under current law EPA lacks the tools it needs to regulate hazardous chemicals. He called TSCA "severely flawed."

Lautenberg also said waiting on modernization leaves business uncertain about the laws by which they must abide, a situation he called untenable.

Cope also has focused on scientific integrity and speeding Superfund cleanup. Superfund sites contain soil that has been poisoned by chemicals, contaminated groundwater or toxic air. The work to clean up these properties has slowed to a crawl since the Polluter Pays fee expired and the fund ran dry.

The majority has pushed to reinstate fees on oil and chemical companies in order to gain more money for cleanups, a proposition that ranking member Sen. James Inhofe, R-Okla., opposes.

Cope has said providing adequate funds for cleanups helps "protect public health, create jobs and revitalize local economies." Another priority for Cope will be coordinating nuclear safety oversight.

When Cope isn't working on environmental issues, he can be found playing Ultimate Frisbee and jogging around the Capital Mall.

SENATE ENVIRONMENT AND PUBLIC WORKS

Kathy Dedrick

Professional Staff Member

410 Dirksen Senate Office Bldg.

Phone: (202) 224-8832

Fax: (202) 224-1273

Personal: Born 07/28/1975 in Newberg, Ore.

Education: B.A., political science, Willamette University (Oregon), 1997.

Professional: 1997–2001, legislative assistant, Vice President Al Gore. 2001–2006, legislative assistant, Rep. Peter DeFazio, D-Ore. 2007–present, professional staff member, Senate Environment and Public Works Cmte.

Expertise: Transportation.

Kathy Dedrick wants to put the nation's infrastructure system on the road to success during the 112th Congress.

Dedrick, a professional staff member on the Senate Environment and Public Works Committee, is a key player on transportation issues, which Committee Chairwoman Barbara Boxer, D-Calif., has said will be a priority this session. Boxer hopes to get a new surface transportation bill enacted by the end of this year.

The senator recently lauded Congress's passage of the Surface Transportation Act of 2011, which extends surface transportation programs under the Safe, Accountable, Flexible, Efficient Transportation Equity Act: A Legacy for Users (SAFETEA-LU) through the end of fiscal year 2011.

Boxer called the extension "especially important because it will give states the certainty they need to award contracts and get projects underway."

Boxer has said a new surface transportation bill will help stimulate the economy through new job creation and will improve air quality and public health, key concerns for Dedrick. The legislation also could reduce congestion, which creates additional costs and time delays and releases pollution, she noted.

Dedrick came to Washington, D.C., after college to work for Vice President Al Gore and then landed a job with her hometown congressman, Rep. Peter DeFazio, D-Ore.

As part of the EPW committee, Dedrick was part of the team that worked to secure more than $8 billion to restore a shortfall in the Highway Trust Fund in 2008. She also worked on the American Recovery and Reinvestment Act of 2009.

The other hat Dedrick wears is as a staff member on nuclear issues; the Nuclear Regulatory Commission falls under EPW's jurisdiction. Oversight of reactor safety and the issue of the safe disposal of nuclear waste has become a hot topic after the March nuclear accident in Japan after the tsunami.

SENATE ENVIRONMENT AND PUBLIC WORKS

Matthew Dempsey

Communications Director

Ranking Republican James Inhofe, R-Okla.

456 Dirksen Senate Office Bldg.

Phone: (202) 224-9797

Fax: (202) 224-5167

matt_dempsey@epw.senate.gov

Personal: Born 07/27/1978 in Denver, Colo.

Education: B.A., history and political science, University of Colorado at Boulder, 2001.

Professional: 2001–2002, organizational director, Wayne Allard for Senate Campaign. 2003–2004, dtaff assistant, Senate Cmte. on Environment and Public Works. 2004–2006, deputy press secretary, Senate Cmte. on Environment and Public Works. 2006–2008, press secretary, Senate Cmte. on Environment and Public Works. 2008–2009, press secretary, U.S. Sen. James Inhofe, R-Okla. 2009–present, communications director, Senate Cmte. on Environment and Public Works.

Expertise: Communications, New Media.

Republican Communications Director Matt Dempsey believes the Senate Environment and Public Works Committee will enter a new phase in the battle over greenhouse gas regulation in 2011.

"Last year, we finally reached an understanding here in the Senate that cap-and-trade legislation was dead," he said. "That has been a result of almost a decade's worth of work by Sen. Inhofe to expose the costs of cap-and-trade."

Dempsey said the next battle will involve halting the Environmental Protection Agency's attempts to move forward with the cap-and-trade agenda.

The committee also will focus on the fallout from the 2010 BP oil spill in the Gulf of Mexico and the March 2011 nuclear accident in Japan resulting from the earthquake and tsunami. Dempsey said spectators also may see an "unholy alliance" between Democrats, Republicans and environmental groups on the nation's ethanol policy. Additional bipartisan efforts will include the passage of a new Water Resources and Development Act, Economic Development Act and highway bill.

"We face an uphill battle on all three given the debate over earmarks is where it is," he noted.

Dempsey, an expert in new media issues, has been instrumental in designing the prize-winning Senate Environment and Public Works Committee's Web site and in creating Facebook and Twitter accounts for Inhofe's press office, along with posting YouTube videos of congressional hearings.

"It's a way to reach out, especially to constituents [or others] who may not always follow the usual ways of accessing information from Congress," Dempsey said.

Dempsey, who hails from Colorado, is an avid ski enthusiast, as are his wife and three-and-a-half-year-old daughter. "I wasn't sure which was more exciting, [my daughter] skiing to me or walking to me," he said.

SENATE ENVIRONMENT AND PUBLIC WORKS

Elizabeth S. Fox

Professional Staff Member

Ranking member Sen. James Inhofe, R-Okla.

415 Hart Senate Office Bldg.

Phone: (202) 224-6176

Education: Bachelor of Arts, Chemistry and Peace Studies; Minor, Biochemistry, Whitworth University.

Professional: 2004–2005, Senate Special Committee on Aging. 2005, Senate Committee on Veterans' Affairs. 2005–Present, professional staff member, Senate Environment and Public Works Cmte.

Expertise: Drinking Water, Clean Water, Public Buildings.

Senate Environment and Public Works Committee Professional Staff Member Elizabeth Fox has seen some major successes during 2011, including the passage of the Reduction of Lead in Drinking Water Act.

Fox, who specializes in water and public building issues, was a key player involved in the enactment of the law, which reduced the allowable lead content in drinking water pipes, pipe fittings and plumbing fixtures. Another critical water bill success was the passage of S. 3481, legislation that amended the Clean Water Act to require federal agencies pay a share of stormwater management fees, lifting a financial burden from local communities.

Fox's boss, EPW ranking member, Sen. James Inhofe, R-Okla., said the laws would "strengthen protections for drinking water [and end] an unfunded mandate on local communities." He also lauded the cooperation between Republican and Democratic members of the committee and Environmental Protection Agency (EPA) Administrator Lisa Jackson, saying the lead bill was an example of what can happen when members on opposite sides of the aisle "keep an open line of communication."

Nevertheless, Inhofe also accused the agency of taking advantage of bipartisan support for certain water programs. Water issues became a contentious topic at EPW's budget hearing for EPA, where Inhofe criticized the agency's fiscal year 2012 budget submission as a "fiscal bait and switch." Inhofe said the agency has proposed "significant cuts that appear fiscally responsible - but in truth they are cuts EPA knows Congress will readily restore."

Inhofe said 83 percent of EPA's proposed budget cuts come from three water programs with strong bipartisan support in Congress, such as the State Revolving Funds, which support the nation's water infrastructure.

During the 111th Congress, Fox worked on S. 1005, the Water Infrastructure Financing Act, which would have reauthorized the State Revolving Loan Fund programs for drinking and waste water. While that legislation has not been enacted into law, it did garner bipartisan support.

Fox joined the EPW Committee's Republican staff in 2005. Prior to joining the committee, she worked for the Senate Committee on Veterans' Affairs and the Senate Special Committee on Aging. She is a graduate of Whitworth University.

SENATE ENVIRONMENT AND PUBLIC WORKS

Kate Gilman

Deputy Communications Director
Chairman Barbara Boxer, D-Calif.
410 Dirksen Senate Office Bldg.
Phone: (202) 224-8832
Fax: (202) 224-1273

Personal: Born 01/16/1979 in Canandaigua, N.Y.

Education: B.A., public relations, Pennsylvania State University, 2001.

Professional: 2000–2001, assistant to director of marketing, WPSU, WPSX-TV (Public television), State College, Pa. 2001–2003, public relations assistant, Association of Blood Banks, Bethesda, Md. 2003–2004, deputy press secretary, Rep. Nydia Velazquez, House Small Business Cmte. 2004–2007, press secretary, Rep. Nydia Velazquez, House Small Business Cmte. 2007–2010, press secretary, Senate Environment and Public Works Cmte. 2011–Present, deputy communications director, Senate Environment and Public Works Cmte. 2011–Present, deputy communications director, Senate Environment and Public Works Cmte.

Expertise: Strategic communications, message development, media relations.

As Deputy Communications Director for the Senate Environment and Public Works Committee, Kate Gilman explains Democratic policy goals and complex environmental statutes to the media.

In the 112th Congress, Gilman and Committee Chairwoman Barbara Boxer, D-Calif., will push an agenda that includes the passage of a new transportation bill, the reauthorization of the Water Resources and Development Act, the reduction of toxic chemicals in drinking water, and management of the aftermath of the BP Oil Spill.

During the 111th Congress, Gilman helped publicize issues including global warming, public health, pollution reduction, transportation and water infrastructure with reporters from nationally known media outlets to trade publications. She said she enjoys helping reporters gain a better understanding of the critical issues the committee covers.

Gilman's background in Rep. Nydia Velázquez's D-N.Y. office and on the House Small Business Committee, where she became familiar with environmental, energy security and green jobs issues, helped prepare her for her roles within the EPW Committee.

Gilman first pursued communications at Penn State, where she wrote for the university's newspaper and worked in the marketing department at the local public radio/television station. Add to that growing up in a family where her dad talked a lot about politics and a career on Capitol Hill, Gillman was a natural.

Gilman said working for the committee is gratifying given the important work Boxer is doing, and noted that one of the Senator's top priorities is protecting the health of families and children.

When she's not working, Gilman spends time running, hiking, and discovering Washington, D.C.'s restaurants with her husband.

SENATE ENVIRONMENT AND PUBLIC WORKS

Alex Hergott

Professional Staff Member

Ranking member Sen. James Inhofe, R-Okla.

415 Hart Senate Office Bldg.

Phone: (202) 210-0681

alex_herrgott@epw.senate.gov

Personal: Born in Phoenix, Ariz.

Education: Bachelor's in Business Administration, , Finance and International Business, George Washington University, 2003.

Professional: 2004–2006, staff assistant, Senate Environment and Public Works Committee. 2006–2008, research assistant, Senate Environment and Public Works Committee. 2008–Present, professional staff member, Senate Environment and Public Works Committee. Jan. 2000–May 2000, intern, The Office of United States Senator John McCain, R-Ariz.. Jan. 2003–Dec. 2004, government affairs assistant, Cultural Property Consulting, LLC. May 2000–Jan. 2003, research associate and intern, National Center for Policy Analysis.

Expertise: Transportation.

Passing legislation that will fund the vast network of federal highways stretching across the United States will be a main priority for Alex Hergott, professional staff on the Environment and Public Works Committee, in 2011.

Hergott believes the highway trust fund, which has been the primary source of funding for surface transportation activities, has been overstressed by its support of non-essential transportation activities. He noted that priorities for the fund should include safety, new capacity and interstate commerce needs such as freight movement.

"If we don't take dramatic action to improve our transportation infrastructure system, growing congestion, and deteriorating pavement conditions it will choke the U.S. economy," Hergott said.

Hergott's boss, EPW Ranking Member James Inhofe, R-Okla., has described infrastructure as a bipartisan issue. But Inhofe said in January the challenges of getting a highway bill completed this Congress are "significant," citing Republican opposition to funding for recreational trails and other items he views as unnecessary. Inhofe has urged members to recognize that the Highway Trust Fund can no longer support spending more than the nation collects in gas taxes.

Hergott's primary responsibilities are the safety, research and federal lands components of the highway program reauthorization. He also advises Inhofe on regulatory implications and legislative concerns affiliated with the National Environmental Policy Act, Endangered Species Act, and streamlining the permitting process for infrastructure design and construction. Hergott serves as primary committee staff in charge of issues concerning the U.S. Fish and Wildlife Service's Lacey Act and the Environmental Protection Agency's environmental justice policies.

Hergott has been with the committee since 2004. Previously, Hergott worked as a government affairs assistant at Cultural Property Consulting, LLC, in Washington, D.C. Hergott also served as a research associate and interned at the National Center for Policy Analysis in the District.

SENATE ENVIRONMENT AND PUBLIC WORKS

Matthew Hite

Minority Counsel

Ranking member Sen. James Inhofe, R-Okla.

415 Hart Senate Office Bldg.

Phone: (202) 224-6328

Fax: (202) 224-5167

matthew_hite@epw.senate.gov

Personal: Born 7/18/1972 in Grand Blanc, Mich.

Education: B.A. (cum laude), University of Rochester, 1996. Oxford University/Free University of Brussels, 1995. J.D., Cleveland Marshall College of Law, Cleveland State University,, 2001.

Professional: 2002–2004, independent contractor. 2004–2005, staff assistant, Rep. Paul Gillmor, R-Ohio. 2005–2006, legislative correspondent, Sen. Mike DeWine, R-Ohio. 2006–2007, legislative assistant, Rep. Don Young, R-Alaska. 2007–2008, senior legislative assistant, Rep. Bill Sali, R-Idaho. 2008–present, minority counsel, Senate Cmte. on Environment and Public Works.

Expertise: Electronic waste, Mining, Brownfields, Eco-terrorism, Coal ash, Recycling, Electronic waste, Mining, Brownfields, Eco-terrorism, Coal ash, Recycling, Superfund, RCRA, Grants, Oversight and investigations.

Republican Counsel Matt Hite said the committee's 2011 priorities include the proposed Comprehensive Environmental Response, Compensation, and Liability Act financial assurance regulation and proposed coal ash regulations.

Hite said action could also take place on legislation related to electronic manifests, Brownfields reauthorization, electronic waste, rare earths, the Equal Access to Justice Act and recycling.

During the past year, Hite produced two reports on the Obama administration's handling of coal mining Clean Water Act Section 404 permits.

"The administration has created an unfair and uncertain regulatory environment in regards to the permits that they review," Hite said. "This is an issue that will have a continued focus."

Hite also predicted the administration will attempt to reinstate the CERCLA, otherwise known as Superfund, taxes, which Senator Inhofe has criticized as targeting those with money rather than those responsible for pollution. Hite attributed the administration's failure to reinstate Superfund taxes in the 111th Congress to Inhofe's efforts.

Hite started his Capitol Hill career as an aide to the late Congressman Paul Gillmor and to former Sen. Mike DeWine. He then moved handle Rep. Don Young's, R-Alaska, natural resources and environment portfolio while he sat on the Committee on Natural Resources. Before joining EPW in 2008, Hite was the senior legislative assistant for former Rep. Bill Sali, R-Idaho, and handled environment, transportation, and natural resources issues.

Hite received his Bachelor of Arts degree from the University of Rochester in 1996 and his law degree from Cleveland Marshall College of Law at Cleveland State University in 2001. He currently resides in Alexandria, Virginia. Hite, a Cleveland native, is an avid Cleveland Browns and Indians fan. He also enjoys fishing and hiking.

SENATE ENVIRONMENT AND PUBLIC WORKS

Ted Illston

Majority Counsel
Sen. Barbara Boxer, D-Calif.
410 Dirksen Senate Office Bldg.
Phone: (202) 202-224-8832
Fax: (202) 202-224-1273
ted_illston@gmail.com

Personal: Born in Syossett, N.Y.

Education: B.A., St. Lawrence University, 1986. J.D., Hamline University School of Law, 1991.

Professional: 1995–1999, project manager and policy advisor, Northeast-Midwest Institute. 1999–2007, senior policy advisor, The Nature Conservancy. 2007–2010, counsel, House Cmte. on Transportation and Infrastructure. 2010–Present, majority counsel, Senate Cmte. on Environment and Public Works.

Expertise: Water resources policy, Ecosystem Restoration, Water Infrastructure, Regional Watershed Policy, Floodplain Management.

Majority Counsel Ted Illston joined the Senate Environment and Public Works Committee at the end of 2010, bringing an expertise in water issues and a determination to see a Water Resources and Development Act (WRDA) of 2011 in the Senate this year.

Illston is well-suited to the task. Previously, he worked for the House Transportation and Infrastructure Committee, where he drafted WRDA 2010. The most recent authorization of WRDA, a bill aimed at supporting water infrastructure projects, took place in 2007 when Congress overrode President George W. Bush's veto to pass the legislation. Committee Chairwoman Barbara Boxer, D-Calif., hopes to return WRDA to a biennial reauthorization schedule this session.

Illston said he also expects to defend Clean Water Act protections. Democrats on the committee have claimed recent Supreme Court decisions like Rapanos v. United States have eviscerated wetland protections by changing the meaning of "navigable waters" in the Clean Water Act. Former House Transportation and Infrastructure Committee Chairman James Oberstar, D-Minn., and former Sen. Russ Feingold, D-Wis., both had championed legislation to roll back the impact of those decisions, but both were ousted by voters during the 2010 election.

Illston's other areas of focus will include: ecosystem restoration; regional watershed policy (including the Mississippi River, Great Lakes, Chesapeake Bay, Gulf of Mexico, Coastal Louisiana, Everglades); Floodplain Management; the U.S. Army Corps of Engineers; and the U.S. Environmental Protection Agency.

Before working for Congress, Illston was a senior policy advisor at The Nature Conservancy and a project manager and policy advisor at the Northeast-Midwest Institute. He earned his juris doctorate from Hamline University School of Law and his Bachelor of Arts degree from St. Lawrence University.
Illston hails from Syosett, New York and his hobbies include flyfishing and his dogs. One of his favorite places in Washington, D.C., is Rock Creek Park.

SENATE ENVIRONMENT AND PUBLIC WORKS

Dimitrios J. Karakitsos

Professional Staff Member

Ranking member Sen. James Inhofe, R-Okla.

456 Dirksen Senate Office Bldg.

Phone: (202) 224-6176

Fax: (202) 224-5167

Education: Bachelor of Arts, Western Michigan University, 2004. Juris Doctorate, University of Miami, 2008.

Professional: 2009–Present, professional staff member, Senate Environment and Public Works Committee.

Expertise: Chemical Regulation, National Environmental Policy Act, Environmental Streamlining, Oil Pollution Act.

Oil pollution issues have kept Professional Staff Member Dimitrios Karakitsos busy in 2010 and promise to fill his schedule again in 2011. Karakitsos spent much of 2010 helping the committee address the BP Deepwater Horizon Oil Spill in the Gulf of Mexico and the Oil Pollution act.

Karakitsos's boss, EPW Ranking Member James Inhofe, R-Okla., has responded to recommendations by the President's National Commission on the BP Deepwater Horizon Oil Spill that included reforms to the Oil Pollution Act and the National Environmental Policy Act (NEPA). Inhofe agreed that safety regulations could be improved in light of the BP spill but urged that more "effective" regulations not impede domestic oil production.

Inhofe has accused the Obama administration of blocking domestic production and increasing the nation's dependence on foreign oil, calling it "the inevitable result of the Obama administration's cap-and-trade agenda." He has warned that such policies will increase energy prices and called for increased domestic production.

Karakitsos also expects to focus on the modernization of the Toxic Substances Control Act (TSCA). TSCA, a 35-year-old statute, addresses the production, importation, use and disposal of chemicals such as asbestos, Polychlorinated biphenyls (PCBs), radon, and lead-based paint.

Inhofe has criticized TSCA's "broad reach over chemical manufacturing" saying the Senate should look into whether EPA is overregulating the industry and stifling innovation. Inhofe urges a risk-based standard for chemical reviews and more rigorous cost-benefit requirements, along with protection of proprietary information and the prioritization of reviews for existing chemicals.

Karakitsos also will work on analyzing the environmental aspects of a new transportation bill, including the Congestion Mitigation and Air Quality Improvement (CMAQ) program, and looking at opportunities to conform and streamline the legislation. Karakitsos also will look at domestic energy production issues.

Karakitsos holds a bachelor of arts degree from Western Michigan University and a juris doctorate from the University of Miami.

SENATE ENVIRONMENT AND PUBLIC WORKS

Mary Kerr

Communications Director
Sen. Barbara Boxer, D-Calif.
410 Dirksen Senate Office Bldg.
Phone: (202) 224-8832
Mary_Kerr@epw.senate.gov

Education: Bachelor of Arts, Political Science and Communications, University of Michigan, 1987. Juris Doctorate, University of Wisconsin, 1991.

Professional: 1995–2007, communications director, Rep. Jim Oberstar, D-Minn.. 2007–2011, majority press secretary, House Committee on Transportation and Infrastructure. 2011–Present, communications director, Senate Environment and Public Works Committee.

Expertise: Transportation, Water Resources, Infrastructure, Media.

Majority Communications Director Mary Kerr is used to being a voice for Democrats on the Hill, but 2011 marks her first time speaking for the Senate.

Kerr comes to the Senate Environment and Public Works Committee from the House Committee on Transportation and Infrastructure, where she began serving as majority press secretary in 2007. Her background in transportation and infrastructure issues will be key as the committee attempts to pass a highway bill and Water Resources Development Act (WRDA), aimed in part at shoring up water infrastructure, in this first session of the 112th Congress.

Boxer has described a surface transportation authorization bill as a bipartisan issue, pointing out that she and ranking member Sen. James Inhofe, R-Okla., are working closely on the issue. Boxer also said she has begun discussions with Rep. John Mica, R-Fla., the new chairman of the House Transportation and Infrastructure Committee.

"Our nation's transportation systems used to be the best in the world, but investments have not kept up with needs, and now we are falling behind," Boxer said at a hearing this year. "The rest of the world is building infrastructure systems to move people and goods - and so must we."

Kerr will be busy will media inquiries too as the EPW committee also will attempt to reauthorize WRDA for the first time since 2007. Previously, Congress had not passed WRDA, which is scheduled for reauthorization every two years, for seven years. A key goal for Kerr and Boxer is getting the legislation back on a regular reauthorization schedule.

While working for the House Transportation and Infrastructure Committee, Kerr was the principal spokeswoman for four subcommittees: Water Resources and Environment, Economic Development, Public Buildings, and Emergency Management; Railroads, Pipelines and Hazardous Materials; and Coast Guard and Maritime Transportation.

Prior to joining that committee, Kerr was the communications director in former Transportation and Infrastructure Committee Chairman Jim Oberstar's, D-Minn., office. She began her career as spokeswoman for Oberstar in 1995.

Kerr earned a law degree from the University of Wisconsin and received a Bachelor of Arts degree in Political Science and Communications from the University of Michigan.

SENATE ENVIRONMENT AND PUBLIC WORKS

David Napoliello

Senior Policy Advisor
Sen. Barbara Boxer, D-Calif.
410 Dirksen Senate Office Bldg.
Phone: (202) 202-224-8832
David_Napoliello@epw.senate.gov

Personal: Born in Omaha, Nebr.

Education: Bachelor of Accountancy, The George Washington University, 1991.

Professional: 1992–1996, budget analyst, Office of Budget and Finance, Federal Highway Administration, U.S. Department of Transportation. 1996–2000, transportation specialist, Office of Policy Development, Federal Highway Administration, U.S. Department of Transportation. 2000–2002, program analyst, Office of Budget and Program Performance, Office of the Secretary of Transportation, U.S. Department of Transportation. 2002–2003, special assistant/program analyst, Office of the Assistant Secretary for Budget and Programs/Chief Financial Officer, Office of the Secretary of Transportation, U.S. Department of Transportation. 2003–2005, chief, Budget Division, Office of Budget and Finance, Federal Highway Administration, U.S. Department of Transportation. 2005–2011, professional staff, Subc. on Transportation, Housing and Urban Development, and Related Agencies, House Cmte. on Appropriations. 2011–Present, senior policy advisor, Senate Cmte. on Environment and Public Works.

Expertise: Federal-aid Highway Program funding and policy.

Senior policy advisor David Napoliello's main goal this year is to help the Senate Environment and Public Works Committee put a highway bill on the road to success.

The legislation also is a top priority for Committee Chairwoman Barbara Boxer, D-Calif., and ranking member Sen. James Inhofe, R-Okla. Boxer has described the infrastructure funding as a way to create construction jobs and accelerate the United States' economic recovery. She also has described it as critical to successfully and safely moving people and goods across the web of roads that connect the nation.

Napoliello brings a host of experience to the issue. He came to the committee after serving as a professional staff member for the House Appropriation Committee's Subcommittee on Transportation, Housing and Urban Development, and Related Agencies for more than five years. In that role, he addressed transportation issues relating to highways, highway safety, pipeline safety, and the National Transportation Safety Board for the Committee and was involved in drafting the American Recovery and Reinvestment Act of 2009.

Previously, Napoliello was Budget Division Chief for the Federal Highway Administration's Office of Budget and Finance in the Transportation Department. In that role, he analyzed proposed and enacted legislation and assessed its impact on apportionment to the states. He also held a number of other roles in the Transportation Department and is familiar with the highway funding shortfalls Boxer and Inhofe are attempting to address. The two senators are attempting to creatively finance infrastructure needs by increasing the amount of cash in the Highway Trust Fund, among other options.

Napoliello received the Founding Father of the Transportation Security Administration Award in 2003 in recognition of his work toward the creation of a new Federal agency in the wake of the September 11, 2001 attacks. He also received a special achievement award in 2001 for outstanding analytical support to the Assistant Secretary for Budget and Programs during negotiations on the initial Finance Plan for the Woodrow Wilson Memorial Bridge project.

When he is not attempting to shore up the nation's crumbling infrastructure, Napoliello also is a comic book writer and publisher. He hails from Omaha, Neb.

SENATE ENVIRONMENT AND PUBLIC WORKS

James O'Keeffe

Senior Economist

Sen. James M. Inhofe, R-Okla.

415 Hart Senate Office Bldg.

Phone: (202) 224-6176

Fax: (202) 224-2322

Personal: Born 07/17/1972 in Rye, N.Y.

Education: B.A., University of Wisconsin, Madison, 1995. M.P.P., Georgetown University, 1998.

Professional: 1997–1998, project asst., The World Bank. 1998–2000, transportation budget analyst, Congressional Budget Office. 2001–2003, senior analyst for transportation, Senate Cmte. on the Budget. 2003–present, senior economist, Senate Cmte. on Environment and Public Works.

Expertise: Transportation, budget issues.

Funding the nation's public works infrastructure is a top priority for senior economist James O'Keeffe and his boss ranking member Sen. James Inhofe, R-Okla., during the 112th Congress.

O'Keeffe's main task is to work on the full reauthorization of the highway bill, a goal he also pursued in the 111th Congress. Challenges for O'Keeffe include the lack of cash in the Highway Trust Fund and the major highway and bridge project backlog across the nation, which some estimate at more than $500 billion.

Yet both Inhofe and Committee Chairwoman Barbara Boxer, D-Calif., are committed to finding funding for the bill, which is a priority for Democrats and Republicans on the committee. Inhofe, however, has suggested that Republicans will only accept the bill if overall expenditures are reduced and items like Capitol Dome repairs and recreational bike paths are struck. He believes the bill should be confined to maintenance, construction, bridges and highways.

Nevertheless, work on the bill is still largely bipartisan.

O'Keeffe also is considering transportation experts' calls for major reforms to the highway and transit programs as the committee tackles the transportation bill, noting that the variety of approaches presents policy challenges for Senators and staff on the committee.

O'Keeffe has been on the committee's Republican staff for more than seven years. Prior to joining the Environment and Public Works Committee, O'Keeffe worked for the Senate Budget Committee and the Congressional Budget Office on transportation and budget issues.

O'Keeffe lives in Washington, D.C., with his wife Deanna and their daughter, Fiona.

SENATE ENVIRONMENT AND PUBLIC WORKS

Bettina Poirier

Majority Staff Director and Chief Counsel
Chairman Barbara Boxer, D-Calif.
456 Dirksen Senate Office Bldg.
Phone: (202) 224-8832
Fax: (202) 224-5167

Education: B.A., Columbia University, 1983. J.D., New York University, 1987.

Professional: 1987–1992, environmental associate, Skadden, Arps, Slate, Meagher & Flom. 1992–2001, deputy assistant general counsel for pollution control, U.S. Department of Agriculture. 2001–2002, legislative assistant for environment and agriculture, Sen. Barbara Boxer, D-Calif. 2003–2005, minority counsel, House Cmte. on Energy and Commerce, Ranking Member John Dingell, D-Mich. 2005–2007, senior counsel, Sen. Barbara Boxer, D-Calif. 2007–present, majority staff director and chief counsel, Senate Cmte. on Environment and Public Works.

Expertise: staff management, global warming, toxics, water.

Senate Environment and Public Works Committee Chairwoman Barbara Boxer, D-Calif., and Majority Staff Director Bettina Poirier continue their historic partnership as they tackle critical environmental issues during the 112th Congress. Boxer is the first woman to chair the Committee while Poirier is its first female staff director.

Key goals for Boxer and Poirier include the passage of a transportation bill, the reauthorization of the Water Resources and Development Act, regulation of chromium-6 in drinking water and oversight of the BP oil spill. The committee also will watch nuclear issues after the March nuclear reactor accidents in Japan following the tsunami.

Poirier said modernization of the Toxic Substances Control Act also is on the agenda, as well as "a bill to improve federal support to communities that are experiencing disease clusters that may be connected to toxic pollution in the environment." The committee will continue its focus on clean energy and climate issues, including renewable fuel issues, energy efficiency in federal buildings, and carbon pollution, she added.

Notable achievement's for Boxer include Congress's passage of the Hiring Incentives to Restore Employment Act, which extended the current authorization for highway, transit and highway safety programs (SAFETEA-LU) through the end of the year and transferred approximately $20 billion from the General Fund into the Highway Trust Fund.

Congress also approved funds for EPA to study black carbon and reauthorized the Diesel Emissions Reduction Act, which established a voluntary national and state-level grant and loan program to reduce diesel emissions. Congress also passed EPW legislation aimed at reducing drinking water in lead and forcing the federal government to pay its fair share of stormwater pollution fees.

"Senator Boxer sets the goals and priorities for the Committee, and my job is to help her accomplish those goals," Poirier said. "Everything we do in this Committee has a direct impact on the health and welfare of every American, and the infrastructure that our economy depends on," she said. "That's a big responsibility, and we keep that in mind when we come to work every day."

Poirier lives in Virginia with her husband of more than 20 years and their young son.

SENATE ENVIRONMENT AND PUBLIC WORKS

Tyler Rushforth

Counsel

508 Hart Senate Office Bldg.

Phone: (202) 224-8056

Fax: (202) 224-1273

Personal: Born 12/01/1972 in Los Angeles, Calif.

Education: B.A., political science, Brigham Young University, 1999. J.D., Vermont Law School, 2006.

Professional: 1999, staff assistant, Sen. Harry Reid, D-Nev. 2000, network equipment sales representative, Sarcom. 2001–2003, research assistant, Management Assistance Corp., Rockville, Md. 2006–2007, staff assistant, Sen. Harry Reid, D-Nev. 2007–present, counsel, Senate Cmte. on Environment and Public Works.

Expertise: Water infrastructure, transportation.

In the 112th Congress, Tyler Rushforth plans to hit the ground running on a major priority for the Senate Environment and Public Works Committee: a new transportation bill.

Committee Chairwoman Barbara Boxer, D-Calif., and ranking member, Sen. James Inhofe, R-Okla., have described the bill as a key legislative goal and are working on ways to creatively finance it. We are "working very closely to come up with a bill that uses funding in the Highway Trust Fund, looks at ways we can agree to make that fund larger, but mostly we're really focused on leveraging dollars," Boxer said.

Boxer identified the Transportation Infrastructure Finance and Innovation Act as the "easiest" option because it is already a law. Another option, she said, is an infrastructure bank capitalized at about $10 billion dollars that would give out both grants and loans. A third option is a "Build America" bond approach for transportation.

Along with his transportation expertise, in 2007, Rushforth was a key staffer on the Water Resources Development Act (WRDA), a major bill that sets water policy for the nation and helps fund water infrastructure projects. Rushforth will likely pitch in on efforts to reauthorize WRDA in 2011.

The Los Angeles native's commitment to environmental issues extends back to his decision to attend Vermont Law School because it was ranked number one in the subject.

Rushforth has always combined a love of politics with his interest in the environment. Between college and law school he did a short stint with now Senate Majority Leader Harry Reid, D-Nev., and again after law school. That cemented his interest in working on Capitol Hill.

When Rushforth is not working, he is spending time with his wife and children and, when he can, taking bicycle rides so he can enjoy the environment he is working to help protect.

SENATE ENVIRONMENT AND PUBLIC WORKS

George Sugiyama

Chief Minority Counsel

Ranking member Sen. James Inhofe, R-Okla.

456 Dirksen Senate Office Bldg.

Phone: (202) 224-0146

Fax: (202) 224-2322

George_Sugiyama@EPW.Senate.Gov

Personal: Born in Baltimore, Md.

Education: Bachelor of Arts, Drake University, 1970. Juris Doctorate, University of Maryland, 1976.

Professional: 1976–1979, attorney-advisor, Office of Enforcement, Mobile Source Enforcement Division, Environmental Protection Agency. 1982–1984, policy analyst, Office of Policy, Planning and Evaluation, Environmental Protection Agency. 1984–1986, supervisor, Office of Policy Analysis and Review, Office of Air and Radiation, U.S. Environmental Protection Agency. 1986–1994, partner, Pillsbury Madison & Sutro. 1994–2006, partner, Dorsey & Whitney LLP. 2007–2009, counsel to assistant administrator for air and radiation, Office of Air and Radiation, U.S. Environmental Protection Agency. 2009–Present, chief minority counsel, Senate Environment and Public Works Cmte.

Expertise: Clean Air Act, Clean Water Act, NEPA, Endangered Species Act, Toxic Substances Control Act, Administrative law, FOIA.

Senate Environment and Public Works Committee Chief Minority Counsel George Sugiyama's own energy expenditures will soar in 2011 as he oversees the economic impacts of environmental regulations on energy projects and looks into electric system reliability.

Sugiyama, who provides the Republican staff with legal and policy advice on a wide range of environmental and administrative law issues, also expects to monitor the Obama administration's "apparent resistance to fossil energy projects," he said. High priority items will include potential greenhouse gas regulations coming through the Environmental Protection Agency (EPA) and renewable fuels issues.

EPW Ranking Member James Inhofe, R-Okla., is pushing the Energy Tax Prevention Act of 2011, as a way to block any cap-and-trade regulations. Inhofe has insisted Congress should be in charge of the nation's energy policies and describes regulatory efforts as "back-door energy taxes."

"EPA's cap-and-trade regime is bad policy that must be stopped," Inhofe said. "Imposing energy taxes through EPA's cap-and-trade regulations and blocking expansion won't make Americans healthier—it will only mean fewer jobs, a higher cost of living, and less growth and innovation."

Sugiyama's extensive experience at the Environmental Protection Agency helps to inform his policy and legal advice to the committee. He served as counsel to the assistant administrator for EPA's Office of Air and Radiation during the George W. Bush administration, where he took a lead on Yucca Mountain environmental standards. Additionally, prior to an extensive career in private practice, Sugiyama also worked as a supervisor in EPA's Office of Air and Radiation and as a policy analyst in EPA's Office of Policy, Planning and Evaluation; Office of Air and Radiation and the Office of Enforcement in the agency's Mobile Source Enforcement Division during the Reagan and Carter administrations.

Sugiyama has won a number of awards, including the EPA Superior Performance Award in 2008 and the EPA Silver Medal in 1983 and 1984. He served as a member of EPA's Clean Air Act Advisory Committee from 1991 to 1993.

When he is not wrangling with climate change and other thorny issues on Capitol Hill, Sugiyama enjoys judo and attending events at the Verizon Center in Washington, D.C.

SENATE ENVIRONMENT AND PUBLIC WORKS

Ruth Van Mark

Staff Director

Ranking Republican James Inhofe, R-Okla.

415 Hart Senate Office Bldg.

Phone: (202) 224-8204

Personal: Born 10/08/1959 in Torrington, Wyo.

Education: B.A., political science, Bethel College (Minn.), 1982. M.A., public administration, George Mason University, 1988.

Professional: 1982–1988, legislative staff, Rep. Daniel E. Lungren, R-Calif. 1989–1991, legislative dir., Rep. James M. Inhofe, R-Okla. 1991–1994, professional staff member, House Cmte. on Public Works and Transportation. 1994–2000, legislative director, Sen. James M. Inhofe, R-Okla. 2001–2002, staff member, Subc. on Transportation and Infrastructure, Senate Cmte. on Environment and Public Works. 2003–2009, deputy staff director for transportation, Senate Cmte. on Environment and Public Works. 2009–present, staff director, Senate Cmte. on Environment and Public Works.

Expertise: Transportation, water resources.

Ruth Van Mark is entering her second session as the Republican staff director for the Senate Environment and Public Works Committee. In that role, Van Mark coordinates minority staff work on committee projects and helps make sure ranking member Sen. James Inhofe's, R-Okla., priorities are on track.

A top priority for Inhofe in the 112th Congress is the passage of a transportation bill. Inhofe expects to work closely with Committee Chairwoman Barbara Boxer, D-Calif., on the bill, which the two hope will zip through Congress this year.

Inhofe and Boxer also want to reauthorize the Water Resources and Development Act, aimed at shoring up the nation's aging water infrastructure, a goal they were unable to complete last session.

Van Mark will also work on the pair's third goal: the passage of the Economic Development Revitalization Act, a bill that would authorize $500 million per year for a limited time period for job promotion and industrial and commercial growth in communities with limited job opportunities, low per capita income, or other economic distress.

Van Mark, a longtime Inhofe staff aide, said the senator has a good working relationship with Boxer despite their disagreement on the climate change issue. Inhofe will be "working closely with her to get these critical infrastructure bills done," Van Mark said.

Van Mark counts the defeat of cap-and-trade legislation in Congress as a minority victory last session.

The director, who is known as Inhofe's "Right Hand," will work with EPW minority staff members and the legislative staff of Republicans on the committee to battle any EPA attempts to move forward with climate change regulations.

SENATE ENVIRONMENT AND PUBLIC WORKS

Jim Wrathall

Senior Counsel

Chairman Barbara Boxer, D-Calif.

456 Dirksen Senate Office Bldg.

Phone: (202) 224-8832

Fax: (202) 224-1273

jim_wrathall@epw.senate.gov

Personal: Born 09/14/1962 in Salt Lake City, Utah.

Education: B.S, business, Tulane University, 1984. J.D., Georgetown University Law Center, 1987.

Professional: 1987–1991, associate in environmental practice group, Skadden Arps Law firm. 1991–1995, associate, Wilmer, Cutler and Pickering. 1996–2007, partner, Wilmer, Cutler and Pickering. 2007–present, senior counsel, Senate Cmte. on Environment and Public Works.

Expertise: Environmental law, oversight, investigations.

Senior Counsel Jim Wrathall brings a wealth of knowledge about the nation's waterways to the Senate Environment and Public Works Committee.

Wrathall, an expert in the Clean Water Act, has mainly focused on water quality and drinking water issues. He saw several major successes during the last session, including the passage of the Reduction of Lead in Drinking Water Act, which reduced the allowable lead content in drinking water pipes, pipe fittings and plumbing fixtures.

Wrathall's boss, Committee Chairwoman Barbara Boxer, D-Calif., also has seen success on the agency front, lauding the Environmental Protection Agency's decision to establish a national drinking water standard for perchlorate, a component of rocket fuel. Boxer and Sen. Dianne Feinstein, D-Calif., recently introduced legislation that would set a deadline for the agency to set an enforceable drinking water standard for chromium-6, which has been linked to cancer.

Previously, Wrathall focused on the Clean Water Restoration Act, legislation aimed at addressing wetland protection issues in the wake of the controversial Supreme Court ruling in Rapanos v. United States. Wrathall, who briefed the case before the Supreme Court, was uniquely suited to tackle the bill.

Wrathall moved from a private law firm to Capitol Hill in 2007. In his previous career, Wrathall represented both private companies and major environmental groups in cases that have gone all the way up to the U.S. Supreme Court.

When Wrathall is not worrying about the environment from his office, he's getting a different view of it—from the air. He has a pilot's license. His six-year-old daughter also keeps him busy on his off hours.

Committee on Finance

219 Dirksen Senate Office Bldg.
Washington, DC 20510-6200
Phone: (202) 224-4515
http://finance.senate.gov

Ratio: 11/13

MAJORITY MEMBERS

Max Baucus, MT, Chairman

John D. Rockefeller, WV
Kent Conrad, ND
Jeff Bingaman, NM
John F. Kerry, MA
Ron Wyden, OR
Charles E. Schumer, NY
Debbie Stabenow, MI
Maria Cantwell, WA
Bill Nelson, FL
Robert Menendez, NJ
Thomas Carper, DE
Ben Cardin, MD

MINORITY MEMBERS

Orrin G. Hatch, UT, Chairman

Charles E. Grassley, IA
Olympia J. Snowe, ME
Jon Kyl, AZ
Mike Crapo, ID
Pat Roberts, KS
John Ensign, NV
Michael B. Enzi, WY
John Cornyn, TX
Tom Coburn, OK
John Thune, SD

SENATE FINANCE

JURISDICTION

(1) Bonded debt of the United States, except as provided in the Congressional Budget Act of 1974.
(2) Customs, collection districts, and ports of entry and delivery.
(3) Deposit of public moneys.
(4) General revenue sharing.
(5) Health programs under the Social Security Act and health programs financed by a specific tax or trust fund.
(6) National social security.
(7) Reciprocal trade agreements.
(8) Revenue measures generally, except as provided in the Congressional Budget Act of 1974.
(9) Revenue measures relating to the insular possessions.
(10) Tariffs and import quotas and matters related thereto.
(11) Transportation of dutiable goods.

SENATE FINANCE

Creating jobs and reducing the federal deficit are major themes for the Senate Finance Committee in the 112th Congress, as Chairman Max Baucus, D-Mont., and Ranking Member Orrin Hatch, R-Utah, pursue tax, trade and health care policy initiatives to try to accomplish both. Baucus believes that reforming the tax code will help create jobs and grow the economy, so in 2011 the committee is undertaking a comprehensive review of the tax system.

In a series of hearings, the committee has received testimony on how the tax code is affecting individual and business decisions, and is considering what changes could be made to incentivize job creation and economic growth. The committee also is reviewing the tax system's effect on household and business debt levels, and is considering whether simplifying the tax code would encourage individuals to save.

The committee was instrumental in crafting and enacting the health care reform law, the Patient Protection and Affordable Care Act of 2010 (PPACA), and it continues to influence the committee's work in 2011. Baucus believes the law will help reduce the deficit and create jobs, and his staff is working to ensure that it is implemented according to Congressional intent. Hatch feels the law is an example of reckless government spending, and his staff is developing targeted reform packages to replace the health care law if it is able to be repealed. They are also promoting several bills Hatch has introduced to repeal individual provisions of the PPACA.

Medicaid reform is another key committee objective in 2011. Baucus wants to cut down on Medicaid and Medicare fraud, which is costing the government billions of dollars each year. The Democratic staff is working to ensure that PPACA provisions which bolster the prevention and prosecution of Medicaid and Medicare fraud are implemented. Hatch wants the Medicaid reform effort to give states flexibility in managing the money they spend on Medicaid, and has targeted PPACA provisions that he believes limit governors' ability to control their states' Medicaid spending.

The Senators' international trade priorities in the 112th Congress include reauthorizing and extending the Trade Adjustment Assistance program, and working to finalize free trade agreements with Colombia, Panama and South Korea. The Colombia and Panama agreements have few remaining hurdles and could be approved quickly, but the Korea agreement is being held up by issues related to U.S. beef exports.

Other issues the committee is working on in the 112th Congress include trying to permanently fix the Medicare physician payment system, developing packages of energy and education tax incentives, and fighting overseas tax evasion. Strengthening tax laws for American Indian businesses and lowering the health disparities faced by American Indians are also on the committee's agenda.

SENATE FINANCE

John C. Angell

Senior Advisor

219 Dirksen Senate Office Bldg.

Phone: (202) 224-4515

John_Angell@finance.senate.gov

Personal: Born 05/23/1953 in Santa Monica, Calif.

Education: B.A., political science, Pomona College (Claremont, Calif.), 1975. J.D., Loyola Univ. (Los Angeles, Calif.), 1980.

Professional: 1981–1988, legislative assistant, Rep. Leon Panetta, D-Calif. 1989–1992, chief of staff, House Cmte. on the Budget. 1993–1994, executive associate director, Office of Management and Budget. 1995–1996, senior advisor, The White House, Office of the Chief of Staff. 1997–2000, assistant secretary, Department of Energy, Office of Congressional Affairs. 2001–2002, Democratic staff director, Senate Cmte. on Finance. 2004–present, senior advisor, Senate Cmte. on Finance.

Expertise: Oversight in the areas of tax, health, retirement programs and trade, general federal budget issues.

Senior Advisor John Angell assists with the Finance Committee's oversight responsibilities and, in the 112th Congress, that will include monitoring the Medicare and Medicaid programs. The committee's goal is to try to address cost increases in those programs and in the health sector generally.

Border security, terrorism financing, and offshore tax evasion are other oversight priorities for Committee Chairman Max Baucus, D-Mont., Angell said. In the area of offshore tax evasion, the committee is continuing its work, which began in 2010, on the tax profile of Transocean Ltd.

Transocean is the owner of the offshore drilling rig that exploded in the Gulf of Mexico, leading to the Gulf spill. Angell and his colleagues are examining the U.S. tax implications of the company relocating its headquarters to the Cayman Islands and Switzerland.

In the area of Medicare oversight, Angell contributed last year to a committee report on Abbott Laboratories and the use of stents at a Maryland hospital. The report found that questionable stent implantations at the hospital by a doctor with ties to Abbott cost the Medicare program $3.8 million from 2007 through mid-2009.

In 2010, Angell also helped with the committee's preparation and release of two reports on the diabetes drug Avandia. The committee uncovered documents suggesting that GlaxoSmithKline, the maker of Avandia, failed to publish in a timely manner studies that found serious health risks associated with the drug, and actively promoted it despite the known safety concerns.

He also assisted with the completion of a GAO report on bulk cash smuggling. The report highlights the need to take action against cross-border currency smuggling, which is estimated at between $18 billion and $39 billion each year across the U.S./Mexico border alone.

SENATE FINANCE

Lily Batchelder

Democratic Chief Tax Counsel

219 Dirksen Senate Office Bldg.

Phone: (202) 224-4515

Lily_Batchelder@finance.senate.gov

Personal: Born 1972 in Brookline, Mass.

Education: J.D., Yale Law School, 2002. M.P.P. in microeconomics and human services, Harvard's Kennedy School of Government, 1999. A.B. in political science, Stanford University, 1994.

Professional: 1994–1995, client advocate, Neighbors Together Corporation. 1995–1997, director of community affairs, Office of New York State Senator Marty Markowitz. 2001, Wiener fellow, Wiener Center on Social Policy, Harvard Kennedy School of Government. 2005–2010, affiliated faculty, New York University Wagner School of Public Service. 2005–2007, assistant professor of law and public policy, New York University School of Law. 2007–2008, associate professor of law and public policy, New York University School of Law. 2008–2010, professor of law and public policy, New York University School of Law. 2009–2010, affiliated scholar, Urban-Brookings Tax Policy Center. 2009, Roscoe Pound visiting associate professor of law, Harvard Law School. 2010–present, Democratic chief tax counsel, Senate Cmte. on Finance.

Expertise: Income taxation, wealth transfer taxation, tax incentives, tax and social policy.

The key issues on the agenda of Chief Tax Counsel Lily Batchelder in 2011 include tax reform, job creation, and tax incentives in the areas of education and energy. The Finance Committee began its review of the tax code in 2010 with an examination of the lessons of the Tax Reform Act of 1986 and a consideration of historical trends in income and revenue.

In 2011, Chairman Max Baucus, D-Mont., convened a hearing to review the changes made to the tax code since the 1986 reform efforts and the extent to which the changes have kept up with transformations in the U.S. and global economy.

In another hearing under Baucus and Batchelder, the committee heard testimony on how the tax code is affecting individual and business decisions and what changes could be made to incentivize job creation and economic growth in light of increasing globalization. The committee is looking at the tax system's effect on household and business debt levels, and whether tax incentives for debt-financing contributed to the financial crisis or hurt the economy in other ways.

Batchelder and the committee's tax team are also considering whether individual incentives for savings in the tax code effectively promote individual savings, and how best to simplify the tax code to encourage Americans to save.

In 2010, the tax staff helped to enact a number of successful job-creation tax packages, including the Hiring Incentives to Restore Employment (HIRE) Act, the Tax Relief, Unemployment Insurance Reauthorization and Job Creation Act, and the Small Business Jobs Act.

The Small Business Jobs Act was co-authored by Chairman Baucus and Senator Mary Landrieu, D-La., and provided that small businesses can carry back general business tax credits to offset their tax burdens from the previous five years. They also can count the general business credits against the Alternative Minimum Tax, freeing up capital for expansion and job growth.

Batchelder received her Master's in Public Policy at Harvard's Kennedy School of Government, where she was president of the Kennedy School's student government. She earned her law degree at Yale, where she was twice awarded the prize for best paper on taxation. While in law school, she was a member of the Yale Law Journal, executive editor of the Yale Human Rights & Development Law Journal, and founded and directed the Pro Bono Network.

SENATE FINANCE

Chris Campbell

Republican Staff Director

219 Dirksen Senate Office Bldg.

Phone: (202) 224-3338

Chris_Campbell@finance.senate.gov

Personal: Born in Redlands, Calif.

Education: B.A. in political science, University of California Santa Barbara, 1998. MBA, Thunderbird, The Garvin School of International Management, 2006.

Professional: 1998–2000, president, Campbell Consulting. 1999–2000, national field director, Orrin Hatch for President. 2000, campaign director, Orrin Hatch for U.S. Senate. 2000–2004, staff director, International Trade Subcommittee, Senate Cmte. on Finance. 2004–2006, president, Campbell Enterprises. 2006–2010, legislative director, Office of Senator Orrin Hatch, R-Utah. 2011–present, Republican staff director, Senate Cmte. on Finance.

Expertise: International trade, international commerce.

Republican staff director Chris Campbell has worked for new Ranking Member Orrin Hatch, R-Utah, for a significant portion of his career, including serving as national field director in Hatch's run for president in the 2000 election. He was the Senator's legislative director for the past five years.

As staff director, Campbell is overseeing the staff's work on Hatch's priorities in the areas of taxation, international trade, health care, Social Security, and oversight of ten federal agencies.

In the 112th Congress, Campbell said that Hatch wants the committee to begin a comprehensive examination of the tax code. The committee has already begun hearings on the issue, and is working on formulating policies for reforming both the domestic and international tax codes.

Campbell said the tax team's 2011 agenda also includes pension reform, a package of energy tax incentives, and the tax title of the highway transportation bill. He said Hatch also wants to find permanent solutions for certain tax extenders, such as the Alternative Minimum Tax and research and development tax credit, so that the Congress does not have to patch them every year.

The Finance Committee is one of two committees of jurisdiction on the health care reform law. Campbell said that Hatch wants the staff to develop a series of targeted reform packages and some smaller bills that would replace the law if it is repealed. The health care team also is starting to look at how to reform Medicare, Medicaid, and Social Security.

Campbell said that the international trade area is where the committee hopes to be most legislatively active in 2011 because of unfinished business from the last session. The staff is working on a customs reauthorization bill, three pending free trade agreements and the renewal of trade preference programs. Consideration of Russia's accession to the World Trade Organization and work on the miscellaneous tariffs bill also could be on the committee's agenda later in 2011, he said.

Campbell hails from California. Early in his career he owned his own consulting firm that specialized in venture capital and the marketing of start-up businesses.

SENATE FINANCE

Alan Cohen

Democratic Senior Budget Advisor and Chief Social Security Counsel

219 Dirksen Senate Office Bldg.

Phone: (202) 224-4515

Fax: (202) 224-5920

Alan_Cohen@finance.senate.gov

Personal: Born 1950 in New York, N.Y.

Education: B.S., physics, Grinnell College, 1972. M.P.P., University of Michigan, 1973. Ph.D., economics, University of Wisconsin, 1979.

Professional: 1979–1983, economist, Dept. of Health and Human Services. 1983–1987, senior economist, Senate Cmte. on the Budget. 1987–1992, assistant staff director for budget priorities, Senate Cmte. on the Budget. 1992–1993, budget economist, Senate Cmte. on Finance. 1993–2001, senior advisor to the secretary for budget and economics, Dept. of the Treasury. 2001–present, senior budget advisor and chief Social Security counsel, Senate Cmte. on Finance.

Expertise: Social Security, budget.

Alan Cohen continues to advise Committee Chairman Max Baucus, D-Mont., on budget and Social Security issues in his eleventh year as Democratic senior budget advisor and chief Social Security counsel. In 2011, Cohen is joining his committee colleagues in developing strategies to promote job growth and economic recovery. Cohen is also working on reducing the federal deficit and addressing the federal debt limit.

Keeping the Social Security Administration's (SSA) administrative budget adequately funded remains a top priority in the 112th Congress. Cohen said that if the SSA is not adequately funded, it means the backlog of disability appeals hearings could start to grow again. The SSA had finally started to make progress on the huge backlog in recent years, he noted.

In 2010, Cohen helped develop a major Finance Committee hearing highlighting the issue of the lack of due process protections in private long-term disability policies covered under the Employee Retirement Income Security Act (ERISA). Chairman Baucus convened the hearing in response to reports of unfair claims denials that threaten the finances of beneficiaries who are unable to work due to disability.

Witnesses cited instances of long procedural delays and the use of in-house doctors by long-term disability insurance companies to avoid claims payments. The committee heard testimony that ERISA, which was intended to address these issues, has been interpreted in ways that further hurt the claims review process for claimants.

Chairman Baucus is committed to finding a solution that gives policy holders the fair process and benefits they deserve. Cohen said the committee is continuing to look at the issue in 2011.

SENATE FINANCE

Amber Cottle

Chief International Trade Counsel
219 Dirksen Senate Office Bldg.
Phone: (202) 224-4515
Amber_Cottle@finance.senate.gov

Personal: Born 1970 in St. Louis, Mo.

Education: BA, St. Louis University, 1993. JD, University of Chicago Law School, 1996.

Professional: 1996–1997, clerk, Judge Francis Murnaghan, Jr., U.S. Court of Appeals for the Fourth Circuit. 1997–2001, associate, international group, Wilmer, Cutler & Pickering. 2001–2003, assistant general counsel, Office of the U.S. Trade Representative. 2003–2007, deputy assistant U.S. trade representative, Office of the U.S. Trade Representative. 2007–2009, international trade counsel, Senate Cmte. on Finance. 2009–present, chief international trade counsel, Senate Cmte. on Finance.

Expertise: International trade issues.

Amber Cottle has been on the Finance Committee's Democratic international trade staff since 2007 and in 2009 was promoted to Chief International Trade Counsel. In that role, she works to promote the international trade-related initiatives of Chairman Max Baucus, D-Mont.

In 2011, the committee is working on Congressional consideration of pending free trade agreements (FTA) with Colombia, Panama and South Korea. Baucus feels that the Colombia FTA is critical to U.S. agricultural producers because Colombia has traditionally been a top export market for U.S. agricultural goods, including wheat. The U.S. is losing wheat market share to Argentina and Canada, and Baucus believes that U.S. farmers could lose the entire market if the Colombia FTA is not approved early in the 112th Congress.

Panama has agreed to eliminate trade barriers and open its markets and, in Baucus' view, the U.S. should act quickly to resolve any issues standing in the way of the FTA. The Korea FTA has been delayed by concerns related to U.S. beef. Baucus is urging the Administration to resolve the issue and work with the Koreans to develop a roadmap towards full market access so that the FTA can move forward.

Cottle this year also is helping Baucus as he works to reauthorize and extend the Trade Adjustment Assistance (TAA) program, which he views as critical in supporting American workers whose jobs have been shipped overseas.

Cottle joined the Committee after serving as chief investment negotiator at the Office of the USTR, where she negotiated the investment provisions of the FTAs with Korea, Thailand, Morocco, and Oman. She also supervised the negotiation of the investment provisions of several bilateral investment treaties.

SENATE FINANCE

Everett Eissenstat

Chief International Trade Counsel

219 Dirksen Senate Office Bldg.

Phone: (202) 224-4515

Everett_Eissenstat@finance.senate.gov

Personal: Born 1963 in Lawrence, Kans.

Education: B.S., Spanish and political science, Oklahoma State University, 1985. M.A., Latin America studies, University of Texas at Austin, 1988. J.D. (cum laude), University of Oklahoma, 1993.

Professional: 1994–1995, associate attorney, Dixon and Dixon. 1995–1996, special asst., U.S. Trade Representative. 1996–2000, legislative director, Rep. Jim Kolbe, R-Ariz. 2001–2006, chief international trade counsel, Senate Cmte. on Finance. 2006–2010, assistant U.S. trade representative for the Americas, Office of the United States Trade Representative. 2011–present, chief international trade counsel, Senate Cmte. on Finance.

Expertise: International trade.

Everett Eissenstat serves as the chief international trade counsel to Ranking Member Orrin Hatch, R-Utah, to whom he provides advice on international trade matters before the committee. His legislative responsibilities include trade agreements, customs authorization, preferential trade arrangements, and sanctions policy.

Eissenstat is also responsible for the oversight of U.S. government international trade agencies. Eissenstat served previously as chief international trade counsel from 2001 to 2006.

Before re-joining the Finance Committee staff, Eissenstat served five years in the Office of the U.S. Trade Representative as the Assistant USTR for the Americas. In that capacity, he served as lead negotiator for the Americas and was responsible for developing, implementing, and monitoring U.S. trade policy in the region.

In 2011, Hatch has asked Eissenstat and his trade team to work on Congressional approval of pending trade agreements with Colombia, Panama, and South Korea. The trade team also is working on the renewal of trade preference programs, which give developing countries duty-free access to the U.S. market for certain products, helping those developing economies grow and emerge from poverty.

The committee's extensive oversight of the U.S. international trade agencies is also on Eissenstat's agenda in the 112th Congress, as is oversight of ongoing international trade negotiations such as the Doha round World Trade Organization negotiations and the Trans-Pacific Partnership negotiations.

Eissenstat received his J.D. cum laude from the University of Oklahoma, an M.A. in Latin American Studies from the University of Texas and a B.S. in Political Science and Spanish from Oklahoma State University. He lives in Alexandria, Virginia, with his wife Janet, former director of the President's Commission on White House Fellowships, and their two sons.

SENATE FINANCE

Antonia Ferrier

Communications Director, Sen. Orrin Hatch

219 Dirksen Senate Office Bldg.

Phone: (202) 224-4515

Antonia.Ferrier@hatch.senate.gov

Personal: Born 10/04/1973 in Bristol, United Kingdom.

Education: B.A., American University, 1996.

Professional: 1997–1999, assistant to associate, IEP Advisors, Barbour Griffith and Rogers. 1999–2001, associate, Shepardson, Stern + Kaminsky. 2001–2002, deputy communications director, National Republican Senatorial Cmte. 2002–2003, deputy communications director, Senate Majority Leader Bill Frist, R-Tenn. 2003–2007, communications director, Sen. Olympia Snowe, R-Maine. 2007–2008, communications director, House Republican Whip Roy Blunt, R-Mo. 2007, vice president, Manning, Selvage & Lee. 2009–2010, Press Secretary/Spokeswoman, House Republican Leader John Boehner, R-Ohio. 2010–present, communications director, Sen. Orrin Hatch, R-Utah.

Expertise: Communications.

Antonia Ferrier is communications director for Senator Orrin Hatch, R-Utah, the Ranking Member of the Senate Finance Committee in the 112th Congress. In addition to handling communications going in and out of Hatch's personal office, she is writing press releases and other communications for the Finance Committee's minority staff.

She moved to Hatch's office after two years as the spokeswoman and press secretary for Speaker John Boehner, R-Ohio, while he was still House Minority Leader. In that position, she was the liaison for House Republicans to the White House and the Pentagon. She also served as communications director for former House Whip Roy Blunt, R-Mo., in the 111th Congress.

Ferrier's Capitol Hill experience goes back 11 years to when she was deputy communications director for the National Republican Senatorial Committee. Her longest stay in one communications director position was from 2003 to 2007 when she worked for Sen. Olympia Snowe, R-Maine.

For the Finance Committee in 2011, Ferrier is helping to get the message out on Hatch's key initiatives, such as reducing wasteful spending in the federal government, reforming the domestic and international tax codes, and overseeing the proper implementation of the health care reform law.

Ferrier is also helping to deliver Hatch's message that the United States needs to finalize free trade agreements with Colombia, Panama, and Korea in the 112th Congress.

Ferrier is highly regarded on Capitol Hill as an effective communicator, according to Bob Stevenson, her boss when she worked for former Senate Majority Leader Bill Frist, R-Tenn. In an interview with Politico, a Capitol Hill newspaper, Stevenson said that she is "more than willing to work with people across the aisle, but is tough as nails when she needs to be."
Born in Bristol, England, Ferrier grew up in Lexington, Massachusetts.

SENATE FINANCE

David S. Johanson

International Trade Counsel

219 Dirksen Senate Office Bldg.

Phone: (202) 224-4515

David_Johanson@finance.senate.gov

Personal: Born 02/25/1964 in Austin, Texas.

Education: B.A, history, Stanford University, 1987. M.Phil., Cambridge University, 1990. J.D., University of Texas, 1993.

Professional: 1988–1989, legislative corresp., Sen. Phil Gramm, R-Texas. 1993–1995, legislative asst. and press secretary, Rep. Wally Herger, R-Calif. 1995–1997, legislative director, Rep. George Radanovich, R-Calif. 1997–2003, associate attorney, Stewart and Stewart. 2003–present, trade counsel, international trade counsel, Senate Cmte. on Finance.

Expertise: International trade law, agricultural trade.

David Johanson serves as the point person on the Republican staff for bills that any Senator wants to include in the Miscellaneous Tariffs Bill (MTB). In 2011, the committee is again incorporating non-controversial miscellaneous tariff bills into the larger MTB, and Johanson is coordinating the process for the minority staff.

The MTB provides an opportunity to temporarily eliminate or reduce duties on imported products and to make technical corrections to U.S. tariff laws. To be included in the MTB, bills must meet numerous requirements and undergo a vetting process by the committee and several agencies. The committee makes the final determination on whether a bill qualifies for inclusion in the MTB.

Johanson also is assisting with the committee's effort to secure approval of pending free trade agreements with Korea, Panama and Colombia. Ranking Member Orrin Hatch, R-Utah, is pressing on the Panama and Colombia agreements in particular, and has asked the U.S Trade Representative to provide the committee with a clear timetable for moving the two agreements through the Congress.

Passing a customs reauthorization bill is a priority for Hatch in the 112th Congress, and Johanson is helping with that effort. Previous attempts at reauthorization have sought to re-balance the duties of the U.S. Customs and Border Protection Agency to ensure that trade facilitation is not overshadowed by homeland security.

In the 112th Congress, Johanson continues to monitor the Doha round of WTO negotiations, which began ten years ago. An agreement that emerges from those negotiations would have to be voted on by the Congress, and he will participate in Hill discussions should an agreement be reached.

The development of a trans-Pacific partnership is ongoing, and Johanson is working with his colleagues to build this trade pact with many Pacific Rim countries.

SENATE FINANCE

Matt Kazan

Health Policy Advisor

219 Dirksen Senate Office Bldg.

Phone: (202) 224-4515

Matt_Kazan@finance.senate.gov

Personal: Born 1983 in Littleton, Colo.

Education: B.A. in political science and English; minor in economics, Uinversity of Denver, 2005. M.P.P., George Washington University, 2009.

Professional: 2005, fundraising and compliance director, Bill Winter for Congress. 2006, fundraising associate, Peggy Lamm for Congress. 2007, campaign manager, Doug Linkhart for City Council At-Large. 2008–2010, health policy associate, Cmte. on Finance. 2010–present, health policy advisor, Cmte. on Finance.

Expertise: Medicare and Medicaid program integrity, Medicare Part C, health care workforce, dual eligibles, medical malpractice.

Given the significant health care legislation enacted in 2010, the first session of the 112th Congress will feature oversight hearings for Matt Kazan and the Finance Committee's Majority health care team. Hearings are focusing on the Obama administration's efforts to implement the policies established in the American Recovery and Reinvestment Act and the Patient Protection and Affordable Care Act according to Congressional intent.

Legislatively, Kazan and the Finance Committee health care team will seek to permanently reform the Medicare physician payment system that threatens to jeopardize access to physician services for tens of millions of seniors and disabled Americans.

Also on the 2011 agenda are several important health care policies within the committee's jurisdiction set to expire at the end of 2011 that may require temporary or permanent extensions. These include relief from caps on Medicare therapy services, protections for rural doctors and hospitals, and the Qualifying Individual and Transitional Medical Assistance programs.

Kazan and his colleagues are also working to reauthorize the Temporary Assistance to Needy Families program. The health care staff was instrumental in 2010 in extending the program for another year.

The program provides aid for low-income families with dependent children. Specifically, it assists with job training and job search support, child care and transportation, and other services that help people transition back to work.

In 2010, the work of Kazan and the committee health care team was dominated by the enactment, and early stages of implementation, of the Affordable Care Act. In particular, the health care staff held the first in a series of oversight hearings regarding health reform implementation, beginning with Don Berwick, administrator of the Centers for Medicare and Medicaid Services. He testified about his agency's efforts to use Affordable Care Act resources to modernize the health care delivery system.

In addition to passage of the health care reform legislation, Kazan and the health care team led successful legislative efforts to stave off deep cuts to physician payments under Medicare's Sustainable Growth Rate formula, culminating with a 12-month fix enacted in December 2010.

# SENATE FINANCE

Jay Khosla

Republican Chief Health Counsel

219 Dirksen Senate Office Bldg.

Phone: (202) 224-4515

Jay_Khosla@finance.senate.gov

Personal: Born in Alexandria, Va.

Education: B.S. in biology, Virginia Commonwealth University, 2001. J.D., University of Richmond, 2005. M.H.A., Medical College of Virginia, 2005.

Professional: 2005–2006, health counsel, Office of Majority Leader William Frist, R-Tenn. 2006–2008, health counsel, Senate Budget Cmte. 2008, senior health policy advisor, John McCain for President Campaign. 2009–2010, legislative director and senior health counsel, Office of Senator Orrin Hatch, R-Utah. 2011–present, Republican chief health counsel, Cmte. on Finance.

Expertise: Medicare, private health insurance market.

Reforming the entitlement programs—Medicare, Medicaid and Social Security—is a priority in the 112th Congress for Ranking Member Orrin Hatch, R-Utah, according to chief health counsel Jay Khosla. For Khosla and the health care staff, the major focus initially is on Medicaid reform.

One goal of the Medicaid reform effort is to give states flexibility in managing the money they spend on Medicaid, Khosla said. Hatch feels that Medicaid maintenance of effort provisions in the Patient Protection and Affordable Care Act (PPACA) limit governors' ability to control their states' Medicaid spending.

Hatch is taking aim at other provisions in the PPACA as well. Khosla and the health care team will help to promote Hatch's Medical Device Access and Innovation Protection Act. The bill provides for the immediate repeal of the excise tax on medical device sales included in the health care reform law. The tax intends to raise money, but Hatch believes it will hinder innovation and force manufacturing jobs to move overseas.

Khosla is also working on the Ranking Member's American Liberty Restoration Act, which calls for the repeal of the provision in the PPACA that requires everyone to have insurance.

Assisting with balanced budget amendments, a signature issue for Hatch, and rigorous oversight, particularly of the PPACA, are also on the 2011 agenda of Khosla and the health care staff. He said that there has not been a lot of transparency in the way the health reform regulations have been implemented, and the committee will work to change that.

Khosla noted that there is always a huge overlap between the committee's health care and tax issues, so he is working closely with chief tax counsel Mark Prater on tax reform and tax policy. Health care tax credits are among the pieces that Khosla and his staff will contribute to the tax reform effort.

Khosla served as Hatch's legislative director and senior health counsel immediately prior to being chosen as the top Republican health care staffer on the Finance Committee. In 2008 he served as senior health policy advisor to Sen. John McCain, R-Ariz., during his run for president.

SENATE FINANCE

Richard Litsey

Counsel and Senior Advisor for Indian Affairs

219 Dirksen Senate Office Bldg.

Phone: (202) 224-4515

Richard_Litsey@finance.senate.gov

Personal: Born in Wright-Patterson Air Force Base, Fairfield, Ohio.

Education: B.A., Oklahoma State University. J.D., Thurgood Marshall School of Law. LL.M., University of Houston.

Professional: 1989–1991, attorney/advisor, Social Security Administration, Office of Hearings and Appeals. 1991–1994, attorney, Baker & Hostetler. 1994–1995, attorney/advisor, Social Security Administration, Office of Hearings and Appeals. 1995–1998, senior attorney, Social Security Administration, Office of Hearings and Appeals. 1998–2000, supervisory staff attorney, Social Security Administration, Office of Hearings and Appeals. 2000–2004, hearing office director, Social Security Administration, Office of Hearings and Appeals. 2004–2007, counsel, Senate Cmte. on Finance. 2007–present, counsel and senior advisor for Indian affairs, Senate Cmte. on Finance.

Expertise: Social Security, Indian health care, Indian tax issues.

Richard Litsey will advise Chairman Max Baucus, D-Mont., on addressing domestic violence and child abuse on Indian Reservations, during the 112th Congress. The topic has been a priority for Baucus, a cosponsor of the Violence Against Women Act, for many years.

In the past, Baucus has secured grants for Indian women under the Violence Against Women Act. The grants helped to provide legal advocacy, support groups, and referrals to area service providers for Indian women who were victims of domestic violence.

During 2011, Litsey also will work on strengthening tax laws for American Indian businesses, and continuing to try to lower the health disparities faced by American Indians. The committee is trying to address the fact that Medicare spends about three times as much per person each year as the Indian Health Service, and Medicaid spends about twice as much.

In 2010, Litsey was involved with the committee's health care reform efforts, and also worked on tax issues such as accelerated depreciation. He also helped with Indian employment tax credits and New Markets Tax credits that were enacted within the Tax Relief, Unemployment Reauthorization and Job Creation Act of 2010.

The law extended the business tax credit for employers of qualified employees that work and live on or near an Indian reservation. The credit is 20 percent of the excess of wages and health insurance costs paid to employees (up to $20,000 per employee) in the current year over the amount paid in 1993.

Litsey is a member of the Muscogee (Creek) Nation. He served on the board of directors of the Houston chapter of the American Indian Chamber of Commerce and the Houston Native American Resource Center. He has appeared on tax panels for the Native American Financial Officers Association and the Native American Finance Conference sponsored by the Information Management Network.

James Lyons

Republican Tax Counsel

219 Dirksen Senate Office Bldg.

Phone: (202) 224-7619

Jim_Lyons@finance.senate.gov

Education: B.S., James Madison University, 1995. J.D, University of Texas School of Law, 2000.

Professional: 2000–2001, law clerk, Judge W. Eugene Davis, U.S. Court of Appeals, Fifth Circuit. 2001–2004, tax associate, Cleary, Gottlieb, Steen & Hamilton, LLP. 2004–2005, Republican tax counsel, House Ways and Means Cmte. 2005–2008, trial attorney, Department of Justice, Tax Division. 2008–present, Republican tax counsel, Senate Cmte. on Finance.

Expertise: Financial products, excise tax, energy, bank and insurance issues, tax law.

In his fourth year with the Senate Finance Committee, Jim Lyons has kept the title of tax counsel but has assumed some new responsibilities. Lyons now handles education tax incentives and has joint responsibility for Internal Revenue Service oversight issues with his colleague Brendan Dunn.

In 2011, his main focus is on comprehensive tax reform, and on developing a package of energy-related tax incentives.

Lyons said he also is working on crafting some federal tax incentives for state and local government bonds. The tax incentives for state and local government bonds would be an alternative to the Build America Bonds program, which is opposed by Lyons' boss, Ranking Member Orrin Hatch, R-Utah.

The program provides tax incentives and federal subsidies to reduce the cost of borrowing for states and local governments. It expired at the end of 2010, but the president proposed to revive the program in his fiscal 2012 budget.

In 2010, Lyons helped to negotiate an extension of the Bush-era rates and tax extender provisions. He also participated in the drafting of most of the tax provisions that were enacted in the Small Business Jobs Act.

Prior to joining the Finance Committee Lyons worked in the tax division of the Department of Justice, where he was a trial attorney for one of the civil trial sections. Lyons also managed tax cases in federal district and bankruptcy courts on behalf of the IRS. He previously served as tax counsel for the House Ways and Means Committee.

Lyons received his law degree from the University of Texas, and studied toward an LL.M in taxation at New York University while working full-time at Cleary Gottlieb Steen & Hamilton. He holds an undergraduate degree from James Madison University in Harrisonburg, Va.

SENATE FINANCE

Mark Alan Prater

Deputy Staff Director and Chief Tax Counsel

219 Dirksen Senate Office Bldg.

Phone: (202) 224-5493

Mark_Prater@finance.senate.gov

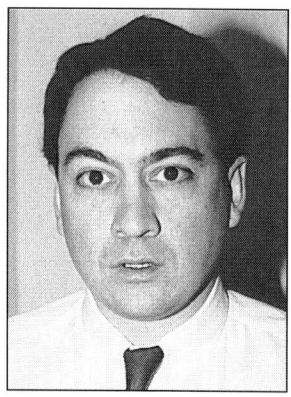

Personal: Born 03/03/1959 in Portland, Ore.

Education: B.S., accounting, Portland State University, 1981. J.D., Willamette University, 1984. LL.M., taxation, University of Florida, 1987.

Professional: 1984–1986, tax associate, Touche Ross. 1987–1990, attorney, Dunn, Carney et al. (Portland, Ore.). 1990–1993, tax counsel, Senate Cmte. on Finance. 1993–1995, Republican chief tax counsel, Senate Cmte. on Finance. 1995–2006, chief tax counsel, Senate Cmte. on Finance. 2007–present, deputy staff director and chief tax counsel, Senate Cmte. on Finance.

Expertise: Tax issues.

Mark Prater has been handling tax issues for the Finance Committee for more than 20 years. At the start of the 112th Congress, new Ranking Member Orrin Hatch, R-Utah, asked him to continue to lead the staff's tax work. Prater remains deputy staff director and chief tax counsel, positions he has held since 2007.

Prater said that his top initiatives in 2011 are tax reform and tax initiatives relating to programs and agencies that will require reauthorization such as the Farm Bill, the Highway Trust Fund and the Federal Aviation Administration. He also is pushing for tax incentives for energy production and conservation.

He is working with a bill co-sponsored by his former boss, Sen. Charles Grassley, R-Iowa, and committee chairman Max Baucus, D-Mont., called the Rural Heritage Conservation Extension Act of 2011. The legislation would permanently extend income tax relief for ranchers, farmers and other landowners who donate agricultural land for conservation.

The tax deduction, which is scheduled to expire at the end of 2011, was first passed in 2006 as part of the Pension Protection Act, and was extended in 2008 and 2010.

Prater is also working on a plan to draft legislation that would extend renewable fuel tax and tariff provisions. In particular, the bill seeks to preserve tax credits for ethanol producers that offer ethanol as a U.S.-produced, renewable alternative to foreign oil.

In 2010, Prater participated in the development of a year-end bipartisan agreement that extended tax relief from 2001 and 2003 bills. The legislation extended 51 tax incentives for different sectors of America's economy.

He also contributed to the 2010 small business tax relief package. Prater said this bill became partisan after it left the committee because of the small business lending facility program added as the legislation was debated on the Senate floor.

SENATE FINANCE

David Schwartz

Acting Chief Health and Human Services Counsel

219 Dirksen Senate Office Bldg.

Phone: (202) 224-4515

David_Schwartz@finance.senate.gov

Personal: Born 1971 in New Hyde Park, N.Y.

Education: B.A., University at Albany, State University of New York, 1993. J.D., George Washington University, 1996.

Professional: 1997–1998, antitrust staff attorney, Collier, Shannon, Rill & Scott. 1999–2002, attorney advisor, Office of Hearings and Appeals, Social Security Administration. 2002–2006, attorney advisor, Office of the Commissioner, Social Security Administration. 2004, Capitol Hill fellow, Senate Cmte. on Finance. 2005–2006, detailee, Senate Cmte. on Finance. 2007–2010, health counsel, Senate Cmte. on Finance. 2010–present, acting chief health and human services counsel, Senate Cmte. on Finance.

Expertise: Pharmacy benefits and pharmaceutical industry issues, Stark Law and anti-kickback statute issues, health information technology, oversight and investigations.

David Schwartz, who was promoted to acting chief health and human services counsel in 2010, was a major part of the Majority health care team's efforts on the health care reform legislation in the 111th Congress. In 2011, he is assisting with the committee's oversight hearings that are focused on efforts to implement the health care policies established in both the Patient Protection and Affordable Care Act (PPACA) and the American Recovery and Reinvestment Act.

Schwartz and his colleagues began their oversight hearings regarding implementation of the PPACA in 2010 with testimony from the administrator of the Centers for Medicare and Medicaid Services (CMS). He told the committee about the CMS's efforts to use PPACA resources to modernize the health care delivery system.

In the 112th Congress, developing legislation to permanently reform the Medicare physician payment system is also on the agenda of Schwartz and the health care team. Without the reform, the payment system could jeopardize access to physician services for tens of millions of seniors and disabled Americans.

The Majority health care team is also working on possible temporary or permanent extensions to policies on protections for rural doctors and hospitals, caps on Medicare therapy services, and the Qualifying Individual and Transitional Medical Assistance programs.

Another important initiative for Schwartz and the health care staff in 2011 is the reauthorization of the Temporary Assistance to Needy Families program. The team helped in 2010 to extend the program, which provides job training and other aid for low-income families with dependent children.

In addition to contributing to the PPACA, in the last session Schwartz and the health care team helped to enact a 12-month fix that staved off cuts to physician payments under Medicare's Sustainable Growth Rate formula.

SENATE FINANCE

Tiffany Smith

Democratic Tax Counsel

219 Dirksen Senate Office Bldg.

Phone: (202) 224-4515

Tiffany_Smith@finance.senate.gov

Personal: Born 1973 in Rockford, Ill.

Education: B.A., political science, University of Illinois at Urbana-Champaign, 1995. J.D., University of Illinois, 1998. LL.M., Georgetown University, 2006.

Professional: 1998–1999, assistant chief counsel, City of Chicago, Department of Law. 2001–2004, attorney/advisor, Internal Revenue Service, Office of Chief Counsel. 2004–2007, assistant to branch chief, Internal Revenue Service, Office of Chief Counsel. 2007–present, tax counsel, Senate Cmte. on Finance.

Expertise: Individual tax law, education tax incentives, tax-exempt entities.

The Democratic tax team helped to enact a number of successful job-creation tax packages in 2010, and tax counsel Tiffany Smith and her colleagues are working to do more of the same in 2011. Job creation, education and energy tax incentives, and tax reform are on the committee's agenda in the 112th Congress.

Contributing tax provisions to the Hiring Incentives to Restore Employment (HIRE) Act was one of the Smith's and the tax team's accomplishments in 2010. The legislation includes an employer exemption from Social Security payroll taxes for workers hired between February 3, 2010, and January 1, 2011, that had previously been unemployed for at least 60 days.

Smith's work and the committee also contributed to the Tax Relief, Unemployment Insurance Reauthorization and Job Creation Act and the Small Business Jobs Act. The Small Business Jobs Act encourages investment in small businesses by allowing investors to exclude the gains from the sale of certain small business stock from their income for tax purposes if it is held for more than five years.

In 2011, the committee has held several hearings on tax reform, including one to review the changes made to the tax code since the Tax Reform Act of 1986 and the extent to which they have kept pace with changes in the global and U.S. economies.

The committee is examining how the tax code could be changed to provide incentives for job creation and economic growth in light of increasing globalization. Smith and the tax team will also look at tax system's affect on household and business debt levels, and whether tax incentives for debt financing contributed to the financial crisis.

Chairman Max Baucus, D-Mont., wants to simplify the tax code to encourage people to save, and has asked the tax staff to consider what individual incentives for savings in the tax code might effectively promote individual savings.

SENATE FINANCE

Russell W. Sullivan

Democratic Staff Director
219 Dirksen Senate Office Bldg.
Phone: (202) 224-4515
Russ_Sullivan@finance.senate.gov

Personal: Born 05/02/1961 in Little Rock, Ark.

Education: B.B.A., Baylor University, 1983. J.D., University of Texas Law School, 1987.

Professional: 1983–1985, staff auditor, Peat Marwick (Dallas, Texas, and Little Rock, Ark.). 1988–1995, tax law specialist/federal income tax planner, Vinson & Elkins, L.L.P. (Washington, D.C.). 1995–1996, legislative asst./tax specialist, Sen. Bob Graham, D-Fla. 1996–1999, legislative director, Sen. Bob Graham, D-Fla. 1999–2003, chief Democratic tax counsel, Senate Cmte. on Finance. 2004–present, Democratic staff director, Senate Cmte. on Finance.

Expertise: Tax law, budget policy.

Job growth is a major focus of Finance Committee Chairman Max Baucus, D-Mont., in the 112th Congress, and Staff Director Russell Sullivan is overseeing the Democratic staff's efforts to develop initiatives to create more jobs. Sullivan also is guiding the staff's work in each of the committee's three major policy areas—tax, health care, and international trade.

In 2011, the committee is continuing a comprehensive examination of the tax code, one of the goals of which is to consider new tax incentives for job creation. The committee is also looking at whether individual incentives could be added to the tax code to encourage individuals to save.

In the area of health care, the committee is following up its major 2010 success, enactment of the Patient Protection and Affordable Care Act, with oversight to ensure the law's provisions are implemented according to Congressional intent. Sullivan is also helping with efforts to enact permanent reform measures for the Medicare physician payment system in 2011.

Baucus's international trade priorities in the 112th Congress include reauthorizing and extending the Trade Adjustment Assistance (TAA) program, which he believes is crucial in supporting American workers whose jobs have been sent overseas. The committee also is working to finalize free trade agreements with Colombia, Panama and South Korea.

Sullivan is overseeing the staff's work on trying to reduce the federal deficit and to address the federal debt limit. Working to ensure that the Social Security Administration's administrative budget stays adequately funded is another committee priority with which he is assisting.

Sullivan is in his 13th year with the committee, and his eighth year as Democratic staff director. The Little Rock native's first job on Capitol Hill was as a legislative assistant in the office of former Senator Bob Graham, D-Fla.

SENATE FINANCE

Kelly Whitener

Democratic Health Policy Advisor

219 Dirksen Senate Office Bldg.

Phone: (202) 224-4515

Kelly_Whitener@finance.senate.gov

Personal: Born 1980 in Orange, Calif.

Education: MPH, UCLA, 2008. B.A. in psychology and Spanish, University of Michigan, 2002.

Professional: 2002–2005, volunteer, U.S. Peace Corps. 2006–2008, mental health case manager, Saint John's Child and Family Development Center. 2008–2009, Winston health policy fellow, Senate Cmte. on Finance. 2009–present, health policy advisor, Senate Cmte. on Finance.

Expertise: Medicaid, CHIP, prevention, mental health, American Indian health care.

Kelly Whitener is a member of the Democratic health care staff, and in the 112th Congress she is helping the team work on temporary or permanent extensions of a number of important health care policies that will expire at the end of 2011 if no action is taken.

These expiring policies and programs include the Qualifying Individual and Transitional Medical Assistance program, relief from caps on Medicare therapy services and protections for rural doctors and hospitals.

Whitener and her colleagues were successful in 2010 in extending the Temporary Assistance to Needy Families (TANF) program for another year, and now are working to reauthorize the program.

TANF gives job training and other assistance to low-income families with dependent children. The program provides job search support, child care and transportation, and other services that help people transition back to work.

In terms of new legislation, Whitener and the Finance Committee health care team are working to reform permanently the Medicare physician payment system. If the system remains unchanged many millions of disabled Americans and seniors could be denied access to physician services.

For Whitener, 2011 also features oversight hearings that are following up on the health care legislation enacted in 2010, the Patient Protection and Affordable Care Act. The subject of the hearings is the Administration's efforts to implement the health care policies established in the reform law and in the American Recovery and Reinvestment Act, which was enacted in 2009.

In the last session, enactment and the early stages of implementation of the Affordable Care Act dominated the schedule of Whitener and the committee health care team. Late in the session, they began a series of hearings on implementation of the law in which the witness offered insight into how the Centers for Medicare and Medicaid Services would use resources provided by the new law to modernize the delivery of health care services.

In addition to passage of the health care reform legislation, Whitener and her colleagues led legislative efforts to prevent severe cuts to physician payments under Medicare's Sustainable Growth Rate formula.

Committee on Foreign Relations

439 Dirksen Senate Office Bldg.
Washington, DC 20510-6225
Phone: (202) 224-4651
Fax: (202) 224-0836
http://foreign.senate.gov

Ratio: 9/10

MAJORITY MEMBERS

John F. Kerry, MA, Chairman

Barbara Boxer, CA
Robert Menendez, NJ
Benjamin L. Cardin, MD
Robert P. Casey, PA
Jim Webb, VA
Jeanne Shaheen, NH
Christopher Coons, DE
Richard J. Durbin, IL
Tom Udall, NM

MINORITY MEMBERS

Richard G. Lugar, IN, Ranking Member

Bob Corker, TN
James E. Risch, ID
Marco Rubio, FL
James Inhofe, OK
Jim DeMint, SC
Johnny Isakson, GA
John Barrasso, WY
Mike Lee, UT

SENATE FOREIGN RELATIONS

JURISDICTION

(1) Acquisition of land and buildings for embassies and legations in foreign countries.
(2) Boundaries of the United States.
(3) Diplomatic service.
(4) Foreign economic, military, technical, and humanitarian assistance.
(5) Foreign loans.
(6) International activities of the American National Red Cross and the International Committee of the Red Cross.
(7) International aspects of nuclear energy, including nuclear transfer policy.
(8) International conferences and congresses.
(9) International law as it relates to foreign policy.
(10) International Monetary Fund and other international organizations established primarily for international monetary purposes (except that, at the request of the Committee on Banking, Housing, and Urban Affairs, any proposed legislation relating to such subjects reported by the Committee on Foreign Relations shall be referred to the Committee on Banking, Housing, and Urban Affairs).
(11) Intervention abroad and declarations of war.
(12) Measures to foster commercial intercourse with foreign nations and to safeguard American business interests abroad.
(13) National security and international aspects of trusteeships of the United States.
(14) Oceans and international environmental and scientific affairs as they relate to foreign policy.
(15) Protection of United States citizens abroad and expatriation.
(16) Relations of the United States with foreign nations generally.
(17) Treaties and executive agreements, except reciprocal trade agreements.
(18) United Nations and its affiliated organizations.
(19) The World Bank group, the regional development banks, and other international organizations established primarily for development assistance purposes.

SENATE FOREIGN RELATIONS

To say that Massachusetts Senator John Kerry has his hands full as chairman of the Senate Foreign Relations Committee would be an understatement.

The veteran lawmakers and former Democratic presidential candidate certainly racked up the miles during the first quarter of the 112th Congress—visiting Pakistan and the Middle East.

"In the coming months and years, the Senate Foreign Relations Committee will address some of the most pressing challenges this nation faces," Kerry writes on his committee's Web site. "America faces momentous challenges: wars in Afghanistan and Iraq, climate change, the spread of nuclear weapons, global terrorism, and an unfolding financial crisis with global implications."

The Foreign Relations Committee has a history of bipartisanship, particularly between Kerry and ranking Se. Richard Lugar, R-Ind. But when it came to the Libya campaign, the two broke ranks.

Lugar fumed over the way President Obama went into Libya without getting Congressional approval. Kerry championed the administration's intervention.

The chairman did listen to Lugar and held a hearing on Libya just days after Obama's address to the nation on his policy.

Kerry plans another bipartisan effort targeted to two nations where protesters toppled long-standing dogmatic regimes. Kerry, Sen. John McCain, R-Ariz., and Sen. Joe Lieberman, I-Conn., plan to introduce bills to create two new enterprise funds for Egypt and Tunisia. The lawmakers are modeling the efforts for those two countries after enterprise funds established in Central and Eastern Europe after the fall of the Berlin Wall in 1989.

Kerry has also been very active on Korea.

"We have all grown weary of North Korea's brinkmanship—a habit of ratcheting up tensions, followed by suggestions of ways to negotiate back from the brink, followed by concessions, and a repetition of the process,"

Kerry said in March in discussing the need to break North Korea's cycle of provocation and nuclear expansion.

Pending free trade agreements are also likely to take up much of the committee's time. Lugar has promised to block the administration's pending pact with South Korea unless the Columbia and Panama trade agreements signed by former president George W. Bush are not also on the table.

SENATE FOREIGN RELATIONS

Dan Diller

Staff Director

450 Dirksen Senate Office Bldg.

Phone: (202) 224-6797

Fax: (202) 224-3612

dan_diller@foreign.senate.gov

Personal: Born 1959 in Princeton, Ill.

Education: B.A., English and history, Augustant College (Ill.), 1982. M.A., international relations, American University, 1986. M.A., English literature, University of Virginia, 1987.

Professional: 1985–1991, writer/editor, *Congressional Quarterly*. 1991–1993, legislative assistant, Sen. Richard Lugar, R-Ind. 1993–2003, legislative director, Sen. Richard Lugar, R-Ind. 2003–2010, deputy staff director, Senate Cmte. on Foreign Relations. 2011–present, staff director, Senate Cmte. on Foreign Relations.

Expertise: Middle East, Russia, the former Soviet Union.

After spending much of his career working as a senior aide for Senate Foreign Relations Committee Republicans, Dan Diller steps into the top staffer spot in the 112th Congress as staff director.

Diller fills the shoes of longtime staff director Kenneth Myers, who left the committee in 2009 to be the director of the Defense Threat Reduction Agency. But Diller, an expert in Middle Eastern and Russian affairs, who has worked alongside Committee Ranking Member Richard Lugar, R-Ind., since 1991, is well-suited for the new role.

In the early days of 112th Congress, much of Diller's work for the panel focused on working alongside Lugar to craft the Senator's response to the revolutions which spread through many Middle Eastern nations, including Tunsia, Egypt and perhaps most notably, Libya. While Lugar maintained he wanted to see Libyan President Moammar Gadhafi out of power, he was skeptical of President Barack Obama's decision to use the military to intervene there, noting that the commander in chief was not clear about the ultimate goals of the action or how much it would ultimately cost taxpayers.

Diller also assisted Lugar on other efforts, including a bipartisan push to help immigrant entrepreneurs secure visas to the United States. The StartUp Visa Act of 2011 would permit an immigrant entrepreneur to get a two year visa if they can show that a qualified U.S. investor is willing to invest in the immigrant's startup venture, according to a press release.

In the 111th Congress, Diller assisted Lugar on similar efforts, and also helped the Senator in his bipartisan push to ratify the new START treaty. One of the few Republicans to come out in favor of START early on in the debate, Lugar's support of its ratification was considered key to its ultimate success.

SENATE FOREIGN RELATIONS

Mark Helmke

Professional Staff Member

450 Dirksen Senate Office Bldg.

Phone: (202) 224-6797

mark_helmke@foreign.senate.gov

Education: B.A., political science, College of the Potomac, 1972. M.A., political science and journalism, Goodard College, 1980.

Professional: 1972–1976, reporter, Piedmont Virginian. 1976–1980, reporter, Fort Wayne News-Sentinel. 1980–1987, staffer, Sen. Dick Lugar, R-Ind. 1987–1995, president, Robinson Lake Strategic Communications. 1995–2002, president and CEO, Helmke Group. 2002–present, senior professional staff member, Senate Cmte. on Foreign Affairs.

Mark Helmke is a true Washington insider and a loyal aide to Senate Foreign Affairs Committee ranking member Dick Lugar, R-Ind. Helmke has worked as a top D.C. lobbyist and a reporter, but his home appears to be with Lugar.

In the 112th Congress, Helmke is serving as Lugar's chief committee spokesman, handling much of the Senator's interaction with the press. In the early days of the session, much of Helmke's work was sharing the Senator's views on U.S. intervention in Libya, explaining that while Lugar supported the work of the troops, he wanted more congressional involvement in the ongoing military engagement.

"He still believes this action requires greater congressional debate: Where is it going? What is the end game? How much will it cost? Who's going to pay? The nation is in the middle of another three-week [funding measure]. What do these new obligations mean?" Helmke told the Washington Post.

Helmke is the best person around to speak for Lugar, considering he's worked on-and-off for the Senator for more than 30 years, including much of the 1980s and on his presidential campaign in the 1990s. An Indiana native, Helmke told his hometown news station WANE TV that although he ran a strategic communications business and a variety of other organizations, his time with Lugar has been especially rewarding, which is what keeps him coming back.

"I'm studying new issues all the time. New events keep on coming at us every day and we have to study them and find out what's going on to articulate [Lugar's] position on it," Helmke said. "[I'm] working for a gentleman and a scholar, somebody who works hard, who treats you well. There's a bunch of us who've worked for the senator for some time. We all get along with each other. Nobody's jealous of anybody else. We're a strong team and a strong family."

Helmke notably opened up about his struggle with depression in a 2003 U.S. News and World Report article. He told the magazine that, at times, his depression was so severe he couldn't get out of bed. Eventually, Helmke found treatment, but explained that he still sees depression in the faces of the homeless people he encounters on the street.

"The difference between me and them is very thin. It's hard for me to see them," he said.

One notable fact about Helmke: his brother, Paul, serves as president of the Brady Campaign to End Gun Violence.

SENATE FOREIGN RELATIONS

Frederick L. Jones II

Communications Director

446 Dirksen Senate Office Bldg.

Phone: (202) 224-4651

Frederick_Jones@foreign.senate.gov

Personal: Born 1970 in San Francisco, Calif.

Education: Howard University, 1992. J.D., University of California, Davis School of Law, 1996.

Professional: 2005–2006, press secretary, National Security Council. 2006–2008, deputy director, Office of Strategic Communications, Department of State. 2008, vice president, Levick Strategic Communications. 2009–present, communications director, Senate Foreign Relations Cmte.

Expertise: Communications.

As Communications Director for the Senate Foreign Relations Committee Frederick L. Jones II had some overseas experience before joining the panel—and it was working for the other political party.

Jones may be touting the policy direction and communicating the views of committee Chairman Sen. John Kerry, D-Mass. But in June of 2003 when Jones joined the National Security Council, first as a deputy spokesman and two years later as press secretary, Republican President George W. Bush was his ultimate boss.

According to a profile of Jones that former *Washington Post* reporter Peter Baker did in 2005, Jones got the foreign relations bug in the mid-1990s when he studied European law in Amsterdam.

Jones told Baker that he was eager to spend more time abroad and after seeing the Foreign Service listed in a book on jobs abroad, he applied.

"I'd never heard of the Foreign Service until I was 25-years-old," Jones told Baker. According to the *Post*, Baker's "foreign service exam led to his first posting in Spain as the U.S. Embassy's deputy press attaché. After two years there, he returned to Washington for a job in the State Department press office, where he worked for then Secretary of State Colin L. Powell.

Since going to Capitol Hill, Jones has worked for a Democrat.

Reporters who cover the Foreign Relations Committee describe Jones as an affable laid-back guy who is responsive to their needs.

And those needs are many. Kerry was determined to pass the START Treaty during the 111th Congress and he got his wish in the lame duck session.

Reporters packed the hearings on the treaty in the Foreign Relations Committee room and Jones had to field questions not just from the domestic press but foreign reporters as well.

Kerry is one of the more active lawmakers when it comes to foreign policy and has close ties with the Obama White House. The former presidential candidate's efforts include going to Pakistan to try and diffuse the bad feelings after a CIA agent shot two men there.

As the United States became involved in the efforts to help the rebels in Libya, Kerry was outspoken and right in the thick of the debate. After meeting with Libyan forces in May, Kerry announced plans to push legislation to fund the rebels.

And after the U.S. killing of Osama bin Laden, Jones was peppered with questions from the media about what his boss' role would be as lawmakers worked to get to the bottom of what Pakistan knew about the terrorist's whereabouts and when they knew it.

SENATE FOREIGN RELATIONS

Edward Levine

Senior Professional Staff Member

439 Dirksen Senate Office Bldg.

Phone: (202) 224-4651

Fax: (202) 224-3612

levine_edward@foreign.senate.gov

Personal: Born in Washington, D.C.

Education: Ph.D., international relations, Yale University, 1971. B.A., University of California, Berkeley, 1964. M.A, Yale University, 1966.

Professional: 1968–1972, lecture, assistant professor, political science, University of Michigan. 1972–1976, assistant professor, political science, Rice University. 1976–1997, professional staff member, Senate Select Cmte. on Intelligence. 1997–present, senior professional staff member, Senate Cmte. on Foreign Relations..

Expertise: U.S. arms transfers, Arms control, Nonproliferation policy.

As a senior professional staff member on the Foreign Relations Committee, Edward Levine is there as the panel's expert on weapons proliferation.

It's a topic Levine will continue to push even as a growing number of crises in the world will compete for the committee's time and attention.

"One major focus, and a major challenge in difficult economic times, will be to secure robust funding for executive branch nonproliferation programs, international organizations that contribute to nonproliferation and nuclear weapons stockpile stewardship," said Levine, who is a veteran Capitol Hill staffer. He came to the Foreign Relations Committee in 1997.

But before that, Levine spent 20 years as a professional staff member of the Senate Select Committee on Intelligence, having moved to the Hill from academia. On the intelligence panel he worked on oversight and helped author the committee's analyses of U.S. capabilities to monitor compliance with the Strategic Arms Limitations Talks II, the Intermediate-Range Nuclear Forces treaty, Threshold Test Ban Treaty, the Treaty on Conventional Armed Forces in Europe, the Strategic Arms Reduction Treaties I and II, the Open Skies Treaty and the Chemical Weapons Convention.

During the 1111th Congress, Levine worked on the new START treaty as well as the U.S.-UK and U.S.-Australia Defense Cooperation Treaties and the implementing legislation that went with those agreements.

Committee Chairman Sen. John Kerry, D-Mass., has urged the administration to continue on with diplomatic efforts on weapons proliferation, particularly when it comes to the dismantling of North Korea's nuclear program.

"We must get beyond the political talking point that engaging North Korea is somehow 'rewarding bad behavior.' It is not," Kerry said in March.

SENATE FOREIGN RELATIONS

Frank Lowenstein

Democratic Chief Counsel
439 Dirksen Senate Office Bldg.
Phone: (202) 224-4651
frank_lowenstein@foreign.senate.gov

Personal: Born 1967 in New York City, N.Y.

Education: B.A., Yale University. J.D., Boston College.

Professional: 1990–1994, foreign policy and defense legislative assistant, Office of Sen. Robert Kerrey. 2003–2004, national security policy director, Kerry-Edwards campaign. 2006–2009, senior foreign policy advisor, Office of Sen. John Kerry. 2009–2010, Democratic chief counsel, Senate Cmte. on Foreign Relations. 2010–present, Staff Director, Senate Cmte. on Foreign Relations.

Expertise: Terrorism, homeland security, nonproliferation.

Given what was going on in the world in the first months of the 112th Congress, Foreign Relations Committee Staff Director Frank Lowenstein had his hands full.

Lowenstein's boss, committee Chairman, Sen. John Kerry, D-Mass., was busy being briefed on, commenting on, and reviewing what happened in Egypt, the broader Middle East, and Libya where the U.S. took the lead in "Operation Odyssey Dawn," the move to enforce the no-fly zone authorized by the United Nations.

Kerry made it clear in March that he wanted the U.S. to view its Middle East policy in a new way.

Amid cries for democracy in the always-volatile region, "a re-adjustment is required," Kerry said during a speech in Washington just days before he left for a trip to the region. "We can no longer view the Middle East solely through the lens of 9/11. Now, we must view it through the lens of 2011."

The 111th Congress was no quiet time for the committee either.

"The START treaty is probably first and foremost, and then we've done a bunch of stuff, foreign trips with Kerry, a lot of work on Sudan, Syria and Pakistan," Lowenstein said. "They are really the three major foreign policy issues we've been working on."

The committee had hearings on Afghanistan, starting in March with questioning of General David Petreaus. The panel also will continue to focus on developments in South Asia.

Lowenstein has been with Kerry on Capitol Hill since September of 2005 but also worked on the Massachusetts Democrats' presidential campaign in 2003 and 2004 when he served as the national security director. Before joining the committee, he was a foreign policy advisor on the senator's personal staff.

When he's not worrying about the problems of the world, Lowenstein's two children keep him busy, but he also enjoys tennis and golf and going to the movies with his wife.

SENATE FOREIGN RELATIONS

David Willkie

Professional Staff Member

450 Dirksen Senate Office Bldg.

Phone: (202) 224-6797

david_willkie@foreign.senate.gov

Education: M.B.A., Columbia University, 1999.

Professional: 2008–present, Professional Staff Member, Senate Cmte. on Foreign Relations.

Expertise: Finance, Economics and Trade.

Although David Willkie is new to Capitol Hill by standards of many of his colleagues on the Senate Foreign Relations Committee—it's common to find panel staffers who have worked along ranking member Dick Lugar, R-Ind., for well over a decade—politics is in Willkie's blood. His grandfather, Wendell Willkie, was the Republican nominee for president in 1940.

While Wendell Willkie had his moment into the political spotlight, his grandson works in a behind-the-scenes fashion, assisting Lugar on issues related to finance, economics, and trade.

Trade treaties have been a dominant priority for Lugar. In the early days of the 112th Congress, Lugar pledged to block President Barack Obama's push for a free-trade agreement with South Korea, unless similar treaties with Colombia and Panama that were signed by former President George W. Bush also were submitted to Congress for approval, according to a press release.

Financing America's foreign relations actions also will be a priority in the session. Willkie likely advised Lugar on his reaction to U.S. intervention in Libya; Lugar expressed concern that by not making clear what the military's priorities and goals will be in the country, it opened up the possibility of a costly war.

Willkie isn't completely behind the scenes, however, as he frequently speaks on foreign relations issues at forums around D.C., including at a 2008 event held by the National Foreign Trade Council.

Willkie appears proud of his political heritage. When a 1992 New York Times article spelled Wendell Willkie's name wrong, his grandson wrote a letter to an editor, noting that his granddad probably would want to be best remembered for his ideas. "Willkie sought international cooperation and understanding. He also championed civil rights and women's rights when it was not popular to do so," David Willkie wrote.

David Willkie also worked to preserve his grandfather's memory by collecting memorabilia related to his campaign. In 2006, he told the Rushville Republican that he had purchased a large collection of Willkie campaign buttons from a collector in New Jersey, hoping to eventually give them to a museum that will honor his grandfather's legacy.

"He is one of the few people to lose the highest office in the land and still leave a long lasting impression on American politics," David Willkie said.

Committee on Health, Education, Labor, and Pensions

428 Dirksen Senate Office Bldg.
Washington, DC 20510
Phone: (202) 224-5375
Fax: (202) 224-5044
http://help.senate.gov
Help_comments@help.senate.gov

Ratio: 10/10/1

MAJORITY MEMBERS

Tom Harkin, IA, Chairman

Barbara A. Mikulski, MD
Jeff Bingaman, NM
Patty Murray, WA
Robert P. Casey, PA
Kay R. Hagan, NC
Jeff Merkley, OR
Al Franken, MN
Sheldon Whitehouse, RI
Richard Blumenthal, CT

INDEPENDENT MEMBERS

Bernard Sanders, VT

MINORITY MEMBERS

Mike Enzi, WY, Ranking Member

Lamar Alexander, TN
Richard Burr, NC
Johnny Isakson, GA
Rand Paul, KY
Orrin G. Hatch, UT
John McCain, AZ
Pat Roberts, KS
Lisa Murkowski, AK
Mark Kirk, IL

SENATE HEALTH, EDUCATION, LABOR, AND PENSIONS

JURISDICTION

(1) Education, labor, health, and public welfare.
(2) Aging.
(3) Agricultural colleges.
(4) Arts and humanities.
(5) Biomedical research and development.
(6) Child labor.
(7) Convict labor and the entry of goods made by convicts into interstate commerce.
(8) Domestic activities of the American National Red Cross.
(9) Equal employment opportunity.
(10) Gallaudet College, Howard University, and Saint Elizabeth's Hospital.
(11) Individuals with disabilities.
(12) Labor standards and labor statistics.
(13) Mediation and arbitration of labor disputes.
(14) Occupational safety and health, including the welfare of miners.
(15) Private pension plans.
(16) Public health.
(17) Railway labor and retirement.
(18) Regulation of foreign laborers.
(19) Student loans.
(20) Wages and hours of labor.

Comprehensive study and review of matters relating to health, education and training, and public welfare.

SENATE HEALTH, EDUCATION, LABOR, AND PENSIONS

After spending much of the 111th Congress preoccupied by controversial and often partisan debates over healthcare legislation, the Senate Committee on Health, Education, Labor, and Pensions is setting a more bi-partisan tone as it turns education during the first session of the 112th Congress.

In March, President Obama put pressure on lawmakers to revamp the Elementary and Secondary Education Act, also known as the No Child Left Behind Act, by fall. Signed into law in 2002, the K-12 federal education law is long overdue for reauthorization and has come under fire from both sides of the aisle for its reliance on standardized testing, requirements that schools meet escalating annual educational benchmarks, and the penalties the law imposes for schools that don't meet those goals.

In January, committee chairman, Sen. Tom Harkin, D-Iowa, and ranking member Sen. Michael B. Enzi, R-Wyo., released a joint statement calling for education reform.

"This Congress," the statement said, "we must rewrite this law to create a better and more flexible education system that prepares our nation's students for success in college, careers and the global economy."

That process will include discussion on school performance ratings, teacher quality requirements, standardized testing, academic standards, and equity for poor and minority students.

Also on the education front, Harkin in the 111th Congress created a new investigative unit of the committee, and its first focus has been the for-profit college sector. In September 2010 the committee released a report showing that over 87 percent of total revenues for the schools investigated came directly from the federal government in the form of federal financial aid and other federal assistance. However, the report found that 57 percent of students who enrolled left without a diploma but with a high probability of debt.

The committee continued a series of hearings this year on the topic, but Enzi criticized the investigation, calling it "flawed" and saying that hearings focused solely on a few problem examples and not solutions.

With an economy that many feel still has not recovered, the committee continues to pay close attention to workplace and employee issues. Early in the session, the committee held hearings on boosting 401(k) investment and on how to improve employment opportunities for people with disabilities.

The Workforce Investment Act is also up for reauthorization. The Act, which oversees federal employment, training and adult education programs for adults, dislocated workers and youth, seeks to promote employment, job retention, increased earnings and occupational skills.

Mine safety continues to be a priority for the committee, particularly after the April 5, 2010, mining accident that killed 29 miners at Massey Energy's Upper Big Branch coal mine in West Virginia. An investigation blamed the fatal explosion on a series of preventable safety violations. Though Harkin is pushing for additional mine safety legislation, Enzi has taken a more "wait and see approach" and has supported voluntary workplace safety programs instead.

Though President Obama's Affordable Care Act was signed into law, controversy over the measure spilled into the first session of the 112th Congress. Republicans repeatedly attacked the measure, attempting to repeal the whole law and portions of it. Oversight and wrangling over its provisions is expected to last throughout the session.

SENATE HEALTH, EDUCATION, LABOR, AND PENSIONS

Beth Buehlmann

Republican Education Policy Director

835 Hart Senate Office Bldg.

Phone: (202) 224-6770

Fax: (202) 224-2311

beth_buehlmann@help.senate.gov

Personal: Born in Chicago, Ill.

Education: B.S., math education, 1966. M.A., curriculum development, 1971. Ph.D., higher education administration, 1974.

Professional: 1979–1991, various positions ending with education policy director, House Cmte. on Education and Labor. 1991–1998, executive director, Washington office, California State University System. 1998–2005, executive director, Center for Workforce Preparation, U.S. Chamber of Commerce. 2005–present, education policy director, Senate Cmte. on Health, Education, Labor and Pensions.

Expertise: Education policy.

Education Policy Director Beth Buehlman is delving into a number of education-related issues during the first session of the 112th Congress: everything from reauthorizations to the area of for-profit schools.

Early in the 2011, Buehlman worked with the committee's Republicans, including Ranking Member Michael B. Enzi, R-Wyo., who called for reforms to the No Child Left Behind Act, also known as the Elementary and Secondary Education Act. The K-12 federal education law is overdue for reauthorization and has come under fire for its reliance on standardized testing, requirement that schools meet annual educational benchmarks that rise each year and the penalties the law imposes for schools that do not meet these annual goals.

In January, both Enzi and committee chairman, Sen. Tom Harkin, D-Iowa, released a joint statement calling for education reform.

"This Congress, we must rewrite this law to create a better and more flexible education system that prepares our nation's students for success in college, careers and the global economy," the statement said.

This will without doubt occupy Buehlman's time this session.

Also early in the session, the committee took a close look at the world of for-profit higher education.

Allegations surfaced that these for-profit schools used improper student recruitment practices, instituted excessive profit taking and had poor student outcomes, but Enzi said the investigation and its conclusions were flawed.

"Unfortunately, by only focusing these hearings on individual examples of a problem in one sector of higher education, we have no understanding of the true extent of the problem, nor have we heard any constructive solutions for solving that problem," Enzi said.

SENATE HEALTH, EDUCATION, LABOR, AND PENSIONS

Charles M. Clapton

Health Policy Director

727 Hart Senate Office Bldg.

Phone: (202) 224-6770

chuck_clapton@help.senate.gov

Personal: Born 05/22/1968 in Boston, Mass.

Education: B.A., history, Boston College, 1990. J.D., Catholic University, 1995.

Professional: 1995–1996, legislative aide, Senate Cmte. on the Judiciary, Subcmte. on Terrorism, Technology and Government Information. 1997–1998, counsel, Rep. Harris Fawell, R-Ill. 1999–2004, health counsel, House Cmte. on Energy and Commerce. 2004–2005, chief health counsel, House Cmte. on Energy and Commerce. 2006–2007, assistant for policy, Office of the Speaker of the House. 2007–2008, Republican chief health counsel, House Cmte. on Ways and Means. 2008–present, health policy director, Senate Cmte. on Health, Education, Labor and Pensions.

Expertise: Health care policy, Medicare, Medicaid.

Health Policy Director Chuck Clapton's time this session is consumed with oversight and implementation of the health care law, the Patient Protection and Affordable Care Act. Signed into law on March 23, 2010, by President Barack Obama, this act and the Health Care and Education Reconciliation Act of 2010 (signed the same month) focus on the reform of the private health insurance market, improved coverage for people with pre-existing conditions, and improved prescription drug coverage in Medicare.

However, since the law was enacted it has come under fire from Republican, including Sen. Michael B. Enzi, R-Wyo., the ranking member of the GOP on the Committee for Health, Education, Labor and Pensions. Early in the first session of the 112th Congress Republicans attempted, unsuccessfully, to repeal the law.

Clapton said much of his time is spent this session examining the impact of the health care law on states, particularly when it comes to exchanges in Medicaid, the impact on health insurance premiums and on employers.

"This was the largest piece of domestic legislation passed by Congress in probably 50 years," Clapton said. "Congress is going to spend a lot of time looking at it, working on it and litigating it."

Clapton has worked on Capitol Hill for years and has held positions with several different committees. He said Enzi and committee chairman Sen. Tom Harkin, D-Iowa have a positive working relationship, which makes the agenda roll along more smoothly.

Clapton said he has stayed on The Hill throughout much of his career because he finds the work exciting and inspiring. "Being able to work on issues I'm passion about gets me motivated and helps me get up and come in here every morning," he said.

SENATE HEALTH, EDUCATION, LABOR, AND PENSIONS

Greg Dean

Republican Chief Counsel/Pension Policy Director

835 Hart Senate Office Bldg.

Phone: (202) 224-6770

Fax: (202) 224-6510

greg_dean@help.senate.gov

Personal: Born 1963 in Montgomery County, Pa.

Education: B.A., Villanova University, 1985. J.D., Widener School of Law.

Professional: 1990–1999, assistant chief counsel for banking and finance, Office of Advocacy, Small Business Administration. 2000–2001, assistant general counsel, NASD Regulation. 2001–2002, banking counsel, Senate Cmte. on Small Business and Entrepreneurship. 2003, finance counsel, House Cmte. on Small Business. 2003–2004, staff director, Subc. on Securities and Investment, Senate Cmte. on Banking, Housing, and Urban Affairs. 2005–2008, Republican general counsel, Senate Cmte. on Health, Education, Labor, and Pensions. 2008–present, Republican chief counsel/pension policy director, Senate Cmte. on Health, Education, Labor, and Pensions.

Expertise: Health, education, labor, pensions, financial matters.

Greg Dean is looking at many issues this year through the lens of the small business owner.

For instance, when it comes to retirement security, Dean and his boss, Sen. Michael B. Enzi, R-Wyo., are examining regulations and requirements surrounding 401(k) programs, particularly regarding to small businesses.

Enzi, a former shoe store owner in his home state, said at a hearing before the Committee of Health, Education, Labor, and Pensions in February that past legislation promoting automatic enrollment of employees in 401k retirement programs has been "tremendously successful." He cited a surge in workers signing up for such programs between 2006 and 2009, but said that spike has now leveled off.

Dean is also working on tax policies that relate to maintaining defined benefit and contribution systems and the type of 401k's and retirement accounts that are available to small businesses.

In addition, he's addressing administration requirements that can snarl small business owners in paperwork and red tape when they use independent contractors.

Healthcare remains a big issue for Dean, who worked on healthcare legislation during the 111th Congress as well. Enzi remains dissatisfied with the healthcare law which passed in the last Congress and said in February that if given the opportunity, he would vote to repeal it. Enzi said the law increases the cost of care and reduces consumer choices.

In February the senate voted 81-17 to strike a provision in the healthcare law that would force businesses to submit a separate 1099 form to the Internal Revenue Service for every business-to-business transaction that totaled more than $600 a year. Enzi supported the measure. At the time of the vote Enzi said, "I hope this repeal is the first of many to come."

SENATE HEALTH, EDUCATION, LABOR, AND PENSIONS

Kyle Hicks

Labor Policy Director

835 Hart Senate Office Bldg.

Phone: (202) 224-6770

kyle_hicks@help.senate.gov

Personal: Born 07/07/1974 in Indianapolis, Ind.

Education: B.A. cum laude, University of Colorado, 1996. J.D., George Washington University Law School, 1999.

Professional: 1999–2001, judiciary counsel, Rep. Spencer Bachus, R-Ala. 2001–2003, counsel, Sen. Tim Hutchinson, R-Ark.. 2005–2010, labor counsel, Senate Cmte. on Health, Education, Labor and Pensions. 2010–present, labor policy director, Senate Cmte. on Health, Education, Labor and Pensions.

Expertise: Labor employment, workplace safety, mine safety.

Labor Policy Director Kyle Hicks said because Republicans are in the minority on the Senate Committee for Health, Education, Labor and Pensions, it's hard to predict what labor issues will be on the agenda during the first session of the 112th Congress.

But Ranking Member Michael B. Enzi, R-Wyo., will continue to look at mine safety, Hicks said. Early in the year a preliminary report from the Mine Safety and Health Administration on the April 5, 2010 mining accident that killed 29 miners at Massey Energy's Upper Big Branch coal mine in West Virginia blamed the fatal explosion on a series of preventable safety violations.

Enzi and other Republicans said they wanted to hold off on legislative action until the investigation into the accident was complete, but a spokesman for Enzi said in January that such legislation was "still a priority."

Though in the 111th Congress, Hicks worked on the committee's hearings on mine safety and worked on the Robert C. Byrd Mine and Workplace Safety and Health Act of 2010, but the legislation failed to pass. At the time, Enzi complained that Democrats were not working on the legislation in a bi-partisan fashion as they had during the development of the Mine Improvement and New Emergency Response Act, also known as the MINER Act, signed into law in 2006. That legislation was widely seen as the most significant mine safety legislation in decades.

Enzi will also continue work on the Voluntary Protection Program Act, which he introduced during the last Congress along with Sen. Mary Landrieu, D-La.

The act encourages voluntary workplace safety programs rather than enforcement-first programs. It would require the Department of Labor to recognize achievements in both the technical and managerial protection of employees from occupational hazards; provide temporary, appropriate protection from inspection, investigation, and citation for employers who are voluntarily working with the government to ensure their site meets relevant standards; and expand voluntary assistance programs to small businesses, which are most vulnerable to being unaware of or confused by complex worksite regulation.

Hicks has been on the committee since 2005, where he started as a counsel on labor issues. He moved up to the Labor Policy Director spot in 2010.

SENATE HEALTH, EDUCATION, LABOR, AND PENSIONS

Andrew Imparato

Senior Counsel and Disability Policy Director

607 Hart Senate Office Bldg.

Phone: (202) 224-8535

andrew_imparato@help.senate.gov

Personal: Born in Huntington, N.Y.

Education: B.A., humanities, Yale College, 1987. J.D., Stanford Law School, 1990.

Professional: 1990–1991, law clerk, U.S. District Judge Robert E. Keeton, Boston. 1991–1993, staff attorney/Skadden Fellow, Disability Law Center, Boston. 1993–1994, counsel, U.S. Senate Subcmte. on Disability Policy, Cmte. on Labor and Human Resources. 1994–1997, attorney/advisor, Commissioner Paul Steven Miller, U.S. Equal Employment Opportunity Commission. 1997–1999, general counsel and director of policy, National Council on Disability. 1999–2010, president and CEO, American Association of People with Disabilities. 2010–present, senior counsel and disability policy director, Senate Cmte. on Health, Education, Labor and Pensions.

Expertise: Disability policy, social welfare policy, civil rights law and policy, labor and employment policy.

As senior counsel and disability policy director, Andy Imparato advises Sen. Tom Harkin, D-Iowa, chairman of the Committee on Health, Education, Labor and Pensions on all disability issues before the panel.

Imparato's work includes drafting legislation, speeches and floor statements, planning hearings, interacting with senior administration officials, working with constituents and a diverse group of stakeholders. He also supervises members of the committee's disability policy team, collaborates with other Congressional staff, and is part of the committee's senior management.

Early in March, during the first session of the 112th Congress, Imparato was preparing for a hearing on employment issues pertaining to people with intellectual disabilities and hoped the event would kick off a series of discussions on disability employment issues.

Imparato is working on disability aspects of the reauthorization of the Elementary and Secondary Education Act, also known as the No Child Left Behind Act, as well as the Individuals with Disabilities Education Act, which governs how public schools provide special education and related services to children with disabilities.

The Workforce Investment Act is also up for reauthorization. This act, which oversees federal employment, training and adult education programs for adults, dislocated workers and youth, includes the Vocational Rehabilitation Act, which requires most private employers with federal contracts to take affirmative action to hire individuals with mental or physical disabilities.

"The economic downturn has had a disparately negative effect on workers with disabilities," Imparato said. "A lot of times they're at the bottom of the pecking order, or are part time, and are the first to get laid off."

Imparato is working to find ways to seek better employment outcomes and opportunities for people with disabilities.

Imparato started working on disability issues after taking a first job out of law school doing Supplemental Security Income advocacy. He also developed bi-polar disorder and manic depression while in law school. "I feel like I was given this condition and a cause or a calling so I could take my experiences and try to make things better for people with disabilities," he said.

SENATE HEALTH, EDUCATION, LABOR, AND PENSIONS

Jenelle Krishnamoorthy

Health policy director

428 Dirksen Senate Office Bldg.

Phone: (202) 224-5375

jenelle_krishnamoorthy@help.senate.gov

Education: M.S., psychophysiology, University of Tennessee. B.S., psychology/biology, Randolph-Macon College, 1994. Ph.d., clinical psychology, Virginia Commonwealth University, 2002. Residency/Post Doc, Pediatric Clinical Psychology, Brown Medical School, 2003.

Professional: 2003–2004, AAAS fellow, Sen. Tom Harkin, D-Iowa. 2004–2005, AAAS diplomacy fellow, U.S. State Department. 2006–2010, health policy advisor, Senate Cmte. on Health, Education, Labor and Pensions. 2010–present, health policy director, Senate Cmte. on Health, Education, Labor and Pensions.

Expertise: Health policy.

Jenelle Krishnamoorthy certainly has the credentials to back her decisions as health policy director for the Senate Committee on Health, Education, Labor and Pensions.

A licensed clinical psychologist, Krishnamoorthy did her residency and post-doctoral fellowship in pediatric clinical psychology at Brown University, but she also has a long history of health policy work to bolster her credentials.

Along with other staff members, Krishnamoorthy helped write the Healthy Lifestyles and Prevention (HeLP) America Act, which Harkin sponsored. The legislation offered initiatives aimed at improving nutrition, increasing physical activity and fighting obesity. The legislation also included a menu labeling provision that later inspired a provision in the more recent health reform law.

That law, President Obama's Affordable Care Act, took up the majority of Krishnamoorthy's time during the 111th Congress. It was signed into law on March 23, 2010, and aims to expand Medicaid eligibility, reform health insurance practices, provide medical insurance to more workers and their families, and improve prescription drug coverage, among other provisions.

But the enactment of the law did not squash the controversy over the controversial healthcare bill, and during the first session of the 112th Congress Krishnamoorthy continued to hold the issue as her main focus. Republicans attempted to repeal the law, in whole and in part, and Democrats like Harkin began to hold hearings that touted its benefits.

The push and pull over the healthcare initiative and its oversight was expected to continue throughout the session. In January, Harkin launched a series of hearings to examine implementation of the act in January, with testimony from Americans who were benefiting from the new law.

At the hearing Harkin said, "I think we can all agree that what this debate needs is more light and less heat."

Krishnamoorthy has also been Harkin's point person on illness prevention and wellness and has published papers in the areas of childhood obesity and tobacco issues.

SENATE HEALTH, EDUCATION, LABOR, AND PENSIONS

Bethany Little

Chief Education Counsel

644 Dirksen Senate Office Bldg.

Phone: (202) 224-0767

bethany_little@help.senate.gov

Education: B.S., foreign service, Georgetown University.

Professional: director of government relations, Children's Defense Fund. associate director, White House Domestic Policy Council. vice president for policy and federal advocacy, Alliance for Excellent Education. 2001–2003, legislative assistant, U.S. Sen. Patty Murray, D-Wash. 2009–present, chief education counsel, Senate Cmte. on Health, Education, Labor and Pensions.

Expertise: Education policy.

Bethany Little has ramped up her focus on reauthorizing the Elementary and Secondary Education Act during the first session of the 112th Congress as chief counsel of the Senate Committee on Health, Education, Labor, and Pensions.

Though the K-12 federal education law, also known as the No Child Left Behind Act, has been overdue for reauthorization for several years, both Little's boss, chairman Sen. Tom Harkin, D-Iowa, and ranking member Sen. Michael B. Enzi, R-Wyo. said early in the session that they planned to make the legislation a priority.

And in March, President Obama put even more pressure on lawmakers, calling for them to rewrite the law by fall. "Let's seize this education moment," Obama said at an appearance in Arlington County, Va. "Let's fix No Child Left Behind."

At an American Enterprise Institute panel discussion in late 2010, Little expressed optimism that the reauthorization would take place this Congress, noting that the last authorization of the law happened under a Republican controlled White House and a divided Congress, but that bi-partisan cooperation still took place.

The ESEA discussions will take on issues including school performance ratings, teacher quality requirements, standardized testing, academic standards and equity for poor and minority students. But lawmakers are likely to raise other issues including merit pay for teachers, the impact of charter schools and school vouchers for students who wish to attend private or parochial schools.

The current version of the law requires that schools and subgroups of students meet annual educational benchmarks, or Adequate Yearly Progress (AYP). If a school or a group of students does not meet these achievement goals for several years in a row, the law puts escalating penalties in place.

Also early in the year Secretary of Education Arne Duncan announced that 82 percent of public schools are in jeopardy of missing those targets in reading and math, up from 37 percent last year.

Before Little came to the committee, she was vice president for policy and federal advocacy at the Alliance for Excellent Education where she led the group's policy work on high school reform, including accountability and school improvement, adolescent literacy and college preparation.

SENATE HEALTH, EDUCATION, LABOR, AND PENSIONS

Frank Macchiarola

Republican Staff Director

835 Hart Senate Office Bldg.

Phone: (202) 224-6770

frank_macchiarola@help.senate.gov

Personal: Born 11/13/1976 in Brooklyn, N.Y.

Education: B.A., College of the Holy Cross, 1998. J.D., New York University School of Law, 2002.

Professional: lawyer, private practice. 2004–2006, counsel, Senate Cmte. on Energy and Natural Resources. 2006–2009, Republican staff director, Senate Cmte. on Energy and Natural Resources. 2009–present, Republican staff director, Senate Cmte. on Health, Education, Labor and Pensions.

Expertise: Domestic policy issues, Senate committee procedures, Senate floor procedures.

Frank Macchiarola has made the move from the Senate Committee on Energy and Natural Resources to the Committee on Health, Education, Labor and Pensions, but he continues to act as staff director for Republicans.

As staff director for the new panel, he manages about 40 professional staff members, helping to schedule hearings and mark ups, and works on staff negotiations and floor strategy on a variety of legislation before the committee.

During the first session of the 112th Congress, Macchiarola turned his attention to the overdue reauthorization of the Elementary and Secondary Education Act, also known as the No Child Left Behind Act. The K-12 federal education law pushes benchmarks for schools higher each year in an effort to ensure that all students receive an adequate education. The law induces schools to close achievement gaps between different groups of students and penalizes schools that do not hit annual goals.

But the bi-partisan law has come under attack from both Republicans and Democrats, and in March, Secretary of Education Arne Duncan announced that more than three-quarters of the nation's public schools could soon be labeled as "failing" under the law. In January, ranking committee member Sen. Michael B. Enzi, R-Wyo. and Chairman Tom Harkin, D-Iowa, issued a joint statement calling for the law to be rewritten to "create a better and more flexible education system that prepares our nation's students for success…"

Macchiarola is also working on reauthorization of the Workforce Investment Act, which covers a broad range of job training activities, among other programs, to promote employment, job retention, increased earnings and occupational skills. Additionally, the committee will look at Food and Drug Administration user feel legislation and oversight of healthcare reform.

SENATE HEALTH, EDUCATION, LABOR, AND PENSIONS

Lauren McGarity McFerran

Labor and Pensions Policy Director

428 Dirksen Senate Office Bldg.

Phone: (202) 224-5375

Education: B.A., Rice University, 1998. J.D., Yale Law School, 2001.

Professional: associate, Bredhoff & Kaiser, P.L.L.C. law clerk, Judge Carolyn King, United States Court of Appeals, 5th Circuit. 2005–2010, labor and employment counsel, Senate Cmte. on Health, Education, Labor and Pensions. 2010–present, labor and pensions policy director, Senate Cmte. on Health, Education, Labor and Pensions.

Expertise: Labor policy, employment policy.

Named in 2010 as the labor and pensions policy director for the Senate Committee on Health, Education, Labor and Pensions, Lauren McFerran's new position has her overseeing the committee's labor and pensions team. She's also serving as the primary liaison with the many constituencies interested in these issues.

During the first session of the 112th Congress, those issues were varied. Workforce issues before the committee included job creation, job security, and retirement. In February the committee kicked off a series of hearings on the retirement security crisis, which focused on what could be done to help Americans save more for retirement and make better decision about their retirement savings.

At the hearing, committee chairman, Sen. Tom Harkin, D-Iowa, said with flat wages, increasing prices and job insecurity, it's becoming more and more difficult for people to save for retirement. He said Congress had taken important steps to improve the 401(k) system, particularly when it came to transparency and automatic enrollment, but he said 401(k)'s are still confusing to many workers. The Pension Protection Act of 2006 helped establish some of these 401(k) reforms, but more are needed, Harkin said.

"Can we do a better job of getting people the information they need to make better financial decisions?" Harkins said.

Harkin called for the creation of periodic statement that would give workers an idea of what their monthly retirement income might be and how much they could expect from their 401(k)'s, similar to the statement that Americans now receive regarding Social Security.

McFerran is also working on unemployment issues. In March the committee launched a series of hearings to examine how to improve employment opportunities for people with intellectual disabilities.

SENATE HEALTH, EDUCATION, LABOR, AND PENSIONS

Craig Orfield

Communications Director

132 Hart Senate Office Bldg.

Phone: (202) 224-8584

Fax: (202) 228-0937

craig_orfield@help.senate.gov

Personal: Born in Bristol, Va.

Education: B.A., University of Virginia, 1985.

Professional: 1993–1994, director of government relations, Household Goods Forwarders Association. 1994–1997, press secretary, House Cmte. on Small Business. 1997–1999, press secretary, Sen. Kit Bond, R-Mo. 1999–2005, communications director, Senate Cmte. on Small Business. 2005–present, communications director, Senate Cmte. on Health, Education, Labor, and Pensions.

Expertise: Media, healthcare, education, labor and workplace safety, food and drug safety, business and finance.

As communication director for Republicans on the Senate Health, Education, Labor and Pensions Committee, Craig Orfield has to be able to converse on nearly every issue that comes before the panel, particularly those that become controversial or attract widespread media attention.

In the 111th Congress, this meant Orfield spent a lot of time talking about healthcare, as the Senate worked on President Obama's healthcare package, which ultimately was signed into law. But Republicans were not happy with the result and have been working to try and repeal the law, or portions of it, in the first session of the 112th Congress.

Orfield's boss, ranking Sen. Michael B. Enzi, R-Wyo., has vowed to fight the healthcare package and said he would vote to repeal it, claiming its provisions actually increase the cost of care and reduce consumer choices.

Orfield is also turning his attention to K-12 education this year. The overdue reauthorization of the federal No Child Left Behind Act, also known as the Elementary and Secondary Education Act, is on the table. Signed into law by President George W. Bush in January of 2002, the law attempts to close the achievement gap between white and minority students and low-income students and their more affluent peers. It relies heavily on standardized testing and penalties for schools that don't hit annual educational benchmarks. Both Republicans and Democrats have criticized the law and Enzi and Chairman Tom Harkin, D-Iowa have vowed to rewrite it in this Congress.

In addition to education and health issues, Orfield is spending time fielding media calls on the Robert C. Byrd Mine Safety Protection Act, which did not pass during the last Congress but is likely to get another look; Food and Drug Administration Prescription Drug User Fee Act reauthorization; and reauthorization of the Workforce Investment Act.

SENATE HEALTH, EDUCATION, LABOR, AND PENSIONS

Amy Angelier Shank

Senior Policy Advisor

835 Hart Senate Office Bldg.

Phone: (202) 224-6770

amy_shank@help.senate.gov

Personal: Born in Annapolis, Md.

Education: B.A., Roanoke College, 1994.

Professional: 1999–2001, Washington rep., Associated Builders and Contractors. 2001–2003, policy advisor, Sen. Don Nickles, R-Okla. 2003–2004, senior analyst for income and labor policy, Senate Cmte. on the Budget. 2004–present, senior policy advisor, Senate Cmte on Health, Education, Labor and Pensions.

Expertise: Budget, appropriations, floor and reconciliation procedure.

Amy Shank is working on a wide range of issues during the first session of the 112th Congress, running the gamut from education to healthcare.

Senior Policy Advisor Shank will continue her work from the previous Congress on healthcare, when lawmakers passed President Obama's Affordable Care Act. The law aims to reform the insurance industry and extend health insurance to those who were uninsured and ease access to healthcare.

However, Republicans have criticized the measure and early in the session were working to repeal the law or portions of it. Ranking member Sen. Michael B. Enzi, R-Wyo., supported a repeal, saying he believes the law hurts small businesses and increases the cost of care and reduces consumer choices.

Shank, on behalf of Enzi, is continuing to focus on implementation of the law and new rulemaking associated with it.

On the topic of education, Shank has spent much of her time this session addressing an investigation into for-profit higher education. Chairman Tom Harkin, D-Iowa, has raised concerns that for-profit colleges are raking in exorbitant profits, while students often don't finish their degrees. A report released by Harkin in the 111th Congress concluded that under current law for-profit schools can be extremely profitable while failing a majority of their students.

But early in this session Enzi blasted the report and said its findings were questionable. Hearings on the issue were continuing.

Also on Shank's agenda is an ongoing review of the Ryan White AIDS Act, the country's largest federal funded program for people living with HIV/AIDS. The law seeks to improve availability of care for low-income, uninsured, and underinsured AIDS victims.

She also is working on the background review and vetting of White House nominees before the committee.

SENATE HEALTH, EDUCATION, LABOR, AND PENSIONS

Pam Smith

Deputy Staff Director

644 Dirksen Senate Office Bldg.

Phone: (202) 224-0767

pam_smith@help.senate.gov

Personal: Born in Ill.

Education: B.A., government and international relations, University of Notre Dame. J.D., cum laude, Notre Dame Law School.

Professional: senior director of government relations, Catholic Health Association. director of Health and Welfare Poilcy, Catholic Charities USA. U.S. Department of Justice. 2005–2009, legislative director, Sen. Tom Harkin, D-Iowa. 2009–present, deputy staff director, Senate Cmte. on Health, Education, Labor and Pensions.

Expertise: Healthcare.

Pam Smith has years of experience helping the chairman of the Senate Committee on Health, Education, Labor, and Pensions manage his legislative portfolio.

After joining the office of Sen. Tom Harkin, D-Iowa, as legislative director, Smith oversaw the development and implementation of Harkin's domestic and foreign policy legislative agenda, including initiatives to promote wellness and disease prevention, support military families, combat child labor, and increase pension security, among other issues.

During her time in Harkin's office the Senate passed several pieces of legislation sponsored by Harkin, including the Americans with Disabilities Amendments Act and the Joshua Omvig Suicide Prevention Act.

When Smith moved over to the committee in 2009, Harkin said her guidance would be key to the agenda. "She brings a unique understanding of the legislative process and a commitment to strengthening laws that benefit Americans' lives," he said.

This session her knowledge on a wide range of issues important to Harkin is coming into play as the committee considers everything from healthcare to education and job security issues.

One of the main items on Smith's agenda is reauthorization of the Elementary and Secondary Education Act, which was known as the No Child Left Behind Act under President George W. Bush. The law was created by a bi-partisan group, but since its enactment in 2002, it has come under fire by both Republicans and Democrats. Critics say the law relies too heavily on standardized testing, calls for schools and students to meet unrealistic achievement goals, and attaches harsh penalties for failure to meet those goals.

In January, both Harkin and ranking member Sen. Michael B. Enzi, R-Wyo. issued a joint statement calling for the quick reform of the law.

Smith is also looking at workforce issues. In that arena, the Workforce Investment Act, which includes a number of job training and adult-education programs, is also up for reauthorization.

In addition, early in the first session of the 112th Congress, Harkin had already started a series of hearings on issues of job security and other workforce issues for the disabled. The committee held a hearing on employment opportunities for people with intellectual disabilities early in the session. Harkin is known as a champion of the Americans with Disabilities Act, which Smith worked on during her time in his office.

SENATE HEALTH, EDUCATION, LABOR, AND PENSIONS

Daniel E. Smith

Staff Director

644 Dirksen Senate Office Bldg.

Phone: (202) 224-0767

daniel_smith@help.senate.gov

Personal: Born 07/31/1961 in Britt, Iowa.

Education: B.A. with highest distinction, University of Iowa, 1983. J.D., Georgetown University Law Center, 1986.

Professional: 1991–1992, director of delegate selection, Americans for Harkin. 1992, Iowa campaign director, Clinton/Gore Campaign. 1993–1997, chief of staff, U.S. Sen. Tom Harkin, D-Iowa. 1997–1999, Democrtic staff director, Senate Cmte. on Agriculture, Nutrition and Forestry. 1999–2006, national vice president, federal and state government relations, American Cancer Society. 2006–2010, president, American Cancer Society Action Network. 2010–present, Democratic Staff Director, Senate Cmte. on Health, Education, Labor and Pensions.

Expertise: Tobacco control, cancer research, Health policy, cancer prevention.

Dan Smith has returned to Capitol Hill after spending years working on advocacy for the American Cancer Society. Smith said he came back to work with the Senate Committee on Health, Education, Labor, and Pensions' chairman, Sen. Tom Harkin, D-Iowa, whom he had worked for in the 1990s.

Smith said he also was drawn back to federal service by a drive to have a positive impact on issues that are so important to Americans. "You have much more direct access to decision-makers and you can affect things much more immediately," he said. "The ability to change people's lives for the better is why I'm in public service."

As staff director for the committee, Smith has his hand in nearly every issue that comes before the panel. He also helped Harkin set up a new investigative unit of the committee which unveiled its inaugural investigation early in the first session of the 112th Congress. That investigation raised concerns about for-profit higher education providers who were charging high-fees from students, even with low graduation and completion rates.

The issue is likely to receive ongoing attention from the committee this session.

Also on the education front, Smith is working on the overdue reauthorization of the Elementary and Secondary Education Act, which seeks to close the achievement gap between white and minority students and low-income students and their more affluent peers. But the law has been criticized by both Republicans and Democrats for the penalties it imposes on schools that fail to meet annual student-achievement goals.

Smith will also focus on the Workforce Investment Act, also due for reauthorization. The Act oversees a number of workforce training and adult education programs and reauthorization should add further enhancements to the law, Smith said. "We want to know how we can make the Workforce Investment Act work better for ordinary people," he said.

Harkin, a champion of the Americans with Disabilities Act, has also made workforce issues regarding people with disabilities a high priority, Smith said. Early in the session the committee held a hearing on ways to improve employment opportunities for people with intellectual disabilities. Smith said hearings on related topics are likely to continue throughout the session.

SENATE HEALTH, EDUCATION, LABOR, AND PENSIONS

Beth Stein

Chief Investigations Counsel

644 Dirksen Senate Office Bldg.

Phone: (202) 224-0767

Education: B.A., University of California, Berkley. J.D., University of California, Hastings College of Law.

Professional: 2004–2010, counsel, U.S. Sen. Tom Harkin, D-Iowa. 2010–present, chief investigations counsel, Senate Cmte. on Health, Education, Labor and Pensions. ss, counsel, Senate Permanent Subc. on Investigations. counsel, Senate Cmte. on Governmental Affairs judiciary committee counsel, U.S. Sen. Maria Cantwell, D-Wash. election counsel, U.S. Rep. Steny Hoyer, D-Md.

Expertise: Fraud, investigations, campaign finance.

The Senate Committee on Health Education Labor and Pensions has created a new investigative unit and Bethany Stein is overseeing its operations.

Stein has a history in the investigative area. In previous jobs as counsels to the Senate Permanent Subcommittee on Investigations and the Senate Committee on Governmental Affairs, Stein played a key role in an investigation into campaign finance abuses in the 1996 election cycle and helped lead investigations into a variety of subjects, including food safety, Medicare fraud, wastes, and abuse, and the relationship between thyroid cancer rates and exposure to nuclear fallout from Nevada testing in the 1940s.

The new committee investigative unit formed in May 2010, kicked off its first effort with a look at the for-profit higher education institution sector. Stein examined federal money that flows to for-profit colleges and in Sept. 2010, the committee released a report showing that over 87 percent of total revenues for the schools investigated came directly from the federal government in the form of federal financial aid and other federal assistance.

However, the report also found that 57 percent of students who enrolled between 2008-2009, left without a diploma but with a high probability of debt.

The committee under Stein has held a series of hearings on various aspects of the investigation, which continued during the first session of the 112th Congress. In February, the committee held a hearing on improper recruiting practices by for-profit colleges, uncovered both in Stein's investigation and cited in an August 2010 Government Accountability Office report which noted deceptive marketing and recruiting practices on behalf of for-profit colleges.

"When these types of deceptive and exploitative tactics are used to enroll students, we should not be surprised to see high dropout and high default rates as a result," Harkin said.

However, the committee's ranking member Sen. Michael B. Enzi, R-Wyo. has blasted the investigation, calling it flawed and saying that the hearings focused on individual examples of a problem of one sector of higher education without constructive solutions for solving the problem.

Committee on Homeland Security and Governmental Affairs

340 Dirksen Senate Office Bldg.
Washington, DC 20510
Phone: (202) 224-2627
http://hsgac.senate.gov

Ratio: 8/8/1

MAJORITY MEMBERS

Carl Levin, MI
Daniel K. Akaka, HI
Thomas R. Carper, DE
Mark Pryor, AR
Mary L. Landrieu, LA
Claire McCaskill, MO
Jon Tester, MT
Mark Begich, AK

INDEPENDENT MEMBERS

Joseph I. Lieberman, CT, Chairman

MINORITY MEMBERS

Susan M. Collins, ME, Ranking Member

Tom Coburn, OK
Scott Brown, MA
John McCain, AZ
Ron Johnson, WI
John Ensign, NV
Rob Portman, OH
Rand Paul, KY

SENATE HOMELAND SECURITY

JURISDICTION

(1) Archives of the United States.
(2) Budget and accounting measures, other than appropriations, except as provided in the Congressional Budget Act of 1974.
(3) Census and collection of statistics, including economic and social statistics.
(4) Congressional organization, except for any part of the matter that amends the rules or orders of the Senate.
(5) Federal Civil Service.
(6) Government information.
(7) Intergovernmental relations.
(8) Municipal affairs of the District of Columbia, except appropriations therefor.
(9) Organization and management of United States nuclear export policy.
(10) Organization and reorganization of the executive branch of the government.
(11) Postal Service.
(12) Status of officers and employees of the United States, including their classification, compensation, and benefits.

Such committee shall have the duty of (a) receiving and examining reports of the Comptroller General of the United States and submitting such recommendations to the Senate as it deems necessary or desirable in connection with the subject matter of such reports; (b) studying the efficiency, economy, and effectiveness of all agencies and departments of the government; (c) evaluating the effects of laws enacted to reorganize the legislative and executive branches of the government; and (d) studying the intergovernmental relationships between the United States and the states and municipalities, and between the United States and international organizations of which the United States is a member.

SENATE HOMELAND SECURITY

Longtime Chairman of the Senate Homeland Security and Governmental Affairs Committee Joseph Lieberman, I-Conn., announced that he will retire at the end of 2012, giving added urgency to his priorities in the 112th Congress. Completing a Department of Homeland Security authorization bill, U.S. Postal Service reform and improving the nation's cyber security are at the top of the list in 2011.

Postal Service reform is a goal that Lieberman shares with Ranking Member Susan Collins, R-Maine. The issue has been on the committee's agenda for the past three Congresses, and in 2011 the staff is working with the Collins's U.S. Postal Service Improvements Act of 2011. The Postal Service has suffered from the recession and the increasing use of digital communications, and the legislation would help it achieve financial stability without undermining customer service.

Lieberman and Collins also see eye-to-eye on cyber security, and co-introduced The Cybersecurity and Internet Freedom Act in 2011 to help secure the nation's most critical cyber infrastructures and protect Internet freedom. The bill provides that the President, the Director of the National Center for Cybersecurity and Communications, or any government officer or employee will not have the authority to shut down the Internet. It also provides for judicial review of the designation of certain sensitive IT systems and assets as covered critical infrastructure.

Other priorities in 2011 for Lieberman include legislation to modernize the Federal Protective Service, which oversees security at most federal buildings, and renewed efforts to pass domestic partnership benefits legislation, which would give same-sex domestic partners of federal employees the same benefits available to the spouses of federal employees.

In keeping with the Republican theme of reducing government spending in the 112th Congress, Collins has asked the committee to clean up redundancies and inefficiencies in federal programs. The several-pronged effort includes promoting The Information Technology Investment Oversight Enhancement and Waste Prevention Act, which is co-sponsored by Collins and Senator Tom Carper, D-Del. The bill seeks to monitor more effectively the $80 billion that federal agencies spend annually on information technology.

The committee also is engaged in aggressive oversight of the implementation of The Improper Payments Elimination and Recovery Act, a law that the committee counts among its achievements from the 111th Congress. The legislation is designed to cut waste due to improper payments by government agencies, estimated by the Office of Management and Budget to be $125 billion annually. The law requires mandatory audits and corrective action plans, and mandates that all agencies spending more than $1 million must perform recovery audits on their programs to recover the overpayments.

SENATE HOMELAND SECURITY

Michael Alexander

Majority Staff Director

340 Dirksen Senate Office Bldg.

Phone: (202) 224-2627

Michael_Alexander@hsgac.senate.gov

Personal: Born 1956 in Griffin, Ga.

Education: B.S., political science, University of Maryland University College, 1996. Master's degree, government, Johns Hopkins University, 2000.

Professional: 1987–1993, legislative director and legislative assistant, Rep. Michael Espy, D-Miss. 1993–1994, executive assistant to the secretary, Dept. of Agriculture. 1994–1997, special assistant to the Director of Civil Rights, Dept. of Agriculture. 1997–1998, acting deputy director, Office of Civil Rights, Dept. of Agriculture. 1998–2001, confidential assistant to the chief information officer, Dept. of Agriculture. 2001–2006, professional staff member, Senate Cmte. on Homeland Security and Governmental Affairs. 2006–2007, minority staff director, Senate Cmte. on Homeland Security and Governmental Affairs. 2007–present, majority staff director, Senate Cmte. on Homeland Security and Governmental Affairs.

Expertise: Homeland security, governmental affairs, government information technology management, emergency preparedness and response.

Committee Chairman Joseph Lieberman, I-Conn., plans to retire in 2012 and has said completing a Department of Homeland Security (DHS) authorization bill before then is a priority. As a result, the DHS authorization bill is near the top of Staff Director Michael Alexander's agenda in the 112th Congress.

Alexander said the staff is also finalizing work on a bill to improve the government's ability to protect cyberspace. Legislation was reported out of committee in 2010, but must be reconciled with bills from other panels before it can be completed, he said. A key provision of the 2010 legislation was the creation of an Office of Cyber Policy in the White House responsible for devising a national cyberspace strategy.

Alexander said legislation to modernize the Federal Protective Service (FPS), which oversees security at most federal buildings, is also on the committee's agenda in 2011. It will address problems outlined in a 2010 GAO report, including that the FPS does not adequately train its contractor guards and that no one is accountable for decisions about each building the FPS protects.

In the new Congress, the committee is working on a bill to reauthorize key grant programs for first responders under the FIRE Act and the SAFER Act. It also is continuing efforts to oversee the significant changes the government has made to protect homeland security since 9/11, Alexander said.

Those efforts include the maturity of DHS, border and transportation security, bio security and weapons of mass destruction preparedness. Of particular importance in this area are efforts to counter homegrown terrorism, he said.

Alexander is in his eleventh year with the committee and his sixth as Democratic staff director. During his tenure with the committee he has worked on many important pieces of legislation including the Telework Enhancement Act, the Improper Payments Elimination Act, the Nuclear Forensics Attribution Act, and the Pre-Disaster Mitigation Act.

SENATE HOMELAND SECURITY

Elizabeth E.R. Anderson

Press Secretary

340 Dirksen Senate Office Bldg.

Phone: (202) 224-2627

ER_Anderson@hsgac.senate.gov

Personal: Born in Barbados.

Education: ABJ in journalism and public relations, University of Georgia, 1988. Masters in mass communications, University of Georgia, 1989.

Professional: 1994–1997, press secretary, Office of Rep. John Linder, R-Ga. 1997–2000, director of program support, International Republican Institute. 2000–2001, director of communications, Financial Services Roundtable. 2001–2006, associate under secretary for economic affairs, U.S. Department of Commerce. 2006–2008, deputy under secretary for economic affairs, U.S. Department of Commerce. 2008–2010, regional media director, Walmart. 2010–present, press secretary, Cmte. on Homeland Security and Governmental Affairs. 2010, public affairs officer, U.S. Department of State for Kaseman LLC.

Expertise: Communications, government relations.

Elizabeth "E.R." Anderson joined the Senate Homeland Security and Governmental Affairs Republican staff in 2010 as press secretary. In that position, Anderson writes news releases, handles all press inquiries that the committee receives, and keeps the minority Web site up to date.

Anderson helps to keep the public informed about the major initiatives of her boss, Ranking Member Susan Collins, R-Maine. In 2011, she is spending considerable time talking about reining in federal spending, and identifying areas of waste and inefficiency in government programs.

Collins has also identified Postal Service reform as a top priority in the 112th Congress, and Anderson is helping to promote the U.S. Postal Service Improvements Act of 2011, which Collins introduced early in 2011. Anderson also will keep the media and public up to date on legislation to extend the law governing security at U.S. chemical facilities, and efforts to improve airport screening technology.

For most of 2010, Anderson was employed by Kaseman LLC to work on a contract basis at the State Department as a public affairs officer. She handled specific media strategy projects in the Diplomatic Security unit, which is the department's law enforcement division.

Anderson worked as regional media director for Wal-Mart for two years, during which she acted as both a national and regional spokesperson for the company. While there, she developed ways to communicate to Capitol Hill staff and media Wal-Mart initiatives on health care, environmental sustainability and community involvement.

Anderson worked at the Department of Commerce from 2001 to 2008. In her last position there, which was deputy under secretary for economic affairs, she managed the Economic and Statistics Administration, including a staff of 40 economists, policy analysts, and other personnel. She briefed top administration officials on economic information, and spoke to national organizations about job creation and U.S. economic growth.

Anderson is an avid golfer and runner—she has completed six marathons.

SENATE HOMELAND SECURITY

Troy Cribb

Senior Counsel

340 Dirksen Senate Office Bldg.

Phone: (202) 224-2627

Troy_Cribb@hsgac.senate.gov

Personal: Born 1965 in Spartanburg, S.C.

Education: B.S., Northwestern University, 1988. J.D., Georgetown University, 1995.

Professional: 1989–1993, legislative assistant, Office of Sen. Ernest Hollings (D-S.C.). 1993–1995, professional staff member, Senate Cmte. on Commerce. 1995–2000, first deputy assistant secretary, Dept. of Commerce, International Trade Administration. 2000–2001, second secretary for import administration, Dept. of Commerce, International Trade Administration. 2001–2005, trade counsel, Steptoe & Johnson. 2005–present, counsel, Senate Cmte. on Homeland Security and Governmental Affairs.

Expertise: Government contracting and procurement, international trade, financial management, emergency communications, Lobbying Disclosure Act.

Promoted to senior counsel at the outset of the 112th Congress, Troy Cribb is busy working on the committee's draft of a Department of Homeland Security (DHS) authorization bill. In particular, she is helping to write the provisions relating to DHS acquisitions and management.

Cribb said she is also assisting with Chairman Joseph Lieberman's, I-Conn., effort to highlight the link between trade and national security. Lieberman is particularly concerned with the nation's trade policy with Asia, where China is using its economic leverage to influence its neighbors on strategic issues, and compromising American security.

In 2010, the committee made a big push on the Lieberman-Collins cyber bill called the Protecting Cyberspace as a National Asset Act of 2010. The legislation sought to strengthen the protection of federal IT systems through better procurement and supply chain management practices. Passage of the cyber legislation is a top priority for Lieberman in 2011, according to Cribb, who is assisting with the effort.

Also on Cribb's agenda in 2011 is ongoing oversight of acquisition reforms being undertaken by the Office of Management and Budget, many of which are in response to legislation passed through the committee.

In addition to the cyber bill, last year Cribb helped to draft the First Responders Protection Act of 2010, which would allocate the D Block of spectrum to public safety. She said the committee is pushing the legislation again in the 112th Congress.

In the last session, she also participated in the committee's oversight of federal contracts that go to companies that are possibly in violation of Iran sanctions laws. This effort helped establish the basis for the procurement provisions of the Comprehensive Iran Sanctions, Accountability and Divestment Act of 2010, she said.

SENATE HOMELAND SECURITY

Gordon Lederman

Associate Staff Director and Chief Counsel for National Security and Investigations

340 Dirksen Senate Office Bldg.

Phone: (202) 224-2627

Gordon_Lederman@hsgac.senate.gov

Personal: Born in Rochester, N.Y.

Education: J.D., Harvard Law School, 1997. B.A., Harvard College, 1993.

Professional: 1997, law clerk, Hon. Robert Cowen, U.S. Third Circuit Court of Appeals. 1998–2003, attorney, Arnold & Porter, national security law and policy practice group. 2003–2004, counsel, 9/11 Commission. 2004–2006, counsel, Senate Cmte. on Homeland Security and Governmental Affairs. 2006–2007, advisor, U.S. National Counterterrorism Center. 2007–2008, attorney, White & Case. 2008–2010, counsel, Senate Cmte. on Homeland Security and Givernmental Affairs. 2011–present, associate staff director and chief counsel for national security and investigations, Senate Cmte. on Homeland Security and Givernmental Affairs.

Expertise: Counterterrorism, interagency reform, intelligence reform, bioterrorism, domestic intelligence.

At the start of the 112th Congress, Gordon Lederman was promoted from counsel to associate staff director and chief counsel for national security and investigations. In his new position, Lederman said he will focus on domestic intelligence issues, inter-agency reform, and various committee investigations.

The inter-agency reform effort began at the end of the 111th Congress and involved an examination of how the many agencies that contribute to national security could more effectively work together on counter-terrorism, radicalization, and other issues. The report on the investigation was finished early in 2011, and now Lederman and the committee are considering drafting legislation that will help enhance inter-agency cooperation.

Lederman's domestic intelligence responsibilities cover issues such as how to strengthen the nation's defenses against nuclear terrorism. The committee also is examining the effectiveness of the Intelligence Reform and Terrorism Prevention Act of 2004, a law with which Lederman is intimately familiar. He served on the 9/11 Commission, whose recommendations formed the basis of the law, and he was one of the primary drafters of the legislation.

The Act created a Director of National Intelligence and the U.S. National Counterterrorism Center. After helping to secure passage of the law as a member of the Homeland Security Committee from 2004 to 2006, Lederman joined the National Counterterrorism Center to assist with the law's implementation.

Lederman said that in 2010 one of his key accomplishments was helping with the investigation and release of a report by Chairman Joseph Lieberman, I-Conn., and Ranking Member Susan Collins, R-Maine, concerning the 2009 terrorist attack at Fort Hood, Texas. Testimony on the incident provided the committee the opportunity to consider the larger issue of the growth in the U.S. of violent ideological extremism.

Lederman graduated magna cum laude from both Harvard College and Harvard Law School, and was inducted into Phi Beta Kappa. In 1999, he published a book on the Defense Department's organizational politics. He has authored or co-authored numerous reports and articles in the areas of counterterrorism strategy, intelligence reform, bioterrorism, and information warfare.

SENATE HOMELAND SECURITY

Rob Strayer

Republican Director of Homeland Security Policy

340 Dirksen Senate Office Bldg.

Phone: (202) 224-4751

Rob_Strayer@hsgac.senate.gov

Personal: Born 1975 in Troy, Ohio.

Education: B.A., Denison University, 1997. J.D., Vanderbilt University, 2000.

Professional: 2000–2001, judicial clerkship, U.S. Court of Appeals for the Eleventh Circuit, Chief Judge Lanier Anderson. 2001–2002, fellowship, State Solicitor's Office, Ohio Attorney General Betty Montgomery. 2002–2005, associate, Wilmer Cutler Pickering Hale and Dorr. 2005–2006, counsel, Cmte. on Homeland Security and Governmental Affairs. 2006–present, director of homeland security policy, Cmte. on Homeland Security and Governmental Affairs.

Expertise: Homeland security, terrorist travel, port security, border security.

Cyber security legislation co-sponsored by Senate Homeland Security and Governmental Affairs Committee Chairman Joseph Lieberman, I-Conn., and Ranking Member Susan Collins, R-Maine, is high on Rob Strayer's agenda in 2011. A bill to develop a national strategy to better protect federal IT systems made it out of committee in 2010 and is being promoted again in the 112th Congress.

As Republican Director of Homeland Security Policy, Strayer is the point person on Collins' efforts to get the Department of Homeland Security (DHS) to deploy whole body imaging technology at airports to improve security while alleviating passengers' privacy concerns. Collins is a proponent of auto-detection technology that is successfully being used at the Amsterdam airport.

Strayer also contributes to the committee's ongoing oversight of DHS. In 2011, this includes addressing Collins' concerns that DHS's long range strategic plans are too broad and unspecific. She has asked the agency to set more detailed priorities to improve preparedness and overall security.

The committee also monitors DHS's decision to change from the system of color-coded alerts to a new notification system. Collins favors the move and has called for a system that makes more information and specific guidance available to citizens and first responders.

Strayer also assists with the committee's work on extending certain anti-terrorism protections designed to safeguard the nation's shipping lanes and seaports from attack. Collins co-authored the original SAFE Port Act in 2005.

With Strayer's help, the committee is continuing its work in 2011 on combating home-based terrorism. Collins' goal is to improve efforts to anticipate and prepare for attacks, possibly including charging one federal agency with responsibility for identifying radicalization and stopping the recruitment of U.S. citizens for terrorism.

SENATE HOMELAND SECURITY

Kenya Wiley

Counsel

340 Dirksen Senate Office Bldg.

Phone: (202) 224-6848

Fax: (202) 228-3792

Kenya_Wiley@hsgac.senate.gov

Personal: Born in Chicago, Ill.

Education: B.A., Stanford University, 1996. J.D., Georgetown University Law Center, 2002.

Professional: 1997–1998, assistant, Office of Alderman John O. Steele and Alderwoman Freddrenna M. Lyle. 1998–1999, legal assistant, Jenner & Block (Chicago, Ill.). 2002–2003, legal honors law clerk, Department of Housing and Urban Development, Office of General Counsel. 2003–2005, attorney-advisor, Department of Housing and Urban Development, Office of General Counsel. 2005–2007, manager, regulatory and judicial affairs, Society for Human Resource Management Government Affairs (Alexandria, Va.). 2007–present, counsel, Senate Cmte. on Homeland Security and Governmental Affairs.

Expertise: Tax and benefits, health care, labor and employment, postal reform, cyber security workforce.

The major issues on Kenya Wiley's agenda in 2011 include renewed efforts to pass domestic partnership benefits legislation, and U.S. Postal Service reform aimed at improving its financial condition. Wiley is also working in this session to find ways to improve the cyber security workforce at the Department of Homeland Security (DHS).

A domestic partnership benefits bill was voted out of committee in the 111th Congress, but did not make it through the Senate. It provided that same-sex domestic partners of federal employees would be entitled to the same benefits available to spouses of federal employees. A similar bill is being put forward in 2011, Wiley said, and its passage is a high priority for Chairman Joseph Lieberman, I-Conn.

In the area of postal reform, Wiley said the committee is looking to address the Postal Service's decline in revenues that has resulted from the electronic diversion of mail and the overall economic downturn.

One problem that needs to be addressed is restructuring retiree health benefit payments for future retirees, which cost the Postal Service approximately $5 billion each year, she said. Bills introduced in the 111th Congress sought to correct the overpayment by the Postal Service to the Civil Service Retirement and Disability Fund and transfer funds into the Postal Service's Retiree Health Benefits Fund.

Wiley and the committee are also examining ways to recruit and retain skilled individuals to improve DHS's cyber talent. DHS has difficulty recruiting and retaining staff in this area because they are in such high demand.

In 2010, the committee helped to pass legislation to cut waste due to improper payments by federal government agencies that added up to $110 billion in 2009. The Improper Payments Elimination and Recovery Act was signed into law in July 2010. Wiley helped to craft the legislation and shepherd it through the Senate.

SENATE HOMELAND SECURITY

Molly Wilkinson

General Counsel

340 Dirksen Senate Office Bldg.

Phone: (202) 224-2627

Molly_Wilkinson@hsgac.senate.gov

Personal: Born in Amsterdam, N.Y.

Education: J.D., Albany Law School. B.A., College of the Holy Cross.

Professional: 2003–2005, several positions, U.S. Department of Defense, Office of the Secretary and U.S. Department of the Army. 2005–2006, associate deputy secretary for management, Office of the Secretary, U.S. Department of Labor. 2006–2008, chief acquisition officer, General Services Administration. 2008–2009, chief of staff, U.S. Small Business Administration. 2009–2010, staff director, Subcommittee on Contracting Oversight. 2009–2010, deputy general counsel, Cmte. on Homeland Security and Governmental Affairs. 2010–present, general counsel, Cmte. on Homeland Security and Governmental Affairs.

Expertise: Acquisition policy and management, federal management issues, election law/ballot security.

Molly Wilkinson joined the committee in January 2009 as Republican deputy general counsel and staff director of the Subcommittee on Contracting Oversight with responsibility for federal acquisition policy issues. She was promoted to general counsel in 2010, and has added federal management issues to her duties.

The upstate New York native brought considerable acquisitions policy experience to the committee, having served as chief acquisition officer at the General Services Administration from 2006 to 2008. Wilkinson's work history also includes nine months of service in Iraq for the Department of the Army.

In the 112th Congress, Wilkinson is helping with the follow up on a major committee achievement in 2010, the enactment of The Improper Payments Elimination and Recovery Act. The committee is working to ensure that the law, which is designed to cut waste due to improper payments by government agencies, is implemented properly.

Ranking Member Susan Collins, R-Maine, a co-sponsor of the legislation, has called for aggressive implementation in light of recent Office of Management and Budget estimates that improper payments have reached $125 billion annually. The law requires mandatory audits and corrective action plans, and mandates that all agencies spending more than $1 million must perform recovery audits on their programs to recoup the over-payments.

Wilkinson also is assisting with Information Technology Investment Oversight Enhancement and Waste Prevention Act, which is co-sponsored by Collins and Senator Tom Carper, D-Del. A version of the legislation passed the Senate in 2010.

The bill seeks to monitor more effectively the $80 billion that federal agencies spend annually on information technology. Collins said that the need for the legislation was underscored by a Government Accountability Office report that found significant cost overruns in a project by the National Archives to preserve and manage the government's electronic records.

In 2010, Wilkinson staffed committee oversight hearings on the role of the Special Inspector General for Afghanistan Reconstruction (SIGAR) in providing independent oversight of reconstruction contracts in Afghanistan. A peer review of the SIGAR found that it did not conform to professional standards in the conduct of its investigations, and the committee heard testimony on the findings.

SENATE HOMELAND SECURITY

Amanda Wood

Republican Deputy General Counsel

340 Dirksen Senate Office Bldg.

Phone: (202) 224-2627

Amanda_Wood@hsgac.senate.gov

Education: J.D., University of Maine Law School, 2001. B.A. in political science, University of New Hampshire, 1997.

Professional: 2001–2006, assistant general counsel, General Services Administration, Real Property Division. 2006–2010, director of governmental affairs, Senate Cmte. on Homeland Security and Governmental Affairs. 2010–present, Republican deputy general counsel, Senate Cmte. on Homeland Security and Governmental Affairs.

Expertise: Government contracting and services.

In keeping with the Republican theme of reducing government spending in the 112th Congress, Ranking Member Susan Collins, R-Maine, has asked the committee to work toward cleaning up redundancies and inefficiencies in federal programs. Republican Deputy General Counsel Amanda Wood, who spent five years as director of governmental affairs for the minority staff, is assisting with that initiative.

The committee is working with a Government Accountability Office (GAO) report that identified many duplicative federal programs such as food safety where 15 federal agencies contribute to a poorly managed effort. The badly coordinated biodefense and northern border security programs are also under scrutiny.

Wood works toward Collin's goal of bolstering the U.S. Postal Service, often identified by the GAO as an agency that is prone to waste and mismanagement. The Postal Service has suffered from the recession and the increasing use of digital communications, but Collins believes it has also been slow to take advantage of the 2006 postal reform law that she authored.

Early in 2011, Collins introduced the U.S. Postal Service Improvements Act of 2011, and Wood and her colleagues are working to secure its passage. The legislation will help the Postal Service achieve financial stability and future cost savings without undermining customer service.

In 2010, Wood helped to prepare a committee report on providing additional personnel authorities for the special inspector general for Afghanistan reconstruction. She also contributed to a report on the Anti-Border Corruption Act of 2010, which sought to provide heightened screening and background checks for all applicants for law enforcement positions with U.S. Customs and Border Protection.

Wood earned her law degree at the University of Maine. While there, she was a member of the Moot Court Board, and was co-chair of the Women's Law Association. She also served as president of the Sports and Entertainment Law Association.

Wood did her undergraduate work at the University of New Hampshire, where she studied political science with a minor in justice studies. She was captain of the school's women's indoor and outdoor track and field teams. In her final year at UNH, she was named the Dean Williamson student-athlete of the year.

Committee on the Judiciary

224 Dirksen Senate Office Bldg.
Washington, DC 20510
Phone: (202) 224-7703
Fax: (202) 224-9516
http://judiciary.senate.gov

Ratio: 8/10

MAJORITY MEMBERS

Patrick J. Leahy, VT, Chairman

Herbert Kohl, WI
Dianne Feinstein, CA
Charles E. Schumer, NY
Richard J. Durbin, IL
Sheldon Whitehouse, RI
Amy Klobuchar, MN
Al Franken, MN
Richard Blumenthal, CT
Christopher Coons, DE

MINORITY MEMBERS

Charles E. Grassley, IA, Ranking Member

Orrin G. Hatch, UT
Jon Kyl, AZ
Jeff Sessions, AL, Ranking Member
Lindsey Graham, SC
John Cornyn, TX
Michael S. Lee, UT
Tom Coburn, OK

SENATE JUDICIARY

JURISDICTION

(1) Apportionment of representatives.
(2) Bankruptcy, mutiny, espionage, and counterfeiting.
(3) Civil liberties.
(4) Constitutional amendments.
(5) Federal courts and judges.
(6) Government information.
(7) Holidays and celebrations.
(8) Immigration and naturalization.
(9) Interstate compacts generally.
(10) Judicial proceedings, civil and criminal, generally.
(11) Local courts in the territories and possessions.
(12) Claims against the United States.
(13) National penitentiaries.
(14) Patent Office.
(15) Patents, copyrights, and trademarks.
(16) Protection of trade and commerce against unlawful restraints and monopolies.
(17) Revision and codification of the statutes of the United States.
(18) State and territorial boundary lines.

SENATE JUDICIARY

With two new subcommittees and a handful of controversial issues to tackle in 2011, it'll likely be another busy and headline-grabbing year for the Senate Judiciary Committee.

The committee began 2011 by passing long-awaited patent reform legislation and by approving a three-year extension of the USA PATRIOT Act, including provisions that would make terrorists who commit a crime using a weapon of mass destruction eligible for the death penalty.

The panel also approved new privacy and civil liberty safeguards for the Patriot Act provisions, but opposed an investigative tool that would compel businesses to turn over customer records without a judge's orders.

The committee has jurisdiction over a broad swath of issues, including oversight of the Department of Justice, the Federal Bureau of Investigation, and the Department of Homeland Security, as well as all judicial nominations and a variety of other issues. In 2011, the committee reorganized, creating two new subcommittees: One on Privacy, Technology and the Law and the other on Constitution, Civil Rights and Human Rights.

The former committee sparked a turf issue early in 2011 when Commerce Committee Chairman Jay Rockefeller, D-W.Va., and ranking member Kay Bailey Hutchison, R-Texas, sent a letter to the committee asserting that any online privacy legislation should be tackled by Commerce, not the Judiciary. The new Judiciary Subcommittee is chaired by Sen. Al Franken, D-Minn., with Sen. Tom Coburn, R-Okla., serving as ranking member. According to the subcommittee's website, its jurisdiction included privacy issues related to social networks, online advertising, and emerging technologies.

The committee also faced the continuing problem of judicial vacancies. Early in 2011, judicial vacancies topped 100, with more than two dozen circuit and district courts facing judicial emergencies. Chairman Patrick Leahy, D-Vt., said he would make filling those vacancies a priority in 2011, but said it could only be done with bipartisan cooperation.

SENATE JUDICIARY

Bruce A. Cohen

Staff Director/Chief Counsel

224 Dirksen Senate Office Bldg.

Phone: (202) 224-7703

Fax: (202) 224-9516

Personal: Born 1950 in St. Louis, Mo.

Education: B.A., Stanford University, 1972. J.D. (Order of the Coif, Editor-in-chief, *California Law Review*), University of California, Berkeley, 1975.

Professional: 1975–1976, law clerk, U.S. District Court Judge Jon O. Newman. 1976–1977, general attorney, Civil Rights Div., Dept. of Justice. 1981–1983, chief counsel, Subc. on Juvenile Justice, Senate Cmte. on the Judiciary. 1983–1988, attorney, Dechert Price & Rhoads. 1988–1994, attorney, Jeffer, Mangels, Butler & Marmaro. 1994, chief counsel, Subc. on Technology and the Law, Senate Cmte. on the Judiciary. 1995–1996, Democratic chief counsel, Subc. on Antitrust, Business Rights and Competition, Senate Cmte. on the Judiciary. 1997–2001, Democratic staff director/chief counsel, Senate Cmte. on the Judiciary. 2001–present, Democratic staff director/chief counsel, Senate Cmte. on the Judiciary.

Expertise: Civil litigation.

In 2011, Bruce Cohen continues his work as Chief Counsel and Staff Director of the Senate Judiciary Committee, chaired by Senator Patrick Leahy of Vermont. Cohen is a Judiciary Committee veteran—he has worked for the Committee since 1981 and has served as the Democratic Chief Counsel and Staff Director of the Committee since 1999.

Cohen is the Chairman's lead staffer in the committee's oversight efforts. He is also a key staffer on national security efforts, and focused much of early 2011 on the Committee's work and the Senate's efforts to extend expiring provisions and improve civil liberties and privacy protections in the USA Patriot Act.

This year, one key focus for Cohen will be supporting Leahy in his goal to enact meaningful patent reform legislation. Leahy has made patent reform a priority, and the Patent Reform Act was the first bill reported by the committee this Congress. Leahy—and Cohen—also will work on advancing legislation in 2011 to combat online infringement. Work on that legislation began during the last Congress.

The Committee will also be working to fill several high-profile vacancies this year, including the Solicitor General, the Inspector General of the Department of Justice, and the FBI Director.

Cohen has extensive experience in confirmation proceedings—he was the lead advisor to Chairman Leahy in the confirmation proceedings of the two most recent Supreme Court Justices, Elena Kagan and Sonia Sotomayor, and also worked on the confirmation proceedings for Chief Justice John Roberts and Justice Samuel Alito.

He has also worked closely on Leahy's other legislative priorities on the committee, including hate crimes legislation, FOIA legislation, intellectual property bills—including patent reform and legislation to combat online infringement—and Leahy's criminal justice work. That work includes efforts to reauthorize the Justice for All Act and to enact meaningful forensics reform legislation.

Besides his work on the Senate Judiciary Committee, he worked in the Civil Rights Division at the United States Department of Justice and clerked for the Honorable Jon O. Newman on the United States District Court for the District of Connecticut.

SENATE JUDICIARY

Kolan L. Davis

Minority Staff Director and Chief Counsel
219 Dirksen Senate Office Bldg.
Phone: (202) 224-5315
Kolan_Davis@finance-rep.senate.gov

Personal: Born 02/17/1958 in Franklin, Ind.

Education: B.A., cum laude, University of Dallas, 1980. J.D., Indiana University School of Law, 1984.

Professional: 1985–1987, counsel, Subc. on Administrative Practice and Procedure, Senate Cmte. on the Judiciary. 1987–1995, counsel, Sen. Charles Grassley, R-Iowa. 1995–2000, chief counsel, Subc. on Administrative Oversight and the Courts, Senate Cmte. on the Judiciary. 1998–2000, legislative director and tax counsel, Sen. Charles Grassley, R-Iowa. 2001–present, staff director and chief counsel, Senate Cmte. on Finance.

Expertise: Tax issues.

After 10 years as Republican Staff Director and Chief Counsel to the Senate Finance Committee, Kolan Davis returned to the Senate Judiciary Committee in 2011 when Sen. Chuck Grassley, R-Iowa, became ranking member.

Davis is a long-time Grassley aide, working for Grassley for almost 26 years.

Davis expects to spend much of 2011 working on oversight. "Sen. Grassley views oversight as important, if not more important than legislation to keep checks and balances on the government," Davis said. "'Congress doesn't do enough oversight,' is always his mantra."

Davis will work on a variety of Grassley priorities, including a long-term extension of the USA PATRIOT Act and the nominations process. Grassley has indicated he wants to process "consensus judicial nominees" that both parties can agree upon.

Those will be two key issues, but a variety of smaller issues will also bubble up in 2011 for Davis and the rest of the staff.

In February, Grassley reintroduced a bill to allow chief judges of the federal trial and appellate courts to permit cameras in the courtroom. "The Sunshine in the Courtroom Act" also directs the Judicial Conference to draft non-binding guidelines for the judges regarding cameras and would direct the Judicial Conference to issue mandatory guidelines for protecting witnesses including victims, victims' families and undercover officers.

In early 2011, Grassley also reintroduced The Lawsuit Abuse Reduction Act that would impose mandatory sanctions for lawyers who file meritless suits in federal court.

Grassley will also be pursuing a money laundering reform bill that will crack down on current loopholes in the law.

Beyond that, Davis expects to work on whistleblower protection for congressional employees as well as on reducing inefficiencies and redundancies within the grant program in the Department of Justice.

# SENATE JUDICIARY

Stephen Higgins

Chief Counsel

224 Dirksen Senate Office Bldg.

Phone: (202) 224-9032

Fax: (202) 228-0623

stephen_higgins@judiciary-rep.senate.gov

Professional: 1999–2001, staff director and chief counsel, Subc. on Technology, Terrorism, and Government Information, Senate Cmte. on the Judiciary. 2001–2003, Republican staff director and chief counsel, Subc. on Technology, Terrorism, and Government Information, Senate Cmte. on the Judiciary. 2004–present, chief counsel, Subc. on Terrorism, Technology, and Homeland Security, Senate Cmte. on the Judiciary.

Expertise: Technology and information issues.

Stephen Higgins returns in 2011 as the general counsel for the Senate Judiciary Committee's Subcommittee on Crime and Terrorism during ranking member Sen. Jon Kyl's, R-Ariz., swan song—Kyl has indicated he will not seek re-election in 2012.

Higgins has worked for the subcommittee as chief counsel since 1999 and assists Kyl in developing and prompting the senator's legislative initiatives. The former chairman of the subcommittee when Republicans controlled the Senate, Kyl said he has long fought for and will continue to fight to improve the federal government's ability to prevent, defend against, and respond to terrorist threats to the nation, according to his Web site. Higgins will monitor these and other issues.

Higgins works on issues within the subcommittee's jurisdiction, which includes the Department of Justice's Criminal Division, the U.S. Drug Enforcement Administration, the Office on Violence Against Women, the Federal Bureau of Investigation, and the Bureau of Alcohol, Tobacco, Firearms and Explosives, among other federal departments. Kyl will spend his last year on the subcommittee working with a new chairman, Sen. Sheldon Whitehouse, D-R.I.

In the two years before the Sept. 11, 2001 attacks, Higgins worked on identity theft legislation and a crime victims' Constitutional amendment that would have given crime victims more power through notification about their perpetrator and access to court proceedings.

The subcommittee has been reorganized several times, recently as the Subcommittee on Terrorism and Homeland Security, and has seen iterations with Sen. Ben Cardin, D-Md., and Kyl himself at the helm.

The 2008 agenda for the subcommittee touched on issues related to border security and immigration, identity theft, and the detention of combatants in the War on Terror.

SENATE JUDICIARY

Matthew L. Johnson

Chief Republican Counsel
Subcommittee on Immigration, Refugees and Border Security
224 Dirksen Senate Office Bldg.
Phone: (202) 224-7840
Fax: (202) 228-2260
matthew_johnson@judiciary-rep.senate.gov

Personal: Born 09/11/1977 in Houston, Texas.

Education: B.S., journalism, Northwestern University. J.D., Notre Dame.

Professional: 2005–2006, Judicial nominations counsel, Sen. John Cornyn, R-Texas. 2006–2007, counsel, Sen. John Cornyn, R-Texas. 2007–present, chief counsel, Subc. on Immigration, Border Security and Citizenship, Senate Cmte. on the Judiciary.

Expertise: Freedom of information laws, Intellectual property, immigration.

Matthew L. Johnson returns in 2011 as the lead counsel for Sen. John Cornyn, R-Texas, the ranking member on the Subcommittee for Immigration, Refugees and Border Security.

The subcommittee's jurisdiction covers all of the immigration functions of the Department of Homeland Security. It's also the panel that would deal with any comprehensive immigration reform—an issue that President Obama has vowed to pursue since the beginning of his term.

Johnson himself worked on the comprehensive immigration reform that stalled in the Senate in 2007, and while Cornyn was supportive of Obama's promise to pursue comprehensive immigration reform in 2009, there hasn't been much agreement on the issue since then. Rather, Cornyn and Johnson have focused on border security, particularly given the rise in drug violence on the U.S.-Mexico border. In 2011, Johnson said he expects to work toward Cornyn's goal of encouraging interagency coordination and cooperation in the fight against Mexican drug cartels.

In April of 2010, Cornyn introduced the Southern Border Security Assistance Act, a bill that would provide $300 million in grants for border law enforcement officials. Cornyn also is continuing to press for passage of the Emergency Port of Entry Personnel and Infrastructure Funding Act, which would help add more pedestrian and vehicle inspection lanes at the border.

Johnson is also likely to continue working for a Balanced Budget Amendment to the Constitution, a longtime Cornyn goal. He'll also work on Cornyn initiatives to reform the Freedom of Information Act and work on oversight for the OPEN Government Act.

SENATE JUDICIARY

Kristine Lucius

General Counsel and Deputy Staff Director
224 Dirksen Senate Office Bldg.
Phone: (202) 224-7703
Fax: (202) 224-9516

Personal: Born 03/04/1972 in Robinsdale, Minn.

Education: B.A., University of Minnesota, 1994. J.D., Georgetown Law School, 1999.

Professional: 1999, clerked for Judge Emily Hewitt, Court of Federal Claims. 1999, clerked for Judge Richard Tallman, Ninth Circuit Court of Appeals. 2001–2002, attorney, Jenner & Block LLP. 2002–2006, counsel, Senate Judiciary Cmte. 2006–2008, deputy staff director & chief counsel for civil justice, Senate Judiciary Cmte. 2009–present, general counsel & deputy staff director, Senate Judiciary Cmte.

Expertise: Federal court system.

Kristine Lucius currently serves as the Senate Judiciary Committee's general counsel and deputy staff director. Prior to that, she served as the committee's point person on issues related to the federal court system.

Her past work for the committee has included successful efforts to reauthorize the Voting Rights Act and enact the Matthew Shepard and James Byrd, Jr. Hate Crimes Prevention Act. Currently, she helps oversee committee counsels in all legislative areas.

Her work also extends to legislation with relevance to the Judiciary Committee's jurisdiction, but which originate in other panels. In the past Congress, these included the Affordable Care Act; the Wall Street Reform Act; and the James Zadroga 9/11 Health and Compensation Act, which was enacted in the closing days of the 111th Congress.

Lucius also serves as Chairman Patrick Leahy's, D-Vt., chief advisor on constitutional issues, and was the lead counsel on the SPEECH Act and the Animal Crush Video Prohibition Act, both signed into law in the last Congress.

Lucius previously served as the committee's chief counsel for civil justice, and worked on initiatives like placement of cameras in the courtroom, addressing the needs of the federal judiciary through legislation to authorize additional judgeships in overburdened districts, and court security. She also worked on such civil rights issues as the repeal of the military's "Don't Ask, Don't Tell" policy.

Lucius has worked on five Supreme Court nominations. While the Judiciary Committee is expected to be busy considering many nominations during the 112th Congress, Lucius will also be a key advisor on a range of issues identified by Leahy as top priorities in the 112th Congress, including fraud enforcement and prevention, national security and privacy issues, and Committee efforts to spur job development and economic growth.

SENATE JUDICIARY

Matthew S. Miner

Chief Counsel

Subcommittee on Administrative Oversight and the Courts

224 Dirksen Senate Office Bldg.

Phone: (202) 224-7572

Fax: (202) 228-0464

Education: B.A., University of Cincinnati. J.D., University of Michigan.

Professional: 2005–2006, counsel, Senate Cmte. on Homeland Security and Government Affairs. 2006–2008, counsel, Senate Cmte. on the Judiciary. 2008–2009, chief counsel, Senate Cmte. on the Judiciary. 2009–2010, deputy staff director, Senate Cmte. on the Judiciary. 2010–2011, staff director, Senate Cmte. on the Judiciary. 2011–present, chief counsel, Senate Cmte. on Judiciary.

After a stint as staff director for Republicans on the U.S. Senate Judiciary Committee, Matthew Miner returns this year to his prior role as chief counsel to Sen. Jeff Sessions, R-Ala, the ranking member on the Subcommittee on Administrative Oversight and the Courts.

This year, Miner anticipates that the overall Senate Judiciary Committee will spend a great deal of time focusing on national security legislation including the Patriot Act and FISA Amendments. Both are due for reauthorization by the end of this Congress.

In the subcommittee, however, the focus will likely be on reforms to bankruptcy laws. The subcommittee's chairman, Sen. Sheldon Whitehouse, D-R.I., has signaled that he wants to have hearings on such reforms. Sessions' focus, meanwhile, has been centered on encouraging the U.S. Department of Justice to examine bankruptcy reform. As a U.S. Attorney, Sessions prosecuted multiple cases of bankruptcy reform. Taking a hard look at bankruptcy fraud would "bring a lot of integrity into the system," Miner said, and would ensure that "folks on both sides of bankruptcy proceedings would have complete faith in all failings, claims and assertions in litigation."

Prior to his time at the subcommittee, Miner worked for the Senate Judiciary Committee's former chairman, Sen. Arlen Specter, R-Pa., on issues relating to detainees, interrogation, state secrets, and habeas corpus. Miner also served as counsel to the Senate Homeland Security and Governmental Affairs Committee. Before his arrival in the Senate, Miner was an Assistant United States Attorney in the Middle District of Alabama, serving as Corporate Fraud Coordinator. He also clerked for the Honorable Richard W. Vollmer, Jr., United States District Judge for the Southern District of Alabama after his time at the University of Michigan Law School.

SENATE JUDICIARY

Joseph Zogby

Majority Chief Counsel

224 Dirksen Senate Office Bldg.

Phone: (202) 224-1158

Fax: (202) 228-0781

joseph_zogby@judiciary-dem.senate.gov

Personal: Born 12/07/1969 in Philadelphia, Pa.

Education: B.A., University of Virginia, 1991. J.D., University of Virginia, 1996.

Professional: 1996–1998, public service fellow, Echoing Green. 1998–1999, attorney, U.S. Dept. of State. 1999–2003, attorney, U.S. Dept. of Justice. 2003–2006, counsel, Senate Cmte. on the Judiciary. 2007–2008, majority chief counsel, Subc. on Human Rights and the Law, Senate Cmte. on the Judiciary. 2009–present, Chief Counsel, Subc. on Crime and Drugs, Senate Cmte. on the Judiciary.

Expertise: Human rights, immigration.

Joseph Zogby returns to the Senate Judiciary Committee, albeit with a different title in 2011: After serving on subcommittees overseeing human rights as well as crime, Zogby is now serving as staff director and chief counsel on the reconstituted Subcommittee on Constitution, Civil Rights and Human Rights.

The panel has changed, but according to Zogby many of the issues overlap. Among key issues he has worked on over the past two years is the Fair Sentencing Act, which reduced the disparity between crack and powder cocaine. Durbin held hearings on the issue while serving on the Crime and Drugs Subcommittee, submitting legislation on the issue later that year. "Frankly, he views it both as a criminal justice and human rights issue," Zogby said. The bill passed the Senate unanimously in 2010.

Zogby also most recently worked on the Human Rights Enforcement Act, which created a new office at the Department of Justice to investigate and prosecute human rights violations. That bill built on legislation that Durbin wrote during previous years that gave the Justice Department the authority to prosecute crimes such as the recruitment of child soldiers, human trafficking and genocide.

This year, Zogby expects to continue work on passage of the DREAM Act, aimed at helping illegal immigrants who meet certain requirements have an opportunity to enlist in the military or go to college and have a path to citizenship. The bill has been a priority for Durbin for eight years and will remain one in 2011.

The constitutional also will be a priority. The panel's first hearing of 2011 was on the constitutionality of the new health care law. Durbin also plans to examine campaign finance reform, the censorship of the Internet and CEDAW, the women's' rights treaty.

"Human rights treaties are an issue he is likely to spend some time on," Zogby said of his boss.

Committee on Rules and Administration

305 Russell Senate Office Bldg.
Washington, DC 20510
Phone: (202) 224-6352
Fax: (202) 228-2401
http://rules.senate.gov

Ratio: 8/10

MAJORITY MEMBERS

Charles E. Schumer, NY, Chairman

Daniel K. Inouye, HI
Dianne Feinstein, CA
Richard J. Durbin, IL
E. Benjamin Nelson, NE
Patty Murray, WA
Mark Pryor, AR
Tom Udall, NM
Mark Warner, VA
Patrick Leahy, VT

MINORITY MEMBERS

Lamar Alexander, TN, Ranking Member

Mitch McConnell, KY
Thad Cochran, MS
Kay Bailey Hutchison, TX
C. Saxby Chambliss, GA
Pat Roberts, KS
Richard Shelby, AL
Roy Blunt, MO

SENATE RULES AND ADMINISTRATION

JURISDICTION

(1) Administration of the Senate Office Buildings and the Senate wing of the Capitol, including the assignment of office space.
(2) Congressional organization relative to rules and procedures and Senate rules and regulations including floor and gallery rules.
(3) Corrupt practices.
(4) Credentials and qualifications of members of the Senate, contested elections, and acceptance of incompatible offices.
(5) Federal elections generally, including the election of the president, vice president, and members of the Congress.
(6) Government Printing Office, and the printing and correction of the Congressional Record, as well as matters under Senate Rule XI.
(7) Meetings of the Congress and attendance of members.
(8) Payment of money out of the contingent fund of the Senate or creating a charge upon the same (except that any resolution relating to substantive matter within the jurisdiction of any other Senate standing committee is to be first referred to such committee).
(9) Presidential succession.
(10) Purchase of books and manuscripts and erection of monuments to the memory of individuals.
(11) Senate Library and statuary, art, and pictures in the Capitol and Senate Office Buildings.
(12) Services to the Senate, including the Senate restaurant.
(13) United States Capitol and congressional office buildings, the Library of Congress, the Smithsonian Institution (and the incorporation of similar institutions), and the Botanic Gardens.

Such committee shall also (a) make a continuing study of, and recommend improvements regarding, the organization and operation of the Congress, with a view towards strengthening it, simplifying its operations, improving its relationships with other branches of government, and enabling it to better meet its responsibilities under the Constitution of the United States; (b) identify any court proceeding or action which, in the opinion of the committee, is of vital interest to the Congress as a constitutionally established institution of the federal government and call such proceeding or action to the attention of the Senate; and (c) develop, implement, and update as necessary a strategic planning process and a strategic plan for the functional and technical infrastructure support of the Senate and provide oversight over plans developed by Senate officers and others in accordance with the strategic planning process.

SENATE RULES AND ADMINISTRATION

Sen. Chuck Schumer, D-N.Y., is in his second term at the helm of the Senate Rules and Administration Committee, one of the oldest panels in the U.S. Congress. In this role, the Senator is charged with leading the committee's efforts to enact electoral reform and conduct oversight of the Capitol campus.

The committee got off to a slow start in 2011. Early on, committee staff handled the task of assigning office space and helping new Senators and their staff get adjusted to life in the chamber. But the panel didn't even hold its first hearing until February 17, the usual meeting that is held every two years to organize the committee. Its second order of official business took place on March 1, when Members met to mark up the legislation providing a budget for other Senate committees. As of March 2011, no other hearings had been announced.

But the panel likely will have plenty on its plate as the year continues. As Congress looked to cut spending from its own budget, several legislative agencies that rely on tax dollars to survive complained their programs might suffer if they lose too much funding. Others complained cutting funding now would do more harm than good in the long run.

A coalition of architects, builders, contractors and engineers wrote to Members urging them to spare the Architect of the Capitol from cuts, the Capitol Hill newspaper Roll Call reported. A House proposal to trim $29 million from the AOC's budget will ultimately cost the federal government more money, they argued, explaining that construction projects to fix and maintain congressional buildings must be completed at some point—and the longer the wait, the higher the repair cost. An effort to repair the Capitol Dome will likely be put off, for example, until additional funding is secured.

Typically, the chairman of the Senate Rules and Administration Committee steps in to chair the Joint Congressional Committee on Inaugural Ceremonies, the special panel formed every four years to plan the presidential inauguration, from security concerns to what guests will eat during the inaugural luncheon. Although the 2013 event is still about two years away, as the date gets closer Schumer and his team will begin preparations; the joint committee is usually formed about a year before the big event.

SENATE RULES AND ADMINISTRATION

Jean Bordewich

Staff Director

305 Russell Senate Office Bldg.

Phone: (202) 224-6352

Fax: (202) 224-1912

jean_bordewich@rules.senate.gov

Education: B.A., classics, Brown University. M.B.A., business administration, George Washington University.

Professional: 1999–2007, regional director, Sen. Chuck Schumer, D-N.Y. 2007–2009, chief of staff, Rep. John Hall, D-N.Y. 2009–present, staff director, Senate Rules and Administration Cmte.

Expertise: Management.

While most Senate committee staff focus on a specific issue for a committee that is charged with overseeing on a particular aspect of the federal government, Jean Bordewich is the woman charged with a very different task. Bordewich keeps the Senate's trains running on time—and doing so during a period of tight congressional budgets isn't always easy.

The Senate Rules and Administration Committee hosted its first hearing of the year in February 2011, to organize the panel. But administrators already were dealing with the repercussions of intense fiscal restraint. Bordewich told the Capitol Hill newspaper *Roll Call* that a project to repair the Capitol Dome might be canceled if a continuing resolution could not be approved by Congress, for example.

In most sessions, the Rules committee is charged with jurisdiction of the Capitol complex, including the Architect of the Capitol, Capitol Police, and Library of Congress. It also oversees presidential inauguration ceremonies (a task Bordewich and her fellow staffers can largely ignore, at least until 2012).

Bordewich came to the Rules panel in 2009, when her old friend, Sen. Charles Schumer, D-N.Y., asked her to serve as staff director. She entered with an impressive background of congressional experience. She is a former city councilwoman and even once ran for Congress herself, challenging Rep. John Sweeney, R-N.Y., in the 1998 midterm elections. Bordewich lost the contest, but soon wound up running Schumer's regional campaign operations.

While Bordewich is a political veteran, her husband, Fergus, is a published author. His latest book, "Washington: The Making of the American Capital" studies how the capital city was built though backroom deals and the work of a variety of unsung heroes, including slaves. It received positive reviews from several prominent D.C. insiders, including Schumer.

Committee on Small Business and Entrepreneurship

428-A Russell Senate Office Bldg.
Washington, DC 20510
Phone: (202) 224-5175
http://sbc.senate.gov
webmaster@small-bus.senate.gov

Ratio: 9/9/1

MAJORITY MEMBERS

Mary Landrieu, LA, Chairman

John F. Kerry, MA
Carl Levin, MI
Tom Harkin, IA
Maria Cantwell, WA
Mark Pryor, AR
Benjamin L. Cardin, MD
Jeanne Shaheen, NH
Kay Hagan, NC

MINORITY MEMBERS

Olympia J. Snowe, ME, Ranking Member

David Vitter, LA
James Risch, ID
Marco Rubio, FL
Rand Paul, KY
Kelly Ayotte, NH
Michael B. Enzi, WY
Scott Brown, MA
Jerry Moran, KS

INDEPENDENT MEMBERS

Joseph I. Lieberman, CT

SENATE SMALL BUSINESS AND ENTREPRENEURSHIP

JURISDICTION

(1) All proposed legislation, messages, petition, memorials, and other matters relating to the Small Business Administration.

(2) Any proposed legislation reported by such committee, which relates to matters other than the functions of the Small Business Administration shall, at the request of the chairman of any standing committee having jurisdiction over the subject matter extraneous to the functions of the Small Business Administration, be considered and reported by such standing committee prior to its consideration by the Senate; and likewise, measures reported by other committees directly relating to the Small Business Administration shall, at the request of the chairman of the Committee on Small Business, be referred to the Committee on Small Business for its consideration of any portions of the measure dealing with the Small Business Administration and be reported by this committee prior to its consideration by the Senate.

(3) Such committee shall also study and survey by means of research and investigation all problems of American small business enterprises and report thereon from time to time.

SENATE SMALL BUSINESS AND ENTREPRENEURSHIP

Chairwoman Mary Landrieu, D-La. and Ranking Member Olympia Snowe, R-Maine, continue to lead the Committee on Small Business and Entrepreneurship in a spirit of bi-partisanship as they look out for the interests of small business owners, who employ approximately 50% of the nation's workforce. Among their shared objectives in the 112th Congress are eliminating waste and inefficiency in Small Business Administration (SBA) programs, reducing the regulatory burden on small businesses, and promoting technological innovation.

Landrieu and Snowe joined seven other senators in introducing legislation to reauthorize the SBA's Small Business Innovation and Research (SBIR) and Small Business Technology Transfer (STTR) programs for eight years. A version of the bill passed the Senate unanimously in the 111th Congress. Through the SBIR and STTR programs, the government partners with small businesses to help them develop technology that can then be used by government agencies.

Landrieu also introduced the Small Business Broadband and Emerging Information Technology Enhancement Act of 2011, a bill that calls on the SBA to help small businesses access broadband and other advanced technologies by creating a new broadband and emerging IT coordinator.

The Government Accountability Office has issued a series of reports detailing waste and abuse in the SBA's Section 8(a), historically underutilized business zone and service-disabled veteran-owned small business lending programs. Landrieu and Snowe have asked the agency to provide a plan to rectify these problems, and the committee is following up on that request in 2011.

The committee's SBA oversight also includes identifying areas of waste and duplication in its programs. Other agencies have programs that overlap with the SBA, and the committee is doing a government-wide search to find out which are working best, with the goal of eliminating duplicative efforts. The committee also is helping the SBA streamline its operations in order to reduce administrative and overhead costs.

Reducing the regulatory burden on small businesses has been a goal of the committee for many years. In 2011, the effort includes trying to repeal the Form 1099 reporting requirement. In addition, Snowe has asked her staff to work to ensure the implementation of a provision that was included in the Small Business Jobs Act of 2010 requiring the Congressional Budget Office to provide a job impact statement on the potential small business job creation and job loss for every bill with an economic impact of $5 billion or more.

The committee's major success from the 111th Congress was passage of the Small Business Jobs Act. Among other things, the law increased SBA loan limits and called for the creation of an online lending platform, and it is the committee's job in 2011 to ensure that those provisions are implemented properly.

SENATE SMALL BUSINESS AND ENTREPRENEURSHIP

Caroline Bruckner

General Counsel

428A Russell Senate Office Bldg.

Phone: (202) 224-5175

Caroline_Bruckner@sbc.senate.gov

Personal: Born in Houston, Texas.

Education: LLM in taxation, Georgetown University Law Center, 2004. J.D., George Mason School of Law, 2003. B.A., Emory University, 1997.

Professional: 2004–2006, associate, Paul, Hastings, Janofsky & Walker LLP-Employment Law and Employee Benefits Group. 2006–2009, senior associate, PricewaterhouseCoopers, LLP-Washington National Tax Services-International Tax Services Group. 2009–present, general counsel, Cmte. on Small Business and Entrepreneurship.

Expertise: Tax, labor and budget issues.

General Counsel Caroline Bruckner came to the Small Business Committee in 2009 from PricewaterhouseCoopers, where she served as counsel in the firm's Washington National Tax Services unit. At PwC, taxation issues, international contract manufacturing arrangements, and Internal Revenue Service-related issues were among her many responsibilities.

Her tax background, which includes a Master of Tax Laws degree from the Georgetown University Law Center, is an asset in 2011 as Chairwoman Mary Landrieu, D-La., pursues a number of tax-related priorities.

Landrieu wants to extend certain tax provisions of the Small Business Jobs Act of 2010. The committee is working to extend the 100 percent capital gains exclusion for investments in certain small businesses for one year, and the deduction of health care costs for payroll tax purposes for the self-employed for one year. The effort also includes extending the increased deduction for start-ups.

The committee also will work on Landrieu's goal of repealing the Form 1099 reporting requirement for small businesses. In late January, she co-introduced legislation with Senate Finance Committee Chairman Max Baucus, D-Mont., to repeal the requirement, which is set to take effect in January 2012. The bill would keep the current reporting requirement in place.

The health care reform legislation passed in 2010 includes this new requirement, and Landrieu feels it is too burdensome for small businesses, which already face many regulatory hurdles that interfere with their day-to-day operations. She also tried to repeal the Form 1099 requirement in the 111th Congress.

Bruckner said she also will help Landrieu try to provide broader regulatory relief for small businesses, which employ approximately 50 percent of the U.S. workforce. Landrieu believes that at a time when job creation is critical, small businesses cannot be over-burdened with regulatory red tape.

A report published by the Small Business Administration's Office of Advocacy found that in 2008 the total annual cost of federal regulations in the U.S. increased to more than $1.75 trillion. Small businesses with fewer than 20 employees incur regulatory costs 42 percent greater than firms with between 20 and 499 employees, and 36 percent greater than firms with more than 500 employees. Bruckner and her colleagues are working to correct that imbalance in the 112th Congress.

Krystal Brumfield

Tax Counsel

428A Russell Senate Office Bldg.

Phone: (202) 224-5175

Krystal_Brumfield@sbc.senate.gov

Personal: Born 1982 in Hammond, La.

Education: LLM in taxation, University of Florida Frederic G. Levin College of Law, 2008. J.D., Southern University Law Center, 2007. B.S. in accounting, Southern University and Agricultural and Mechanical College at Baton Rouge, 2004.

Professional: 2008–2009, attorney, Louisiana Department of Revenue. 2009–present, tax counsel, Cmte. on Small Business and Entrepreneurship.

Expertise: Tax law.

Hammond, Louisiana, native Krystal Brumfield moved to Washington, DC, in 2009 to serve as an advisor to Small Business Committee Chairwoman Mary Landrieu, D-La., on tax issues and on the Small Business Administration's (SBA) business development programs.

Brumfield said her top priority in 2011 is to cut down on fraud, waste, and abuse in several SBA programs and look for ways to improve them.

These programs include the Historically Underutilized Business Zones or HUBZones, the 8(a) program, named for Section 8(a) of the Small Business Act, that aims to help small companies owned by socially and economically disadvantaged persons, as well as programs designed to help small businesses owned by women and service-disabled veterans.

Brumfield also will work on the committee's investigation of whether to change to the preference provided to Alaska native corporations in the SBA's 8(a) program. Alaska native corporations receive a "super preference" over other participants in the program, she said, and legislation to eliminate it has been introduced and referred to the committee. Brumfield is helping to determine what, if any, changes are needed.

During the 111th Congress, Brumfield assisted with the committee's work on the Small Business Jobs Act of 2010. She said that most of law's provisions came out of the committee, including the economic development programs, the exporting and trade provisions, and the contracting parity provisions.

The parity provisions were developed out of a bill co-sponsored by Landrieu and Senator Richard Durbin, D-Ill. They give small businesses participating in any of the SBA's preference programs an equal chance to win federal contracts.

Misinterpretation of a court ruling and Government Accountability Office reports created a situation where small businesses in the HUBZone program were being given a priority over firms participating in other SBA programs in the awarding of federal contracts. Landrieu helped to develop the piece of the Small Business Jobs Act designed to change that practice, and in the 112th Congress, Brumfield is working to ensure that all federal agencies implement the new contracting provisions.

Brumfield holds a master of law degree in taxation from the University of Florida. After earning that degree she worked at the Louisiana Department of Revenue for one year before joining the Small Business Committee staff.

SENATE SMALL BUSINESS AND ENTREPRENEURSHIP

Richard Carbo

Democratic Press Secretary

428A Russell Senate Office Bldg.

Phone: (202) 224-5175

Richard_Carbo@sbc.senate.gov

Personal: Born in Alexandria, La.

Education: B.A. in communications, Louisiana State University and Agricultural and Mechanical College, 2006.

Professional: 2008, communications director, Don Cravins Jr. for Congress. 2008, deputy finance director, Kopplin for Congress. 2009–present, Democratic press secretary, Senate Cmte. on Small Business and Entrepreneurship.

Expertise: Communications.

Richard Carbo is in his third year as Democratic press secretary for the committee. As the Majority staff's liaison with the press, he writes many of the releases and communications the committee puts out on behalf of committee Chairwoman Mary Landrieu, D-La.

Carbo studied communications at Louisiana State University, and then sharpened his skills prior to joining the committee by working as communications director for Don Cravins, Jr. in his bid for the House seat in Louisiana's 7th Congressional District.

Cravins lost that race, and following the campaign, Cravins and Carbo moved to Washington to work for Landrieu on the Small Business Committee. Cravins now works as the Democratic staff director for the committee.

As press secretary, Carbo helps to shape the message that the committee puts forth on Landrieu's many initiatives on behalf of the nation's small businesses. In 2011, Carbo will work to get the word out on priority to reauthorize the Small Business Innovation and Research and Small Business Technology Transfer programs.

The committee believes that the reauthorizing legislation has a good chance to make it to the Senate floor in 2011. It would be the second committee-generated bill to make it to a vote in as many years following 2010's enactment of the Small Business Jobs Act.

Oversight of the implementation of that law's provisions is a committee priority, and Carbo is keeping the press and the public informed of the progress. The law provided that the Small Business Administration (SBA) must implement the SBA-specific provisions of the Act in 2011.

Carbo is working to ensure that Landrieu's work to provide adequate access to capital for small businesses is being communicated to interested parties. Likewise, he is trying to keep small businesses aware that Landrieu is their advocate on the issue of securing government contracts.

In her view, contracts that go to small businesses lead to immediate job creation, whereas larger companies that win contracts absorb the work with their existing staff. Nearly 25 percent of government contracts are supposed to go to small businesses each year.

Carbo is a native of Alexandria, Louisiana. Early in 2008, prior to joining Cravins' campaign, he assisted Andy Kopplin in his bid for the Congressional seat in Louisiana's 6th District.

SENATE SMALL BUSINESS AND ENTREPRENEURSHIP

Donald Cravins

Democratic Staff Director

428-A Russell Senate Office Bldg.

Phone: (202) 224-5175

Donald_Cravins@small-bus.senate.gov

Personal: Born 1972 in Houston, Texas.

Education: B.A., Louisiana State University, 1994. J.D., Southern University Law Center, 1998.

Professional: 1998, deputy campaign manager, Sen. John Breaux, D-La. 1998–2000, associate attorney, McGlinchey Stafford APLC. 2000–2003, associate attorney, Domengeaux Wright Roy & Edwards, LLC. 2004–2006, state representative, State of Louisiana. 2006–2009, state senator, State of Louisiana. 2009–present, Democratic staff director, Senate Cmte. on Small Business and Entrepreneurship.

Expertise: Insurance issues, Small business issues.

Former Louisiana state Sen. Don Cravins is helping Chairwoman Mary Landrieu, D-La., carry out her legislative agenda, and in 2011 that involves ensuring that the Small Business Jobs Act of 2010 is being implemented properly.

Cravins said that one-third of the Act is focused on the Small Business Administration (SBA), and that piece of the legislation was developed by the committee. In 2011, the staff working to ensure that the SBA implements the law's provisions.

The committee also is continuing its general oversight of the SBA. Cravins said that other agencies have business development programs that overlap with the SBA's, and Sen. Landrieu has asked the staff to do a government-wide search to find out which ones are working best and where, with the goal of eliminating duplicative and wasteful programs.

There is a renewed focus on innovation and technology in the committee in the 112th Congress, which Cravins said includes trying to reauthorize the Small Business Innovation and Research (SBIR) and Small Business Technology Transfer (STTR) programs. The programs provide funding to small high-tech businesses to develop technology that then can be used by the government.

Cravins believes that legislation on SBIR and STTR could make it to the Senate floor in 2011 because the mood on Capitol Hill is that innovation is something on which everyone can agree.

In addition to the Small Business Jobs Act, the committee counts among its 111th Congress successes the American Reinvestment and Recovery Act. The law included committee-developed provisions to eliminate fees on SBA-backed loans, which caused SBA lending to reach all-time highs.

When not on Capitol Hill, Cravins teaches intellectual property in the Master's paralegal studies program at George Washington University. He is the father of three children, including a daughter born early in 2011.

SENATE SMALL BUSINESS AND ENTREPRENEURSHIP

David Gillers

Counsel

428A Russell Senate Office Bldg.

Phone: (202) 224-5175

David_Gillers@sbc.senate.gov

Personal: Born 1976 in Tucson, Ariz.

Education: J.D., Boston College Law School, 2006. B.A. in English, Columbia University in the City of New York, 2000.

Professional: 2006–2009, associate, Goulston & Storrs. 2009–2010, counsel, House Cmte. on Financial Services, Domestic Monetary Policy and Technology Subcommittee. 2010–present, counsel, Senate Cmte. on Small Business and Entrepreneurship. 2010–present, counsel, Office of Sen. Mary Landrieu, D-La.

Expertise: Banking, small business lending, commercial real estate finance, Monetary policy.

David Gillers is counsel for banking and lending issues on the Small Business Committee and in Chairwoman Mary Landrieu's, D-La., personal office. He was a member of the committee team that produced the Small Business Jobs Act of 2010. Gillers helped to negotiate the lending provisions that went into the legislation.

In 2011, Gillers is helping to examine the challenges faced by minority-owned businesses trying to get venture and other forms of capital funding. The committee is looking into ways to strengthen the Small Business Administration's Section 8(a) contracting program, which helps to promote minority entrepreneurship.

Gillers also is participating in the oversight of the implementation of certain provisions of the Dodd-Frank Wall Street Reform and Consumer Protection Act. In particular, the committee is trying to ensure that the federal banking agencies, the Secretary of Housing and Urban Development, and the Director of the Federal Housing Finance Agency adhere to the legislative intent of the qualified residential mortgage (QRM) provisions.

There have been efforts to impose a high down payment requirement for any mortgage to meet the QRM exemption standard, and Landrieu feels that would have a disproportionately negative effect on small lenders. Gillers is helping her deliver the message that the QRM framework specifically allows for the inclusion of low-down payment loans, provided they have mortgage insurance or other forms of credit enhancement, to the extent that the insurance or credit enhancement reduces the risk of default.

Gillers brings prior real estate financing experience to his work on this issue. As a corporate attorney in Goulston & Storrs' Boston office, he worked on commercial real estate financings and acquisitions. He assisted a real estate investment trust in its acquisition and financing of a $7 billion piece of the $36 billion Blackstone/Equity Office buyout, which at the time was the largest buyout ever.

Gillers worked on the House Financial Services Domestic Monetary Policy Subcommittee before joining the Small Business Committee in 2009. Prior to his congressional work, he volunteered for the Obama presidential campaign.

Gillers is a graduate of Columbia College, and received his J.D. from Boston College Law School where he was a Weinstein Scholar.

SENATE SMALL BUSINESS AND ENTREPRENEURSHIP

Wallace Hsueh

Republican Staff Director

428-A Russell Senate Office Bldg.

Phone: (202) 224-5175

Wally_Hsueh@sbc.senate.gov

Personal: Born 1971 in Los Angeles, Calif.

Education: B.A., California State University, Long Beach, 1993.

Professional: 1995–1996, professional staff member, House Government Reform Oversight Cmte. 1997–2004, legislative assistant and senior policy advisor, Office of Sen. Gordon Smith, (R-Ore.). 2005–2006, staff director, Senate Cmte. on Commerce, Subcommittee on Trade, Tourism and Economic Development. 2007–present, Republican staff director, Cmte. on Small Business and Entrepreneurship.

Expertise: Commerce, small business issues, intellectual property, economic development.

In the 112th Congress, the Small Business Committee gained five new Republican members, so Minority staff director Wally Hsueh said the committee is very active with energetic new Senators looking for opportunities to help small businesses succeed. The top issues on the agenda of Ranking Member Olympia Snowe, R-Maine, include small business health reform, ensuring small business access to capital, and a budget deficit overhaul.

Hsueh said he is also overseeing the Republican staff's work on reducing small business regulatory burdens and maximizing small business opportunities in federal contracting. Snowe also seeks to reauthorize and improve the Small Business Administration's (SBA) entrepreneurial development programs, and to reauthorize the Small Business Innovation and Research (SBIR) and Small Business Technology Transfer (SBTT) programs.

In the area of health care, the committee works to address health care issues affecting small business that were not addressed in the Patient Protection and Affordable Care Act (PPACA). They will also examine provisions of the PPACA that cause uncertainty and can negatively impact small business job creation, Hsueh said.

Oversight duties in 2011 include monitoring the effective implementation of the Small Business Jobs Act, including increased SBA loan limits and the creation of an online lending platform. The staff will also work to ensure that there is rigorous oversight of the newly created Small Business Lending Fund, the small business provisions from the Dodd-Frank Wall Street Reform and Consumer Protection Act, and the SBA's lending programs.

During the 111th Congress, Hsueh and his colleagues did extensive work on the stimulus bill, the Small Business Jobs Act and the Dodd-Frank Act. They also helped to make significant progress toward reauthorizing the SBIR and STTR programs.

SENATE SMALL BUSINESS AND ENTREPRENEURSHIP

Christopher Lucas

Counsel

428-A Russell Senate Office Bldg.

Phone: (202) 244-5175

Fax: (202) 224-5619

Christopher_Lucas@sbc.senate.gov

Personal: Born 09/18/1980 in New York, N.Y.

Education: B.A., University of Rochester, 2002. J.D., Brooklyn Law School, 2007.

Professional: 2001–2002, assistant finance director, Congressman Tom Reynolds, R-NY. 2003–2004, legislative assistant, Monroe County, NY Legislature. 2008–2009, research analyst, Senate Cmte. on Small Business and Entrepreneurship. 2009–present, counsel, Senate Cmte. on Small Business and Entrepreneurship.

Expertise: Small business lending and banking issues.

Chris Lucas is in his third year with the committee, and in 2010 began to cover banking issues for Ranking Member Olympia Snowe, R-Maine. In that role in 2011, his top issue is lender oversight legislation.

Senator Snowe introduced lender oversight legislation in the 110th Congress, and Lucas said the current draft of the bill follows the senator's previous work on the issue. Among other things, the earlier bill sought to require borrowers under the Small Business Administration's (SBA) 7(a) and 504 loan programs to report on their economic performance, and to create a 7(a) and 504 portfolio default rate that can be compared directly to commercial lenders' default rates.

A second priority for Lucas in the 112th Congress is trying to pass a comprehensive reauthorization of the SBA's access to capital programs. He said a reauthorization is giving Congress the opportunity to examine the SBA's entire access to the capital program roster to ensure that all its programs are cost-effective and not duplicative.

Lucas also is examining the impact of the Dodd-Frank Wall Street Reform and Consumer Protection Act of 2010 on small banks and small businesses. The committee wants to ensure that the bill does not harm the ability of banks to lend to small businesses and does not raise regulatory compliance costs for small banks, he said.

In 2010, Lucas worked extensively on increasing access to capital for small businesses through the SBA loan programs. He noted that Senator Snowe did not support final passage of the Small Business Jobs Act of 2010 because of the inclusion of the small business lending fund, but made a major contribution to the SBA lending provisions of the law.

In particular, all of the key provisions of Snowe's Next Step for Main Street Credit Act of 2009 were included in the legislation. These included larger 7(a), 504 and microloan sizes and an online lender platform for 7(a) loans. Snowe also was responsible for a provision that extended fee relief for SBA loans until the end of 2010, which was credited with leading to the largest spike in SBA lending history, he said.

On banking issues, Lucas helped Senator Snowe with several amendments to the Dodd-Frank bill to reduce intrusive reporting requirements for community banks. The amendments also removed small businesses that do not supply credit from the Consumer Financial Protection Bureau and gave seasonal businesses continued access to credit.

SENATE SMALL BUSINESS AND ENTREPRENEURSHIP

Cheryl Miller

Deputy Staff Director for Technology and Innovation

428A Russell Senate Office Bldg.

Phone: (202) 224-5175

Cheryl_Miller@sbc.senate.gov

Education: LL.M in intellectual property law, George Washington University Law School, 2010. J.D., The Catholic University of America, Columbis School of Law, 2005. B.A. in English, Georgetown University, 2000.

Professional: 2000–2002, legislative assistant, Sun Microsystems, Inc. 2004, legal intern, U.S. Department of Justice. 2004, summer associate, Kalik Lewin, LLP. 2005, law clerk, Senate Judiciary Cmte. 2006–2007, manager, regulatory affairs, France Telecom, North America. 2006, associate, regulatory affairs, France Telecom, North America. 2007–present, professor of intellectual property law, George Washington University. 2007–2010, assistant chief counsel for telecommunications and technology, U.S. Small Business Administration, Office of Advocacy. 2010–present, deputy staff director for technology and innovation, Senate Cmte. on Small Business and Entrepreneurship.

Expertise: Technology issues, Intellectual property issues, telecommunications law.

Making broadband Internet more accessible to small businesses is an important agenda item in 2011 for committee Chairwoman Mary Landrieu, D-La., and Cheryl Miller is working to help her accomplish that goal. As deputy staff director for technology and innovation, Miller is a key advisor on the Small Business Broadband and Emerging Information Technology Enhancement Act of 2011, which was co-introduced by Landrieu and former committee chairman John Kerry, D-Mass.

This bill calls on the Small Business Administration (SBA) to help small businesses access broadband and other advanced technologies by creating a new broadband and emerging IT coordinator. The coordinator would help develop small business broadband initiatives within the SBA and act as a liaison with other agencies.

Miller will work on this legislation, which would require small business development centers and other SBA partners to provide technical assistance related to accessing and using broadband and emerging technology. Landrieu believes broadband access will enable small businesses to reach a huge pool of customers located outside the United States.

Miller also is working in the 112th Congress to reauthorize the SBA's Small Business Innovation and Research (SBIR) and Small Business Technology Transfer (STTR) programs. Through the programs, the government partners with small businesses to help them develop innovative technology that can then be used by government agencies.

The last full reauthorization of the SBIR program occurred in 2000, when it was reauthorized for eight years. It has received many temporary extensions since October 2008. The STTR was last reauthorized in 2001, also for eight years.

The SBA's programs are very familiar to Miller who served as assistant chief counsel for telecommunications and technology in the SBA's Office of Advocacy from 2007 to 2010. Prior to that, Miller worked in the regulatory affairs unit of France Telecom North America where she focused on satellite, wireless, wire line, international telecommunications and competition issues.

Miller holds a Master of Law degree in intellectual property from George Washington University. Since 2007, she has been a professor of intellectual property law in that school's Master's paralegal studies program.

SENATE SMALL BUSINESS AND ENTREPRENEURSHIP

Matthew Walker

Deputy Republican Staff Director and Counsel

428-A Russell Senate Office Bldg.

Phone: (202) 224-7884

Fax: (202) 224-9746

Matt_Walker@sbc.senate.gov

Personal: Born 05/04/1972 in Bangor, Maine.

Education: B.A., University of Maine. J.D., Maine School of Law.

Professional: 1990–present, reservist, Army National Guard. 1995, Washington representative, Coalition for Fair Atlantic Salmon Trade. 1995–2000, staff member, Sen. Olympia J. Snowe, R-Maine. 1999, legal intern, Bath, Maine, District Attorney's Office. 2000, consultant, Government Affairs. 2000, associate, Pierce Atwood. 2001–2003, attorney, Pierce Atwood. 2003–2006, oversight counsel, Senate Cmte. on Small Business and Entrepreneurship. 2006–2007, liaison officer, Operation Enduring Freedom (Afghanistan). 2007–present, deputy Republican staff director and counsel, Senate Cmte. on Small Business and Entrepreneurship.

Expertise: Small Business Administration, small business issues, manufacturing and trade, SBA lending, economic development, veteran entrepreneurship.

Matt Walker, Republican deputy staff director and counsel, helps formulate and implement the Small Business Committee's agenda and oversees the work of the committee's staff. Walker has over 12 years of Senate experience.

He is also a veteran whose service included a 15-month deployment in support of Operation Enduring Freedom (Afghanistan). While deployed, he was the U.S. Liaison Officer to the South Korean and Polish contingents and the project manager of those countries' construction operations.

In 2011, Walker and the Small Business Committee will focus on a broad array of economic growth measures for America's small businesses. The committee will work on tax and regulatory reform; assisting small businesses with trade; and ensuring that entrepreneurs have access to credit. Walker said the committee also will continue its oversight of the Small Business Administration (SBA) to help make certain that it is cost efficient and runs effectively.

Ranking Republican Senator Olympia Snowe of Maine has introduced and co-sponsored legislation to improve access to trade loans and counseling programs for small exporters and to improve inter-agency coordination of existing federal export assistance resources. Some of these provisions were included in the Small Business Jobs Act of 2010.

In the area of regulatory reform, Snowe intends to continue her efforts to require the Congressional Budget Office to estimate in a "job impact statement" the potential job creation or job loss attributable to each bill or joint resolution reported by a Congressional committee that exceeds $5 billion in costs.

Many of the legislative items Walker worked on in 2010 were signed into law. The Small Business Jobs Act of 2010 includes numerous provisions that Walker helped to craft and negotiate into the bill. In particular, he worked on provisions to increase SBA loan limits, enhance small business trade, and provide small businesses greater access to federal contracting opportunities.

SENATE SMALL BUSINESS AND ENTREPRENEURSHIP

Meredith West

Professional Staff Member
428A Russell Senate Office Bldg.
Phone: (202) 224-7884
Meredith_West@sbc.senate.gov

Personal: Born 1979 in Baton Rouge, La.

Education: B.A. in political science, Rhodes College, 2001.

Professional: 2001–2002, legislative correspondent, Office of Sen. Fred Thompson, R-Tenn. 2002–2003, legislative aide, Office of Sen. Fred Thompson, R-Tenn. 2003–2007, legislative assistant, Office of Senate Majority Leader William H. Frist, M.D., R-Tenn. 2006, senior policy advisor, Bob Corker for U.S. Senate. 2007–2008, senior advisor to the administrator, U.S. Small Business Administration. 2007, assistant director of congressional and legislative affairs, U.S. Small Business Administration. 2008–2009, assistant administrator for policy and strategic planning, U.S. Small Business Administration. 2009–present, professional staff member, Cmte. on Small Business and Entrepreneurship.

Expertise: Trade policy, SBA issues, government reform, economic policy, education policy, budget and appropriations.

Meredith West worked at the Small Business Administration (SBA) for several years before joining the committee in 2009 and she is putting that experience to good use in 2011. Her boss, Ranking Member Olympia Snowe, R-Maine, has asked West to lead the staff's examination of the status and effectiveness of each SBA program to identify areas of inefficiency and duplication.

West said she will work on the committee's focus on how the SBA can streamline its operations in order to reduce administrative and overhead costs, including carefully analyzing the SBA's budget and performance reports.

Reducing the small business regulatory burden is high on West's agenda in the 112th Congress. The staff is trying to ensure the implementation of a provision that was included in the Small Business Jobs Act requiring the Congressional Budget Office to provide a job impact statement on the potential small business job creation and job loss for every bill that would have an economic impact of $5 billion or more.

Snowe also has asked the committee to work toward instituting small business advocacy review panels at every federal agency. West worked for the Dodd-Frank Wall Street Reform and the Consumer Protection Act to include a provision that requires the new Consumer Financial Protection Bureau to convene a small business advocacy review panel to scrutinize a new rule before it can be published.

The Small Business Act has been operating under a series of short term extensions, and West and the staff will work towards a full reauthorization of the programs in the 112th Congress.

In 2010, West assisted with provisions of the Small Business Export Enhancement and International Trade Act of 2010, which were included in the Small Business Jobs Act and improved export opportunities for small businesses. The Small Business Jobs Act also included an additional $50 million in funding in place for small business development as a result of West's work.

Upon learning that many women's business centers had to accept less federal funding because they were not able to raise matching funds, West worked with the majority staff to craft a proposal to provide temporary waiver authority to help the centers receive their full grants. The provision was included in the Small Business Jobs Act and helps struggling non-profits avoid layoffs and service disruption to women's business clients, while protecting the crucial matching component.

SENATE SMALL BUSINESS AND ENTREPRENEURSHIP

Kevin Wheeler

Democratic Deputy Staff Director

428-A Russell Senate Office Bldg.

Phone: (202) 224-8496

Kevin_Wheeler@sbc.senate.gov

Personal: Born in Houston, Texas.

Education: B.A., University of Houston, 1989.

Professional: 1990–1993, research assistant and legislative correspondent, Sen. Lloyd Bentsen, D-Texas. 1993, junior legislative assistant, Sen. Bob Krueger, D-Texas. 1994, policy advisor and research staff, gubernatorial campaign of Bill Curry, D-Texas. 1995–1998, reporter and assistant editor, *Business New Haven*. 1998–2005, professional staff member, Senate Cmte. on Small Business and Entrepreneurship. 2005–present, Democratic deputy staff director, Senate Cmte. on Small Business and Entrepreneurship.

Expertise: Small business issues.

Kevin Wheeler joined the committee in 1998 and has earned a reputation as a tireless behind-the-scenes advocate for small businesses. In 2008, the Small Business Technology Council named her SBIR Person of the Year for her work on trying to reauthorize the Small Business Administration's (SBA) Small Business Innovation and Research (SBIR) program.

That same year, the National Small Business Association selected her as one of its Small Business Stars, an award given to ten of the most influential, small-business friendly members of Congress, their staff, members of the Administration and the media.

Reauthorization of the SBIR and Small Business Technology Transfer (STTR) programs is on the table again in 2011. Wheeler is working on the initiative, which is supported by both Chairwoman Mary Landrieu, D-La., and Ranking Member Olympia Snowe, R-Maine. The Senate passed a reauthorization bill in 2010, but the House was unable to consider the legislation before the end of the 111th Congress.

Wheeler is also assisting with efforts to reauthorize other key SBA entrepreneurial development programs. Landrieu has asked the staff to examine closely the effectiveness of each program, considering areas of duplication within the SBA and with other government programs. The committee's goal is to streamline the programs at the same time they are renewed.

Early in the 112th Congress, the Administration launched its Startup America Initiative, which has the strong support of Landrieu. Wheeler and other committee staff are promoting the program, whose goals include expanding access to capital for high-growth startups and expanding entrepreneurship, education, and mentoring programs.

The initiative also seeks to strengthen commercialization of the $148 billion in annual federally-funded research and development to generate startups and new jobs.

Committee on Veterans' Affairs

412 Russell Senate Office Bldg.
Washington, DC 20510
Phone: (202) 224-9126
Fax: (202) 224-8908
http://veterans.senate.gov

Ratio: 7/7/1

MAJORITY MEMBERS

Patty Murray, WA, Chairman

John D. Rockefeller IV, WV
Daniel K. Akaka, HI, Ex Officio
Sherrod Brown, OH
Jim Webb, VA
Jon Tester, MT
Mark Begich, AR

MINORITY MEMBERS

Richard Burr, NC, Ranking Member

Johnny Isakson, GA
Roger F. Wicker, MS
Mike Johanns, NE
Scott Brown, MA
Jerry Moran, KS
John Boozman, AR

INDEPENDENT MEMBERS

Bernard Sanders, VT

SENATE VETERANS' AFFAIRS

JURISDICTION

(1) Compensation of veterans; life insurance issued by the government on account of service in the Armed Forces.
(2) National cemeteries.
(3) Pensions of all wars of the United States, general and special.
(4) Readjustment of servicemen to civil life.
(5) Soldiers' and sailors' civil relief.
(6) Veterans' hospitals, medical care, and treatment of veterans.
(7) Veterans' measures generally.
(8) Vocational rehabilitation and education of veterans.

SENATE VETERANS' AFFAIRS

Sen. Patty Murray, D-Wash., made history at the start of the 112th Congress when she was named the first woman to ever chair the Senate Committee on Veterans' Affairs. In her historic role, Murray is tasked with conducting oversight of the Department of Veterans Affairs, passing legislation designed to improve the lives of veterans and just keeping an eye on how the nation's 22 million veterans are doing.

Murray appeared to be the obvious choice for the position, having served on the committee since 1995 and making veterans' issues one of her top legislative priorities as a senator. (Her merely being on the committee was a historic first; no other woman had ever done so.) When talking about veterans' issues, Murray often speaks from personal experience, as her father used a wheelchair most of his life after being wounded in World War II.

Early on in her tenure, Murray appeared to be tough in her oversight duties. In March, she questioned VA Secretary Eric Shinseki regarding his decision to limit a benefit provided to caregivers of veterans from the wars in Iraq and Afghanistan. A stipend for people who quit their jobs to care for injured loved ones full time, the benefit was approved by Congress during the 111th session. Eligibility rules for the stipend are too strict and include too many bureaucratic hurdles, making it tough for folks who need it to receive it, Murray argued.

Murray had the backing of the committee's Republican ranking member, Sen. Richard Burr, R-N.C., in this effort, as well as their counterparts in the House. Both committees sent President Barack Obama a letter urging him to act on the issue. "This legislation was originally designed to provide a path forward for caregivers who are already sacrificing their own aspirations in order to make the lives of severely wounded veterans easier to bear," Burr said in a statement. "I urge the President to work with VA to get this bill right."

There won't be a shortage of other issues for the committee to tackle during the rest of congressional session. Although Obama's budget proposal included a small increase in funds for the VA, the challenging fiscal climate guaranteed Members will have to take a serious look at which veterans programs receive federal funding.

SENATE VETERANS' AFFAIRS

Bill Brew

Staff Director

412 Russell Senate Office Bldg.

Phone: (202) 224-9126

Fax: (202) 224-9575

bill_brew@vetaff.senate.gov

Personal: Born 10/14/1945 in Washington, D.C.

Education: B.B.A, Notre Dame, 1967. J.D., Catholic University, 1976.

Professional: 1978–1997, Senate Cmte. on Veterans' Affairs. 2001–2002, staff director, Senate Cmte. on Veterans' Affairs. 2002–2003, counselor, President's Task Force to Improve Health Care Delivery for Our Nation's Veterans. 2003–2004, staff, CARES Commission. 2004–2006, consultant, various clients (principal focus on VA issues). 2006–present, staff director, Senate Cmte. on Veterans' Affairs.

Expertise: Veterans' issues.

The Senate Committee on Veterans' Affairs saw significant leadership changes at the start of the 112th Congress, when Chairman Daniel Akaka, D-Hawaii, left the panel for another committee post. But with committee staff director Bill Brew at the helm, new Chairwoman Patty Murray, D-Wash., likely can take comfort in knowing she'll be brought quickly up to speed.

If there ever was a staffer with vast institutional knowledge, it's Brew. The Arlington, Va., native has been with the Veterans Affairs committee on and off for decades, having first joined in 1978. He retired in 1997, but returned in 2001 when the Democrats took control of the Senate. Brew left again in 2002 when Republicans took back the chamber, but he didn't stay away for too long. Brew rejoined the Senate's staffer ranks in 2006 at the bequest of Akaka, who asked him to be staff director.

With nearly 30 years of experience behind him, Brew has worked on an eclectic mix of issues during his Senate tenure. In the 111th Congress, Brew tackled care legislation that is designed to ensure that the cost of war is not unfairly paid by families whose loved ones were injured in service to the nation. He also worked on legislation to address problems in the veterans' benefits system and to create necessary new benefits. Brew also engaged in the committee work on backlog, including a claims processing bill reported by the committee.

Brew should stay busy in the 112th Congress as well, considering the focus that has been placed on veterans' issues. In a time of budget cuts, President Barack Obama's budget request included a $2.7 billion increase for health care programs at the Department of Veterans Affairs, for example.

"The truth of it is, working on these issues just seems to be what I was supposed to do," Brew told Politico in 2007.

SENATE VETERANS' AFFAIRS

Kim Lipsky

Deputy Staff Director

412 Russell Senate Office Bldg.

Phone: (202) 224-9126

Fax: (202) 224-9575

kim_lipsky@vetaff.senate.gov

Personal: Born 07/13/1969 in Miami Beach, Fla.

Education: B.S., public relations, University of Florida, 1991. M.A., public administration, George Washington University, 1993.

Professional: 1993–1994, legislative aide, Senate Cmte. on Veterans' Affairs. 1994–1995, staff asst., Alliance for Helath Reform. 1995–1997, consultant, Birch & Davis Health Management Corporation. 1997–2003, professional staff member, Senate Cmte. on Veterans' Affairs. 2003–present, deputy staff director, Senate Cmte. on Veterans' Affairs.

Expertise: Health.

With more than a decade of experience at the Senate Committee on Veterans' Affairs, Kim Lipsky has worked on a slew of issues designed to help military veterans and their families. In 2010, she was recognized for her years of work when the Washington-based group The Military Coalition honored her with its "Freedom Award."

Lipsky and her fellow Capitol Hill staffers "expend huge amounts of effort in crafting the legislation, working with the military associations to fill in the details, and coordinating our mutual efforts to get other legislators and the public on board," group president Michael Cline said in a statement. Cline, who is also the executive director of the Enlisted Association of the National Guard of the United States, noted that Lipsky's work on wounded warrior caregiver legislation was particularly impressive.

As the No. 2 Democratic staffer on the panel, Lipsky helps oversee many of the issues analyzed by committee members during the congressional session. In the 111th Congress, Lipsky joined fellow panel staffers in working on caregiver legislation designed to help families whose loved ones were injured during their military service. She also oversaw legislation for veterans' health care and worked on the committee's administrative backlog.

Lipsky likely will stay busy in the 112th Congress, considering her expertise is health care. When Sen. Patty Murray, D-Wash., was named the committee's chairwoman in January 2011, she said ensuring veterans have access to health benefits will be among her top priorities.

SENATE VETERANS' AFFAIRS

Dahlia Melendrez

Chief Benefits Counsel

412 Russell Senate Office Bldg.

Phone: (202) 224-9126

Fax: (202) 224-9575

dahlia_melendrez@vetaff.senate.gov

Personal: Born 09/13/1974 in San Leandro, Calif.

Education: B.A., University of San Francisco, 1996. J.D., Catholic University of America, 2002.

Professional: 1997–1998, staff asst., National Hispanic Scholarship Fund. 2002–2003, Democratic counsel, Senate Cmte. on Veterans' Affairs. 2003–2004, senior legislative asst., Rep. Corrine Brown, D-Fla. 2005–present, Democratic counsel, Senate Cmte. on Veterans' Affairs.

Expertise: Compensation, pension, insurance, housing, military exposures.

Dahlia Melendrez has spent much of the past decade with the Senate Committee on Veterans' Affairs, working alongside past Chairman Daniel Akaka, D-Hawaii, and new Chairwoman Patty Murray, D-Wash., on a wide range of issues.

In the 111th Congress, Melendrez was among the staffers who assisted on caregiver legislation designed to help families whose loved ones were injured in military service. She also worked on legislation to address problems in the veterans' benefits system and to create necessary new benefits, and tackled committee work on backlog, including a claims processing bill reported by the panel.

In June 2010, Melendrez joined Republican committee staffer Amanda Meredith on a trip to Fort Carson, Colo. The two staffers visited Army base Fort Carson to be briefed on the status of a Disability Evaluation System pilot program, which is designed to evaluate whether service members who are wounded or suffer an illness should remain in the Army or transition to civilian life. Creators of the new program hope it will make the evaluation process easier in part by eliminating duplicative practices by the Department of Defense and Department of Veterans Affairs, according to an Army press release.

For Melendrez, who also worked on veterans' issues as a staffer to Rep. Corrine Brown, D-Fla., serving the committee is not just a job. Two members of her family served in Iraq, and in the past complained to her about the lack of supplies they received, including food, Melendrez told the newspaper *Stars and Stripes*.

Melendrez made sure to do something about it. While working for Brown, Melendrez helped her boss lead an effort to get necessary supplies to the troops, including everything from food to Interceptor flak vests, according to *Stars and Stripes*.

Amanda Meredith

General Counsel

825A Hart Senate Office Bldg.

Phone: (202) 224-2074

amanda_meredith@vetaff.senate.gov

Personal: Born 1972 in Binghamton, N.Y.

Education: B.S., accounting, State University of New York at Buffalo, 1994. J.D., State University of New York at Buffalo School of Law, 1997.

Professional: 1997–2000, judicial law clerk, Judge Kenneth Kramer, U.S. Court of Appeals for Veterans Claims. 2000–2004, executive attorney, Chief Judge Kenneth Kramer, U.S. Court of Appeals for Veterans Claims. 2004–2005, director, Task Force for Backlog Reduction, U.S. Court of Appeals for Veterans Claims. 2005–2007, benefits counsel, U.S. Senate Cmte. on Veterans' Affairs. 2007–present, general counsel, U.S. Senate Cmte. on Veterans' Affairs.

Expertise: Claims process, vocational rehabilitation, education.

While having a law background isn't unique on Capitol Hill, Amanda Meredith uses her legal expertise to help her boss, Senate Committee on Veterans' Affairs ranking member Richard Burr, R-N.C., find ways to help veterans with education, vocational and health benefits claims.

The New York native is an expert on veterans' claims issues, having worked in the U.S. Court of Appeals for Veterans Claims for nearly a decade. She's worked on a variety of veterans' claims issues during her time with the committee. She also helped out with the Post-9/11 Veterans' Educational Assistance Act, one of the first measures championed by Burr when he took leadership of the committee after former ranking member Sen. Larry Craig, R-Idaho, left the chamber.

In the 112th session, Meredith likely will work to pass a measure Burr introduced in March that is designed to help veterans receive faster decisions on their disability compensation claims. The bill lets vets who file "fully-developed claims" receive compensation for up to one year prior to the date the claim was filed, so the veteran will not lose any benefits while the VA is collecting evidence, which can often be a lengthy process.

Meredith joined the committee's counsel from the other side of the aisle, Democratic staffer Dahila Melendrez, on a visit to Fort Carson, Colo., in 2010 to study a disability evaluation system pilot program. The pair met with officials from Evans Army Community Hospital and received briefings on the status of the program at Fort Carson, according to a press release from the hospital's public affairs office.

Meredith also spoke on a panel alongside other congressional staffers during a veterans conference sponsored by the American Legion and others veterans groups held in Washington, D.C. in 2010.

SENATE VETERANS' AFFAIRS

Maureen O'Neill

Professional Staff Member

825 Hart Senate Office Bldg.

Phone: (202) 224-2074

maureen_oneill@vetaff.senate.gov

Personal: Born 1967 in Philadelphia, Pa.

Education: B.A. Political Science, Trinity College, 1990.

Professional: 1990–1997, legislative assistant, Nuclear Energy Institute. 1997–2007, budget analyst, Senate Budget Cmte. 2007–2010, legislative affairs representative, Parsons Brinckerhoff.

Expertise: Budget, appropriations.

After working several years as the legislative affairs representative with a construction management organization, Maureen O'Neill returned to her career roots in the Senate at the start of the 112th Congress. These days, O'Neill is offering up her knowledge of budget and appropriations matters to the Senate Committee on Veterans' Affairs.

O'Neill, who worked for the Senate Budget Committee for nearly 10 years before leaving for the private sector in 2007, will be charged with helping ranking member Richard Burr, R-N.C., find ways to help veterans while also managing a tough economic climate.

O'Neill can also lend expertise on a wide portfolio of other issues related to veterans' health and health benefits, including long-term care, health facilities, procurement and acquisitions, health care for spouses and family members, emergency preparedness, homelessness and women's issues, according to a committee spokesman.

The 112th session will certainly be busy for O'Neill. Burr and his colleagues must find a way to balance the needs of America's growing ranks of veterans from the wars in Afghanistan and Iraq with the movement to cut federal spending. Although President Barack Obama's fiscal year 2012 budget proposal included a small increase to the Department of Veterans' Affairs budget, all federal agencies were under enormous pressure in 2011 to tighten their purse strings.

O'Neill is likely to have some ideas how to achieve such a balance between helping vets and cutting spending. During her decade with the Senate Budget Committee, O'Neill served as the policy, budgetary, and appropriations advisor for a number of areas, including the Veterans Affairs, International Affairs and Social Security portions of the budget.

She also worked as an advisor to the chairman on State and Foreign Operations Appropriations Bill, the Iraq Emergency Supplemental Appropriations Bill and the Veterans Affairs and HUD Appropriations bills. During her time in the Senate, O'Neill also worked as an advisor to former budget Chairman Judd Gregg, R-N.H., and a budget analyst for ex-Sens. Don Nickles, R-Okla, and Pete Domenici, R-N.M., according to the veterans' affairs spokesman.

SENATE VETERANS' AFFAIRS

Marie Guadalupe (Lupe) Wissel

Staff Director

825A Hart Senate Office Bldg..

Phone: (202) 224-2074

lupe_wissel@vetaff.senate.gov

Personal: Born 01/30/1956 in Piedras Negras, Mexico.

Education: Boise State University.

Professional: 1978–1982, rehabilitation counselor, Idaho Division of Vocational Rehabilitation. 1978–1995, talk show host, KJCY Radio (Mountain Home, Idaho). 1982–1985, Spanish teacher, Children's House of Montessori. 1985–1999, assistant rehabilitation manager, Idaho Division of Vocational Rehabilitation. 1999–2001, state director, Idaho Commission on Aging. 2001–2005, staff director, Senate Special Cmte. on Aging. 2005–present, staff director, Senate Cmte. on Veterans' Affairs.

Expertise: Aging issues.

As staff director for Republicans on the Senate Committee on Veterans' Affairs, Lupe Wissel is charged with supporting Ranking Member Richard Burr, R-N.C., as he works to find ways to help American veterans.

An Idaho native, Wissel first came to the committee in 2005 when it was chaired by then-Sen. Larry Craig, R-Idaho. During her time with Craig, Wissel assisted the Senator as he worked to increase benefits to veterans, including through the Veterans Benefits, Healthcare and Information Technology Act, which former President George W. Bush signed into law in 2006.

Since Burr has taken the helm, he's continued to push for veterans' benefits. In the 111th Congress, Wissel assisted the senator on the Post-9/11 Veterans Educational Assistance Improvements Act, which was designed to improve the Post-9/11 GI Bill, and on the Veterans' Benefits Act of 2010.

Signed by President Barack Obama, the measure included several provisions Burr and his team spearheaded, including offering the highest level of "aid and attendance" benefits for vets with severe brain injuries, a second to reduce the delay severely-injured vets face in receiving veteran's benefits as they transition to civilian life, and a provision to enhance disability compensation for some veterans who have trouble using prostheses.

In the 112th Congress, Wissel will work with Burr and the rest of the staff as they are expected to continue their effort to improve veteran care. In March 2011, Burr introduced a measure that would help veterans receive faster decisions on their disability compensation claims, for example. The Senator also introduced a measure to designate March 30th as "Welcome Home Vietnam Veterans Day," because March 30th is the anniversary that combat and combat support units completely withdrew from South Vietnam, according to a press release.

Select, Special, and Other Committees

Committee on Indian Affairs

838 Hart Senate Office Bldg.
Washington, DC 20510
Phone: (202) 224-2251
Fax: (202) 224-5429
http://indian.senate.gov

Ratio: 6/8

MAJORITY MEMBERS

Daniel K. Akaka, HI, Chairman

Daniel K. Inouye, HI
Kent Conrad, ND
Tim Johnson, SD
Maria Cantwell, WA
Jon Tester, MT
Tom Udall, NM
Al Franken, MN

MINORITY MEMBERS

John Barrasso, WY, Ranking Member

John McCain, AZ
Lisa Murkowski, AK
John Hoeven, ND
Michael Crapo, ID
Mike Johanns, NE

SENATE INDIAN AFFAIRS

JURISDICTION

(1) To conduct a study of any and all matters pertaining to problems and opportunities of Indians including, but not limited to, Indian land management and trust responsibilities; Indian education, health, special services, and loan programs; and Indian claims against the United States.
(2) To report to the Senate, by bill or otherwise, its recommendations with respect to matters referred to it or otherwise its jurisdiction.

SENATE INDIAN AFFAIRS

As the Senate Select Committee on Indian Affairs continues to grapple with the perennial business of tribal health-and-welfare legislation and such pressing new business as uncertainty over the federal land trust process, the panel has entered a transitional period in its leadership.

With North Dakota Sen. Byron Dorgan's retirement after the 111th Congress, 88-year-old Sen. Daniel K. Akaka, D-Ha., succeeded him as chairman of the panel for the 112th Congress—in part to continue to push legislation that would give indigenous Hawaiian Islanders the semi-autonomous status that American Indians and tribes of Alaska Natives hold in this country.

Meanwhile Akaka, too, announced early in the 112th Congress that he would not seek reelection, so more change looms for his committee, even as Indian County continues its relationship with a presidential administration that has been unusually active in Native American affairs.

One milestone accomplishment of the Obama administration was the enactment late in 2010 of a $3.4-billion settlement of the Cobell v. Salazar case, a longstanding claim by American Indians that the government had mismanaged the trust funds that it handled on behalf of tribes. The legislation included a separate settlement of a decades-old claim against the government by black farmers.

At the instance of the committee's Republican vice-chairman, Sen. John Barrasso of Wyoming, part of the price of the Cobell compromise was reductions in federal spending on certain tribal social programs to offset the cost of the settlement.

But another important legal initiative in Indian Country was left unfinished. Late in the lame-duck congressional session of 2010, opponents killed the so-called "Carcieri fix," a measure to reverse Carcieri v. Salazar, a 2009 Supreme Court decision named for then-Gov. Donald Carcieri of Rhode Island and Interior Secretary Ken Salazar. The decision prevented Rhode Island's Narragansett Indians from having the Interior Department take into trust a parcel of land they had purchased for a housing project, because the tribe was not federally recognized until decades after the enactment of the modern trust system. Tribal advocates, along with Chairman Dorgan, asserted that the decision clouded the status of many initiatives—from law enforcement to natural resources management—on Indian lands across the country.

Indian rights advocates made clear that they would again look for the committee to move the Carcieri fix legislation in the new Congress, while opponents reiterated their concerns that it could lead to the expansion of tribal gambling.

Some pressing bread-and-butter issues are also on the committee's agenda for the new Congress. These include the drafting of provisions to accommodate the needs of tribes and reservations in two major federal programs that are due to expire, the authorizations for the federal highway trust fund and for public school programs including the "No Child Left Behind" system of testing and improving the performance of pupils and schools.

SENATE INDIAN AFFAIRS

Lenna Aoki

General Counsel

838 Hart Senate Office Bldg.

Phone: (202) (202) 224-2251

lenna_aoki@indian.senate.com

Personal: Born 07/07/1959 in Venice, Fla.

Education: B.A., Yale College, 1981. J.D., University of Pennsylvania, 1984.

Professional: 1987–1989, legislative assistant, Sen. Alan Cranston, D-Cal. 1991–1994, counsel, Senate Cmte. on Indian Affairs. 1995–1999, staff director, Senate Democratic Policy Committee. 1999–2001, director, Office of Congressional and Legislative Affairs, Interior Department. 2001–2011, private law practice.

Expertise: Indian affairs policy and law.

Sen. Daniel K. Akaka took on an experienced legal and political hand, Lenna Aoki, to be his general counsel when he assumed the chairmanship of the Indian Affairs Committee for the 112th Congress early in 2011. After years in private practice, Aoki returned to Capitol Hill to assist Akaka as he took over the committee's leadership from the retiring Sen. Byron Dorgan, D-N.D.

Akaka made clear that one of his top agenda items would be to continue his campaign for legislation that would confer upon Native Hawaiians a semi-autonomous status comparable to that of American Indians and Alaska Natives who are organized into tribes.

"He had strong feelings, understandably, on the future of Native Hawaiian self-determination and the rights of all indigenous people in America," Sen. Daniel K. Inouye explained as Akaka gave up another chairmanship in order to head the Indian Affairs Committee. Inouye, a former Indian Affairs Committee chairman, and Akaka are both Hawaii Democrats with high seniority in the Senate.

Akaka, who has announced that he will not seek reelection in 2012, faced significant challenges as his committee reorganized for a Congress in which Republicans held significantly more power after the 2010 elections.

Some opposition to Akaka's Native Hawaiian legislation was likely to come from the new House majority of Republicans. Meanwhile, Rep. Don Young, R-Alas., the incoming chairman of the key Indian affairs subcommittee in the House, has made clear his own distinct priorities, including a streamlining of the Bureau of Indian Affairs.

The change of command in the Indian Affairs Committee came against the backdrop of strenuous efforts to reduce federal spending. In statements early in the new Congress, Akaka indicated his determination to protect crucial programs in Indian Country against excessive cuts.

Aoki, a graduate of Yale and the University of Pennsylvania law school, served for several years as an attorney for the committee early in her career. She is broadly experienced in legislation and party politics, having directed the Democratic Policy Committee under Sen. Harry Reid of Nevada, who is now Majority Leader. Aoki is well-connected in the executive branch as well, having run the Interior Department's congressional affairs office during the last years of the Clinton administration.

SENATE INDIAN AFFAIRS

Jesse Broder Van Dyke

Deputy Communications Director, Sen. Daniel K. Akaka

141 Hart Senate Office Bldg.

Phone: (202) 224-6361

jesse_brodervandyke@akaka.senate.gov

Personal: Born in Honolulu, Hawaii.

Education: B.A., Boston University, 2001.

Professional: 2002–2006, news producer, KHON2 television. 2006, communications deputy, Sen. Daniel K. Akaka.

Expertise: Communications.

As a spokesman for Sen. Daniel K. Akaka, Jesse Broder Van Dyke assumed communications responsibilities for the Select Committee on Indian Affairs when the veteran Hawaii Democrat became chairman of the panel in 2011.

A graduate of the prestigious Punahou School, just like President Barack Obama, Broder Van Dyke brought deep Hawaii roots to the job.

Broder Van Dyke has been with Akaka's press staff since 2006. During the 111th Congress, he closely tracked the progress—and the last-minute demise—of legislation that will be high on Akaka's agenda for the Indian Affairs Committee in the 112th Congress, the Native Hawaiian Government Reorganization Act, which he has introduced since 2000.

"The bill would simply put the State of Hawaii on equal footing with the rest of the country in the treatment of its indigenous people," Akaka told Senate colleagues as time ran out on his measure during the waning days of the lame-duck congressional session in 2010. "It provides a process for the reorganization of a Native Hawaiian governing entity," said Akaka, who pressed for a study to prepare for the eventual passage of his bill, which cleared the full House and the Senate Indian affairs panel before it died.

"The idea is to do this study so that if the Native Hawaiian Reorganization passes in the future, the state of Hawaii can hit the ground running in beginning that process," Broder Van Dyke said at the time. "Native Hawaiians are the last major indigenous group in the United States of America which doesn't have this sort of recognition."

"The people of Hawaii have waited for far too long" for the legislation, Akaka said in 2010. Indeed, if he can overcome Republican opposition—and some home-state controversy—to steer it into law during the new Congress, it would be a fitting cap to his four terms in the Senate. Akaka announced early in 2011 that he would not seek reelection.

Broder Van Dyke studied film, history, and journalism at Boston University, graduating in 2001. He began his professional life as a news producer for KHON2 television of Honolulu. He also has a family connection of sorts to Akaka's Native Hawaiian bill. Both of his parents, lawyer Sherry Broder and University of Hawaii law professor and author Jon Van Dyke, are prominent supporters of the initiative.

SENATE INDIAN AFFAIRS

Rhonda Harjo

838 Hart Senate Office Bldg.

Phone: (202) 224-2251

rhonda_harjo@indian.senate.gov

Rhonda Harjo, deputy chief counsel for Republicans on the Senate Indian Affairs Committee, is a committee veteran who first began working on Indian Affairs issue under former Sen. Ben Nighthorse Campbell, R-Colo.

Harjo's focus on the committee has been largely centered on health care issues: She was the lead Republican staff member for the committee on Indian Health Care Improvement Act reauthorizations and had a hand in components of the Indian health care provisions in the massive health care overhaul bill that passed Congress in 2010.

In 2011, the committee will continue work on health care and economic development issues under Sen. John Barrasso, R-Wyo., vice chairman of the committee.

The committee has a reputation for being one of the most bipartisan committees in the Senate, and this year, with Vice Chairman Daniel Akaka, D-Hawaii helming the Democratic side of the committee, that does not look likely to change.

The committee also will likely continue to focus on issues with Indian Health Services management. A Senate investigation started under former North Dakota Sen. Byron Dorgan found serious management problems in Indian Health Services in the Aberdeen area, which serves 18 tribes across the upper Midwest. That investigation found severe management problems including a lack of employee accountability, several key staff positions remaining vacant for long periods and other problems. The committee will likely continue oversight as the Indian Health Services seeks to rectify those problems.

Harjo and the committee also will eye provisions in last year's health care bill to see whether court challenges have an impact on them. The Indian Health provisions in the health care overhaul were not considered controversial but court challenges could impact whether they are enacted.

Barrasso has also signaled an interest in non-gaming economic development and job creation.

The committee also will likely focus on law enforcement improvements and housing initiatives in 2011. Harjo has also had a hand in the former issue: In 2010, she worked on the Tribal Law and Order Act, a bill aimed at giving tribes and the federal government improved tools to address the complex jurisdictional issues they face. That bill was signed into law on July 29, 2010.

SENATE INDIAN AFFAIRS

David A. Mullon Jr.

Republican Staff Director and Chief Counsel

838 Hart Senate Office Bldg.

Phone: (202) 224-2251

Fax: (202) 224-5429

david_mullon@indian.senate.gov

Personal: Born 12/27/1951 in Minneola, N.Y.

Education: B.A., University of Arizona, 1975. M.A., Thunderbird School of Global Management, 1977. J.D., University of Tulsa, 1980.

Professional: 1993–1995, director of legal division, Cherokee Nation. 1996–1999, attorney general, Muscogee Nation of Oklahoma. 1999–2003, associate general counsel, Cherokee Nation. 2003–2004, deputy chief counsel, Senate Cmte. on Indian Affairs. 2005–2006, general counsel, Senate Cmte. on Indian Affairs. 2007–present, Republican staff director and Chief Counsel, Senate Cmte. on Indian Affairs.

Expertise: Indian legal issues, trust reform.

Republican Staff Director and Chief Counsel David Mullon will spend 2011 focusing on a key priority for Republican vice chairman, Sen. John Barrasso, R-Wyo.: energy and non-gaming economic development for tribal lands.

"Energy and non-gaming economic development are [things] (Barrasso) has always been concerned about," said Mullon, who has worked for the committee since 2003.

The committee has a new Democratic vice-chairman in 2011—Sen. Daniel Akaka, D-Hi.,—and Mullon said the committee will continue to be one of the most bipartisan committees in the U.S. Senate.

Even one of the most controversial bills to be passed in recent history— the massive health care overhaul passed in 2010—was received with comity in the Indian Affairs Committee. The bill contained provisions for Indian Health Care, and Mullon said both parties largely agreed on those provisions. However, it's unseen whether court challenges to the law will have an impact on those provisions, which Mullon said are not considered controversial.

Mullon is largely known for work on natural resource, land, and energy development issues, but he also expects to work on law enforcement and public safety issues for Barrasso in 2011. Education and health care, he said, will also be priorities for Barrasso in 2011. He has worked for the committee for seven years, following a decade in private law practice and several years as a tribal lawyer.

Mullon acted as associate general counsel for the Cherokee Nation, of which he is a member, from 1999 to 2003. His mother was a Cherokee from northeastern Oklahoma. He also was the attorney general for the Muscogee Nation of Oklahoma and head of the Cherokee Nation's legal division during the 1990s.

SENATE INDIAN AFFAIRS

Loretta Tuell

Democratic Staff Director and Chief Counsel

838 Hart Senate Office Bldg.

Phone: (202) (202)224-2251

Loretta_Tuell@indian.senate.gov

Personal: Born in Idaho.

Education: B.A., Washington State University, 1988. J.D., U.C.L.A., 1992. Senior executive program, Kennedy School of Government, Harvard University, 1999.

Professional: 1993–1998, Counsel, Senate Cmte. on Indian Affairs. 1998–1999, Special Assistant and Counselor to the Assistant Secretary-Indian Affairs, Department of the Interior. 2000–2001, Director, Office of American Indian Trust, Department of the Interior. 2001–2007, law practice, Monteau & Peebles. 2007–2011, law practice, Anderson Tuell.

Expertise: Native American legal issues, gaming law, environmental law, land trust issues.

When Sen. Daniel K. Akaka rose to the chairmanship of the Senate Indian Affairs Committee in 2011, he tapped as his staff director and chief counsel Loretta Tuell, a woman whose legal career fulfilled her childhood ambition as a daughter of the Nez Perce tribe in Idaho, and who came of age as a lawyer for the committee in the 1990s.

"She grew up on the reservation and is familiar with many of the issues you experience in your own communities," Akaka told the National Congress of American Indians at their legislative summit early in the 112th Congress. Tuell, who left the Washington law firm she co-founded in order to return to Capitol Hill, brought to the new job a "wealth of knowledge and experience in Indian law," and a familiarity issues facing Native Americans, Native Hawaiians, and Alaska Natives, Akaka has said.

Akaka, who plans to retire at the end of the 112th Congress, gave up his chairmanship of the Veterans Affairs Committee in order to take the reins at the Select Committee on Indian Affairs.

Among the items on Akaka's agenda for the new Congress: preserving the budgets for key federal programs affecting Native Americans, legislation to secure semi-autonomous status for Native Hawaiians, and reauthorization of highway and education programs that serve Indian reservations.

Tuell first joined the committee under another Democratic senator from Hawaii, longtime Chairman Daniel K. Inouye, in 1993, the year after she took her law degree from U.C.L.A. This was a time of ferment in Indian Country, as a number of tribes explored the opportunities available under Inouye's landmark Indian Gaming Regulatory Act of 1987.

Tuell has extensive experience with Native American policy in the federal government and in private practice. In 1998, President Bill Clinton appointed Tuell a counselor to the Interior Department's assistant secretary for Indian Affairs. Later she directed a key tribal agency within the department, the Office of American Indian Trust. Tuell spent seven years with an Indian affairs-oriented law firm, Monteau & Peebles. In 2007, she became co-founder of Anderson Tuell in Washington, D.C., one of the first law firms owned by an American Indian woman.

Special Committee on Aging

G31 Dirksen Senate Office Bldg.
Washington, DC 20510
Phone: (202) 224-5364
Fax: (202) 224-8660
http://aging.senate.gov
mailbox@aging.senate.gov

Ratio: 10/11

MAJORITY MEMBERS

Herbert Kohl, WI, Chairman

Ron Wyden, OR
Bill Nelson, FL
Bob Casey, PA
Claire McCaskill, MO
Sheldon Whitehouse, RI
Mark Udall, CO
Michael Bennet, CO
Kirsten Gillibrand, NY
Joe Manchin, WV
Richard Blumenthal, CT

MINORITY MEMBERS

Bob Corker, TN, Ranking Member

Susan Collins, ME
Orrin Hatch, UT
Mark Kirk, IL
Jerry Moran, KS
Ronald H. Johnson, WI
Kelly Ayotte, NH
Richard Shelby, AL
Lindsey Graham, SC
Saxby Chambliss, GA

SENATE SPECIAL ON AGING

JURISDICTION

(1) It shall be the duty of the special committee to conduct a continuing study of any and all matters pertaining to problems and opportunities of older people, including, but not limited to, problems and opportunities of maintaining health, of assuring adequate income, of finding employment, of engaging in productive and rewarding activity, of securing proper housing, and when necessary, of obtaining care or assistance. No proposed legislation shall be referred to such committee, and such committee shall not have power to report by bill, or otherwise have legislative jurisdiction.

(2) The special committee shall, from time to time (but not less than once year), report to the Senate the results of the study conducted pursuant to paragraph (1), together with such recommendation as it considers appropriate.

SENATE SPECIAL ON AGING

There's no shortage of issues for the Senate Special Committee on Aging to tackle in the 112th Congress. As a special committee, it has no legislative authority, meaning that any aging-related measures a Senator seeks to introduce must make its way through other congressional panels. However, it does serve as a place for Senators to study the problems facing older Americans, a group that is rapidly going to grow over the next decade as the Baby Boomer generation reaches retirement age.

The aging committee certainly will study how a push to cut federal spending could affect seniors, as many of the government programs that could be slashed benefit the elderly, such as Medicare and Social Security. The panel is charged with conducting oversight of both entitlement programs, as well as the Older Americans Act, one of the measures passed as part of President Lyndon Johnson's "Great Society" reforms. The act created and funds a variety of smaller programs designed to benefit Americans 60 and older.

Not everything the committee oversees requires significant federal spending. Early on in the 112th Congress, longtime Chairman Herb Kohl, D-Wis., took up the issue of elder abuse. It was the focus of the first hearing of the new session, which featured testimony from 90-year-old actor Mickey Rooney. The legendary Hollywood performer shared how a family member took advantage of him, explaining that the unnamed person denied him food and medicine and even sold his awards. Kohl used the hearing to promote his Elder Abuse Victims Act, which would create an Office of Elder Abuse at the Department of Justice and strengthen elder abuse enforcement.

Kohl also planned hearings on other senior-related topics, including one studying assisted living facilities and another looking at how the economic crisis affected how people fund their personal retirement plans, such as 401(K) plans.

There is perhaps no other Member who has a better knowledge of senior issues than Kohl, who has chaired the aging committee for several sessions. In that time, he's led efforts to reduce the cost of prescription drugs and increase access to affordable generic brands; helped create a nationwide grant program designed to improve background checks for people working with the elderly in nursing homes or long-term care; and fought to strengthen Social Security and 401(K) programs for retired Americans.

The committee's ranking member, Sen. Bob Corker, R-Tenn., is relatively new to the panel, at least compared to Kohl. Corker took over as the Republican leader on the committee after the 2009 retirement of Sen. Mel Martinez, R-Fla. Thus far, Corker has used the committee to further his legislative agenda, including his own push to cut federal spending and repeal health care reform legislation.

SENATE SPECIAL ON AGING

Ashley Glacel

Press Secretary

G37 Dirksen Senate Office Bldg.

Phone: (202) 224-7752

Fax: (202) 224-8660

ashley_glacel@aging.senate.gov

Personal: Born 12/29/1980 in West Point, N.Y.

Education: B.A., public policy, College of William and Mary, 2002. M.A., liberal studies, The New School for Social Research, 2004.

Professional: 2005–2007, communications director, Rep. Gwen Moore, D-Wisc. 2007–present, press secretary, Senate Special Cmte. on Aging.

Expertise: Communications.

While some Senate staffers come to the chamber with a rather wonky past, Ashley Glacel's resume is a little different. Prior to starting work as an aide on Capitol Hill, Glacel wrote for publications such as *The Village Voice* and *Ms. Magazine*.

These days, Glacel serves as the on-the-record spokeswoman for Special Senate Committee on Aging Chairman Herb Kohl, D-Wisc., ready to chat with reporters on a vast array of topics affecting America's seniors. During the 111th Congress, she had to be ready to speak on an array of issues, including housing for low-income seniors, health care, elder fraud and abuse, and even a resolution that designated Sept. 23, 2010,—the first day of fall—as "National Falls Prevention Awareness Day."

Glacel served as Kohl's voice in the press in December 2010 when he temporarily held up the nomination of Michelle Leonhart to be head of the Drug Enforcement Administration. Kohl wanted the agency to agree to allow nurses to give painkillers to nursing home patients, a request that the DEA granted, and Leonhart eventually was confirmed.

Glacel said in 2009 that the diversity of the issues the aging panel studies each congressional session is one of the reasons she likes working on the committee. "I love that the committee covers a lot of ground, which affords me the opportunity to always learn something new," she said.

Aside from her work on the aging panel, Glacel has been an active member of the Senate community. She served several terms on the board of the Senate Press Secretaries Association, a bipartisan forum for press secretaries in the chamber to meet and discuss ideas. Glacel takes an active role in organizing the group's annual trip to New York, according to the group's Web site.

SENATE SPECIAL ON AGING

Chuck Harper

Press Secretary

G31 Dirksen Senate Office Bldg.

Phone: (202) 224-5364

chuck_harper@corker.senate.gov

Education: B.A., political science, Rhodes College, 2003.

Professional: 2004–2006, deputy press secretary, Senate Majority Ldr Bill Frist, R-Tenn. 2007–present, deputy press secretary, Sen. Bob Corker, R-Tenn. 2009–present, press secretary, Senate Cmte. on Aging.

Expertise: Communications.

Chuck Harper is charged with handling press matters for the Senate Special Committee on Aging minority team, but it's not his only full-time job. He also serves as deputy press secretary to the committee's ranking member, Sen. Bob Corker, R-Tenn.

As press secretary, Harper is tasked with taking phone calls and e-mails from journalists who have questions about the committee's work. He also is charged with helping Corker with his messaging strategy. It's a task that requires Harper to have knowledge on a variety of topics, considering the aging committee handles such a wide range of issues.

Since taking the helm from retiring Sen. Mel Martinez, R-Fla. in 2009, Corker has partly used his leadership position on the panel to further some of his top legislative priorities, making Harper's dual role in the Senator's personal office important. In the 111th Congress, for example, much of Corker's priorities with the committee included a push for the repeal of health care reform legislation.

In the 112th Congress, Corker has used his position to further his goal of cutting federal spending. One press release on the aging committee website, for example, promoted the Commitment to American Prosperity Act, or the "CAP Act," which Corker introduced alongside Sen. Claire McCaskill, D-Mo. The measure is designed to force cuts by capping federal spending and eliminating the "off-budget" distinction for Social Security.

Not everything handled by the committee is so partisan. The first hearing of the 111th Congress staffed by Harper focused on ways to combat elder abuse, and even featured a celebrity appearance by 90-year-old entertainment legend Mickey Rooney. The actor testified that he had been a victim of such abuse when a family member took advantage of him and stole some of his money.

A graduate of Rhodes College in Memphis, Harper also is a member of the Sigma Alpha Epsilon fraternity. Prior to his stint with Corker, Harper worked on the press staff for another Tennessee Senator, former Majority Leader Bill Frist, R-Tenn.

SENATE SPECIAL ON AGING

Debra Whitman

Staff Director

G31 Dirksen Senate Office Bldg.

Phone: (202) 224-5364

debra_whitman@aging.senate.gov

Personal: Born 06/02/1970 in Phoenix, Ariz.

Education: B.A., economics, Gonzaga University, 1992. M.A., economics, Maxwell School of Citizenship and Public Affairs, Syracuse University, 1996. Ph.D., economics, Maxwell School of Citizenship and Public Affairs, Syracuse University, 1997.

Professional: 1997–2001, economic analyst and project director for the Retirement Research Consortium, Social Security Administration. 2001–2003, Brookings Institution LEGIS Fellow, Senate Cmte. on Health, Education, Labor and Pensions. 2003–2007, researcher and aging initiative leader, Domestic Social Policy Division, Congressional Research Service. 2007–present, staff director, Senate Special Cmte. on Aging.

Expertise: Senior issues.

As staff director of the Senate Special Committee on Aging, Debra Whitman puts in plenty of hours on Capitol Hill working to advance the agenda of her boss, Chairman Herb Kohl, D-Wisc. But Whitman also has been known to speak off the Hill about aging issues...say, halfway around the world.

In June 2010, Whitman was among the speakers at the International Federation on Ageing 10th Global Conference in Melbourne, Australia. The multi-day event studied a vast range of issues that affect older people, from health care to the global economic downturn to climate change and even human rights. Many of the topics discussed likely related to Whitman's work on the aging panel, which in recent years has paid significant attention to how the retirement of the baby boomer generation will affect programs such as Social Security and Medicare.

Whitman and her team also have looked at ways to provide long-term care for needy seniors, help low-income seniors acquire housing, and even help older Americans adjust to the recent digital television transition. The committee's first hearing in the 112th Congress was scheduled to study how best to stop elder fraud and abuse.

During the 2008 presidential election, Whitman served as an advisor on health and long-term care to future President Barack Obama's campaign. While working as a fellow at the Brookings Institution, Whitman was a health policy advisor to one of Obama's mentors, Sen. Edward Kennedy, D-Mass., who passed away in August 2009.

Aside from working on aging issues, Whitman is an avid traveler who spent a year studying abroad in Florence, Italy. She told *The Hill* newspaper in 2007 she hopes to visit 50 countries and all 50 states.

Select Committee on Ethics

220 Hart Senate Office Bldg.
Washington, DC 20510
Phone: (202) 224-2981
Fax: (202) 224-7416
http://ethics.senate.gov

Ratio: 3/3

MAJORITY MEMBERS

Barbara Boxer, CA, Chairman

Mark Pryor, AK
Sherrod Brown, OH

MINORITY MEMBERS

Johnny Isakson, GA, Vice Chairman

Pat Roberts, KS
James E. Risch, ID

SENATE SELECT ON ETHICS

The Senate Select Committee on Ethics is charged with investigating allegations of rule-breaking by senators, and even though a large majority of the complaints are dismissed, the committee generates headlines either way.

Membership is evenly split between the two major parties in an effort to avoid the appearance of political influence in its inquiries and rulings. Complaints can end in dismissal, referral to law enforcement, public admonition, disciplinary sanctions, or adjudicatory review.

Recently, the committee appointed a special counsel to handle the complaint against Sen. John Ensign, R-NV. Former federal prosecutor Carol Elder Bruce was appointed to head the inquiry into Ensign's affair with an aide and related payments to her family.

The committee handled high-profile cases involving former Sens. Roland Burris, D-Ill., Christopher Dodd, D-Conn., and current Sen. Kurt Conrad, D-N.D., in the past term.

Burris received a public letter of qualified admonition "for actions and statements reflecting unfavorably upon the Senate in connection with your appointment to and seating in the Senate," the committee wrote in November 2009. Burris was appointed by former Illinois governor Rod Blagojevich, who faces federal corruption charges, to fill the vacancy left by Barack Obama, who was elected president in 2008. The committee found that Burris made "misleading" statements, but added that it didn't find evidence that a law was broken.

The committee announced in August 2009 that after a year-long investigation, which involved 18,000 documents and subpoenas, it had dismissed complaints against Dodd and Conrad. Both senators had been accused of violating the Senate's gifts rules because of home mortgages they obtained from Countrywide Financial.

Despite the dismissal, the committee said they "should have exercised more vigilance" to avoid appearance of preferential treatment.

The Dodd-Conrad cases brought the committee into the world of home mortgages for the first time. It noted in its dismissal letters to the senator that it "has not previously offered specific guidance to senators, officers, and employees on the matters they should consider when negotiating mortgages and other financial transactions. The committee should proactively provide more guidance to the senate community about issues surrounding mortgage negotiations."

It also encouraged all "to seek prior guidance concerning participation in any programs like the one addressed here."

The committee's work is traditionally handled in private—indeed, most complaints don't make it to the preliminary inquiry stage—but as such it can become a very public target.

When the committee rejected a separate complaint about Dodd receiving a discount price for an Irish cottage, the nonprofit Judicial Watch, which had filed the complaint, lashed out. It criticized the "despicable handling" of the case, claiming the committee "sat on our complaint" and then "dismissed it out of hand days before Dodd's Senate career ends." Dodd did not seek re-election in 2010.

The committee rarely comments publicly on its business, preferring instead to issue statements like this one from 2008: "The Senate Ethics Committee does not comment on pending matters or matters that may come before the committee."

In the committee's annual report for 2010 activities, it said it received 84 complaints of violations, down from 99 the prior year. Most were dismissed because they didn't violate Senate rules or for lack of evidence.

SENATE SELECT ON ETHICS

In 12 cases, the committee staff conducted a preliminary inquiry, including six cases carried over from 2009. None of them resulted in disciplinary sanctions and no letters of admonition were issued. There was one letter of admonition (Burris) in 2009, two in 2008, and none in 2007.

The staff received 11,137 telephone inquiries and 1,227 inquiries by email for ethics advice and guidance, and wrote 769 advisory letters and responses, among which 540 were related to travel and gifts.

Sen. Barbara Boxer became chairwoman in 2006. Though the US Constitution gives both the House and Senate the power to discipline its members, it wasn't until the 1960s that the Senate had a standing committee to deal with ethics violations. Prior to that, ad hoc committees were appointed.

Congress established its permanent ethics committee on July 24, 1964. It was called the Select Committee on Standards and Conduct. In 1977, its name was changed to the Select Committee on Ethics.

SENATE SELECT ON ETHICS

Annette Gillis

Deputy Staff Director

Phone: (202) 202-224-2981

Education: George Mason University, 2007.

Professional: 1995–2004, Chief Clerk, Senate Select Committee on Ethics. 1995–2004, Chief Clerk, Senate Select Committee on Ethics. 2004–present, Deputy Staff Director, Senate Select Committee on Ethics.

Annette Gillis has served more than 16 years on the Senate Select Committee on Ethics. She took on the title of the deputy staff director in 2004, after a lengthy run as the committee's chief clerk.

Gillis was chief clerk during the committee's high-profile probe of former Sen. Bob Packwood, an Oregon Republican who resigned from office in 1995. The committee had unanimously voted to recommend a full investigation of Packwood after finding credible evidence of a pattern of sexual misconduct between 1969 and 1990, as well as evidence that Packwood had improper financial gains while in office. The committee's membership at that time included Sen. Larry Craig, R-Idaho, who in 2008 was admonished by the committee in the fallout of his arrest for allegedly soliciting sex in a men's bathroom at a Minnesota airport.

More recently, Gillis, the rest of the committee's staff, and a new special counsel appointed by the committee have been investigating allegations against Sen. John Ensign, R-Nev., who allegedly routed $96,000 to the family of a woman, one of his former aides, with whom he had an affair.

Most of Gillis' work stays out of the public spotlight. The committee in 2010 wrote 769 ethics advisory letters, which included 540 letters related to travel and gifts, according to the committee's annual report. The committee also issued 3,527 letters concerning financial disclosure filings by senators, staffers and Senate candidates.

Gillis is listed as a graduate of George Mason University.

SENATE SELECT ON ETHICS

John C. Sassaman Jr.

Staff Director and Chief Counsel

220 Hart Senate Office Bldg.

Phone: (202) 224-2981

Fax: (202) 224-7416

Education: J.D., Albany Law School, 1992.

Professional: 2001–2004, counsel, House Cmte. on Standards of Official Conduct. 2004–2008, senior counsel, House Cmte. on Standards of Official Conduct. 2008–2009, senior counsel, Senate Select Cmte. on Ethics. 2009, staff director and chief counsel, Senate Select Cmte. on Ethics.

Expertise: Ethics advising and investigation.

Capitol Hill veteran John Sassaman joined the staff of the Senate Select Committee on Ethics in 2008 as senior counsel and a year later became staff director and chief counsel. In that position Sassaman investigates complaints about ethics violations by senators, staff members and campaigns. He and his staff advise the six-member committee about whether complaints should result in dismissal or disciplinary action.

While most cases are dismissed for lack of evidence, others stir up controversy. Sassaman's staff and a special counsel appointed by the committee in early 2011 examined allegations against Sen. John Ensign, R-Nev., who allegedly routed $96,000 to the family of a former aide, with whom he had an affair. Also on the committee's radar was a complaint against Sen. Claire McCaskill, D-Missouri, who used taxpayer funds to pay for flights on a private jet. She has said it was a mistake and repaid the funds.

An Albany Law School graduate, Sassaman told the school's alumni magazine in the spring 2008 edition that working on Capitol Hill affords him the "non-traditional legal career I wanted." He said he enjoys researching new ethical issues. "I like the role of advisor."

Sassaman and his staff have increased their public education role in recent years. They conducted 43 ethics seminars, 21 campaign briefings, and 10 international ethics briefings in 2010, according to the panel's annual report. He also is a faculty member at the Practising Law Institute, a nonprofit legal-education organization that updates lawyers on current practices. He's a panelist at the institute's annual seminal on corporate political activities.

Sassaman clerked in the District of Columbia Court of Appeals and was a special counsel for the District of Columbia Attorney General's before coming to Capitol Hill.

Select Committee on Intelligence

211 Hart Senate Office Bldg.
Washington, DC 20510
Phone: (202) 224-1700
Fax: (202) 224-1774
http://intelligence.senate.gov

Ratio: 9/10

MAJORITY MEMBERS

Dianne Feinstein, CA, Chairman

John D. Rockefeller IV, WV
Ron Wyden, OR
Barbara A. Mikulski, MD
Bill Nelson, FL
Kent Conrad, ND
Mark Udall, CO
Mark Warner, VA
Harry Reid, NV, Ex Officio
Carl Levin, MI, Ex Officio

MINORITY MEMBERS

Saxby Chambliss, GA, Vice Chairman

Olympia J. Snowe, ME
Richard Burr, NC
James Risch, ID
Daniel Coats, IN
Roy Blunt, MO
Marco Rubio, FL
Mitch McConnell, KY, Ex Officio
John McCain, AZ, Ex Officio

SENATE SELECT ON INTELLIGENCE

JURISDICTION

(1) Created pursuant to S.Res. 400, 94th Congress: to oversee and make continuing studies of the intelligence activities and programs of the United States Government, and to submit to the Senate appropriate proposals for legislation and report to the Senate concerning such intelligence activities and programs. In carrying out this purpose, the Select Committee on Intelligence shall make every effort to assure that the appropriate departments and agencies of the United States provide informed and timely intelligence necessary for the executive and legislative branches to make sound decisions affecting the security and vital interests of the Nation. It is further the purpose of this resolution to provide vigilant legislative oversight over the intelligence activities of the United States to assure that such activities are in conformity with the Constitution and laws of the United States.

SENATE SELECT ON INTELLIGENCE

The Senate Select Committee on Intelligence convened in the 112th Congress with six fresh faces and a new vice chairman, Sen. Saxby Chambliss, a Georgia Republican.

Bipartisanship is being promised by the panel's chairman, Sen. Dianne Feinstein (D-Calif.), as lawmakers' oversight of the intelligence community faces challenges relating to shrinking budgets, growing instability in several Muslim countries, and terrorist threats to the homeland.

Tumult in North Africa and the Middle East, where widespread demonstrations have sought democratic reforms, reverberated through the panel's opening days of this Congress.

Feinstein might have revealed one of her initiatives for the 112th when she criticized the nation's spy bosses for failing to provide intelligence on Egyptian unrest, which she said could be gleaned from social Web sites like Facebook. Those sites should be monitored, Feinstein said, to provide advance notice to policymakers.

"I think we were at fault in that regard," Feinstein told a panel of intelligence chiefs in February 2011.

Other priorities are expected to include legislation around cyber security and oversight of counterterrorism operations. Chambliss has expressed concern about U.S.-detained terror suspects returning to Al Qaeda groups upon release. Another priority for him will be ensuring intelligence agencies work effectively with smaller budgets.

"The days of bloated budgets, including for the [intelligence community], [are] behind us," said Chambliss, who replaces former Sen. Christopher Bond (R-Mo.) as vice chairman.

The committee was created in 1975 under Senate Resolution 400 during the 94th Congress to monitor and oversee the intelligence activities and programs of the federal government and to ensure that those activities are within the bounds of the Constitution.

SENATE SELECT ON INTELLIGENCE

David Grannis

Majority Staff Director

211 Hart Senate Office Bldg.

Phone: (202) 224-1700

Fax: (202) 224-1772

Personal: Born 1975.

Education: B.S., chemistry, Cornell University. M.A., public policy, Harvard University.

Professional: 2001–2003, senior policy advisor, Rep. Jane Harman, D-Calif. 2003–2005, professional staff member, House Cmte. on Homeland Security. 2005–2009, professional staff member, Senate Select Cmte. on Intelligence.

David Grannis will help oversee a funding deceleration of the intelligence community in the 112th Congress, as spy agencies face flattening budgets compared to the booming spending sprees of the last decade. The budget brakes are being tapped after intelligence funding roughly doubled since 9/11.

Grannis, the majority staff director for the Senate Select Committee on Intelligence, is witnessing the funding slowdown two years after rising to the panel's upper deck. Sen. Dianne Feinstein, D-Calif., elevated him to the position when she became chairman in 2009. Grannis previously worked with the committee as Feinstein's designee, a role he assumed in March 2005.

Grannis helped develop the Intelligence Authorization bill of 2010, marking the first time since 2004 that the spending blueprint was adopted. The legislation authorizes new authorities, and restricts others, for the intelligence community. A classified annex to the bill recommends funding levels for the spy agencies.

A priority for Grannis will be to advance authorizing bills for fiscal years 2011 and 2012 as the panel tries to reestablish a tradition of success on that topic. Intelligence authorizations passed in an unbroken streak between 1978 and 2004.

Tightening budgets come as intelligence agencies cope with the threat of terrorism at home. Grannis helped steer the committee through investigations of high profile attacks during the 111th Congress. The panel studied intelligence effectiveness related to a series of dangerous events, including an attempted Christmas Day attack in 2009.

An unclassified report by the panel revealed "systemic failures" across intelligence agencies to identify the threat posed by that incident, when an explosive failed to detonate on a Northwest flight from Amsterdam to Detroit.

SENATE SELECT ON INTELLIGENCE

Martha Scott Poindexter

Republican Staff Director

211 Hart Senate Office Bldg.

Phone: (202) 224-1700

Personal: Born in Morgan City, Miss.

Education: B.S., Mississippi State University, 1989.

Professional: 1997–2001, professional staff member, Subc. on Agriculture, Senate Cmte. on Appropriations. 2002–2003, director of government relations, Monsanto. 2003–2004, legislative director, Sen. Saxby Chambliss, R-Ga. 2005–2010, staff director, Senate Cmte. on Agriculture, Nutrition and Forestry. 2011–present, Republican staff director, Select Committee on Intelligence.

Expertise: Agriculture.

Martha Scott Poindexter's background resembles a spook's alias. The new Republican staff director for the intelligence panel studied home economics near her family farm in Mississippi and later became a registered dietitian.

Since 2005, Poindexter has led the Republican staff on the Agriculture Committee for Georgia Republican Sen. Saxby Chambliss, where she used her expertise on farming issues to help develop energy provisions in the 2008 Farm Bill. She also spent time reviewing the Commodity Futures Trading Commission and regulatory reforms.

But when Chambliss replaced Missouri Republican Sen. Christopher Bond as vice chairman on the intelligence panel for the 112th Congress, he brought along his trusted aide. Poindexter will help Chambliss fulfill his emphasis on monitoring intelligence capabilities with regard to suspects who are released from the U.S. detention center in Cuba and reduce spending in the spy agencies.

Poindexter also could take a central role in investigating intelligence related to terrorist attempts in the United States. Chambliss says more needs to be done.

"There are going to have to be some major changes," he said of intelligence capabilities.

Chambliss and Poindexter have worked together on and off since 1995, when she left a job lobbying for Louisiana sugar cane farmers to become his legislative aide in the House for agriculture and natural resources policies.

Poindexter began her career with Sen. Thad Cochran, R-Miss., for whom she helped develop the nutrition title of the 1990 Farm Bill. She left three years later to accept an internship in nutrition at the University of Maryland and later became a registered dietitian.

Joint Committees

Joint Committee on the Library

305 Russell Senate Office Bldg.
Washington, DC 20510
Phone: (202) 224-6352
http://www.senate.gov/general/committee_membership/committee_memberships_JSLC.htm

Ratio: 3/4

REPUBLICANS

Dan Lungren, CA-3rd, Chairman

Lamar Alexander, TN
Thad Cochran, MS

DEMOCRATS

Charles Schumer, NY, Vice Chairman

Robert Brady, PA-1st
Richard Durbin, IL
Patrick Leahy, VT

JOINT LIBRARY

JURISDICTION

(1) The Library of Congress, management of the Congressional art collection and the U.S. Botanic Garden.

JOINT LIBRARY

The Joint Committee on the Library was established 1800 and is Congress's oldest continuing joint panel. It is tasked with the job of overseeing the Library of Congress, the oldest federal cultural institution and the research arm of Congress. The committee's jurisdiction also includes management of the Congressional art collection—most notably the National Statuary Hall Collection—and the maintenance of the U.S. Botanic Garden.

The panel is made up of Members of the House Administration Committee and the Senate Rules and Administration Committee and chairmanship of the joint committee rotates each year between the chairmen of those two oversight panels.

This year, the joint library panel will play an advisory role in the selection of one of the Library's top posts. After 17 years as director of the Congressional Research Service, Daniel P. Mulhollan retired in early April. CRS serves as the nonpartisan research arm of Congress and provides policy and legal analysis to Members as they create and review legislation. Librarian of Congress James H. Billington has appointed Mary B. Mazanec as acting director of CRS until a new director is appointed.

The Joint Committee on the Library has also been busy in recent years overseeing changes to the National Statuary Hall collection. A new statue of President Gerald Ford, who died in 2006, was set to be unveiled in early May after the panel approved a plan for the state of Michigan to replace one of its two contributions to the collection with a statue of the former president.

Meanwhile a group of Maryland lawmakers have been moving a bill through the state legislature this year to include prominent abolitionist Harriet Tubman to the Statuary Hall collection. Some lawmakers are seeking to have Tubman added to the collection without removing the statues of either Charles Carroll or John Hanson, two Colonial American revolutionaries. But such a rare move would have to be approved by the joint panel.

Delegates from the District of Columbia and U.S. territories continue to push for legislation that would allow them to add their own statues to the collection. Last year a measure passed the house that would have allowed D.C. and the territories to add one statue to the collection but that bill did not make it to the Senate floor before the end of the 111th Congress.

Joint Committee on Printing

1309 Longworth House Office Bldg.
Washington, DC 20515
Phone: (202) 225-2061
Fax: (202) 225-7664

Ratio: 2/3

REPUBLICANS

Lamar Alexander, TN
Saxby Chambliss, GA

DEMOCRATS

Charles Schumer, NY, Vice Chairman

Patty Murray, WA
Tom Udall, NM

JOINT PRINTING

JURISDICTION

(1) The principal purpose of the Joint Committee on Printing is to oversee the functions of the Government Printing Office and general printing procedures of the federal government. The authority vested in the Joint Committee on Printing is derived from Title 44 of the U.S. Code, and the committee is thereby responsible for ensuring compliance by federal entities to these laws and the Government Printing and Binding Regulations.

JOINT PRINTING

The Joint Committee on Printing oversees the Government Printing Office, the legislative branch agency that is charged with printing the official documents of the United States federal government. The panel acts almost as a board of trustees for the GPO, with members of the Senate Rules and Administration and House Administration committees keeping a watchful eye on the agency.

Part of the work of the joint committee in the 112th session will be getting to know the new public printer, William Boarman. Having officially taken office on Jan. 5, 2011, Boarman brings more than four decades of printing experience to his new leadership role. His first job at the GPO was in 1974, when he was hired as a journeyman printer, a position he earned after taking part in an apprenticeship with the International Typographical Union. Boarman was active in the union throughout his career, and rose to become union president in 1987; he subsequently was elected to seven consecutive terms.

Boarman oversees a changing federal agency, as the government moves to put most of its documents online. Despite its printing legacy, the GPO has been a leader in this effort through the launch of its "Federal Digital System." This online database allows visitors to search and download an array of government documents and publications from multiple federal agencies.

There is one lingering challenge for the joint committee to study: What to do with the agency's massive headquarters located just off Capitol Hill on North Capitol Street. The GPO has been headquartered in the historic building since its founding more than 150 years ago, but as much of the agency's work becomes digitized, much of the space sits empty. GPO officials have long pushed to move into a small location, but thus far, no concrete plans have been made.

Joint Committee on Taxation

1015 Longworth House Office Bldg.
Washington, DC 20515
Phone: (202) 225-3621
Fax: (202) 225-0832
http://www.jct.gov

Ratio: 5/5

REPUBLICANS

Dave Camp, MI-4th, Chairman

Wally Herger, CA-2nd
Sam Johnson, TX-3rd
Charles E. Grassley, IA
Orrin Hatch, UT

DEMOCRATS

Max Baucus, MT, Vice Chairman

John D. Rockefeller IV, WV
Kent Conrad, ND
Charles B. Rangel, NY-15th
Sander Levin, MI-12th

JOINT TAXATION

JURISDICTION

(1) Investigate the operation and effects of internal revenue taxes and the administration of such taxes.
(2) Investigate measures and methods for the simplification of internal revenue taxes.
(3) Make reports to the House Committee on Ways and Means and the Senate Committee on Finance on the results of investigations and studies.
(4) Review any proposed refund or credit of income or estate and gift taxes or certain other taxes set forth in Internal Revenue Code section 6405 in excess of $2,000,000.

JOINT TAXATION

Established under the Revenue Act of 1926, the Joint Committee on Taxation is a bicameral panel tasked with providing independent tax analysis and advice for lawmakers.

One of four joint panels on the Hill, the Joint Committee on Taxation is made up of 10 members of Congress, five from the Senate Finance Committee, and five from the House Ways and Means Committee. During the first session of each Congress the House has the Chair of the panel and the Senate holds the vice-chair. During the second session those roles are reversed. For 2011, the committee's chairman is Rep. Dave Camp, R-Mich.., and the vice-chairman is Sen. Max Baucus, D-Mont.

The Joint Tax staff does not operate as a majority or minority staff. The Committee's independence and nonpartisan nature are designed to facilitate exchanges of information between Congress and the Internal Revenue Service (IRS), Treasury, other government agencies, interest groups, and taxpayers. Any member of Congress may request a revenue estimate for a tax proposal from the committee.

Generally, a response to a request is released only to the member making the request and the response remains confidential unless the member decides to release the information to the public. Along with helping lawmakers study and craft tax legislation, the committee is also charged with investigating the operation and effects of internal revenue taxes, examining measures and methods for tax simplification and assisting Congress in writing tax treaties.

In the early days of the 112th Congress, the many economists, accountants, and attorneys that make up the committee staff were particularly busy as Republicans moved quickly after taking over the House to try to repeal various tax provisions included as part of the controversial health care law that was passed last year. That effort came after a very busy 2010 in which the committee saw plenty of work on the ongoing stimulus effort, the various versions of the health care bill, the cap and trade bill that eventually failed and a late frenzy in the lame duck session to extend the Bush era tax cuts.

Meanwhile the committee continues to conduct its annual studies to track yearly tax expenditures and expiring tax provisions, and analyze revenue provisions in the president's budget proposal.

JOINT TAXATION

Thomas A. Barthold

Chief of Staff

1625 Longworth House Office Bldg.

Phone: (202) 225-3621

Fax: (202) 225-0832

Thomas.Barthold@mail.house.gov

Personal: Born 11/23/1953 in St. Louis, Mo.

Education: B.A., mathematics and economics, Northwestern University, 1975. M.S., mathematics, Northwestern University, 1975. M.A., economics, Harvard University, 1978. Ph.D., economics, Harvard University, 1980.

Professional: 1977–1980, teaching fellow, Dept. of Economics, Harvard University. 1980–1987, assistant professor, Dept. of Economics, Dartmouth College. 1987–1996, economist, Joint Cmte. on Taxation. 1996–2004, senior economist, Joint Cmte. on Taxation. 2004–2009, deputy chief of staff, Joint Cmte. on Taxation. 2009–present, chief of staff, Joint Cmte. on Taxation.

Expertise: Tax law and economics.

As chief of staff, Thomas Barthold oversees the bi-cameral panel that helps shape tax policy at the request of the House Ways and Means and Senate Finance committees.

The committee's economists, accountants, and attorneys work behind the scenes to assist lawmakers in developing tax proposals and provide qualitative and quantitative analysis on past and future legislation.

The committee works to determine how tax-cut proposals will affect the budget deficit and that effort can occasionally make it a focal point of partisan pressure. Barthold needs to ensure that his staff sticks to the data and remains nonpartisan body.

Barthold occasionally ventures outside Capitol Hill to defend the panel's work and conclusions when outside institutions question its findings. Last summer, in a letter to the *Wall Street Journal*'s editorial board, Barthold took the paper to task for misstating the committee's methodology for estimating the revenue effects of tax legislation and for exaggerating the revenue impact of previous investment tax cuts.

In the 112th Congress, Barthold expects the committee to spend a lot of time on tax bills aimed at deficit reduction and job creation. His committee saw plenty of action during the final days of the 111th Congress in the late push to extend the Bush tax cuts for two more years. And after spending much of the last two years conducting studies on the tax provisions included in the high profile health care bill that passed in 2010, Barthold's panel was back at it during the first few months of 2011 as Republicans pushed a variety of proposals aimed at repealing various provisions from that bill.

Prior to his arrival in Washington, he was a member of the economics faculty of Dartmouth College. His publications include studies of capital gain realizations, charitable bequests, and measuring the distribution of the tax burden.

JOINT TAXATION

Bernard A. Schmitt

Deputy Chief of Staff
Joint Committee on Taxation
1015 Longworth House Office Bldg.
Phone: (202) 226-7575
Fax: (202) 225-0833
bernard.schmitt@mail.house.gov

Personal: Born 03/19/1948 in Idaho Falls, Idaho.

Education: B.S., Weber State College (Ogden, Utah), 1971. M.S., Florida State University, 1975. Ph.D., Florida State University, 1977.

Professional: 1976–1977, consultant, Florida State Dept. of Commerce. 1977–1986, economist, Joint Cmte. on Taxation. 1986–1989, chief of revenue analysis, Joint Cmte. on Taxation. 1989–94, associate chief of staff, Joint Cmte. on Taxation. 1994–present, deputy chief of staff, Joint Cmte. on Taxation.

Expertise: Public finance, taxes, economic modeling.

Bernard Schmitt has worked for Joint Committee on Taxation since 1977 and served as deputy chief of staff for the panel since 1994. His job is to help oversee the committee's army of economists, lawyers, and accountants who work to determine how much various tax bills and proposals would cost the government.

Joint Tax is a bicameral and nonpartisan committee that works directly with the tax-writing House Ways and Means and the Senate Finance committees. Its mission is to offer guidance to any member of Congress, armed with a fledging tax proposal, who seeks its expertise. Members look to Schmitt and his team to provide data, develop cost models and estimate revenue effects of proposed tax law changes.

This year, Schmitt said he expects the committee will spend the lion share of its time analyzing tax proposals that deal with deficit reduction and job creation as well as more general tax reform bills and the usual budget estimates.

In the early days of the 112th Congress, Joint tax was particularly busy as House Republicans sought to move several bills aimed at repealing key parts of the health care reform law that became the most high profile piece of legislation passed by the 111th Congress. One bill that the panel issued a slew of studies on during the opening weeks of the 112th Congress was the Comprehensive 1099 Taxpayer Protection and Repayment of Exchange Subsidy Overpayment Act. That bill sought to amend the Internal Revenue Code to repeal the expansion of information reporting requirements for payments made to corporations.

Last year, Schmitt and his team were busy with the health care bill and with ongoing effortsto assess the tax-related components of the stimulus legislation that was championed by Democrats and the White House. In the lame duck session that followed the 2010 election Joint Tax was particularly busy as Congress and the White House hammered out a plan to extend the Bush-era tax cuts until the end of 2012.

Joint Economic Committee

G-01 Dirksen Senate Office Bldg.
Washington, DC 20510
Phone: (202) 224-5171
http://jec.senate.gov
webmaster@jec.senate.gov

Ratio: 12/12/1

REPUBLICANS

Kevin Brady, TX-8th, Vice Chairman

Michael C. Burgess, TX-26th
John Campbell, CA-48th
Justin Amash, MI-3rd
Mick Mulvaney, SC-5th
Sean P. Duffy, WI-7th
Sam Brownback, KS
Jim Demint, SC
Dan Coats, IN
Pat Toomey, PA
Mike Lee, UT
James E. Risch, ID

DEMOCRATS

Robert P. Casey, PA, Chairman

Charles Schumer, NY
Jeff Bingaman, NM
Amy Klobuchar, MN
Jim Webb, VA
Mark Warner, VA
Carolyn Maloney, NY-2nd
Maurice Hinchey, NY-22nd
Baron Hill, IN-At Large
Loretta Sanchez, CA-47th
Elijah Cummings, MD-7th
Vic Snyder, AR-At Large

INDEPENDENT MEMBERS

Bernard Sanders, VT

JOINT ECONOMIC

JURISDICTION

(1) Review the condition of the national economy.
(2) Recommend improvements to the national economy.

JOINT ECONOMIC

When the economy is humming, the Joint Economic Committee is easily overlooked. But in the current and last session of Congress, as the nation has struggled out of a recession and tried to address stubbornly high unemployment, the committee's research and hearings have enjoyed special attention.

The new chairman for the 112th session is Sen. Robert Casey, D-Pa., who joined the committee after his election to the Senate in 2007. He succeeds Rep. Carolyn Maloney, D-N.Y., the first female chair of the committee. As a bicameral committee, the chairmanship alternates between the House and Senate every two years. The Vice Chair of the committee for the 112th Congress is Rep. Kevin Brady, R-Tex.

As a non-legislative committee, its members hold hearings, conduct research and advise other members of Congress. The panel regularly reviews the latest unemployment statistics, for example, and its portfolio includes issues as diverse as energy, fiscal responsibility, gas prices, health care, income inequality, labor and the sub prime mortgage crisis.

In the current Congress, the committee will pay close attention to monthly job reports, and suggest ways of boosting employment. Both leading Democrats and Republicans on the committee have vowed to cut federal spending, but they are sure to clash on the specifics. Casey can be expected to use the committee as a platform to defend President Obama's approach, while Brady uses it to tear it down.

Since Democrats remain at the helm of the committee, despite the Republican takeover of the House, many of its priorities are likely to remain, including investigations into how the financial regulatory system failed to prevent the most recent economic crisis and how Congress can improve its oversight.

The committee was established by the Employment Act of 1946 to review economic conditions and to analyze the effectiveness of economic policy. As a joint committee, it includes ten members each from the House and Senate.

JOINT ECONOMIC

Gail Cohen

Chief Economist

Phone: (202) 224-517

gail_cohen@jec.senate.gov

Professional: 2007–2009, senior economist, Joint Economic Cmte. 2010–present, deputy staff director and chief economist, Joint Economic Cmte.

Expertise: Energy security, women in the workforce.

As the Democrat's deputy staff director and chief economist on the Joint Economic Committee, Gail Cohen oversees much of the committee's research and publications, tracking unemployment and other economic trends. Cohen is also involved in preparing the committee for its hearings on monthly job reports, and for helping the Democrats articulate their agenda for economic recovery.

In the 112th Congress, Cohen works for Sen. Robert Casey, D-Pa., the committee's chairman, who was first elected to the Senate in 2006.

During the 111th Congress, when Rep. Carolyn Maloney, D-N.Y., chaired the committee, Cohen worked on, among other issues, the Healthy Families Act, which would establish a basic workplace standard of seven paid sick days. JEC research concluded that if implemented, the legislation would give 30 million additional workers paid sick leave.

Also in recent years, with colleagues Frederick Joutz of George Washington University, and Prakash Loungani of the International Monetary Fund, Cohen authored, "The Determinants of Energy Vulnerability and Security: An Empirical Analysis." The paper was discussed at a 2010 meeting of the Allied Social Science Association.

Also during the 111th Congress, in March of 2010, Cohen was a speaker at Feminist Majority Foundation's National Young Feminist Leadership Conference in Washington, D.C. Her topic was women, employment, and the economy.

She spoke on similar topics weeks later at a Washington meeting of Corporate Voice for the Working Family, a group of public and private sector leaders looking to grow the workforce.

Cohen joined the panel in 2007 serving as chief economist before adding deputy staff director to her title in 2010.

JOINT ECONOMIC

Jeffrey L. Schlagenhauf

Senate Republican Staff Director

G-01 Dirksen Senate Office Bldg.

Phone: (202) 224-5171

Jeff_Schlagenhauf@jec.senate.gov

Personal: Born 02/12/1958 in Batavia, N.Y.

Education: B.A., history, The College of William and Mary, 1980.

Professional: 1985–1992, legislative director/chief of staff, Rep. Tom Bliley, R-Va. 1992–1998, president, The Smokeless Tobacco Council. 1998–2001, senior vice president, Maguire Woods Consulting. 2001–2004, government relations consultant, self-owned business. 2004–present, Republican staff director, Joint Economic Cmte.

Expertise: Economic research.

As Republican staff director of the joint economic committee, Jeffrey L. Schlagenhauf works with Vice Chairman Kevin Brady, R-Tex., to push for conservative solutions to the nation's deep deficit and stubborn unemployment.

Schlagenhauf is one of the few returning key staffers on a committee that underwent significant turnover at the outset of the 112th Congress, in its membership, leadership and staffing. Having served as Republican staff director since 2004, Schlagenhauf is relied upon by Republicans to provide the numbers and the arguments for less government spending on social programs.

Schlagenhauf plays an important role in organizing the committee's monthly hearings on job reports, a task made more difficult in the beginning of the 112th Congress since the committee was not fully organized before March. Schlagenhauf's first job in the first session of the 112th Congress was to help Republican members on the Joint Economic Committee voice their ideas about how to help the nation through the current economic crisis and evaluate overall fiscal policies.

Schlagenhauf also oversees minority publications on the JEC, both paper and online. This includes monthly reports on the economy as well as year-end reports, which summarize the Republican take on what policies helped or hindered the economic recovery.

In all these tasks, Schlagenhauf draws upon his experience as a former independent businessman and lobbyist, for both Maguire Woods Consulting and The Smokeless Tobacco Council.

Name Index

NAME INDEX

A

Adamo, Christopher John, 406
Adler, Ann, 306
Albritton, Jason, 520
Alexander, Michael, 594
Allen, Michael, 365
Amerling, Kristin Lawes, 148
Anderson, Allyson K., 486
Anderson, Doug, 188
Anderson, Elizabeth "E.R", 595
Anderson, John T., 307
Anderson, Kyle, 212
Andres, Gary J., 149
Andringa, Tara, 442
Androff, Blake J., 308
Angell, John C., 546
Aoki, Lena, 646
Apelbaum, Perry H., 220
Apostolou, Carolyn E., 416
Arcangeli, Paul, 94
Ash, Michelle, 150
Ashbrook, John, 6
Avant, Lanier, 200

B

Bailey, Steve, 464
Baker, Andrew, 46
Balkham, Dennis, 417
Barnett, Phil, 151
Barnette, James D., 152
Baron, Dena, 66
Barr, Patricia, 47
Barrett, Murphie, 521
Barron, Dan, 522
Barthold, Thomas A., 682
Batchelder, Lily, 547
Batkin, Gabrielle, 418
Becker, Ben, 407
Beckerman, Michael M., 153
Beirne, Kate, 7
Bergeron, James, 130
Bernards, Stacey Farnen, 8
Berquam, Tanuja, 67
Bertoson, Todd, 478
Billingsley, Tara, 487
Billups, Karen K., 488

Bingen, Kari, 95
Bingham, Jeff, 479
Bjorklund, Cybele, 346
Black, Barry C., 375
Black, Jonathan, 489
Blair, Rob, 68
Bloomquist, Michael D., 154
Blumenthal, Rob W., 419
Borden, Michael, 172
Bordewich, Jean, 616
Bowers, Mandy L., 201
Bradley, Neil L., 9
Brady, Lawrence J., 246
Branson, Cherri L., 202
Brenckle III, Joseph J., 480
Brew, Bill, 634
Brinck, Mike, 332
Broder Van Dyke, Jesse, 647
Brooks, David, 490
Browyn, Maryam Sabbaghian, 155
Bruckner, Caroline, 620
Brumfield, Krystal, 621
Buehlmann, Beth, 576
Burkett, Alex, 309
Burroughs, Harry F., 236
Buse, Mark, 376
Byers, Dan, 266

C

Cabannis, Dale, 420
Cain, Hilary, 267
Calabro, Rosemarie, 491
Calemine, Jody, 131
Campbell, Chris, 548
Campbell, Doug, 189
Campbell, McKie, 492
Caputo, Annie, 523
Caravelli, Margaret E., 268
Carbo, Richard, 622
Carr, Michael, 493
Cecil, Guy, 10
Chapla, John D., 96
Cheshire, Jamie, 97
Chotvacs, Anne Marie, 69
Christian, Lisa, 286

Clapp, Douglas, 421
Clapton, Charles, M., 577
Clinger, Jim, 173
Cohen, Alan, 549
Cohen, Bruce A., 606
Cohen, Gail, 688
Cohen, Howard, 156
Cohen, Rosaline, 203
Collins, William, 333
Condon, Joan O., 190
Cooke, Alyson, 524
Coon, Jim, 310
Cope, Grant, 525
Coppess, Jonathan William, 408
Cottle, Amber, 550
Coughlin, Daniel P., 11
Cravins, Donald, 623
Cribb, Troy, 596
Cuaderes, John, 247

D

Davies, Rebecca, 422
Davis, Kolan L., 607
Dawson, Liz, 70
Dawson, Thomas III, 287
Day, Michael, 288
Dayspring, Brad, 12
Dean, Greg, 578
DeBobes, Richard D., 443
Dedrick, Kathy, 526
Delgado, Martin, 71
Dempsey, Matthew, 527
Diller, Dan, 566
Dillon, Robert, 494
Dimarob, Michelle, 347
Donnelly, Kellie A., 495
Dotson, Gregory J., 157
Drew, Whitney, 496
Duhnke, Wiliam, 454
Duncan, Jeff, 237
Dunlap, Mike, 48

E

Eastman, Sage, 348
Edwards, Isaac, 497
Eissenstat, Everett, 551

NAME INDEX

Ellard, Angela Paolini, 349
Elling, Dan, 350
Elshami, Nadeam, 13
Emerson, Jeff, 174
Epstein, Jonathan, 498
Erickson, Nancy, 377
Estes, Deborah M., 499
Evans, Bruce M., 423
Evans, Christina, 424

F

Fallon, Brian, 14
Fasteau, Jamie, 132
Fatemi, Erik, 425
Feddeman, Ed, 269
Ferrier, Antonia, 552
Fettig, Dwight, 455
Fieldhouse, Richard W., 444
Fishman, George M., 221
Fite, David, 191
Fleet, Jamie, 213
Flores, Daniel M., 222
Fluhr, Christopher, 238
Flynn, Timothy, 114
Foley, Martha, 72
Foltz, Nicole, 465
Fonnesbeck, Leif, 426
Fountain, Galen, 427
Fowler, Sam E, 500
Fox, Elizabeth S., 528
Fried, Neil, 158
Friedlander, Liz, 49
Friedman, Joel, 466
Friedman, Ruth J., 133
Froehlich, Kaleb D., 501
Frumin, Alan S., 378

G

Gage, Mark, 192
Gainer, Terrance W., 379
Gallegos, Chris, 428
Garibay, Marisol, 175
Gilbert, Leslie, 270
Gillers, David, 624
Gillis, Annette, 660
Gilman, Kate, 529
Gilroy, Edwin J., 134
Giovinazzi, Giles, 311
Glacel, Ashley, 654
Gladics, Frank, 502
Gluck, Carolyn, 380
Goehner, Brad, 193
Goldberg, John J., 50

Gorski, Jenny, 256
Graffeo, Jonathan, 456
Grannis, David, 666
Graziano, Dena, 204
Greco, Kristie, 15
Greenawalt, Bob, 381
Greene, Creighton, 445
Grooms, Susanne Sachsman, 248
Grove, Paul, 429
Gwyn, Nicholas C., 351

H

Haas, Karen Lehman, 16
Hall, Jennifer L., 312
Hallahan, Kate, 73
Halpern, Hugh Nathanial, 257
Hammill, Drew, 17
Hammond, Tom, 271
Hannel, Eric, 334
Harclerode, Justin, 313
Hardy, Johanna, 314
Harjo, Rhonda, 648
Harper, Chuck, 655
Hartz, Jerry, 18
Hartz, Joe, 289
Hayes, Colin, 503
Healy, Richard J., 239
Hearn, Jim, 467
Helmke, Mark, 567
Herbert, Martin, 335
Hergott, Alex, 530
Hermann, Megan, 504
Herz, Jim, 115
Hicks, Kyle, 579
Higgins, Michael R., 98
Higgins, Stephen, 608
Hildred, Kim, 352
Hill, Frederick R., 249
Hing, Jennifer, 74
Hinton, Tamara, 51
Hite, Matthew, 531
Hogshead, Laura, 75
Holmes, Stewart, 430
Homendy, Jennifer L., 315
Houy, Charles J., 431
Hoy, Serena, 382
Hsueh, Wallace, 625
Hughes, Brian, 505

I

Illston, Ted, 532
Imbergamo, Bill, 409
Imparato, Andrew, 580

Inglee, William, 76
Ivancic, Charlotte, 116

J

Jagger, Craig, 52
Jarvis, Adam, 258
Jawetz, Tom, 223
Jentleson, Adam, 383
Jesmer, Rob, 384
Jester, Julia, 272
Johanson, David S., 553
Johnson, Joshua, 506
Johnson, Matthew L., 609
Jones, Amy, 135
Jones, Clinton C., 176
Jones III, Frederick L., 568
Juola, Paul, 77

K

Kahn, Thomas, 117
Karakitsos, Dimitrios J., 533
Karr, Barrett, 136
Kazan, Matt, 554
Keenan, Alex, 432
Kerr, Mary, 534
Kholsa, Jay, 555
Kieffer, Charles, 433
Kiefhaber, Peter, 434
Kiko, Philip, 214,
Kim, C. Morgan, 300
King, Bruce, 385
King, Christopher, 273
Kleeschulte, Chuck, 507
Knudsen, Patrick L., 118
Kolb, James, 316
Kramp, Kevin, 53
Krishnamoorthy, Jenelle, 581
Kuehl, Sarah, 468
Kugajevsky, Alex, 99
Kumar, Rohit, 386
Kundanis, George, 19

L

Lachmann, David, 224
Lackey, Miles M., 259
Lara, Juan, 336
Larew, Rob, 54
Lavender, Larry, 177
Lawrence, John A., 20
Lederman, Gordon, 597
Leeling, Gary, 446
Lenihan, Keagan, 260

NAME INDEX

Leone, Kate, 387
Lesley, Turner
LesStrang, David, 78
Levine, Edward, 569
Levine, Peter K., 447
Lewis, Mark R., 100
Lierman, Terry, 21
Lightfoot, Karen L., 159
Lipsky, Kim, 635
Litsey, Richard, 556
Little, Bethany, 582
Livingood, Wilson, 22
Lofgren, Mike, 469
Long, Ryan, 160
Loskarn, Ryan, 388
Lowenstein, Frank, 570
Lowery, Leon, 508
Lucas, Christopher, 626
Lucius, Kristine, 610
Lynch, Caroline, 225
Lynch, Mike, 23
Lyons, Holly Woodruff, 317
Lyons, James, 557

M

Macchiarola, Frank, 583
MacDonald, Don, 194
MacKenzie, Tom, 101
Maney, Jo, 261
Marrero, Alexa, 161
Martens, John, 79
Martz, Stephanie A., 226
Mathews, Daniel W., 318
May, Tina M., 410
Mays, Janice A., 353
McAfee, Karen Brown, 354
McBride, Stacy, 435
McCallum, David, 389
McCarragher, Ward W., 319
McCarthy, David, 162
McElroy, Catherine, 102
McFerran, Lauren McGarity, 584
McGinnis, Colin P.J, 457
McLaughlin, Sean P., 227
McLemore, Tom, 80
Medina, Frank, 178
Melendrez, Dahlia, 636
Mercier, Stephanie, 411
Meredith, Amanda, 637
Merritt, Blaine, 228
Millar, Gail, 119
Miller, Cheryl, 627
Miller, Pam, 55

Miller, Richard D., 137
Miller, Scott, 509
Miller, Stephen, 470
Miner, Matthew, 611
Molino, Heather Moeder, 366
Monahan, Bill, 448
Monroe, Ken, 274
Moore, Stephanie, 229
Morton, Andrew S., 120
Moss, Dorinda, 390
Mullon, Jr., David A., 649
Murray, John, 24
Myrick, Gary, 391

N

Napoliello David, 535
Naylor, Mary, 471
Neasham, Duncan, 290
Nelson, Karen, 163
Nevins, Kyle, 25
Newby, Darek, 81
Newhouse Mullen, Suzanne, 320
Nicholson, Ben, 82
Nickel, Ryan, 83

O

O'Keeffe, James, 536
Obermann, Richard, 275
Ogilvie, Clark, 56
Olander, Dave, 355
Oliver, Janet L., 291
Olmem, Andrew, 458
Olson, Kathryn, 356
Olson, Scott R., 179
O'Neill, Maureen, 638
O'Reilly, Megan, 138
Orfield, Craig, 585
O'Shea, John S., 164
Overbeek, Kimberly, 121

P

Palarino, R. Nicholas, 205
Paul, Christopher John, 449
Pawlow, Jonathan R., 321
Payne, Warren, 357
Peacock, Marcus, 472
Pearce, Michael A., 103
Pearson, Dan, 276
Peller, Julie, 139
Peterson, Tim, 84
Piazza, John, 277
Pierson, Jay, 26

Pinder, Joe, 180
Pineles, Barry, 292
Pittman, Lisa, 240
Poindexter, Martha Scott, 667
Poirier, Bettina, 537
Pomerantz, David, 85
Poppleton, Janet, 278
Prater, Mark Alan, 558
Price, Reva, 27
Primus, Wendell, 28

R

Rangaswami, Viji, 358
Rapallo, David P., 250
Rayfield, John, 322
Reich, David J., 86
Reinhard, Courtney, 122
Rennert, Kevin J., 510
Renz, Brandon, 262
Restuccia, Paul, 123
Rieser, Timothy S., 436
Ringler, Michael, 87
Ritchie, Donald A., 29
Roach, Douglas C., 104
Romick, Brian, 30
Rose, Joyce, 323
Roslanowick, Jeanne M., 181
Ross, Kimberly, 337
Rothschild, Tara, 279
Rushforth, Tyler, 538
Russel, Mike, 206

S

Safavian, Jennifer, 359
Salley, Lori, 293
Samuelson, Drey, 459
Sarmiento de Poblete, Yleem, 195
Sass, Paul, 294
Sassaman Jr., John C., 661
Schaumburg, Amanda, 140
Schiappa, David, 392
Schlagenhauf, Jeffrey L., 689
Schmitt, Bernard A., 683
Schnittger, David, 31
Schwartz, David, 559
Scott, Nicole, 57
Seiger, Ryan, 324
Sepp, Steven, 88
Shahinian, Dean, 460
Shank, Amy Angelier, 586
Sheehy, Thomas P., 196
Sherman, Roger C., 165
Shorter, Malcom, 338

NAME INDEX

Sienicki, David, 105
Simler, Jenness, 106
Simmons, Anne, 58
Simmons, Bob, 107
Simon, Robert M., 511
Simpson, Kevin, 512
Slattery, Tim, 295
Slobodin, Alan M., 166
Smith (Steinmann), Amy B., 325
Smith, Daniel E., 588
Smith, David A., 182
Smith, Kevin, 32
Smith, Pam, 587
Smith, Tiffany, 560
Smith, Will, 89
Smythe, Austin, 124
Snow, Andi, 215
Soderstrom, Sharon, 393
Sokolov, Dahlia, 280
Sommers, Mike, 33
Souders, Patrick, 394
St. Martin, Jo-Marie, 34
Stayman, Allen, 513
Steel, Michael, 35
Stein, Beth, 589
Stephenson, Mark, 251
Stewart, Don, 395
Stivers, Jonathan, 36
Stombres, Steve, 37
Straughn, Pelham, 59
Strayer, Rob, 598
Strickland, Kelle, 301
Sugiyama, George, 539
Sullivan, Gael, 481
Sullivan, John V., 38
Sullivan, Russell W., 561
Summers, Jon, 39
Suruma, Askia M., 360
Sweeney, Conor, 125

T

Taylor, Bettilou, 437
Taylor, Paul, 230
Teitz, Alexandra, 167
Thiessen, Pamela B., 396
Thompson, Darrel, 397
Thomson, Pete, 60
Tolar, Helen, 339
Towers, Jonathan, 340
Traub, Jon, 361
Trujillo, Tanya, 514
Tucker, David, 341
Tucker, Sara, 515
Tuell, Loretta, 650
Turner, Lesley, 90
Tymon, Jim, 326
Tyron, Warren, 183

U

Ungerecht, Todd, 241
Upton, Marianne, 438

V

Van Mark, Ruth, 540
Varnhagen, Michele, 141
Vassar, Bobby N., 231

W

Wada, Debra S., 108
Walker, Matthew, 628
Wall, Anne, 398
Wallner, Judith, 399
Walsh, Brian J., 400
Walsh, Dick, 450
Waring, Greg, 126
Wasniewski, Matt, 40
Watkins, KerryAnn, 207
Watkins, Yelberton, 41
Weaver, Kiel, 242
Weber, Michelle, 61
Weidinger, Matt, 362
Weiss, Daniel, 142
Wender, Joseph A., 327
West, Meredith, 629
Wheeler, Kevin, 630
Whitener, Kelly, 562
Whitman, Debra, 656
Whitney, Pamela, 281
Wiblemo, Catherine Cecilia, 342
Wicker, Bill, 516
Wiggins Jr., Mason E., 401
Wiley, Kenya, 599
Wilkinson, Molly, 600
Williams, Lynn, 109
Williams, Mele, 282
Willkie, David, 571
Wissel, Marie Guadalupe (Lupe), 639
Wolfe, Shane, 208
Wolski, Lisa M., 402
Wood, Amanda, 601
Wood, Sally, 216
Wooten, Todd, 412
Wrathall, Jim, 541
Wroe, Elizabeth (Liz), 473

Z

Zakheim, Roger, 110
Zogby, Joseph, 612
Zoia, James H., 328
Zola, Michael C., 143